ROOM 21

Martina Purdy is political correspondent for BBC Northern Ireland and has been reporting on the peace process since 1996. She covered the multi-party talks that led to the Good Friday Agreement, the subsequent efforts to achieve devolution and the ups-and-downs of political life at Stormont during the years 1999-2002. Before joining the BBC in 1999, she worked for *The Irish News* and the *Belfast Telegraph*. She has won several awards for journalism.

Born in Belfast in 1965 and raised in Toronto, Canada, Martina holds a Bachelor of Arts degree in International Relations from the University of Toronto and a post-graduate degree from the Ryerson School of Journalism. She trained with the *Toronto Star* before returning to Belfast in 1990. Her articles have been published in the *Globe and Mail* newspaper, the *L.A. Times* and the *Christian Science Monitor*. This is her first book.

ROOM 21

STORMONT – BEHIND CLOSED DOORS

MARTINA PURDY X

THE BREHON PRESS
BELFAST

First published 2005 by The Brehon Press Ltd
1A Bryson Street, Belfast BT5 4ES
Northern Ireland

ISBN: 1 905474 01 6

Design: December Publications
Printed and Bound by J H Haynes & Co. Ltd., Sparkford

For my loving parents, Al and Margaret Purdy

When through the woods and forest glades I wander
And hear birds sing sweetly in the trees;
When I look down from lofty mountain grandeur,
And hear the brook and feel the gentle breeze.

Contents

Acknowledgements

This book was started in late 2002 and has taken longer than anticipated to complete, and a great debt is owed to a number of people for their support and assistance. First, I would like to thank all those who consented to be interviewed – both on and off the record. A number of people asked not to be named in the book but were extremely helpful, for which I am very grateful. I would especially like to thank my good friend Louise McCall and Peter Cardwell; they assisted by interviewing a number of the committee chairmen. Thanks also to Johnsons Solicitors in Belfast, particularly Paul Tweed and Sarah Loughran.

A big thank you to the Political Unit at the BBC, particularly my understanding line manager, Lena Ferguson, and my very supportive colleagues: Mark Devenport, Gareth Gordon, Robin Sheeran, Mark Armstrong, Jim Fitzpatrick, Naomi McCafferty, Linda Ruddy and the ever-helpful producer Louise Duffy. Also to Seamus Kelters, Vincent Kearney and Paul Clements for their excellent feedback; Jeremy Adams, Andrew Colman, Angelina Fusco, Kathleen Carragher, Chris Kelly, Chris Buckler, Daragh McIntyre, Mary Kelly, Siobhan Savage, Ian McTear, Damien Magee, Noel Thompson, Maurice Hawkins, Noel McCartney, James Kerr, Dot Kirby, Jacqueline McIntyre, Maggie Taggart, Mike McKimm, Martin Cassidy, Richard Wright, David Dunseith, Seamus Boyd, Michael Cairns, Brian Rowan, Brendan McCourt, Kevin Magee, Aisling Strong, Nuala McCann, Mandy McAuley, Mark Simpson, Kevin Connolly, Denis Murray, Paul Doran, cameramen Sam Wilson, Brian Elliott, Sam Thompson, John Otterson and William John Crawford, Controller Anna Carragher, Gerry Allen, Clare Blankley, Pauline McKenna, Cheryl Cander, Fionnuala Wilson, Fiona Moore, Fionuala Boyd, Seamus McKee, Leslie Van Slyke, Shane Harrison, Mary Campbell, Noel Russell, Conor MacAuley, Yvette Shapiro, Sarah Travers, Jacqui Quinn, Marie Irvine, Kevin Kelly, Camilla Carroll, Gwyneth Jones, Stephen Walker, Maurice Hawkins, Salena Gamble, Eddie Fleming and Donna Smyth in Graphics. I'm also grateful to my former colleagues in the political unit: Ioan Bellin, who has returned to Wales, and Stephen Grimason, former BBC political editor.

Colleagues across the media have been extremely helpful, particularly David McKittrick and John Devine, who kindly read the manuscript, Anne Cadwallader, William Graham, Brian Feeney, Steven McCaffery, Gerry Moriarty, Eamonn Mallie, Dan McGinn, Fionnuala O Connor, UTV political editor Ken Reid and reporter Fearghal McKinney, *Belfast Telegraph* reporters Gail Walker, Nigel Gould, Chris Thornton, Noel McAdam, as well as reporters Suzanne Breen, Michael Appleton and Henry McDonald. Also to Derek Henderson, Tommy O'Gorman and my former editors Terry McLaughlin, Nick Garbutt, and Ed Curran.

The BBC librarians provided invaluable help in assisting with research – special thanks to Danny Cooper, Neal Sutherland and Marinda Hamill. Thanks also to the IT department, particularly Jonny Harvey.

Thanks to all the Stormont Assembly officials and civil servants who kindly assisted when facts needed to be checked, including Joe Reynolds, Dermot McCreevy and Paddy Price. Also to Seamus Magee from the Electoral Commission. I am also very grateful to the party press officers, Sinn Féin's Richard McAuley, Ned Cohen, Mark McLarnon, and Colm Delaney; the UUP's press office, particularly Alex Benjamin; the DUP's Timothy Johnston; and the SDLP's James Dillon and Ronan McKay.

I would also like to thank the staff at the Linenhall Library and *The Irish News* library, particularly Kathleen Bell and Mark Boylan, and also Kathleen Magee for her kind assistance. Many thanks to the newspaper's photographic department for assisting with photographs, particularly Picture Editor Ann McManus and photographers Brendan Murphy, Hugh Russell, Margaret McLaughlin, and Bill Smyth. I am also indebted to John Harrison Photography. *The Irish News* kindly provided the cover photograph, as it was a pool shot taken on the day by Paul Faith of Press Association, to whom I'm also grateful. Thanks also to Seán Moran for providing the cover image of Stormont.

To publishers Brendan Anderson and Damian Keenan of Brehon, who got me into this, and editor Rachel Pierce, of Verba Editing House, for her hard work, patient assistance and invaluable suggestions; special thanks to Damian for working so hard to get the book out on time, and also to Nicola Pierce who burned the midnight oil.

Finally to my family and friends for their love and support, particularly my mother and father and Mark, Emma, Connor, Cameron, Alexis, Logan, Grant, Lisa, Mikalya, and Ryan Purdy and Riva Dany; also Paddy, Veronica, Louise, Margaret, Patrick and Martin Burns, who took in a waif in 1987; and all the Logans, especially Geraldine, Al, Liam, Christopher, Jennifer, Bridie, Mary, Anthony, Jean and Margaret; and the Buntings, especially Frank and Peter; and Seamus McCafferty; and my Eastwood relations, especially my three aunts, Florence, Betty and Edith; and to those who have gone before: Francis, Monica and William Logan, and Daisy Smith and George Purdy and Matt Rosbotham; also to Jacquie Castel, Christine de Lima and Susie O'Rawe; and all the gang from the Beaches, Kristie, Jason, Sabrina and Wayne Sills, Rita Picard, and Lydia Stante.

Humble apologies to anyone I have overlooked.

Foreword

From Donegal and Down, Foyle and Fermanagh, Antrim and Armagh, the ministers came, unionists, nationalists and republicans, to form the most representative government in Northern Ireland's history and the first power-sharing Executive in a generation. This is their story. The tale of the men and women who tried to write a new history for Northern Ireland, who carried the burdens of their parents and grandparents, who laboured to ensure their children and grandchildren escaped the noose of the past.

The true beginning of this story is 10 April 1998, the day the Good Friday Agreement was ratified. It was a day many feared would never come, a day when even former combatants would declare they had found the elusive compromise that would provide them with a map out of the past and into a new future. The negotiations officially lasted two years, but in reality they were rooted in years of dialogue, years when even talking seemed impossible, and often was. Those who spoke of a hopeful compromise were drowned out by the cries of despair during what had become known as the Troubles, twenty-five years of bitter conflict that claimed more than 3,600 lives.

The Agreement was negotiated by eight parties, the largest being the Ulster Unionist party (UUP), led by David Trimble, and the nationalist Social Democratic and Labour party (SDLP), led by John Hume. Both men would receive the Nobel Peace Prize for their efforts. Their power-sharing deal was unique, and not without its flaws, but it represented a massive compromise by all sides: unionists who had set their face against power-sharing, nationalists who would have preferred to join a Dublin Parliament in a 32-county Ireland, republicans who had taken up arms and vowed never to participate in a Northern Ireland administration, and loyalists who had violently opposed a formal relationship with Dublin.

Stormont, the old Northern Ireland Parliament, which had sprung from the partition of Ireland, was reopened following the deal, allowing unionists and nationalists to seize some control of their new destiny. The price was a twelve-member, power-sharing Executive, drawn from a 108-member Assembly and led by a First and Deputy First Minister who were elected by a majority of unionist and nationalist members. The Assembly was formally linked to the Irish Republic and Great Britain through a North South Ministerial Council and a British Irish Council of Ministers, underpinning relationships and giving both sides the confidence to proceed.

This book was inspired by the first image taken of the new Northern Ireland ministers, seated together in Room 21 in Stormont's Parliament Buildings. Paul Faith, of the Press Association, was the only photographer invited into the meeting and he captured the joy and excitement of that historic day, a day that proved a turning point in the lives of the Ulster Unionist members – David Trimble, Sam Foster, Michael McGimpsey and Sir Reg Empey – and of the SDLP members – Seamus Mallon, Bríd Rodgers, Mark Durkan and

Sean Farren – and of the Sinn Féin members – Martin McGuinness and Bairbre de Brun.

This book attempts to tell two stories: that of the political events that defined and ultimately destroyed the Northern Ireland Executive of 1999–2002, and the lives, emotions and difficulties of the people behind the politics. What shaped these people? How did they get to be ministers? Why did they go where others – namely the DUP – refused to tread? They understood only too well the meaning and possible repercussions of crossing the threshold into Room 21, yet they took that step, together and as individuals. That courage, that conviction is the starting point of this book and of an intriguing story. (Accordingly, the biographical information on the DUP ministers is condensed into one chapter and less attention is paid to their personal journeys because the book is intended to profile those who entered Room 21.)

The Executive took around eighteen months to form and began with the election, on 1 July 1998, of a First and Deputy First Minister, David Trimble and Seamus Mallon. They led a shadow administration until December 1999. During this period the new Departments were agreed, but the Ulster Unionists refused to nominate Executive ministers until the issue of IRA weapons decommissioning had been addressed to their satisfaction. Their agreement was required before any nationalist ministers could be appointed. It took longer than expected to break the stalemate over guns and government. It was not until 29 November 1999 that the other ministers were nominated. Power was then devolved from London on devolution day, 2 December 1999. The ministers struggled to succeed against the odds until Stormont's last suspension, on 14 October 2002. Why, one might ask, bother to write about a failed, short-lived Executive?

First, it was an Executive that once would have been unimaginable – the fact that it happened at all was a miracle in itself. It was a political institution that emerged from three decades of bloodshed and turmoil in a conflict that has caused damage on a massive scale. During most of those years, Northern Ireland was ruled directly from Westminster, with a succession of British MPs appointed as ministers to the Northern Ireland Office (NIO), to take decisions on behalf of the people. Direct rule was imposed in 1972 and was expected to be a temporary measure. Indeed, it appeared as such when the Ulster Unionist leader, Brian Faulkner, reached an agreement with his SDLP counterpart, Gerry Fitt, at Sunningdale in 1973. The terms of that deal envisaged a devolved, power-sharing administration between unionists and nationalists. The administration would stand in marked contrast to the original Stormont government, which had been initiated after Partition in 1921 and comprised one-party unionist rule. The Faulkner–Fitt Executive took power on 1 January 1974, but had collapsed by 28 May 1974 when direct rule was resumed. And yet twenty-five years after that failed enterprise, these men and women again forced themselves to the edge, to jump together into the unknown. That is the primary impetus for this story.

A second reason for writing this book is that the Trimble–Mallon Executive was born out of the Good Friday Agreement 1998, a treaty that has given hope to countries around the world which are either engaged in conflict or emerging from conflict. The Executive was the heartbeat of that Agreement and its rise and fall contains lessons for other peacemakers. Although devolution was expected to come six months after the Good Friday Agreement, it in fact took three times as long – some eighteen months – before direct rule ceased and power was handed back to Stormont.

Initially, this book was to focus exclusively on the Executive, but it quickly became apparent that the pre-Executive shadow period was a crucial part of the story. It was during the days of shadow government that these men and women learned about each other and alliances and enmities were formed. It was this period, too, that helped define the central relationship of the Executive – that of David Trimble and Seamus Mallon.

Thirdly, the Trimble–Mallon dynamic was a fascinating relationship, a fascinating struggle and, like the other ministers in Room 21, they were fascinating personalities. Politically, they were strong-willed, determined and focused. As people, they came from very different backgrounds and held very different beliefs. In this, Room 21 provided a microcosm of Northern Irish society: two opposing viewpoints struggling to find a common language. Among the ministers who entered Room 21 were two who had fought in the conflict: one on the side of the security forces; the other on the side of the IRA. For many years and certainly during the final, dark days of the Sunningdale Executive, when the Ulster Workers' Council strike saw armed loyalist paramilitaries terrorising the populace, Martin McGuinness – who would go to Room 21 as Minister of Education – was an active member of the IRA. In contrast, Sam Foster, the Ulster Unionist Minister of Environment, was a member of the security forces and determined to defend the Union. Two decades later these men had to sit across a table from each other and find some way to let go of the past.

Others had been politically active in one way or another as well, either pro- or anti-Sunningdale. Indeed, the First Minister, David Trimble, had a role in bringing down Sunningdale, while his new partner in government, Seamus Mallon, Deputy First Minister, was an elected member of the Sunningdale Assembly and had been devastated by its failure.

Even if power-sharing once again becomes a reality in Northern Ireland, there will never again be another Executive quite like this one. The ministers were pioneers and because their endeavour was so new and unique, it was something special, an unparalleled period in Northern Ireland's history. For a while they made sweet music for those who longed for a new tune. "It was history every day," recalled the SDLP's director of communications, Barry Turley. The Ulster Unionist minister Dermot Nesbitt put it another way: "It was an effing time. It was fascinating, fulminating, fatiguing, frustrating, farcical. Above all, it was fun."

Room 21 is not intended as an academic study; it is instead a dramatic human story that brings to life the characters and the times, the tragedy and comedy, the joys and rages, the defining moments of a Stormont Executive that Gerry Adams dubbed a "Humpty-Dumpty Parliament": destined to be irreparably broken. In all, Stormont was suspended for the first time in February 2000, twice for twenty-four hours in 2001, and for the fourth and last time in October 2002. This story examines the successes and ultimate failure of a remarkable political and personal journey into a new future for Northern Ireland. These ministers shattered shibboleths that had prevented change and laid the foundations for a return to power-sharing on a sounder basis, if two new tribal leaders can find the will, and the way, to forge another elusive compromise.

Chapter 1
Room 21

Shortly before 3.00pm on 2 December 1999, just a month shy of a new millennium, William David Trimble took a gamble no unionist leader had been prepared to take for twenty-five years. On his heels and heading for the same destination was Martin McGuinness, Northern Ireland's new Minister of Education and one of the most notorious IRA figures of the past three decades.

Like McGuinness, Trimble was going to Room 21 in the East Wing of Parliament Buildings at Stormont. It was here that the new power-sharing Executive would meet for the first time. As he made the historic, rather dangerous political journey through the marble corridors of Stormont, Trimble was not sure if the Executive was going to work. As First Minister and leader of the Ulster Unionist party, he carried a heavy burden. The SDLP minister Mark Durkan once said that Trimble had two groups on his back: those in his party trying to bring him down and those in the rival Democratic Unionist party who were happy to piggyback on his efforts. Despite these twin pressures, Trimble was fairly confident that he would take the majority of his party with him, however slight that margin might be. Only one Ulster Unionist member from his twenty-eight-strong Assembly team had openly rebelled over the decision to share power with republicans, although many, at least another third, were unhappy with the prospect of dealing with a group of people they considered terrorists.

Pro-Agreement Ulster Unionists saw devolution as a chance to secure the Union and to stabilise Northern Ireland after years of bloody conflict, years when they saw their influence ebbing away. One of Trimble's lieutenants, Sir Reg Empey, declared – perhaps more for sceptical unionist than republican ears – that Sinn Féin had now entered a partitionist administration and their IRA forefathers would be "spinning in their graves".

Sinn Féin President Gerry Adams saw it differently. He declared that this was the end of the Government of Ireland Act which had partitioned the island. Of course it did not end partition, but Adams claimed it was a stepping-stone. Around this time he was asked why it took so many years, so many deaths before this compromise came about. He answered: "I don't know why it didn't happen earlier. It is a question I am intrigued by." Curiously, lost for an answer, the republican quoted an English bard, Shakespeare: "There's a tide in the affairs of men…" The late Sir Robert Cooper, a former minister in Sunningdale, had his own reasons why early compromise had failed, paving the way for years of conflict: "People were not exhausted. They thought there were other ways."

While unionists remained divided about the latest compromise, in the guise of the Good Friday Agreement, the majority of nationalists and others were excited by the deal and the new power-sharing arrangement. Among them was the new Deputy First Minister

Seamus Mallon, the deputy leader of the SDLP, which had played a key role in achieving the Agreement. "I had a very distinct sense," said Mallon, "that if we got this right, it would change things very fundamentally." President Bill Clinton, who had done so much to encourage compromise, said the people of Northern Ireland now had the power to shape their own destiny. With characteristic American optimism he declared: "It's now possible to believe the days of the gun and the bomb are over."

Civil servants watched in anticipation as Trimble made his way to Room 21 with the other ministers – seven men and two women – following closely behind. One civil servant, who was among those who peeped from inside a doorway to witness the arrival of the first power-sharing ministers for a generation, was struck by the sense of history in the making: "It was pure theatre."

As First Minister, Trimble was occupying the office once used by Brian Faulkner, who as Ulster Unionist leader had led the first power-sharing administration in 1974, a move that had proved politically fatal for him. It was from this same ground-floor office in the West Wing that Faulkner had watched in horror as the Sunningdale administration was snuffed out by loyalist wrath in May 1974. Faulkner's sin had been to share power with the late SDLP leader, Gerry Fitt. A working-class Catholic and self-proclaimed socialist, Fitt – later Lord Fitt of Bell's Hill – led a party that rejected violence and sought Irish unity through consent of the unionists. One civil servant, aghast at the prospect of Fitt in government, memorably dismissed him as a "rebel" – a description laughable by the standards of the 1999 power-sharing Executive. Faulkner and Fitt had shared power while the IRA bombing campaign raged all around. Back then the IRA's political wing, Sinn Féin, barely registered on the political radar: even if the party had wanted to – and it certainly did not – there was no question of it participating in the Sunningdale power-sharing arrangements.

Trimble found himself in a very different situation from Faulkner. Twenty years after Sunningdale's collapse, on 31 August 1994, the IRA had declared a "complete cessation of military operations". While the ceasefire had broken down sixteen months later when multi-party negotiations failed to start, it was restored in July 1997, enabling Sinn Féin to enter the talks leading to the Good Friday Agreement. As a result of the peace process, and that compromise, Sinn Féin's popularity with nationalists had increased and it had become a formidable political force, strong enough to claim two of the twelve seats in the new Executive. But many unionists were not convinced by Sinn Féin's promises of peace. Only a tissue-thin majority of unionists had backed the Agreement when it was ratified in the 22 May referendum that followed the deal. And at a subsequent Assembly poll, on 10 June, anti-Agreement unionism, although fractured, had gained ground.

Many unionists, including senior members of Trimble's party, were horrified that the unionist leader was about to share power with Martin McGuinness, an IRA leader who had reputedly spent most of his life engaged in a bloody campaign to drive the "Brits" out of Ireland. By those standards, Fitt was no rebel; Trimble was about to sit down face-to-face with the real thing. In fact, Lord Fitt, at seventy-two years of age, had been so excited by this dramatic event that he had travelled to Stormont on devolution day to see the new regime for himself.

Trimble's motives for his political gamble became the subject of much speculation. Was his foray into Room 21 merely a tactical manoeuvre to outwit his republican opponents? Was he appearing flexible to appease the British government in the certain knowledge that power-sharing would soon fail, with republicans taking the blame for not decommissioning? Or was he genuinely interested in sharing power and testing the republican movement's willingness to disarm? Perhaps he recognised the arrogance of the former Stormont Prime Minister Johnny Andrews, who once declared Ulster was safe for 1,000 years. Perhaps Trimble understood that to preserve the Union he had to share power with nationalists and Catholics, who were growing in number and influence in Northern Ireland.

Trimble defended his decision to accept the Agreement and power-sharing with Sinn Féin by insisting it secured the Union, arguing that power-sharing with republicans was the key to getting the IRA to decommission its weapons.

Under the terms of the Agreement the Irish government was required to remove from its constitution its territorial claim over the Six Counties. It also had to revoke the Anglo-Irish Agreement (AIA), negotiated over the heads of unionists in 1985 by the Thatcher government. The Irish government had complied that very morning in Dublin when a new treaty was signed by Irish Foreign Minister David Andrews and Secretary of State for Northern Ireland Peter Mandelson. In a tangible symbol of the new era, a few hours later the Irish President, Mary McAleese, lunched with the Queen at Buckingham Palace.

Removing the territorial claim and replacing the hated *diktat*, as unionists described the AIA, had given David Trimble the confidence to share power with nationalists and to take part in cross-border cooperation through the new North South Ministerial Council (NSMC), which was due to be formed later that month.

Trimble already had an historical link with Room 21, and an ironic one at that. A generation earlier he had raised eyebrows in that room for advocating power-sharing just a year after Sunningdale had collapsed. As a member of a newly formed coalition of like-minded unionists, the United Ulster Unionist Council (UUUC) – which had defeated Faulkner – Trimble was attending a group meeting in Room 21, then numbered Room 17. (Numbers were re-jigged after the 1995 fire at Stormont.) Satisfied that Sunningdale and its unpalatable North–South arrangements had been defeated, Trimble had advocated power-sharing with the SDLP in a new devolved assembly. The other UUUC members gathered in "Room 21" were appalled and he was thrown out of the Council for making the audacious proposal. "That was in my so-called right-wing days," he remarked wryly, years later.

A quarter century on, those ready to cry "sell-out" still hovered. A potent reminder of anti-Agreement unionist sentiment was the lone protestor who sailed through Stormont's Great Hall on devolution day, holding aloft a placard that read: "For sale: Ulster. Contact D Trimble." He shouted "traitor" before being escorted from the building.

Ignoring these cries, David Trimble entered Room 21. It was a rather elegant chamber, with panelled walls, chandeliers and patterned burgundy carpet and its east window faced the burial plot of Lord Craigavon, Stormont's first Prime Minister. That day, it was dominated by a round, blue-trimmed mahogany table, set with eleven glasses and bottles of water alongside eleven nameplates, one for each of the ministers present – the First Minister David Trimble, the Deputy First Minister, Seamus Mallon, the Ulster Unionist ministers Michael McGimpsey, Sam Foster, and Sir Reg Empey, the SDLP's Bríd Rodgers, Mark Durkan, Sean Farren and Sinn Féin's Martin McGuiness and Bairbre de Brun – and one for the head of the civil service, Sir John Semple. In this unique coalition of unionists, nationalists and republicans there should have been twelve ministers from either side of the divide. But the DUP ministers were refusing to come to the power-sharing table with Sinn Féin. Therefore, the nameplates of the two DUP ministers, Peter Robinson and Nigel Dodds, had been quietly removed. In the referendum campaign of May 1998 Paisley's Democratic Unionist party had campaigned against the Good Friday Agreement and lost. Nevertheless the party had adopted a policy of taking ministries, but not attending power-sharing meetings. So instead of twelve ministers around the table, there would be only ten.

The order of the nameplates had been carefully worked out in advance by civil servants, who were primarily concerned with the other ministers' reaction to McGuinness and de Brun. It was arranged that the two Sinn Féin ministers would sit together in the circle. Sir John Semple would sit between McGuinness and Trimble, who had Mallon to his left along with the other SDLP ministers. De Brun, wearing a green suit, was placed between McGuinness and the unionists as some kind of buffer. According to a senior Stormont official: "A lot of thought went into how the seating should be arranged. But nobody ever asked about it. The ministers didn't."

McGuinness was among the last to arrive. After a quick glance at the nameplates he nervously grabbed the chair he believed had been allocated to him. He had, however, misread a nameplate bearing the same initials of a name roughly the same length as his own. Trimble, who was already seated and waiting for his colleagues, smiled, almost to himself, and shyly ventured, "Hello, Mr McGimpsey." At first McGuinness was confused, then blushed and released a hearty laugh. "First mistake," he grinned. It broke the tension, as the old foes laughed nervously together.

The first meeting of the Northern Ireland Executive lasted around seventy-five minutes and was basically a formality. Mark Durkan, SDLP minister, remembered there was a degree of excitement in the room: "But it was more a matter of relief to be there rather than any big sense of anticipation." The SDLP's Sean Farren was overheard to remark that anyone listening to the proceedings would not have been able to separate the parties along their old divisions. A civil servant described a good atmosphere: "People were delighted that they had got where they had got to."

Not everyone shared this sense of possibility, however. DUP leader Ian Paisley struck a sour note when he declared: "This is not a daybreak, not a new dawn. This is a new night and one does not know what the midnight will be." Paisley always liked to say he was neither a prophet nor the son of a prophet, but in this summation he was correct. The midnight hour would prove a bedevilling one in the days and months to come.

Nonetheless, the ten ministers gathered in Room 21 allowed themselves some cautious hope, some sense of potential – reasons to take the first step on this unpredictable political journey. Each had travelled their own unique path and they had around them that day many well-wishers, as well as political commentators and curious observers. Stormont was packed with people, among them reporters from around the world, camera crews crushed beside American politicians, such as Congressmen Peter King and Richard Neal, and a few figures from the Sunningdale era, including Gusty Spence, a former loyalist paramilitary leader who, from his prison cell, had sympathised with loyalist efforts to destroy Sunningdale over the Council of Ireland. He had been jailed for the 1966 murder of a Catholic teenager, but had eventually broken with his violent past and embraced the Good Friday Agreement. He was spotted standing in the corner, talking to one of his old enemies, John Kelly, once a well-known figure in the IRA and now a member of the Assembly. Amid this odd melee, looking almost like a tourist, was Gerry Adams. The Sinn Féin leader had brought his own camera to capture the day's events.

But it was Press Association photographer Paul Faith who got the official portrait of the ministers; he was the only stills photographer permitted into Room 21. Posing for the camera, Deputy First Minister Seamus Mallon spun around in his chair, turning towards Trimble. Camera poised, Paul Faith pressed the button, and the moment was recorded for posterity.

Mallon looked particularly pleased, his smile as wide as Trimble's. He had been deeply affected by the magnitude of the events that day. Mallon could be contrary and his manner was often gruff, but he was a highly emotional and sensitive man. Twenty months earlier, on the morning the Good Friday Agreement had been signed, an agreement he had spent half his life trying to achieve, Mallon had emerged exhausted and exhilarated. Tears welled in his eyes as he answered questions about the significance of the deal, declaring it the proudest day of his political career. He told a *Belfast Telegraph* reporter that he would go home and have a pint of Guinness, or a large whiskey or two, in quiet celebration.

While Mallon had allowed himself to be carried by the moment, a cautionary note was struck by the Irish government official Dermot Brangan, who knew Mallon's journey was far from over. He told the same *Belfast Telegraph* reporter that it would take at least three to five years to implement the Agreement. When he was branded a pessimist, Brangan was taken aback and protested, "I was being optimistic." He did indeed prove to be an optimist. Mallon, in turn, would be sobered by his own experiences between the signing of the Agreement on 10 April 1998 and devolution day on 2 December 1999 when powers would be transferred from Westminster to Stormont, finally opening the door to Room 21.

Chapter 2
Assembling in the Shadows

Seamus Mallon passed through the gates of the Stormont estate, motored up Prince of Wales Avenue, lined with yew and lime trees, and stopped at the roundabout where Lord Carson beckoned. Immortalised in bronze, with his right hand raised in triumph, the architect of the union stood high on a plinth, surveying his domain. Carson was a familiar, if unwelcome, sight to nationalists such as Mallon. Behind Carson, high on the hill at the peak of the estate, was another reminder of the old Northern Ireland: Parliament Buildings, a neo-classical structure of Portland stone, dazzling white under the July sun. Parliament Buildings had long been a symbol of the past, of one-party unionist rule. "Mallon hated the building," said a colleague. "Hated it. Hated the architecture, hated what it represented."

Even so, Mallon felt optimistic that Stormont could come to represent a new order. Mallon had journeyed to Stormont almost thirty years earlier, as a young man, passionate about the prospect of change. He was heartened by the power-sharing deal between his party and the Ulster Unionists, but the partnership forged at Sunningdale, in Berkshire, in December 1973 lasted just a few short months. By the spring of 1974 it had collapsed. Power-sharing had proved too little for republicans wedded to violent revolution, and too much for loyalists threatened by change.

A generation on, Mallon, now white-haired, was desperate for another chance to try, another chance to shake off the burden of the past and move forward into a new future. It was the morning of 1 July 1998, and the new power-sharing Assembly was due to meet at Stormont for the first time. The most important item on the agenda was the election of a First and Deputy First Minister to lead the new administration. One a unionist, the other a nationalist, they would be jointly nominated and jointly elected. However, the Assembly chamber at Parliament Buildings was no more ready than some sections of the Northern Ireland population for the changes about to occur – the chamber was still being refurbished after a fire in 1995. So instead of heading up the hill to the steps of Stormont, Mallon circled Carson's statue and turned down towards the more austere Castle Buildings, where a make-shift debating chamber had been arranged for the new power-sharing Assembly's inaugural meeting.

For some days there had been speculation that Mallon would be nominated Deputy First Minister that afternoon. But inside Castle Buildings, drinking tea and reading the morning papers, Mallon found no clue as to his destiny and was uncertain what his party leader, John Hume, intended to do. The *Irish News* was not alone in reporting that Hume would most likely fill the post.

As he perused the papers, Mallon was wondering why his Assembly colleagues were so late when he was spotted by the Ulster Unionist deputy leader John Taylor. "You're in the wrong place," Taylor advised him. The Ulster Unionist informed Mallon that the SDLP was meeting in the Wellington Park Hotel in South Belfast. Irritated and muttering under his breath, Mallon made his way across the city to the hotel, where it had been arranged that the SDLP leader and deputy leader would make a triumphant entrance into the conference room to the cheers of their Assembly team. By the time Mallon arrived, there was a bit of a panic over his whereabouts. As he was hustled into the room, Mallon felt a tug at his elbow. It was his party leader. "This Deputy First Minister thing," whispered Hume. "You'd better do it. The doctors tell me I shouldn't do it. You had better do it."

Mallon's jaw tightened. He had been wondering when Hume was going to get around to this subject. Despite past experience of his leader's secretive nature, Mallon had presumed that Hume would have given him more than a few hours' notice. In fact, Hume had been with him in Dublin for the past few days, but throughout the trip had kept his deputy guessing as to his intentions regarding the Deputy First Minister's post.

Hume had been informed – belatedly apparently – that under European Union rules he could not be both a Euro MP and the Deputy First Minister of Northern Ireland. David Trimble believed Hume had been lobbying in vain in London and in Europe to try and change this but when this was put to Hume, he was aghast: "Not at all. Such nonsense! It couldn't happen." Hume knew he would have to choose between Strasbourg and Stormont – and there was no question of his giving up his seat in Europe, a position he cherished. Even if he was minded to, there was uncertainty over his health and the Deputy First Minister's job would have been extremely taxing, both mentally and physically. These factors had fuelled speculation that Mallon would be nominated and elected Deputy First Minister, but Hume had made no statement on the matter, nor had his party.

Mallon himself knew, and had known for some weeks, about the rules barring Hume from holding office and remaining an MEP. But, bizarrely, with the election of the First and Deputy First Minister looming, Hume had kept his counsel during their business trip. While in Dublin, Mallon had been summoned by the Taoiseach, Bertie Ahern, who had sent his driver around to collect him. On the eve of the Assembly's first session the Taoiseach wanted to be briefed by Mallon on the unfolding political situation. But if the Taoiseach knew that Mallon was going to be the new Deputy First Minister, he too said nothing.

On their last evening in Dublin, Mallon dropped into the bar of the Merrion Hotel and he bumped into a bevy of Irish officials, holding court with none other than Hume. Mallon would, on occasion, recount the story, pausing for effect and speaking in rhythmic tones, first clipped, then droll and slow: "My leader was there – in taciturn form. I went over and asked him what he'd like to drink. Hume said, 'Nothing thanks' and I knew right off something was going on!" It was not the first time Hume had failed to inform his deputy about what was happening.

Now, in the Wellington Park Hotel, with hardly a moment's notice on his new posting, Mallon was seething. He protested to Hume, through clenched teeth, that he had been given no time to prepare and told Hume that he had seen him in Dublin the night before and he had not even mentioned it. But Hume insisted, "I have to announce it now."

Mallon could hardly have refused. Even so, some in the party suspected he resented the way Hume had handled the matter. "It really wasn't right," said a senior party source.

"There was such an historic speech to be made [that day]. Seamus hadn't even a speech written. I think John had difficulty coming to actually accept he wasn't going to be the Deputy First Minister." A former SDLP chairman and Member of the Legislative Assembly (MLA), Joe Byrne, explained Hume's reluctance to cede power to Mallon: "He likes to be totally in control."

At the time, it was not reported how Mallon had been treated and in an early interview for this book he was diplomatic when questioned about it: "I'd have much preferred if something was said to me, or he had said to me that night in Dublin, 'Will you think about this?' But it didn't happen that way." Mallon would not be drawn on Hume's motives. Why did he behave this way – did he harbour the notion of taking the job himself? Mallon's reply was a terse, "I don't know." In a later interview for *Room 21*, he was more forthcoming about Hume's behaviour:

> "Let's put it this way, and whatever the reason, and whatever the set of circumstances, it could have been done the night before, the day before, two hours before, three hours before – a week before. Because I knew for six weeks that because of his European Parliament membership he couldn't [take the job] … Let anybody judge it."

Asked why he waited until the last possible minute to tell Mallon his fate, Hume seemed taken aback by the question: "I assumed he knew. It was known that it wasn't going to be me. Who else was it going to be?" But on the morning of the crucial vote the SDLP spokesman could not confirm to reporters which of them would be Deputy First Minister – and an early edition of the *Belfast Telegraph* suggested it would be Hume.

A veteran of the party was not alone in thinking Hume had an understandable desire to stay centre stage. Like any successful politician he had a healthy ego, and no leader, especially one of Hume's standing, relinquishes power easily. He had enjoyed a remarkable political career by any standards, by the end of which he had helped to forge the peace process through talks with Sinn Féin leader Gerry Adams, which ultimately led to the Good Friday Agreement.

One party insider told a story that illustrates how difficult it was for Hume to stand aside after so many years at the centre of political events. Despite his delight at devolution, it was claimed Hume was feeling a little left out when power was finally transferred to the new Executive in December 1999. Hume, who had laid the foundations for the Agreement through his talks with Adams, was stung by the reality that he was not going to be a player in the new administration. Adams, too, had decided against taking a place in the Executive. Their absence was underscored when the power-sharing Executive's picture was splashed all over the newspapers and on television, both at home and abroad, with articles on the new ministers and all the new committee chairmen and deputies. The source recalled Hume roaming the corridors of Stormont, and wandering into the office of the party's director of communications, Barry Turley. Hume pointed at the newspaper's front-page image of the new ministerial line-up and complained: "You know, there are two faces missing there." Turley, a huge admirer of Hume, no doubt knew what he meant, but feigned ignorance. "Who's missing?" he enquired.

"Me and Adams," Hume muttered, "and we started the whole damn thing!" He went out and slammed the door behind him.

While there had been doubt about Mallon's fate, there was no question about who would become the First Minister. The leader of the largest party was David Trimble and as Ulster Unionist leader he was widely expected to take the post. Even so, Trimble claimed to have been a reluctant First Minister. Astonishingly, he said he would have preferred to concentrate on Westminster. Sitting in the Europa Hotel, sipping tea on a winter's afternoon in 2004, Trimble recalled trying to coax his deputy, John Taylor, to take the post. Taylor was an MP, a former minister in the old Stormont and had helped negotiate the Agreement. "I tried very hard to persuade John Taylor to become First Minister," Trimble said. "I thought he had the experience and the personality and in many respects he would do a better job or have the right talents."

Taylor, later Lord Kilclooney, was a wily politician and was appalled at the notion that anyone other than the leader should be First Minister. He firmly resisted Trimble's overture and also rebuffed efforts to encourage him to accept a ministerial post. Then aged sixty-two, he insisted he wanted to focus on his responsibilities in Westminster and Europe and suggested that younger party members be given a chance. "That's the reason – age," he said, musing that Sam Foster, who was older than he, did accept a ministerial post. Taylor instead had the honour of proposing Trimble and Mallon for the top posts.

Trimble's apparent reluctance to take on the role of First Minister no doubt reflected the nervousness felt by many unionists about the new power-sharing administration. As unionist leader, Trimble was not only haunted by the ghost of Brian Faulkner, whose ill-fated attempt at power-sharing had cost him his leadership and split his party, but he also had to endure the ridicule of Faulkner's old nemesis: the Reverend Ian Paisley. The leader of the Democratic Unionist party, a powerful orator whose uncompromising brand of politics was mixed with a deep-rooted Protestant fundamentalism, remained an influential figure in Northern Ireland politics. Like Hume, he was a member of the European Parliament as well as being a Westminster MP and a member of the new Assembly. Paisley had made a career out of saying "no" and crying "sell-out" and had been instrumental in Faulkner's fall from grace. While Trimble knew the latest compromise forged through the Good Friday Agreement was a painful step for unionists, he was acutely conscious that it was unthinkable for almost half the unionist electorate, who had followed the DUP lead in vehemently opposing the Agreement.

Paisley, who had left the multi-party talks in protest when Sinn Féin gained entry without IRA weapons being decommissioned, appeared determined to destroy the Agreement, just as he had helped smash Sunningdale. What was different this time, however, was that the loyalist paramilitaries, chastened by years of conflict, had opted to give the Agreement a chance. Two former members of the Ulster Volunteer Force (UVF) had been elected to the Assembly on a pro-Agreement ticket. They represented the Progressive Unionist party and Trimble would need their backing if he were to be elected First Minister because anti-Agreement unionists remained a potent force in the new 108-member Assembly.

The Assembly poll three weeks earlier, on 10 June, had delivered a fractious result for unionism, which had collectively taken 58 of the seats. Trimble's Ulster Unionist party did not have a majority of these seats, having won just 28. This was significant because Assembly rules dictated that a majority of unionists, as well as a majority of nationalists, had to take key decisions, one being the election of the First and Deputy First Minister. The Ulster Unionists were two short of a majority. The PUP could be relied upon to provide the extra votes, but the DUP and their anti-Agreement allies collectively had 28 seats – just short of a majority. The balance of power in the Assembly was not a good omen, particularly when a number of Trimble's Assembly team were deeply sceptical about the new arrangements.

While unionism was split over the deal, an overwhelming majority of nationalists and republicans backed the Agreement. The SDLP had taken 24 seats, giving it a comfortable majority on the nationalist side, while Sinn Féin's 18 seats gave it a minority role. Unlike Trimble's party, the SDLP was solidly pro-Agreement and would be strong enough to pass decisions independent of their tribal rivals. Sinn Féin, however, had enough support to command two seats at the power-sharing table: a prospect that horrified many unionists who had suffered fiercely at the hands of the IRA.

Persuading the IRA to decommission its arsenal of weapons was just one of the massive challenges facing the new administration. Trimble's party had tried and failed to pin down the arms issue on the last day of GFA negotiations. It had almost resulted in no deal, but after assurances from Prime Minister Tony Blair – who wrote a side-letter pledging to exclude from power-sharing those not exclusively committed to democratic and peaceful means – Trimble had accepted the Agreement, even as one of his key negotiators, Jeffrey Donaldson, walked away from the talks and the deal.

Donaldson had protested that the decommissioning part of the deal left unionists with no guarantees that the IRA would ever give up a single weapon. However, Trimble was not prepared to abandon the negotiations – not least because he wanted to avoid unionism being blamed for yet another failed deal. He also dreaded unionism being further marginalised. Trimble feared that the Prime Minister would, like Thatcher before him, punish unionists by moving closer to the nationalist position and pursuing closer relations with Dublin over the heads of unionists.

Trimble refused to accept that decommissioning, as outlined in the Agreement, was merely aspirational, with all parties committed to using their influence to bring it about by May 2000 in the context of the full implementation of the Agreement. For republicans, this meant power-sharing before decommissioning. For unionists, it meant the opposite. As a consequence, David Trimble's party had made an election promise not to share power with Sinn Féin without IRA decommissioning, a move the Sinn Féin leadership regarded as a tactical error that stunted political progress for years.

Republicans suspected that demands for decommissioning were a red herring and that unionists were using the weapons issue to mask their distaste for power-sharing with Sinn Féin. They continually questioned Trimble's commitment to the deal. Sinn Féin's chief negotiator, Martin McGuinness, recalled observing Trimble on Good Friday, the last day of the talks, when the party leaders were asked to vote "yes" for the Agreement. In the formal final plenary session, McGuinness claimed Trimble had used a pencil, rather than his finger, to press the button on the intercom system to declare his approval for the deal. According to McGuinness, "His pencil almost broke and in my view this was a man who was experiencing great difficulty and I remember saying to Gerry Adams at the time that this was only the beginning of our troubles." Trimble said this was nonsense. The Ulster Unionist leader, in turn, was deeply sceptical about the commitment of the republican movement to the Agreement, which required everyone to use exclusively peaceful and democratic means to achieve their political aims. The Ulster Unionist leader believed that the IRA was still preparing for war while Sinn Féin talked peace and would be prepared to return to conflict if their demands for Irish national reunification were not delivered by the new arrangements.

As he made his own way to Stormont that day, Trimble was brooding over the decommissioning issue; he had already concluded that devolution would only be possible if decommissioning were forthcoming. He had time to make his arguments as it would be some months before the other ministers were appointed. The structure of the new devolved administration had to be settled first, and only then could the Executive be formed and power transferred from London. The Assembly had no power as yet. It was meeting in shadow form until devolution and the First and Deputy First Minister would, in effect, be shadow ministers.

Journalist Frank Millar, in his book on David Trimble, *The Price of Peace*, provided some insight into Trimble's thinking at the time. The Ulster Unionist leader admitted he viewed the Agreement as being like a constitution and therefore as a "work in progress" and that he intended to use the shadow period after the Assembly elections to achieve decommissioning. Trimble also confirmed in that book that initially he had thought he could form an administration with the SDLP and leave out Sinn Féin. Indeed, one senior republican believed Trimble had misinterpreted Sinn Féin's slogan, "No return to Stormont", which referred to the old one, not the new one. The exclusion of Sinn Féin could not be delivered because the SDLP refused to cut the republican party loose, believing this would undermine the stability of the new arrangements and be contrary to the Agreement. While the SDLP insisted it was committed to the letter of the Agreement, Trimble also told Millar he did not regard the Agreement as "Holy Writ".

This fundamental difference in approach can be likened to two people buying a property together and then fighting over the contract they have drawn up. It did not make for smooth relations. Mallon would ultimately conclude that Trimble was politically and emotionally afraid of the Agreement, even though he supported it intellectually.

In the hours before his election Trimble had more than decommissioning on his mind. More immediately there was Drumcree, the annual marching dispute in Portadown that was another symptom of the old conflict between unionists and nationalists, Catholics and Protestants. Members of the Protestant and Unionist Orange Order were demanding the right to march along their traditional route on the Garvaghy Road, despite vehement opposition from local Catholic nationalist residents. Tensions over the parade – which was due to take place within days of the new Assembly's debut – were running as high as ever that summer. While the North's new future beckoned, Drumcree was becoming a rallying point for anti-Agreement unionists still wedded to the past.

Drumcree lay in the heart of Trimble's Upper Bann constituency, and he was worried. His mood – captured by a documentary TV crew travelling with him to Castle Buildings that day – appeared sullen and in stark contrast to the overwhelming excitement at home and abroad about the new administration. Headlines around the world boasted of a new peaceful era in Northern Ireland. Inside the chamber, where the new First and Deputy First Minister would be elected, the atmosphere was thick with an odd mixture of history, hatred and hope. Old enemies, some of whom had been directly involved in armed conflict and had only ever viewed one another via their television screens, eyeballed each other from across the room. The makeshift chamber with its functional pine furniture and plum-coloured chairs seemed all too ordinary given the events unfolding.

After more than ninety minutes of business the new presiding officer, Lord Alderdice – initially appointed, amid some controversy, by the Secretary of State and kept in post when no other candidate came forward – called for nominations for the First and Deputy First Minister. Taylor rose to his feet to make the joint nomination. "I am proposing two men who have shown vision and leadership," Taylor told the Assembly, naming David Trimble and "my good friend" Seamus Mallon, who he said would work for the good of Northern Ireland. The proposal was seconded by John Hume. "I accept," said Trimble. His words were swiftly echoed by Mallon.

It was the "I do" in a political marriage of convenience, where neither partner had time to build any kind of rapport after years of bitter opposition. Like any wedding, the speeches began immediately, first the Sinn Féin president and then the DUP leader. Paisley had tried to speak first, but Gerry Adams had beaten him to it. Earlier, the Sinn Féin leader, unschooled in the ways of Parliamentary procedure never having taken up his seat at Westminster, was chided from the DUP benches for failing to stand as he raised a point of order. Adams mumbled an embarrassed "sorry" before recovering his composure and declaring lightheartedly: "I thought I was standing up… I am certainly standing up for the rights of the people who sent me here."

In his formal speech, Adams became the first person to speak in Irish in the new Assembly – to even greater mutterings from the DUP benches. Lord Alderdice called order, but Paisley protested, "If we could understand him, we might give him order!" Lord Alderdice chastised the DUP, and Adams began again:

> *"Agus as seo amach, agus b'fhéidir má éisteann an Dochtúir Paisley liom, beidh a fhios aige faoinár dteanga féin, agus b'fhéidir go gcuirfidh duine éigin* 'manners' *ar an fhear udaí. Go raibh míle maith agaibh."*

While Paisley sat scowling, Adams spoke in Irish about putting manners on the DUP leader. Adams also offered his support to the new office-holders, wishing them well, and then focused on the need for change: the very thing Paisley did not want. Adams indicated that his party would be abstaining in the vote for the top posts out of concern for the unionist leader: "We might not be doing Mr Trimble any favour by voting for him. Other unionists would be only too pleased to beat him up."

When it was his turn to speak, Paisley led a chorus of opposition from unionists who neither supported the Agreement nor the anticipated inclusion of Sinn Féin in any devolved administration. He railed about the past brutality of the IRA, and demanded decommissioning.

When Trimble spoke, he did not underestimate the difficulties ahead nor the terrors of the past, but declared his intention to lead the community out of the morass of political violence. By reversing direct rule he wanted to put unionism back at the centre of influence and reconnect the community with the rest of the body politic. He stressed the importance of establishing a firm and lasting commitment to the democratic process. He acknowledged that some present in the chamber had done terrible things, but pointed out this was not confined to one corner – a clear reference to those involved in loyalist violence. He wanted to give space for people to change and, looking directly at Sinn Féin, he declared: "We have never said … the fact that someone has a certain past means he cannot have a future." He concluded with an assertion that his party would not be blamed for want of effort if the process failed: "We have started on the long march to a better future. The opportunity must not be discarded."

When Seamus Mallon rose to speak he thanked the members who had nominated him for their kind and generous words. "All true," he declared to a ripple of laughter. Turning to the opposition unionists, he said his party stood by the promise of the Agreement, which envisaged decommissioning, and insisted devolution would help bring it about. And in a jibe to those unionists, some within Trimble's own party, who had opposed him, Mallon added, "I look forward to working with Mr Trimble. I have known him a long time. We have not always agreed, and there will still be times when we disagree, but the disagreements will be sorted out face to face, for I am sure that his back is sore enough."

Mallon, characteristically, also talked in idealist terms that afternoon. Some observers noted he had referred to "Northern Ireland" rather than the "north of Ireland", as was his custom, but he insisted this was not deliberate. Unionists, however, who found the latter term grating, thought it was important. Mallon spoke of a "new vision, and a new imagination for a new century". Also characteristically, he tempered his remarks with a note of realism: "There will be difficulties. But we can all help each other. My difficulties are David Trimble's and David Trimble's are mine."

Minutes later, in their first official photograph as shadow First and Deputy First Minister, Trimble and Mallon were shaking hands, looking at each other with rather tight, mistrustful smiles as an approving Assembly speaker looked on. The clock read 18:01, as if time had moved on from the Act of Union of 1800. But both would soon find that the past is never very far away, drawing Northern Ireland into old battles and threatening to make time stand still. As leaders of the new administration, Trimble and Mallon carried the burden of history, the burden of the new order and the burden of two conflicting personalities.

Chapter 3
The Odd Couple

Two men, one Catholic, the other Protestant, made the headline news that day. Theirs was a rare relationship, one that refused to be chained by prejudice. Perhaps it was their simple friendship, coupled with flickering hints of a new future that spring, which made what happened to them so cruel, so callous and so criminal.

On the evening of 3 March 1998 the two men were enjoying a drink together in the Railway bar in Poyntzpass, a village outside Newry with a population of just 300 and a reputation for religious tolerance. Philip Allen was planning to marry his sweetheart soon and Damian Trainor was to be his best man. The men were chatting over a pint when masked loyalist gunmen burst in. "Get down on the floor, you bastards," they screamed, spraying the little country pub with bullets.

Seamus Mallon was among the first to hear the news. Poyntzpass was on the edge of his constituency and the MP for Newry and Armagh knew the bar well. It was owned by the brother of an SDLP colleague, Armagh councillor Tom Kavanagh, who immediately telephoned Castle Buildings to tell Mallon of the horrific shooting. The SDLP deputy leader was working late that night, engaged in the talks aimed at hammering out an historic compromise with unionists. Deeply distressed by the news, Mallon made his way to the village.

The philosopher Friedrich Nietzsche famously wrote that it is the painful experiences, burned in our memory, that stay with us because they never cease to hurt. Years after Poyntzpass, Mallon would let out a deep sigh as he recalled the tragic events and the fate of Trainor and Allen. "Oh, it was a very bleak night. I remember standing at the corner, talking to a number of people there and a senior police officer took me aside to tell me the men were both dead."

The morning after the murders Mallon returned to the village to pay his respects to the families of his murdered constituents. It was a stark reminder of the darkest days of the past with its unremitting violence, when he would wake to news of the latest killing, when there was no hope in the air, times he called "the dog years of political vacuum". For much of Mallon's life such bloody murders had been virtually unrelenting and he had spent years, an era spanning more than three decades, walking behind coffins, comforting the bereaved and arguing to convince gunmen that there was a better way.

In Poyntzpass the media presence was gradually swelling and Mallon was being interviewed by a reporter in the street when he spotted a solitary red-headed figure. David Trimble, Ulster Unionist leader and MP for Upper Bann, had also felt compelled to go to the village, which was near the boundaries of his own constituency. Apart from his police driver, Trimble was alone. Mallon went to speak to him and they agreed to go together to pay their respects. Mallon suggested they journey on foot, leaving the cars behind; the shrewd politician knew what a potent image the pair walking together would make.

These two politicians had known each other for years, as they were both Westminster MPs. They had shared cups of tea and worked on various pieces of legislation, sometimes at cross-purposes but not always. More recently they were used to being together at the talks table. They had long been on opposite sides of the divide and politically they were polls apart. However it was not an unfriendly relationship, according to Mallon.

Despite being fierce opponents politically, a sense of duty, a common purpose and a shared outrage united them in Poyntzpass. Inside the homes of the dead men's relatives, Mallon was impressed by Trimble, a man he felt was uncomfortable with emotion, afraid of it. "He would have seen it as a sign of weakness," Mallon would say. Looking back years later, he believed the real David Trimble surfaced that day in these private meetings with grieving families: "I will never forget sitting in both those houses and that emotion was actually raw. If we could have translated that emotion somehow back into the political process in a more public way, then I think his problems and indeed the problems of Northern Ireland might not be as deep as they are today."

After the condolences, they gave an impromptu news conference to the media in the village and their message was clear: the murderers may have killed two men, but they would not kill the future that politicians were trying to map out at the multi-party talks. Trimble, the voice of unionism, and Mallon, the voice of nationalism, spoke with harmony, promising that this "deliberate" attempt to block any agreement would fail. "The people who carried out these murders," Mallon declared, "will not be able to drive a wedge between us."

One eye-witness recalled the power of their joint presence. "It was palpable," he said, "watching Mallon with his arm around David Trimble, taking him to meet people." The SDLP negotiator Mark Durkan was also watching that day. Seeing Trimble and Mallon together inspired him. He returned to the talks table with the concept of a First and Deputy First Minister in the new Executive. "Literally, binding the wounds," Durkan would later say.

However, others close to the negotiations insist that a myth has grown up around the significance of Poyntzpass and the inspiration it provided to the concept for the twin ministers. A senior Sinn Féin figure claimed the idea of a binary department was, in fact, inspired by what negotiators had learned in South Africa some months earlier. Mitchel McLaughlin pointed out that the model was similar to the one that operated in the South African government for national unity. Whatever the inspiration, Poyntzpass had shown with cruel clarity the price paid for failure. It also held out the promise of what was possible, if they worked together. "We are going to do our best to bring peace," Trimble pledged to reporters.

The two men left the village that day with a powerful resolve. They may have sensed it, but they could not have known it at the time, not for sure, that within five nerve-wracking weeks they would deliver the Good Friday Agreement. And within four months they would be jointly elected by a majority of nationalists and unionists in a new assembly, to head the first power-sharing Executive in a generation. Indeed, this was Trimble and Mallon at their best. Adversity threw them together, and once united they projected a powerful image to a divided society. In truth, however, the unity was more symbolic than real. The pair never really got on nor did they ever develop a warm rapport or understanding as they came to share power. "This bonding was a media invention," said a senior civil servant who worked at the heart of their administration.

Such moments of unity, while necessary, would be unusual in this uneasy political alliance, which like the history that bound them would be at times tense, at times turbulent and at times unbearable. "The chemistry between Trimble and Mallon, when it worked well, was brilliant," recalled one official. "You'd nearly have a tear in your eye. But when it didn't work, it was bad."

It was not surprising that theirs was a turbulent relationship. These were two very different people, already set in their ways and rather wary of each other when they were joined in a political marriage of convenience on 1 July 1998. The power-sharing deal gave them another chance to resolve the ills in their society and forge a new beginning. But their challenge of working in harmony – Herculean in historic terms – was made all the more difficult by the complexities of the new regime in which they had to manoeuvre. By the time they came to office, each had firm views about the other – and they were not terribly positive impressions from either perspective.

"Personality-wise they didn't like each other," says one senior civil servant. "David Trimble had a very historic view of Mallon and Mallon had a very historic view of Trimble and added to that was the personality thing. They were just totally different." An SDLP source who had observed their relationship up close during power-sharing said the chemistry was simply lacking: "They didn't like one another. Mallon couldn't stand Trimble." The pair had little in common and 800 years of history to separate them. They were not just a political contrast, but a physical, emotional and intellectual one as well. "Chalk and cheese," was how the SDLP higher education minister Sean Farren put it. An official in the administration had another description: "Mallon had the air of the old schoolmaster; Trimble the slightly-off-the-wall academic." They were literally an odd couple, as different as today and tomorrow.

When they took up their posts, Trimble was fifty-three and Mallon sixty-one. Trimble had the energy of a younger man; Mallon was reported to be suffering from angina and low blood pressure. Perhaps prematurely aged by the stress of the Troubles, Mallon had the look of a man whose shoulders had carried a lot of burdens and his face was deeply lined. Trimble was fresh-faced for a man of his age, with a ruddy complexion and dark auburn hair. Beside him, Mallon's ivory face, capped with snowy hair, seemed bloodless and he resembled a grandfatherly figure. Mallon would later joke that it was the strains of the process that had turned his complexion the colour of his hair.

There were other marked contrasts between the two men. Mallon tended to speak in lyrical colour, Trimble in clipped black-and-white; Mallon in poetry, Trimble in prose. With an actor's easy movement and a dramatist's gift for oratory, Mallon was extremely eloquent. "Mallon has an intrinsic set of values," observed one Irish diplomat. "That's why he is so articulate. He has a very clear sense in his head of what he wants." He loved poetry and often quoted favourite lines from Shakespeare or Joyce. One of his favourites was 'Ulysses' by Lord Tennyson. 'Old age hath yet its honour and its toil; Death closes all: but something ere the end, Some work of noble note, may yet be done' is a line he would often quote, according to SDLP colleague, Denis Haughey. "Seamus saw himself very much in that character of a man who has yet one more huge task to undertake," said Haughey.

Mallon had a flair for the dramatic and was slow, reflective and methodical in his manner, always choosing his words carefully. "Pipe-smoking steady," is the evocative phrase SDLP veteran Ivan Cooper used to describe him. Although moody, Mallon was much more constant in public, unlike the mercurial Trimble, who could be fidgety and helter-skelter in his movements, almost manic at times. One colleague likened Trimble's movements under pressure to "a hen on a hot griddle."

Colleagues and political opponents found Trimble to be a very impulsive character on occasion. Said one SDLP source in the administration: "He would agree to things you would think he would never agree to if you got him on the right day in a good mood." Nonetheless, Trimble had a fiery temper and a short fuse. "It descends like a red mist," said one former colleague. His face would flush and anti-Agreement unionists in the Assembly unkindly dubbed him "the purple turtle." One insider who worked closely with Trimble remembers him "losing it a lot … The finger wagging would then start," he said.

These outbursts also extended to the media. Sometimes he did not bother to argue, but simply exited abruptly. During a joint interview with Mallon for the BBC's "Good Morning, Ulster" programme in the autumn of 2000, Trimble revealed his impetuous side. The presenter, Seamus McKee, was pre-recording the interview in Belfast with the First and Deputy First Minister, who were in an office in Paris. The two ministers were in France to promote the Northern Ireland economy and the new administration and this was the intended subject of the interview. McKee let Trimble know that he also wanted to ask about an unfavourable court decision involving his ban on Sinn Féin. It would have appeared odd if he did not ask. Trimble – under intense pressure trying to juggle the peace process, his divided party and his duties as First Minister – insisted the interviewer stick to the subject at hand. He told McKee in no uncertain terms that he did not want the question asked – even if all that was required was a "no comment".

McKee made an effort to persuade him and then proceeded with the interview, but heard no response to his first question – just silence at the other end. After a reasonable pause McKee, fearing technical problems, made another attempt to speak to the First Minister. "Mr Trimble, are you there?" he asked. Silence. "Mr Trimble?" he persisted. More silence. Then he heard another voice saying, "I'm still here." It was the Deputy First Minister, who explained that the First Minister had departed. Mallon did the interview alone, and at the end McKee apologised for any misunderstanding that had occurred. "It's not a perfect world, I'm afraid," McKee told Mallon, who replied dryly, "Not the one I'm in, anyway."

A unionist colleague of Trimble's who worked with him during the turbulent years of his leadership found the unionist leader extremely intense. He could not imagine him relaxed and listening to classical music at home, something he said he did to unwind. "His hands were always moving, his face was always red, and when he was reading the paper, he'd just flick through it in two or three seconds and scan the page like a computer."

When he did get the chance to relax a little and enjoy a glass of his favourite red wine, Trimble could be perfectly pleasant. And when he was in good form, he could be rather droll. In 2004 he made headlines in *The Sun* newspaper following its revelation that it had sneaked an undercover reporter with a hoax bomb into the Palace of Westminster. Disguised as a waiter, the reporter had served the Ulster Unionist MP on the terrace and in his article had boasted: "I could have killed Trimble." When this headline was reported to Trimble, he joked, "I'll add him to the long list."

Flashes of humour aside, in the main Trimble was regarded as a cold fish, somewhat awkward and something of a loner. "He is not in politics to be popular," said a veteran journalist who had long observed him. "He is in it for the right reasons, to do the right thing, not to make friends." Trimble could be very formal. When he took up his post as shadow First Minister, one official remembered how different his approach was from Mallon's. The Deputy First Minister insisted on being called by his first name, instead of "Minister". "I was christened Seamus and I've always been known as Seamus. I'm not going to change now," he said. When Trimble was asked how he would like to be addressed, the official said the reply was, "We'll see."

Often uncomfortable in social settings, Trimble was essentially a shy person according to some who got to know him, including Maura Quinn (now Maura Campbell), who worked for him as his private secretary. She also found him to be very gracious and appreciative of staff. He was impatient with her only once, when she had forgotten to do something, and afterwards was apologetic that he had snapped at her. "I found him quite gentlemanly," she said.

Other civil servants also found him relatively easy to work for, although some noted that he was different, more difficult, around certain party colleagues and advisors. One said he could be quite moody. "Some days Trimble would come in quite touchy-feely and talk to you about the opera and the other days he would come in with a face like thunder and not speak." Several who have worked with him found his manner could be very brusque. Hugh Logue, who would become one of Mallon's advisors, recalled Trimble's personality as "dreadful". But another SDLP figure who occasionally encountered him always found him polite, quite reasonable and open to persuasion. Others in the party grew to admire him. One said: "I had great respect for him. He's a hard man to like but to be fair he was doing his best."

Even within the Ulster Unionist party, Trimble tended to keep to himself, or at least keep his ideas to himself, according to party colleagues who complained that policy was often dropped on them at the last minute. "No one around him knows what's going on," one UUP man would complain in frustration. "He does have vision but he doesn't articulate it."

Despite his weaknesses, Trimble was a man of great strengths, if not natural leadership abilities. Many politicians would have folded under the pressures he faced. His stamina and his ability to continue in the face of adversity were remarkable. His strongest qualities were his guts, determination and intelligence. Trimble was certainly intellectually gifted in the academic sense, but possibly lacked what is now known as emotional intelligence, an ability to relate well to other people – a sense or quality that charismatic politicians, such as former president Bill Clinton, have in abundance. Some found Trimble unfeeling, but Mallon's description of a man uncomfortable with emotion was probably more accurate. Some people who had worked closely with him formed the impression that Trimble failed to fathom why others became upset by his erratic or rude behaviour. Trimble has insisted he was quite well-mannered and that sometimes, because he coloured easily, people wrongly believed he was about to explode. "I've heard some people say I'm very rude. But I'm direct you know. I don't like beating around the bush," he is quoted as saying in *The Price of Peace*. Some of this behaviour may have been down to the stresses of the job, coupled with an impatient nature, but he insisted he was cool in a crisis and it was when he was less pressured that his irritation showed.

Some who had experienced Trimble's odd ways gave up trying to work him out, dismissing him as insensitive, rude, or just plain peculiar. Trimble shocked some onlookers at a ceremony in Washington in 1998 when the former talks chairman, Senator George Mitchell, was being awarded the highest honour in the United States: the Congressional Medal. President Clinton was leading the ceremony. Trimble had been reluctant to attend as he had lingered in private talks with Clinton and Adams, and the ceremony was now running late. Hoping to leave discreetly during an ovation he made his way out of the auditorium along with his wife, Daphne, but was surprised to discover he had to run a media gauntlet. Asked later by a curious observer why he had left, he said he had dinner reservations. The inquisitor, a prominent journalist, wondered who he was meeting for dinner, presuming it must have been someone especially important to cause him to leave in the middle of a Presidential address. But to his surprise, he discovered the dinner reservations were for Trimble and his wife. Trimble simply did not want to be late and leave Daphne waiting. "He could be very loyal that like in an odd kind of way," said one source. It would not be the last time the politician would surprise onlookers by failing to remain in his seat for President Bill Clinton.

Trimble's supporters insist he could be very sensitive to others. Mark Neale, one of his aides, recalled his kindness to him when he failed to win a seat in the Assembly poll in Upper Bann: "He can have an immense capacity for being compassionate. I remember after the Assembly election when I wasn't elected, and he said to me, 'This is all about you getting elected at a future date. You got the same vote I got [in 1975]'."

Unlike Trimble, Mallon had an easy charm and what could be called the common touch, so essential in a politician. "He knew how to talk to the boys in the bookies who backed horses," as one SDLP veteran put it. When he was in the mood, he liked company, storytelling and holding court into the wee small hours. Mallon could be stern and some in the administration found his manner cutting. He was, however, generally regarded as a more sociable character than Trimble, not as serious, someone who could communicate his emotions well and who had a well-developed sense of fun.

Mallon was renowned for his wit and his humour, which could be both entertaining and devastating. When loyalists daubed graffiti on a gable wall near his home with the message, "F— the Pope and hang Mallon", Mallon liked to say that the Pope got the better deal. One SDLP veteran described Mallon, who adored cowboy films, in macho terms: "Mallon is very, very much an old-fashioned man's man, a drinker, and gambler – horses, dogs, cards. He would sit up to play cards for three days and three nights." He was a renowned tipster and many a politician or official of varying shades has benefited from his gambling tips over the years. An oft-told story in SDLP circles involved a party weekend event in Donegal that coincided with the Grand National. Mallon had weighed the odds and was placing a carefully worked out bet of £60. Others in the party followed his lead with more modest wagers of £5 and £10. Cash on the horse tipped by Mallon was mounting in the town bookmakers when Hugh Logue, an SDLP member who worked for the European Commission in Brussels, arrived with his driver and suitcase. He too was redirected to the bookies by an enthusiastic party colleague. However, when Logue stepped into the betting shop carrying his suitcase, a panicked bookie, fearing a major sting was underway, slammed the shutters down, declaring: "We're closed!"

Trimble and Mallon's contrasting personalities were highlighted in their approach to the late Secretary of State, Mo Mowlam, who helped forge the Good Friday Agreement and was the first woman to hold the post in Northern Ireland. She was working class, earthy and totally informal. Her Christian name was Marjorie, but she preferred to be called Mo. Mallon felt she was a sympathetic character and found her informal irreverence refreshing after years of stiff-upper-lip British ministers. But Trimble regarded her as pro-nationalist, scatty and vulgar. He loathed her touchy-feely approach as much as Mallon loved it – and her. One official recalled: "When Mo would come up to see them, Mallon would throw his arms around her and kiss her and Trimble's reaction would be 'get away from me'."

For all his gregariousness, enjoyment of a drink and a flutter, especially on the horses, Mallon could be a prickly character and something of a loner, at times deeply unhappy or disgruntled. One SDLP colleague commented: "No one really knows him." For a politician, Mallon was intensely private and always shied away from discussing his personal life. For example, in December 1998 he was scheduled for a gall bladder operation at Daisy Hill Hospital and had instructed his family and close aides not to breathe a word: no one was to know.

The secret seemed safe until Sinn Féin press officer Dominic Doherty wandered over to a group of journalists standing with Mallon's press officer, Colin Ross, in the Great Hall of Parliament Buildings during a break in a bout of negotiations. Making small-talk, he mentioned Mallon and innocently ventured, within earshot of reporters: "I believe he's for the hospital." Doherty, not realising the sensitivity of this information, was immediately chided by Ross: "You've super-grassed!" But it was too late. Ross was hit with a barrage of questions about the state of Mallon's health. He had to come clean, but won the agreement of the press pack not to report it. It was not exactly world news, they agreed. All seemed well until the BBC's political correspondent, Mark Simpson, filling time during BBC's "Talkback" programme, was put on the spot live on air about Mallon having to leave and ended up mentioning his departure was due to a gall bladder operation. Before long Simpson found himself in the office of a rather stern-looking Deputy First Minister. Mallon sat behind his desk, scraping his pipe as Simpson slumped into a chair before him. "What do you have to say for yourself, then?" Mallon demanded. Simpson, hands going like a windmill, apologised and explained what had happened. "It was like being in with the headmaster," recalled Simpson. "I got everything but the cane." Later, on reflection, Mallon was perhaps concerned he had been a bit hard on Simpson and telephoned him from his sick bed to smooth things over. "Ah, sure, we'll forget about it," he told Simpson.

A Stormont civil servant, puzzled by Mallon's behaviour, recounted the story to a long-time associate of Mallon's. "I don't understand it. Seamus Mallon is so intelligent, well-travelled, artistic, funny, so cultured and urbane..." "No," replied the other man. "Seamus Mallon is not urbane. Inside there is still the country schoolmaster and the country man at heart and in the country you don't tell your business or talk about your illness and don't make yourself look weak."

What Trimble and Mallon did have in common did not always serve them well. Both were stubborn, opinionated and strong-willed. Mallon once said: "David Trimble has a personal need always to be right." No doubt Trimble would have found this remark particularly rich. Both were known for their plain-speaking, but while this could be an admirable trait, it did not always make for easy relations. And although they shared a background that could be considered relatively humble, they were poles apart in their upbringing and outlook, with one as committed to the union as the other was to a united Ireland. In effect, they were representative of the communities from which they hailed: one staunchly Protestant and fiercely loyal; the other traditional Irish Catholic.

William David Trimble was born into a lower middle-class Presbyterian family on 15 October 1944. The Second World War was drawing to a close in Europe and the seaside town of Bangor, on the Down coast, offered a tranquil setting for a young child and his family. It was largely Protestant, British in character and staunchly unionist. The Trimbles were a respectable Presbyterian family. His father, William, earned a modest living as a clerk in the civil service; his mother, Ivy Jack, busied herself raising David and his brother and sister. William Trimble's civil service post did not allow for too many luxuries. The family were careful with their money and lived frugally – "Middle class going down," was how Trimble put it. Ivy was a strong, socially ambitious woman and felt disappointed that her family had not prospered.

The young David, who had inherited his father's red hair and argumentative nature, lived at first in a small terraced house in the town at King Street and then in 1948, at the age of four, moved to a larger home on Victoria Road in Bangor. He had pleasant memories of playing by the sea, sheltered from the simmering tensions in 1950s Belfast and other towns where a resentful Catholic population would soon rebel against the political regime at Stormont. He attended Central Primary School and later Ballyholme Primary. A bookish boy with a skinny frame, he was a shy, awkward child, clumsy and uncoordinated – or handless, as his father rather unkindly put it. Trimble would describe his father as "emotionally illiterate", a characteristic others would later attribute to him*.

A bright and capable child, he passed the Eleven-plus qualifying exam and won a scholarship to attend the non-denominational Bangor Grammar school, where, after an initial period of adjustment, he thrived. He was a school prefect, as well as a sea scout and when he grew old enough joined the Air Training Corps. At sixteen he entered the Orange Order, in spite of his mother's distaste for the loyal institutions, which she regarded as vulgar*.

He had intended to pursue a degree in History, but found circumstances were against him – not least his family's financial difficulties. Under pressure from his father to earn a wage packet, he joined the civil service and took a junior position, eventually pursuing his studies part-time. By 1968, aged twenty-four, he had earned a first-class honours degree from Queen's Law Faculty, where he would become a lecturer. He was also married that year to a Donaghadee woman, Heather McComb, whom he had met through working in the civil service. The two were mismatched, however. She was as outgoing as he was shy

* sourced from Dean Godson's *Himself Alone*

and did not share his interest in books. The relationship was damaged irreparably when Heather gave birth prematurely to twin boys, neither of whom survived. The marriage faltered and ended in divorce in 1976*.

Trimble subsequently married Daphne Orr, a law graduate whom he first met at Queen's University when she enrolled in his law class. After she graduated the pair began to date and within a few years were married, on 31 August 1978. They had four children: Richard, Victoria, Nicholas and Sarah. Daphne combined child-rearing and family life with an active role in running her husband's constituency office. She also provided invaluable guidance and political advice to her husband. It was Daphne who shrewdly surmised that each time he faced his Ulster Unionist ruling council he would muster just enough support to get through. Party insiders say his wife's influence was necessary at times when Trimble would not accept what they regarded as reasonable advice: "He can be totally obsessed with an issue … There would have been certain things that you would have used Daphne as an avenue [for] because you knew she would have a lot more influence than any of us." Daphne Trimble said she could only recall party people asking her to remind her husband about something that might have slipped his mind. She did not agree he was obsessive. Some party colleagues regarded Daphne as both a driving force and a calming influence in Trimble's life and one government official who came across them both found her extremely pleasant. "I never got any warmth from him, but she is totally the opposite."

During the civil rights movement in the 1960s, Trimble became more interested in politics. While not active himself, he was critical of the then unionist Prime Minister, Terence O'Neill, who introduced modest reforms. Trimble preferred instead the hardline firebrand William Craig, but was dismissive of Ian Paisley, whom he regarded as a crank. As Northern Ireland descended into violence at the end of the 1960s, Trimble was horrified by the street disorder. Although he was not sufficiently stirred to get involved in politics, he did campaign on behalf of unionist Basil McIvor in 1969, but mainly because a work colleague had asked him to help. Subsequently he applied to join the Ulster Unionist party.

An event in March 1972 proved the catalyst for Trimble's entry into political activism. Ted Heath's Conservative government suspended the Stormont Parliament a few weeks after Bloody Sunday in Derry, when the Parachute Regiment shot dead thirteen civilians. The move came amid serious violence and an escalating IRA campaign. Trimble, like many unionists, regarded Heath's move as a betrayal and feared its consequences for the union. He told his biographer, Dean Godson, "I am a product of the destruction of Stormont."

Uninspired by the Ulster Unionist elite and what he regarded as complacency in a crisis, Trimble turned to Bill Craig, a fiery orator who infamously called for the liquidation of the enemy. In the aftermath of the suspension of Stormont, Craig – who had founded a pressure group within the Ulster Unionist party in a bid to influence the leadership and policy – held a series of spirited rallies that were also attended by a paramilitary style group, the Vanguard Service Corps. Its critics called it Fascist. When Vanguard split from the UUP to form a party in its own right, Trimble defected from the UUP to become

* sourced from Dean Godson's *Himself Alone*

Craig's deputy. The new party, opposed to the fledgling power-sharing deal forged at Sunningdale in December 1973, backed the Ulster Workers' Council (UWC) strike, which ultimately unseated the Sunningdale Executive some months later.

Trimble, a gangly young law lecturer with Buddy Holly-style spectacles, seemed out of place with the rough-and-ready masked loyalists who were manning illegal roadblocks. Former Sunningdale SDLP minister Ivan Cooper remembered Trimble from those days, when he dismissed him as a "red-haired non-entity". But Trimble was determined to destroy Sunningdale and did his bit by co-editing *The Bulletin*, a daily news-sheet published by the loyalist strike committee which outlined exactly which roads were closed and what steps would be taken to disrupt daily life in Northern Ireland. He also provided political and legal advice to the UWC, which was using the muscle of the paramilitaries in a trenchant bid to carry out its aims. The Ulster Defence Association (UDA) was then a legal back-street group made up of thousands of disgruntled loyalists. Trimble played a backroom, but significant role in the strike. The UWC used widespread intimidation to destroy the power-sharing deal, which was fervently supported by Mallon and his party.

The threat of force by the loyalists was completely anathema to Mallon, who never abandoned his commitment to non-violence, not even in the darkest days of the Troubles when many nationalists found themselves ambivalent about IRA violence in the face of loyalist bloodshed and what they regarded as gross British injustice. Mallon was repulsed by violence and the violent men on both sides, whom he regarded as thugs and bullies. He had an abhorrence of violence and how it brutalised communities and individuals. He would say: "I know all the excuses for violence. But there's no reason for the awful loss of life."

He was deeply touched by the injustice of the Troubles and its victims, those who were killed and those who were unjustly abused. Mallon was very affected by the murder of Dinny Mullan, an SDLP friend who was killed in 1975 outside the County Armagh village of Moy. Mullan's body was lying outside his house when Mallon came upon the scene. His little daughter was sitting on the step, while his wife had gone across the fields on foot to get help. "A stark scene," he would confide later.

Trimble, too, was deeply affected by the violence around him, not least by the IRA murder of his law faculty colleague Edgar Graham, an outspoken and effective Ulster Unionist Assemblyman. Just weeks before Christmas 1983 the IRA assassinated the twenty-nine-year-old law lecturer, shooting him several times in the head. Trimble had to identify his body. He never forgot how some republican students cheered when Graham's murder was announced over the public address system at the university.

It was through electoral politics that Trimble and Mallon came into occasional contact throughout their careers, starting with Sunningdale. Trimble stood as a Vanguard candidate in the 1974 Stormont election. Mallon was an SDLP candidate. His journey to Parliament Buildings contrasted sharply with Trimble's, as did the forces that shaped them.

The Mallon family came from Markethill, each successive generation living out their lives in that rural village. The local townland is named Lurga Uí Mheallain after the clan of Mallon, and the family enjoyed a privileged role as keepers of St Patrick's Bell, a much-prized relic of the saint who drove the snakes out of Ireland and overcame paganism, bringing Christianity to Irish people: a legacy the Mallons were protecting.

Seamus Mallon was born on 17 August 1936 into a large Catholic family in the "Hungry Thirties", just three years before the outbreak of the Second World War. Markethill, in County Armagh, was just a few miles from the border, a physical reality that Irish Catholics found hard to accept; emotionally and intellectually most Catholics looked to Dublin, not London, as their nation's capital. Markethill was overwhelmingly unionist, reinforcing the minority status of Catholic nationalists within Northern Ireland. Partition was less than twenty years old when Mallon born. Although Catholics and Protestants worked alongside one another in the village mill, enjoyed ploughing matches and endured hard times together, beneath the surface there was always acute division. Recalling village life, he said: "There was nothing idyllic about it. You had your raw sectarianism that you had right throughout the north of Ireland. It was there the day you learned to walk."

From an early age, Mallon was conscious of the different cultures. Traditional Orange marches were a familiar sight in his boyhood, a colourful reminder of tribal divisions in the town. Even as a youngster Mallon was conscious of his minority status as an Irish Catholic, aware that not being a unionist somehow made him inferior – "not deemed a full person in Northern Ireland."

Markethill was home to Gosford Castle, a potent symbol of Irish history and the traditional power of the landed gentry dating back to the plantation of Ulster. The castle belonged to the Earls of Gosford, the Acheson family, until 1921. Years later, Mallon sat at a table taken from Gosford Castle when he attended round-table talks at Stormont. The talks delegates never forgot how Mallon pounded the table in frustration at then Secretary of State Sir Patrick Mayhew, an Anglo-Irish, aristocratic, stiff-upper-lip figure who did not seem to comprehend nationalists such as Mallon.

"You don't understand!" Mallon told him across the table. "You don't understand how it feels for me sitting down at this table. You couldn't understand could you? You don't know where this table comes from, do you?" While Sir Patrick sat dumbstruck, Mallon went on: "This table comes from Gosford Castle. My grandmother's friend, Nettie, served at this table. I think about how she served food any time I come down and sit at this table." On one occasion Mallon was reputed to have said: "All the Gosfords are gone – but I'm here." Later, the same table was used for Executive meetings post-devolution.

Mallon never forgot where he came from and had a deeply ingrained sense of nationalism, which he had inherited from his parents who were republicans: longing for Irish unity, but totally opposed to bloodshed to achieve it. "They gave no quarter on that to anybody," he said.

His mother, Jane O'Flaherty, was a nurse before she married and became a housewife. According to her son she was a quiet and unassuming woman, strong in everything, with a devout faith. His father, Frank, was headmaster of the local primary school, and played a prominent role in the life of the village. His son recalled: "He was the guy who filled in forms for people, wrote references, pleaded their cases when they were in trouble. So strangely, in a different kind of way, when I went into politics I was continuing what he had been doing in a non-elected way."

Frank and Jane Mallon already had three daughters when Seamus came along in 1936. He was followed by another daughter, the last child, and so was the only boy in a household of girls. Mallon recalled his childhood as being a happy time. He grew up with a strong sense of his Irish nationalist identity, as fierce as David Trimble's sense of Britishness. He excelled at Gaelic games and played Gaelic football for County Armagh. He enjoyed a variety of sports and was a keen rugby and soccer fan. His boyhood friends came from both sides of the divide. Many believed his experiences growing up in a mainly Protestant community gave him a better insight and understanding of unionists than most of his Assembly colleagues.

As well as being an accomplished athlete, Mallon was also a scholar. Growing up in the days before television, books were a popular pastime. "Ours was a reading house," was how he put it. "There were always books coming in and out. Dickens, or the classic novels." He performed well at school and sat the Eleven-plus, which must have been a daunting test for a young boy from a rural village. He was among the first batch of pupils to take the exam and his pass opened the door to third-level education. Before the exam was introduced, such schooling was on offer only to those who could afford to pay. Thanks to the Eleven-plus, Mallon was able to enter Abbey Grammar School in the border town of Newry, where he was educated by the Christian Brothers. For a young, educated Catholic in Markethill the options were limited: it was the priesthood, or education. Mallon opted for the latter and attended St Joseph's Training College in Belfast, where he qualified as a schoolteacher.

Looking back years later, Mallon would say that his parents' generation could scarcely have taken in the changes that would occur in their son's lifetime, never mind any notion of their son reaching high office at Stormont. How that must have been brought home to him when, as shadow Deputy First Minister, alongside Trimble, he went to Markethill and jointly launched a new £500,000 business centre.

In 1966 he married Gertrude Cush and they had a daughter, Orla. Mallon was pursuing a career in teaching and was absorbed in work and family and his other interests, such as literature and the theatre. He produced plays for the Newpoint Players in Newry and the Armagh theatre group. One of his plays, "Adam's Children", a one-act production that focused on man's inhumanity to man, won an all-Ireland drama festival in 1969.

He maintained scriptwriting, not politics, was his first love. For Mallon, politics had always been a form of drama, as stimulating as it was frustrating and as challenging as it was despairing. He could not ignore the political turmoil that was beginning to grip the north of Ireland in the 1960s any more than Trimble could. Inspired by Martin Luther King, the North's Catholics began to march for their civil rights, demanding the right to vote and equality in housing provision.

"I suppose it touched everybody at the time," said Mallon. "You saw what was happening living in a place like Markethill. I saw it in the injustices that were prevalent."

He emulated his father and became headmaster of St James' Primary School in Markethill, and was pushed into politics when the plight of one his pupils' family caught his attention. The family was desperately trying to get out of a horribly dilapidated dwelling and into a council house. He explained: "At that time councillors had the power of allocation. That family was turned down by a [unionist] councillor who said, 'No Catholic pig and his litter will get a home in Markethill while I am here'."

Mallon was moved to try to do something to address the situation. By 1963 he was chairman of the Mid-Armagh anti-Discrimination Committee, a post he held for five years. Within ten years he had taken that unionist councillor's seat. By then, violence had taken deep root and Mallon's political career took off in earnest in 1973 with his election to Armagh Council and his successful bid for a seat in the Sunningdale Assembly shortly thereafter. A unionist who worked alongside Mallon at the Council, where he remained until 1989, came to respect him: "He was always straight. And no matter how much we disagreed in the chamber, he never let that get in the way of our personal relationship."

However, politics cost Mallon both in personal and financial terms. He quit his job as a school headmaster, but failed to secure a stable career as a politician after Sunningdale was over-thrown. He regarded the collapse of Sunningdale as a tragedy for Northern Ireland, a missed opportunity not just for himself but for society as a whole. Later, with the signing of the Good Friday Agreement, in a barbed reference to all those who had opposed Sunningdale, Mallon dubbed the 1998 Agreement, "Sunningdale for slow-learners".

The irony cannot have been lost on him, then, that the man who helped destroy Sunningdale was his partner in a power-sharing Executive a generation later. Trimble viewed Sunningdale, with its promise of a Council of Ireland and its all-Ireland dimension, as a threat to union with Britain; he viewed the Good Friday Agreement as cementing that union. Their parallel politics, which narrowed with the Agreement, contributed to the wide gulf that separated them for years as both pursued their political ambitions, poles apart.

After the failure of Sunningdale, which saw Mallon elected as an SDLP member and Trimble as a Vanguard candidate, both won places in the 1975 Convention, which also faltered. By the end of the 1970s Mallon had been elected deputy leader of the SDLP and Trimble was back in the fold of the Ulster Unionists, having rejoined the party in 1978. In 1982 both were elected to the Prior Assembly, yet another failed initiative. Mallon was forced to resign from the Assembly, however, because of his appointment to the Senate in Dáil Éireann by Taoiseach Charles Haughey.

Four years later the Anglo-Irish Agreement, which formally gave the Irish government a say in the affairs of Northern Ireland, deepened the political divisions between Trimble and Mallon. Some regarded this deal as the SDLP's revenge for Sunningdale's destruction. The pact – signed by Taoiseach Garret FitzGerald and Prime Minister Margaret Thatcher – sparked widespread protests. Unionist politicians resigned their seats at Westminster to force a series of by-elections. Ironically, this brought Mallon some much-needed political good fortune. Having tried and failed three times to win a Westminster seat, he caused a major upset for the Ulster Unionists and their Anglo-Irish protest when he defeated UUP MP Jim Nicholson in the 1986 by-election in Newry and Armagh. The victory secured for Mallon a stable income after years of having to teach part-time to provide for his family.

At Westminster, he had a powerful platform from which to criticise republican and loyalist paramilitaries, unionist politicians and the government of the day. He was the SDLP's policing and justice spokesman and he used his role as an MP to distinguish himself by asking tough questions. He campaigned against what he regarded as a "shoot-to-kill" policy within the security forces. While he had no love for the IRA, Mallon regarded such a policy as anti-democratic and sought justice, not revenge. His probing led to death threats, anonymous phone calls and verbal abuse and his home was petrol-bombed on occasion – an acute reminder of the dangers posed to his wife and daughter by extremists on both sides.

His criticism of the police meant he was not always welcome at the homes of murdered officers who lived in his constituency. Sometimes when he arrived to pay his respects, he was turned away at the door. He found this hurtful, but carried on. Mallon also used the Commons to intensify his battles against injustice, in particular for Gerry Conlon who was wrongfully jailed for the Guildford pub bomb. Mallon visited Conlon in prison and helped to win his release on appeal. Conlon described Mallon as "a single voice that echoed in the wilderness" and recalled the words of his father, Giuseppe, who was also wrongly imprisoned and had faith in Mallon: "It's better to have one good man working for you than ten who don't care." When Conlon repeated this tribute to Mallon in an address at the party's 2005 conference, he took Conlon's head in his hands afterwards and, fighting back tears, said, "God bless you".

Mallon had been an MP for four years when Trimble was finally elected to Westminster. The failure to overturn the Anglo-Irish Agreement had drawn Trimble deeper into political activity and by 1990 he had succeeded Harold McCusker as MP for Upper Bann, winning a by-election after the deputy unionist leader passed away. By 1995 Trimble would be Ulster Unionist leader, although he was conscious that the old guard of the party would never have fully accepted him in this role. He did not win the leadership through their patronage. In fact, it was Trimble's role in a disputed Orange march at Drumcree, County Armagh, that was widely credited with his election as party leader in the autumn of 1995 – although Trimble himself downplayed the significance of Drumcee in his leadership victory.

That summer, in the heat of July, Trimble led what would become known as the Battle of Drumcree, during which thousands of Orangemen converged on the grounds of the little church and demanded the right to march back to Portadown along the Garvaghy Road, as they had done for years. The march was opposed by Garvaghy Road's Catholic residents, led by a former republican prisoner. Trimble stood defiant, both as an Orangeman and as the local MP. When the march was finally allowed to proceed, after a stand-off lasting several days, Trimble incensed nationalists when he rejected any suggestion that it was the result of compromise with them.

Nationalists were also deeply offended by his behaviour when the parade arrived back at its destination in Portadown. Trimble was pictured hand in hand with the DUP leader Ian Paisley, their arms jointly raised in glee. Nationalists regarded the display as triumphalist; Trimble has always denied this. But the result – a procession down the Garvaghy Road – impressed hardliners in the Unionist party, many of whom were also Orangemen. These loyal Order members had influence in the UUP's ruling council and would deliver a decisive victory for Trimble in the leadership battle of 1995.

The following year the stand-off was repeated and Trimble was once again present at Drumcree, now as leader of the UUP. This time nationalist protestors were more determined than ever to have the march re-routed. Unionists and Orangemen regarded the challenge as a "Sinn Féin/IRA" plot to destroy their culture and were equally determined to proceed. In fact, in 1996 the Drumcree protest was backed up by loyalist paramilitary muscle and it escalated into street disorder, with Orangemen blocking roads.

While Trimble led Orangemen in their demand to march, Mallon found himself trapped in his Markethill home. He had to be airlifted out of Armagh by helicopter in order to reach the House of Commons for a debate. How he resented that, and the role Trimble had played at Drumcree. Indeed, Mallon was a committed parliamentarian. A former associate of Mallon's recalled: "Even though he was an Irish nationalist at heart and wanted to live to see democracy achieved and a united country, he loved Westminster to the very depths of his being, loved the Commons, loved the debates, couldn't see Gerry Adams' problem with it."

Respect for Parliament was one of the few things Trimble and Mallon had in common, despite the fact that their points of view on the floor of the House were often polarised. Although Trimble would have been glad to hear Mallon condemn the IRA in the fiercest of terms, he would have been appalled at Mallon's attacks on the police and British Army. Asked if Trimble and Mallon shared any kind of rapport while at Westminster over many years, the Ulster Unionist MP and deputy leader John Taylor, who occupied an office with Trimble, replied tartly: "I don't think so – I think they had even less when they shared power."

Chapter 4
Walking Shadows

The new era got off to an unfortunate start. When the new shadow ministers emerged from the temporary debating chamber, having taken the pledge of office, they found little to cheer about. Their election did not seem to have registered with the civil service. Not only was the head of the civil service, Sir John Semple, not there with his senior staff to greet them but their offices were not ready. "It's not that you were expecting an entourage," said Mallon. "But I mean, there was nobody. Believe you me, there was nobody!"

Mallon and Trimble were eventually brought to a single room that had a telephone in it. They had to scramble around looking for office equipment and both were furious about it. Mallon told a senior civil servant that he wanted an office of his own. He said he was given an ill-equipped room with no telephone. "I had another scrap," recalled Mallon. "To get a bloody phone was a scrap."

One insider recalled how Trimble and Mallon would continually complain about the situation, to the point where the experience seemed wildly exaggerated. When referring to what greeted him when he took office, Mallon, shaking his head, declared with incredulity: "A chair, just a chair." Trimble remembered well the early battles with the civil service: "I had quite a row for a week or two to try to get some people to come and provide support for the transition and there were, I'm afraid, a few bruised egos."

In fact, the day after they were appointed Sir John Semple seconded his own private secretary, David Crabbe, to work for them. Trimble and Mallon spent the subsequent days battling for more support and services. A senior unionist described the early shadow period as "shambolic", with only derisory support for the new ministers. "It was a disgrace," he said. The speed of political events seemed to have caught the civil service off-guard – it was still operating under direct rule. Many had doubted that there would actually be a successful election of two new shadow ministers, and no contingency plan was in place to deal with them if they were elected. No one knew what their status would be nor how to deal with them pre-devolution. "There was uncertainty about the role of the shadow ministers," said a senior civil servant.

Indeed, this whole situation was new to the civil service. The political status quo had suddenly shifted from decades of stalemate to the new Agreement and then, within a few weeks of that, to a shadow administration. Perhaps the civil servants did not believe there would be devolution, assuming friction over arms would smother the new regime. A senior NIO official, describing the situation, lamented: "They basically had a phone between them. The system wasn't prepared. I'm sure the system just didn't know how to respond. In hindsight it could and should have done more."

There was also a presumption that during the shadow period they would use their own party offices. Trimble felt civil servants did not believe the new Agreement would last: "The received wisdom after the Agreement was it was never going to work, so what on earth do they do with these fellows with no clearly defined role and no power?"

Mallon was unforgiving about the apparent lack of preparedness for the arrival of two shadow ministers: "Well, everybody else knew it was going to happen that day. They [the civil servants] were all sitting clocked in Castle Buildings anyhow. Now even if they hadn't been expecting [it], somebody, anybody, might have come to the door and said, 'You are welcome, here is your room'." However, a senior government official insisted there was no offence intended: "They were given an office, but the presumption was that in shadow form they would not be doing that much work … It was a very bad start, but it picked up very quickly after that."

Whatever the reason, Trimble and Mallon never forgot what they both regarded as a snub by the system. "It was one of the few things they agreed on," sniffed one senior official. Given that the two politicians were already generally suspicious of civil servants, whom they felt had too much power for too long, it was a regrettable start. It would take time to learn to trust the administration and to accept that this pool of men and women were there to work on their behalf. There were other teething problems to overcome first, however. Trimble and Mallon clashed almost immediately with the system over press releases, perhaps not realising that the government information service could not issue political statements. "That was a learning curve for them," one insider recalled.

A statement in the name of the shadow First Minister was deemed inappropriate because it attacked the Sinn Féin leader, Gerry Adams, and was therefore political. Mallon was in the process of putting out a press statement as shadow Deputy First Minister when an official informed him of an objection. Frank Woods, a senior NIO media official, who was then acting as press director for the shadow ministers, had dutifully and properly objected on the grounds that Mallon's statement was political. Already vexed by the treatment he had received upon his arrival, Mallon set off in search of Woods, determined to give him a piece of his mind. As he stormed down the corridor he bumped into Sir John Semple and told him, "John, you come with me because, you'll want to see, I am going to kill this fellow!"

Sir John, a rather gentle soul, whom Mallon liked very much, was rather startled by the outburst. Mallon never found Woods, which would explain why the official recalled some sensitivity around press releases in the new shadow period but could not remember any serious objections from the Deputy First Minister: "I certainly don't recall Seamus Mallon coming at me in a towering rage."

Later, Mallon saw the comical side of the row and rather enjoyed recounting the tale. In the end, his statement went out and Mallon got his point across very forcibly to the head of the civil service. "John," he said, "tell those people, never again. I mean literally, never again!'"

Mallon also informed Sir John Semple of his problems with the lack of facilities. Semple was told, in no uncertain terms, what was required and Mallon put him on notice – warning that he would hold a press conference in his spartan office and tell the media exactly what had been going on. Semple was horrified: a news-hungry press pack would devour the story. He made sure that the press conference was never called and made great efforts to fix the problems. Gradually the trappings of office were assembled. While David Crabbe continued to work for Trimble for a time, Geoff Beattie was temporarily brought in as Mallon's private secretary. Trimble and Mallon were asked to interview suitable permanent candidates to serve in these posts. Mallon chose Billy Gamble, a Protestant from a loyalist, working-class background, while Trimble hired Maura Quinn, an Irish-speaking Catholic. Mallon said it was a coincidence that each chose someone from the opposite community.

Semple also ensured that when devolution day arrived in December 1999 the problems were not repeated and the transition went smoothly, which it did. However, the tussles with the system continued in the weeks after the election of shadow First and Deputy First Minister. Mallon sought to second two special advisors from the European Commission, Hugh Logue and Colm Larkin. He was entitled to one advisor but felt this was insufficient. He told the Secretary of State, Mo Mowlam, that he would require three advisors in total. For various reasons the demand for two, and then three advisors was resisted. One reason given was that the UK civil service would be compromised if European officials were brought in and paid by the European Commission.

There were objections from other politicians, including his new partner, David Trimble. But Mallon was not for turning. In his words, he "brought out the heavy hitters and prepared for battle ... I just said, 'Okay boys, if that is the way you want to play it, this is the way we will play it'." He got the Taoiseach and the Prime Minister involved and this time he did more than threaten to hold a news conference. He threatened to quit as Deputy First Minister. Recounting his discussion with Tony Blair, Mallon said: "I made it quite clear ... either they come in my door or I go out your door, one or the other!"

Mallon got his way. By the end of the summer the EU officials were settling into the administration. Hugh Logue was a veteran of the SDLP, while Colm Larkin was a Dublin-based EU mandarin. Reflecting on the battle to get the advisors appointed, Logue recalled: "The civil service was saying it was impossible. They just went the wrong way about it and as soon as you say to Mallon 'you can't do something', he's determined to do it. Winning is important to him and he won it."

As well as the advisors, two experienced press officers – Colin Ross and Don McAleer – were despatched to assist the new ministers, while Trimble recruited his own inner circle. The Ulster Unionist press chief David Kerr, aged just twenty-four, became the First Minister's official spokesman. There was a notion in the shadow First Minister's office that Kerr would be the equivalent of Alistair Campbell, the head of communications in Downing Street, but Kerr soon learned that he could not tell the other party's press officers what to do in this quirky, multi-party Executive.

David Campbell, the cerebral, Oxford-educated Antrim farmer who helped run the Somme Association, was appointed Trimble's chief-of-staff. When Mallon was asked if he, too, would like a chief-of-staff, he replied archly, "No. I think the North has had enough chiefs-of-staff" – a none-too-subtle reference to the IRA.

However, their skirmishes over administrative support paled in the face of battles that were taking place away from Stormont that summer, battles that would lead to tragedy and a renewed resolve to make the Agreement work.

Chapter 5
Despair

Tension was spreading on the wind when David Trimble and Seamus Mallon first took up their posts in the shadow period. A row over an Orange march linked to Drumcree church, in Trimble's constituency, was undermining the new era of reconciliation. Drumcree was like a volcano, which threatened to spew a toxic mix of hatred, fear and prejudice. It was about to erupt with deadly force.

Drumcree had preoccupied both Trimble and Mallon almost from the moment they were elected. The police and Army had erected barriers at the site and security was extremely tight. Drumcree looked like a war zone, completely at odds with the new peace they were trying to foster. For the previous three years the row over the march had been attended by violence and July 1998 promised to be no different. Angry at being re-routed from the Catholic Garvaghy Road following opposition from residents, members of the Orange Order were busily planning a mass protest to demand their right to march. Catholic, nationalist residents of the Garvaghy Road were just as defiant about their right to prevent the parade passing through their area. In this they had the support of the Parades Commission, which had ruled that the parade should take an alternative route.

The dispute polarised Catholics and Protestants right across Northern Ireland and impacted severely on daily life: workers were sent home early, restaurants closed and by tea-time the streets were deserted. Belfast was like a ghost-town – just as it had been during the height of the Troubles in the 1970s. Drumcree was rife for exploitation by bigoted extremists and anti-Agreement elements; there was nightly violence on the streets.

Prime Minister Tony Blair was also preoccupied with the dispute, fearing it could undermine the hard-won Agreement. Blair knew that nationalist faith in the new order would be damaged if the march were forced through, but he was also conscious that unionists were resentful of some of the changes being made and needed to have confidence in their place in the new Northern Ireland. In an attempt to achieve a resolution, Blair had travelled to Stormont the day after Trimble's and Mallon's historic election as shadow ministers, stopping on his way at Aldergrove, County Antrim, to view the charred remains of a 200-year-old Catholic church that had been destroyed in a sectarian attack. It was an ominous reminder that the legacy of hatred in Northern Ireland was not going to be washed away overnight by the tide of an historic agreement.

As shadow ministers, Trimble and Mallon had no power to wield and even if they had, security would have remained the preserve of Westminster. What they lacked in real power, however, they made up for in moral authority and both did their best to defuse the situation. Trimble sent an open letter to the Garvaghy Road residents, appealing for compromise and both ministers met with members of the Orange Order. Even though they disagreed fundamentally on the issue, the two ministers tried to work out a resolution.

Trimble, it emerged, was also applying pressure on the government to allow a parade. Rumours abounded that he had threatened resignation on this point, and he was forced to deny this. When pressed about the matter in an interview for this book he stood by his denial, but showed some regret at not having threatened to resign: "Maybe I should have."

Trimble roundly condemned the violence being perpetrated by loyalist protestors, while Mallon insisted the law of the State must be upheld. Trimble and Mallon were pictured together at a joint news conference, looking extremely weary. On 7 July, at the height of the stand-off at Drumcree, Mallon – now shadow Deputy First Minister for less than a week – travelled to the Garvaghy Road with local SDLP representative Bríd Rodgers to appeal to the local residents, who were under siege but refusing to give in and allow a parade. It was reported, and denied by the SDLP, that Mallon asked them to accept a small number of Orange marchers. Mallon wanted to test opinion to see if a solution was possible, but any talk of compromise was quickly rebuffed by those he met. As Mallon departed, he was heckled by a few locals who shouted, "Go back to Trimble" and "No sell-out". He found it a nasty and intimidating experience.

Depressed by the lack of progress, Mallon accompanied Bríd Rodgers to her home in nearby Lurgan where they had a cup of tea. He then made his way home in his ministerial car. The roads were eerily quiet and there was a palpable sense of anxious anticipation. As his car neared the comfortable bungalow he shared with his wife, Gertrude, Mallon spotted a roadblock manned by loyalists in front of his house. Realising he was driving into a dangerous trap, Mallon screamed at his driver, "Swing round!" The driver turned and they went back along the Armagh Road and stopped at the home of a friend of Mallon's. He was extremely resentful that he had been blocked from getting to his home and anxious about his wife, who was alone in the house.

There was worse to come as the Twelfth approached, and some nights Mallon was forced to stay in Belfast. For days there were violent clashes as a result of the Drumcree siege: scores of vehicles were hijacked, homes were damaged and hundreds of petrol bombs were thrown. Several dozen policemen were injured and there were several hundred arrests. This prompted some Orangemen to rethink their support for the protest and those not wanting to be associated with attacks on the police and Army stayed away.

On 8 July, Trimble and Mallon appeared at separate press conferences. This was noted by the media, but neither recalled it being an issue or remembered a strong clash on the parades issue because they had worked together as best they could. "We had discussions about what was the best thing to do," said Trimble. "Mallon was all for going and meeting people together but I was not in favour of that. I had some idea of the temperature which was down there and if we had gone down it probably would have precipitated a riot." Looking back, Mallon still maintained they should have gone together: "That was a mistake."

By the eleventh night it was clear this had been one of the most tense Twelfth fortnights on record, but the worst was yet to come. On the Carnany estate, in Ballymoney, County Antrim, while Twelfth bonfires blazed across the North, three young brothers were asleep in their beds when loyalist thugs set up a burning barricade at the entrance to their estate.

The Quinn brothers, Richard, 11, Mark, 9, and Jason, 8, lived in a terraced house with their Catholic mother, Christine Quinn, and her Protestant partner, Thomas Craig. Not content to intimidate the Catholic residents of this predominantly loyalist estate, a loyalist gang targeted their house with petrol bombs. The petrol bomb that hit the Quinns' home sparked a deadly inferno and all three young boys burned to death. The community awoke to shock, horror and shame. Some Orangemen were too sickened to march, and there were calls for the Drumcree protest to end immediately.

The shadow First and Deputy First Ministers were devastated. As soon as they could, they held a joint news conference. In a show of unity they asked the Orangemen to end their protest and appealed to the Garvaghy residents to "positively recognise" the significance of such a decision. Trimble said the only way the Portadown brethren could distance themselves from the Quinn murders was to leave the hill and go home. It was a significant and brave move by the shadow First Minister, himself an Orangeman, but it added to his woes in Portadown, a key area of his constituency. "It will be a long time before he is welcome in the town," said one Portadown unionist.

Trimble had broken with tribal politics – always a risky move in Northern Ireland. Lord Craigavon, Northern Ireland's first Prime Minister, had proudly boasted that he was an Orangeman first and Prime Minister second. Trimble had clearly shown that he put his role as minister, and his promise to serve all, above narrow tradition. "This was a test for him and he has lived up to it," said Monica McWilliams an Assembly member who had helped negotiate the Agreement as a member of the Women's Coalition.

Trimble's stance on the Drumcree protest was backed by a senior Orange chaplain, and the impetus for the protest was lost. Defiance had turned to disgust. Nationalist residents on the Ormeau Road who had planned to oppose a controversial march on this route instead held a silent protest as the Orangemen marched past. Some Orangemen remained unrepentant, insisting it was not Orangemen who bore responsibility for the tragedy. At Drumcree there were whispers that this was not sectarian murder but that there was another motive, due to a grudge. Still there could have been little doubt that sectarianism had caused the children's deaths. On the weekend of the killing, five Catholic families living on the estate reportedly received death threats from the loyalist terror group, the UVF. At the time the Chief Constable, Sir Ronnie Flanagan, made clear the attack was sectarian, a view echoed by the shadow First Minister.

From the age of seventeen Trimble had donned an Orange sash and taken part in Orange marches, but this Twelfth he dressed in a sombre suit and went instead to visit the Quinn family. Mallon, also devastated by the tragedy, made his own visit to the Quinn home. He wanted to accompany the shadow First Minister but they were unable to co-ordinate their schedules. The sight of the three tiny white coffins is an enduring image of the Troubles, and one that haunted Mallon.

By then Mallon was working extremely well with his private secretary, Billy Gamble. The pair would discuss the problem of loyalist alienation from the current process. Gamble had some insight due to his own background, as he was a Protestant raised in a working-class, loyalist area. "It was a remarkable relationship," said Mallon. "Billy was superb. We disagreed about a lot of things, but I don't think we had a cross word." Aided by Gamble, Mallon began to hold private meetings in North Belfast on an ongoing basis.

He met with working-class people, including former loyalist and republican paramilitaries who were now working for peace in the community. Even after he had left office, Mallon gave little detail about the process, which had never been disclosed to the media. He did not claim to persuade the loyalists, but was happy to keep dialogue going, something he was able to do during the shadow period. It may also have helped him to keep things in perspective during these dark days of his administration.

While the deaths of the Quinn children had led to soul-searching on the loyalist side, another atrocity had a similar impact on nationalism, this one perpetrated by extremist republicans opposed to the Good Friday Agreement. On 15 August 1998 the Real IRA – a splinter group of the pro-Agreement Provisional IRA – exploded a bomb in the heart of Omagh town. It was a Saturday afternoon and the streets were crowded with shoppers, many buying school uniforms and other school supplies for the new term.

Trimble was in Germany with his family and news of the tragedy was slow to reach him. He later complained that no one from the NIO had thought to ring him. This was disputed by a NIO official, who insisted efforts were made to contact him on his mobile telephone. In the end, Trimble's party aide, David Campbell, who was himself in Toronto, telephoned him late on Saturday night to break the news. Trimble was deeply shocked. He wanted to get back to Northern Ireland as quickly as possible and became frustrated by what he regarded as the indifference of the NIO. He claimed the Prime Minister had to intervene, but this was also disputed by a senior official who said Trimble failed to understand the difficulties involved. Both Mallon and the NIO official stated that strenuous efforts were made to get Trimble back and that a flight was arranged at the earliest opportunity to return him home in time to meet Tony Blair. However, a unionist source, still annoyed at the memory of it, recalled being met with casual indifference and the question: "Why should the civil service do anything to bring David Trimble home?"

Mallon was in Donegal that Saturday, golfing. Earlier in the day he had played a round with a man from Omagh. A security person arrived and informed him about the bombing. Mallon was deeply distressed and could scarcely take in the news. "You have to get on the road," he was told. When Mallon arrived in the County Tyrone town, he witnessed the full horror of the bomb, first at the scene of the explosion, where he spoke to police, and then at the hospital, where he stayed until 3.00 or 4.00am observing the blood-splattered floors, the grieving relatives and the trolleys carrying the casualties:

> "I think the hospital part of it was the most startling, startling in the sense that people in a total panic situation were carrying out their work with no panic. And yet to the outside and to someone like me, standing watching it, the question was, how in the world does anybody cope with this?"

At the leisure centre in Omagh, families gathered to hear the roll-call of the dead, the missing and the injured. The final death toll was twenty-nine men, women and children and two unborn babies; Spanish tourists had been amongst those massacred in the atrocity. Trimble and Mallon became a walking, breathing symbol of hope in a time of great pain and despair. They were the embodiment of the new era, standing shoulder to shoulder in public. Together they attended the funerals of the victims. In the face of violence aimed at destabilising the new Stormont, they remained resolute, walking with dignity through the streets of Omagh, along with the Prince of Wales who came to the bombsite to pay his respects.

Among the victims were three little boys from Buncrana in County Donegal: Oran Doherty, 8, Sean McLaughlin, 11 and James Barker, 12. David Trimble and Seamus Mallon were at their funerals together, along with other dignitaries, including the Irish President Mary McAleese, who had also made an emotional journey to the town days earlier. "It was just funeral after funeral after funeral – just desperate," said David Trimble's aide David Kerr. A Stormont insider recalled, "David and Seamus were deeply affected by Omagh. It was such a sickening blow after the initial election."

Following the Buncrana funerals, Trimble went to the burial of Unionist party member Fred White and his son, Brian, who had been shopping in the town when the bomb went off. The day after there were yet more services, in the morning and in the afternoon. Kerr particularly remembered Samantha MacFarland's funeral. She was just seventeen and had been killed alongside her best friend, Lorraine Wilson. "Samantha's funeral was very, very difficult," said Kerr. "Her friends were there and they were playing a violin piece and it was just haunting and it was kind of the peak of grief. [David Trimble] would have had a tear in his eye, he didn't break down, but he was very upset."

On the way to a memorial service after the bombing, Trimble called into the Royal Victoria Hospital in Belfast to visit the injured. Donna Marie McGillion's parents were there at their daughter's bedside as she lay in a coma. The young woman had been out shopping for her wedding dress when she was caught up in the blast. She suffered serious burns.

The Prime Minister and the Taoiseach both visited the Royal within twenty-four hours of the blast. Blair later commented that what he had seen at the hospital would stay with him his whole life. An official remembered he was so overcome that he went into a quiet room on his own for a short while to compose himself. The blow was felt far and wide, even in the White House. President Bill Clinton had also been watching the tragedy unfold. He had been involved in the peace process for several years and had personally pressed the politicians to conclude the Agreement when negotiations faltered in the final hours of talks. He wanted to help. Just as he had made a difference in the Good Friday negotiations, Clinton, the political evangelist intended to do the same now to safeguard the new regime.

Chapter 6

Hope

President Clinton's visit to Northern Ireland had been planned for some months when the Real IRA bomb exploded in Omagh. Undeterred by this turn of events, he was anxious to put his personal seal of approval on the new Agreement and the new administration. Mallon had in fact already convinced White House officials that the President should visit the city of Armagh, which lay in his constituency. "I fought like a wildcat to get him there," Mallon recalled.

However, after the bombing Clinton was determined to visit Omagh, meet the survivors and provide what comfort he could. His itinerary was altered: Omagh was put on the agenda and Armagh was removed. When Mallon heard the news, just days before the Clinton visit, he was horrified – not that Omagh was included, but that Armagh had been dropped. He immediately got on the phone, seeking to influence the decision-makers. "Look, you are daft!" he told American officials, explaining that in Omagh the president would be in a mourning situation and would have to be sombre and constrained and he therefore needed to also go somewhere else where he could meet people in a more upbeat atmosphere to send a positive message. Beleaguered by a crisis in his Presidency, Clinton needed positive, happy images, urged Mallon, as did the people of Northern Ireland. Mallon's argument swayed the officials and the administration decided to proceed with the "Gathering For Peace" in Armagh.

Even before Clinton arrived there were signs that the politicians were going to make progress that autumn towards establishing the new power-sharing Executive. On 31 August 1998, the anniversary of the 1994 IRA ceasefire and just three days before President Clinton's arrival, Sinn Féin president Gerry Adams made a ground-breaking statement: "Sinn Féin believes the violence we have seen must be for all of us now a thing of the past, over, done with and gone."

His remarks were widely welcomed. Some regarded them as an implicit "war is over" statement, although Adams would continue to be pressed on the issue for some years. Trimble welcomed the words, but felt Adams should have gone further and continued to demand more concrete, less aspiring assurances. Adams' statement was swiftly followed by the appointment of Martin McGuinness as Sinn Féin representative to the de Chastelain Arms Commission (IICD). A senior SDLP source remembered Trimble being unhappy with the appointment of a Sinn Féin representative, claiming the Ulster Unionist leader would have preferred someone who was overtly IRA. According to this source, Blair and Ahern had to convince Trimble the move was important and credible and that the republicans meant business: "They urged Trimble to back off." Trimble denied this had been an issue.

In the aftermath of Omagh and in the face of huge pressure, republicans finally responded with a compromise move. While their gesture fell short of this, it placated London for the time being and left Trimble under pressure to make a groundbreaking move of his own. It was the see-saw pattern of the peace process: when one side moved, the other was expected to follow, or take the blame. In this game it was especially important not to alienate Washington, and Clinton was all too aware of the power of his presence in the North.

On the morning of 3 September 1998, Clinton arrived at Belfast International Airport on Air Force One from Moscow and was greeted by the Prime Minister and other dignitaries. He headed for Parliament Buildings at Stormont, where he was welcomed on the steps by the shadow First and Deputy First Ministers. Inside he met the new Assembly members. From there his cavalcade travelled to the Waterfront Hall, where he addressed an audience of MLAs and other dignitaries; the DUP boycotted the event. It was here that President Clinton delivered his keynote address, along with Prime Minister Tony Blair, David Trimble and Seamus Mallon.

The First and Deputy First Ministers arrived together and waited in a side room at the showpiece hall where they were served coffee and sandwiches. Mallon recalled the President was edgy when he arrived. At the time he was being threatened with impeachment amid allegations that he had lied about his relationship with a young White House intern, Monica Lewinsky. Two weeks earlier he had endured the humiliation of testifying before a Grand Jury. He was experiencing probably the most difficult period of his presidency, but he cared deeply about Northern Ireland and wanted to help. Behind the scenes at the Waterfront Hall, Irish-American democrats hovered and huddled because back home the well-respected Democrat Senator, Joe Lieberman, had publicly condemned Clinton's affair with Lewinsky. Clinton was under pressure to apologise, which he did before he left Ireland. Initially, Clinton sat on the stage looking every inch a humiliated and downtrodden man: hunched over, legs crossed, his head bowed. But he was among friends in that crowd and he would soon draw warmth from the 2,000-strong audience, which gave him two standing ovations.

Mallon, a natural performer, also won plaudits for his oration. The next morning's *Irish News* called it the performance of his life. He had worked hard on the speech, finessing it the Sunday before Clinton's arrival. His address began with a warm welcome for the President: "A man from a town called Hope in Arkansas has come again," said Mallon, "to a place where hope lives again as a result of your interest, encouragement and help." The inspirational speech was enlivened with a quote from Maya Angelou, an African-American poet who hailed from St Louis, Missouri. At Bill Clinton's inauguration as President in 1993 she had recited a moving poem; Mallon felt that the Waterfront Hall event was the equivalent of his and Trimble's inauguration ceremony. He repeated Maya Angelou's words from her poem, "On the Pulse of Morning". Mallon's voice, sometimes raspy from years of pipe-smoking but enriched with emotion, filled the auditorium as he declared, "History, despite its wrenching pain, cannot be unlived, but if faced with courage, need not be lived again." Mallon spoke not of the problems facing Northern Ireland but chose instead to speak of what might be, declaring, "Tomorrow is another country".

(His new aide, Hugh Logue, who had been seconded from Brussels, had sourced the

Maya Angelou poem for Mallon, at his request. The speech won such praise that Logue continued to pepper Mallon's speeches with her work, to the point where the Deputy First Minister began to complain, "If he comes to me with another Maya Angelou line…")

Lacking Mallon's panache and always the more practical nuts-and-bolts politician, Trimble struck a sour note in his address despite its merits. The shadow First Minister's speech declared his goodwill towards peacemakers and, significantly, he spoke of a "pluralist parliament for a pluralist people." This remark was, of course, a reference to the infamous comment by Northern Ireland's first prime minister, Lord Craigavon, whose limited vision saw only a "Protestant Parliament for a Protestant people". But Trimble's newsworthy soundbite was overshadowed by his focus on decommissioning. He argued that if the "so-called war was really over", then there was no need for weapons:

> "Mr President, the path ahead is for true democrats only. As First Minister and leader of Northern Ireland, I cannot reconcile seeking positions in government with a failure to discharge responsibilities under the Agreement to dismantle terror organisations … I will speak to anyone who has the good of Northern Ireland at heart, but no democrat can tolerate coercive threats."

Mallon, listening from a few feet away, thought Trimble had pitched his address all wrong. While Mallon liked to articulate a vision, Trimble liked detail and tended to focus on the practical problems on the immediate horizon. "He had a hang-up about what he called 'the vision thing'," Mallon would say years later. "He thought it was not real politics."

Whatever the poker-playing Mallon thought of Trimble's negotiating skills, Trimble's speech was not without vision, but it was regarded as patchy and was certainly much more political than the shadow Deputy First Minister's; Sinn Féin members in the audience were most unhappy with the tone. Unlike Mallon, who received compliments from both Blair and Clinton, Trimble did not enjoy widespread praise for his performance.

Deáglán de Bréadún, writing in *The Irish Times* the following day, described Trimble's remarks to republicans as an "olive branch wrapped in barbed wire". *The Irish News* concluded the First Minister's speech was "ungenerous". A *Belfast Telegraph* report carried some criticism also. One insider recalled David Trimble not being best pleased with the criticisms: "Trimble and Mallon were quite competitive with each other and Mallon got the accolades for his speech and the tenor of it, whereas David was lambasted … His speech was seen as mean-minded at the Clinton visit." Trimble's senior unionist party colleagues, however, were satisfied. And for a politician who was constantly concerned about rebellion in the ranks, this was perhaps more important than plaudits in newspapers.

Clinton – who had arrived humiliated, with many noticing the frostiness between him and his wife, Hillary – seemed to draw strength from the warmth of the reception he received, particularly in Armagh. Observers noticed his demeanour changing; the shoulders were no longer hunched. By the end of the visit, having drawn thousands of well-wishers, he stood tall, looking refreshed and relaxed.

Mallon had vivid memories of the Armagh visit, not least how the evening sun set through the spires of the Cathedral as the president rose to speak. At first Clinton used his speaking notes, but after a page or two he realised he was not striking the right chord. He swept the papers aside and spoke from the heart. It was an impressive performance. Mallon watched Blair, as competitive as any politician, strive to match the achievements of the American orator: "Blair made a remarkable effort trying to top Clinton in Armagh, which he nearly did. He made a damn good speech."

It was a speech as finely balanced as the one Clinton had made earlier that day, in Belfast's Waterfront Hall, when he had delivered a mixture of soft inspiration and hard advice for the road ahead. Clinton told the audience: "Remember that in the early days of the American republic the Gaelic term for America was Inis Fáil – Island of Destiny. Today Americans see you as Inis Fáil and your destiny is peace." He borrowed from W.B. Yeats, paraphrasing the poet's words to suit his message about shoring up the pro-Agreement politicians: "Help them to prove that things can come together ... that the centre can hold." President Clinton also added his voice to the calls for decommissioning by the IRA, while urging all the political parties to form the Executive and to adopt a police force that had the confidence and respect of all members of the communities.

Decommissioning did not follow Clinton's visit and it would be some time before policing won widespread support or the Executive was formed; but there was a remarkable change. As Clinton departed, it was reported that Trimble would hold his first face-to-face meeting with Gerry Adams the following week, on 10 September. Although they had sat across a table from each other during multi-party talks, their remarks had been addressed through the Chair and Trimble had always kept Adams at arm's length. In his book, *Hope and History*, Adams recounted a scene in the toilets of Castle Buildings during the multi-party talks. Standing next to Trimble he jokingly suggested they must stop "meeting like this". "Grow up," was Trimble's curt response.

Before his first official meeting with Adams – a calculated risk for the unionist leader – Trimble told his party that he would confront the Sinn Féin leader on the arms issue. He also made clear that he would not shake hands with Adams, not while the IRA still possessed weapons. No doubt irked by this, Adams was making clear that decommissioning was not a pre-condition to power-sharing. Meanwhile, there was also some annoyance in the office of the Deputy First Minister with regard to the historic talks. Approaches were made to Trimble's staff, and among the points put to them was that the Office of First and Deputy First Minister was a single unit, therefore Mallon ought to be included in a meeting involving the First Minister before the one-to-one meeting between Adams and Trimble. The twosome became a threesome.

Once the three men had finished their meeting, Trimble met Adams immediately afterwards in a small ante-room in his capacity as unionist leader. This meeting had been negotiated by Trimble's private secretary, David Crabbe, and Sinn Féin's Siobhan O'Hanlon. It lasted thirty-three minutes. Journalists were desperate for information, but were only able to glean that the wallpaper was cream and pink; a NIO official joked that there were a few chairs whose arms had been decommissioned. Afterwards both sides said the meeting had been constructive. Adams later confided that when he first met Trimble he was so concerned about media intrusion, he went and closed the curtains to prevent any photographs being taken by powerful lenses. A source close to Trimble said the unionist leader was also uneasy about meeting Adams, and how it would be viewed: "He was pragmatic and he knew he had to talk to this guy, but he was slightly worried it would spook the troops." Another official remembered that "Sinn Féin wanted to make a big deal of it, but Trimble wanted to play it down." Trimble did not recall the curtains being closed on this occasion, but did admit to closing them when meeting Adams in his West Wing office, where the windows were quite exposed and window-cleaners were sometimes present.

Standing in the Great Hall at Parliament Buildings after his meeting with Adams, Trimble tried to provide historic context for the encounter and he pointed behind him to the statue of the dour Lord Craigavon which was perched at the top of the staircase. As he approached waiting reporters in the Great Hall, Trimble paused at the statue ever so briefly and during the news conference he spoke of parallels between himself and Craigavon and how, at the foundation of the Northern Ireland state, the unionist hero had met the Irish rebel leaders Michael Collins and Éamon de Valera, the latter while he was still on the run.

Strangely enough, it was not only unionists who felt a connection to the deceased unionist leader. Craigavon is buried on the Stormont estate, in a plot guarded by a well-trimmed griselinia hedge grown in the shape of a cross. The cruciform plot lies just yards from the east wing of the Parliament. This unionist shrine was not a natural place to find republicans, but Gerry Adams and Martin McGuinness found it an ideal spot to hold confidential discussions during negotiations leading to the Agreement. McGuinness claimed Craigavon was the only unionist who was privy to their secrets: "Gerry and I often found ourselves ... walking around the grave and discussing our policy and strategies in relation to the talks."

After his first historic meeting with Trimble, Adams said that the unionist leader was a man with whom he would and could do business. However, Adams had already calculated that Trimble had made an error when he promised decommissioning before devolution to his party. Adams was also conscious of what McGuinness claimed he had observed on the last day of the negotiations: Trimble almost breaking his pencil as he gave his verdict.

Trimble, on the other hand, was equally suspicious of Adams' intentions. He recalled what the Sinn Féin leader had said to his party's *Árd Fheis* after the signing of the Good Friday Agreement and Trimble's success in gaining his party's approval. "Well done, David," Adams had declared. His republican audience had hesitated, then applauded timidly, unused to plaudits for any unionist leader. Perhaps the praise was genuinely meant, but Trimble felt that Adams was trying to "wind up" unionists, to sow confusion and dissent. With minds so suspicious, it is little wonder that the formation of the Executive, like peace itself, would come dropping slow.

Chapter 7
Poor Players

Seamus Mallon sat on the brick wall outside Castle Buildings with his head in his hands, desolate, bone-weary and deeply frustrated. It was the first anniversary of his election as shadow Deputy First Minister, but instead of celebrating he was caught in a web of mind-numbing talks aimed at breaking the stalemate over guns and government. While the deadlock remained, neither he nor David Trimble could share power. Instead they were condemned to walk the corridors of Stormont as little more than shadow ministers, poor players on the political stage. "Both of us," said Mallon, "were responsible for administrative decisions, without any real authority. And the worst of any world is to have responsibility without authority."

The First Minister and his Ulster Unionist party refused to set up an Executive involving Sinn Féin ministers until the IRA decommissioned its weapons. Sinn Féin insisted it had a right to Executive posts and that Trimble must move first in order to convince the IRA to decommission. Mallon was trapped in the middle. He suffered the added burden of speculating about what secret deals unionists and republicans were trying to hammer out in London, Dublin and Washington. With arguments over guns and government ringing in his head, Mallon sat on the wall at Castle Buildings, strained with the misery of it all. He was struggling with the physical exhaustion of working days that stretched from twelve to fifteen hours, a schedule that would have taxed a man half his age.

Mallon's plight, as he sat hunched over, head in hands, caught the eye of a nearby press photographer, who snapped his picture. The image appeared in *The Irish News* the following day under the headline: "Talks Agony". Mallon liked the photograph. He seemed to like it so much that the SDLP's director of communications, Barry Turley, commissioned an artist to paint it and presented it to Mallon as a gift. For Mallon it eloquently summed up his experience of shadow government.

He could scarcely believe he had spent a year as shadow Deputy First Minister, with no devolution in sight. Such a time-frame had never been envisioned in the Good Friday Agreement. The twelve months since 1 July 1998 had been at times exhilarating, and at times excruciating. High points included the visit to Parliament Buildings by Taoiseach Bertie Ahern, the first Irish Prime Minister to do so in thirty years, and the unprecedented address to the Irish Parliament by Prime Minister Tony Blair. Another milestone had been the passing of the Settlement Bill, giving legal form to the Agreement.

The shadow First and Deputy First Ministers had also represented the fledgling administration on a number of foreign trips, including the autumn investment drive to the United States. It was not a high point, however. Mallon found no respite in the United States on the eleven-city tour to promote Northern Ireland and woo investors from corporate America. The New York launch was attended by the Secretary of State Mo Mowlam, the NIO economy minister Adam Ingram and Chancellor Gordon Brown. As in Poyntzpass, the unity of purpose between old adversaries was impressive. Less impressive, as far as Trimble and Mallon were concerned, was the tour itself. Mallon felt it was failing to exploit the new Executive relationship and that the opportunities to reach potential investors were being wasted. "Performing fleas!" Mallon recalled with fury. "They tried to treat us like performing fleas."

Both Trimble and Mallon became frustrated fairly quickly. In New York, Mallon was annoyed when a woman came up to him and handed him a piece of paper and told him it was his speech and he was to keep it to one minute. Mallon looked at the speech, which in his view was full of "stuffed shirt" remarks, and told the woman to take it back. "I will make my own speech," he added, "and I am telling you, darling, I will speak for as long as I frigging want to speak." As the tour progressed, Ingram was forced into the role of peace-maker between Trimble, Mallon and the Northern Ireland jobs promotion agency, the IDB, which was organising the tour. "It all got quite tense," said the official. "On one occasion Trimble bawled out an official and then stomped off and then Ingram bawled out of one Trimble's officials."

Trimble and Mallon were not known to enjoy a warm relationship, but misery loves company and one official recalled the pair going off together and having dinner in Philadelphia. "They just said, 'A plague on both your houses – go away!'" He watched them go into a restaurant and share a bottle of wine over their meal. Mallon took issue with the facts of this story. "No," he mused. "We hadn't a bottle of wine – we had two or three."

The Denver leg of the tour was memorable because it was where the news broke that David Trimble and John Hume had won the Nobel Peace Prize, following days of speculation about it. Trimble had gone to bed at 1.00am, before the news was confirmed, and had instructed his officials not to wake him as he had an early morning appointment. But by 6.00am the world's media was clambering and his private secretary Maura Quinn was forced to go and wake him. A bleary-eyed Trimble was relieved to hear that Gerry Adams had not shared in the prize. "The nightmare hasn't happened," he was reported to have said. Mindful of the hurdles ahead, Trimble also hoped that the accolade would not prove premature, and his cool public reaction was in marked contrast to that of the jubilant Hume.

Back home, the excitement of the Nobel win was tempered by the ongoing row over guns and government and the delay in agreeing the shape of the new administration and nominating ministers to head the new departments. Agreement on the number of ministers and their departments became a source of contention, as did the number and scope of the north-south bodies under the umbrella of the North South Ministerial Council (NSMC). The Executive and the Council were interlocking. The price of the Stormont Assembly for nationalists was the north-south dimension and to ensure both sides kept faith with the deal, one could not operate without the other.

The Good Friday Agreement contained few concrete dates, but 31 October 1998 was one of them. By that date a meeting of the NSMC ought to have occurred, involving ministers from Dublin and Belfast. However, that required northern ministers to be appointed. Trimble and Mallon clashed over the issue. Trimble's refusal in the absence of IRA decommissioning to even appoint shadow ministers put the NSMC meeting in peril. Trimble tried to go ahead with the meeting without the Executive, arguing that he and Mallon were more than capable of representing the Executive and thereby meeting the 31 October deadline. Mallon disagreed. In a very public rebuke to Trimble, Mallon gave an interview to *The Irish News* political correspondent William Graham that autumn, making clear his opposition to such a move. "There can be no substitute for the [Executive]," he insisted.

As Trimble and Mallon were split on the way ahead, the 31 October deadline came and went without a resolution, but with much acrimony. The tension escalated on 30 October when loyalist gunmen, under the guise of the Red Hand Defenders, a cover name for the LVF, murdered Brian Service, a North Belfast Catholic man. Mallon was increasingly worried about the damage the row was causing to the Good Friday Agreement and to the stability of the whole peace process. He decided to take the initiative and offer his own solution at the SDLP's annual conference that November, at the Canal Court Hotel in Newry. The conference was designed to celebrate the hard-won Agreement, but Mallon put a twist into the proceedings by offering a guarantee to the Ulster Unionists and Sinn Féin: he told unionists that if, after two years of power-sharing, Sinn Féin sought to pocket gains from the Agreement without honouring the commitments of decommissioning, the SDLP would throw them out of office. To republicans he made a similar pledge, that if unionists tried to exclude Sinn Féin from power-sharing or offered new pre-conditions once the arms issue had been addressed, the SDLP would refuse to cooperate with them.

Well-placed sources suggested SDLP members, including John Hume, were upset by this proposal. They felt Mallon had gone too far in trying to meet Trimble's precondition of decommissioning. Sinn Féin, too, was unhappy that the SDLP had offered to exclude them over the arms issue. Mallon felt republicans had overlooked the flipside of his offer while unionists had acted hastily and foolishly in rejecting a chance that would not come again. Pro-Agreement unionists would later come to regret not exploring the opportunity presented by Mallon. "I always thought," said Mallon, "it was very short-sighted of the unionists not to [take it up]. It was over a year before they discussed it with me."

By then, Mallon felt it was too late. Had the offer been accepted in the autumn of 1998, there might have been a lot less grief and frustration, but as the row deepened so did sympathy for Sinn Féin's position among nationalists and the SDLP's strong position post-Agreement appeared to be diminishing as time went on. Once Mallon's offer had been rejected by both sides, the pass-the-parcel arguments over decommissioning and power-sharing grew louder and more furious through the autumn and winter, disrupting another deadline. February 1999 was the date set for devolution. To meet that deadline the parties would have to at least agree the number of departments and bodies for north-south cooperation by the end of November 1999. If not, Westminster would be unable to pass the appropriate legislation. But in the climate of disharmony, these negotiations proved more onerous, infuriating and complex than expected. Ulster Unionists complained that Northern Ireland was being asked to do in six months what Scotland and Wales had eighteen months to do – design a government.

The task of the negotiators was to reshape six direct rule departments, responsible for issues such as Health and Education. The Good Friday Agreement envisaged up to ten departments, but the unionists were holding out for six or seven, which would curtail Sinn Féin's allotted ministry to one instead of two. Dublin and the SDLP supported the argument for ten departments, although Mallon personally was not keen. "Probably for my own reasons," he said. "Six would have been easier handled." Mallon felt the UUP opposition to ten departments was a futile position: with four parties involved in the Executive, ten was always going to be the more attractive number, both to the parties and to the civil service, which would have ten permanent secretaries instead of six.

As the new 30 November deadline approached the Ulster Unionists finally agreed to ten departments, but friction continued over the function of those departments. The SDLP and UUP were at loggerheads about whether finance should be a stand-alone department. The SDLP thought it should be, and also wanted tourism to come under the department called CHATS (Culture, Heritage, Arts, Tourism and Sports). The Ulster Unionists, on the other hand, wanted to keep tourism within the Department of Enterprise, which they expected to control. But if Ulster Unionists took Enterprise, the SDLP would surely take the Department of Finance. Trimble was uncomfortable with this notion and was pressing for the Office of First and Deputy First Minister to have a say in finance matters.

There was also much disagreement over the number of north-south bodies and their respective functions. Dublin wanted seven cross-border bodies; the Ulster Unionists no more than six. The SDLP, working in conjunction with the Irish government, also wanted a cross-border body on tourism, however the Ulster Unionists, nervous about the political sensitivities involved, were not keen on such a high profile area having its own north-south body. Indeed, this sensitivity was one of the reasons the issue had not been pinned down during the Good Friday Agreement negotiations. The Ulster Unionists were willing to have the bodies deal with issues such as environmental and veterinary research, inland waterways, transport planning, food safety and Carlingford Lights, but were resisting Dublin's demand for a trade body as well as a tourism body. Unionists could see that the Irish desire for the tourism body could be a powerful negotiating chip for them and they hoped to use it to get their own way on finance, pushing it into the centre department and therefore away from the SDLP's control. On the opposite side of the table the SDLP was sticking to its demand for a separate Department of Finance.

Mallon remembered pushing for a cross-border body on Agriculture, but being over-ruled by Dublin, which had other preferences. Dublin also vetoed SDLP proposals – opposed by the unionists anyhow – that inward investment should be part of the cross-border body on trade. According to the SDLP negotiator Mark Durkan, Mary Harney, the Minister for Enterprise, let it be known that that was a non-starter. Unionists exploited the differences between northern nationalists and the Irish government, which wanted a cross-border body for EU programmes.

Amid mounting fears of a protracted stalemate, the Prime Minister and the Taoiseach got directly involved in the talks. Blair had decided he wanted to do all his negotiating with the SDLP through Seamus Mallon, to the consternation of others in the party. Mallon and Blair got on well, although Mallon felt Blair would "do a deal with the devil to get his way".

They began to make steady progress, but a number of sticking points meant the 30 November deadline slipped into December. Blair flew to Stormont for talks and on the evening of 1 December, after painstaking work, it appeared as if the outstanding matters had been resolved. But the Prime Minister left before the deal had been concluded and with his departure went any understanding reached between unionists and nationalists. Nationalists, particularly Mallon, were furious and felt betrayed by Blair. Privately, Mallon was suspicious of Ulster Unionist deputy leader John Taylor, who appeared unconcerned, grinning and telling everyone to relax. "It's going very nicely," he told confused reporters.

Anxious to have a deal, nationalists were alarmed by the unionist go-slow attitude, fearing that the devolution deadline would also be missed. Mallon felt the UUP had failed to honour its word and wondered what Taylor was up to. Was he at odds with David Trimble? The party strongly denied a split in the UUP leadership. Indeed, Trimble blamed the SDLP for the impasse. Taylor's role in the negotiations became increasingly important as Trimble had to leave the country on various trips, including a visit to Oslo on 10 December to accept his Nobel prize.

A new deadline, Monday, 13 December, was set for a deal, but it too slipped away. It was not until 18 December, just a week before Christmas, that a spirit of generosity broke out between the parties. By 4.00am on the morning of 18 December the sticking points had gradually been resolved as the Ulster Unionists and the SDLP hammered out the shape of the new administration, leaving Sinn Féin feeling the party had been sidelined in the negotiations. Ten departments were agreed, with six cross-border bodies. Dublin's demand for a cross-border body on tourism did not materialise, but a compromise was reached that saw the formation of an all-Ireland corporate body to deal with the issue. The SDLP got its way on the Department of Finance: it became a stand-alone department. The compromise was the acceptance of an Economic Policy Unit (EPU) within the Office of the First and Deputy First Minister, a move that would create significant friction between Finance and the OFM/DFM when devolution got underway.

Trimble would later regret not taking Finance for his own party: "I remember people saying to me that finance doesn't matter, that they're just bean-counters and the real decisions were taken elsewhere. We were wrong. Finance runs everything." Trimble was, perhaps, overlooking the fact that the Minister for Finance is required to achieve consensus in the Executive, but it certainly proved to be a lynch-pin of the administration.

Mallon was disappointed that the deal was eventually sealed without him. He had to depart the building the day before it was finalised to prepare for an operation. Before leaving, he had left written instructions that nothing was to be agreed without him. "He actually left us a note," laughed colleague Sean Farren. "He was very firm, nothing was to be agreed in his absence." Eddie McGrady, the SDLP MP and chief whip, continued the negotiations in Mallon's stead, but Mallon, like a worried parent, kept in constant contact by telephone, even calling in for an update at 3.00am. Party leader John Hume was also in touch by telephone.

The spirit of compromise did not last beyond the Christmas holidays, however. There had been hope that the deal meant devolution in the New Year, but 1999 brought fresh troubles. The IRA murdered Eamon Collins, a former IRA member who had written a book, *Killing Rage*, that was critical of the organisation. He was killed by elements of the

Provisional IRA on 27 January. In the face of this brutal murder, unionists once again questioned the authenticity of the stated peaceful intentions of the republican movement. Trimble stepped up his demands for decommissioning and an end to paramilitarism before power-sharing commenced. One party official said establishing the Executive without decommissioning would be like turning the ignition in a booby-trap car – it would lead to disaster. For its part, Sinn Féin insisted Trimble's party would have to swallow the "bitter pill" of having republicans in government with them.

The February target date for devolution moved to 10 March due to delays in reaching agreement over the shape of the institutions. The Office of First and Deputy First Minister had drawn up a report on the new structures, which had to be ratified by the Assembly. Trimble was nervous about getting it through as the deal required a majority of unionists as well as nationalists and several members of his Assembly team were openly threatening to vote against the new structures, fearing such an endorsement would lead to power-sharing by 10 March, without decommissioning. This was despite the fact that the UUP executive had backed the arrangements by a majority of 70 per cent.

It was late February before the Assembly endorsed the deal. After assurances from Trimble that voting for the package would not lead to power-sharing without decommissioning, all but one of his Assembly team remained loyal. The North Down MLA Peter Weir – who would ultimately join the DUP – defied his party and voted against. There was now intense pressure on the IRA to decommission, including an acknowledgement by Taoiseach Bertie Ahern that there could not be power-sharing without it, but republicans still refused to bend. Mallon warned that republicans could not keep on saying an "absolute no" to decommissioning. Yet when the 10 March deadline for devolution came and went, nationalists were upset that Secretary of State Mo Mowlam, facing unionist objections and pressure from London, failed to trigger the mechanism for selecting ministers, as promised. She pledged to do so within weeks. Sinn Féin leader Gerry Adams warned that her decision had caused problems: "We're into crisis – big time."

Little wonder, then, that the parties were in no mood to celebrate St Patrick's Day in Washington. The festivities were further overshadowed by another brutal murder. This time it was the human rights lawyer Rosemary Nelson, one of David Trimble's constituents, who was murdered by anti-Agreement loyalists. Trimble expressed his horror; Mallon said her killing was grotesque and underscored the need to implement the Agreement.

During their American visit, President Clinton held one-to-one meetings with a number of party leaders, pressing them to compromise. Adams and Trimble also held a meeting in Washington where they devised a potential solution to their "after you" approach to the guns and government argument. They talked about "jumping together". Another set of intense negotiations followed as the first anniversary of the signing of the Good Friday Agreement approached. Effectively the anniversary became the next deadline for compromise amid concern among nationalists that if Easter came and went without a deal, the Agreement would be imperilled.

The demands for decommissioning persisted while Sinn Féin continued to insist there would be no decommissioning. Martin McGuinness told reporters in early March, "IRA defeat is not on offer." To underline their point, republicans painted a mural in West

Belfast depicting David Trimble along with the words: "The Waster, wasting time, wasting your vote, wasting the opportunity for lasting peace."

While holding out for IRA weapons, Trimble told his party's ruling council there was no alternative to the Agreement: "The time has come to take control of our future. We must not let it go." In the face of heckling from anti-Agreement elements in his party, efforts were made to avoid a scene when everyone was called upon to sing the national anthem; it temporarily defused the situation. John Taylor attempted to inject some hope into the process by declaring that unionists would enter power-sharing within hours of decommissioning, while Trimble warned that without it, any attempt to trigger devolution would prompt a call from the Ulster Unionist party for a vote to exclude Sinn Féin.

Mallon began to urge republicans to come up with a form of words that could resolve the issue. In response, Sinn Féin's Gerry Kelly went to the Maze prison days before the negotiations and spoke to IRA prisoners about the decommissioning issue. He had little good news to report afterwards. "Not a single prisoner suggested there should be a goodwill gesture on decommissioning," he said. Talks were called involving the Prime Minister and the Taoiseach, but there seemed little reason to hope they would succeed and produce what the two governments were calling a "synchronised compromise".

As March slipped into April, Hillsborough Castle became a hothouse of negotiations, with Tony Blair settled in the Lady Grey room, while other parties had their own spaces for talks. The negotiations were likened to musical chairs as politicians came and went, dropping in periodically to see the Prime Minister or the Taoiseach. Like so many talks marathons that occurred in Hillsborough, rooms were divided up for the parties and negotiators slept where they could. Ulster Unionist MP Ken Maginnis, later Lord Maginnis, remembered grabbing a much-needed nap in the Prime Minister's quarters, only to be disturbed by Tony Blair, who had stayed awake all night, nipping into his room for a shower. Mallon was found stretched out on the floor of the Throne Room, on the dais, snoozing. "His hands were folded across his chest," recalled Mark Durkan, "and he looked like he was lying-in-state." Mo Mowlam took a photograph.

There were other odd scenes in the Castle, the Queen's official residence in Northern Ireland: rough-looking men in leather jackets and dark glasses were seen wandering in the Throne Room, or queuing for their breakfast while the negotiators tried to sort out the arms issue. A number of well-known senior IRA members were also present. It was a bustle of activity at all hours. Day and night the British and Irish prime ministers came and went. Many ideas were thrown up and hope was fuelled when the IRA issued a statement suggesting that if the political will existed, the peace process contained the potential to resolve the conflict and deliver durable peace. Trimble suggested that a commitment from the IRA – one that provided certain knowledge decommissioning was going to be carried out in a credible way – might be acceptable.

By Friday, 1 April, after seventy-eight hours of roller-coaster negotiations, a deal was finally taking shape. It involved elaborate choreography and sequencing. In effect, republicans and unionists would jump together into a new future. Under the proposals decommissioning was not a pre-condition but rather an obligation that had to take place before actual power-sharing. Trimble saw this as a victory for his position. Under the new proposals, ministers would be nominated for ministerial office, but weapons would have to be destroyed within one month of the nomination day when the head of the Decommissioning Commission, General John de Chastelain, would announce a date for an act of reconciliation that would put arms beyond use on a voluntary basis. Then, and only then, would devolution take place.

The collective act of reconciliation would involve not just the IRA but other armed groups, including the British Army, a move designed to make the decommissioning process more attractive to republicans despite unionist distaste for equating the security forces with paramilitaries. The complex document also proposed a ceremony of remembrance for all victims of the Troubles – a controversial proposal for unionists who would not have wanted to see police officers and civilian victims given the same status as IRA volunteers. While some elements in the Sinn Féin leadership were thought to be disposed towards the idea, the leadership was not in a position to sell it to the IRA, especially at Easter time – the anniversary of the 1916 Rising. An Irish government source remembered that the IRA was being asked for a gesture only. He also recalled, with mock tones, how unionists were pleading for such a move. "'Just one act and we'll never mention it again,' was what the unionists told us. But the feckers [the IRA] wouldn't do it." Trimble, however, insisted this description of his party's attitude was nonsense and stressed he had made it clear that there had to be a process, a beginning and an end to decommissioning.

During the talks Mallon became concerned when he learned that republicans had requested and were being granted more time. Mallon was horrified. "I had become convinced that maybe it could have been nailed that day. I went to Blair and I went to Ahern – oh, late on – and I said don't leave, don't let this stop. Run it through the night, run it through the next night and the night after that. Keep it going for a week if you have to, but don't let it stop." Mallon feared that if the talks ended without the republicans making a firm commitment to the arrangements, the deal would be lost. He recalled that a number of senior British and Irish officials were in agreement with him and he felt he had succeeded in convincing Blair and Ahern. But for some reason the talks ended at 4.00pm on 1 April. Mallon's understanding was that the unionists were on board for the deal, so he thought perhaps republicans had turned on the Taoiseach:

> "I suspect Ahern had some very big row with the Shinners that day. I suspect that – now nothing more – he was very flustered at a certain point. Now what changed it I don't know but I am still convinced had we stayed … The Shinners missed a deal."

When the talks ended, the Prime Ministers, the parties and General de Chastelain addressed the media about the developments. In a clear sign that all was not well, Sinn Féin members, including Gerry Adams, sat on the steps looking glum. The only light moment came when Adams congratulated a blushing Martin McGuinness on becoming a grandfather. Sinn Féin did not want to get the blame for failure and did not publicly reject the deal outright on the day, but republican sources privately told reporters that the deal was a non-starter, that it was built on sand.

Within days, as Mallon had feared, the deal had evaporated. Nonetheless it had stirred the political waters and introduced the notion of synchronised decommissioning and power-sharing. The view had been formed in London and in Dublin that republicans were obliged to decommission in order to initiate a power-sharing institution. This pleased Trimble, who felt he was making progress on unionists' behalf. While Trimble was not enthusiastic that the IRA and the security forces were both involved in the symbolic remembrance ceremony, suggesting moral equivalence, he said he had an open mind on the proposals if they could achieve the primary goal of decommissioning.

The republican leadership remained wary of the deal. Without a sustained period of power-sharing, how could they ask the IRA to give up its weapons? Republicans – possibly under pressure from some hardline elements – argued this would smack of surrender and defeat, and the IRA would never agree.

Further negotiations took place at Downing Street in mid-May. A pattern had been established where pressure was brought to bear on the various players at different stages, and this time it was Trimble's turn to be squeezed. These talks also failed, with Trimble getting the blame when his Assembly party rejected the offer. Trimble's biographer, Dean Godson, gives a critical account of this, suggesting Trimble did not negotiate well, was isolated and settled for too little on decommissioning. The final proposals did not make it abundantly clear that there was an obligation on the IRA to disarm before power-sharing. There was an acknowledgement that the arms issue must be finally and satisfactorily settled, but there were no cast-iron guarantees. Sinn Féin was committed to trying to achieve this within the time-frame set out in the Agreement and the IICD was to consult with all parties by 30 June. The deal proposed that all parties, without prejudice to their clear positions on the issue, anticipated devolution by this date. In effect, devolution was just six weeks away with only a promise, not a guarantee, on the crucial arms issue.

According to Trimble, the negotiations were incomplete and scrappy and promises made to him did not materialise. He claimed he anticipated a draft amendment to the Assembly's Standing Orders that would allow the ministers to be named under the d'Hondt rule of proportionality, but without giving them any status, and that devolution would only occur after decommissioning. He claimed amendments to this effect were drafted during the Hillsborough negotiations, but the proposals did not appear in the final draft – which explained why he was optimistic early in the day, but left the talks in bad form: "I never committed to anything during that day and the most I would say was I would consider it and I told Blair in the garden I didn't like it."

While Trimble acknowledged that he had shown enthusiasm for devolution early in the discussions, he said it was not because he was over-anxious to conclude a deal but rather because he had made progress at Hillsborough. He saw that one outcome of Hillsborough was that decommissioning had become an obligation and was accepted as an integral part of the process of devolution. This, coupled with the fact that Hillsborough had ended with the republicans under pressure, may have caused him to be slightly off-guard and over-optimistic about the outcome of the London negotiations.

Once the negotiations got under way in Downing Street they immediately hit a number of snags. Trimble claimed republicans tried to drag out the talks, knowing that the Prime Minister was impatient to conclude a deal because he had other pressing issues, including the Kosovo conflict. When Trimble left Downing Street that evening he headed for Pizza

Express, where he spoke by telephone to the Ulster Unionist party chairman Denis Rogan who, he said, "registered my foul temper".

Downing Street had been expecting Trimble to sell the deal to his Assembly team and the Ulster Unionist leader – always conscious of shielding unionists from blame – no doubt felt obliged to at least go and outline it to his team. He resisted efforts by Downing Street to get him to come to a 5.00pm press conference the following day. When they called he was en route to the airport and refused to turn back, suggesting that having slept on it he was no more inclined towards the proposals than the night before. Quite possibly, the closer he got to home, the less enthusiastic he felt about the deal.

Trimble had been outnumbered by republicans in Downing Street and got burned in the negotiating pressure-cooker. He may well have put too much faith in Blair, with whom he wanted to maintain a good relationship. But if he was enamoured of the Prime Minister's powerful status, it did not stop him from saying no. It was during these talks that Blair noticed Trimble studying a picture of the war Cabinet by the stairway. Trimble told the Prime Minister, "This is the sort of Cabinet you should have." Trimble was making the point that two Ulster Unionists, Edward Carson and Walter Long, were in the war Cabinet with Lloyd George. Blair seemed to have got the impression Trimble was hinting at having a place in his Cabinet, but Trimble said he was simply trying to impress upon Blair that, historically, Ulster Unionists had always been part of the British national political scene.

By now Blair was used to Northern Ireland politicians remarking on photographs in Downing Street. Gerry Adams, on his first trip to Number Ten for "unfinished business", had also paused by the stairway, where the wall was adorned with black-and-white portraits of previous British Prime Ministers. Adams, contemplating how Blair's predecessors, such as Gladstone and Thatcher, had handled the Irish Question, mused: "Do you put all your failures on the one wall?"

Following the failure of the mid-May Downing Street talks, a deadline of 30 June was set for agreement. By this time the British and Irish governments were hosting negotiations at Castle Buildings. It was these talks that coincided with the first anniversary of Trimble's and Mallon's election as shadow ministers, by which time the Deputy First Minister was feeling the strain. This time round the proposals – presented as "take it, or leave it" by London and Dublin – were acceptable to Sinn Féin because decommissioning was not required before devolution. But the Ulster Unionists dug in, wary of the revised arrangements: just as Easter had not been a good time for republican compromise, the July marching season was not going to be a time of compromise for unionists. The new formula, entitled "The Way Forward", involved all parties reaffirming their commitment to the principles of an inclusive Executive with devolved powers and to the decommissioning of all paramilitary weapons by May 2000. Decommissioning would be carried out in a manner determined and prescribed by the de Chastelain arms commission, which would have urgent talks with the paramilitary groups' representatives. The IICD would ensure that decommissioning would start within a specified time, with progress reports in September, December and May 2000. Prior to decommissioning, ministers would be nominated on 15 July. The devolution order would be laid before parliament the following day, to be implemented on 18 July.

It was proposed that the de Chastelain commission would confirm a start to the process of decommissioning within a specified period. But unlike the Hillsborough proposals, there would be no firm date for the actual destruction of IRA weapons, mainly because republicans had always insisted this must be a voluntary act on their part. To ensure that unionists were not trapped in an Executive while the IRA dithered on decommissioning, the proposals also included a "failsafe": the institutions would be suspended if there were a default on decommissioning or devolution. Unionists still objected that this did not constitute a "cast-iron" guarantee that the republican movement would disarm. Trimble was not convinced by the "safety net" of suspension legislation. "A cure just as bad as the disease," he told reporters.

Recalling the events years later, Trimble reiterated that there was no point accepting "The Way Forward" proposals, even with suspension, because he could see no change in republican attitudes. The Ulster Unionist leader was under pressure from his party, with several members of his Assembly team publicly opposed to the proposals, and as he could not afford to lose even one member, this was a serious situation for him. Trimble was also mindful of criticism from the DUP. Ian Paisley's anti-Agreement unionists were ready to accuse him of reneging on his "no guns, no government" election promise. DUP deputy leader Peter Robinson declared: "We want product, not promises."

Trimble expressed a willingness to go into government with Sinn Féin, but was insistent that unionists and republicans "jump together" – that is, they enter into government when the IRA destroyed its weapons. "The Way Forward" proposals required government before guns. Mallon and the SDLP were suspicious that Trimble's dilemma had more to do with timing than anything else – that he did not wish to ask unionists to compromise during the Orange marching season when, as some nationalist commentators put it, the unionists were in the grip of "Orange fever". One SDLP observer told *The Irish News*: "As Sinn Féin becomes more flexible, the unionists are becoming more tense."

However, the SDLP did share the Ulster Unionist concern that Tony Blair's government was attempting to spin the magnitude of the republicans' apparent shift on the arms issue. Much was made of the fact that republicans had moved towards accepting that decommissioning was going to happen. "Seismic shift" was how it was described by the Prime Minister's official spokesman and spin doctor, Alastair Campbell. Sinn Féin's Pat Doherty dismissed the claim as "a cod", but it is not clear what, if anything, the party leadership told the governments inside Castle Buildings to justify the claim. Trimble called it "bluff and counter-bluff" by republicans. "They [the governments] were spinning it as a seismic shift but in our discussions with republicans we could see no evidence of that."

The SDLP, too, concluded that the reality was more seismic spin than seismic shift. During the course of talks with the Prime Minister, a sceptical SDLP – mindful that Sinn Féin had signed up to an Agreement in 1998 that envisaged decommissioning – challenged Tony Blair. The Prime Minister had spent many hours in meetings with the parties during this talks session and was no doubt impatient for progress. In a private session with him, the SDLP leadership demanded to know the exact nature of this "seismic shift". The party was concerned about attaching too much significance to what seemed a small, incremental move. Their question received no satisfactory reply, so John Hume challenged the Prime Minister over his official's spin. "You can't do this to our peace process," he said. At that point, it was claimed, Blair lost his patience and snapped, "This is *my* peace process! I'm the Prime Minister and I guided this through. Nothing happened until I became Prime Minister." An SDLP source said that after about five seconds Blair became composed again. "It was as if he had wiped the memory of losing his temper and then went on with the meeting."

Blair's relationship with the unionists was not faring much better. Although he did not show it in public, he was thought to be very unhappy with the Ulster Unionist leader's attitude to the proposals, especially since he had taken a risk and annoyed republicans in the days after the talks by beefing up the suspension legislation. He may also have been annoyed by the way Ken Maginnis, the Ulster Unionist, had spoken to him during the talks. Maginnis had told Blair rudely, "Prime Minister, this is a load of shit."

As the days passed and the date for the appointment of Executive ministers crept closer, Trimble declined to give his answer and pressure mounted on the unionists to accept the proposals. Blair spoke to a delegation of Ulster Unionists at Downing Street. He publicly urged everyone to accept "The Way Forward". "Don't just say no," he beseeched.

The Ulster Unionists were still adamantly refusing to either reject or accept the proposals. In the meantime, Mallon made clear his position. He could not understand how the unionists had rejected "The Way Forward" proposals, with their suspension safety net, when they had endorsed the Hillsborough ones, which he described as a "piddling little thing" in comparison. The Deputy First Minister claimed that the outside world would not understand it either. In a biting interview, Mallon said it was quite remarkable that some politicians – meaning unionists – thought it was the "wrong time" to form the Executive. "There has been no good time. One seriously has to ask the question, do people want decommissioning to happen or do they want to win the argument about decommissioning?"

After listening to circular arguments over arms day after day, Mallon had had enough. He suspected the row was not about decommissioning at all. He had become convinced that Trimble was in fact trying to renegotiate the Agreement. In particular, Mallon thought the Ulster Unionist leader was unhappy with the notion of parallel consent and "jointery" – giving nationalists and unionists and the two First Ministers equal say over key decisions. Mallon recalled that during the negotiations leading to the Good Friday Agreement, Trimble had argued for a weighted majority in decision-making. Mallon stuck to his demand for parallel consent. Mallon told the governments that the issue was a deal-breaker as far as he was concerned. "I made it clear on the second last night before Good Friday that, if that ain't there, I am going to get into my little car and I am going to Markethill and I am going to bed."

Mallon got his way in the end, but claimed Trimble was determined to reverse parallel consent later. "That is what all this stuff with Blair was about," he insisted. "That was at the heart of the decommissioning thing. I told that to Blair and I told that to Ahern and I told that to everybody involved and I says, 'You are going to f— it up unless you understand that'."

When Mallon's claims were put to him, Trimble grinned. "I think decommissioning came up the list," he said. But he did admit to disliking the notion of jointery in the office of First and Deputy First Minister, saying: "I grumbled a bit." He claimed it was SDLP negotiator Mark Durkan who convinced him to accept the titles of First and Deputy First Minister. "I was opposed to having any titles at all," said Trimble. "Mark Durkan sold it to me on a false basis. The Agreement doesn't give any status to these posts at all and then comes the legislation and the legislation introduces the bloody jointery thing and I didn't want that. And if Durkan had been more forthright in what he was proposing, there would never have been an agreement on this."

Durkan remembered it differently. He thought Trimble fell for the idea of being First Minister and knew exactly what he was signing up to with the joint and equal ministers. Durkan recalled Trimble talking about the power of patronage when the concept was explained to him. Whatever the truth, Trimble has always insisted he wanted the Agreement to work but that he needed unequivocal evidence that the IRA was going to decommission. He did not believe that republicans, at the time the Agreement was signed, had any intention of carrying out decommissioning: "In terms of their grassroots, they were saying 'not a bullet, not an ounce' and I think they meant it."

Trimble has long maintained that he was fighting for a genuine peace, not a sham one. He had still not given a public answer on "The Way Forward" when he and Mallon were bestowed with honorary doctorates from Queen's University, Belfast. They appeared in their robes, smiling, but as was often the case with this political duo, they were sending out different signals. Mallon, almost willing it to be true, declared: "We will form the Executive and we will solve the problem." Trimble's response to the question about the formation of the Executive on 15 July was: "Let's see."

The following week began with the devolution Bill in the Commons, when Trimble highlighted his dilemma: "If I gamble and the gamble is a mistake, then we lose the process and we lose the current leadership of the UUP." Trimble became adept at convincing the Prime Minister – who hosted an Ulster Unionist delegation on 12 July – that the process could not succeed without him. His precarious position, whether exaggerated or not, was useful in getting Downing Street's attention. Eventually, Sinn Féin cynically labelled the political efforts as the "Save Dave" process. Mallon, too, believed Trimble – to his own cost and the cost of the process – exploited his weaknesses within unionism to win concessions from London instead of honouring and selling the Agreement more forcefully. "Oh, he played on that [his vulnerability]," said Mallon. "He was in Downing Street every week asking for more changes. And it had to stop. Dublin should have stopped it." Trimble, however, took particular exception to suggestions that he failed to sell the Agreement, insisting the opposite was the case.

Matters came to a head on 14 July, the eve of the Assembly meeting at Stormont Parliament at which the d'Hondt mechanism for nominating ministers was to be triggered. After an Assembly meeting at Stormont, the Ulster Unionist Executive, a 100-strong body made up of constituency and elected representatives, gathered at the Ulster Unionist headquarters, then situated in an antiquated building on Glengall Street, just behind Belfast's Grand Opera House. Reporters gathered outside to hear the verdict. They expected a long, tedious night standing on the pavement while Trimble attempted to persuade his party. They were therefore taken aback when Trimble, surrounded by colleagues, emerged after just fifteen minutes to give a news conference on the doorstep of Glengall Street. The answer was no.

Seamus Mallon was fuming. His mood turned blacker when he switched on the news and saw UTV political correspondent Ken Reid offering analysis, having just interviewed the Prime Minister in the garden of Downing Street. Reid said it was his understanding that the process had been put "on ice" until the autumn. Mallon knew that Reid would only have said this if he had got the nod from Downing Street. Mallon got on the telephone to the Taoiseach's Office to complain and then spoke to Downing Street. "Look," he said, "you can't play it like this. This is not acceptable what you are doing. You are taking something that we have been negotiating on and at the request of one of the participants you decide unilaterally to [sideline it]." Mallon told Downing Street and Dublin he would not accept it, warning: "I will take steps."

Faced with the belief that Downing Street and Trimble were acting in bad faith, Mallon followed through on his threat. The following day the Assembly was due to meet to select ministers for a shadow Executive; Mo Mowlam was proceeding with the d'Hondt mechanism despite objections from Trimble that it would be nothing more than a charade. Mallon was at the Wellington Park Hotel in Belfast, where he had summoned two of his key advisors, Brian Barrington and Hugh Logue. When they arrived he informed them that he was resigning as Deputy First Minister and was drafting a speech that he would deliver at the Assembly the following day. The speech was worked on into the wee small hours while phone calls came from London and Dublin. Mallon said the same thing to both governments: "I've told you what I think, I can do no more."

Logue claimed he also tried to change Mallon's mind. "I tried to persuade him it was wrong, that it was foolish, but he was very determined." Mallon's other close aide, Colm Larkin, was in Brussels on business and insisted he too would have tried to convince him not to resign. Mo Mowlam, also alarmed at the news, was among the influential politicians who tried to dissuade Mallon. He was in no mood to listen. A senior civil servant who had worked closely with Mallon summed up just how stubborn he could be once he had made up his mind: "Trying to turn Seamus Mallon – you had more chance turning the *Titanic* from the iceberg."

In the hours leading up to the d'Hondt process, Trimble heard that Mallon was going to resign. He urged Mowlam to use her influence with the Deputy First Minister to try to dissuade him. "I remember phoning up Mowlam and saying, 'This is daft. Go and get hold of him and stop this,'" Trimble said. Trimble's legal opinion was that Mallon's resignation would have no impact in terms of his own status, so if Mallon had any thought of forcing the First Minister from office, such a notion should be dismissed. Ignoring the obvious political implications of Mallon's resignation, Trimble told the Secretary of State that it would not force him from office as he was determined not to go, a move that some regarded as a crass attempt to cling to power. Trimble claimed Mowlam agreed with him that the resignation was a mistake, but she got nowhere with Mallon.

Logue remembered telephone calls coming through from the Taoiseach and even from Downing Street. He also remembered Mowlam, having herself suffered from Downing Street's machinations, being sympathetic to Mallon's plight. Mowlam told Mallon that if anybody should resign, it should be her. Mallon, Logue believed, was still teetering on his decision and might have been persuaded not to resign if Trimble himself had telephoned him. Trimble laughed at this notion. "I was encouraging other people who I thought might have some chance of persuading him." In a telling insight into the true nature of their relationship, he said: "I thought if I speak with him, it ain't going to happen." He laughed again. "I would have been the last person to talk to him."

Mallon agreed an intervention from Trimble would have made no difference. What he required were assurances from London and Dublin that a review would be called in the wake of the latest crisis, one that was properly constituted and capable of breaking the stalemate without descending into renegotiations of the Agreement. "They were resisting having a review other than them handling it," said Mallon. He wanted someone from outside London and Dublin to conduct the review, someone of the calibre of Senator George Mitchell. Without those assurances, Mallon was determined to resign. Sources also suggest Mallon became absolutely certain that he was doing the right thing when he arrived at the Assembly for the debate and the d'Hondt procedure and found that the Ulster Unionist party Assembly team were not going to leave Glengall Street, effectively boycotting the Assembly that day. "That was the final straw," said one SDLP source. "We had an inkling ... they were in Glengall Street and weren't coming. Going to the chamber and just seeing these empty benches on the other side. That made up his mind very clearly."

Mallon said he was already convinced that he was taking the right course and the boycott by unionists did not influence him. Nor was he influenced by other last-ditch appeals. Hours before his resignation the political development minister, Paul Murphy (who would later become Secretary of State), came to see him in his office. But Murphy, like everyone else, got nowhere. Mallon informed the minister that he was tired of Downing Street making side-deals with the shadow First Minister: "I have told the Prime Minister this messing has been going on with Downing Street on a weekly basis and I said, 'you can't work in this type of joint arrangement if you have Downing Street playing games and so as far as I am concerned that is that'." Mallon repeated his complaint that the Prime Minister had let it be known through a reporter, without consultation, that the process was going to be sidelined until the end of October. Mallon was blunt with Murphy. "I am not taking it," he said.

Mowlam also came and went that morning without success. The Prime Minister himself rang Mallon on his mobile phone as he sat in the chamber waiting for proceedings to begin. Mallon might have changed course then, but Blair did not give him the assurances he needed in relation to the review. Another source close to Mallon at the time said: "Right up to the last moment Seamus' mind was reasonably open, but he felt Number 10 hadn't come through. He hadn't got what he wanted and felt the only way to defend the Agreement was to remove himself."

Before he could deliver his resignation speech, the Assembly had other business to address, mainly ministerial nominations. During the proceedings a hand-written Standing Order was delivered from the Secretary of State's office to Lord Alderdice, the Assembly speaker, authorising him to trigger d'Hondt.

Soon the Assembly had descended into farce because, according to the rules, the Speaker had to call on Trimble to nominate and give him five minutes in which to make up his mind. The difficulty was that Trimble had not shown up, nor had his Assembly team, and in effect the speaker was addressing rows of empty Ulster Unionist benches.

Laughter erupted in the chamber as the speaker, careful to ensure the unionist leader was given his lawful five minutes to nominate, shouted: "Clerk, check the clock."

Thus began the pretence of nominating a doomed Executive. It could not last because it lacked a single unionist participant. Ian Paisley announced he would not be taking part as he wanted to keep Sinn Féin out of government. The Alliance leader, Sean Neeson, condemned the nomination process as outrageous and lambasted the UUP absence as unforgivable. Nonetheless, one by one the ministers, all nationalists, were nominated, first by John Hume and then by Gerry Adams.

The SDLP MLA Mark Durkan became the first minister appointed, to the post of Finance, followed by Sinn Féin's Bairbre de Brun, to Enterprise, Trade and Investment, and then the SDLP's Sean Farren, to Regional Development. The SDLP's Bríd Rodgers was nominated Minister of Higher Education, while Sinn Féin's Pat Doherty took Minister of Education.

John Hume then attempted to nominate Eddie McGrady as Minister of Health, but he refused to accept it. McGrady had realised that his nomination was well down the pecking order, thereby ruling him out of the three ministerial posts the SDLP would get if this were a real nominating process. He wanted to be a minister and would have liked Finance, according to SDLP sources.

Hume went on to nominate Joe Hendron for Health and Denis Haughey as Minister of Social Development, before Sinn Féin's Mary Nelis took up Culture, Arts and Leisure. Finally, Alban Maginness was nominated Minister of the Environment. With six SDLP ministers and four Sinn Féin Ministers and not a single unionist (the rules stated there must be no less than three unionists and three nationalists), the Executive was immediately dissolved.

Then, in dramatic style, Seamus Mallon rose to deliver his personal statement.

A unionist who was in the UUP's Glengall Street headquarters that day recalled how some unionist Assembly members called out to the television in vain as they watched Mallon rise to make his resignation speech, "Don't do it, Seamus."

The Deputy First Minister lambasted the failure to implement the Agreement and set up the institutions, his weary frustration plain for all to see. "Deadline after deadline has been missed ... Permutation after permutation has been tried. We have tried and I have tried every move in the book and outside it," he said. Mallon, whose relationship with the First Minister was now strained to breaking-point, accused Trimble's party of spurning and scorning the efforts of the British, Irish and American governments, of dishonouring the Agreement and of "bleeding the process dry". He spoke of the need for a fundamental review, where all the parties entered as equals without "the trappings of office or the benefits of title". And in a pointed comment to Trimble, he declared that he could not enter a review "from the privileged position of First Minister of the Assembly". Apologising for being a little long-winded, he finished with another barbed comment that was clearly aimed at Trimble's absence that day: "I do not treat this Assembly with contempt."

To Mallon, the UUP's failure to turn up at the Assembly that day was a grave insult. A senior civil servant observed that Mallon had come to regard himself as the guardian of the Agreement and had begun to feel a fraud. Representing the new administration, Mallon was out in public talking of a bright future, while all the while trapped in an old argument. Nonetheless, Mallon's resignation did shake the process, if not Trimble himself, who refused to leave office. The next day's headlines warned: "Peace in Tatters as Mallon steps down". Almost immediately Mowlam announced a wide-ranging review and within a few days Senator George Mitchell had been recruited to chair it. The review was expected to get under way in earnest that autumn.

The resignation did not improve Mallon's relationship with Trimble, which was already fractious, but the unionist insisted it was not a turning-point in their partnership. "I didn't pay any attention to what he said," Trimble insisted, and then laughing added: "If I paid attention to all the negative comments people made about me, I'd stay in bed." Indeed, years later Trimble was dismissive of the episode, suggesting Mallon was unable to resist a bit of drama: "Seamus had got himself into a very strange state of mind at that stage and he was just going to go ahead. Bear in mind, Seamus was at one stage a playwright so he did the marvellous scene for himself and he is a very good actor."

Trimble's flippant dismissal of the resignation failed to appreciate the enormous pain that Mallon was feeling, according to SDLP colleagues. His advisor, Brian Barringon, said the shadow Deputy First Minister had become deeply pessimistic about the political process: "At that point he no longer believed a solution was around the corner. And he really did see himself as the defender of the Agreement." Barry Turley concurred that the resignation decision was not taken lightly:

> "I remember Seamus saying he had a conversation with himself and that it was most interesting and he came to the view that he had absolutely no choice. Seamus had no leverage in office, no power, and the two governments did not have the wit to listen to him. What Seamus was doing was using his office as political leverage. It was the only leverage he had. He wanted a proper review and he wasn't getting it and he used [his resignation] to draw attention to it and to blow the whole thing out of the water."

Mallon was acutely conscious of the impact his decision would have not only in London and Dublin but also in Washington. He conducted a series of media interviews aftwards, insisting on starting with the Atlanta-based US network, CNN. Turley recalled, "He wanted Bill Clinton to hear why he had done what he had done and he wanted to go on CNN first."

Turley also remembered being in the lift at Stormont a few hours after the resignation speech, when the pair had time to draw breath. He recounted the story to illustrate how deeply Mallon felt at the time:

> "Don't underestimate how little appetite he had for it. He didn't want to do it. And it hurt him deeply to do it. Seamus took a lot of personal knocks during that time, a lot of them. And I remember shaking hands with him in the lift and I had tears in my eyes, and he said, 'don't you start, or I will'. It was an awful day, but it achieved what it set out to achieve because it was back to the drawing board with Mitchell and we got what we wanted."

With the benefit of hindsight, Mallon has remained resolute about his decision: "I did the only thing open to me at the time. I didn't want to do it, but there would have been no Mitchell review, no review of that nature. Things would have got worse."

The reaction of the government was swift, and appeared unforgiving. The trappings of office were withdrawn immediately. While Mallon was on his feet delivering his speech, his driver got a call requesting him to go to another job. "The system dropped him immediately," said an SDLP source. "He had to get a lift home with John Fee that day."

Chapter 8
Mitchell's Return

Senator George Mitchell, the smiling diplomat from Maine, was reluctant to get involved in the political stalemate over guns and government. He had chaired two years of talks leading to the Good Friday Agreement, when hours, days even, would be spent arguing over the tiniest detail – where a comma should go, or the exact meaning of a particular word. He did not wish to repeat the experience. He knew the best brains in London, Dublin, Belfast and Washington had been unable to resolve the deadlock over weapons.

Despite these reservations, Senator Mitchell, who was a skilled diplomat, may have decided the parties were closer to a resolution than everyone thought. He had learned the art of compromise on Washington's Capitol Hill and he believed that the Good Friday Agreement was still the best hope for peace in Northern Ireland. He also remembered how difficult it had been to achieve the Agreement. Preparing to return home at Easter 1998 after helping to negotiate it, Senator Mitchell had memorably told reporters, "I hate to leave, but I'm dying to go." Whatever the final impetus, he decided to chair the review after some consideration. His wife, Diane, supported his decision, telling him, "You've got to go because if you don't and the conflict resumes, you'll never forgive yourself."

During the summer the Ulster Unionists had been unsuccessful in their attempts to coax Mallon back to his post as shadow Deputy First Minister. It was hoped the review would prove fruitful, but as it got underway in September 1999 the omens were not good for a deal between the Ulster Unionists and Sinn Féin. Unionists were furious with republicans amid allegations of ongoing violence by the Provisional IRA (PIRA), which was widely believed to have been behind the murder of a Catholic man in July. The body of Charles Bennett was found on waste ground behind a social club on the mainly nationalist Falls Road. He had been bound and shot dead. The Bennett murder coincided with allegations of republican involvement in gun-running in Florida. Again, suspicion pointed to the PIRA. Unionists pressed the Chief Constable, Sir Ronnie Flanagan, and the Secretary of State, Mo Mowlam, to clarify whether the ceasefire remained intact. To the chagrin of unionists and others, Mowlam ruled that the ceasefire had not been breached. The murdered man's grieving family asked that politicians not use his murder as a political football, but tensions were running high.

Sinn Féin claimed to be reluctant participants in the review after unionist rejection of "The Way Forward" proposals some weeks earlier. The review's remit was very specific: it involved the establishment of an inclusive, power-sharing Executive with devolved power and the decommissioning of weapons by May 2000 in a manner determined by the Independent International Commission on Decommissioning (IICD).

The first day of the review attracted pro-Agreement supporters to the gates of Castle Buildings. Politicians who had negotiated the Good Friday Agreement passed placards with the words: "We still say yes." These enthusiastic cheerleaders for the Agreement would grow thinner on the ground as the process stalled repeatedly over the years.

The review got off to a slow start. Mitchell knew he was not going to get anywhere immediately and was astute enough to let the parties vent their spleen at each other, to air their grievances before the real negotiating began. According to one account, when McGuinness made a statement blaming unionists for the problems in the process, Trimble responded by quoting Oliver Cromwell: "I beseech thee in the bowels of Christ, brethren, to think that ye may be mistaken." Outraged, McGuinness hit back that it was a hell of a thing to quote Cromwell at an Irish republican, when he had been sent to Ireland in the seventeenth century to quell rebellion. When Trimble responded along the lines that Cromwell had at least fought a clean fight, there were further heated exchanges.

There were also tensions within the Ulster Unionist party, which erupted into open dissent on the question of participation in the review. In one interview, John Taylor suggested the party should pull out. David Trimble subsequently appeared on the defensive at the Labour party conference, where he was forced to reject suggestions that his party was preparing to set up government without decommissioning. It was around this time that Trimble, often accused by nationalists of failing to sell the Good Friday Agreement, gave one of his most impassioned defences of the deal. He was in Bangor addressing young unionists, who generally tended to be on the right of the party; "the *herrenvolk*" was how *The Irish News* columnist Brian Feeney liked to describe them. Before Trimble signed the Agreement, the young unionists had flocked around him. No longer, though. In Bangor that autumn they passed a resolution calling for Sinn Féin's exclusion from government. Trimble was very angry when he arrived at the meeting. In his speech he was frank about his displeasure, revealing some of his motivation for signing the Agreement. He chided the young unionists that this resolution was not party policy, arguing that the Good Friday Agreement was necessary to sustain the union in the face of growing numbers of Catholics within its borders. The unionist majority, he said, was in decline and Northern Ireland would one day need the support of pro-Union Catholics to sustain its place in the United Kingdom. Alienating this group, which was overwhelmingly pro-Agreement, would put the union at risk, he argued: "The destruction of the Agreement will undermine the union faster than any other course of action you can think of." For his part, Gerry Adams had already warned that the Agreement was finished if the UUP failed to live up to its responsibilities.

Initially, Senator Mitchell appeared to be getting no further than the governments had. For weeks all that the unionists and republicans seemed able to agree on was that there was no progress to report. Senator Mitchell spoke of great stress on the process. Irish government sources, however, were predicting that a deal would be hammered out, and one that was close to "The Way Forward" proposals. This seemed remote until Senator Mitchell announced he was taking the parties to an undisclosed location, away from Northern Ireland, away from the news media and away from the paralysing fears that prevented them from taking risks.

The Senator imposed a news blackout, but word soon leaked out that he had taken them to Winfield House, the London residence of the US ambassador. Only a small number would take part in this intense dialogue, among them: Gerry Adams, Martin McGuinness and Aidan McAteer on the republican side; and David Trimble, Sir Reg Empey, Fred Cobain, Danny Kennedy and Ken Maginnis on the unionist side. The party's respective press aides were there, republican Richard McAuley and unionist David Kerr. Trimble's chief-of-staff, David Campbell, was also present.

It appeared Mallon had been cut out of the very review he had fought to bring about. He denied this, however, saying: "I wasn't cut out in the sense that I sat there for how many bloody months almost on a daily basis, almost always on my own. I wasn't letting anybody cut me out as I was part of the discussion the Shinners were having. I was also having daily – three times a day – discussions with Senator Mitchell. So I had a good idea what was going on."

Winfield House proved to be a turning-point according to some, although others felt its importance was exaggerated. At a dinner on the first night, Senator Mitchell broke the ice by warning the participants sitting around the imposing dining-room table that they could talk about anything other than politics. One diner recalled a bizarre evening: "All of us were sitting around a table, sworn enemies basically, and trying to be polite just so George wouldn't feel put out."

Senator Mitchell used his status as an outsider to good advantage. Ken Maginnis, a former UDR major, was looking across the table at Martin McGuinness, whom he had once described as "the godfather of godfathers". Mitchell helped ease the tension between them when he looked at the opposite side of the table and gently teased, "Well, Ken, Martin McGuinness, Ken Maginnis – you must be related." Maginnis good-humouredly pointed out that his own name was an old Celtic one, whereas McGuinness was "very much Anglo-Irish". McGuinness laughed and answered, "Well, you might be right." The pair ended up talking about their grandchildren and then Martin McGuinness brought up one of his favourite subjects: fly-fishing.

Senator Mitchell was sitting between McGuinness and Trimble, a known opera buff, and McGuinness admitted he tried to engage the Ulster Unionist leader in conversation on the subject. Weeks earlier McGuinness had received an Andre Bocelli CD from Richard McAuley. McGuinness had quite enjoyed listening to the Italian opera singer and asked Trimble what he thought of him. McGuinness was taken aback when Trimble described Bocelli as "third division". The republican, who knew more about fly-fishing than opera, did not argue. But McGuinness was most amused a few weeks later to hear another verdict on Bocelli. As he sat watching television at home, he heard the announcer introduce "the man that opera superstar Luciano Pavarotti considers to be the greatest tenor in the world". McGuinness moved forward in his chair to hear who this might be. When the announcer introduced Andre Bocelli, McGuinness leaned back with great satisfaction, telling himself: "Well, that just shows what you know about opera, David Trimble." Trimble does not dispute calling Bocelli third division, but was extremely dubious about McGuinness' claim that Pavarotti would have rated Bocelli so highly. "I don't believe a word of that," he chuckled.

The Winfield House dinner was reported in the media as a watershed moment when, in the words of one of the participants, "Trust crept in." In truth, trust was an overstatement, but a spirit of compromise did permeate the talks with the Sinn Féin and Ulster Unionist leaderships appearing to move closer to understanding one another's predicament. By mid-November, after an eleven-week review, two jubilant governments and a coterie of nervous political leaders had drawn up a formula they believed would end what Mallon had called, with considerable understatement, a "miserable dispute". Before departing for home, Mitchell declared: "I say to you with all my heart and soul, this is the best opportunity in many years to put the bitterness of the past behind you."

Effectively, Trimble had let go of his demand to have the Ulster Unionist party and Sinn Féin jump together. He would jump first, but would expect Sinn Féin to follow swiftly.

A number of carefully choreographed steps were laid out as part of the Mitchell review. These were to be taken between the end of November and the first weeks of December 1999. As a first step, the various parties issued statements about their intentions. This would be followed by the appointment of an IRA representative to the IICD. Within days a meeting of the Ulster Unionist ruling council would be held, followed by the nomination of Executive ministers and devolution. Then there would be the inaugural meetings of the Executive and its interlocking bodies, the North-South Ministerial Council and the British-Irish Council.

As part of the choreography, Sinn Féin issued a statement on 16 November. Echoing what the Sinn Féin leader had said the previous autumn, it insisted that violence "must be for all of us now a thing of the past, over, done with and gone". Sinn Féin stressed its opposition to the paramilitary beatings that had continued, despite the ceasefire. While insisting decommissioning must be voluntary, the party suggested the arms issue would be settled "finally and satisfactorily under the aegis of the IICD".

The Mitchell proposals did not seem vastly different from the terms of "The Way Forward". They still involved the unionists moving first. In his book, *Himself Alone*, Godson reveals that Trimble almost gave up on the review, amid disappointment at the republicans' statements and fears that his party would split. What does appear to have been different was that the Ulster Unionist leader, after a crisis of confidence, decided there was more to lose if he did not proceed. Two other changes that may have encouraged him to take a leap of faith was that the marching season was over and Mo Mowlam had been forced out of office and replaced by Peter Mandelson, who was considered much more sympathetic to unionists' concerns. In the event, it was Mandelson who helped persuade unionists that they had nothing to lose. He personally addressed the Assembly team, persuading doubtful and nervous MLAs that suspension legislation would provide a safety net.

David Kerr, the Ulster Unionist director of communications and a close aide of Trimble's, remembered feeling unconvinced that the Mitchell review was going to work. He was concerned that republicans were bluffing unionists, particularly David Trimble and Sir Reg Empey, who had engaged in the secret talks. He feared these two politicians were no match for "the likes" of Gerry Adams and Martin McGuinness. Kerr said: "It was like sending in your school principal and the local reverend to negotiate with the two biggest hoods in the neighbourhood who will say anything and do anything to get what they want and you had these two inherently decent blokes in negotiations with these two guys."

Kerr claimed Sinn Féin played the game of negotiations masterfully, much better than unionists, staging their approach to the talks very cleverly.

> "Every time we'd ask for decommissioning they [Sinn Féin] would say 'no, no, no, no, no. We can't do that.' Then they would spend an hour-and-a-half on Bloody Sunday. Martin would talk about Bloody Sunday, British injustice and inequality and how he couldn't get a job when he was sixteen and all this and they would more or less drag this into every discussion … and redirect every question about decommissioning onto something completely ridiculous, or some useless discussion about human rights or somebody who had been abused in Derry in 1972 or whatever. And this went on and I can remember seeing Reg [Empey]coming back from some bilaterals looking very grey and tired and thinking, 'These guys are a bloody nightmare. They aren't engaging at all'."

Sinn Féin negotiators would have argued that they were merely trying to get unionists to understand the republican mindset, the difficulties republicans had with the process and why decommissioning before power-sharing was so impossible for them.

Towards the end of the review Kerr remembered Trimble and Empey coming back from talks in more upbeat form, insisting there had been a change in the mood. But Kerr believed the Sinn Féin leadership merely gave the impression that decommissioning was now possible: "The Provos had changed tack from saying, 'no, no, no, no' to 'well now, let's just think about that now… hmmmm'. The Provos had not said they were going to do it, they had changed from no to hmmm … They sucked us in. It was a propaganda war at the time. Who was going to get the blame? Who are the good guys and who are the bad guys and who is going to take the rap?"

Ulster Unionists, Kerr claimed, seized on the hope of decommissioning, but failed to get firm guarantees. Others believed they did get promises, but were let down. The voice one would most like to hear on this is that of Senator Mitchell, but unfortunately he declined to be interviewed for this book.

Sir Reg Empey insisted Ulster Unionists would not have embarked on the Mitchell compromise if they believed republicans were bluffing, but other unionists talked about "calling the republican bluff". A NIO source said: "I do believe it was more than a promise [from republicans] to do their best. It was a commitment in principle. The tragedy was nothing was put on paper. That's the only thing that let us down."

Another source close to the negotiations believed there was a lot of spin around the review on the part of the unionists and the government, talking up decommissioning when in fact the outcome was a very elaborate gamble in which everyone would do their best. This was the view of an SDLP insider who remarked: "It was a gamble. But in my view the Provos did double-cross the unionists. It's what they do. They gave David Trimble enough so that the nationalist people would think the unionists had got enough." Mallon, who was briefed regularly by Senator Mitchell, was careful about what he said in this regard, but certainly he was in no doubt that the unionists were double-crossed.

Trimble's explanation would suggest things were not so straightforward, that there were perhaps no guarantees. He said Adams knew very well that 31 January was the final cut-off for an act of decommissioning:

> "We had gone through that again and again and again and he knew we were proceeding on the expectation that within a period of time after the formation of the administration, action would begin on the decommissioning front. Adams' position was that he was going to work very, very hard to achieve that, but he couldn't absolutely guarantee it would happen."

Indeed, Adams himself may have been gambling. According to Godson, at a lunch in the final days of the review, Adams tried to persuade unionists to extend the 31 January deadline, but got nowhere. The difficulty facing Trimble was that his party's ruling council demanded guarantees from him when he met them to ratify the deal and, feeling unable to give them, he took another tack by promising to quit the Executive within weeks if there were no progress. Perhaps this upset the balance of the understanding with Adams, who used the term "consenting adults" in an interview about the Mitchell review. The less benign explanation was that Adams never had any intention of following through. Trimble later suspected this may have been the case: "I have my suspicions. But I don't know. There is no point in me speculating."

Fuelling suspicions about republican intentions were two critical interviews in the United States in the aftermath of the Mitchell review. On 22 November Sinn Féin's vice-president, Pat Doherty, gave an interview to the *Boston Herald*'s editorial board. It caused a furore. The *Herald* intimated that Doherty had cast doubt on decommissioning, while suggesting that power-sharing would be secure because "no one will want to go back". A few days later the former IRA gunrunner-turned-senior Sinn Féin member Martin Ferris also reportedly gave interviews in the United States in which he was quoted as saying he did not think the IRA would decommission weapons. Republicans claimed these reports were misleading and inaccurate. In Sinn Féin's defence, Adams insisted his party had no hidden agenda and repeated that decommissioning must be voluntary.

Whatever really happened, these interviews unnerved pro-Agreement unionists and made it more difficult for David Trimble to sell the Mitchell proposals. Kerr, who came up with the media strategy for the Mitchell sequencing, also remembered feeling alarmed when he saw the IRA statement that followed the review. It did not specifically state that the organisation was going to decommission. Instead, the statement said the IRA was willing to further enhance the peace process and that following the establishment of the institutions outlined in the Good Friday Agreement, its leadership would appoint a representative to enter into discussions with the IICD. Kerr started asking questions. He said his concerns, which were shared by others in the party, were brushed aside. When he was told by a senior party colleague to read the IRA statement again he replied: "I have a law degree. I know what it says and it doesn't say they are going to decommission."

Even if those around him had accepted his concerns, it was probably too late anyway. The media was already reporting elements of the deal, with 2 December 1999 set for devolution. Plans were in motion for a special meeting of the Ulster Unionist ruling council. Trimble would have to persuade a majority of the 800-odd members to accept the terms of the Mitchell review. Anti-Agreement elements in the party, led by MP Jeffrey Donaldson, were determined to block the move. The showdown was set for Saturday, 27 November, just five days before devolution was due to take place.

Trimble had decided to heed republican insistence that decommissioning was possible only in the context of power-sharing. He would now argue there was a corollary to "no guns, no government" – a phrase dreamed up by his advisor, Steven King. The flipside was that if there were no government, there would be no guns. He would tell his party: "The choice is simple. Do we want devolution and decommissioning? If we do, this is the only way to get it."

For the showdown Trimble chose the futuristic, space ship-shaped Waterfront Hall, a symbol of Belfast's urban renewal. Some in the anti-Agreement camp were the same people who had dumped Faulkner a generation before; others were on the youth wing of the party, full of youthful exuberance and known as the "Baby Barristers" because a number were young lawyers whom Trimble had taught at Queen's University. He had once been their pin-up, their great hope for the future of unionism. Some of these youths were just as staunch as their parents, who had opposed Sunningdale. Wholly committed to blocking power-sharing with Sinn Féin without IRA decommissioning, they had believed Trimble would be just as uncompromising on this issue as they were. They had forgotten the lessons of Room 17, and Trimble's pragmatic streak.

Like Faulkner, Trimble could not even be sure of support from all the members of his Assembly team. The UUP member for West Tyrone, Derek Hussey, had quit the Assembly's deputy whip post when he saw the outcome of the Mitchell review – although he refrained from public criticism of the party leader. The situation was certainly not helped by the republicans' contribution. In the face of media speculation about an imminent arms move, Sinn Féin – either concerned about rebellion among the republican grassroots, or else trying to be deliberately difficult – began to insist that there had been no secret deal on weapons. The veteran Ulster Unionist, Ken Maginnis, was sanguine, saying: "Maybe it will work and maybe it won't. But we can't be any worse off than we have been for the past thirty years."

Trimble also held his nerve in the face of a rather nasty protest a few days before the UUC meeting. Accompanied by Secretary of State Peter Mandelson, he went to Edenderry Orange Hall, Portadown, where a group of protestors jeered Mandelson, who had recently been denounced by DUP leader Ian Paisley as having a "love-in with terrorists". Dermot Nesbitt, the pro-Agreement Ulster Unionist for South Down, claimed he was punched in the back outside a meeting in the seaside town of Newcastle.

A group of protestors was also on hand outside the Waterfront Hall for the UUC meeting, shouting "traitor" and other insults when they spotted Trimble arriving with his wife, Daphne. However, the Trimbles were also greeted by a small but lively group of well-wishers singing, "Trimble, Trimble, he's our man!"

In his jacket pocket David Trimble had an unstamped letter that had been hand-delivered to him just hours earlier. It was from the widow of the murdered unionist politician Robert Bradford and its contents helped reassure him that he was doing the right thing. In fact, as revealed by Frank Millar in *The Price of Peace*, the Ulster Unionist leader showed the letter to his party's ruling council president, the late Sir Josias

Cunningham. When asked if he would use it in the meeting, Trimble indicated he would not. Inside the hall, Trimble spent several hours trying to convince his party to embark on power-sharing. He faced stiff opposition, not just from elements of the old guard but from most of his Westminster colleagues. The meeting became particularly emotive when references were made to those murdered by republicans, including Ulster Unionists Robert Bradford and Edgar Graham.

Trimble said nothing about the letter of encouragement, but during his summing-up he heard one of his former supporters roaring from the back row, accusing him of betraying Robert Bradford. It was then that Trimble pulled out the letter and read it. Whether it changed anybody's mind or not is a matter of conjecture, but it did silence his critics. Fearing retribution from the no-men of his party and conscious of Faulkner's fate, Trimble was careful not to push his luck with the Council. He calculated that grassroots unionists would not accept the new Executive involving Sinn Féin unless there was certainty that IRA guns would follow swiftly. The unionists' concerns were many: what good was a promise of a report on 31 January from General de Chastelain? What if no guns were decommissioned? Would unionists be trapped in the Executive? Could they trust the British to suspend the institutions?

Trimble attempted to reassure the meeting. He told the 860-strong body of unionists that if there were no guns by February 2000, he and his three ministers would resign. It is thought this decision was prompted by a *Daily Telegraph* report which had predicted a 50-50 split in the council. Without Trimble's promise of resignations, it is possible he would have been defeated. However, with guarantees that all the Ulster Unionist ministers would resign should decommissioning not occur within weeks, the resolution was passed. The ministers' letters of resignation were placed in the care of party president Sir Josias Cunningham. Trimble won the day at the Waterfront Hall by a margin of 58% to 42%: just sixty votes separated the winners and losers. Trimble had taken a risk and won.

The UUC meeting coincided with the DUP annual conference, held several miles away at the La Mon Hotel, the scene of one of the worst IRA atrocities of the Troubles. At his conference that day the DUP leader, Ian Paisley, an orator few could match, shouted out insults aimed at Trimble and his ideas of new unionism. Predictably, just as he had done to Faulkner and others before him, Paisley accused Trimble of treachery, of selling out, painting him as a salesman who was prepared to "besmirch his heritage, split his party, and destroy his country".

Some of those at the Waterfront Hall may have agreed with Paisley in that moment. Outside the Hall the mood had turned nasty as more protestors gathered to challenge the Ulster Unionists. One woman screamed bitterly that the Ulster Unionist party had sold Ulster, spitting out the words: "May God forgive them, may God forgive them!" Inside, a rather flushed Trimble, with his wife by his side, had held a news conference and delivered a sharp message to the Sinn Féin president: "Mr Adams, it's over to you. We've jumped. You follow."

When Senator Mitchell was informed of what had occurred at the Ulster Unionist Council, he was pleased. He declined to be interviewed for this book, but according to a well-placed source he saw nothing wrong with the decision to recall the Council because, like Trimble, he believed it would not be necessary. Perhaps the Senator did not fully appreciate the republican mindset, which would balk at the unionists' threat to resign if decommissioning failed.

Certainly there was no positive response from Gerry Adams, who was also listening intently to the live broadcast. Plagued by a bout of 'flu, Adams listened to the proceedings from his sickbed. When he heard Trimble's announcement, he did not so much jump as nearly fall out of bed. Decommissioning, republicans had always maintained, had to be voluntary. To Adams' ears, Trimble's tactics smacked of ultimatum: disarm or else. Adams insisted he could not, indeed would not, sell this to the IRA hardliners, whose mindset from the first mention of decommissioning back in the 1990s was "not a bullet, not an ounce". Even in the context of power-sharing and the full implementation of the Agreement, the weapons issue was always going to be a massive obstacle. Adams immediately rang the "Talkback" programme and went live on air, telling presenter David Dunseith that he could not believe his own ears.

Republicans would later contend that the North's new beginning was soured by Trimble. Trimble has consistently stood by his actions, claiming they concurred with the Mitchell review. Before the promises turned to disagreement, there would be a frenzied political dance when, in the words of Seamus Heaney, 'hope and history would rhyme'.

Chapter 9
Out of the Shadows

The Sinn Féin leader Gerry Adams rose from his seat in Stormont's debating chamber with all sides straining to hear what he had to say, especially the unionists. Although the chamber was unusually crowded, both with Assembly members on the benches and visitors in the galleries, the only sound that could be heard was Adams' voice. The Sinn Féin leader, as was his custom, spoke first in Irish: "*Ainmnim Mairtin MacAonghusa mar Aire Oideachais.*"

At that moment, outside of Sinn Féin, only a smattering of Irish speakers in the chamber, such as the SDLP's Bríd Rodgers and Sean Farren, understood the significance of what Adams had said. It sank in when he translated his words: "I nominate Martin McGuinness as Minister of Education."

Those members who had been holding their breath in anticipation released a collective gasp of disgust. This was followed by hisses and cries of "shame". The presiding officer, Lord Alderdice, in line with the formality of the occasion, tried to ask McGuinness if he would accept the nomination, but he could hardly be heard, his words drowned out by the rising cries from the unionist benches and from some in the visitors' gallery above. Lord Alderdice threatened to clear the gallery and insisted he would not be interrupted, booming, "Order!"

The outcry faded for a moment, but then the anti-Agreement member, Cedric Wilson – who had built his reputation as a placard-waving serial protestor following the Anglo-Irish Agreement – declared, "I can't sit through this obscenity. I am leaving." He was the only one to walk out.

Speaking first in what little Irish he knew, McGuinness accepted the nomination, which gave him control of all children's education. Unionists were aghast at the prospect of the sworn republican being responsible for the education curriculum and their children's schools. McGuinness' alleged role in the IRA over several bloody decades had made him a hate figure for most unionists. Despite firm denials, McGuinness was reputed to have spent most of his life leading the Provisional IRA, which had been responsible for the deaths of hundreds of police and Army personnel and civilians.

The peace process, and McGuinness' growing electoral base, did not alter the fact that many unionists still regarded him as chief executioner: the man who had waged war and cynically exploited the ballot box while employing the bomb and bullet. During the shadow period, after the DUP made allegations about his continuing IRA role, McGuinness brought part of a loyalist hand-grenade used in an attack on a constituent into the chamber to remind everyone that republicans were not the only armed group. When unionists complained, the Speaker ruled that McGuinness' action was not a breach of protocol.

Now, McGuinness was the fourth minister to be chosen for the new Northern Ireland Executive, and without question he was the most controversial.

The ministerial selections had begun at 5.40pm on 29 November 1999, after Mallon's resignation of the previous July had been dramatically reversed. Under Assembly rules more than 50 per cent of both unionists and nationalists had to agree the joint election of a First and Deputy First Minister. Nationalists' votes in favour were secure, but without guns up front it was uncertain whether Trimble could muster the support required from his benches. Mallon's resignation was deemed invalid by the government on a technical point and was reversed following a decision by the Secretary of State to rewrite Standing Orders. The resignation was declared not to have taken place because the Assembly had not formally accepted it – even though Mallon had formally tendered his resignation and given up the trappings of office.

Mallon was uncomfortable with the reversal procedure and had made it clear to the government that he was not going to tell any lies. In fact, he insisted he would be stating very clearly that he had resigned. However, the government had found a loophole in the law and was determined to proceed with his "unresigning". Mallon said he had no choice but to go along with it: "The law was against me. I was not happy but I could do nothing about it." A source close to him said the fact that no one challenged the move in the courts showed the law was sound on this point: "It was Trimble who should have been embarrassed. He was the one who couldn't deliver his side of the house, but he always took the view these were problems for other people to solve."

With the law against them, the best the anti-Agreement unionists could do on selection day was point-score over several hours of debate. Mallon's pride was sacrificed for the process and he had to put up with some teasing from the anti-Agreement members, not least Peter Robinson, who suggested he should be re-elected as "Minister for Loopholes".

The selection process took place three days before the first meeting of the power-sharing Executive, with the posts distributed according to party strengths. There were ten ministerial posts on offer. That meant three each for the Ulster Unionists and SDLP, and two each for the DUP and Sinn Féin.

After a delay of more than a year during the shadow period, the whole nominating process took just forty-four minutes. The procedure resembled a political chess game. The nominations were made by each of the party leaders, who had worked out in advance which of the ministries they would most like to have, while at the same time second-guessing what the other parties might choose. The failed nomination attempt back in July 1999 had given a few clues, but had also thrown up some red herrings, giving unionists a false sense of security that McGuinness would not take Education and with it the control of their children's school lives. A "natural assumption" was that McGuinness would select the Department of Agriculture because that was the portfolio he had ended up with in the aborted Executive. "That was a ruse on our part," confessed McGuinness, "to confuse the DUP." Much black humour had attended that occasion as the Agriculture portfolio would have put the republican in charge of agricultural fertiliser: a key ingredient in some IRA bombs.

But unionists saw nothing funny about McGuinness seizing Education. They had wrongly assumed that Sinn Féin's Bairbre de Brún, the other party nominee, was the obvious choice for Education. Sinn Féin stayed quiet about what it would take and let others surmise that de Brun, a former teacher, would take either Education or Culture. The DUP MLA Sammy Wilson remembered seeing Bairbre de Brun at all the briefings on education issues. "The natural assumption was she was going to be the one who took [it]," he said.

Trimble was as surprised as everyone else when McGuinness took Education and he made a mental note to select the chairmanship of the Education Committee for his party at a later stage in the process. The Ulster Unionist party could have taken Education as its first choice, as it had the first, fifth and eighth nominations. However, when he was invited to make his first selection, Trimble nominated Sir Reg Empey to the post of Minister of Enterprise, Trade and Investment. This choice came as no surprise. Empey had wanted the job and Trimble said there had been a strong lobby within the party on his behalf: "A lot of people in the party thought he deserved it." Strategically, it was seen as a high profile ministry, and comprised industry, energy and tourism.

The SDLP leader John Hume had the second choice. Earlier that morning he had met his party Assembly team and together they had worked out which ministries best suited them. Typically, Hume had written the choices on the back of an envelope. He got to his feet and announced he was appointing Mark Durkan as Minister of Finance, in part to prevent it falling into the hands of either the DUP or Sinn Féin.

The third choice was the DUP's and it too failed to select Education. As widely predicted, DUP leader Ian Paisley appointed his deputy, Peter Robinson, to Regional Development. It was a big budget department, putting him in charge of roads and rail transport. Robinson told the Assembly he would be scrupulously fair in office, and read out his own ministerial pledge.

At that point Education was still on the table; Sinn Féin claimed it. According to party sources, there had been energetic debate within Sinn Féin about which two ministries the party should take. It is claimed that initially only a few shared McGuinness' desire for the Education portfolio; many considered Culture, Arts and Leisure, or some other department, a far more attractive proposition. "The number of people who would have argued Education in the weeks before d'Hondt was run wouldn't have been that many," McGuinness recalled. Having listened to advice from all sides about what choice his party should make, an exasperated Gerry Adams finally said, "Martin, you are going to do the job, you choose."

McGuinness chose Education, taking his inspiration from the sixteenth US president, himself a didactic. He had read that in his first speech Abraham Lincoln had said that education was the most important issue facing the people of the United States. McGuinness had decided that Education was the department for him: "Depending on how you shape a department of education, you can bring about huge social, political and economic change." He was mindful of the fact that this portfolio would put him in the heart of both government and community, whether it was the Falls or the Shankill. The Department of Education controlled a £1 billion budget – one of the largest in the Northern Ireland administration. As minister, he would be responsible for the education of almost 350,000 children and young people in almost 4,000 nursery, primary, secondary and grammar schools.

The republican would have been bitterly disappointed had the DUP seized Education, but would have settled for the Department of Further and Higher Education. When he heard Ian Paisley declare his preference for Regional Development, as many expected, McGuinness was filled with relief. Oddly, it had not occurred to the unionists, or to the majority of commentators, that Sinn Féin would put Martin McGuinness in charge of their children's future. Even some Sinn Féin Assembly members claimed to be taken aback; one party source said he thought McGuinness was supposed to take Health. "There was no big debate. McGuinness would take Health and de Brun would take Education and at the last minute it was switched. It was McGuinness who forced the issue. He didn't want Health." McGuinness insisted this was never the plan.

Once Sinn Féin had selected Education, six were left: Health, Environment, Higher Education, Agriculture and Social Development. By this point all four party leaders had made one choice and were now moving onto their second selections. Two more nominations followed swiftly.

Trimble named Sam Foster as Minister of the Environment. Senior unionists later confided that it was a strategic mistake to take this portfolio, a view shared by Sir Reg Empey: "We were more concerned with the politics of local government. If we were looking at it again, we would revisit these issues. But planning issues were hugely important. That was the rationale."

Hume then named Sean Farren as Minister of the Department of Further and Higher Education and Training, no surprise given that he was a former college lecturer and a close associate of Hume's.

Paisley requested an adjournment to consider which of the remaining portfolios to take. After the permitted fifteen-minute break the DUP leader chose Nigel Dodds for Social Development, eschewing Health and Agriculture, particularly important to the rural heartland from which the DUP drew its vote. Peter Robinson later claimed Social Development was chosen because it did not require too much contact with other departments and contained important issues, such as housing. But it is also possible the DUP, recognising that both Health and Agriculture were in crisis, preferred the less contentious portfolio. The DUP leader's son, Ian Paisley Jr, would also later claim that the DUP realised early on that there was a possibility Sinn Féin would take Education, but that the DUP allowed the party to do so as a means of further eroding unionist support for the Agreement. This has been dismissed by others as spin.

For his third choice Trimble selected the brand new Department of Culture, Arts and Leisure (D-CAL), calculating that Sinn Féin would be anxious to get this portfolio. It had responsibility for issues such as the Irish language – and Trimble wanted to keep it from Sinn Féin. The Ulster Unionist leader snapped it up and named Michael McGimpsey, who was thrilled: "I think a lot of people were stunned when we chose D-CAL. But it was very important to us." The Ulster Unionists and the DUP would later blame each other for the fact that Education fell to Sinn Féin. Sir Reg Empey said Ulster Unionists were relieved not to get the blame for Culture falling to republicans: "We felt if Bairbre had been let loose in D-CAL, it would have been hugely unpopular."

An Irish official claimed that Sinn Féin's key players, who had sent their nominees to Dublin to learn the art of running a government department, had never been interested in the tiny Culture department, which had a small budget and little influence. The official felt the Ulster Unionists had actually managed to make it more significant than it was ever intended and that McGimpsey made the best of a bad choice. It was long thought, however, that Bairbre de Brun would have liked the post and would, according to McGimpsey, half-joke to him some months later: "Can we swap jobs?"

When Adams rose to make his second choice there were two portfolios left: Health and Agriculture. The Speaker had to call order once again and Adams complained about the protests, insisting he had been quite tolerant of what he called "latchecos" – an expression used in the Hollywood westerns of Adams' youth, meaning cowboys. Then, like Paisley, Adams decided to call time while he worked out what to give Bairbre de Brun – a sign, perhaps, that Sinn Féin had not, as some would later claim, settled hungrily on Health before the proceedings even began. The Assembly proceedings were suspended at 6.07pm.

They had weighed the options: Health, or Agriculture? After a brief discussion about the pros and cons, Sinn Féin decided to choose Health for de Brun. It had the biggest budget, but was also the biggest challenge. It was plagued by bureaucracy, chronic shortages and years of under-funding. Hospital waiting lists were at record levels. It was a Department that could sink a minister, but crucially it was also the kind of Department where a capable and determined minister could make real strides and initiate changes that would have an immediate impact on the lives of the electorate. Despite the difficulties posed by Health, Sinn Féin was drawn to it over Agriculture. "We thought we could make a difference," said the party's press aide Richard McAuley.

As the Sinn Féin Assembly team, having been briefed on the decision, re-entered the chamber, Bairbre de Brun passed by the SDLP's Bríd Rodgers, who had been tipped for the last post. Rodgers said de Brun whispered in Irish that she was taking Health. Rodgers was dejected because she knew then that Agriculture was hers. She had been dreading getting that portfolio and over lunch that day had confided to her leader's wife, Pat Hume, that she had a "funny notion" she was going be lumbered with Agriculture. Mrs Hume had reassured her, "Don't be daft! The DUP won't let Agriculture go!"

By the time Hume rose to make the final nomination, there was no choice but Agriculture.

It could be argued that Sinn Féin took risks and got the selection right. Republicans seized the departments that others either could not, or would not take. As a consequence, Martin McGuinness and Bairbre de Brun ended up with the best choices: high spending departments that focused on people and gave the new ministers a strong public profile. It was a chance for Sinn Féin to shine and they grabbed it, while other ministers seemed to be reduced to bit players.

Graham Gudgin, David Trimble's economic advisor, said he was not consulted about the selection and was appalled when Sinn Féin walked out with control of more than half the budget: "My blackest day up there was the day he chose the portfolios." The DUP's Peter Robinson, on the other hand, was not exercised about the size of the Sinn Féin departments because he felt a lot of their millions were predetermined by teachers' and nurses' salaries, for example, and that his department had more spending discretion.

Of course, Robinson's input to the Executive was going to be limited in any case because he and his DUP colleague, Nigel Dodds, although claiming two ministerial positions, were refusing to actually attend any meetings. When the Secretary of State Peter Mandelson heard this he accused the DUP of "breath-taking hypocrisy".

After the ministers had been selected the party leaders, including Ian Paisley, selected their nominees to head the Assembly's various committees. This allocation was also carried out according to relative party strengths. Bríd Rodgers' mood was not improved when Paisley nominated himself to chair the Agriculture committee. Not only had she received a portfolio most considered the short straw but now Paisley himself would be keeping a sharp eye on her.

Once the selection process had been fully completed, the ministers' first task was to greet the waiting media and their Department officials. Sean Farren had another priority, however, and he sprinted past a delegation that included the permanent secretary from his Department and ran up the stairs to hug his wife, Patricia. After years of frustrating stalemate, he, like the other ministers, was overjoyed.

It was dark before any of the ministers left Stormont that evening. None was yet a fully fledged minister – that would not happen until midnight the following evening. Legislation ending direct rule was rushed through both houses of Parliament the following day. Trimble welcomed the end of direct rule, while Gerry Adams welcomed the legislative changes that came with it. The ministers were now headed for Room 21 on 2 December.

Having fulfilled his side of the bargain, Trimble awaited the IRA's response. It came within hours. In a statement that fulfilled the choreography of the Mitchell review, the IRA announced it was appointing a representative to the IICD. The unnamed man turned out to be Brian Keenan, a veteran republican ex-prisoner whose nickname was "the Dog". Keenan was wiry and small and had a fierce reputation that made him feared by other IRA men. He had once famously declared that the decommissioning he envisaged was "the decommissioning of the British State in our country". It was not clear whether his appointment was a signal of defiance, or a signal to the hardliners that a staunch republican was willing to support a decommissioning process, therefore they should too. The former seemed more plausible given the sour tone of the IRA statement, signed with the traditional pseudonym: P. O'Neill. The statement expressed concern about the conditions on arms laid down by Trimble, i.e. that weapons must be decommissioned by February 2000. The IRA said it was carefully considering the implications of this proposal. At that point, what that actually meant was anyone's guess.

Chapter 10
"Call me Martin"

Martin McGuinness fingered the sheaf of papers in his lap as he was driven along the M5 at speed, clad in his best dark suit and amber tie. It was 30 November 1999 and he was making the eighty-five-mile trip from the Bogside to Bangor, a two-and-a-half-hour journey to Rathgael House that had taken a lifetime along a troubled road to complete.

The bundle of papers, his first ministerial brief, had been given to him the night before at Parliament Buildings, after he had finally been nominated as a minister. As he headed for his first day at the office as Minister of Education, he was anxious about how he would be received in his Department – especially given the hissing in the Assembly chamber the previous day when his nomination was announced. McGuinness was given to understand that the Education Department was dominated by unionist attitudes and unionist personnel; he had heard Catholic educationalists complain privately that it was sectarian. "It never struck me that there would be any republicans in there at all and I wondered how we could make this work," he said later.

McGuinness had been somewhat reassured, upon leaving the Assembly chamber, when he was immediately surrounded by a knot of friendly officials led by his new permanent secretary, Nigel Hamilton. Hamilton had the appearance of a kindly but fastidious professor and, like McGuinness, came from working-class stock. Unlike McGuinness, however, he came from the other side of the divide. Hamilton was a consummate professional. "A smooth operator," said one official. Trained to work with whichever minister came his way, Hamilton expected the same level of professionalism from his staff. To his delight, McGuinness was informed that the permanent secretary would personally come out and greet him when he made his debut at the Department the following morning. On top of that, his new officials had already anticipated his desire to use the Irish language in formal statements, and press releases had been prepared in English and Irish. It seemed a good start. En route to Rathgael House with his aide, Bríd Curran, McGuinness reflected that the Gaelic translation of Rathgael was Fort of the Irish. "Probably a most appropriate headquarters," he mused.

McGuinness' driver that day was Gerry McCartney, a fellow Derryman, whose brother, Raymond, had played a prominent role in the first H-Block hunger strike in 1980. There was a sense of adventure as the republicans travelled along the breathtaking Glenshane Pass, down into the valley below and on towards the motorway. Flicking through his briefing notes, McGuinness was conscious that his life was about to change fundamentally and he struggled to maintain his concentration as he neared his destination. From the front passenger seat of the dark green Ford, he looked out at the drizzly grey day and peered into a corner of County Down that had once been alien to him. Bangor was about as far away from the republican Bogside as you could get, politically, socially and culturally. It was British in outlook and character and loyal to the Crown. Set in the heart of affluent North Down, an area known as the Gold Coast, it was home to the privileged: wealthy businessmen, senior civil servants, as well as many police officers. As far as he knew he had never been there before, and he was struck by the irony that a Bogside republican was about to take up residence in this bastion of unionism. What a contrast McGuinness presented to Northern Ireland's first Minister for Education under the old Stormont in 1921: Lord Londonderry was the scion of privilege, educated at Eton and Sandhurst.

James Martin Pacelli McGuinness had started life in Derry's Bogside, in relative poverty, on 23 May 1950 at Waterside General Hospital. He was the second son of William and Margaret (Peggy) McGuinness, whose family would soon swell to seven children: six boys and one girl. McGuinness' unusual middle name, Pacelli, was in honour of the Italian Pope at the time, Pius XII, previously Eugenio Pacelli.

McGuinness' father was a foundry worker, eventually progressing to foreman in Brown's Iron Foundry in Foyle Street. His mother had come to Derry from Buncrana in Donegal in the 1940s and had found work in the shirt factories before devoting herself to being a full-time mother and housewife. The family lived in Elmwood Street, in a tiny terraced house with two bedrooms. In those days it was common for nine people to be squeezed into such small quarters and many were living a hand-to-mouth existence in appalling conditions. The McGuinness family was more fortunate than most because the head of the household had a steady job. The foundry's workforce was mixed and Willie McNeill, a Protestant from the Fountain Estate, was a close family friend. McGuinness later said this friendship had a positive impact on his own attitudes and made him aware of the evils of sectarianism. He always regarded his long battle with the State and its forces as political, not religious. While he was taught to be tolerant of other religions, his upbringing was steeped in Catholic tradition and culture. The family said the Rosary each evening and William McGuinness attended daily Mass. "A deeply religious man," was how McGuinness described his father. McGuinness professed a belief in God, but respected other faiths, saying: "I am not so foolish as to think we have it all right and everybody else is wrong."

As a child he attended the Victorian-era St Eugene's Convent School, known locally as the "Wee Nuns", before transferring, at the age of seven, to the Christian Brothers' Brow of the Hill School, which had a reputation for corporal punishment, or what the pupils called "a good thumping". McGuinness said his experiences of school were "not that great". While he remembered good and decent teachers, he was discouraged by a "tiny minority" who were not suited to teaching. "Some of them effectively turned me off education. I couldn't get away from school quickly enough," he said. Some of his teachers were excellent and he enjoyed their classes. One, Jack Hanna, remembered a well-mannered, industrious and disciplined boy. "Martin was very much a team player," said Hanna, who taught him mathematics. "He was probably one of the quieter boys, which in some ways is why he stood out."

Peggy McGuinness described him as the quietest of all her children. As a child, despite his poor eyesight, McGuinness was athletic and liked Gaelic games and soccer, often playing matches at the bottom of his street. In the summer he relished trips to his Granny

Doherty's farm in Donegal, in the Illies area, just five miles from Buncrana on the banks of the Crana River, where beech, lime and maple trees lined its brown waters. It was there he learned to fish. His passion for fly-fishing came later when a friend told him it would be a therapeutic pastime. He learned how to cast a line in a football field. When he tried it with water, he caught a salmon on his second cast. He liked to say his dream job would be "Minister for Fly-fishing". While he loved Donegal, his heart lay in the Bogside. He married local girl Bernadette Canning in November 1974 and raised two girls and two boys at Westland Terrace, just a few streets from his childhood home. "This is where I feel at home," he said. "It is important to me."

Growing up in the Bogside, McGuinness was always conscious that people in his community were treated as inferior. "They were taught to know their place and not reach for the stars," he recalled. When he left school and applied for a job as a mechanic, McGuinness got to interview stage but was quickly shown the door when it became clear from his schooling that he was a Catholic. Derry writer Eamonn McCann remarked drily that it was the most expensive "thanks-but-no-thanks letter" in history. According to McGuinness, the rejection impacted deeply on him, but not immediately. "It was only afterwards, whenever my consciousness was raised by the civil rights protest, that I realised how rotten the State was," he said.

Unlike Gerry Adams, McGuinness was not raised in a republican household. His parents were nationalists and more likely than not would have voted for the old nationalist party leader, Eddie McAteer, or SDLP founder John Hume. "Politics," said McGuinness, "were never really discussed at all in our house and we could certainly not have been described as being a republican family."

Derry became the focus of the civil rights movement in the 1960s when Catholics and nationalists challenged discrimination in voting, housing and employment. Unwilling to bend, the system dealt with the civil rights protestors in a heavy-handed fashion and rallies were often forcibly broken up by the security forces. Like other young Catholic men, McGuinness became involved in contests with the police and the British Army in what they regarded as a battle for justice: "Nearly all of my generation were drawn into the Battle of the Bogside. I was involved with everybody else in throwing [stones] and whatever else we could get our hands on at the RUC and the B Specials."

By 1970 he had signed up with the IRA. McGuinness said he joined after one of his neighbours was murdered by the security forces. It was the police, not the IRA, he insisted, who claimed the first casualties: "That's the reality." He had watched teenager Desmond Beattie die at the bottom of his street after being shot by the British Army in disputed circumstances. McGuinness decided to hit back with what he would later call "the cutting edge of the IRA": "There are limits to what you can do with a stone. And at the same time lead bullets were being used against the people."

Although McGuinness was already involved with the IRA when the British Army shot dead thirteen civilians in Derry on 30 January 1972, Bloody Sunday doubtless had a profound impact on him. He would later tell the Bloody Sunday Inquiry that he had wanted to shoot back at soldiers that day and actually went looking for a gun. But he controlled himself and instead decided "to let the world see what the British had done". He said his role at the time, aged twenty-one, was to maintain the integrity, discipline and structure of the IRA. McGuinness, along with others, vehemently disputed claims by the undercover agent "Infliction" that he may have fired shots on Bloody Sunday, dismissing the allegation as dirty tricks. Despite widespread condemnation of the IRA's campaign as immoral and futile, McGuinness was always defiant. He refused to accept sole responsibility for the burden of history and the bloodshed of the Troubles, laying blame at the doors of Stormont and Number 10, Downing Street.

He became more and more involved in the struggle against the State, eventually entering politics through the IRA's political wing, Sinn Féin. Politics and armed struggle dominated his life. The two roles fused in 1972 when he was a member of a top-level IRA delegation that met with Secretary of State Willie Whitelaw in London. It was claimed that McGuinness went to those political talks armed with a gun, although he has refused to comment on that allegation. In the years leading up to the 1994 IRA ceasefire he met secretly with British government representatives, in spite of official claims the government did not "talk to terrorists".

In the 1980s Sinn Féin began to seriously contest elections and McGuinness first stood in 1982 in Derry, after playing a role in overturning Sinn Féin's ban on taking part in elections to "partitionist" bodies. In line with party policy he did not claim his seat, but it did raise his profile and he continued to defend the IRA in public. In 1986 he was quoted in *The Irish News* as stating: "Freedom can only be gained at the point of an IRA rifle and I apologise to no one for saying that we support and admire the freedom-fighters of the IRA."

McGuinness' alleged role in the IRA made him a hate figure for many unionists. Members of the security forces feared and also loathed him. Once, McGuinness was detained at a checkpoint in Tyrone for four hours. The RUC man who stopped him called him a bastard and when McGuinness got out of his car to complain to the senior officer, he was told: "I think you are a bastard, too." He was even named in "The Cook Report" as "Britain's Number One" terrorist. He denied the programme's claim that he had lured an IRA informer, Seamus Hegarty, back to Derry from a safe house outside Ireland by assuring the man's mother that he would not be harmed. Hegarty returned, and was soon found with a bullet in the back of his head, his hands bound behind his back and his eyes covered with black tape. Such was McGuinness' reputation and association with the IRA that for years he was banned from travelling to England and his voice, like that of Gerry Adams, was banned from the airwaves.

But things changed, society moved on and eventually he turned away from the "long war strategy", which had led to stalemate. As he reached middle-age his views shifted and he embraced the "peace strategy" as a means of driving Irish unity. One Belfast republican remembered that when others became despondent or wanted to give up, McGuinness was always resolute about the future of the movement. The Belfast republican claimed that in the latter days of the Troubles, McGuinness was the visionary, ever confident of Sinn Féin achieving power. McGuinness denied he ever envisioned the party at Stormont, but said he did have faith that Sinn Féin would triumph in the end:

> "I have been arguing within Sinn Féin, going back more than a decade, that the day would come when we would have the ability to become a major political force, not just in the north, but all over the island."

By the time the Good Friday Agreement was signed in 1998 he was already an MP, although he had not taken his seat in Westminster because he refused to swear an oath to the British monarch – a prerequisite to sitting in the Commons. His decision to go to Parliament Buildings at Stormont was a milestone in his political career. After Bloody Sunday McGuinness had declared bitterly, "They [unionists] want their Stormont and we will not give them their Stormont." By laying claim to his ministerial post in a new power-sharing Stormont that was linked to Dublin, McGuinness perhaps felt it was a stepping-stone to his goal of Irish unity. He declared: "My war is over. My job as a political leader is to prevent war." Describing the peace process as one of the most significant things to have happened in his life, he added: "Where we are now is a far, far happier place."

McGuinness had known many darks moments, as had so many others who had endured and survived the Troubles. Some who observed him in those times saw him as very serious, intense and forever frowning. A press photographer was once asked by Sinn Féin press officer Richard McAuley if he would take a "smiling" picture of McGuinness. "I would," said the photographer, "if you could get him to smile." When this observation was put to McGuinness during an interview for this book, he seemed genuinely perplexed by it. After some brief reflection he said his disposition reflected troubled times: "There was little to smile about many years ago."

McGuinness' unauthorised biography, *From Guns to Government*, claimed that during the Troubles his mood would fluctuate between black depression, when the IRA campaign was going badly, and great elation, usually associated with Sinn Féin victories. Certainly there was no mistaking McGuinness' elation on the morning of 30 November 1999 when he arrived at Rathgael House for his first day as Minister of Education. His grin was as wide as it could stretch, his blue eyes lit with pure joy as he observed the large gathering of reporters and cameras and the row of civil servants waiting outside for him. McGuinness straightened his tie before rushing forward to greet Hamilton. McGuinness was never sure when he extended his hand that it would be taken, and to avoid embarrassment on either side he often waited for others to make the first move. But as he approached his new permanent secretary, he was confident of a handshake.

"Welcome to Rathgael House," Hamilton greeted him, his hand outstretched.

"Thank you very much. It's great to be here," McGuinness answered.

Two senior officials, Stephen Peover, deputy permanent secretary, and Tom Shaw, chief inspector of schools, greeted their new boss, appearing rather awkward in front of the cameras. Their public welcome filled the new minister with confidence and it helped win his trust, particularly in Hamilton. "For a civil servant," McGuinness said, "to come and extend a welcome to a republican minister, with my history in the struggle and so forth, was a huge thing for me. And in many ways it was probably a bigger thing for him." To McGuinness, Hamilton had demonstrated more than mere bravery. "Leadership. That's what it showed, leadership," he maintained. Conscious of the hostility and horror felt by some in his Department at the prospect of "Minister McGuinness", Hamilton believed it was the right thing to do. He wanted to show McGuinness that he was prepared to work professionally with him and he knew it would serve as an example to the entire staff. When it had become clear that the Department of Education would be headed by a devolved minister, Hamilton had gathered members of staff together to remind them of their duty to serve the new minister, whomsoever it might be.

McGuinness gave a news conference in the lobby of Rathgael House while some curious staff members listened from their doorways. Some smiled; some did not. Maggie Taggart, BBC Northern Ireland's education correspondent, posed the first question: "What do you think in your own school background will guide you in this department?" It was a question McGuinness had anticipated. "Well, I left school when I was fifteen. I think in the course of the last thirty years I've been through the political education of a lifetime," he said. He also made clear that he was there to learn and was aware some people feared he would not serve all children equally. "They couldn't be more wrong," he insisted. As his civil servants looked on, some looking distinctly nonplussed, McGuinness talked of a history of discrimination and declared it was not something he intended to repeat. He was looking forward to a new future and described the formation of the Executive as a powerful step forward. Asked about IRA decommissioning, he said it was now over to General de Chastelain, who was expecting a statement from the IRA. "Steady as it goes," McGuinness declared. Peover looked over at Shaw, but failed to catch his eye. At that point it was still not clear if the price of power-sharing was going to be paid. As he moved away, a reporter asked McGuinness if it felt strange to have the trappings of office. He seemed irritated by the question: "I'm not interested in the trappings of office. ... I'm interested in treating people with respect."

McGuinness and his entourage of civil servants and republicans crushed into the lift and headed for his second-floor office, where he greeted his diary secretary and other staff. As a minister, McGuinness was entitled to earn what was a fortune for someone living in the Bogside – around £70,000 a year. Most of his salary went to Sinn Féin, however, and the party said his take-home pay was equal to those who answered his telephone.

"Nice place," McGuinness declared on entering the room. Once again he fixed his tie before diving for his desk, taking to the burgundy leather chair like a child to a new toy. He joked about his workload and someone suggested there might be a red or green box for the minister. "Nigel, is there such a thing as a red box or a green box?" McGuinness inquired. "There'll be a box somewhere," Hamilton bantered back.

While McGuinness got used to his Department and his new role, others were going to have to get used to him and his new advisor, Aidan McAteer. McAteer was a Derry-born republican raised on the Falls Road, who was sentenced to twelve years in jail for possession of arms and explosives. "I left school at eighteen and went straight to jail," McAteer would say matter-of-factly. His father, Hugh McAteer, was a former IRA chief-of-staff who had once staged an escape from Crumlin Road jail in Belfast. Incarcerated in the Maze prison, his son performed a different kind of escape by applying himself to the study of politics, economics, history and Irish. It did not take long for the Assembly's education committee to order a copy of his CV. McAteer had worked closely with McGuinness during the Good Friday Agreement negotiations and, like the new minister, had pre-conceived notions about civil servants, who at one point during the Troubles were on the IRA's list of "legitimate targets". McAteer's view of senior civil servants was informed by the BBC satire "Yes, Minister", in which officials manipulated bumbling politicians into doing things their way. He may not have been far wrong. Former head of the civil service, Sir David Fell, once joked that he thought "Yes, Minister" was a documentary. Nonetheless, McAteer had much to learn about the men and women who worked for and supported the minister.

McGuinness went out of his way to try to build good relationships with his officials and anyone else with whom he came into contact. There was a gathering in one of the conference rooms soon after he arrived, an opportunity for the new minister and his staff to get to know each other. The minister made his way around the room and spoke to anyone who wanted to talk. "It was very heartening so many turned up," he said. "They could have chosen not to." McGuinness immediately told them he did not want to be called "Minister", as was Civil Service tradition. "'Just call me Martin', that was his catch phrase," said one civil servant.

McGuinness preferred informality. Asking everyone to use his Christian name was a conscious decision on his part: he thought it would break down barriers. He denied there was any political discussion in Sinn Féin about this: "I just thought it was a sensible way to proceed, dealing with people on a human level rather than behind these very grand titles, such as minister." His officials gradually got used to the informality, but it took a while. "Initially, they lapsed into 'Minister'," he said. "That showed how well trained they were." After a few months the vast majority, especially officials with whom he worked closely, were calling him by his first name. "It was very human. I liked it and I think they liked it, too," he recalled.

While many civil servants may have been both curious and courteous, there was a backlash within unionism. McGuinness had been in office only a few days when Protestant schoolchildren began protesting. The first reported protest was in the fishing village of Kilkeel in County Down, but the demonstrations soon spread to Belfast, Portadown, Newtownards and other areas. Seventy pupils from Ballymoney High School marched into their town centre in school uniform, singing "The Sash" and shouting, "McGuinness out, Paisley in." Some, draped in the union flag, were reported as stating that "No Fenian will teach us Irish." Some DUP members and some other anti-Agreement unionists supported the protests, while the Office of First and Deputy First Minister condemned the walk-outs, which were discussed at the Executive table. McGuinness said he would not be deflected from his job

The Presbyterian Church claimed the children were being manipulated for political purposes and condemned the walk-outs. Opposition to the schools protest also came from an unexpected quarter when Shankill UFF leader Johnny Adair urged children in North Belfast to go back to school, while his associate, John White, was reported to have spoken to students from Mount Gilbert and Model Boys' in Ballysillan. A protest also took place at Regent House Grammar in Newtownards, where almost 200 pupils staged a two-hour protest in the staff car park. Students held up posters decrying the new minister: "Say no to directors of murder and mutilation in charge of our schools." To add insult to injury the poster spelled his name wrong: "Maginnis out!" Students interviewed by the *Ulster News Letter* included fifth-formers David Ennis and Martine Armstrong, who said she believed McGuinness would eventually impose policies objectionable to Protestants: "We don't want to learn Gaelic." The students were supported by the DUP's Strangford Assembly member Jim Shannon, who said he had heard about the protest that morning and decided to come along to back it.

Sinn Féin was keen to defuse the situation quickly. The minister held a discussion with staff and advisors and agreed to a suggestion that he attempt to meet with concerned pupils. It was not reported while he was a minister, but a number of young people involved in the protests did choose to come and meet McGuinness; their identity has not been disclosed. Accompanied by their teachers, some students went to Rathgael House where the minister offered them biscuits, tea and fizzy orange. McGuinness poured the tea himself and the groups engaged in robust dialogue. "We tried to make the situation as warm as possible," said McGuinness. "They sat in my office and I was very honest with them. [I] explained where I was coming from, what my politics were and how I saw my responsibilities as Minister of Education."

The young people were forthright but dignified, according to the minister. Aidan McAteer said that initially the meetings were strained, with the young people expressing fears that they would be forced to learn Irish. The minister had to persuade them that he had no such intention. "Martin didn't win them over," said McAteer, "but I think he reassured them. Martin said, 'If you think I'm doing things wrong, come back and talk to me. I will listen to you. My door is open.' That was his approach."

The schools protests soon melted away, but a more sinister confrontation came in June 2000 following his failure to fly the union flag at his Department's headquarters. On his return to Rathgael House, he was confronted by a mob of angry loyalists, some masking their faces with scarves while others shouted "IRA scumbag". Lampposts outside his headquarters had been festooned with red, white and blue bunting and paramilitary UVF flags. The sight of the loyalist protestors was chilling for McAteer and other republicans, but McGuinness brushed it off.

Soon thereafter the minister moved out of Rathgael House. It was reported the decision was linked to the loyalist protest, but this was denied by the Department and by republicans, who insisted the move had been decided months earlier on the basis of convenience. McGuinness was working long hours – he left Derry at 5.30am so he could be at his desk first thing – and going to Bangor lengthened his journey time. Consequently, he opted instead to use an office at Castle Buildings while still attending to business at Rathgael House when necessary. "It's my headquarters, and remains my headquarters," he said. But the suspicion lingered that the decision to conduct some work at Stormont was taken partly for security reasons. When this was put to a senior Department official long after the final suspension, he blanched and refused to discuss it. Another went quiet and then said: "I couldn't be definitive about that. Everybody was putting their own interpretation on it."

The flags protest coincided with primary pupils withdrawing from an event attended by McGuinness. The minister had been visiting the regional heat of the Engineers for Britain competition at Balmoral when it was reported that Aughnacloy Primary School had pulled out. The school principal, Billy Tate, had received a telephone call from a staff member who was concerned about the school's involvement as some of the children's parents had served in the security forces and had been killed by the IRA. Tate realised the pupils would never have attended had they known McGuinness would be present, and one parent who had gone along was furious. Tate felt it was grossly insensitive not to inform the school of McGuinness' presence and urged the Department to introduce a suitable protocol for such events. He claimed a number of schools followed his lead that day. McAteer thought an attempt had been made in this instance to arrange a meeting, but Tate said this was not so, although he would have met the minister as he supported bridge-building. He said he was acting in the parents' interest and his decision had their support. Interestingly, he was complimentary about McGuinness as a minister, saying: "I think he was the best Minister of Education we have had up to that date. Many of my colleagues have praised his professionalism." Tate's one criticism was the vacuum left when there was nothing to replace the Eleven-plus after McGuinness, having scrapped it, was forced out of office by suspension.

Throughout his term in office McGuinness remained a controversial figure for some educationalists, although the public protests dwindled as time went on. For his part, McGuinness did make an effort to reach out to all sides, always striving to prove that he was a minister for all schools. A department insider recalled the contrasting responses from each community to the minister's entreaties, particularly evident when McGuinness invited those schools that had been allocated Budget funding to visit him at Stormont. During direct rule the practice had been for the minister to go to a school that was benefiting and make the announcement there. But McGuinness decided to bring all the schools to Stormont. Some were reluctant, but one official recalled watching as a big cross-section of children and teachers arrived for the "meet and greet" session: "On the one hand you had this hesitancy about meeting him and on the other you had a complete contrast, you had this hero-worship – he was almost god-like to some of them."

The new minister was inundated with invitations to visit Catholic schools, some of which had never before issued an invitation to a government minister. By the time he left office there were around 200 invitations outstanding, according to McAteer. His first official visit was to his old primary school, St Eugene's, in the Bogside. The visit appeared to go well at the time. McGuinness had a natural affinity with children and the cameras soaked up the image of excited eight-year-olds mobbing the minister and being told, "Call me Martin". Unlike some civil servants, the children at St Eugene's had no trouble adjusting to using his first name. "Hello Martin!" they chanted in unison.

McGuinness entertained the children with anecdotes of his own time at the school some forty-four years earlier and spoke of Sr Xavier, the nun who was principal in his time. He also told the children that he wanted to build an Ireland where there was no division, no hatred and no conflict. But McGuinness faced controversial headlines afterwards. He had told waiting journalists that he had met Sr Xavier's nephew while "on the run" in County Leitrim. When this was reported he was immediately criticised by the DUP for the remark, although he insisted he had not referred to his republican past when talking to the children. The DUP member for Foyle, William Hay, complained, "It is frightening to think this is the man in charge of our education system." McGuinness later admitted he had forgotten himself and let his guard down during what he took to be a private conversation. "That's another lesson you learn. There's always people ear-wigging with microphones," he said. McGuinness claimed he did not realise the comment was being picked up as a story. Asked if he would repeat the tale knowing what he knew now, he muttered, "Probably not."

The minister was anxious that his visits not be limited to Catholic schools, so he was thrilled to receive an invitation from Methodist College Belfast, which had links to the Methodist Church. It was the school's custom to invite direct rule ministers. Anticipating devolution, the board of governors had discussed whether or not to invite the new Stormont minister, whomsoever it might be. After consulting the school headmaster, Wilfred Mulryne, it was agreed an invitation would be extended on the basis that it was a private visit. Mulryne telephoned Nigel Hamilton, himself a Methodist, with the news and had found the permanent secretary extremely receptive. McGuinness, like the Methodists, wanted to build bridges. "It was tremendously courageous [of them]," he said.

Mulryne, who strongly opposed what McGuinness had stood for and his IRA involvement, remembered looking forward to the visit with a mixture of curiosity and apprehension. He found the minister to be personable, genuinely interested in young people and well-briefed: "What was impressive was that within a very short time, two or three weeks, he had clearly learned a great deal about the more intricate aspects of Education."

The school had a mixed intake and many pupils were glad to meet McGuinness. Those who did not wish to make his acquaintance simply stayed out of the way. There were some complaints afterwards about his visit, however, from parents, a few students and some unionists who claimed the school had sneaked McGuinness in and out. The headmaster dismissed this accusation, insisting that the same conditions of privacy had applied to visiting direct rule ministers and were employed for reasons of security only. Mulryne respected the concerns of parents and pupils, but was more robust when dealing with complaints from unionist politicians, pointing out that both the UUP and DUP could have taken the departments. There were some in Methodist College who felt a chill from other educationalists over the invitation.

McGuinness, on the other hand, described the visit as being one of the highlights of his time in office. "It was completely free of tension and stress and worry that someone would say something out of place," he said.

Another highlight for McGuinness was his visit to Lagan College, the first integrated school to be established in Northern Ireland. The invitation – to mark the school's twentieth anniversary – was sent by a former education minister in the Sunningdale Executive, Basil McIvor, a Faulkner unionist who had gone on to chair the school's board of governors. McIvor posed happily with McGuinness for a photograph and allowed it to be published in the newspapers. Not everyone was so accommodating. A source at an organisation where the minister was made welcome said internal staff complained about having McGuinness in a photograph and his image was cut out of the picture before it appeared in an in-house publication.

The same applied in his own department: some learned to adjust to McGuinness as Education minister; others could not see past his earlier role as an IRA activist. McGuinness said the only negative experience he had was the small minority of people who resented his presence and would not say hello. "They would pass you in the corridor and that was okay … I understood that and didn't make a big deal about it," he said.

In the early days of devolution DUP Assembly member Edwin Poots claimed there had been a dramatic rise in sick-leave due to McGuinness' presence because staff felt intimidated by him. This was denied by the Department and by McGuinness. McAteer insisted there was little negativity displayed within the department over McGuinness' appointment, whatever any individual's personal feelings might have been. "Civil servants, not without exception, but for the most part, worked professionally, efficiently and diligently," he maintained.

In fact, McGuinness found the Department more progressive than he had imagined. Both he and McAteer were delighted by the relationship they developed with senior officials. One insider said the minister and Hamilton enjoyed a good working relationship and "got on fine". When Hamilton moved on, McGuinness issued a press statement paying tribute to him and after leaving office said: "At a senior level, there was a very, very good working relationship." Hamilton was succeeded by Derry-born Gerry McGinn.

From day one the minister made it clear that he wanted to hear his staff's views. "He did not want them to tell him what they thought he wanted to hear. He said he would respect their views no matter how much they differed from his own," said an insider. McGuinness concluded that most civil servants recognised that he shared their passion for education, if not their politics, and it was not long before officials were speaking well of him. One described him as extremely personable and "the most down-to-earth, friendly minister I've ever worked with." Another, from a unionist background, was also impressed. At first, this official had to be coaxed into working for him, but had a very positive experience in the long run. "I found him quite winsome," he said. "On a person-to-person basis he was very agreeable and from an operational point of view we got the job done in a very effective way. All you had to do was get over the initial barrier of, 'Can you trust this man?' Obviously the first thing you saw was this commander from Derry and you had to get over that." The civil servant was less enamoured with McGuinness' entourage of bodyguards and party members, however. "They were almost overbearing, in terms of "the heavies" and the search people who were there and, running in parallel, the advisors and things. It was almost over-powering in terms of politics," he said.

McGuinness spoke to everyone he met, from the top to the bottom of the Department, and this openness was appreciated, even by those who would previously have regarded him with contempt. One Stormont official remembered very junior staff from loyalist backgrounds praising him for taking the trouble to speak to them and ask them how they were getting on. Unlike some British direct rule ministers, who did not always take time to personally thank or get to know staff, when McGuinness heard a good idea he wanted to know who had come up with it. He would single out the official in question for special praise. He did the same with those who drafted policy papers.

The Sinn Féin minister was anxious to overcome his controversial image and both he and McAteer tried to avoid causing offence. Following IRA decommissioning, the strategy might have been called "charm and disarm". McGuinness deliberately refrained from bringing any political symbols into the office and immediately replaced his green ribbon – worn in solidarity with republican prisoners – with the badge of the National Society for the Prevention of Cruelty to Children (NSPCC). In truth, there were not too many Provisional IRA prisoners left behind bars, but he wanted to be seen as a minister for all by wearing the NSPCC's circular green badge. Soon other senior members of Sinn Féin were wearing the badge, along with senior officials in his Department. The charity's patron, Prince Andrew, was taken aback one day when he was watching the news and saw the badge on Gerry Adams' lapel.

To his annoyance, McGuinness' charm offensive was undermined when Sinn Féin councillor Finbar Conway announced that the Duchess of Abercorn was not welcome at a school in Pomeroy. Conway condemned her as a member of the Royal family; she was not, although she moved in those circles. For many years she had organised a schools prize competition in honour of one of her ancestors, the Russian writer Alexander Pushkin. Now Conway was saying she was no longer welcome. The objection caused a storm in the media and the Sinn Féin education minister was very embarrassed. The Ulster Unionist chairman of the education committee, Danny Kennedy, gleefully recounted the episode in the Assembly as if it were a humorous fairytale, prompting a caustic reply from McGuinness that the unionist might himself take the Pushkin Prize for his creative writing. It was thought that McGuinness intervened and smoothed things over. While the Duchess was pleased, the republican Conway was not. He was extremely vexed when a BBC reporter telephoned him to say the party had issued a statement saying he was now welcoming her visit. He denied this and felt betrayed and abandoned by the leadership. He did not stand for the party at the next council elections.

When an Ulster Unionist member of the education committee passed away, McGuinness wrote to the man's widow, Anne, who was surprised to receive a handwritten card from the republican minister. She appreciated the gesture, and his words about her husband: "I admired the fact that in his dealings with me he was always dignified and cordial."

McGuinness proved to be a good performer when he was out representing the Department. Even those from unionist backgrounds found themselves warming to the new minister. When he visited UTV to speak to schools about an environmental initiative, one member of the audience, who had slipped in just to observe McGuinness, recalled how he faltered at first. "He was clearly not used to reading speeches by civil servants, and he was a bit stiff and dull. The unionists in the audience were sitting with their arms folded, waiting to be unimpressed. But then he started to come alive when he spoke off-the-cuff. He talked about the Red American Indians and about his experiences as a fisherman and by the end he seemed to have won them over." As a minister, McGuinness had an easy way with children and thought nothing of squatting on the floor to speak to them or read them a story. He would recite poetry he had written and was even pictured playing table tennis at St Josephine's Primary School.

Several unionist sources from the Assembly said he was both industrious and conscientious. "He was everything one would look for in a politician – except his party label," said one. The Ulster Unionist minister Michael McGimpsey said McGuinness seemed to want the same things as the other pro-Agreement ministers: "We all wanted to get away from the past violence and create a better future for everybody." Another unionist admitted: "As a minister, I couldn't fault him. It is what they [republicans] do after dark that worries me." He added: "In one sense, McGuinness was trying too hard to be nice and that was resented, I think, by unionists. They didn't want to be drawn into a matey relationship. They were quite content to be professional about it."

The SDLP finance minister claimed he was taken aback when McGuinness forfeited £3 million in education money to give the Ulster Unionist Minister of Enterprise a bigger budget. Durkan said he chided McGuinness, telling him he actually had a good case for having more funding, not less. "McGuinness just said something like, 'In that case I know you'll be good for it'," Durkan said. However, McGuinness said this was nonsense, adding: "I was always asking for more money."

Others found it hard to match the approachable, affable pragmatist with his reputation as a ruthless republican. One SDLP source admired McGuinness' political skills and, acknowledging his charm, said: "I think he is a great politician. I think he is a man who has moved on. But [to me] he's always the man who sent Patsy Gillespie to his death. I don't forget that when I talk to him." (Gillespie was a Catholic civilian worker at a British Army base who was kidnapped by the IRA and used as a human bomb to kill five soldiers.) McGuinness would firmly reject any allegation of involvement in Gillespie's murder. Such allegations arose from his reputation as an IRA leader at the time of the murder. How did the man who was reputedly chief-of-staff of the IRA fit in so well with the political system? For one civil servant in the administration, the answer was fairly straightforward:

> "Martin McGuinness is incredibly bright. He's a natural born leader. Some of his officials are extremely loyal to him. He can run an army and he can run a department. When he only thought about the war, he was brutal, but with peace … he's charming, witty and charismatic."

An ex-IRA prisoner and veteran republican also claimed McGuinness underwent a personality change with the peace process, "He absolutely changed … he grew up if you like and he grew into that personality. I don't know how you explain it, it's as if he became another person once he got into that position, that platform of being a minister." The source then whispered in quiet tones of how cold and frightening McGuinness could be. When asked which was the real McGuinness – the friendly minister, or the ruthless republican – he cited the latter. But another man who has long observed McGuinness insisted it was wrong to label him as one just thing or another: "Human nature is complex. McGuinness is both of those things."

Even the father of a twelve-year-old boy killed in an IRA bomb attack found something positive to say after meeting McGuinness at a reconciliation concert. Colin Parry, whose son, Tim, died in the Warrington bomb in 1993, met the Sinn Féin minister, as did Wilf Ball, whose three-year-old son, Jonathan, had died in the same blast. Parry said the meeting was just something that "had to be done" if understanding was to be forged. McGuinness said he was sorry that Irish republicans were involved in the deaths of the children in Warrington. It was wrong, he said. Parry went away from the meeting convinced that McGuinness' desire to make the peace process work was very strong. "The man gives a very strong impression," he said. Wilf Ball was less impressed, saying: "I shook his hand but it was only in politeness. In all honesty I wanted to break his fingers."

McGuinness' ministerial colleagues also formed differing opinions of the man and the politician. Sam Foster, the Ulster Unionist Environment minister, found McGuinness preferable to the Sinn Féin leader: "Adams, to me, was quite arrogant and pompous and McGuinness, if you didn't know him, could maybe fool you, until he gets his back against a wall and you can see the bristles come out." Ulster Unionist David Trimble also formed a more positive view of McGuinness than he ever did of the Sinn Féin President.

"McGuinness is much more open in terms of expressing his views. [With] Adams you get the feeling that everything is a matter of calculation," he said. One insider remembered being taken aback when he spotted Trimble and McGuinness deep in conversation in Room 21. Both were leaning back on their elbows, their heads tilted in the same direction and seemed very relaxed. "I would love to have taken a picture," he said.

Relations with political unionism – especially with the DUP – were the most difficult to manage and were always fraught.

In keeping with DUP policy of "shunning Sinn Féin," the party's MLAs wrote to the Department of Education's permanent secretary with a constituency matter, rather than to the minister. This was the case, too, with the Sinn Féin Health minister. Ulster Unionist MP Jeffrey Donaldson recalled: "I wrote to the permanent secretary and got a response from the minister and I would just write back to the permanent secretary." Similarly, Ian Paisley Jr always prefaced his letters to the permanent secretary with an explanation as to why he would not deal with the minister. He cited his IRA background and twice, he said, the permanent secretary, due to expediency, answered but not always. "I kept all my letters from McGuinness," said Paisley Jr. "They started, 'Dear Ian' and finished 'yours ever, Martin'." The DUP MLA Sammy Wilson, deputy chair of the Education committee, recalled McGuinness writing him "Dear Sammy" letters, too. "He didn't quite finish it 'Love, Martin', but you got the impression he wanted to," Wilson said.

The Assembly education committee had a role in scrutinising the Department. Along with Wilson, Ulster Unionist committee chairman Danny Kennedy, member for Newry and Mourne, pledged to keep a keen eye on the minister: both wanted to show grassroots unionists how tough they could be on McGuinness. In his first weeks in office, Kennedy complained that the minister failed to keep members informed about a meeting he was having with Dublin Education minister Micheal Martin. The Department said the minister was not obliged to do so and that the First and Deputy First Minister had been informed. McGuinness accused the unionists of politicking. McGuinness did apologise, however, for the "oversight" in not informing the committee of his announcement on pre-school education. As time went on meetings with the committee could often be cordial, especially when the cameras were not present. The SDLP MLA for Lagan Valley, Patricia Lewsley, a committee member, said McGuinness made an effort to be open and approachable in meetings, but as often as not Wilson would attempt to provoke him: "It didn't happen all the time, but most of the time Wilson would have a fair go at him. It would just be hammer and tongs. Some of it was nasty and then McGuinness would have taken control and said just move on to something else."

Kennedy recalled the pair trading insults fairly frequently: "It was my job to keep the discussion on a more even keel." Occasionally, said Kennedy, there would be lighter moments, with some witty repartee. The most contentious issue was the allocation of school funding. The DUP and UUP both accused McGuinness of bias, of treating Catholic maintained schools more favourably than State schools, which were largely Protestant. The minister insisted money was distributed according to need and that even if he had wanted to favour Catholic schools, his officials would not have allowed him to do so. Wilson wound him up by insisting that the minister had the final say. Wilson stood by his claim and was especially pleased to have upset the minister during a closed session of the committee. "He [McGuinness] must have been having a bad morning because normally he would be fairly cool. Even when you tried to provoke him, he was fairly cool. But this day he thumped the table and he said, 'This is so much bullshit!' and then he kind of went into a two- or three-minute rant," said Wilson. McGuinness could not remember ever losing his temper in this way with Wilson.

The DUP politician raised what he called the minister's "loutish behaviour" in an Assembly session the following week. During a rather fractious debate, McGuinness insisted he had nothing to apologise for and would not be allocating money on some kind of sectarian headcount. Referring to Wilson's claims of discrimination, he said: "The member is speaking absolute nonsense, which is, of course, his *forte*."

McGuinness generally tried to avoid confrontation with Wilson. He found his DUP colleague in the committee, Oliver Gibson, member for West Tyrone, more constructive. The opportunity for public confrontation was, naturally enough, exploited during ministerial question time on Mondays. McGuinness enjoyed the despatch box and only regretted that he did not get to field questions more often. A Department official recalled how sharp he was when dealing with a surprise question. "He was a master at that. He would make a seamless transition while you rustled up the answer," he said. Kennedy, acknowledging that McGuinness performed well when under pressure from political opponents, said: "He was no slouch at the despatch box or in debate or in response to committee hearings that we held. But I think the problems surrounding his personality and his background, that was never going to be properly overcome."

Lord Alderdice, the Assembly speaker, singled McGuinness out, along with the DUP's Nigel Dodds and Peter Robinson, as particularly impressive ministers at the despatch box. Alderdice said he found McGuinness very easy to deal with and respectful of the rules, adding: "He took to the parliamentary chamber and he came in and behaved respectfully. He didn't rise inappropriately to the bait when people tried to tease him. He had a sense of humour and he was very good at taking his brief and responding to questions."

McGuinness seemed a natural public speaker and was extremely articulate. In his first parliamentary speech, in July 1998, he spoke with all the passion of a man who had waited thirty years to have his say. Face-to-face for the first time with the DUP's Ian Paisley and Peter Robinson, he lashed out, challenging unionists over their own past misdeeds. Some of what he alleged about certain unionists was so contentious it was removed from the Hansard Report for legal reasons. McGuinness could not resist humiliating Wilson, who was mortified when a tabloid newspaper published nude pictures of him taken on holiday. "It's great to see him today with his clothes on," McGuinness declared. A red-faced Wilson had no comeback that day. But when McGuinness took office, Wilson sparred frequently with the minister and memorably told the Assembly that he would be like a Doberman at the minister's heels. During his despatch box debut McGuinness replied: "I would remind everyone the place for a Doberman is at the heels of the master."

Wilson inspired much mirth in the chamber when he accused McGuinness of being evasive over questions. Referring to his IRA background and his interrogation by police at Castlereagh, Wilson declared: "Mr Speaker, perhaps you would inform the Minister that he is in Stormont and not Castlereagh and that he is permitted to answer questions." When Wilson discovered the curly-haired McGuinness was sensitive about suggestions he

looked like the singer/songwriter Art Garfunkel, he worked the theme into his attack on
the minister's spending plans: "Although he might look like Art Garfunkel, [he's] sounding
more like Abba singing 'Money, Money, Money'." Wilson claimed to have observed a few
discreet smiles on the Sinn Féin backbenches.

Neither Kennedy nor Wilson warmed to McGuinness' informal style and insisted on
calling him "Minister". Kennedy said he had to strike a balance between the minister's IRA
background and his position in the Executive. He described relations as reasonably
civilised and businesslike, saying, "I regarded him as a minister of the Crown and had to
treat him with that level of authority. I think he wanted a more 'matey' relationship and I
preferred to keep it on a more formal basis."

Kennedy said the minister offered access to the Department and suggested the
Department and committee should "co-manage" issues, but Kennedy remained very
conscious of his scrutiny role. Only once did Wilson refer to McGuinness as anything
other than "Minister" and that was after McGuinness gave evidence to the Bloody Sunday
Inquiry and admitted to being second-in-command of the Derry IRA at the time.
McGuinness' admission sparked a DUP no-confidence motion in the Assembly and
Wilson sarcastically referred to the minister as "Commander McGuinness". The deputy
Speaker, Sir John Gorman – a decorated officer who had served as captain in the Irish
Guards during the Second World War – was presiding that day and was not amused.
"McGuinness," said Wilson, "didn't seem to take exception to it at all. But Sir John
Gorman took great exception to it and upbraided me and when I refused to withdraw it,
he then said that he would have to punish me ... It was about six weeks before I got
speaking again in the Assembly."

After hearing McGuinness' confession, Ian Paisley tabled a motion that the republican
minister be thrown out of office and into jail. The Ulster Unionist minister Sir Reg Empey
tried to defuse the controversy by pointing out that his party was more focused on
McGuinness' present and future intentions. But Kennedy fuelled the debate when he
demanded to know if McGuinness was still in the IRA. This issue resurfaced in October
2001, around the time of IRA decommissioning, when it was reported that McGuinness
had moved into position as IRA chief-of-staff to facilitate the change. McGuinness called
these reports "bogus, malicious, rubbish".

During the Assembly debate the DUP's Peter Robinson called McGuinness the
"Bogside butcher" and linked him to the deaths of at least twelve soldiers. Defending his
minister, Adams pointed out that McGuinness had made it clear, through the Speaker's
Office, that he had left the IRA. The Sinn Féin leader challenged the DUP's motives,
saying, "Is this not about having a Catholic, an uppity Fenian, about the place? Let's get
real." The motion, which was designed to embarrass the Ulster Unionist party, failed
because it required cross-community support.

The only time McGuinness lost office was through suspension, and indeed his reaction
to the first suspension surprised observers. His passionate tirade on the night of the
February 2000 suspension may have been due to a combination of anger, frustration and
exhaustion, but there was no mistaking his misery as he railed against the injustice of
suspension in an emotional press conference. He spoke of how "gut-wrenching" it had
been for him to compromise and come to Stormont in the first place. But one MLA,

observing him from the upstairs balcony of Stormont's Great Hall, was not alone in thinking it was the loss of Office that was gut-wrenching: "I think he enjoyed the power. Martin was nearly in tears … I remember him looking down at the floor and he was almost crying." First Minister David Trimble contrasted the Education minister's tearful display with his joy on his first arrival in Room 21. "His pleasure at being there was palpable," said Trimble.

It was obvious to many that McGuinness adored being Minister of Education. He glowed wherever he went, even though he worked very long hours, sometimes falling asleep in his ministerial car before he made it home. A republican who was once close to McGuinness said he clearly revelled in the job: "It was an extension of his ego, if you like. He enjoyed doing it, liked getting out and meeting people."

McGuinness had had a tantalising taste of government and the power of making decisions that affected society. Although he had been in Office just seventy-four days when the first suspension called a halt to his power, he felt he had made a difference. He was no unionist, but he did share one trait with the first Stormont Education minister, Lord Londonderry: a desire for reform. With the passing of the Government of Ireland Act 1920 education had ceased to be administered from six offices in Dublin Castle and it was widely agreed reform was necessary. However, the hierarchy of the Catholic Church was anxious to protect its hold over Catholic education and therefore opposed change. As a result, education developed along sectarian lines in Northern Ireland, with the Catholic Church maintaining its own schools, separate from State schools, which were collectively known as the controlled sector. Lord Londonderry believed the system was badly in need of reform and was remembered for his attempts to do so. McGuinness was the first locally elected Education minister in a generation, and the first republican to hold the post. He came into Office after a succession of twelve direct rule ministers. Reform was at the top of his agenda and he took immediate steps. During his first conference meeting with his officials, he told them he had an agenda of change and looked forward to their cooperation in achieving it. "He wanted to tackle difficult issues which had lay unaddressed for years, in some cases decades," said McAteer.

Within weeks the new minister had announced the largest ever provision for pre-school education. This investment was going to be announced by the direct rule minister but fell into McGuinness' lap with devolution, and through the Executive he increased it. He also announced a £500,000 trust for Irish-medium schools modelled on the Integrated Education Fund. This was a milestone in Irish-medium education and provided assistance for those wanting to establish Irish-language schools. He launched a review of the "strict criteria" demanded of those seeking State funds for Irish-medium schools, ultimately making it easier for children to be educated in Irish by relaxing the funding guidelines. Similar steps were taken for integrated schools. In fact, McGuinness recalled that his first big decision when he took office was to fund two integrated schools – one in Belfast, the other in Carrickfergus.

Before the first suspension, he also announced a massive investment in schools of £72 million – the largest ever package allocated by the Department. It included funding for eleven new primary schools. His time in office overall is marked by investment in school building stock. In fact, no minister in the history of the State spent more on this over a comparable period. McGuinness' approach on this issue also highlighted his pragmatism. In order to build much-needed new schools and replace old stock, he agreed to private sector involvement through the Public Private Partnership (PPP). McGuinness decided to accept this measure despite his personal reservations and his own party's traditional opposition to it, believing it to be the only way he could get the required funding for the schools building programme. One Department of Education official recalled hearing how the minister's staff had made a presentation to him on the subject, not expecting him to agree; some wrongly perceived him as a Marxist. One source claimed the minister was reminded that his party's election manifesto had opposed the initiative and that this could pose problems. The source said officials were rather surprised when he agreed to the policy and insisted on adopting the proposal. There was some debate within Sinn Féin about breaking this pledge. Several republicans were reluctant to concede the principle and in internal party meetings argued that students might have to be prepared to put up with poor conditions until public funding became available. But McGuinness did not agree with educating children in "what amounted to hovels". He said: "The department officials made a convincing case."

The minister pointed to one school in particular which had benefited, Dominican College, Fortwilliam, where hundreds of children had been educated in "temporary", makeshift classrooms for years. Nonetheless, at least one former Sinn Féin representative remained disappointed and cynical about the decision, insisting PPP should have been challenged more forcefully: "I think it all boiled down to [Sinn Féin] wanting to see Martin cutting a ribbon for a new school or Bairbre cutting a ribbon for a new [hospital] extension. It was all opportunism, political expediency, cutting out principle."

In his desire to reform education, McGuinness was also struck by the plight of special schools and this too became a priority. He recalled that, pre-devolution, the norm was for one special school to make it onto the list of the school building programme. He increased this number to three. He never forgot what he had seen at one of the first special schools he visited – Rathfriland Hill in Newry. It had been converted from an old hospital and the building was then around fifty years old. McGuinness spotted a young girl on crutches with a brace on her legs and she was at the top of the staircase, struggling to get down the steps. "That was an eye-opener for me," he said. He happily announced approval for proposals to provide a new school in Newry on a green-field site.

The Alliance member for North Down, Eileen Bell, who had been a staunch critic of the IRA and Sinn Féin for years, was impressed with how McGuinness came to the aid of the Clifton Special School in Bangor. Like others in and out of the Assembly, she lobbied him for funding for Clifton. He in turn asked about the possibility of visiting the school and, after some discussion about the sensitivities involved, the board of governors invited him. The school was subsequently awarded £4.8 million for a new building. While a number of his predecessors had visited the school, McGuinness was the first to come up with the funding.

The reform programme was sweeping and comprised many different elements. For example, McGuinness commissioned reports into dyslexia and autism and he and Dublin counterpart, Michael Woods, announced plans, through the NSMC, for an all-Ireland autism centre at Middletown – a much-needed facility. The minister also took the controversial step of scrapping school league tables, which were unpopular with the trade unions but supported by the Labour government. Critics claimed the tables did not reflect accurately the merits of individual schools because they were based solely on academic performance, failing to take into account other pertinent factors, such as whether the school was operating in an area of deprivation, or offering an excellent sports or music programme. The tables system meant schools were motivated to give out qualifications, even if they were rather poor, which did not always serve the pupils' best interests. McGuinness' decision was influenced by his visit to Holy Trinity School in Cookstown, where the pupils staged an impressive concert. During the interval someone tapped him on the shoulder and asked pointedly, "How do you put that in a school league table?"

Sammy Wilson claimed the minister had surrendered to pressure from trade unions and that the decision to scrap the tables would be regretted in time: "You can't raise standards if you don't measure what schools are doing. And while the league tables may not have been the best measure … they were the only measures we had at the time. We have nothing in place now." McGuinness had no regrets over the decision, however, saying: "The fact that the Welsh Assembly followed us and abolished league tables was very gratifying indeed."

McGuinness' best-known reform proposal was the abolition of the Eleven-plus qualifying exam. Introduced in 1947, the exam was taken by ten- and eleven-year-old boys and girls from all backgrounds, and success was a passport to the more elite grammar schools and, more often than not, a university education. Those who failed the exam were placed in what were perceived as the more mediocre secondary schools and they often felt stigmatised by their failure. When it was first introduced, the exam transformed education because it provided free quality education to those who had ability but lacked means; the SDLP's John Hume and Seamus Mallon were examples of this. As time went on, however, the exam became increasingly controversial, with critics arguing that it was out-dated and unfair because middle-class parents were able to afford tutors for their children to help them prepare for the exam. Only one-third of pupils passed, while the other two-thirds had to endure the trauma of failure as well as the likelihood of an inferior education. Many people who failed the Eleven-plus claim it deeply affected them and speak of the shame of failure – even those who went on to distinguish themselves academically. Research also showed that children from poor backgrounds were more likely to fail and that the exam put undue pressure on children at a formative age. One unionist politician, who actually supported the system, denied in an interview he was traumatised by his own failure, but then asked the reporter not to publish the fact that he had not passed the exam. The Education minister and his special advisor, Aidan McAteer, made no secret of their respective failures and their opposition to the exam. McGuinness blamed nerves for his poor performance; one wonders if his path might have been different had he reached his potential on the day.

As soon as McGuinness took Office he made the issue of the Eleven-plus a priority. He branded it an unfair means of selection, or rather "academic rejection", saying, "No education system and no society have the right to tell any child at the age of eleven or ten that they are a failure." While he was clearly determined in his views, McGuinness had to tread carefully as the grammar schools represented a powerful lobby. There was also resistance from other quarters, including the Churches, some parents and unionist politicians. He promised to consult with all interested parties before taking a decision. His direct rule predecessor, Tony Worthington, had already commissioned an academic study on the Eleven-plus when both the exam and the grammar school system had re-emerged as a political issue with the election of New Labour in 1997. It is a matter of debate whether the scrapping of the Eleven-plus would have happened under direct rule, but it is arguable that devolution fast-forwarded the process. McGuinness was not alone in believing such change was unlikely under direct rule, mainly because of the unionist parties' opposition and the perceived reluctance of NIO ministers to upset their unionist colleagues. Kennedy, too, doubted a direct rule minister would have made such a dramatic change, saying: "I don't think a direct rule minister would have had the courage to have gone ahead and made such a wide-ranging decision."

McGuinness, on the other hand, displayed the will to drive change and he extended the remit of the academic study being undertaken by Professor Alan Smith of the University of Ulster and Professor Tony Gallagher of Queen's University to include researching systems in other countries, such as America, England and Scotland. Following the publication of the study, which confirmed the selection procedure's shortcomings, the minister immediately launched a massive consultation. He appointed a Review Body on Post-Primary Education, nominating the former ombudsman, Gerry Burns, to lead it. Burns' remit included making recommendations. McGuinness described the Burns review as one of the biggest debates in education for 100 years. It lasted longer than anyone expected. The much-anticipated Burns report took a year to conclude and when it was finally published, in the autumn of 2001, it also reached the conclusion that the Eleven-plus was out-dated. It recommended that the exam be scrapped at the earliest opportunity, along with selection itself. It also recommended pupil-profiling and a new "collegiate" system for schools that encouraged clusters of schools to work together. Of course, the report was the subject of much debate, with some critics complaining that it was complex and overly bureaucratic.

The minister welcomed the recommendation to scrap the exam, but knew the issue had to be handled carefully. He promised legislation after a further round of consultation. Comments were invited from all sections of Northern Ireland society, including parents, young people and other interested parties. Every household in Northern Ireland was surveyed and the returns were exceptionally high: around 200,000 people filled in the survey. It showed widespread support for change, but relatively little support for the Burns model in its entirety. There was strong consensus on the need to abolish the Eleven-plus, but it was less clear what to put in its place. Although most of those involved in education supported the ending of academic selection, there was nonetheless substantial opposition to this. Key interest groups, such as the grammar schools and unionists parties, and a majority of those who took part in the household survey were still arguing for some form of selection. The DUP, the UUP and some educationalists were also arguing against abolition until a suitable replacement was identified. As a mark of their opposition, a number of grammar schools spent thousands of pounds on newspaper advertisements condemning the Burns report.

The minister – whose own quest for a better system led him to Finland and Germany on fact-finding missions – had promised he would act on consensus. Indeed, he announced that no final decision would be taken until after the consultation and after he had conferred with the Assembly, the Education committee and the Executive. The process was still ongoing when it was interrupted by suspension. In one of his last ministerial acts, McGuinness published the findings of the consultation on Burns and then, just before leaving Office, unexpectedly announced that the Eleven-plus was being scrapped and would end in two years' time. Even though he had not found an alternative he justified his defiant decision by saying: "I wanted to make it impossible for any future direct rule minister to reverse my decision to abolish the Eleven-plus."

The other parties dismissed his unilateral action as a "stunt" that undermined his earlier pledges to reach consensus. Wilson called it a blatant piece of political opportunism. David Trimble dismissed the move as pure theatre, a dramatic gesture to leave the impression of an all-mighty republican minister who could do whatever he liked. The reality, according to SDLP minister Mark Durkan, was that McGuinness would have had to achieve consensus at the Executive table for his plans because the change would have required significant funding.

Wilfred Mulryne, the Methodist principle who had welcomed him to his school, expressed disappointment that McGuinness had taken the decision in the way he did, believing it tarnished his time in Office. In the aftermath of suspension, Downing Street and the Department of Education were flooded with demands from outraged unionist representatives to reverse the decision. His immediate direct rule successor, Jane Kennedy, refused to do so and more consultation followed.

McGuinness recalled educationalists from various quarters advising him against tackling the controversial issue so early in his administration. "Some people said to me, 'Don't even think about doing anything about the Eleven-plus because the powers-that-be will come down on you like a tonne of bricks', and I was trying to work out who the powers-that-be were," he said.

The minister soon found out that the powers-that-be represented various interest groups: the Catholic bishops, the Protestant Churches, the Ulster Unionist party and the grammar schools. He used his powers of persuasion and his natural charm to try to influence these interest groups and enjoyed mixed success. By the time he left Office, it was clear that arguments against the exam had persuaded some opponents to modify or rethink their position. Ulster Unionist Education committee chairman Danny Kennedy found that his opposition to Burns, for example, did not meet with universal approval when he addressed the Assembly of the Presbyterian Church. His party became more conscious of the strength of opposition, but continued with its policy on the Eleven-plus.

During the course of the debate the chief executive of the Council for Catholic Maintained Schools, Donal Flanagan, praised McGuinness' courage and vision for giving priority to a "running sore within the education system". McAteer also boasted that the debate influenced the Catholic Church, which moved to a much "more progressive position than [it] had ever had". But critics complained that McGuinness had approached the debate with a closed mind and was determined to scrap the Eleven-plus, no matter what. Indeed, Wilfred Mulryne became concerned about the future of grammar schools such as Methodist College. He accused the minister of downplaying the performance of such schools to bolster his agenda. McGuinness was sanguine about the criticism, saying it was to be expected given the enormity of the change being proposed. When McGuinness warned that grammar schools that refused to fall into line with the new proposals might have to go it alone, Wilson accused him of employing a "financial Armalite".

McGuinness was also accused of intervening in the debate when he appeared at the annual conference of the Irish National Teachers' Organisation (INTO) and tackled what he claimed were three myths about the selection system. He rejected the notion that selection was a ladder of opportunity for working-class children. "If this is a ladder," he said, "it is an extremely narrow one." He pointed to the loyalist, working-class Shankill Road where only 2% of children would achieve a place at grammar school. The two PUP Assembly members, both ex-prisoners from working-class, loyalist areas, represented a minority voice in unionism when they joined the attack on the exam. David Ervine said it created "social apartheid" in education. He also believed that working-class Protestants were inhibited from speaking out because of a traditional reluctance to criticise the State coupled with the "McGuinness factor". McGuinness' case against the exam was bolstered when five teaching unions, representing a cross-section of the community, issued an unprecedented statement attacking the grammar schools and accusing them of seeking to perpetuate a cold-house for children.

Throughout the consultation McGuinness sought dialogue with all the interested parties, particularly the fabled "powers-that-be". McGuinness credited his Department officials with managing the situation skilfully. As the debate raged he was heartened by the fact that some of the most progressive statements came from within the Catholic and Protestant Churches. However, critics still argued that the minister's consultation was geared towards a predetermined outcome and cite as evidence his "petulant" announcement before he left Office. In his defence, McGuinness insisted that he had listened to all views and was guided by consultation, which indicated a desire for change, as well as by academic research. He pointed to an OECD report that showed that countries without selection, such as Canada, Korea and New Zealand, were outperforming those with it. "The arguments for change were very powerful and in my opinion undeniable," he said.

McGuinness recognised not just the intellectual arguments but was also keenly aware of the emotions involved. He focused particularly on how children were affected. While attending the launch of a Save the Children report on the issue, he was struck by what one ten-year-old girl said of the exam: "If I pass, I go to a good school and if I fail, I go to a stupid school and I'm stupid. I think I'm going to fail." McGuinness would quote this little girl's words on occasion when making his pitch. He recognised that the views of children could not be the sole consideration, but he believed some critics, such as Sammy Wilson, were not affording them due weight. In one interview, McGuinness said he may have been the best friend these children ever had and it was probably this sense of urgency, of responding to a pressing need that precipitated his sudden decision before leaving Office.

He was, without question, the most controversial minister in the Executive. But one insider who had watched them all at close-quarters described him as the "surprise star". A republican, who has been critical of him privately, paid tribute to McGuinness thus: "He performed as if he had been all his life waiting to be Minister of Education. In a public relations sense he was outstanding. He got on very well with his civil servants. There was this perception he was a good people-handler, that was his *forte*, I guess."

The fact that his time in office was relatively brief and ended prematurely complicates an assessment of his performance as Minister of Education: his report card was mixed. His decision to tackle the Eleven-plus issue was seen as brave by some, although it would not have been terribly risky from the point of view of his own republican constituency. The SDLP also favoured scrapping the test. Suspension curtailed McGuinness' plans and left observers wondering how he would have handled the controversial issue. Would he have achieved consensus in the end? One source, in the office of the First Minister, said he was certain he would have and was already consulting along those lines before suspension.

A number of his initiatives would not have been undertaken had direct rule been in place, not least his decision to scrap the league tables. Critics complain that while this may have been the correct decision, he should have replaced the tables with some kind of measure before he scrapped them. It is probably too soon to assess the ultimate impact of this decision. On the plus side, he used his contacts with the USA administration for the benefit of local education. The peace process had opened up routes to the United States, especially on St Patrick's Day, and on one memorable occasion McGuinness was invited to ring a thirty-tonne peace bell in Kentucky, where he was also made an honorary Kentucky Colonel. In Washington he met with the Education Secretary Richard Riley who, like so many Americans, had Irish roots, in this case County Cavan. Riley offered his assistance and one tangible result was a memo of understanding signed by McGuinness, the Higher Education minister Sean Farren, and the Dublin Education minister Michael Woods. This provided US support for research and other projects.

McGuinness' relations with the trade unions were good, although he was dubbed "Scrooge of the Year" by the Low Pay Campaign because of his handling of a dispute with term-time workers. McGuinness was sympathetic but told the workers – who wanted salary adjustments to cover the summer months after their unemployment benefit was cut – that they had to negotiate with the education boards. It was eventually settled and the minister, ever keen to win over his critics, even invited the low pay campaigners into his office for a chat when they turned up to protest at his offices. Frank Bunting, northern secretary of the INTO, described him as an "education minister who listens and is sensitive to the concerns of teachers".

Neither Kennedy nor Wilson gave McGuinness much credit for his performance. When asked what McGuinness got right as a minister, Kennedy – perhaps not surprisingly given the political climate – preferred to say what he got wrong. He cited McGuinness' move to scrap the Eleven-plus as an error. He also continued to insist that in the distribution of funds McGuinness was biased in favour of the maintained and Irish sector. "He might say it was never proved, but a careful study of the figures confirms it. Whether or not it was quite deliberate is another issue," Kennedy said. This is denied by republican and independent sources. McAteer dismissed the claims as propaganda and argued that if the unionists had really believed there was discrimination, they could have sought a judicial review of the minister's decisions. "They knew they wouldn't win a judicial review. It would have vindicated Martin," he said.

The Department of Education stood over the figures and education sources outside the department, with no political axe to grind, dispute the claim of bias. They point to the strict criteria laid down for funding and the fact that recommendations for school funding come from the boards. A senior member of an education board, from a unionist background, did not lend any weight to the claims made by Kennedy and Wilson and did not recall any of his colleagues taking the allegations seriously either.

Graham Gudgin, the First Minister's economic advisor, was asked by David Trimble to investigate and he went through the figures with officials from the Department of Education. "It was clear to me that the allocation was being done objectively by civil servants," he said. Bríd Rodgers concurred with this assessment, saying: "He may well have been stung by Kennedy and Wilson, but the reality was he was allocating funds to where there was the most need."

On a more positive note, Kennedy did recognise that McGuinness was pragmatic when it came to adopting PPP for the schools building funds, but insisted that the credit for this investment should go to the Executive as a whole. "I don't think he can claim exclusive credit for that," he said. Kennedy also alleged that McGuinness relied heavily on officials for the detail of his work, making him a "good firms man". Wilson agreed with this, saying: "He allowed himself to be guided by his officials. He always gave the impression he was his own man doing his own thing, but sometimes I think he was a prisoner of the officials." Sinn Féin dismissed this suggestion as political point-scoring. For his part, Wilson acknowledged that McGuinness was a skilled politician when it came to dealing with teachers' unions and other interest groups: "He sold himself very well and came across very plausibly. He certainly had the ability to be a cosy cuddly-type politician when he wanted to and if people had a lapse and forgot about his background they would have taken him for something different than he was."

When asked what he wished he had done differently in Office, McGuinness was a bit stumped before finally expressing regret: "I wasn't in Office long enough to do more." He was proud of his plans to build eighty new mainstream and special schools, but would have liked to finish the job of replacing the Eleven-plus. He regretted not being able to intervene as minister to resolve the Holy Cross dispute, although he did announce a £150,000 support package for Holy Cross and nearby Wheatfield Primary School due to the unprecedented level of stress caused in the area. He wanted to walk with the beleaguered Holy Cross children as they faced loyalist protestors outside their school, but concluded that even a visit to the Ardoyne area would have exacerbated the situation. Instead he appealed for talks and met with the Holy Cross families in a private capacity, away from the cameras.

On his last day in Office, just hours before the final suspension, Martin McGuinness left Stormont and declared: "I'm saddened … that it has come to this. It's all so unnecessary."

At Rathgael House he bid farewell to his staff. The republican minister said he had come to respect the civil servants with whom he had worked, many of them from the opposite tradition: "They had all assembled in my office and I told them what I felt was going to happen and I encouraged them to carry on with the great work they were doing." There was disappointment in the Department that devolution had come to an end and some were even sorry to see McGuinness leave. He told a story of a woman – whom he had been told was cool about his appointment initially – who became visibly upset during his leave-taking: "There were tears streaming down her face, so I said to myself, I must have had some impact here."

Whatever that impact, and whatever his legacy, plaques bearing his name remain at a number of schools in Northern Ireland, including the school in his native Derry attended by his first grandchild.

Chapter 11
North, South, East and West

It was mid-morning in Armagh. The winter air was dry and crisp, the lingering autumn leaves browned and stuck to the ground, and in the distance, under a grey sky, a most unusual sight appeared. It was a scene that witnesses would recall vividly, one dreaded by unionists and desired by nationalists. It was 13 December 1999 and a convoy of about two dozen black Irish government Mercedes, packed with Dublin ministers and officials, was weaving its way through the grounds of the eighteenth-century Palace Demesne, now home to Armagh Council.

The convoy had crossed the border from Monaghan at Middletown, one of the many villages along the 200-mile border separating Northern Ireland from the Republic. At Middletown the Garda outriders had given way to the RUC, who led the Dubliners deep into the heart of Armagh where the new Northern Ireland Executive ministers waited to greet them. It was only as the Irish delegation crossed the border that some ministers realised the historic significance of their journey. A government aide later recalled: "You suddenly realised that this really was pretty awesome." Justice Minister John O'Donoghue found humour in the occasion. "Tiocfaidh ar Mercs," he joked – a reference to the republican slogan, "*Tiocfaidh ar lá*", meaning "Our day will come". It wasn't quite the day the republican movement had in mind, but it was a day to remember all the same.

The convoy stopped at Council headquarters and the ministers and officials, in their smartest suits, unfolded themselves from the vehicles and surveyed their new environment. Reporters waiting in the cold watched as one by one the official vehicles opened and closed. "It's like a mafia wedding," quipped one. The Ulster Unionists did not make an issue of it at the time, but they were annoyed with the display, which was subsequently condemned by Ian Paisley. One Dublin minister later expressed sympathy with the unionist view, saying, "It was ridiculous." First Minister David Trimble did not see the fleet of vehicles himself as his ministerial car was delayed en route, but he was most unhappy with the news and his sentiments were shared by the Enterprise minister Sir Reg Empey: "The Irish claimed it was on the advice of the police. But it looked bad. It wasn't thought through very well."

The new Stormont Executive had met for the first time just eleven days earlier. Now, the nationalist price for taking part in a Stormont administration was being paid. That morning in Armagh there was no mistaking the historic significance of the North-South Council, even though it was but a pale imitation of what had been drawn up years before. In 1921, when Ireland was partitioned, a Council of Ireland had been envisaged with a view to establishing a parliament for the whole of Ireland. Its initial remit included railways, animal disease and fisheries. Remarkably, it was not the unionist government that had blocked it. The Stormont government of the day had selected a twenty-strong delegation to attend the Council of Ireland, but the fledgling independent Irish government, which had aspirations for a single parliament, refused to recognise the new northern administration, or rather its territory. Dublin delayed the Council of Ireland until a Border Commission had submitted its report. As a result of these procrastinations the Council never met.

A second Council of Ireland had been agreed at Sunningdale in 1974, comprising ministers with executive and harmonising functions. Key areas of cooperation were identified, such as natural resources, environment, agriculture, trade, tourism, culture and electricity. There was also agreement for a consultative assembly of sixty members, drawn from both sides of the border and having advisory and review functions. It, too, floundered, this time in the face of unionist objections. Its demise was widely blamed as a key reason for Sunningdale's collapse.

The modern North South Ministerial Council (NSMC) had more modest aims and required careful handling. Under the terms of the Good Friday Agreement six cross-border bodies and six areas of cooperation had been agreed. The cross-border bodies were: the Food Safety Promotion Board; the Foyle, Carlingford and Irish Lights Commission; the Language Body (known as an Foras Teanga, or in Ulster Scots as Tha Boord o Leid); Special EU Programmes; Trade and Business Development; and Waterways Ireland. The six areas of cooperation were: transport; agriculture; education; health; environment; and tourism. It was not as extensive as the Sunningdale remit, but apparently it was all that was possible at the close of the twentieth century on the island of Ireland. Unionists, a minority on the island, were nervous about looking south, but nationalists and republicans had demanded a robust north-south relationship. During the multi-party talks SDLP negotiator Mark Durkan had colourfully warned that his party was not interested in a "day-release scheme for nationalists". At the Palace Demesne in December 1999 there was a stark reminder of past tensions. RUC marksmen stood guard on the roof of the palace but there was not a single protestor in sight. Bríd Rodgers was struck by this: "If [the Council meeting] had happened four or five years earlier, the road would have been blocked – that is what was really historic about the day, that it was regarded as just routine. There was no trouble."

This made the armed security presence seem out of place, but the governments were taking no chances. Tens of thousands of unionists had protested at Belfast City Hall in 1986 over the signing of the Anglo-Irish Agreement, a concord that gave the Dublin government a say in Northern Ireland affairs – a proposal unpalatable to most unionists. In those days of mass protest, and in the face of rising loyalist violence, Anglo-Irish meetings between ministers of the Crown and ministers of the Republic were held amid tight security for many years. Maryfield secretariat, set up under the terms of the Anglo-Irish Agreement, was a fortress on the outskirts of East Belfast, where the civil servants from Dublin operated behind barbed-wire. It was dubbed "the Bunker" by some unionists. Little wonder, then, that the First Minister was tense as he set out for the plenary session in Armagh. One official recalled he was rather sharp that morning, in bad form and demanding to know where his papers were: "He was very edgy – a bit stroppy." Asked if he was, in fact, feeling uptight that day, Trimble replied: "Well, a little bit. The thing that everybody remembers is the black Mercedes ... They [the Irish government] really did make themselves look rather silly."

However, Trimble insisted the NSMC was not a problem for unionists at that stage because the balance of relationships and structures was correct. Even though Unionists were outnumbered at the table five to one by nationalists, they had agreed to these new institutions because they believed they had a veto over any decisions taken. In the new political climate, the key was cooperation and consent, not coercion.

Trimble liked to recount how the north-south arrangements had finally come to be agreed in the autumn of 1998 after some serious tension. Most of the final, key elements had been worked out beforehand and the deal was to be formalised at a meeting in Dublin, in Government Buildings. Trimble had brought colleague Michael McGimpsey along and they discussed with the southern Irish officials what unionists were offering.

The Irish officials knew what to expect and were anxious that all went well. But somehow their bold anticipation irritated Trimble, who thought them grasping and greedy. He became increasingly uncomfortable each time he reached into his coat pocket for another proposal for a specific north-south body that was acceptable to unionists. Trimble recalled: "We put our series of proposals one by one. We would have cooperation on this and this and this and they said, 'Good, good, good, what else have you got?'" As he heard these words, Trimble turned mischievous. He knew that the sixth and final proposal, for a Special EU Programmes Body, was the most attractive of all as far as Dublin was concerned, so he kept it in his pocket and left the meeting without tabling it. Trimble laughed at the memory: "I went straight to the British embassy and I told them I didn't like the atmosphere and I had held the one on European programmes back. And they said, 'Yes, [the Irish] were wondering why you did that.'" The "problem" was soon worked out and the sixth body was formally agreed.

Again, the Irish government could not hide its enthusiasm at the inaugural meeting of the NSMC. Arriving by helicopter, Taoiseach Bertie Ahern got a bird's-eye view of the Palace grounds, which included a chapel, an obelisk and the ruins of a Franciscan priory. Ahern, Tánaiste Mary Harney and Minister for Foreign Affairs David Andrews travelled to the meeting in an Irish Air Corps red-and-white Dauphin chopper, with a tricolour emblazoned on its tail. A flurry of autumn leaves rose to greet Ahern as his helicopter touched down at around 10.55am, blasting cold air all around. He came with a warm smile and was greeted by Tony McCusker, a senior Stormont official. This was a day unprecedented in Ahern's career and the result of much effort on his part. He had helped negotiate the Good Friday Agreement, leaving the talks at Castle Buildings during Holy Week for only a matter of hours to attend his mother's funeral. Now, in Armagh, there was emotion in his voice when he declared, "This is a day quite unlike any other."

The First and Deputy First Ministers' plans to arrive sequentially had not worked out due to traffic congestion, but they were together in time to jointly greet the Taoiseach and his colleagues. Inside, Tony Canavan, Mayor of Armagh, formally welcomed the Irish delegation and the Stormont ministers to the city, long the ecclesiastical capital of Ireland.

On one side of the table sat the northern ministers: David Trimble, Seamus Mallon, Sir Reg Empey, Sam Foster, Michael McGimpsey, Sean Farren, Mark Durkan, Bríd Rodgers, Bairbre de Brun and Martin McGuinness. Trimble sat directly across the table from the Taoiseach, while Mallon faced the Tánaiste. There were fourteen Dublin ministers at the table, including Minister for Public Enterprise Mary O'Rourke, Minister for Marine and

Natural Resources Michael Woods, Minister for Foreign Affairs David Andrews, Minister of Agriculture Joe Walsh, Minister of Health Brian Cowen, Minister of Finance Charlie McCreevy, Minister of the Environment Noel Dempsey, Minister of Justice John O'Donoghue, Minister of Defence Michael Smith, Minister of Social Security and Family Affairs Dermot Ahern, Minister of Tourism, Sport and Recreation Jim McDaid, Minister of Education Micheal Martin and Junior Minister at Foreign Affairs Liz O'Donnell. Also present to witness the new *détente* was Síle de Valera, Minister for Arts, Heritage and the Gaeltacht and granddaughter of Éamon de Valera, the ex-prisoner and former rebel who founded Fianna Fáil and served for many years as president of the Republic.

Surveying the faces at the table, the Taoiseach said ministers had had their backs to each other for too long because of conflict and division. "That era is now over, and today marks its end," he said. But two DUP ministers had chosen to turn their backs on the new era: Peter Robinson and Nigel Dodds declined to attend, instead going to Armagh to visit victims of the Troubles – a potentially risky move because the NIO had refused to provide police protection. The DUP claimed the NSMC was an embryonic united Ireland. As such, they refused to have meetings within the formal north-south structures of the Good Friday Agreement.

It is believed the Office of First and Deputy First Ministers had in the course of the administration worked on a plan to get the DUP to go to the NSMC, but it did not work out. Just like the Executive some days earlier, the historic meeting therefore went ahead without the DUP. When a photograph was taken of the ministers seated around the table, the DUP's absence highlighted in even starker terms the unionists' minority status at the NSMC. Trimble warned that the two ministers could not avoid engaging with the north-south bodies and that they would be better attending rather than "sending in memoranda".

Inside the meeting room, which was rather cramped given the number in attendance, the atmosphere was jovial, if a little stilted. Martin McGuinness thought it an exciting, joyous occasion and remembered being asked to sign a small booklet, a programme of the historic day which the Armagh Council had prepared and distributed to each of the ministers, along with a framed photograph of Armagh. McGuinness was happy to oblige, "But I had no sooner signed it than another one came, and then another one." One source remarked, "It helped alleviate the boredom of the speeches."

Stormont officials had toiled the previous weekend to ensure a smooth plenary meeting, but this was all new to them and inevitably there were a few minor difficulties. The papers relating to the plenary had been completed only the night before and couriered to the ministers around 11.00pm. "That was par for the course," said one minister. "There were always papers flying around at the last minute." On the day, to the embarrassment of the northern delegation, it became clear that some of the northern ministers did not have speaking notes, unlike their southern counterparts, who were used to such summits. A Stormont official put it down to inexperience and said the problem was never repeated. Bríd Rodgers recalled that it was not a big issue. When she suddenly realised she was expected to speak, her permanent secretary, who was sitting nearby, quickly jotted down a few notes. "I spoke off the top of my head – first in Irish and then in English."

It had taken almost eighty years for this kind of formal meeting to occur. It lasted around forty-five minutes, with the First and Deputy First Ministers acting as joint-chairmen. Seamus Mallon spoke of an idea whose time had finally come, while David Trimble predicted that the DUP's absence was likely to be temporary. Trimble also spoke in encouraging tones about the new north-south relationship: "Nobody should be scared of cooperation."

There was, however, a last-minute snag. Bairbre de Brun was unhappy that she had not been consulted regarding the appointment of the Chair of the Food Safety body. The appointment had been agreed by Trimble, Mallon, Durkan and Dublin, and all the appointments to the new bodies were due to be announced that day. De Brun passed along a note outlining her objection. The First and Deputy First Ministers wanted to avoid any difficulty, so another note was sent around the table to Bertie Ahern, instructing him to move on when he got to the part about the nominations. The Executive resolved the issue later.

Despite Trimble's insistence that no one should be afraid of cross-border cooperation, after the rather liturgical meeting ministers observed him blanching at David Andrew's suggestion that everyone pose for a group picture to mark the occasion. The unionist ministers politely laughed off the suggestion. Durkan recalled: "He didn't want the family photo-style picture because the family photo then would have been like a Council of Irish Ministers." Trimble confirmed that he did not want the group photo, but he did consent to a photograph being taking of the NSMC ministers seated around the table.

After that first, historic day the north-south meetings soon became a matter of routine. Indeed, Trimble would sometimes emerge complaining they had been "boring". This secretly pleased at least one official who said: "They were supposed to be boring. It meant things were running smoothly." Trimble was not the only minister to complain about the staid nature of the meetings, although he accepted that was how much of government worked. Some Dublin ministers, too, were annoyed that the meetings were too choreographed, that there was no room for spontaneity. It became a common feature that rows happened beforehand, rather than inside the formal meeting.

One memorable exception occurred at the NSMC meeting in Dublin Castle. The meeting was delayed for up to an hour because the First and Deputy First Ministers were at loggerheads. According to Durkan and Mallon the disagreement concerned Trimble's refusal to have a NSMC meeting in institutional format. The Good Friday Agreement provided for that, as well as for an intersectoral format, but Trimble dug in very hard and it turned into a stand-off on the morning of the meeting.

"We couldn't get Trimble and Mallon to agree," said a senior civil servant. "Mallon said, 'That's the paper we agreed,' and Trimble said, 'I've changed my mind.'" They went into separate rooms and had separate meetings to work it out. Durkan suggested it was a case of Trimble getting cold feet: "I think he thought he was being hustled. Trimble said he did not see the point of having the meeting at that stage. "I was not interested in having a meeting for no good purpose."

Durkan recalled that such a meeting took place later in the life of the administration, after Mallon retired. Trimble agreed to it when it was explained to him that the reason for the meeting was to allow the Irish Foreign Minister to attend a north-south meeting in the sectoral format, as other ministers tended to meet in this format on issues related to their brief. Trimble acknowledged that there were sensitivities for unionists around north-south issues. He recalled that when the meeting did finally take place in this format, it was at a time when the bodies were more developed and he could see a practical purpose. His early objection in Dublin Castle was because he could see no practical purpose. To end the row, Trimble and Mallon were persuaded that they only had to agree what was said in the joint communiqué after the meeting – during the meeting they could say what they liked. The Taoiseach and the entire Irish Cabinet were kept waiting, sipping tea. If Bertie Ahern was annoyed, he didn't show it. Said an official: "He would have regarded this as the children growing up, you have to give them a bit of space."

During the course of the administration, Trimble realised that there were benefits for unionists in having a formal structure to relations with Dublin because it meant unionists had accountability. Where there was no formal area of cooperation, ministers had a freer hand in dealing with Dublin. This was why he suggested exploring the expansion of the north-south function, but soon retreated when the DUP attacked the notion. Trimble complained he had been misunderstood.

Despite his polite presence at the first plenary, Trimble was aware that many unionists would not be as enthusiastic about the new arrangements as nationalists were. He looked forward to the meeting of the British Irish Council (BIC), also established by the Good Friday Agreement, describing it as the truly revolutionary institution. The inaugural meeting of the BIC took place on Friday, December 17 1999 in London. There had been some disagreement as to how it would operate. Unionists wanted the NSMC to come under the umbrella of the BIC, but this was opposed. Instead the BIC became a separate but interlocking entity. Like all the institutions born out of the Agreement, it was designed to operate only while the others were functioning. It comprised ministers from all sections of the British Isles – England, Wales, Scotland, the Republic, Northern Ireland, the Channel Islands, Guernsey, Jersey and the Isle of Man – and would deal with matters of mutual interest and cooperation.

The BIC was an invention to appease unionists, and Trimble was determined to get his own back on the DUP for its ministers' decision to spurn the NSMC. In this act of revenge he had an enthusiastic accomplice in Mallon. The two might have had their disagreements, but they shared a frustration: how to deal with the DUP? "They didn't get on and they played games with each other occasionally," said one senior official, "but one thing they really enjoyed together was doing down the DUP. That made them both happy and they joined gleefully together in that."

What to do about the DUP had been a source of some debate between the two men. It was the responsibility of the First and Deputy First Minister to jointly nominate ministers to attend both the NSMC and the BIC. They ensured that the DUP could not attend the inaugural BIC meeting. Robinson reacted as if he did not care, dismissing the BIC as a show performance for the cameras: "If Sinn Féin were there, we wouldn't be there, even if we received an invite on gold paper." Robinson insisted he did not feel left out of British-Irish relations. He set up his own meetings with his counterparts in Scotland and Wales and spoke "frequently" with the UK minister. "I never felt starved of contact."

In fact, Robinson may have got the last laugh. The Executive chose transport as its area of special interest within the BIC – a brief with which he would have been comfortable.

Without Robinson's participation, Trimble and Mallon struggled with the unfamiliar concepts involved. Robinson gave them only the information he would have given a journalist in terms of his portfolio, and informed them that they could neither enter agreement nor take decisions on behalf of his Department: "I made very clear in writing to them that they were not speaking for my Department," he said.

Trimble insisted that he and Mallon did not do "too badly", but in retrospect came to regret the decision. "Tactically, it would have been better to suck the DUP further in. It wouldn't have been too difficult to set up (BIC) plenaries and invite the DUP and Sinn Féin to them." Trimble calculated that if the DUP had refused to accept the invitation, he would have attacked them for failing to support a UK institution and if they did come along, he would have attacked them as hypocrites by joining in even more ministerial functions.

For the BIC's inaugural meeting a five-strong Northern Ireland delegation was chosen to attend: Mallon and Trimble, Mark Durkan, Sir Reg Empey and Bairbre de Brun. The arrangement was that all five would arrive at Lancaster House together for a photo-call, but it did not work out as planned. The Health Minister got caught in traffic around the Mall and the men reached the venue before her. Her private secretary telephoned to say she was not too far behind, but the other ministers went in without her. Inside Lancaster House the question was raised as to how to manage de Brun's arrival. A source claimed that the Prime Minister's official spokesman, Alistair Campbell, was not keen for the Prime Minister to go back out and meet de Brun and repeat the "meet and greet". However, another official pointed out that if Blair failed to go out, the media would say the Prime Minister had snubbed de Brun and that would become the story of the day.

Tony Blair decided to go out and greet de Brun. When the minister arrived, late, she stole the spotlight. Cameras flashed as the Prime Minister greeted the republican minister, her green scarf blowing in the breeze. It was the first public handshake between Tony Blair and a member of Sinn Féin. The media lapped it up, but according to one insider the other ministers did not: "They felt they'd been upstaged."

As they entered Lancaster House, de Brun apologised to Blair for her tardiness. He was very gracious, and joked, "It wasn't British Rail, I hope?" Exchanging pleasantries, the Prime Minister asked her which portfolio she had received. Observing the scene, Finance minister Mark Durkan was amused by her response: "Health, the poisoned chalice." Durkan recalled: "It was the real martyr culture. And I just said, 'Well, I got the poison decanter'."

One wonders if that public handshake would have occurred had Martin McGuinness been the Sinn Féin minister in attendance. As she had no record of IRA involvement, it was easier for Blair to shake hands publicly with de Brun. Even if he did not look entirely sure that he was doing the right thing, Blair later brushed aside media interest in the event. Part of the whole peace process, he said, involved people starting to treat each other like normal human beings in a normal society. "It would be strange if I was not able to shake hands with her in public since I have shaken hands with her in private ... If it's a milestone, so be it," Blair said. According to de Brun, Gerry Adams had another view. She said: "Someone had commented to him that the big story was that Blair had shaken my hand, and Gerry said the big story was that I had shaken Blair's hand."

Once de Brun had arrived and there was a full complement inside Lancaster House, the ministers settled down to business. The meeting was carefully choreographed. De Brun remembered the British ministers striving to make her feel welcome. "The unionists were much happier and much more relaxed and I do remember a special effort being made that I felt at home there," she said.

During the formal part of the proceedings, the Prime Minister spoke first, followed by the Taoiseach and the Tánaiste, then by Trimble and Mallon. The Deputy First Minister spoke of the gathering as leaving a legacy of peace, a deeper, truer peace than ever before. He quoted the poet Louis McNiece who wrote in "Autumn Journal": "I note how a single purpose can be founded on a jumble of opposites." One of those witnessing the scene recalled that "Mallon made a grand speech. David Trimble's was not so good by comparison." Another witness concurred: "Mallon made the big speech and this should have been Trimble's big day, but it was awful."

Speeches followed by the late First Minister for Scotland Donald Dewar, the First Secretary of the Welsh National Assembly Alun Michael and the Channel Islands representatives. The point was made that each administration could learn from the other. "Dewar thought it would be a good way to exchange ideas and pilots," said Durkan. "He said he always thought that plagiarism was an undervalued art form." Sir Reg Empey, too, was very impressed by Dewar's speech. "He gave a very powerful address. He was very keen." In fact, Sir Reg was taken aback by the level of commitment for the new body displayed by all the ministers, especially those from the Channel Islands, who were constitutionally independent of the United Kingdom. "It was unbelievable. I couldn't understand the enthusiasm from the island governments and I was saying, 'What the hell do these people want to be bothered with this for?'"

In truth, the other regions and Channel Islands – who, according to an Irish official, were not even consulted when the body was first drawn up in the talks – adored the BIC and used it to "gang up" on London: "It was an excuse for a whinge." One minister from the Isle of Man was most enthusiastic: "Before the BIC we would be lucky if we got a second-rate official in Whitehall to speak to us on the phone. Now we got face-time with the Prime Minister." The BIC also gave the island governments a chance to network with European heads of state, such as the Taoiseach. Indeed, Bertie Ahern was later invited to the Isle of Man and spent an evening there dining with the island's ministers.

Although initially lukewarm, according to Trimble, the Scottish Parliament became very interested in the BIC, particularly as it offered a chance to build relations with Dublin. The relationship had suffered after the Republic won independence from the UK. "The warmest relationship in the BIC was between Dublin and Edinburgh," noted one Irish diplomat.

Following the Good Friday Agreement, the Irish government opened consulates in Cardiff and Edinburgh. Trimble, ignoring nationalist sentiment, resented the fact that the Irish did not open a consulate in Belfast. "We got grumbling to them about that," he said. In turn, Donald Dewar made a ground-breaking trip to the Irish capital. An Irish diplomat said the Scottish ministers were keen to learn from the structures of the Dáil because it, like their own Parliament, had evolved out of Westminster. De Brun said the Council did not always reflect the intensity of east-west relations: "It was a public thing the unionists needed, but for my particular portfolio east-west was far more than that. We had this constant stream of correspondence in terms of regulation, in terms of appointments, in terms of a variety of positions being taken." She claimed the four Health ministers from Belfast, Edinburgh, Cardiff and London were constantly in touch with one another and signing-off on documents. "I didn't see it as anybody's job to harmonise with the British government position, but I did believe it made sense to look at what other ministers were doing. Basically we all had the same NHS structures and we were able to come up with different ways of doing things."

Sinn Féin's Martin McGuinness, who attended some BIC meetings as Minister of Education, found them enjoyable. He said republicans were relaxed about the meeting, regardless of unionist perception: "I think the unionists thought it would have scared us off, but we were quite comfortable with it, plus you were meeting quite interesting people from the Isle of Man and Jersey." One Irish official recalled that the Scottish were so taken with the BIC that they deeply resented the interruptions posed by the various suspensions to the Northern Ireland power-sharing Executive. The official said:

> "I don't think the Stormont officials realised how unpopular Northern Ireland was in the Council because of suspension. Scotland at one point got so annoyed with David Trimble because of the stop-start over suspensions that one of them asked, 'Could we throw Northern Ireland out?' This was the founding member!"

Before Trimble and Mallon could return home from the first BIC meeting, they had another historic engagement that same day. The inaugural meeting of the British-Irish Intergovernmental Conference was being held in Downing Street and the two ministers headed to London to attend it. Also set up under the Good Friday Agreement, this new body replaced the old Anglo-Irish Intergovernmental Conference and its brief was to promote bilateral cooperation on areas of mutual interest. It dealt with a more limited range of matters than the old structure because issues of cross-border cooperation relating to devolved matters were now in the hands of the Assembly. Another crucial difference was the presence of the Ulster Unionist minister at the table, in contrast to the old days when unionists picketed the meetings of the old Anglo-Irish Secretariat. To the public eye, the inaugural Conference meeting went smoothly. Trimble would later report to the Assembly that it had been an interesting experience for himself and Mallon. A programme of work had been agreed that included asylum and immigration, drugs policy and combating organised crime. The First and Deputy First Minister had also raised the matter of fuel duty and its impact on the Northern Ireland economy, a matter it was agreed could be considered at future meetings. Trimble told the Assembly, with a particular nod in the direction of anti-Agreement unionists: "We would not have had the opportunity to raise issues in that way under the ancient regime."

At the press conference in Downing Street after the inaugural BIC meeting, Taoiseach Bertie Ahern was in jovial form. Asked if the new closeness in relations would lead to the Republic rejoining the Commonwealth, the Taoiseach responded lightheartedly, "Would you wait 'til we get this one to work?"

Chapter 12
The Politics of Power-sharing

Sir Reg Empey was among those in Room 21 who would have struggled to recognise himself if, in 1974, he were given a glimpse of things to come. What would the young unionist hardliner have thought about his future – sharing power at Stormont in 1999 with Martin McGuinness? "Inconceivable," he answered without hesitation.

In fact, not only did he find himself at the Executive table with Martin McGuinness but as Minister of Enterprise, Trade and Investment he was battling to do business with the Irish government. He was struck by the irony of his position: as a leading opponent of Sunningdale in 1974 he was appalled by the Council of Ireland, yet now he had helped negotiate north-south institutions for the Good Friday Agreement and was determined to achieve benefits for Northern Ireland through cooperation with Dublin.

Empey's greatest achievement in office was the planning of a gas pipeline between the Republic and Northern Ireland. In co-ordinating this cross-border initiative, he became the first minister to travel officially to Dublin to meet his southern counterpart. Within five days of devolution the Unionist minister was welcomed to Kildare Street, on 7 December 1999, by Mary O'Rourke, Minister for Public Enterprise and Transport, and the Tánaiste and Minister for Enterprise, Trade and Employment, Mary Harney. The meeting had in fact been set up for the direct rule minister, John McFall, but Empey decided to go ahead with the discussion because he had a particular project he wished to discuss with O'Rourke.

Empey intended to develop and link, for the first time, the gas networks north and south of the border. Both Northern Ireland and the Republic were already connected to Scotland via costly cross-channel pipelines but, oddly for a small, landlocked island, they were not connected to each other. The gas supply into Northern Ireland was limited to the Greater Belfast Area. A previous attempt in the 1980s, under direct rule, to pipe gas into Northern Ireland from Kinsale in County Cork had collapsed due to the prohibitive cost. The massive capital investment required was still an obstacle, one which Empey needed to overcome: not only would he have to persuade his own cash-strapped Executive to invest in it but Dublin, too, would have to make it a funding priority. However, Empey believed the rewards – a cheaper, more secure gas supply – would more than justify the multi-million-pound expenditure. Over tea and sandwiches in Kildare Street, Empey made small-talk before turning the discussion to serious business. The ministers discussed the creation of an all-Ireland energy market, a policy that the departments in Belfast and Dublin were already pursuing. Indeed, there were proposals on the table for the completion of a £15 million north-south electricity interconnector. The unionist minister wanted a gas network as well, and was certain that O'Rourke would agree. The Fianna Fáil minister did recognise the merits of Empey's proposal, but her great enthusiasm was tempered by political realities. Empey recalled: "Mary O'Rourke could see the long-term advantages to both parts of the island from a technical point of view, but … the departments of finance on both sides of the border were edgy, naturally."

As well as the financial constraints, O'Rourke's department was already pursuing the development of a second Scottish-Irish pipeline, between Gormanstown in the Republic and Beattock in Scotland. Persuading the Minister for Finance to agree to a north-south project as well would be tricky. Scotland was the priority because the Republic was anxious to ensure it had a secure supply. "I wanted them to build between north and south first," said Empey. "So our pipeline could reinforce [their system]. Their concern was their lights had nearly gone out the previous winter and they were in an awful state of worry." The two ministers developed a close working relationship and pressed the issue with their respective Finance ministers, Mark Durkan and Charlie McCreevy. The First and Deputy First ministers and the Taoiseach were also involved. Given the financial complexities, the decision would ultimately be a political one.

By September 2000 they were steadily making progress towards their goal of an all-Ireland energy market, a plan advocated in the 2010 strategy document Empey had inherited from direct rule. At a news conference in Dublin, Empey and O'Rourke announced that they had commissioned consultants to prepare information papers on the energy situation on both sides of the border. They confirmed that their plans for a north-south electricity link were proceeding apace and agreed to explore further initiatives. "We are laying the foundation stone to a process that we hope will provide significant economic opportunity in the years ahead," said O'Rourke.

Empey was delighted with the progress and determined to maintain the momentum for the gas project by ensuring O'Rourke received the support she needed. He continued to build alliances and approached the Chairman of his Stormont committee, whom he knew would be enthusiastic. Pat Doherty, a leading member of Sinn Féin, recalled a tongue-in-cheek plea from Empey: "It was hilarious. He said he was a unionist and an Orangeman and he wanted an all-Ireland gas pipeline and he wanted Mary O'Rourke from the great republican Lenihan family to agree and could I do something about it and take a delegation down?"

Doherty led a committee delegation to Dublin on two occasions, in November and December 2000, to press the case with O'Rourke. The committee raised concerns about her Department's plans to impose a public service levy on natural gas pipeline projects and pointed out this could prove detrimental to the north-south project. O'Rourke said she shared their concerns. She viewed the delegation's visits as an expression of Empey's commitment and practicality and continued to pursue the project. The Stormont Enterprise committee announced it was conducting its own inquiry into the energy market. With his committee and O'Rourke on board, Empey also formed a powerful partnership with the Fianna Fáil tourism minister, Jim McDaid. Empey knew that McDaid, whose constituency was in economically disadvantaged rural Donegal, wanted the gas supply. He knew that the cost of running a pipeline up the western coast of Ireland would be astronomical and that the most cost-effective way to deliver gas to Donegal was via Northern Ireland. McDaid in turn, pressed the case with the Finance minister in

Dublin. At Stormont, Empey worked on the proposal with Durkan, a native of Derry, who had long wanted gas for the northwest. The finance minister, along with Deputy First Minister Seamus Mallon, lobbied Taoiseach Bertie Ahern, who was receptive, according to Damien McAteer, Durkan's special advisor: "Bertie readily agreed. Dublin was quite keen to explore how you get the gas into Letterkenny and the cheapest way of doing it was to take it across the border from Derry."

In fact, Dublin contributed £8 million towards constructing a pipeline within Northern Ireland. By September 2001 the north-south gas pipeline project was edging towards approval in Stormont and Dublin, but there were still problems. The civil servants in Finance could not justify the cost under their own guidelines and would risk being chastised by a Parliamentary probe if the deal was approved and then proved untenable. The deal required a ministerial direction. This was given by Empey and Durkan, who willingly took responsibility.

There was another hiccup, however, in its final stages when one of the companies involved in the consortium to build the project, KeySpan, reconsidered its commitment just days before construction was to be announced; this followed the 11 September attack in New York. According to McAteer, such moves were not uncommon among North American companies at the time. McAteer said few knew about the problem, but it was raised in discussions with him, Durkan, the Taoiseach and senior civil servants. Dublin, he said, was very supportive and told the northern administration: "No matter what happens, we will build the pipeline." O'Rourke said the Irish government realised the importance of having a large project that would benefit north-south cooperation:

> "We were very conscious that north-south relations was a young child and had to be encouraged and wherever we could give practical expression we would. The Taoiseach and I and Charlie McCreevy talked the matter through quite reasonably at Cabinet and I think all in the Cabinet had come to the conclusion that this was a good thing that should be encouraged."

Before the deal was finally announced, on 21 September 2001, Empey claimed to have met resistance from another, unexpected quarter: the Deputy First Minister. In September 2001, as acting First Minister and Enterprise minister, Empey had taken Seamus Mallon through the finer points of the venture. Their meeting was also attended by a clatter of civil servants. Empey naturally assumed that Mallon, a border nationalist, would champion the project and was disappointed by his attitude that day:

> "The officials' mouths were hanging open. Here we had a unionist from East Belfast, and a member of the Lenihan family pushing for this deal and we found ourselves facing all these obstructions and obfuscations over procedures and papers for this and papers for that. I couldn't understand it. Maybe he wasn't well that day, I don't know."

Mallon had concerns that the project would not reach some rural areas. He was also aware of an opportunity to bring Newry into the deal at a cheaper cost, but this had been rejected as it would not have benefited Craigavon, where Empey hoped the manufacturing base could benefit. A SDLP source thought Mallon was just in contrary form that day. Despite some awkwardness between Mallon and Empey, the deal was announced in the Newry headquarters of Inter-Trade Ireland. The gathering included Empey, Durkan and O'Rourke. The £60 million initiative involved a joint-venture construction of a pipeline from Dublin to Antrim/Belfast by Bord Gáis Éireann Northern Ireland (BGENI). A northwest pipeline would also be built, stretching from Carrickfergus to Derry. The northwest pipeline within Northern Ireland was to be completed by October 2004 and the north-south pipeline by 2006, targets which turned out to be fairly realistic.

For Empey, this joint venture was one of the great achievements of devolution – a concrete example of how the new system could deliver real benefits. According to McAteer the deal would not have been sealed without Empey, but he did stress that it was a joint production with the Department of Finance. The deal meant that 75% of the population of Northern Ireland would be able to access natural gas. While some rural towns, such as Strabane, complained at being left out in the medium term, there was no doubting that the project would benefit thousands of households. Plus the construction of the pipeline into the northwest also gave rural areas of Donegal an opportunity to have a gas supply in future. Empey envisaged that, with time, the network would mature into a dynamic, wide-ranging system. Furthermore, the pipe's construction secured the development of Coolkeeragh power station in Derry, which was converting to gas-fire electricity. "The two projects," announced Sir Reg, "will attract well in excess of £250 million investment in the Northern Ireland economy over the next four years."

By championing the project Empey showed that unionism need not fear cross-border relations. In fact, one of the reasons his party chose the Department was its scope for practical cross-border cooperation though energy, tourism and trade. Another motive was to keep it out of the hands of Sinn Féin's Bairbre de Brun, who had taken the post in the ill-fated selection of July 1999. Some nationalists were suspicious that unionists would stymie cooperation, but this proved groundless. Empey made quite sure of that, pointing out: "It turned out to be the biggest area of north-south cooperation."

Tourism became another priority of Empey's Department through Tourism Ireland, an all-Ireland company set up to market the island abroad. It was agreed jointly as part of post-Agreement negotiations. In 2002, in conjunction with Dublin's tourism minister, Jim McDaid, Empey drew up an ambitious plan to achieve a growth rate of around 25% over three years. The Department also embarked on a review of tourism policy, which included widespread consultation in the industry.

Despite his enthusiasm for north-south cooperation, Empey blocked the SDLP proposal to create another new cross-border body within his Department. Following the gas-pipeline deal, the SDLP pushed for a new all-Ireland energy body. The approach came through the Department of Finance and Personnel, led by the SDLP's Mark Durkan. It was firmly rebuffed by Empey: "I just sent a one-pager and said, 'Not as long as there is breath in me and in this department'." While the SDLP was "chancing their arm", as one party source put it, Empey was obviously sensitive to the political reaction within unionism to such a move. But he said this was not the main objection. He claimed an energy body would have been counter-productive as it would have adversely affected the negotiations that achieved the gas-pipeline deal: "If we had put north-south bureaucracy in the middle of all that, it would have been ruined." O'Rourke agreed with this assessment, saying: "He is right. Maybe nothing would have happened if there had been an energy body."

That a unionist should be so enthusiastic about north-south relations was a sign of a growing maturity in community attitudes to the Republic, a change that was made possible in part by the Good Friday Agreement and the growing trade links being forged by the private sector. As one of the Agreement's negotiators, Empey was one of the deal's strongest advocates, embracing it confidently and, some felt, more enthusiastically than David Trimble. Empey and his fellow unionist ministers, Michael McGimpsey and Sam Foster, embodied the new unionism so despised by the old guard. Empey, in particular, was regarded as quite crucial in party meetings when Trimble had to persuade his party to move in a certain direction. Graham Gudgin, Trimble's economic advisor, was privy to Assembly team meetings, even though he was not actually a party member. He recalled that Trimble would behave like a lawyer, saying as little as possible and not getting into arguments, while Empey expressed disapproval as the issues were thrashed out until finally Empey would side with Trimble. "I'm not sure if it was a deliberate double act, but Reg was essential. It was very effective," said Gudgin.

Empey had learned lessons from the violent history of the Troubles and was pragmatic enough to recognise that unionism had to adapt and alter. He had changed over the course of his own life, slowly coming to believe that the best way to preserve the union and defend Northern Ireland was by demonstrating that the state could work and serve all sections of society. By the time he became a minister, aged fifty-two, Empey was describing himself as an Irish Unionist, a point of view not shared by many in his tribe.

Empey's pragmatism and commitment to compromise was in sharp contrast to the politics of his youth, when he entered politics to maintain the status quo. His attitudes then were not dissimilar from those of many of his peers, firmly in keeping with traditional unionism. He was the scion of a middle-class Presbyterian family that was active in business and unionist politics. Members of his family were involved in retailing and other business interests and several were prominent in the Ulster Unionist party. His maternal uncle, Joe Morgan, was a Stormont MP for nine years until his death in 1962, once commenting, "The Irish are doing so well in Britain that Paddy Reilly will not go back to Ballyjamesduff." Morgan was a fiercely conservative, anti-socialist small businessman who owned Morgan's Fashions in Wellington Place in Belfast. Like his Uncle Joe, Empey would devote his energies to politics and business.

Born in post-war Belfast on 26 October 1947, Reginald Norman Morgan Empey was the second child of Samuel and Emily Empey. Their daughter, Pat, had been born in 1933. Their son was named after Emily's brother, Norman Morgan, an officer in the Royal Ulster Rifles who had joined airborne services and was killed in action just as the Second World War drew to a close.

Samuel Empey, who was originally from County Louth, ran a gentlemen's outfitters, S. Empey Ltd, at the corner of Donegall Place and Donegall Square in the heart of Belfast, just opposite the City Hall. His mother worked nearby in Morgan's Fashions. The Empeys lived in East Belfast's relatively prosperous Shandon Park and the young Reg attended

Hillcrest Preparatory School just a few streets away. At the age of nine his narrow world was turned upside-down when his uncle, Temple Lundie, suggested sending the boy to the Royal School in Armagh. Lundie, a Presbyterian minister who would serve as moderator of the Presbyterian Church in the 1970s, was on the board of that rather prestigious school. The young Reg became a reluctant boarder. The school was founded in 1608 by decree of the Privy Council of King James I and its purpose was to educate the children of English and Scottish planters who had settled in the northeast of Ireland following the flight of the Earls in 1607. The eminent institution had educated generations of Anglo-Irish establishment figures, including Lord Castlereagh, who had served as British foreign secretary at the defeat of Napoleon in 1815, and Isaac Corry, a former Speaker of the Irish Parliament. The Ulster Unionist veteran John Taylor, later Lord Kilclooney, was also a former pupil. The school was originally sited outside Armagh City, but the murder of its headmaster in 1641 was believed to be a factor in its relocation to St Columba's Abbey. By the time Reg was a boarder, the Royal School was located in College Hill, outside Armagh City. The Duke of Wellington, who went on to defeat Napoleon at Waterloo, had reputedly run away from the school during his tenure there, and the young Reg was no more impressed when he arrived and viewed the walled Victorian institution. "It was really like a prison camp," he recalled. "You couldn't go out. You were in these barrack rooms … with lines of beds and cold water in the middle." With just a hint of humour, he added: "If a place like this existed now, the human rights people would be in."

As a child, Empey had never been away from home and initially he was distraught and homesick. "It was a very tough experience. It was fairly brutal stuff," he said. He saw his parents two Sundays per term, between the hours of 2.00pm and 5.00pm. He went home at Christmas, Easter and July, but the rest of the year he boarded at the school. With no telephone, he relied on the kindness of his Aunt Eileen, Temple Lundie's wife, who lived nearby. The youngster would meet her in secret and she would pass food parcels over the wall while he would slip out letters.

Empey eventually learned to adapt and found school-life became more bearable as he got older. The headmaster chose him to be a prefect when he was eighteen and that gave him more freedom. As a rake-thin teenager he was not built for rugby, but he played hockey and enjoyed history. He graduated to Queen's University and studied economics, delighted to be back home and mixing freely with a more diverse group of people. At Queen's, Empey stood out more for his relative wealth than for his politics. Said one former student: "He was quiet, but he had a very exotic car, a 1600E Ford Cortina." Empey laughed at the memory. He was only the second person in Northern Ireland to have the gold-and-black car. "It used to draw crowds," he said.

At Queen's in the mid-1960s he was exposed to the radical politics of the era. Northern Ireland was gripped by civil rights protests and Empey recalled "great contemporaries". These included BBC veteran Nick Ross and civil rights campaigners such as Michael Farrell and "Red" Rory McShane. Another contemporary was Bernadette Devlin, who would go on to represent mid-Ulster as the youngest MP in history. Devlin – a fiery republican who was once famously described as "Castro in a mini-skirt" – was the polar opposite of the pin-striped conservative who had joined the Young Unionists and who would become their vice-chairman. It was through the Young Unionists that Empey met his wife, Stella, whom he married in 1977. The couple had two children, Christopher and Julie-Anne.

As a Young Unionist, Empey had little sympathy with the civil rights campaigners, whom he regarded with suspicion. He recalled making little distinction between them and the republicans who were out to overthrow the State: "At that age, things are very black and white." He visited impoverished streets off the Albertbridge Road in East Belfast and soon discovered that poor Protestant homes were no different from poor Catholic homes: small, cramped, damp houses with outdoor toilets. He remembered being verbally attacked at a party discussion for trying to raise the housing problem and was puzzled to be accused of bringing politics into the meeting, which was largely exercised with organising a jumble sale. "It was clear the party needed a radical shake-up," he said.

After graduating, Empey remained active in politics while pursuing his career. He considered joining his uncle's auction business, John Ross and Co. in Belfast's May Street, but instead went to work at Goodyear tyremakers in Craigavon, before moving into retail with the House of Fraser in Belfast. In the early 1970s he was managing Newell's Department Store in Royal Avenue. The daily lives of those in Belfast became fraught with tension and danger when the IRA began to plant no-warning bombs in the city centre. In July 1972 Empey was in the city when the IRA carried out one of the worst atrocities of the Troubles and exploded twenty-one bombs. Although warnings were given, they were totally inadequate and the result was devastation. Nine people were killed in two of the explosions, the worst of which claimed six lives at a Belfast bus station. A police officer interviewed by the BBC at the time recalled the screaming, crying and moaning. In March 1974 the store Empey was working in, opposite Grand Central Hotel (at the time serving as an Army barracks), was twice damaged in bomb explosions. By the second attack Empey was furious. The store was looted under the noses of the Army and he complained that the barracks should be removed as it was drawing attacks: "I am not prepared to play Russian roulette with my staff any more. We were lucky to get out this time and we may not be so lucky to get out again." In 1986 he opened his own retail clothing company which has since ceased trading.

As the Troubles deepened, so did Empey's interest in politics and, like many unionists, he was alarmed by events and fearful that London would give in to republican demands. As a member of the Young Unionists he aligned himself with the more hardline elements of the Ulster Unionist party. Along with David Trimble, he joined the Vanguard movement in spring 1973 and helped form the Vanguard Unionist Progressive party, under the leadership of Bill Craig. Empey was the Chairman of Vanguard during the anti-Sunningdale period, a time when Vanguard's links with paramilitarism led critics to denounce it as a Fascist movement. Empey vehemently opposed the Sunningdale power-sharing Executive and the fact that the Irish Constitution laid claim to Northern Ireland's territory. He admitted power-sharing was a factor in his hatred of Sunningdale. He was concerned that the SDLP had secured the plum posts in the administration; John Hume, for example, had taken Economy. "There was a feeling," he said, "that the mix wasn't balanced, but what destabilised it politically was the Council of Ireland and the way [it] was handled."

Although Empey was not in the frontline of street politics during the Ulster Workers'

Council strike, he did play a backroom role. "I would have been in Vanguard House and seen what was going on. I wasn't on the frontline committee. I was aware of what was going on and I would have been around." His satisfaction at Sunningdale's collapse was shortlived as the Troubles quickly intensified and politics stagnated. The Convention of May 1975, to which Empey was elected as a Vanguard member aligned to the UUUC coalition, failed to bring stability. Following this, he split from Vanguard that autumn after Bill Craig advocated voluntary coalition with the SDLP. Empey said Craig had brought forward the policy without consultation: "I was Chairman of the party and I didn't know about it."

Empey was among those who suspected that Craig was being set-up by the Ulster Unionist party, which in fact had no intention of supporting such a coalition but merely wanted to discredit him. "Looking back, it would have been worth a try," said Empey. "Whether it would have survived, I don't know. The question of the north-south dimension had never been resolved and I find it hard to believe it would have been." Along with other disaffected Vanguard members, Empey formed a new group in 1977, the United Ulster Unionist party. Its leader was Ernest Baird and Empey was his deputy. The party failed to make an impact electorally and was wound up by 1984.

Ulster Unionists asked Empey to stand in the 1985 council election. He was elected to Belfast City Council, then a bear-pit where republicans and unionists clashed ferociously. Relations became particularly strained that year with the signing of the Anglo-Irish Agreement by Taoiseach Garret FitzGerald and PM Margaret Thatcher. Empey was apoplectic at this unwelcome development and stood on the platform with the DUP leader Ian Paisley when he made his famous "Never, never, never" speech at Belfast City Hall in front of tens of thousands. But Empey was the voice of moderation in terms of political tactics. When unionists wanted to boycott Belfast City Council, Empey argued against it, pointing out that it would be easy to leave but hard to return. When Secretary of State Tom King came to the City Hall a few days after the signing there was bedlam and the British minister was physically attacked by angry loyalists. Empey was among the protestors and recalled feelings were running high.

Fisticuffs also broke out at the Council on a number of occasions. One unforgettable incident occurred when a republican draped a very long tricolour, like a sort of a sheet-ladder, in the public gallery and John Carson, a unionist, attempted to pull it down and ended up swinging like a pendulum across the Council chamber. "It was wild," said Empey.

His career as a councillor was marked by two stints as Lord Mayor, the first of which began in 1989 and thrust him into massive controversy. "I was the victim of circumstances," he smiled wryly. Empey had been asked by Sir John Gorman, later Deputy Speaker of the 1998 Assembly, if he would open a business conference Gorman was organising at the Europa Hotel. Empey was informed it would involve Taoiseach Charles Haughey in his role as President of the European Community. Although Haughey was a hate figure for many unionists who were still embittered by the Anglo-Irish Agreement and deeply resentful of Dublin, Empey agreed to open the conference as he was assured he would be away long before the Taoiseach arrived. However, Empey overestimated his unionist colleagues' tolerance. A negative story appeared in a local newspaper and Empey came under pressure from Council members to withdraw. He refused, even when instructed formally to do so. As Lord Mayor, Empey wanted to show that he was above party politics and did not want to be regarded as little more than a "party hack" while in office. "It wasn't a case of me just being thran [awkward], but I just wasn't going to roll over," he said. "I didn't think it would do the office any good, being pushed around like that." The Ulster Unionist party was polarised at the Council, with a few colleagues, including Ian Adamson, supporting Empey. He lost the whip, as did his supporters. The atmosphere deteriorated further when two UDR men were killed by the IRA and their funerals were scheduled to take place on the same day as Haughey's visit. Empey asked his DUP deputy if he would step in for him at the funerals, fearing his presence might inflame an already tense situation. "It just got worse and worse and worse," said Empey, who was by now receiving threatening phone calls and letters.

At the Europa Hotel on the day of the Haughey visit a hostile crowd had gathered, waving union flags, and there was a protest demonstration on the roof of Ulster Unionist headquarters, then located in Glengall Street, just opposite the hotel. Haughey was a particular hate figure for unionists, not least because he had been at the centre of IRA gun-running allegations in the early 1970s. He was acquitted at his subsequent trial, but unionists still regarded him with suspicion. David Trimble and Ian Paisley were among the rooftop protestors on the Ulster Unionist premises that day. Empey was furious that Paisley had been let into his party headquarters. He suspected Trimble let him in, but could never prove it. Security blanketed the area and police informed Empey they were going to have to take him into the Europa Hotel in a Land Rover. Empey refused, ignoring their warnings and insisting he would travel in a Council vehicle or not at all. After some discussion it was agreed he would use the Council car and the police would follow in a bullet-proof vehicle. Empey arrived at the Europa's back entrance to jeers and protestations. Within seconds he was shuttled inside and a security shutter had slammed behind him. His visit lasted twenty minutes and his remarks to the audience included a pointed message to the Taoiseach about Dublin's claim to Northern Ireland. "You're not on, Mr Haughey," he declared without any bluster.

Fortunately for Empey, a majority of his party colleagues backed his stance and he was subsequently elected honorary secretary. It took longer for his Council colleagues to forgive him, however, and he was frozen out of committee places. But he outmanoeuvred them. The gas committee was poorly attended and Empey and his supporters realised they could stage a *coup* if they turned up and got councillors opposed to the hardline unionists to vote with them. Empey seized the chairmanship of the committee and laughed for a long time after at the memory of his unionist colleagues' sour faces when they heard the news.

By 1991 he was involved in the Brooke–Mayhew talks. Unaware of the SDLP leader's secret initiative with republicans, Empey believed a deal was close and blamed the DUP opposition for scuppering it. "Ian Paisley and Willie McCrea went to the Ormeau Park and put up a big tent and that was the end of it," he said. But when he learned of Hume's initiative with republicans he doubted that the deal would have occurred, regardless of the DUP. Frustrated by the continual lack of progress and keen to break out of council politics, Empey made a bid for Westminster, but failed to get the nomination for North

Down in 1995. In the 1997 general election he secured a nomination in East Belfast, but failed to unseat Peter Robinson.

The Good Friday Agreement brought new opportunities and in 1999 Empey's fortunes improved. In fact, by the end of that year he was a Stormont minister and had received a knighthood in the New Year's Honours list in recognition of his contribution to public life. While other unionists balked at sitting at the power-sharing table with republicans, Empey proved more pragmatic. He had worked with Sinn Féin members at Belfast Council and had gained some insight into the party and learned, of necessity, how to deal with republicans on day-to-day issues. "Those who are most opposed to the peace process," Empey noted, "tend to be people who have no experience of talking to Sinn Féin. Sinn Féin is a world away if you are in Bangor."

Relations at the Council thawed with the IRA ceasefire and Sinn Féin's acceptance of the Agreement. Empey may have been very pragmatic, but he still continued to challenge republicans, particularly over the issue of IRA weapons. Even so, when it was first speculated in 1998 that Empey would be the new Enterprise minister, the normally caustic Máirtín Ó Muilleoir, a former Sinn Féin councillor, paid tribute to him and declared he would be "damned good at the job".

The DUP were scathing about Ulster Unionists for taking seats in the administration, labelling Empey a unionist jellyfish. He, in turn, taunted the DUP about their decision to take their ministerial posts. Nonetheless this notion of weakness gained some currency, especially when he later resisted pressure to challenge Trimble for the leadership. One unionist critic privately echoed the words former Labour PM Harold Wilson used about Tory PM Ted Heath, calling him "a shiver without a spine".

Empey may have had a mild-mannered exterior, but at critical times he showed he also possessed a steely resolve, as witnessed when he refused to back down over Haughey's visit. His refusal to seize the leadership from Trimble may have resulted from pragmatism rather than nerves: the party was deeply divided at the time and pushing out Trimble would not have united it. Empey said that when, in the autumn of 2003, he conducted talks with Jeffrey Donaldson which led to another challenge by Trimble's critics, his actions were rooted in his concern to keep the party together, not leadership ambition. Party sources suggested he would have taken the leadership had it been offered, but he had gone on record as saying he would not challenge Trimble. Yet the criticisms persisted.

In Office he stood up to the SDLP over the proposed creation of a north-south body and refused to be rail-roaded by civil servants. As minister, he quashed a proposal to create a new quango. "One of the first things I was asked to do was agree to this and I refused. It was an advisory body dealing with broadband and they wanted to turn that from an advisory group to a full-blown public body and I refused," he said.

His permanent secretary was Gerry Loughran. The pair had been friends for years – Empey was quite accomplished at mimicking Loughran's mannerisms – and it was a good working relationship. Their mutual respect for one another helped ease the transition from devolution to direct rule. Loughran advised Empey to adopt a formal approach. "I was quite happy to have an informal relationship, but his strong advice was I should be addressed as 'Minister'." Loughran's time at the Department was shortlived, however. After his promotion to head of the civil service, Bruce Robinson took over. Empey had also known Robinson for years; by coincidence, Robinson had attended Empey's *alma mater* and the two had boarded at the same time, although Robinson was a few years younger.

Some party insiders claimed Empey got the job he cherished in the Executive, but he insisted he would have been satisfied with any of the portfolios. Others in the party were lobbying David Trimble for him to be appointed Enterprise minister, but Empey said he was not aware of this. "I would have taken anything I had been given, I was happy to do the job I got," he insisted. Certainly, there was no doubting that he was very comfortable with the Enterprise portfolio, as he already had a good understanding of the issues through his Council work. It was not, however, until a few months before he became minister that he was invited to a jobs announcement. "I think they were afraid of politicians then, nervous about them getting involved," he said.

Empey's first weeks in Office were marked by devastating job losses in the textile industry. In mid-January around 340 jobs were lost within twenty-four hours, with employment under threat elsewhere. Empey was extremely sympathetic. He recognised the problems the industry faced as it grappled with cheap imports from the Far East. Northern Ireland's flax and linen mills had dominated the textile industry in the late nineteenth and early twentieth century, but if it was to survive in the modern economy it would have to adapt and specialise. To encourage the industry to take a strategic view, Empey's Department set up a task force that commissioned leading consultants Kurt Salmon to examine the problems and recommend solutions.

Another project commissioned by Empey and supported by the DUP minister Maurice Morrow was the West Belfast Task Force and the Greater Shankill Task Force, which dealt with deprivation in those areas. The community had been demanding such an initiative for years, but their pleas had been ignored. Empey said he wanted to show people on the Falls Road as well as the Shankill that devolution could deliver for them. He received a warm welcome from the Sinn Féin MP for West Belfast, Gerry Adams, when he visited the Falls Road and toured the Culturlann complex, which fostered both enterprise and the Irish language. Empey said he had no qualms about visiting and had even considered using a bit of Irish in his speech, but decided it would be corny: "I hadn't got it right. I find it a very difficult language."

He impressed nationalists with his approach to north-south matters as well as community relations. "He would have won a lot of respect at the Executive table for that," said a SDLP source. He won the Channel Four Parliamentarian of the Year award and was well regarded by members outside his own party and across the divide.

In the early days of the administration Empey was proud to be representing the Assembly and appreciated the goodwill shown to Northern Ireland. He had been shrewd about involving his committee on various foreign trips, realising it would underscore the cross-community approach of the new administration. He also wanted to encourage its role in policy development: "I believed in the committee and I didn't see it as a nuisance or an opposition like some ministers. I didn't take that approach," he said. "If you fell out with your committee you could do a lot of damage." Pat Doherty, his Sinn Féin committee chairman, was also anxious to build bridges and Empey thought the committee came up with good ideas, assisting with the gas-pipeline project, health, safety and consumer issues, as well as investment. The committee helped shape legislation with its amendments and over time Doherty believed it would have come forward with its own legislation.

The committee undertook a tour of America and Canada and the rapport between Empey and Pat Doherty was evident, particularly at an event in Washington's Tower Club when the political symbolism of the two working together was appreciated by the audience. There, Empey spoke of the need to exploit the rich heritage of Northern Ireland's shipbuilding industry, which had built the *Titanic*. He joked: "I suppose before the film there was a reluctance to highlight the fact the ship was built in Belfast. But as people say in the city, it was floating when it left Belfast docks and, yes, it was being steered by an Englishman!"

Empey was amazed at the access Northern Ireland was given to America's political and business elite. "It was incredible. We had a virtual open-door policy and it was beginning to annoy a number of the interest groups in the United States. I heard that the Polish lobby and others were concerned we were getting the lion's share of access," he said. The minister appeared on CNN and the Department of Enterprise received assistance from the US Secretary of Commerce, Don Evans.

Another major issue for the minister was the crisis at the Harland and Wolff shipyard, whose industrial cranes, affectionately known as Samson and Goliath, had dominated the Belfast skyline for decades. The shipyard had been in danger of sinking under its debts for some time and the company was struggling to keep what was left of its once-massive workforce. The shipyard was located in Empey's constituency and he recognised its symbolic importance to the wider economy and to Northern Ireland's heritage. But the order book was thin and debts were mounting, forcing it to issue a jobs loss warning. The cash-flow problem was made worse by a dispute with a US company over payment for a contract. Throughout his time in Office, Empey tried to support the yard. During one Christmas holiday he was constantly on the telephone, trying to ensure that Ministry of Defence orders promised by the Prime Minister would be forthcoming; Empey had lobbied Geoff Hoon, Minister of Defence, to get the £80 million orders in the first place. "Tony Blair came in on a helicopter, all pillars of fire, and made the announcement," he recalled.

As Christmas 2000 approached, however, there were still loose ends to be tied up before the end of the year, when government subsidies to shipyards were going to be removed. He worked with officials in his department and Hoon pushed the deal through at his end. Empey suspected Hoon may have had to issue a ministerial direction, over-ruling objections by civil servants and risking an auditor's report if something went wrong with the deal he had underwritten. While that situation was resolved, the yard's future remained precarious and by spring 2002 more distress signals were going out to the minister. Shipyard owner Fred Olsen wanted to change the terms of his lease, which had been agreed when the yard was privatised. The yard was located on acres of land leased from the Belfast Harbour Commissioners, a public trust. The land was earmarked for ship-building, but its owners wanted to use some of the land for industrial development. The yard presented a business plan that would see multi-million-pound proceeds from land development put back into a streamlined shipyard, with a new facility built on the old site. Empey was approached, but he needed the agreement of Regional Development Minister Peter Robinson, whose Department had the final say on land. Empey said the ministers' interests were overlapping: "I was interested in salvaging some kind of a business and Robinson was interested in putting the land to proper use while recognising the public interest had to be protected."

They held several meetings with shipyard executives, including its chairman, Sir David Fell, and were persuaded of the merits of the deal. Instead of operating on 160 acres of shipyard land, the core would be scaled back to 80 acres and the other half developed. While it did not require any additional resources from the Executive, critics complained the shipyard was benefiting from a seven-figure gift. The ministers vowed there would be "no smash and land grab" and Empey presented the deal to a sceptical Executive without Robinson, who refused to attend Executive meetings. "There was a lot of scepticism and they [ministers] were unconvinced the company would actually deliver on it," Empey recalled.

Robinson was responsible for getting the land valuation and took great care to ensure that it was accurate lest it should lead to accusations later that the property had been undervalued. Empey recalled: "We didn't want to get our eye wiped and we ended up getting six valuations and they all converged more or less around the same figure." Empey told the Executive the yard would surely close if the deal did not go ahead, and several hundred jobs would go with it. He argued that it would be better to make use of the land, a view shared by Robinson, and hope the yard would survive. The Executive stipulated that a loan from the Department of Employment and Learning to cover earlier redundancy costs would have to be repaid. Once that was agreed, the plan went ahead. However, the Executive's fears were realised when, within a few months of the deal, Harland and Wolff announced plans to make redundant another 265 core workers, leaving just twenty-five manual operators. The result was that the shipyard was effectively no more, but it had cost millions of pounds in a quick land sell-off. Trade unionists made accusations of bad faith, but the company said the orders were simply not there. While the land would at least be put to good use by developing a commercial and entertainment area known as the *Titanic* Quarter, Empey was most annoyed.

There was sympathy for the ministers within the administration. "It's difficult to see what else they could have done in the circumstances," said one SDLP source. Peter Robinson agreed there had been no choice. "What was the decision, to allow the land to lie derelict, or have something on it to bring jobs to the people of East Belfast and Northern Ireland? It was a no-brainer. You can't sit back and say we want a shipyard here when nobody builds ships." As time went on Empey was happier with the decision and the outcome, as the shipyard survived by diversifying.

Empey also became involved in efforts to assist the Belfast operation of aerospace company Shorts during an industrial dispute among its workforce. Talks between management and trade unionists had broken down. Empey intervened and was credited with bringing both sides back to the negotiating table. He also lobbied the Treasury to assist the aerospace company when hundreds of jobs were axed following 9/11. But it was the political crisis forming around the administration that was most disruptive to his efforts to promote investment and economic stability in Northern Ireland. His overseas trade missions became more difficult as he became more embarrassed at the Assembly's failure to achieve stability amid rows over decommissioning and allegations of IRA activities in Colombia and in Castlereagh. When an aide suggested another investment trip in 2002 he balked: "It was soul-destroying. We were consistently interrupted by events and we all knew we didn't have permanency and a hold on the place and that has an impact after a while. I felt we were using up our credit."

Nonetheless, Empey agreed to address the US–Ireland economic summit in September 2002. The event had the backing of US Secretary of Commerce Don Evans, and President George W. Bush was due to make an address at the opening breakfast. Empey would be joined by Tánaiste Mary Harney. He insisted the trip was worthwhile in driving economic investment and lamented the small-minded politics back home that saw it derided as a "jolly". This was the least of his problems, however. As the conference got underway, the controversy back home became more embarrassing. There was a furore over allegations of IRA involvement with FARC guerrillas in Colombia, and a raid on police headquarters at Castlereagh, leading to Ulster Unionists fighting once again about whether to remain in the administration:

> "I knew that stage was rocking under me … And you know, I just felt such a prat being there with all this crisis at home. The top people are prepared to sit and listen to you and they are all looking at this paper to say there is a crisis and the place [Stormont] might be closed and it just makes you look so foolish. It was soul-destroying."

Empey viewed the Assembly as vital if Northern Ireland's economy were to develop and therefore was gutted when Stormont was finally suspended. However, he had always recognised that its stability was tenuous and had refused to give up his seat on Belfast City Council. In the summer of 2000 he had spoken of the necessity for ministers to relinquish their posts, but soon realised the Assembly was not stable enough and ignored demands by Seamus Mallon to quit the Council. "Wasn't I right?" he said long after the 2002 suspension.

Empey had an engagement the evening Stormont was suspended, and he returned home around 10.30pm full of regret. He briefed his direct rule successor, Ian Pearson, as best he could. "I was angry and sad. I would like to have done more. Even if I had another six months, I would have liked in particular to do more around Invest Northern Ireland."

His biggest regret was that having merged the three economic development agencies – IDB, Ledu and IRTU – into Invest Northern Ireland, he was unable to finish the job. This merger was one of his first big decisions as minister. The new one-stop shop offered a streamlined service, something that business interests had been promoting for years but no minister had ever implemented. It was a massive undertaking, involving hundreds of civil servants. Empey was conscious that it could prove controversial and not only brought his committee on board but forged good relations with the trade union leaders to manage the change smoothly. He recalled that the upheaval was "a nightmare", particularly in terms of managing personnel. "It took a lot of time and energy," he said. "We had to have new structures and we had consultants and then there was the design of the logo and instead of three heads of department, there would only be one. And then there was a huge piece of legislation at the end of it." Some criticised the INI as being too bureaucratic, but in

Empey's eyes such criticisms were premature: "We never got an opportunity to see it through."

Nonetheless, the First Minister's economic advisor, Graham Gudgin, was critical of Empey for simply "moving the furniture around". An economist and member of the Labour party, Gudgin felt Empey should have done more to shake up economic policy rather than continue with what he regarded as an outdated focus on state grants for the private sector. "Reg's main thing was to defend his budget," asserted Gudgin. In response, Empey was dismissive of Gudgin, whom he believed was a right-wing economist. Empey believed the wider business community was satisfied to see the agencies merge. Empey said he was right to defend his budget, even though he was never short of money to attract inward investment. He found it frustrating that he was always unsure of his budget when pursuing overseas investment. When Mark Durkan was looking for extra cash, Empey claimed it was to his Department that he turned: "It was the first port of call for the Department of Finance."

His time in Office was marked by a downturn for the tourism industry as a result of the foot-and-mouth crisis, as well as the problems plaguing shipbuilding, aerospace and textiles. Empey enjoyed some success in terms of inward investment, although some of this was likely to have been in the pipeline before he took Office. Despite the economic problems, investment from foreign companies into Northern Ireland peaked during Empey's time. "The middle year I was there was a record that has not been broken, so we were doing pretty well." However, an *Irish News* headline in June 2002 suggested investment was drying up following 9/11 and companies with international owners, such as Nortel, were shedding staff. The paper reported that the enterprise minister was struggling for photo opportunities under the headline, "Reg running on Empey". A few days later the minister was especially pleased to announce 300 jobs in a multi-million-pound investment.

Aside from spats with Durkan over finances, the other ministers were generally positive about his contribution at the Executive table. "Reg was respected," said one insider. "People listened to what he had to say in a way they may not necessarily have listened to Trimble." Others, including his committee chairman Pat Doherty, concluded that he was a good minister. Doherty singled out the north-south gas pipeline as an example of Empey's very real contribution as a minister.

Perhaps the most ironic plaudit came from republican MLA John Kelly, an IRA veteran. Kelly found the Unionist minister very approachable and reasonable and said Empey's style of energetic politics reminded him of Brian Faulkner, a politician whose decision to compromise was appreciated only in retrospect. The young Empey, who had joined anti-Sunningdale unionists to oppose Faulkner, would have been deeply offended by the comparison; the political veteran took it as a compliment.

Chapter 13
Millennium Minister

It was Easter 1966, the fiftieth anniversary of the 1916 Rising. While the Irish Republic celebrated its independence from Britain, its neighbour in the North watched with a mixture of envy and enmity. Belfast's twin ideologies of unionism and nationalism were observing the anniversary from their uneven perspectives when seventeen-year-old Michael McGimpsey returned to Newtownards from Dublin for an Easter break. The Trinity College student was keen to witness for himself the contrasting attitudes. McGimpsey and his teenage friends were curious about a firebrand preacher who was making headlines and whipping up unionist fears about the anniversary, warning of treachery, take-over and imminent doom. On Easter Sunday they headed for the Ulster Hall in Belfast city centre, where Ian Paisley was holding a special service. The hall was packed, so they stood outside, listening on the loudspeaker.

Soon bored with the rhetoric, they headed west to the "trouble spot". Motoring up the Falls Road in McGimpsey's Sunbeam Rapier, they observed republicans crowding the footpath en route to Milltown Cemetery to mark the anniversary. Traffic was moving very slowly, but as the boys neared the cemetery they finally saw some security to deal with the "rebels" Paisley had described: a solitary, rotund constable, wearing an ill-fitting uniform. McGimpsey watched as the red-faced policeman held up his chubby hand and stopped traffic and, with a wave of his other one, invited people forward. The teenage McGimpsey, with Paisley's warning still ringing in his years, was struck by the scene:

> "Unionists were supposed to be sold out and the State on the brink of destruction and yet you go to the seat of the so-called republican insurrection and a fat policeman is standing on his own directing traffic and pedestrians into Milltown. And that was the Belfast and the Northern Ireland I remember as a child growing up in."

Around thirty-five years and 3,500 deaths later, McGimpsey paid another visit to West Belfast to mark another historic occasion, but this time he was a Stormont minister flanked by two Presidents. In February 2000 McGimpsey, the newly appointed minister for Culture, Arts and Leisure, along with 700-odd guests, went to Clonard monastery, which sat on the peaceline between the Falls and the Shankill, where the seeds of the peace process had been nurtured by Redemptorist priests. There, alongside President Mary McAleese and Sinn Féin President Gerry Adams, he attended a Requiem concert to mark the millennium. It was one of the highlights of his time as minister and one of many events he attended to mark the year 2000.

The minister's responsibilities included arts, culture, sports, leisure, libraries and museums, the Armagh Planetarium, the Ulster Historical Foundation, inland waterways and fisheries, Ordnance Survey, the Public Records Office and the Lottery. He was not directly involved in choosing the portfolio, but he saw the logic of the choice, even if his Department did have one of the smallest budgets in the administration. McGimpsey himself acknowledged that some people were stunned by the unexpected selection of such a small department, but he pointed out that the Department enjoyed a pivotal role in a society where the cultures were at war. It also controlled two cross-border bodies, one on language and one on waterways. But there could be no denying that the Unionists' choice of Culture was driven more by fear than desire: they were determined to keep the portfolio from the Irish-speaking Bairbre de Brun. "I think as culture minister she would have been speaking Irish every night and would have driven [unionists] nuts," McGimpsey said. As a consequence, he found himself speaking Irish, learning the words phonetically so he could deliver a few phrases whenever appropriate.

Unlike many unionists, McGimpsey was comfortable with a British-Irish identity and once astonished party colleagues by declaring he would have no problem with the Wolfe Tone principle of uniting Catholic, Protestant and Dissenter under the common name of Irishman. However, his liberal attitude masked a staunch unionism. He did not count himself among the Irish political nation, but recognised that his ancestry lay in County Offaly in the Republic. His last name was derived from the Gaelic, Macdhiomsaigh. "It's a bit difficult with a name like McGimpsey saying you ain't Irish," he said. "You can be Irish and British. As far as I'm concerned, Irish is not a non-word. It is a heritage I am proud of."

McGimpsey was raised in an area of County Down where the Ulster Scots culture was predominant. He believed that some of his forebears found their way to Newtownards some time in the Middle Ages, perhaps stopping in Monaghan, which features a townland called Toneymcgimpsey. The McGimpseys were originally Roman Catholics but converted following the Cromwellian Census, when they joined the reformed Protestant Church. "It was to hell or Connaught," he grinned, "and they took the soup."

Michael McGimpsey was born into one of the oldest families in Newtownards on 1 July 1948. The town, nine miles east of Belfast, rested under the Scrabo Hills to the north and west. It was a mainly working-class market and industrial town, with a number of linen mills and factories and surrounded by a railway track. His parents had met and married as the Second World War was drawing to a close. His mother, Isabel White, had been living in Duncairn Gardens in North Belfast when Hitler's *Luftwaffe* dropped its deadly cargo of bombs over her street and the surrounding district on the night of 15 April 1941. More than 900 people were killed and the White family were evacuated to Newtownards, where Isabel met Harry McGimpsey.

Michael's paternal grandfather James was a blacksmith. It was a family trade and the McGimpsey forge at Six Road Ends was said to have made pikes for the rebellious United Irishmen in 1798. James eventually found work in the shipyard, building the ill-fated *Titanic*. Coincidentally, his maternal grandfather, Joseph White, was a joiner and he had also worked on the ship. As a result, the young Michael was raised on stories about *Titanic* and the shipyard. The family exhibited some early political leanings. Joseph White was sacked for trying to set up a trade union for apprentices and was never again able to work as a joiner. His grandson Michael recalled, "His father had done the same thing as a cutter in Ewart's textile mill on the Crumlin Road and he too was black-beaned and had to return to farm in Ballymena because he couldn't get a job in Belfast."

Michael's father, Harry, had few advantages in life, as his own father, James, died when he was eight months old. Harry had worked in the shipyard, too, as an apprentice blacksmith but he was ambitious and enrolled in evening classes at the local technical college, eventually obtaining a scholarship to Regent House, a secondary school that opened the door to Queen's University. An intelligent man, Harry studied Medicine and was in his third year when the war interrupted his studies. In a quirk of fate, the bomb attack that forced Isabel White out of her house in 1941 also prompted Harry McGimpsey to sign up for the Army Medical Corps, as did all but one of his fellow students. Many young men enlisted that day, including Jim Molyneaux, later Lord Molyneaux, who eventually became leader of the Ulster Unionist party. As a medic with the Enniskillen Fusiliers, Harry McGimpsey administered to the dying and the injured, including Canadians brought from Dieppe to Chester with horrific wounds. "I think he had enough of medicine after that," said his son. After the war, he went into teaching, moving his new bride from his mother's home at number 69 into number 71 William Street. It was in this modest two-up, two-down terrace that Michael began life. When his father's brother, who lived next door, married his mother's sister, he had neighbouring cousins to play with. "There's a very strong family resemblance and my cousin Bill, who is a policeman in New York, often gets mistaken for my brother," he said.

Michael was four by the time his brother Chris came along. His sister, Janet, the middle child, died tragically as a baby. The family moved out of William Street in the early 1950s and into a brand new bungalow built on land acquired by Harry who had, according to his son, a head for business and tremendous stamina for work. After a few successful ventures he was able to take over a corner shop, which he operated between his teaching hours. Sunday was his only day of rest, when the family worshipped at Strain Presbyterian Church, a tradition Michael kept up. Michael recalled a happy childhood, although strict by today's standards. He was a bright child and passed the Eleven-plus, enabling him to attend Regent House school. Encouraged by their father, Michael and his siblings read books in the days before television. "I remember us getting a black-and-white set, and that was a major event," said Michael McGimpsey.

The family was relatively moderate unionist. Harry McGimpsey was briefly an Ulster Unionist councillor in the old North Down Rural District Council and was a member of the Orange Order. He fell foul of the organisation, however, when he defied its ruling and attended the wedding of Lord Londonderry's daughter to an English Catholic, Lord Berry. Years later he rejoined at the behest of his son, Chris.

Michael knew few Catholics growing up in a town that was 90 per cent Protestant and was aware of unionism rather than nationalism from an early age: "You grew up not conscious of anybody's affiliation, but at the bonfire on the eleventh night you knew they [Catholics] weren't there. You realised that afterwards, but not at the time."

Politics was debated at the kitchen table, where Isabel regaled her sons with tales of the 1930s when tensions over partition were still fresh. In one incident, as a young girl Isabel was forced to duck for cover when the IRA shot at a tram in which she was travelling. The

first time the IRA impacted on Michael's life was during a family holiday in 1957, which
coincided with the IRA's border campaign. He was around nine or ten years old at the time
and his father, who had hired a caravan so the family could tour the Irish Republic, was
disturbed to hear about an IRA attack. "My father packed us up one morning and drove
us all up north. He wasn't going to stay there if [the IRA] were active."

By the time he was a teenager, in the 1960s, his father's business ventures had expanded
to property development and he and his brother were recruited to work during their summer
holidays. "I wasn't over industrious," said McGimpsey, "but coming up to holidays my father
was always quite keen to see me in the van." In truth, the teenage McGimpsey was more
interested in rock and roll and would tune into Radio Luxembourg to listen to The Beatles
and The Rolling Stones. He did join the Ulster Young Unionists in Newtownards at the age
of fifteen, but at that point it was more for social than political reasons: the young
McGimpsey enjoyed the away weekends. "We played poker and had glasses of beer," he said,
laughing at the notion that Seamus Mallon would have felt right at home.

McGimpsey was just seventeen when he met his future wife, Maureen, a Bangor girl, at
an eleventh night bonfire. "I'm still trying to put the fire out," he joked. When he met her
he was in his final year at Regent House, after which he headed for Trinity College,
Dublin, where he studied History, English and Economics. He went to Dublin with all
the trepidation one might expect from a Protestant unionist from small-town
Newtownards. But his apprehension was unfounded and he loved college life in Dublin,
finding the people very warm and friendly. He travelled home regularly and kept a close
eye on events north of the border, watching the news with increasing interest as civil rights
marchers clashed with police. "I went down to Dublin in 1966 and basically Northern
Ireland was a peaceful place and I came back to the Troubles in 1970," he said.

At first he was confounded by the events that took place, but with hindsight he came
to understand the forces that led his society into such terrible conflict. But at the time he
was not terribly sympathetic to the grievances of the civil rights movement:

> "There were complaints about housing conditions where people were living in
> a two-up, two-down with no bathroom and no running water but that is the
> house I started life in, in William Street, Newtownards. I was born under gas
> lights with no electricity and the reaction among a number of us was 'what is
> all the fuss about, it is the same for everybody'."

Later he better appreciated the fact that grievances in housing were based on unfair or
sectarian allocation of property. "Looking back now, Catholics kept their heads down and
didn't cause trouble," he said. He insisted the bias was not all one-sided, however, pointing
to the same sectarian allocation of housing in Newry, where Catholics had the advantage
over Protestants, albeit on a smaller scale relative to the number of councils controlled by
unionists. McGimpsey also acknowledged that Catholics were more likely to be
unemployed than Protestants, who had better opportunities to progress, but was not
certain that this was the result of conscious or unconscious discrimination:

> "There was clearly a need for a remedy and there was discrimination, basically

yes. Protestants did better and Catholics did poorly, but the portrayal of it all totally overlooked the plight of working-class Protestants in the Shankill and Sandy Row where conditions there were as bad as anything you could get anywhere in Northern Ireland."

By 1970, when peaceful protest had given way to unremitting violence, he had graduated from Trinity, married his girlfriend and joined the family business. Life in Northern Ireland, now over-shadowed by the Troubles, was never the same. Belfast's fearful population avoided the city after dark and it quickly became a no-go area, a ghost-town. As more people chose to stay close to home, the McGimpseys explored new business outlets, running dances and discos at their hotels: the Town and Country Inns in Newtownards and in Cloughey, near Portavogie. He recalled: "We got very large crowds because the Provos were busy bombing premises all over Belfast." But by 1978, with violence becoming more widespread, the IRA had bombed their premises in Newtownards; five years earlier, the Town and Country Inn in Cloughey had been bombed by loyalists.

Mercifully, says McGimpsey, none of his family was killed in the Troubles, unlike so many who suffered great tragedies. Nonetheless, McGimpsey recalled the stresses of raising two children, Judith and Gareth, in such violent times, always worrying for their safety. He managed to prosper, however, making his fortune in construction and property development, but was modest about his success. He still managed to shock middle-class colleagues on occasion with his salty language. When others would look at him aghast, he would shrug and smile: "What? I'm from William Street in Newtownards!"

As an affluent, middle-class businessman McGimpsey could have taken the same route as so many of his ilk and avoided politics, but he had a desire to change the society in which he lived. While he had remained active in the Ulster Unionist party throughout the 1970s, he saw little opportunity for advancement amid all the convulsions and splits that marked that decade. He had supported Terence O'Neill from 1963 until 1969, when the Stormont Prime Minister's attempts at reform finally cost him his post. For a time McGimpsey had also backed Ulster Unionist leader Brian Faulkner as he attempted to restore devolution and stability. However, he ultimately opposed Faulkner's Sunningdale Agreement, aggrieved by the north-south dimension, which was never put to a plebiscite. "Power-sharing didn't bother me. But the Council of Ireland concerned me. A lot of that was down to presentation and immaturity maybe on both sides," he said.

Despite his views, he did not actively oppose Sunningdale and was appalled by the street violence and lawlessness that some unionists and loyalists engaged in during the UWC strike. "I wasn't out blocking the streets, no way was I opposing the police. But I did support the strike." McGimpsey was always on the left of the party and often not in step with the organisation's approach. He chaired the unionist labour group and joked that he was long regarded as a "dangerous liberal power-sharer".

His liberal reputation was cemented in the 1980s when he defied popular unionist opinion and travelled to Dublin to put the unionist case to the New Ireland Forum, a conference of leading nationalist parties that was attempting to forge an agreed approach to a Northern Ireland settlement. Years later he would become the first unionist to address a Fianna Fáil gathering in Dublin. In fact, he and his brother Chris were trailblazers for unionism, according to the novelist Sam McAughtry, a socialist who hailed from loyalist Tiger's Bay in North Belfast and who himself became an Irish senator. "They were both ahead of their time in going to Dublin," McAughtry said. "They just did it because it seemed the right thing to do. They were both intrinsically brave."

The McGimpsey brothers were members of the Irish Association, which promoted cross-border reconciliation and understanding. Through their contacts they had got wind of a deal that was being put together by then Taoiseach Garret FitzGerald and his British counterpart, Margaret Thatcher. They privately warned their party leader, Lord Molyneaux, that the deal would give the Republic a say in the affairs of Northern Ireland for the first time, but their advice was rebuffed. "We were told we were talking nonsense, that Thatcher would never betray Northern Ireland," says Michael, "that she would be drummed out of the Tory party if she attempted joint authority."

The McGimpseys were as furious as other unionists when the Anglo-Irish Agreement was unveiled in 1985 and their warnings proved accurate. While unionists took to the streets in mass protest, the brothers opted to challenge the pact through the Dublin courts. They argued that the AIA was unconstitutional, but eventually lost their case in the Supreme Court. Nonetheless, the case won them greater profile and a central role in their party's negotiating team in the ill-fated 1990–1991 Brooke–Mayhew talks. Their remit was the strand two section, dealing with north-south relations. Frustrated by the stalemate and the appalling violence, Michael McGimpsey joined the Peace Train movement, which chartered and travelled on trains between Belfast and Dublin in an effort to challenge the IRA's continual sabotage of the rail link between the two cities. McGimpsey also protested with placards outside Sinn Féin's Ard Fheis, which prompted a counter-protest by Sinn Féin members, Alex Maskey among them. McGimpsey said: "We had signs saying, 'Give peace a chance' and the republicans had placards saying, 'No peace without justice.' Republicans would also take pictures of us close-up, trying to intimidate us." He also staged a protest outside UDA headquarters in Belfast: "That was the scariest thing. The locals weren't too pleased to see us."

Sam McAughtry worked closely with McGimpsey when they worked in the Peace Train Movement and encouraged him to become an elected representative. By then, unionism was evolving and power-sharing had become more acceptable. Ulster Unionist leader Lord Molyneaux had made his groundbreaking trip to Dublin to put the party's case there. Consequently, McGimpsey's politics could no longer be regarded as too liberal for the mainstream. Both McGimpsey brothers were elected to Belfast City Council in 1993, while efforts were being made to broker the loyalist and republican ceasefires.

Michael made headlines in February 1994 when he agreed to address a seminar that included leading members of the Combined Loyalist Military Command (CLMC), an umbrella body for the various loyalist paramilitary groups. At that time his party did not speak to Sinn Féin because it was linked to the IRA, a position nationalists criticised as a double standard. A DUP member had declined to attend the event, but McGimpsey saw it as an opportunity to encourage loyalists along a political path, calming and reassuring the gunmen about the implications of the Downing Street Declaration – a newly published framework from London and Dublin aimed at encouraging a settlement. He presented a rational response to the document at a time when the DUP were shouting sell-out.

When the IRA and the CLMC subsequently called their ceasefires in 1994, McGimpsey viewed the development with a mixture of relief and deep scepticism, particularly the IRA's cessation coming, as it did, just months after a devastating bomb attack on the Shankill Road. Although the bomb's intended target was loyalist paramilitaries, nine civilians (and the bomber) lost their lives in the attack. Some believed republicans wanted to weaken loyalism, but in other quarters there was speculation that the attack was motivated by a different agenda: to discourage loyalists from calling a ceasefire first. "I thought an organisation that would murder someone as a public relations exercise needed to be taken with a huge dose of salt," said McGimpsey, who also stated after the IRA cessation: "Three weeks ago, we were 'legitimate targets'. Now we are 'brothers and sisters'. It is no wonder unionists are sceptical." But unlike most unionist politicians, he did not dismiss the initiative altogether, saying: "I was cynical, yes. But having run around with a placard saying give peace a chance, I couldn't be completely deaf to their attempts to give peace a chance."

Ultimately, however, he did not participate in the talks that resulted in the Good Friday Agreement. "I thought they would fail and I thought there was an agenda of destroying unionism." By that time David Trimble was leader of the Ulster Unionist party and McGimpsey would not have been regarded as a natural supporter, given that Trimble was initially the darling of the party's right. Although the two were not friends, McGimpsey said they "were not foes either". He recalled one party conference when Trimble proposed a motion on the need to end direct rule. "I amended it, but David agreed with the amendment."

He supported the leader's decision to stay in the negotiations once Sinn Féin entered them in the autumn of 1997. From a comfortable distance he watched negotiations unfold and when the Agreement was forged, he eagerly sought out a copy: "The first thing I looked at was Strand Two (north-south relations) and I was impressed … This was Sunningdale without the Council of Ireland." He was less impressed with the release of prisoners and police reform, but on balance he decided to support the deal, having been reassured by colleagues, wrongly as it turned out, that there would be no question of prison releases before decommissioning. Abandoned by former allies, Trimble now found support in McGimpsey, who was elected in South Belfast as a pro-Agreement member of the Assembly in 1998. It was a turning-point in his political fortunes. He was soon regularly seen with the leader, having joined the party's senior team in negotiations aimed at delivering devolution and decommissioning. He defended both the Agreement and his leader, declaring in March 2000: "Everybody runs him down, but there is nothing else on offer." McGimpsey's extreme loyalty through the various leadership challenges and party upheavals was later lampooned in the BBC television series, "Folks on the Hill". "Yes, Leader," his caricatured puppet would repeat *ad nauseam* in a monotone voice.

As party leader, Trimble could be difficult and he tested the loyalty of his closest allies. One party insider said he remembered McGimpsey and Sir Reg Empey going to Downing Street with Trimble, only to be left in an outer office while the leader went in alone to talk to the Prime Minister. McGimpsey declined to comment on this. Regardless of how

Trimble conducted himself as leader, he did reward loyalty and McGimpsey received a ministerial post in the millennium Executive. His name was on a shortlist for one of the three posts, although he thought he would end up with a junior post because Trimble's deputy, John Taylor, was higher up the list. McGimpsey did not learn his fate until just before the selection and was thrilled with his portfolio, his smile brightening up his normally serious expression – an expression described as funereal by some, prompting party colleagues to refer to him affectionately as "The Undertaker".

Mindful of his reputation, the DUP mocked McGimpsey as an unlikely "Minister of Fun". Sinn Féin's Mary Nelis, deputy chair of the Culture, Arts and Leisure Committee said of him: "He has a very peculiar sort of personality. Deadpan is the word I would use. There is no great enthusiasm or excitement about him. My overall impression of Michael McGimpsey was of a man who didn't want to be disturbed." The committee chairman, SDLP's Eamonn O'Neill, was kinder and said he was pleased with what was accomplished given all the challenges faced by the minister in a new Department with a small budget: "I know what people mean about a funereal expression, but on a person-to-person basis he was easy to get on with." O'Neill said his main concerns were that McGimpsey could perhaps have done better in terms of drawing funds from Finance and too often papers requested by the committee were not forthcoming quickly enough: "I had to almost use my power to call for papers, which I as a committee chairman was entitled to do. And I had to threaten to do that in order to get meetings and get things going and that did not strike me as terribly efficient, despite all the problems of a new department. That would have been my main criticism." McGimpsey said he could not recollect this particular problem and suggested the committee may have been demanding documents that the department felt were inappropriate to release at that stage: "The fact is, you may not want to show all the papers and he [O'Neill] may have seen this as inefficiency."

Those who worked in the department with him spoke very highly of him. Said one: "This dour image that comes across, it is just not him. He was very committed and very enthusiastic." Blessed with a droll, self-deprecating sense of humour, McGimpsey would often poke fun at his serious image. In a speech given while launching a book, he joked about having met the author in a bar: "It was happy hour, so of course I had to leave." He could also be a quick-witted and sharp debater and the Ulster Unionists considered him particularly good at winding up DUP deputy leader Peter Robinson. "Take is easy, Peter," he liked to say calmly as Robinson rose to the bait; Robinson's "Folks On The Hill" puppet was as angry as McGimpsey's was loyal.

As a minister, McGimpsey had the double challenge of learning a new brief and overseeing a brand new department that was drawn from disparate areas and in a constant state of flux. Compounding his problems, when he took over he had only a skeletal staff. His permanent secretary, Aideen McGinley, had only just been recruited externally and was still working out her notice as CEO of Fermanagh District Council; therefore for the first few weeks she was working just two days a week. There was also the logistics of moving into the new headquarters and centralising the department, which became known as D-CAL. His office space took in the old debating chamber used by the Northern Ireland Forum from 1996 to 1998.

McGimpsey was acutely aware of the building's other past. For years it had housed the old Cooperative Department store where generations of Belfast children eagerly travelled every Christmas to visit Santa Claus and get a toy. The store's grotto, McGimpsey found out, was roughly on the same spot as his new office and when people lobbied him for money he would joke: "I'm in Santa's old grotto but don't think I'm Santa."

The committee chairman, who recalled a pleasant and cooperative relationship, was sympathetic to the minister's plight in terms of funding and having to start from scratch:

> "This was a new department and it was quite interesting and exciting, but they were trying to draw together a programme for department with no baseline. They had nothing on which to build or measure themselves against and the first year was largely taken up with establishing a base level on which to work; the second year was a trial year and then by the time we got into the third year, we were just beginning to get going when we were disrupted by suspension."

McGimpsey's new role became a voyage of discovery, not all of it thrilling. He soon learned that 90 per cent of the paintings in the Ulster Museum were stored away due to lack of display space. He also discovered that the annual allocation for sport was appallingly low. He calculated that spending would be just 25p per person. "The price of a packet of crisps," he declared incredulously.

McGimpsey was determined to effect change, but the first obstacle was funding. Having taken the portfolio many believed Bairbre de Brun had coveted, McGimpsey found himself competing with her Health Department for scarce resources. Funding was always a source of frustration for ministers, but McGimpsey found it especially difficult to attract Budget funds for the arts in the face of chronic hospital waiting lists. "D-CAL was always starved of money," he said. He was critical of Durkan's Finance department, claiming it lacked vision and was too quick to dismiss funding for his department. "They couldn't understand that D-CAL was the golden thread that ran through everybody's department," he said.

Arts funding had been frozen for five years when McGimpsey inherited the portfolio. In his first year in office he announced an 8% increase in his budget, which included an extra £1 million for the arts and a similar amount to enhance safety features at sports facilities, as well as funding for modest capital works at public libraries and museums. But it was hardly adequate. At the time, he said the extra money was a sign that devolution was working and evidence of a renewed focus on the arts, which had been sorely lacking. Nonetheless, he was disappointed that more funding was not made available. The failure of Belfast's bid to become European City of Culture during devolution was a blow for the sector, serving only to highlight the lack of infrastructure within the arts. McGimpsey's department did get annual rises in its budget during devolution, but some of the funding he fought for only came through post-suspension. In McGimpsey's opinion, the new administration lacked overall strategic planning: "Joined-up government didn't exist. We found ourselves being forced to bid for money against each other. We should have been building joint projects rather than competing."

Finance Minister Mark Durkan complained that McGimpsey was too quick to demand money and did not take time to argue and prepare his case adequately.

McGimpsey's department, however, was not well-resourced initially and lacked the skilled personnel to put together a case for funding. In fact, later in the administration personnel were seconded from Finance to assist in this. McGimpsey felt his Executive colleague failed to see the importance of the arts department and the positive mood it could create on the ground. In his view, Finance was blinded by figures and had no vision: "My view was, and remains, that the bureaucratic system in Finance didn't want D-CAL and was upset D-CAL was created and looked forward to it being reabsorbed into the other departments. Durkan to me was a prisoner of the bureaucrats."

McGimpsey complained that Finance would not listen to a business case and he cited as an example the Sports Institute in Northern Ireland, which was created following a deal with the University of Ulster. The institute matched gifted athletes with leading coaches to ensure their talents were fully developed. McGimpsey said he could not get the funds he needed and had to obtain the funding from Sport England. "These sports institutes were being set up all over the UK and we were short £2 million. I had done the deal, but I had to go to Sport England for support ... they recognised the importance of having the institute in Northern Ireland at a time when the UK was making its Olympic bid," he said.

One cross-departmental project that was a source of pride for him was the "Unlocking Creativity" scheme. It was initiated by his department and attempted to encourage and harness innovation across culture, education, training and the economy. Like some of his fellow ministers, McGimpsey felt there should have been more such projects. He believed his department could complement Health, for example, as sport could promote exercise, producing fitter, healthier citizens, which would reduce the burden on the health system. But this was a long-term project in an administration that was short-lived and continually interrupted.

He became frustrated with the attitude of other departments, including Finance, towards his attempts to restore and redevelop the Ulster Canal. The original canal, built in 1841, linked the Erne and the Shannon rivers with Upper Lough Neagh, but had enjoyed only shortlived success, in part because the locks were the wrong size. They had been built 4.5 metres wide, but barges required a 6-metre width. The locks were built on sandstone, which in turn presented another problem in that the Northern Ireland Heritage department was arguing for sandstone to be used in the reconstruction of the locks, which would have increased the cost tenfold in comparison to using concrete, as the Republic had done when it updated its canals. The issue led to a clash between McGimpsey and his party colleague, Environment minister Sam Foster. "I had a meeting with Sam and laid down the law. It is one of the lessons you learn ... the over-protective preciousness of Heritage. If you go to these lengths and insist on prohibitive costs you are destroying your heritage, not preserving it," he said. Neither Sam Foster nor his special advisor, Stephen Barr, who was sympathetic to McGimpsey's viewpoint, recalled any particular friction with McGimpsey. "The riot act may have been read to officials, but there was no set-to between Sam and Michael," Barr said. Foster, however, did not agree that Environmental Heritage should leave his department. At one point, according to McGimpsey, officials in Environmental Heritage suggested that it might be better to create a cottage industry to manufacture smaller barges to get around the problem of environmental heritage. "That was crazy," said McGimpsey.

McGimpsey thought the canal would bring multiple benefits, including a much-needed boost to leisure and tourism. He wanted to develop the canal to allow boating enthusiasts to travel inland from north to south, starting with the River Lagan. Aside from the size of the old canal, there were other problems, including the £100 million cost. The Department of Finance conducted a survey and concluded it was not economically viable, but McGimpsey argued that the economic benefits that would flow to rural communities had been ignored. He cited the success of the Shannon–Erne Waterway, which had transformed the old Ballinamore and Ballyconnell Canal and had boosted tourism. McGimpsey found his southern counterpart, Síle de Valera, very supportive of the project, which could have been financed jointly on a 50-50 basis with the cross-border body, Waterways Ireland. McGimpsey believed that, given more time, he might have been able to forge ahead with the joint initiative, but the final suspension prevented any further progress. Like Sir Reg Empey, he was happy to foster cross-border relations, but resisted attempts by nationalists to create further north-south bodies. There was a proposal in the summer of 2002 for an all-Ireland sports body. "I said no. We had our agreed allocations and that was enough to keep us going. I was having enough trouble funding my Northern Ireland Sports Council," he said.

Tourism remained in Sir Reg Empey's Department of Enterprise, but as time went on McGimpsey began to see this as a mistake, believing his department should have had responsibility for tourism; Empey did not agree.

As for the arts sector, the appointment of a minister with special responsibility for the issue was widely welcomed by interested parties; the Chairman of the Arts Council, Brian Walker, wrote McGimpsey an open letter through the newspapers wishing him well. Like many others, Walker was delighted to have a devolved minister to deal with. He found McGimpsey accessible, approachable and well-disposed towards the arts: "I can't complain about the hearing I received from him and we received some additional funding from his department." McGimpsey said the arts budget was doubled when he took over and that the rises which were announced after suspension should be credited to the devolved administration, including the renovation carried out on the Grand Opera House.

As well as the Irish language, he also inherited responsibility for Ulster Scots, which even among some unionists was regarded as a waste of cash in terms of providing funding for bilingual job advertisements or a translation service. McGimpsey approached it with a broader definition of culture and history, including an appreciation of the role played by Ulster Scots settlers in the United States. This, he felt, could be exploited by the tourism sector. He said he tried to remove the notion that the Irish language and Ulster Scots were mutually exclusive: "I took the view that things like languages aren't a competition, that this is a shared heritage. Culture enriches everybody and I was the minister for all cultures within Northern Ireland."

His department's website boasted various languages, including Chinese. Initially, the Irish-language sector was cool towards McGimpsey, believing a unionist minister would not deliver the support it wanted. Former Sinn Féin councillor Mártín Ó Muilleoir, who chaired Forbairt Feirste, a body that fosters employment opportunities for Irish-speakers, expressed dismay when he heard of McGimpsey's appointment. "In Belfast City Hall he voted repeatedly to ban the use of Irish, so McGimpsey has much to prove," he said. After

McGimpsey left office, Ó Muilleoir's most severe criticism was that he had been too slow to develop initiatives: "Michael McGimpsey was fair but plodding as a minister for arts and culture. In terms of the Irish language he was a safe pair of hands. His heart wanted to do more I suspect, but his head wouldn't let him for fear of boosting the Shinners."

Irish-language activist Gearoid Ó Caireallain did not find McGimpsey's approach sectarian or anti-Irish, but he did share Ó Muilleoir's view about slow progress. He felt Sinn Féin education minister Martin McGuinness had done more for the Irish language, for example, by making funding easier to obtain for Irish-medium schools, and was among those in arts and culture sectors who felt the minister was more interested in sport. Both O'Neill and Nelis credited McGimpsey for his contribution to sport and did not fault him over his attitude to the Irish language, although the Sinn Féin member suspected some in the department were engaged in a "foot-dragging" exercise on the issue. "I wouldn't say he was sectarian. He certainly pushed along the issue of sectarianism in the football grounds and he tried his best to get money to upgrade facilities," Nelis said.

Like any minister, McGimpsey had his priorities. He launched a strategy on road-racing to encourage motor sports and provided funding of £138,000 over two years to the North West 200 motorcycle event, in part to improve safety. He was particularly proud of his Department's soccer strategy. The day he took office his hometown football team, Ards, was facing the threat of closure and crisis talks were being held by its managers. The minister wanted not just to reverse this trend but to develop and encourage the sport as a means of breaking down barriers between the communities. He was acutely conscious that Northern Ireland had produced some talented players, such as Danny Blanchflower and George Best, and believed the lack of support was stifling talent. He also wanted to do something about the fact that Northern Ireland had not qualified for soccer's World Cup since 1986. He wanted to tear down the sectarianism that had debilitated the sport over many years and regenerate the infrastructure. Within months of taking office he had secured an extra £3 million, one-third from the Lottery Fund, and announced a Safe Sports Grounds Scheme. This project, which was the main beneficiary, assisted a variety of sports, including soccer. In his final year in office, McGimpsey channelled a further £1 million into this initiative and grounds such as Mourneview in Lurgan, home to Glenavon, were able improve their facilities. When he launched the scheme McGimpsey spoke of it as a new dawn for sport, but acknowledged that significantly more resources would be required, as much as £20 million, in order to bring them to the same standards as Great Britain.

The minister led the condemnation against sectarianism in sport, particularly soccer, and pledged to introduce legislation to control unruly or sectarian behaviour. Critics complained that he ultimately failed to enact a single piece of legislation to tackle sectarianism in football while he was in office. This, he said, was not due to a lack of commitment but because he wanted it tied to the overall soccer strategy, which was hampered by suspension. McGimpsey did establish the Football Task Force, to develop a soccer strategy and to identify ways of tackling long-term problems, such as low attendance, inferior grounds and under-funding.

The minister boasted that the initiative was the biggest of its kind ever undertaken in local football in Northern Ireland. By the autumn of 2001 a report with 160 recommendations had been presented to McGimpsey. These included: implementing a new league structure; expanding youth development through a new football academy; and playing Sunday football, subject to agreement of the leagues. Controversially, it also recommended the formation of a new governing body, combining the Irish Football Association and the Irish Football League. It further recommended a national stadium in a neutral venue, which could be used by all the leading sports in Northern Ireland. The task force also suggested the game's governing body develop an initiative to stamp out sectarianism in sport. The minister, after consultation, broadly endorsed the recommendations of the advisory panel, although he dodged the issue of Sunday football. While a majority of those with a direct interest in the sport supported the move, the minister noted it was an emotive issue after receiving a large number of letters from those opposed to it. Not wanting to become embroiled in a politically controversial issue, he told the Assembly: "This is a matter for sport to decide upon."

McGimpsey appeared less than enthusiastic about the notion of a national stadium, arguing that scarce resources would be better spent developing the sport and encouraging participation and spectators before indulging in prestigious but costly capital projects. McGimpsey acknowledged the need for a football ground that met international standards and suggested that the sport's governing body put forward detailed options on this. His direct rule successor, Angela Smith, was much more enthusiastic about the proposal and has been making progress towards such a project. Unfortunately for the minister, he was unable to secure the £8 million funding for the strategy before he left office. He was still in the process of reaching consensus on the strategy when suspension interrupted him. The funding was promised under direct rule, however. Praising McGimpsey's efforts, O'Neill said: "That was a nice piece of work and he was to reciprocate that with similar work on rugby and GAA."

While some in the GAA – which was better funded than soccer due to well-organised support within the nationalist community – resented the minister's initial focus on soccer, McGimpsey was credited with making efforts to build bridges and break down historic barriers. In fact, in June 2000 he welcomed the annual Gaelic games festival for young people to Northern Ireland: the first time the Feile na nGael had crossed the border in thirty years. "I think he adopted a fairly even-handed approach," said O'Neill.

McGimpsey had been planning to host a reception at Stormont in October 2002 to mark the achievements of the Armagh senior and Derry minor Gaelic football teams following their all-Ireland victories. But after the collapse of devolution the Secretary of State, Welshman Paul Murphy, welcomed the Gaelic teams instead. Suspension was heartbreaking for the unionist minister.

Two years later, in October 2004, still disappointed over the power-sharing Executive's failure, McGimpsey watched with interest and amusement as Ian Paisley took the road to Dublin for a landmark meeting with the Taoiseach Bertie Ahern in Government Buildings. In the post-suspension gloom, McGimpsey could not resist a wry smile as he reflected on his teenage memories of Easter 1966.

Chapter 14
Surreal Stormont

The New Year, and the Executive, was in its infancy when the first public crisis hit the fledgling administration – a severe dose of the 'flu. The epidemic strained a healthcare system already stretched to the limit and pitched the NHS into its most severe crisis in decades. Hospital emergency rooms were overcrowded with patients, often frail and elderly, who spent many miserable hours on trolleys before being treated in corridors. The Chairman of the Assembly's health committee, Joe Hendron, likened conditions to the Third World. The system simply could not cope with such emergencies.

Stormont Health Minister Bairbre de Brun believed the crisis would have been played down had direct rule prevailed because the British minister would not have wanted to embarrass his Labour party government. As a home-grown minister independent of New Labour, de Brun complained loudly about under-funding. By the time the Executive met for its first discussion of 2000, the Minister had been out visiting hospitals – some felt belatedly – and the issue was dominating the media.

The Executive had funds of £32 million to allocate to various departments, and ministers agreed that a substantial portion should go towards alleviating the hospital crisis. Such funding rounds would later become a frequent source of fierce infighting, normal for any government where money is concerned. One civil servant remarked, "People got on here and there, but there were some fantastic spats over money." The Finance minister Mark Durkan recalled that on this occasion the Ulster Unionists ministers did not complain about funding going to a "Sinn Féin" department. "Even the Ulster Unionists would have found it hard to argue over 'flu money," he said. As a result, de Brun left the meeting with an extra £6 million, about half of which was earmarked to help combat the epidemic.

The consensus on hospitals was not mirrored in other areas. There was much friction at the Executive table about the flying of the Union flag, a divisive issue in Northern Ireland. Just after devolution, in December 1999, de Brun was being briefed by her officials on various procedures when the issue of flags protocol came up. She interrupted sharply: "Come again?" It was explained that the building she occupied was shared by the Secretary of State and the NIO, which was anxious that the UK flag be flown. This required her consent, however, and she refused to agree. The Ulster Unionists were incensed, but as the incident occurred before the Christmas holiday period, the issue was swept into the New Year's Executive meetings.

The Ulster Unionist ministers viewed the republican position on flags as a breach of the Agreement, and rounded on the Sinn Féin ministers at the first opportunity. It was, according to a senior civil servant, one of the relatively few occasions in Room 21 where ministers were not prepared to leave their baggage at the door. The ensuing row illustrated how differently each of the communities interpreted the Agreement. Ulster Unionist Minister Sam Foster recalled a tense situation when he read from a prepared statement, with the odd interjection from David Trimble. The point was made very strongly that the Good Friday Agreement meant Northern Ireland was part of the United Kingdom for as long as a majority consented and that while there was equality *within* the system, it was not *of* the system.

The First Minister tried to argue that Martin McGuinness and Bairbre de Brun had no power to remove the flags from their departments and that the Union flag was flown at the command of the Queen. According to an insider's account, Trimble complained bitterly that Sinn Féin ministers were insulting Her Majesty. "I'm sure Martin McGuinness didn't give a f— whether or not it was insulting to the Queen," the insider said. Sir Reg Empey was also annoyed, insisting that the emblem was the legal flag of the UK and there should be no question about whether or not to fly it. Empey was not impressed with the SDLP's "divided loyalties" speech on flags. "The flying of the flag was very important. It was lights out without it. The issue had the potential to blow the whole thing apart," he said.

McGuinness and de Brun countered that the Agreement gave nationalists the right to equality and that meant both the Union flag and the Irish Tricolour together, or neither. Unionists insisted nationalists were misinterpreting the Agreement, which made clear that sovereignty remained with the British. In an admission that betrayed a certain naivety, de Brun recalled being surprised by the extent of unionist anger over her decision: "I didn't expect it to erupt the way it did. It wasn't the top of my agenda."

As it was prone to do when it could not agree on a matter, the Executive set up a sub-committee to discuss the issue. The ministers involved were Sinn Féin's Martin McGuinness, the SDLP's Bríd Rodgers and the Ulster Unionist Michael McGimpsey. The committee was chaired by a senior civil servant, Gerry Loughran. Rodgers said the committee became deadlocked pretty quickly: "We argued that you either have two flags or none and that was the view of republicans." Despite being outnumbered by nationalists, McGimpsey remained forthright on the issue. Rodgers said the sub-committee met only a few times. "Everyone knew we weren't going to come to an agreement. It was just a long-fingering exercise."

Trimble decided to quietly pursue the issue with the Secretary of State and Downing Street. But to his consternation the DUP raised the issue very publicly on the floor of the Assembly on 17 January. The party tabled a motion and de Brun became the first minister to be formally censured by the Assembly. Although McGuinness was also refusing to fly the flag over his department, de Brun was probably targeted specifically in this way because her department was also the headquarters of the NIO. De Brun was lambasted not just by the DUP member Ian Paisley Jr but, more worryingly, by her fellow pro-Agreement minister Sam Foster, who denounced her actions as "very devious, subtle and totally reprehensible".

His very public attack on a ministerial colleague was a breach of the convention that ministers do not publicly criticise one other. It was a sign of the depth of emotion that had been aroused by the dispute. Foster was frustrated by what he regarded as a constant thrust towards a united Ireland by nationalist politicians. He said: "Instead of saying, 'Let's make a base here, let's get this steadied up on a concrete base and then we can think about it some time in the future,' they just never stopped." The Ulster Unionists, already anxious that they had taken risks by entering power-sharing in advance of decommissioning, could not afford to be seen to be weak on what unionists regarded as a fundamental issue.

The SDLP wanted to avoid a row by setting up another cross-party committee that would report to the Assembly and eventually to the Secretary of State. In the interests of stabilising the new institutions, the SDLP decided to allow the flying of the Union flag in departments controlled by its ministers, although one SDLP source said that would not have gone on indefinitely and was only done to give time and space for the institutions to bed down: "The SDLP would eventually have taken the flags down. We didn't like having them up." Mark Durkan said his party wanted consensus, not confrontation, adding that Sinn Féin ministers were more affected than SDLP ministers: "We didn't have any flagpoles we had discretion over, well, very few anyway. In my own private office the flagpole was Martin's and once he took his stance, Rathgael House became a theme park for flags [as loyalist protestors moved in]." De Brun felt the SDLP should have supported her party more forcefully on the issue.

The spat over flags was swiftly followed by another, this time between David Trimble, Seamus Mallon and the Agriculture minister, Bríd Rodgers. Rodgers was incensed when she learned that Trimble, without directly consulting her in advance, had raised with the Prime Minister the possibility of getting support for a £100 million relief scheme for farmers. Rodgers regarded this as a breach of protocol and an attempt by the First Minister to interfere in her department and undermine her authority. She also considered Trimble's proposals as "off the wall" and "totally against European regulations". She recalled: "The first I heard of it … I hit the bloody roof." Once again, the DUP got wind of the tiff. Ian Paisley Jr questioned Trimble in the Assembly about the incident, insisting that the First Minister owed Rodgers an apology and accusing him of running a "half-baked administration". Trimble accused Paisley Jr of playing politics and informed the DUP member that he had asked his party colleague, George Savage, deputy chairman of the Agricultural Committee, to brief the Minister on his proposals. Savage found himself drawn into a rather nasty row. In fact, when Rodgers met Savage as part of Trimble's efforts to placate the SDLP, she expressed her disapproval, as Pat Toal, a senior civil servant in her department, sat and listened. Rodgers long remembered that Toal turned to her afterwards and said, "I hope I never get on the wrong side of you."

The First Minister had his own confrontation with Rodgers in Room 21. Although he did not apologise, he did back down when Rodgers rounded on him, supported by Sinn Féin ministers and Seamus Mallon. Trimble insisted he was trying to be helpful and suggested that the ministers were overacting, but Rodgers was not having it. "We tore strips off him," she said. "David Trimble ended up with a lot of egg on his face over that one. He was embarrassed and I think he knew he had goofed. He wanted to trump me, but Trimble learned a lesson there."

Mallon – who had been on the phone to Downing Street complaining the minute he heard about Trimble's intervention – was equally forceful at the Executive table, insisting the First Minister had no business dabbling in farming schemes without the approval of the Agriculture minister. Trimble's frequent trips to Downing Street over issues such as decommissioning were already irritating the SDLP. Mallon knew he could do little about these solo runs, but was not going to tolerate Trimble going to the Prime Minister about Assembly matters. Mallon could not recall exactly what he told the First Minister, but "I don't think it was too polite". One SDLP source remembered it a little more clearly: "Mallon ambushed David Trimble very effectively by basically asking David Trimble to elaborate and report on his meeting with the Prime Minister. The story is that David Trimble found it difficult to report." Empey, who witnessed the scene, remembered the Deputy First Minister making his point very forcefully. "Seamus was at his most condescending. He got the boot in and got it in very well and very subtly."

The First and Deputy First Minister had to face the media at a post-Executive news conference. Trimble arrived looking rather flushed; Mallon sat beside him in frost-faced silence, his thin lips pressed into an angry seam. The reporters raised the question of the farming row. While the First Minister did not take the opportunity to apologise, he pledged to spare the Minister of Agriculture from any future embarrassment, suggesting arrangements for consultation would work better in future. Trimble then spoke of an "initiative", but Mallon forcefully repeated that there was no initiative from the Executive, or from the Department.

According to an SDLP source, the nationalist view was that Trimble had overstepped the mark and had been forced to back down, establishing a very important principle: "Trimble always thought of the First and Deputy First Ministers as being like the prime minister. But they're not, because they can't hire and fire their other ministers so they can't control their departments. Trimble thought he could but learned a lesson that he couldn't." Rodgers agreed that Trimble needed to change his attitude about the other ministers' roles: "He didn't realise or understand that you couldn't do that, maybe Blair can do that with his ministers, but we were different. He thought he could undermine me."

Such tensions were to be expected in the early days of an administration of political opposites, who were essentially engaged in a very unusual experiment. Even in an administration where all ministers are of the same party, personality and policy clashes are commonplace. Trimble appeared to have absorbed the lesson because he told reporters at the news conference: "We have to understand this is a different animal to normal Westminster, single-party government." A ministerial code had been drawn up to avoid such difficulties and was ratified by the Executive soon after.

Although the administration faced an uncertain future, plans continued to be made and new staff were appointed to fill new posts. Stormont had an almost surreal atmosphere, as if creating a working Parliament would ensure decommissioning. Empey put his anger aside over the IRA's failure thus far to decommission, and went to Newry to launch the new cross-border trade body with the SDLP's Sean Farren and Tánaiste Mary Harney. "I was out to prove a point – plus I believed in what we were doing," said Empey.

While Empey proved that unionists were prepared to keep their side of the bargain on power-sharing, the First Minister was preparing to prove a point of his own over guns and government.

Chapter 15
The First Suspension

David Trimble was travelling through Brussels airport with his delegation, feeling the pressures of office, when he bumped into one of the people he believed was responsible for his political woes: Chris Patten. The Conservative politician, now an EU commissioner, had chaired the Patten Commission on the future of policing, an issue that was at least as controversial as IRA decommissioning. Patten's Commission, set up under the terms of the Good Friday Agreement, had reported in September 1999, just weeks before power-sharing began, and had made a number of controversial recommendations on the future of the Royal Ulster Constabulary. The RUC had policed Northern Ireland since the foundation of the State, but had never won nationalist approval. It was overwhelmingly Protestant in its make-up and unionist in its ethos, leading unionists to regard it as "our force". More than 300 RUC officers had been killed in the Troubles, mostly at the hands of the Provisional IRA. Sinn Féin had wanted the force disbanded; unionists had fought to save it. Patten, by way of compromise, did not advocate disbandment, but radical change: renaming the police and replacing the original RUC badge and oath with new ones.

Unionists felt betrayed by Patten's recommendations. Trimble had called Patten's report shoddy and claimed, long after power-sharing had failed, that policing was the one issue that killed support for his party and the Agreement. So it was not surprising that Trimble, already under pressure over decommissioning and the burden of office, was less than pleased to see Patten in the Executive lounge.

Heading to board his plane, Trimble was about to rush through set of a tinted-glass sliding doors when they opened automatically to reveal Patten, who had just disembarked his aircraft. For an instant both men froze. They were quite literally stunned to see each other and at that moment neither seemed sure what to do. Standing nose-to-nose with the man he felt had let him down badly on the policing issue, Trimble, or so the story goes, saw red and accused Patten of destroying the RUC. Not deigning to respond, Patten had to step around the Ulster Unionist leader and his delegation to pass through the doorway. Trimble claimed this was an exaggerated account of the encounter. He did not recall any exchanges passing between him and the former Police Commissioner, claiming Patten knew by his demeanour not to speak to him.

The hugely sensitive and controversial issue of policing fuelled the tensions in the new administration in January 2000, making life more difficult for the pro-Agreement forces.

In the House of Commons on 19 July, Peter Mandelson, the Secretary of State who was responsible for the policing issue, had made a statement endorsing the Patten recommendations, handing Ian Paisley's DUP yet another chance to assault the beleaguered Ulster Unionist leader. Continuing its trench warfare in the Assembly, the DUP immediately tabled a motion condemning the Patten Report. Nigel Dodds, DUP minister for Social Development, told the Assembly that of all the issues in the Agreement, policing really touched a "raw nerve". He was right. The DUP motion divided the Assembly along sectarian lines: the motion was passed by 50 votes to 42, with the Ulster Unionists and DUP once more voting together.

While Trimble worked steadily to reverse the government's decision to implement Patten, his partner in government, Seamus Mallon, was striving to achieve the opposite. Mallon calculated that power-sharing could not last if policing failed to win nationalist approval. Obviously this placed a lot of strain on the relationship between the two men. In one memorable scene, around the time the Patten recommendations were unveiled, the First and Deputy First Ministers were invited to breakfast with Mandelson at Hillsborough Castle. Inside the eighteenth-century County Down castle, built in the style of an English manor, the dining-room table was laid with traditional silver and bone china, and a sausage, bacon and egg breakfast was served. The ministers were not half a sausage into the breakfast when Trimble accused Mandelson of destroying the RUC. Mallon recalled Mandelson responded angrily: "I thought the knives were going to fly, quite literally. They were squealing at each other, and I mean squealing." Mallon sat and watched, savouring the spat while he enjoyed his breakfast. When he had heard enough sniping and felt it was beginning to tail-off, he rather mischievously scolded the pair for their manners. "I didn't get up at this time of the morning to listen to you two," he complained. "Then they both rounded on me, which was exactly what I wanted. It gave me an opportunity to have a right go at Mandelson."

Policing was only one half of a twin scourge that was undermining the new power-sharing Executive. It was the question of decommissioning that was really clouding the peace process at that point. Indeed, the issue of IRA arms threatened to extinguish the administration completely. With each passing day debate about bread-and-butter issues was increasingly drowned out by the heated rows over the bomb and the bullet. The Ulster Unionists were demanding that IRA weapons be put beyond use – a new euphemism for decommissioning – by 31 January 2000 if the new power-sharing experiment were to survive.

Trimble had risked his leadership by entering a coalition with armed republicans, but there was little to comfort him in the IRA's New Year message, which accused him of breaching the Mitchell review by promising to quit the Executive and recall his party's ruling council in February 2000 to review progress on the arms issue. Republicans had always insisted decommissioning must be voluntary and their opinion had not changed. From their viewpoint, Trimble's decision to entrust post-dated letters of resignation for the party's ministers to the late Ulster Unionist president Sir Josias Cunningham was nothing short of an ultimatum. The newly knighted Sir Josias had been instructed to present the letters to the Speaker of the Assembly, Lord Alderdice, if there were no progress on arms.

Time was short. The Ulster Unionist ruling council was due to be recalled on 12 February and so far the IRA had only committed to further talks with the IICD, nothing more. As the deadline approached and the IRA showed no sign of decommissioning, Sir Josias warned that his party would accept no more drift on the crucial arms issue.

Despite ominous signs that the administration was on an unavoidable collision course, the IRA's ongoing engagement with the IICD fuelled faint hopes of a resolution. Some commentators even speculated that the IRA would allow some of its weapons to be placed under the IICD's control. Another claim was that the IRA might allow General de Chastelain to witness a controlled explosion. At the time there was certainly discussion among grassroots IRA members about the possible methods of decommissioning, but a republican source insisted this did not mean it was imminent. One Belfast IRA man spoke privately of the organisation keeping its guns but destroying the firing mechanisms, thereby rendering the weapons useless. However, any speculation that the IRA was about to decommission was met by stringent official denials from republican sources, who insisted decommissioning would not come in any form demanded by unionists.

As the verbal warfare intensified, the business of government struggled forward. In a tangible sign of these parallel tracks, Sinn Féin's Gerry Adams and Martin McGuinness left for Washington to discuss the peace process with President Bill Clinton, while Bairbre de Brun cancelled her plans to accompany them so she could focus on her duties as Health minister. In a remark that may offer insight into republican thinking at the time, McGuinness suggested it was "inconceivable" that the power-sharing Executive could collapse over disarmament. McGuinness likened the new administration to a boat that was just moving away from its berthing position: "We are still in the harbour but we are still moving forward. And I think anyone who jumps off at this stage would drown."

Were he and others in the Sinn Féin leadership gambling on the unionists not having the guts to walk away from power-sharing for fear of suffering the blame, or having joint authority from London and Dublin imposed as a consequence? Some Ulster Unionists certainly thought so. Indeed, one senior Ulster Unionist said he became increasingly suspicious that republicans were trying to bluff their way through the arms crisis in the hope that unionists would not have the nerve to quit the Executive: "They seemed to think we were bluffing, that we were selling them a line. They assumed unionists were so daft to see Stormont back they thought we would pay any price."

This was not the case. Ulster Unionists were coming under increasing pressure from anti-Agreement unionists, who saw decommissioning as an opportunity to regain the ground they had lost when they failed to defeat the Good Friday Agreement. The anti-Agreement DUP was determined to unseat the Ulster Unionists as the main voice of unionism and to this end used the Assembly as the new battleground. They steadily cranked up the pressure on the Ulster Unionist leadership by calling for an immediate withdrawal from the Executive in the face of IRA recalcitrance. When it was put to the DUP by other unionists and by the media that it could quit the Executive any time it wished, the party refused to budge, claiming it would not abandon its rightful posts but would "happily" follow the Ulster Unionists out of Office.

At the first meeting of the Assembly that year, on 17 January 2000, the DUP succeeded in tabling a motion calling for immediate decommissioning. Leading the debate, Paisley attacked the IRA and Sinn Féin but was just as scathing about the Ulster Unionist leader, claiming he had "twisted, turned and digressed" over the arms issue. He quoted an article that had appeared in the *Belfast Telegraph* in July 1998, in which Trimble had promised that his party would not serve alongside those who had not proved their commitment to peaceful means through decommissioning. Questioning Trimble's integrity, Paisley added:

"Lines have been drawn in the sand by Mr Trimble, but he always drew the line where the tide could reach it."

Trimble was determined to prove his critics wrong – that he could not be bought off with a ministerial car, a hefty pay packet and a grand title. He did not speak during the debate. Instead his party chose its most liberal Assembly member, Duncan Shipley-Dalton, to declare that even he could not support power-sharing without decommissioning. This time, the line had been clearly drawn.

The SDLP tabled an amendment to the DUP motion, urging that the issue be left to the IICD, a position echoed by the Sinn Féin members. But with support from the Ulster Unionists, the DUP motion was carried by 51 votes to 32. The fact that the Assembly had divided once again along traditional lines – with the Ulster Unionists siding with the DUP – was not a good omen for the administration: it was clear the arms issue was polarising the pro-Agreement parties, exposing a faultline within the Executive that everyone had tried so hard to bury.

It was two days after this debate, and with the arms crisis deepening, that further pressure was brought to bear on the Ulster Unionist leader, and on the Executive, by Mandelson's announcement that the government intended to transform policing, a move that would have seen the name of the RUC consigned to history. Even so, it was to be decommissioning, not policing, that would seal the fate of the Executive. The normally mild-mannered Empey gave vent to his growing frustration with the IRA's failure to decommission: "The time has come for Martin McGuinness, instead of giving platitudes, to deliver. That's the way to keep the Executive." Empey was genuinely angry and said McGuinness had "a cheek" when he urged the Ulster Unionist leader to hold his nerve: "There is not a single thing that we are obligated to do under the Good Friday Agreement that we have not done."

The Ulster Unionist leader was also angry and frustrated by the lack of progress on decommissioning. He was further irritated by reports that Sinn Féin MPs, who had refused to swear an oath of allegiance to the Queen, were about to be granted facilities in the House of Commons. He wrote a letter to the government, objecting and describing Gerry Adams and Martin McGuinness as "unreconstructed terrorists". However, this only inflamed Trimble's internal critics further and they demanded to know why he was giving these "terrorists" an opportunity to share power.

In this tense, brittle atmosphere fears grew that decommissioning would never be realised. One SDLP source said that doubt over the arms issue really took hold when Christmas 1999 came and went without any progress: "I think we felt that if the Provos were going to do something, they were going to do it at Christmas. And it didn't happen and from the moment we came back in January we knew we were going down."

By the end of January 2000 there was speculation that the institutions were about to be suspended. It is believed that it was the promise of suspension, should republicans fail to decommission, that prompted the Ulster Unionists to accept the Mitchell compromise. Around this time David Trimble told the BBC's "Breakfast with Frost" programme that any suspension would not be permanent: "I think actually it will be a temporary one."

Although it seemed doomed, the power-sharing system continued as normal all the while, the ministers clinging to a faint hope that somehow it would all work out. The First and Deputy First Ministers even launched an information leaflet explaining the new structures, which was distributed to every household in Northern Ireland. Mallon, ever the poker player, publicly reminded everyone that it was not over until the last card was played. Martin McGuinness, who had made his debut at the despatch box that month, reiterated the warning that the IRA would not decommission if the Executive were not in operation. While the SDLP was firmly against suspending the institutions, the party began to show some impatience with the republican refusal to decommission any weapons. Mallon was soon embroiled in a public battle with Sinn Féin on the issue. He accused republicans of hedging their bets: organising street protests and exercising Executive authority while denying the imperative to decommission. He said it was time for republicans to choose which path they were taking, and to take it.

The 31 January deadline came and went with no sign of decommissioning, despite wild and bogus media reports that the IRA had sealed some of its arms dumps in the Republic. A report from General de Chastelain was due that day, but it was delayed because the IRA's representative to the IICD, Brian Keenan, wanted to meet him in secret that evening. When it was released to the governments, the de Chastlelain report made grim reading and its publication was delayed. Instead, it was hoped that progress could still be made in what little time was left.

The UUC was not due to meet until 12 February and, like all such negotiations over guns and government, this one went down to the wire. For the next eleven days the crisis worsened, filled with intense shuttle diplomacy involving British, Irish and American officials, Prime Ministers and Presidents, the leadership of the Ulster Unionists, the SDLP, Sinn Féin and senior figures in the IRA.

Those outside the republican movement could only guess as to its mood. There was speculation of a split over decommissioning among the more hardline units of Tyrone, Armagh and north Louth. Was this republican manipulation, or reality? What is more certain is that Sinn Féin leader Gerry Adams was having to manage the peace process cautiously, taking risks but trying to avoid any damaging splits. Adams, it was said, had a morbid fear of splits given the history of the republican movement and the murder of former IRA leader Michael Collins when he sought to compromise the republican ideal. Republican sources insisted decommissioning was still achieveable: it was just a matter of timing. In the absence of significant progress, the British government moved to introduce emergency suspension legislation. Appeals from John Hume and senior Catholic and Protestant clergy for the IRA to decommission for the sake of patriotism, peace, or both were rebuffed.

While the government prepared a "soft landing" in the form of suspension, Gerry Adams emerged from hours of crisis talks in Downing Street looking exhausted. He issued a warning of his own, telling the waiting media that he was fed up being the messenger "who continually gets shot". He wearily told reporters: "No process can limp from crisis to crisis the way this one has. I don't intend to spend the rest of my life trying to shore up a process that is going to be in perpetual crisis." Whether this was bluff or genuine frustration, Adams stuck with the process. But his claims that Sinn Féin had done its best failed to move Ulster Unionists, who insisted the price for power-sharing was a definitive start to decommissioning.

The Secretary of State had told the Commons that suspension was necessary to avoid the whole process collapsing into a black hole. "It's a choice between pause, or bust," was how Mandelson put it. The suspension legislation was passed in the Commons by a vote of 352 to 11. According to a former colleague in the administration, Trimble had always held the view that power-sharing would not be a smooth road: "I heard him say several times that this thing would hit the buffers not once, but twice or three times before it settled." In the last hours of the administration, diplomacy continued. President Bill Clinton spoke to Prime Minister Tony Blair and the Deputy First Minister's office was frantic. According to one SDLP source, "There were phone calls all the time. Clinton was on the phone, Mandela was on the phone, several times." At Stormont, ministers scrambled to make decisions before the final curtain fell. Martin McGuinness announced the largest ever funding package from his department, some £72 million in investment for schools. Sean Farren, the Minister of Higher Education, raced to announce a review of student tuition fees and loans. Even the anti-Agreement DUP minister Peter Robinson admitted: "I took as many decisions as I could in the hope that the direct rule minister wouldn't want to un-take them."

When Friday, 11 February dawned, there was just one day to go until the UUC was due to be recalled. Although there was no arms decommissioning to report, hope of a breakthrough remained alive, albeit with a weak pulse amid fervent speculation that a suspension was imminent. Republicans and Irish government officials, meeting through the night in Belfast, thought they had finally achieved a breakthrough. Dublin officials Paddy Teahon, Tim Dalton and Dermot Gallagher engaged in intense negotiations, along with Adams, McGuinness and Gerry Kelly, a North Belfast MLA who had bombed the Old Bailey in 1972 and had a long history of IRA involvement. At around 4.30am the Irish officials were handed a document outlining a new IRA position on decommissioning and within hours had boarded a plane to brief the Taoiseach in Dublin.

By mid-morning Taoiseach Bertie Ahern had telephoned the Prime Minister and the document was faxed through to Tony Blair, confidentially. In the document the IRA offered to put weapons beyond use, but only in the context of the full implementation of the Good Friday Agreement and after the causes of the conflict had been addressed. It suggested that any move on weapons would only be dealt with following political change. It also pointed out that the May 2000 date outlined in the Good Friday Agreement for the decommissioning of weapons was supposed to come after two years of power-sharing. As it happened, power-sharing had only been operating for weeks. The statement was an important move in republican terms because it committed the IRA to actual decommissioning. There was renewed confidence in Dublin and in nationalist and republican circles that this would be enough to stall suspension. Bairbre de Brun, for one, recalled being fairly sure that suspension would be avoided. "I felt it might work," she said. "I remember that afternoon telling people not only would it work but it was working and that a way had to be found through."

But the IRA offer fell far short of Trimble's and unionists' requirements. The Secretary of State believed the IRA was too vague on when it would actually decommission and the NIO told Sinn Féin it was up to republicans to persuade unionists if a suspension were to be avoided. At 2.30pm that afternoon Martin McGuinness visited David Trimble in his

Stormont office. Trimble was expecting him. He had "heard a whisper" of a new initiative and was informed that McGuinness would come to talk to him about an offer. Their discussion lasted around fifteen minutes, but it was the dialogue of the deaf. "Surreal" was how Trimble described it. Trimble remembers the Sinn Féin chief negotiator coming in with a lot of demands.

> "He was telling me what I should do … that the threat of suspension would have to be lifted and the ministerial resignations would have to be withdrawn, and he told me there could be no question of UUC meetings and I found this amusing."

Trimble sat impassive as McGuinness spoke. He deliberately did not ask questions about any new initiative, knowing that to do anything more than listen might encourage republicans to believe he was softening. "I wasn't going to give the impression, 'I am desperate for a way out of this'," Trimble said. McGuinness quickly assessed that Trimble was not going to be moved. The Ulster Unionist leader said the republican's instincts were right.

> "I had to prove a point. The first time I met Adams I said to him, 'this business of decommissioning…is deeply important.' I didn't think he took the issue seriously enough. And I didn't think he would take it seriously enough until things had gone off the edge."

"Smoke and mirrors," was how he viewed Sinn Féin's endeavours on the arms issue that day. Trimble felt things had gone too far to reverse suspension – he had reached a point of no return: "We would have had to have something really, really dramatic." Already Ulster Unionist party president, Sir Josias Cunningham, was threatening to invoke the letters of resignation if the Secretary of State did not act. Republicans found this ironic as Cunningham's family had financed the import of weapons for the UVF in 1912 during the Home Rule crisis.

At 5.03pm the Secretary of State ignored a second report tabled by General de Chastelain, based on the IRA's latest position, and signed the suspension order at Castle Buildings. Martin McGuinness, speaking in the Great Hall at Parliament Buildings, was visibly upset, close to tears and choked with emotion as he vented his anger at the unionists and the British government. He said it had been "gut-wrenching" for him to come to Stormont and yet he had done it and had tried very hard to make the institutions work.

Trimble acted as if the latest crisis was merely a blip and spoke of a return to power-sharing on the basis of equality; his words seemed premature. Meanwhile the Deputy First Minister spent the evening in his office with his staff, drinking whiskey and lamenting the mess the political process was now in. He took time out to speak by telephone to SDLP junior minister Denis Haughey, who was in the Basque country promoting the peace process. He gave Haughey the bad news: he was no longer a junior minister.

The other ministers also resigned themselves to their fate. Bríd Rodgers and Michael

McGimpsey attended a dinner at Stormont in place of the First and Deputy First Ministers, jointly launching a fundraising drive for the Special Olympics. Rodgers told her audience that she felt like Cinderella, about to be turned into a pumpkin at the stroke of midnight when the suspension order took effect. "By six o'clock in the evening we knew it was gone," she said.

Power-sharing was laid to rest after just seventy-two days. Stormont was now at risk of becoming an enduring symbol of political failure. But David Trimble felt it had achieved something: "Not a lot happened within the administration within those ten weeks, but the main success was that it happened." The Ulster Unionist deputy leader, John Taylor, did not appear to share his leader's view of an imminent resurrection. A former minister in the old Stormont before direct rule in 1972, he warned that suspension would last twenty years.

Chapter 16
Muinteoir, Minister

Bairbre de Brun was chatting at the west door in Parliament Buildings when she spotted Ulster Unionist Dermot Nesbitt. A polite and affable man, he was in particularly good form as he had just been appointed junior minister. De Brun interrupted her conversation with the chairman of her committee, the SDLP's Joe Hendron, to go over and congratulate Nesbitt. She offered him her hand, but it was refused. Nesbitt explained that he could not shake hands with a republican minister while the IRA remained armed. De Brun was deeply offended, even more so when Nesbitt then shook hands with Hendron. Turning away, more in sorrow than in anger, she fled. As Nesbitt realised the impact of his behaviour, he followed de Brun, catching her near the lift. "She was very emotional," Nesbitt recalled, "and in a tearful manner she said something like, 'When are you going to treat us like equals?'" She told the Ulster Unionist that his attitude could not continue: "We have to find some way of working together."

De Brun's vulnerability surprised the unionist. She had always appeared so composed. Nesbitt, along with many unionist politicians, regularly refused to shake hands with Martin McGuinness, who seemed to accept the no-handshake policy without a fuss. At a Labour party conference when the republican had extended a hand in front of the cameras, Nesbitt had good-humouredly chided him, "Catch yourself on, Martin." De Brun's reaction showed Nesbitt another side to the situation, and gave him pause for thought.

De Brun's encounter with Nesbitt was also a lesson for the republican minister, who now realised the new era heralded by the Good Friday Agreement was still some way off. This was underscored a month later when she again met Nesbitt, this time at a function in the US consulate in Belfast. He came over and shook hands with a senior official from Washington, but did not extend the same courtesy to her. This time she met his rebuff with steely resolve. The incident made her more determined to win acceptance and not to be subjugated.

At every opportunity the Sinn Féin minister appeared to be challenging unionists, defending her rights and entitlements as well as those of her party and her constituents. As a consequence, she came to be viewed as the more inflexible and dogmatic of the two Sinn Féin ministers. Whether she wore her republican badge as a defensive shield, or as a form of armoury in the battle-a-day politics of the Assembly is a matter of conjecture. Perhaps she was simply passionate about her cause. Whatever her motivation, according to insiders she often confronted unionists and others over decisions and slights, both real and imagined, at the Executive table and in her role as minister. Accordingly, unionist ministers found her strident. "She argued about what I found were trivial issues," said Michael McGimpsey, "and it seemed to me the Executive was the place to discuss the important stuff. Items would jump on the agenda about something somebody said or didn't say in a press release." Empey concurred: "Oh, it was like a meeting of the *politburo*. Bairbre was difficult, terribly formal and it was almost like the old Soviet system … very, very rigid procedurally."

Another source recalled: "Bairbre used to hold the Executive up by referring to minutes and documents and so on, wringing little issues to death over wording. 'I didn't use this word, I used that word'." Pedantic was how another insider described her: "Bairbre was inflexible whereas McGuinness rolled with the punches. She had to have every 'i' dotted and every 't' crossed. That was unfortunate, but she wasn't a bad minister."

In the course of being interviewed for this book, de Brun stated that she did not wish to go into the detail regarding discussions conducted in Room 21, regarding it as a breach of the ministerial code. She seemed taken aback that other former ministers were openly discussing such issues with the author. When it was put to her that a number of sources had complained she was obsessive about the minutes, often querying what was recorded, she insisted that minutes were meant to be correct. "They are written with an eye to accuracy," she asserted.

While de Brun's approach annoyed some, she was blessed with a sharp intellect and was reputed to have a photographic memory. When asked about this ability, she was characteristically self-deprecating: "Oh that was many, many years ago." Durkan, too, had a phenomenal memory and would challenge her when he felt she was being inconsistent. "The two people who clashed more than most were Bairbre and Mark," said one insider. "Mark has a memory way back and could remember what Bairbre said two years ago and he would remind her of it."

Her sharp mind did win her respect, however, even among detractors. One official concluded that "She was a lot smarter than McGuinness in the way she could absorb a paper or great detail." Consequently, she was sometimes compared to David Trimble, whose ability to absorb facts in a brief was praised by civil servants. On the other hand, attention to detail could be a drawback for ministers who were expected to look at the broad sweep, too. "That could," said one official, "be a little bit irritating at times when she was down to the fine detail."

Her eye for the finer points of a document meant she was sometimes more alert than those around her. It was de Brun who spotted a questionable line in the draft Northern Ireland legislation requiring the First and Deputy First Ministers to nominate ministers to attend NSMC. In a meeting with British direct rule ministers she had complained that this procedure was open to abuse by the First Minister. When Trimble later imposed his ban on Sinn Féin and a court case ensued, which found that the First Minister was acting unlawfully in applying his discretion, de Brun felt vindicated and annoyed that the Secretary of State had not listened to her.

On occasion de Brun would clash with Ulster Unionist minister Sam Foster, who was particularly outspoken on constitutional issues and had clashed with Sinn Féin ministers over the flying of the Union flag. Foster found her harsh. "She was absolutely dogmatic with a capital D," he said. "McGuinness was more placid. I would leave the Executive with her voice ringing in my ears for hours." De Brun insisted she was defending her constituents against opposition from traditional, unyielding unionism, and brushed the criticisms aside saying: "I found a couple of the unionist ministers weren't terribly bothered about whether they were supposed to criticise me or not."

Graham Gudgin, who attended Executive meetings as an observer, sympathised with de Brun's plight, believing it was more difficult at the table for de Brun, being both a woman and a republican. He recalled she was sweet one moment and tough the next: "Martin was relaxed and appeared to want to compromise, but Bairbre was feisty." De Brun's response was that she and McGuinness had a different style and suggested that some people may have found it more difficult to deal with a challenge from a woman.

One SDLP member felt that Trimble tended to pick on de Brun, with whom he had little rapport. "Her mannerisms provoked combat a little bit," he said. "When Trimble would speak, or other people would speak, she would pull faces. I don't think she would even know she was doing it. She'd have scowls on her face." Claiming de Brun had rows when she did not need to, he went on: "McGuinness was much more effective. He gave when he needed to give and worked around problems, whereas Bairbre put her head down and dug in."

On one occasion de Brun clashed with Trimble over a joint ministerial council meeting, a sectoral meeting held under the BIC. It was thought Trimble was pressing for the meeting to be held in Belfast, but de Brun felt it inappropriate or suspected another agenda was at work. She refused to hand over her department's health papers to the First Minister. Some in the administration felt Trimble was entitled to the papers despite de Brun's suspicions about his motives. Empey felt it was a trivial matter, but conceded de Brun was procedurally right as the meeting was being called at short notice. "She had not adequate time to look at the papers," said Empey. While Trimble could not recall the detail of the incident, de Brun declined to comment. Another time, a BIC meeting in Dublin was held up for at least an hour over her objections to a review paper she had not agreed. She was unhappy that the Executive as a whole had not been consulted.

One might have expected McGuinness, the reputed hard man, to be the more difficult of the two for unionists, but it was in fact de Brun, not McGuinness, who was most likely to clash with Trimble and his ministers in Room 21. While McGuinness tried to avoid conflict, if possible, de Brun was often in the thick of it. When the Executive argued about flags or the Sinn Féin north-south council ban, it was de Brun who came across as the more aggressive of the two Sinn Féin ministers. One SDLP source felt she paid more attention to equality issues than McGuinness did and was more effective in that regard. So marked was McGuinness's pragmatism compared to de Brun's dogmatism, that one unionist insider formed an erroneous suspicion that she was there to keep an eye on the education minister, or that there was a deliberate "good cop, bad cop" routine. "She was the most political of all the ministers," said one insider. "Martin was more flexible," another added, "but he had no choice but to back her."

The general perception in the administration that de Brun was somehow more hardline or inflexible than McGuinness was ironic given that she was not burdened with the same IRA baggage. "Maybe she felt she had more to prove than McGuinness," said an SDLP insider. "McGuinness and Adams were around for thirty years. She was a 1980s production."

De Brun was arrested only once in her life, during a May Day trade union rally at

Belfast City Hall in 1981. She was one of a number of protestors who displayed a banner supporting the H-block campaign. She was accused of disturbing the peace and held overnight. There were no charges in the end. In terms of the republican movement, she was regarded as strictly Sinn Féin. Certainly she did not command the same authority as McGuinness and was perceived as being more likely to refer decisions back to the party. De Brun was not a typical member of the movement, which was dominated by working-class northerners. McGuinness was a street-wise republican raised in relative poverty in an urban ghetto with little formal schooling. A rare rebel, de Brun was a well-educated, middle-class woman from the Republic and something of an outsider in that regard. While he was generally relaxed and personable with an easy manner that could be quite disarming, de Brun was very shy and awkward in social situations. Of the two Sinn Féin ministers, de Brun was regarded as having the more serious nature. McGuinness was more inclined to enjoy a joke and a bit of banter.

Empey said he was not fooled into thinking McGuinness was any less hardline than de Brun. "They were both pursuing the republican agenda," he said. "Like any individuals, they just had a different way of doing things. Just because someone is easy to get along with doesn't mean they are any less dangerous than somebody who is awkward."

De Brun was not only shy, but often masked it with an authoritarian air. She was generally called "Minister", unlike McGuinness. As a former schoolteacher she was perhaps accustomed to a certain hierarchy. A former pupil recalled a formidable but effective teacher: "She was the scariest of them all – but my French went down after she left." One senior health board official said his first impression was of a rather rigid personality: "Initially I found her quite a stand-offish person, somebody who would have reminded me of a nun who was quite strict and straight-laced. And basically that was her demeanour within the department." However, as this official came to know de Brun better over a number of years, he found her to be friendly and quite engaging and, perhaps significantly, more laid back after she left office in 2002.

Her intensity was evident when she was in front of reporters or television cameras, although her media performances improved over time as her confidence grew. At times she stared ahead in stony silence when reporters were casually cracking jokes. Supporters insisted she was simply insecure and mistrustful of the media, fearful of saying the wrong thing and embarrassing her party. While McGuinness was viewed as being accommodating and affable, de Brun was thought to be a bit sharp. One reporter recalled that "She could be very friendly and chatty and be lovely, and then as soon as you switched the tape recorder on she was like a different person. I remember one time her staff were in a frenzy that I was going to doorstep her, but she was fine when I did it." The reporter also noted she had a fine grasp of her brief, but that she sometimes hid behind the finer points: "She also would preface nearly every sentence with 'clearly'."

De Brun was viewed as a demanding minister, but she drove herself as hard, if not harder, than those around her. "I do have high standards," she said, "and I do expect a lot of others. I try to expect less, but it doesn't come naturally." She could be unforgiving when she found a mistake in a brief, according to one-well placed source. As minister she would be in the firing line if there was an error and she was acutely conscious that her information had to be accurate. She was quite strict with her press operation and demanded to see almost all press releases before they left the department. She was also very firm about having documents in Irish as well as in English. According to some her bossy style was more suited to the classroom than the debating chamber. One department insider concluded that she was gripped by a desire for perfection and a fear of failure. "She was afraid of making a mistake. She wants to be perfect. Fear drives her." Yet even this civil servant had good things to say about her, pointing out that she was under constant pressure and worked extremely hard. The official praised her commitment, her strength and her intellect: "She was bright and able and that is the most important thing you want in a minister."

De Brun's brittle exterior hid a sensitive nature and one colleague described her as "warm and cold" and as having the capacity to switch between the two temperatures very quickly. Many noticed that she could be extremely thoughtful of others, kind and caring. The minister remembered the birthdays of her private office staff, for example. One source remarked: "She is very sensitive underneath it all, very shy. She comes across on television as very hard-bitten and very strident and if you do something she doesn't like, you will see that side coming out, but if she feels people are being honest and open with her she becomes very open and responsive."

Even some of de Brun's republican colleagues found her zeal to get things done and to muster change a little trying. In the 1980s she lectured republicans from the podium at an Ard Fheis, chiding delegates for not speaking Irish language more frequently. It won her no favours with the hard men of the party. Her passionate promotion of the Irish language was a source of resentment among some unionists, and even some nationalists, who felt she was using the language as a political tool. But de Brun refused to sacrifice what she regarded as her culture and her right to suit the sensibilities of others. She was disappointed when the Assembly members would not agree to allow a simultaneous translation service. During debates she would speak first in Irish and then in English. The DUP members used to cough and splutter all through the Irish segment. She recalled the DUP's Peter Robinson challenging the Speaker once to say whether he could confirm what the minister was saying. Lord Alderdice could not, and he then was given simultaneous translation.

De Brun's insistence on using Irish also posed problems for some of her department officials. Said one: "We were a bit surprised by how much she wanted to use Irish. She used it a lot and every speech she made she would start in Irish and we had to translate all the press releases. We didn't really expect to have to do that." When two representatives from the health sector came to see the minister about an issue, they were impressed that she had taken the liberty of drafting a joint statement for them to agree. When the minister's aide returned with only an English version of the statement, de Brun insisted on having one brought in Irish as well. One of the representatives was from the unionist tradition and joked, "Don't rush it on my account." But the minister's aide, who was described as being in a fluster, by way of apology explained, "Sorry Minister, there is no *fada* on the computer."

De Brun's upbringing had fostered her love of the Irish language. She had a deep love for her Irish heritage and was determined to protect her cultural identity when she moved north of the border. Although a Dubliner, she had strong links with Northern Ireland. Her parents had moved to Dublin from the Glens of Antrim before her birth on 10 January 1954. She was born plain Barbara Brown, but later chose to use the Irish version of her name. Her mother came from the Falls Road area of West Belfast. Albert Street was typical of the area, its tiny terraced houses lined up under the shelter of St Peter's Cathedral's twin towers. It was a tightly-knit, Catholic, working-class community that had felt the full impact of the Troubles. Her father was from Cork, but was raised in England. De Brun's grandfather was a Protestant, although rumour had it – incorrectly – that it was her father who was the non-Catholic.

She was raised in Terenure, a comfortable south Dublin suburb, and was the youngest of four children, two boys and two girls. Her family was not republican and her upbringing was in sharp contrast to that of northern republicans such as Gerry Adams and Martin McGuinness. Her father worked for the Confederation of Irish Industries; her mother ran the family home. At the exclusive St Louis High School in Rathmines, Bairbre showed an aptitude for languages. Her school counsellors attempted to press her into a career as a translator, but she had her own fixed ideas about her future. An intelligent, quiet girl, Bairbre knew her own mind as a youth: "I was absolutely certain from the age of twelve I wanted to be a schoolteacher."

Despite being removed from West Belfast both geographically and socially, she nurtured a political interest in the northern conflict. As a teenager in the late 1960s she was transfixed by the upheaval north of the border, where many of her relations still lived. At home she heard about the suffering of families who hailed from her mother's district. The personal connection to the turbulent Falls Road and its people brought the Troubles home to her: "I can remember my mother listening to every news bulletin on the hour and watching the big stories of the day from the north on the television news. She was intensely interested and I became so as well."

She passed her school exams and headed for University College, Dublin, where she studied modern languages. It was the early 1970s when flares and feminism were all the rage and the Troubles were at their bloodiest peak. Her focus then was on reviving interest in the Irish language. Also, as a young feminist in the heyday of the women's movement, she turned her attention to issues associated with the inequalities facing women. She was active in community work, with the young and old. After completing her degree she was offered a teaching post in Newry, but was unable to take the job because the Northern Ireland authorities refused to recognise her southern qualification. She went to Germany instead, where she taught English for two years. In her final summer there, in 1979, as she looked forward to coming home, her life was shattered: her parents were killed in a horrific car crash. The shocking news came in a telephone call. Her father and mother had been involved in a crash just outside Limerick, while en route to Kerry. The young woman had been close to her parents and it took many years for her to come to terms with the trauma. "When you lose your parents at that stage of your life, you lose a safety net," she confessed in a rare moment of candour in an interview with the *Belfast Telegraph*. An intensely private person, she did not often speak about herself or her past. Many colleagues in Sinn Féin were not aware of the tragedy that had marked her life.

After her parents' death she went ahead with plans to study at Queen's University in Belfast. She earned a teaching qualification that would be recognised in the North. Living in Belfast, she no longer watched the Troubles unfold on her television set, but was witnessing and experiencing the conflict at first-hand. She became absorbed by the events that were scarring Northern Irish society and was increasingly drawn into republican politics. Industrious by nature, she threw herself into efforts on behalf of the H-block committee, set up to support the hunger strikers in the Maze and Armagh Women's prison.

Republican politics is a way of life and de Brun dedicated most of hers to it, sacrificing what may have been an easier existence in Dublin's suburbia, or even a relatively peaceable life as a schoolteacher in a sheltered Malone suburb of Belfast rather than Andersonstown. Initially, de Brun's involvement was limited to single issues centred around the hunger strikes, which culminated in the deaths of ten men in 1981, including Bobby Sands. By 1982 she had taken a further step into politics and joined Sinn Féin. She juggled politics with her teaching career, taking on various supply teaching posts. Joining Sinn Féin was something she felt compelled to do. "A big decision," is how she described it. Although not believed to have been active in the IRA, de Brun had seen at first-hand the impact of the conflict and, like many republicans, justified her defence of violence by pointing to her own community's suffering at the hands of the State. In 1980 she sat in a Belfast hospital with a teenage girl who had been injured when a plastic bullet was fired. De Brun believed the police had aimed deliberately at the fifteen-year-old's head. It was one of a number of experiences that, after careful consideration, convinced her to join Sinn Féin.

As a full-time Sinn Féin activist her responsibilities were varied. She worked for a while in the Sinn Féin press office, campaigned for greater use of the Irish language and was elected to the party executive. Contrasting her community work in Dublin with her efforts on behalf of republicans, she described life then as "relatively easy", adding: "It was only in Belfast that I realised if you worked to improve people's lives, you inevitably came up against the forces of the State like a brick wall."

De Brun was outside Sinn Féin headquarters, Connolly House in Andersonstown, on 12 August 1984 when she and her fellow nationalists smashed into that brick wall in an incident that would stay with her forever. That was the day Sean Downes was killed. Downes had been attending an anti-internment commemoration rally organised by Sinn Féin. There was a massive security presence. There was nothing remarkable about the event until Martin Galvin appeared on the platform to address the crowd. Galvin was the director of Noraid, a Sinn Féin support group based in the United States, and he had been barred from attending the rally. Police moved in to arrest Galvin, firing plastic bullets into the crowd. Downes was caught up in the mayhem. Television cameras captured his last moments: running towards police lines waving a white stick. He was hit by a plastic bullet fired at close range by a RUC reserve constable; the constable was later acquitted of manslaughter. At Sean Downes' funeral, a priest said media reporting of his IRA conviction at the age of sixteen gave a misleading impression and that he was not involved in paramilitarism when he died. He was twenty-two-years old and married with one child. The memory of his corpse as he lay still, with his shirt open, never left de Brun. "I saw him dying on the ground," she said. "It was sheer brutality. An attack on a peaceful demonstration."

During the years when hundreds of people, many innocent civilians, were maimed and killed by the IRA, de Brun remained unrepentant for supporting the republican movement. As a member of Sinn Féin she was condemned by unionists as an apologist for terrorism. She responded with defiance: "The conflict was not of my community's making. [They] would have chosen another avenue for political change if it had been open to them."

She acknowledged that republicans, like all the other players, must hold some responsibility for the length of the Troubles, but she credited Sinn Féin with helping to bring it to an end. In a thoughtful interview given in 2004, de Brun, whilst defensive of her party, was more reflective: "I'd be very much aware that I, as much as anyone else who lives here, have been part of that conflict, either by things that we did, or things that we failed to do, or both." The pain of the conflict has strengthened her resolve to build peace, she said.

Her back-room role became elevated with the peace process. On 31 August 1994, the day the IRA announced its historic ceasefire, de Brun introduced Adams and McGuinness to the waiting media and a crowd of well-wishers that had gathered in Andersonstown. Following the ceasefire Sinn Féin's role within the republican movement was elevated as the party became more powerful at the ballot box and politics began to have greater influence over the direction of the IRA. She assisted Sinn Féin's negotiating team and behind the scenes was asked to research and formulate policy papers. The party's slogan then was "Disband the RUC". De Brun drafted a paper on how to transform the RUC into a new police service that could win the allegiance of nationalists and republicans as well as unionists. Increasingly she found herself in the limelight. Ideologically the party was committed to promoting women; pragmatically it recognised that women candidates attracted female voters. Whenever Sinn Féin wanted to get a newcomer elected the neophyte appeared at Gerry Adams' side in news conferences. De Brun was soon glued to Adams' shoulder and the Sinn Féin president was credited with promoting and encouraging her, despite her unpopularity in some quarters of Sinn Féin.

By 1997 she had taken a year of absence from her teaching job to become a full-time member of the Sinn Féin negotiating team. After the Agreement was signed de Brun stood for election for the first time, having been unable to stand for local council due to citizenship rules. As a candidate in West Belfast she was elected alongside Adams and two others in the constituency, Alex Maskey and Sue Ramsey. Her victory led to another important change in her life because she could not take an indefinite leave of absence from her teaching job. Once again she had a big decision to make: full-time politics, or education? After some soul-searching she opted for politics, reasoning cheerfully that at least the choice was between two things she loved.

Only later did she realise the cost of public life. She valued her privacy highly and at times lamented the loss of anonymity. As Minister of Health she could no longer go unrecognised. Aside from the security implications of even a simple shopping trip in Belfast, she had the added burden of being lobbied constantly: in the hairdressers, or at the corner shop. "It's relentless," she said at the time. No longer did the Falls park offer sanctuary from the stresses of life. It had been a favourite place to walk and reflect, but after her appointment she would invariably meet someone who had a problem, or who had a relative with a problem about a hospital waiting list. Even in Dublin there was no escape, as she would inevitably be recognised by northerners out for the day. The pressures of office began to take a toll. "It was hugely onerous," she admitted later. "I ... had to be careful about my personal health and personal regime and doing yoga and time management and stress management."

Despite the drawbacks, she was thrilled to have been made a minister, less so perhaps with the portfolio. When she realised it was going to be Health, not Education, or Culture, Arts and Leisure, she was thought to be disappointed. She denied this, however, insisting she had already been attending various seminars organised by the departments to brief the MLAs on issues: "There was one specifically on public health and I remember coming out of that one feeling very animated and excited. I felt I could do that." De Brun recalled senior officials in the department being anxious, fearing Health would be left sitting at the end of the selection process. In most governments Health is the one portfolio that is coveted; de Brun claimed there was surprise in government circles that some northern parties "ran away" from it: "We had one of the main British officials the very morning after saying to us, 'How did they let you get education and health?' But the SDLP opted for other choices and unionists were afraid of it." One senior Ulster Unionist called it the "ministry for closing hospitals".

De Brun had been tipped to become a minister as early as August 1999, when *The Irish News* reported that Gerry Adams was not interested in a ministerial portfolio. The newspaper's source suggested that de Brun would go to Education. Her elevation was less controversial than McGuinness', despite unionist hostility towards her politics. Unionists found it ironic that someone aligned to the violent republican movement would be put in charge of health and public safety. She bristled when BBC correspondent Dot Kirby asked her in an early interview about the impact of IRA punishment attacks on the healthcare system and the irony of Sinn Féin holding the public safety portfolio. Particularly controversial was her choice of advisor, Leo Green, an ex-prisoner who had taken part in the 1980 hunger strike, having been jailed for life for the killing of RUC Inspector Harry Cobb in 1977. Green was not chosen for his knowledge of health policy, rather his appointment was an important gesture by republicans in that his presence at Stormont could help seal IRA approval for the new administration. He was also there to provide the minister with sound political advice. "I think she found him a very helpful, strong adviser on the political angles," said one insider. "He was very astute on the politics."

The officials in the department were trained to work with whomever the democratic system delivered, but some found it difficult to work with republicans and there was a bit of shadow-boxing at the start. However senior management reminded civil servants that a professional attitude was required, and was necessary: "It was made clear if people didn't want to work with this minister then they were out of the department ... but nobody transferred out and people got used to it."

While McGuinness faced open opposition outside his department, with school walk-outs and street protests, de Brun's appointment was relatively low-key, albeit with a few notable exceptions. One particularly nasty incident occurred when she visited Lagan Valley Hospital in Lisburn. DUP supporters surrounded her car and banged on the roof. "It was pretty unpleasant," said a senior department source. "She was pretty upset by that." The experience did not deter her from visiting a children's home in the mainly unionist town of Newtownards the following day.

The DUP MLAs wrote to her permanent secretary with questions and, just as McGuinness had done, she wrote back as minister. De Brun noticed that one of the DUP members was using Tippex to blot out her name and signature at the bottom of the letter before circulating it. "After that I used to put a line at the end of the letter saying, 'I, as minister', but the Assembly member ignored that and still Tippexed me out." One SDLP source recalled that de Brun was fussy about correspondence and the use of the term "Northern Ireland":

> "There was a directive that went out that you couldn't refer to Northern Ireland in memos. You had to say 'here'. All the correspondence had to be neutral. We used to joke when Northern Ireland was playing a football match that 'here was playing there'."

Overall, the health sector greeted her appearance as health minister with relief more than anxiety. The sector desperately needed stability and a home-grown minister who would take the tough decisions. There was certainly no public outcry from the sector to compare with the criticism meted out to McGuinness by some educationalists. Even in private, those involved in healthcare claimed they could recall no adverse remarks about the new minister. A senior member of one of the boards said the overwhelming response was relief that a devolved minister might actually bring some decision-making to a beleaguered sector. "I can't speak for the department," said one health board official, "but among the boards, her appointment was met with a mixture of panic and happiness. They were getting a local and there would be some continuity."

Opinion inside the department appears to have been mixed: some were eager or curious, others were apprehensive or unhappy that Sinn Féin had taken the post. Good relations with staff appear to have taken more time to build compared to McGuinness' experience at the Department of Education. Immediately after her appointment, de Brun met her new officials. She was accompanied by Upper Bann MLA Dara O'Hagan and they worked out her first visit to the department and how to manage things. The officials had already anticipated her desire to use the Irish language and the draft press release was ready to be released in both English and Irish – it was believed to be the first time in the history of the Northern Ireland administration that this had occurred. Initially Craig Allen was her private secretary, later replaced by Emer Melarkey (later Morelli), whom de Brun personally appointed, as was customary for ministers. "We had a very special working relationship together and we just gelled," said de Brun. Melarkey declined to be interviewed.

One of Melarkey's tasks was to ensure that ministerial visits were spread evenly, both geographically and socially. De Brun was not interested in just visiting institutions, she also wanted to take part in community events. She was much more accessible than any direct rule minister had been. Early in her administration she went to a community meeting in Newry and stayed for two-and-a-half hours, discussing the impact of poverty on the health of working-class communities. Those present were impressed that she had stayed so long.

Despite the long hours she put in, she was frustrated by the lack of results over many months on issues such as waiting lists. "I think her confidence suffered," said one insider. "I remember watching her on policing issues before she became a minister and she was very formidable, much more comfortable." Her frustrations in office notwithstanding, she always maintained that she would choose health if she had the opportunity to do so again. "It is an absolutely fascinating portfolio," she insisted.

De Brun inherited the most challenging of all the departments, the one with the biggest budget and the biggest problems. "I feel daunted," she said at the time, "but also very excited." Her budget in 1999 was around £2 billion, much of it eaten up by salaries for healthcare workers. That left relatively little flexibility to tackle the big issues, such as spiralling waiting lists, trolley waits, staff shortages, out-dated infrastructure and demands for modern hospitals. When de Brun took office the sector was in perennial crisis. This meant she was on the defensive almost from the start, not just for her republicanism but also for her health policy. She pointed out that her department had more consultations pending than any other because direct rule had not tackled the difficult issues.

Her permanent secretary was the mild-mannered Clive Gowdy. Gowdy and other officials had been used to direct rule and working under successive British ministers. Before devolution in 1999 there had been five direct rule ministers in the Department of Health in as many years. These ministers were not in office long enough to take any significant decisions. The really difficult issues were either fudged or long-fingered through consultation, which proved costly to the health sector. "I wanted to get stuck into the issues straight away," recalled de Brun. Her health officials were encouraging her to visit places and raise her profile. "I remember laughing and saying, 'Look at the number of issues pending, the one thing I am going to have is profile. I don't need to raise my profile'."

One of these pending issues was whether to site maternity services at the Belfast City Hospital in South Belfast, or at the Royal Victoria Hospital in West Belfast. The two hospitals were within walking distance of one another and it was not cost-effective to have the services so close together. The passion which marked the debate might have suggested to a stranger that the choice was between two hospitals that were miles apart. In truth, it was a close-run thing and the arguments had been raging for years, kicked from one direct rule minister to another, with one sometimes reversing the decision of the other. In December 1999 it landed in de Brun's lap. Her immediate predecessor, Tony Worthington, had ruled in favour of the Royal, only to have his decision successfully overturned in the courts after he was accused of failing to consult adequately. What made it so difficult was that both hospitals had a good case. As soon as she took office, de Brun met all the interested parties, determined to take a decision as quickly as possible. "The urgency came from talking to people. Everybody I met said this has gone on long enough, we couldn't wait any longer." She was conscious that the indecision was impacting adversely on the plans for a new cancer centre in Belfast. "Everybody I met said that whatever the decision taken, they wanted the decision taken early." The matter was complicated for de Brun by the fact that the Royal was based in her West Belfast constituency and she was vulnerable to cries of bias from the rival hospital's supporters. Within weeks of taking office de Brun had made her decision on the maternity hospital, even as she juggled problems stemming from the peace process and the 'flu crisis. She followed medical advice and chose the Royal. As expected, this infuriated campaigners for the City and provoked a backlash at Stormont. Critics claimed she had chosen the Royal because it was in her constituency, ignoring the fact she was acting on medical opinion. She was dismayed to find it had become a sectarian issue in some quarters. The DUP member for Strangford, Iris Robinson, a member of the health committee, accused the minister of building "a Catholic hospital for a Catholic people". Robinson refused to retract the remark, having made it to underscore the fact that Protestant members of the security forces and police were nervous about going to the hospital. In fact, her party colleague Nigel Dodds' police minders suffered an IRA attack there.

De Brun was not alone in finding the remark offensive, but she recognised the intensity of emotion that people felt towards their health service. She attributed the controversy over the decision in part to the public's attachment to services and in part to the fact that the issue illustrated how powerful she was as a minister. Unionists realised, perhaps for the first time, that they would not have control over a Sinn Féin minister, that ministers had a great deal of autonomy within the power-sharing administration. An official, who appeared to be acting on behalf of the First Minister, told an Assembly correspondent that de Brun could not make the decision herself. It turned out to be an inaccurate statement. De Brun had not consulted the Executive about the decision – she was not required to because the ruling did not cut across another department. An insider said: "She announced it without telling the Executive ministers and it raised questions about what she was entitled to do in legal and political terms." She was not obliged to tell the Executive because she did not need approval through legislation, nor did she require finance.

Officials had warned de Brun that her decision would be challenged in the courts, so there was no surprise when it went to judicial review. "What took her back," said one insider, "was how strongly entrenched the views were of any issue we dealt with." The minister was criticised in the courts for the process of her decision-making, but an allegation of political bias arising out of her membership of Sinn Féin was dropped. Her initial decision ultimately prevailed and the Jubilee Maternity Unit at the City Hospital was demolished in favour of the Royal.

It was an early lesson for the minister in just how controversial her role was going to be. She knew she would be challenged quite forcefully on the Assembly floor and, unlike McGuinness, did not relish the despatch box. As health minister, de Brun was asked more ministerial questions than any other minister. "We were getting as much in questions and debates as almost every other department combined," said a department insider. This was partly due to the nature and size of her portfolio, and applied even under direct rule. But de Brun noted that around 30%–40% of the questions came from the DUP. "We thought it was political football stuff, some of it was kind of, 'Let's play overload'," she recalled. She said it took her some time to get used to question time. "The bit in the Assembly was actually one of the most stressful parts of the job."

In her first ministerial question time, de Brun, who had been feeling unwell, looked at one point like she was going to pass out as the colour drained from her face and she searched for her notes while Ian Paisley Jr thundered that she was showing contempt for the house. The DUP relished challenging her, and her nervousness was an invitation for attack. The problems might have been worse had her committee been chaired by a member of the DUP, but it was jointly headed by the SDLP's Joe Hendron and his deputy, Tommy Gallagher, another SDLP man. The committee also included the DUP's Iris Robinson and Paul Berry. Relations could be fairly fraught at times. "There was a fair bit of politicking," said a department official. "The minister had a torrid enough time."

De Brun clashed with her committee again over GP fund-holding and it became a big-battle issue within the Assembly. On that occasion Hendron, who had supported her decision on the maternity hospital, took issue with her decision-making. GP fund-holding enabled practitioners to buy services directly from hospitals which got their patients a hospital appointment much faster. Its critics complained it created a two-tier system within the NHS because doctors who were fund-holders were seen to have an advantage. Sinn Féin was opposed to fund-holding and the minister was determined to do away with it, a move that had been promised in the Programme for Government. She thought she could count on her committee for support in this. The problem for her committe was not scrapping fund-holding per se, but the speed at which the minister wished to move on the issue. They felt it necessary to consider the opinion of powerful interest groups, such as the Royal College of Nursing, which opposed scrapping the scheme by 31 March 2001. When it came to an Assembly debate and vote, de Brun did not get the backing from her committee she had anticipated. "She was ambushed," was how a health department source put it. "Those around the Executive table were running away from it."

The committee tabled an amendment to de Brun's Health and Personal Social Services Bill, urging that the decision be delayed for one year. Sinn Féin MLA Sue Ramsey raised hackles when she blamed the "anti-Sinn Féin" politics of the DUP and questioned why some SDLP members were prepared to support the amendment when Hendron had insisted fund-holding was wrong and that this was their party's policy.

The Health minister, who had been prepared to agree a six-month transition period, made an appeal in the chamber for members not to support the amendment. But Hendron said the transition would not work because it came in the middle of a financial year. He was also concerned that a credible replacement should be identified before fund-holding was abolished. Ultimately, the minister announced a new system of Local Health and Social Care Groups, which involved general practitioners and other care professionals. The groups were designed to commission services and give communities a bigger say in health, diluting the role of the boards. The arrangements were condemned by the British Medical Association as adding to the crippling bureaucracy, but de Brun insisted it was a more effective way of dealing with problems.

Observers who had watched the vote on the committee's amendment would have noticed a very telling pattern in the SDLP vote that day. The SDLP ministers and their Assembly team voted with the health minister against the amendment, as did the Women's Coalition committee member Monica McWilliams. But Hendron and SDLP committee colleague Carmel Hanna defied a three-line whip imposed by Seamus Mallon, Deputy First Minister and deputy leader of the party, and voted with the DUP, Alliance and Ulster Unionists in favour of the amendment. The First Minister David Trimble and his ministerial colleagues Sam Foster, Michael McGimpsey and junior minister Dermot Nesbitt did the same, as did the DUP. It represented a clear split in the Executive and another example of a lack of collectivity but the minister did not make an issue of it in public. Nor was she aware, she said, of the extent to which it had divided the SDLP.

Hendron blamed de Brun for the problem. He claimed that the night before the debate, Mallon had suggested a compromise to de Brun's officials. "Nobody was saying to me, 'Joe, back down.' Mallon had never said that to me. She was asked, 'Could you not postpone it for a few months?' That's all. Then we would have withdrawn the bloody motion, but she wasn't prepared to do that." De Brun confirmed a meeting took place aimed at seeking compromise. But she felt further delay was inappropriate as GP fund-holding was inequitable. "It had to end," she said. Hendron also recalled that his SDLP colleagues had sympathised with him, yet when Mallon imposed the whip they did not want to rebel. But Hendron did: "I was on the committee and there was no way I was going to make a fool of myself. They [the SDLP] voted with Sinn Féin on this thing only because Mallon had sympathy for de Brun in principle, of not gutting her."

He also said the three-line whip proved to be a "farce" because Hanna was subsequently promoted to the Executive following a reshuffle in 2002. Hendron said he was sympathetic to the plight of the health minister and the difficulties of her portfolio, but ultimately concluded that this "able woman", as he put it, had become imprisoned by bureaucracy. "I just think she seemed to fall into line with senior civil servants and the status quo." Complaining of endless reviews, Hendron said: "There seemed to be an awful lot of reports coming out. Report after report, and the word 'review' almost turned my stomach. I was fed up. Every problem, there would have to be a review. Everything was bloody reviewed." Citing as an example the review of cardiology and cardiac surgery, he continued: "That's fair enough because there was a huge waiting list for cardiac surgery, but there's a terrible lot of heart disease in Northern Ireland. We all know that. Smoking and being overweight. The figures were there. You don't need some bloody genius from university to come down and do it. Once the department had a review they would sit back on their backsides for another six months or a year."

The DUP's Iris Robinson also accused the Department of Health of hiding behind reviews. De Brun saw real value in the reviews and in consulting as a means of achieving consensus and rejected the notion that her department, and others, were suffering from "consultationitis". She wanted to take the communities with her, and consultation was her best plan for doing so, plus she was required to do it under the terms of the Good Friday Agreement. "Almost everything she did was challenged by somebody," said one senior department official. One of the biggest problems for health was the ever-growing waiting lists. When de Brun took office they were the worst in the UK; it was not long before they were described as the worst in Europe. The minister got very downhearted about the apparent lack of progress and the constant negative headlines, which a health official called "a minefield of horror stories". In response to the problem, de Brun recruited a nurse manager – a common sense move that was in part a cosmetic exercise. It reduced the list immediately by simply striking off those who appeared on it in error, or who had had surgery privately, or who had since died, or who had moved house and were being counted twice. Efforts were also focused on ensuring that patients kept their hospital appointments. Tackling waiting lists required more than finance as some problems were down to a lack of skilled personnel. As a starting point, de Brun increased the number of training places for nurses, announcing in 2000 that 300 extra places would be created. She also pledged to reduce waiting lists by around 10,000 by 2004.

The perpetual cry from the health minister was that her department was badly under-funded. An insider described her attitude at the Executive when it came to funding as "I dare you not to give it to me." Efforts were made by the finance minister to redress the millions of pounds that had been taken out of Health under direct rule. As finance ministers go, de Brun found Mark Durkan to be rather sympathetic: "Mark had a good understanding of the pressures in Health and had a lot of empathy." She described his approach as principled and felt his attitude improved over time. When challenged at the Executive table over her department's performance, de Brun would simply point to the lack of resources. She had, in fact, inherited debt-ridden hospitals that were continually battling with staff shortages and spiralling drug costs. One minister said that when challenged, she would read from a brief and outline the problems and if questioned further would sigh and read aloud again from her brief, as if it had not been understood the first time. Some ministers found this exasperating and she was conscious that she "may have sounded like a broken record". De Brun said she felt more hostility from the other ministers as time went on. When criticised at the Executive table she sometimes pointed out to the other ministers that their parties could have chosen health. "She had a desperately difficult brief," said Empey. "She would say, 'Any one of you could have taken it, but you hadn't the guts.' She was right. Having said that the health department was a complete mystery, no matter how much money went in, the outputs never seemed to get better."

"We were always treading water," de Brun agreed. She said it was unrealistic to expect the service to be transformed in one Executive term, particularly one that was in constant crisis and chronically under-funded. She admitted to feeling frustrated and referred to "sound-bite politics" as a particular problem. Part of the difficulty, too, was that the other parties may have been reluctant to give a Sinn Féin health minister any credit for transforming Health. First Minister David Trimble, in particular, took an interest in Health, regretting that his own party did not take it when the chance arose. "So much of the budget is there," he would sigh with regret, but de Brun, was always quick to respond that most of her funding was swallowed up by staff salaries, which took a large and ever-increasing chunk of her budget.

As time went on Trimble became convinced that funding was not the answer and that there were fundamental flaws in health structures which included nineteen trusts and four boards. He recalled, with some mirth, a presentation given to the Executive on how the health service actually worked: "There was this huge big flow chart that people constructed on the inputs and outputs and the health officials were purring with pleasure. I got the impression from that they had never got to pull together in one bit what the department did. But it was purely descriptive, there was no analysis or critique."

That presentation had come about because the Department of Health was one of several chosen by the Executive to undergo a Needs and Effectiveness Survey, which would benchmark it with its counterparts in Britain. Durkan had sought the surveys as part of his bid to challenge what he regarded as a lack of funding from the Treasury. Sinn Féin viewed the survey as an attempt to undermine the minister's assertion that under-funding was the problem and to highlight inefficiencies. If that was the intention, it did not succeed, according to a department source: "It backfired, not on the Executive, but on some ministers who believed they could shut de Brun up by having this study and demonstrate she was talking rubbish." In fact, the survey vindicated the minister, confirming her department suffered a funding short-fall. "We had a gap of around £300 million," said the department official, "and the game was won by us – if there was a game."

There were constant demands for the minister to cut bureaucracy. Her failure to tackle it was in part due to the decision by the Office of First and Deputy First Minister to embark on a review of public administration, which would include the trusts and boards. The criticism persisted, however, and her committee chairman said she ought to have tackled it. There has been some debate about the actual level of the cost-savings that could have been derived from such a shake-up. De Brun said suspension came before she could deal with it and suggested that a document she launched in 2002, *Developing Better Services*, dealt with proposals for restructuring the sector. This was part of a wide-ranging strategy that also included Investing For Health, an initiative of which she was particularly proud. It focused on prevention by trying to ensure, for example, that the population was fit and would not be susceptible to heart disease. By tackling social need, she hoped to encourage well-being and reduce stress. "That was a major achievement," she said, "one I think can be built on with political will."

De Brun was viewed by some in the sector as being more comfortable with the community side of her portfolio. She always insisted on using her full title, Minister of Health and Social Services and Public Safety. "I always refused to allow myself to be referred to as minister for health … as if the social services didn't exist. It got to the point where one of my officials said to me, 'I suppose we are going to have to start calling [you] the minister for social services and health?' and I said, 'You may just have to'."

One former health official felt this was where she had the most impact and praised her recognition of the links between poverty and health, although he regretted that a more radical solution was not adopted to tackle the structures in healthcare. "It seemed the policies that operated in England and Wales were transplanted here," he said. "Scotland was very different. Structures were worked out to suit a Scottish solution. In Northern Ireland we never arrived at finding a Northern Ireland solution for Health."

Criticism of de Brun was particularly sharp during the debate over the future of acute hospitals – a controversial issue for any minister. The department had to decide where to situate hospitals and how to allocate scarce resources. While most communities wanted hospitals on their doorsteps, experience suggested that it was better to centralise services and expertise rather than spread them out thinly. De Brun inherited plans for the "Golden Six", a group of hospitals clustered around Belfast, with one in Derry. A review conducted by Dr Maurice Hayes suggested a seventh hospital was needed, and should be located in either Fermanagh or Tyrone. Once again, the minister was caught between equally vociferous campaigners, only this time it was even more difficult as she was being pulled in different directions by competing interests within her own party. As minister she had to choose between Enniskillen in Fermanagh and Omagh in County Tyrone: only one could get an acute hospital. Feelings were running extremely high on both sides and as Sinn Féin had strong support in both areas, the MLAs were frantically lobbying her on behalf of constituents. Sinn Féin's Francie Molloy, MLA for Mid-Ulster, and Barry McElduff, MLA for West Tyrone, were supporting Omagh, while Fermanagh MLAs Gerry McHugh and Michelle Gildernew were fighting for Enniskillen. The minister was already finding it tough to deal with external critics and was pushed to breaking-point by pressures from her own party regarding her performance. A Sinn Féin source recalled that de Brun got very emotional and tearful at internal meetings if she were censured or disapproval were expressed: "She was very arrogant in many ways and very self-opinionated but not tough-minded. She used to break down in tears at party meetings if she was asked the hard questions or if she was criticised. There were a few occasions when she broke down when she was being criticised about the Omagh versus Tyrone debate and most of us would have been critical of her. Adams was very supportive of her."

Another Sinn Féin source did not deny de Brun got very emotional at times in party meetings. Asked about this, she said people felt very strongly about the issues. In a newspaper interview in 2001 she remarked about the problems in Health: "It is not a situation that doesn't touch me personally. There are real people facing real problems and there are real people working very heroically to the best of their ability who feel frustrated. It's unacceptable to me as a minister that people face this."

Sinn Féin was a well-disciplined party and any friction tended to be kept under wraps. But behind the scenes de Brun had to endure the wrath of colleagues who felt frustrated with the state of healthcare. Some complained they found it more difficult to get a meeting with her than a direct rule minister, or a minister from another party. They claimed she was concerned about being seen to give them special access. "This was absolutely true," said one Sinn Féin member, "and that same applied for McGuinness." When asked about this, de Brun confessed to being puzzled, as did McGuinness. She acknowledged that she had always striven to follow proper procedure, but doubted she was less accessible to Sinn Féin MLAs than ministers from other parties. "It was a matter of people in the party getting used to the system," said Leo Green, "and getting used to proper practice."

As the hospital debate raged back and forth, within the chamber and outside, Hayes' ultimately recommended that the new hospital for the west should be located in Enniskillen, not Omagh. It was thought Sinn Féin had its own think-tank of party advisors and the minister drew on this pool, as well as her department's advisors. She had long faced serious criticism within the party over health care and the situation was not helped by the Hayes report. One source recalled "heated exchanges" at internal meetings. The party was not able to deliver for both areas and one source said de Brun walked off the platform at a Sinn Féin Ard Fheis when Molloy criticised her department's policy. She faced a major backlash not just from Omagh campaigners but from her own party colleagues. When the report's recommendation was made public, Sinn Féin MP for West Tyrone Pat Doherty immediately visited the Omagh hospital to show solidarity. De Brun was being lobbied in the corridors of Stormont and beyond about the issue. Ulster Unionist Sam Foster recalled meeting her in the corridor after he had left office and she greeted him warmly as they shook hands. He had been diagnosed with Parkinson's disease and de Brun offered to help in any way she could. He said there was nothing he needed, but as he walked away he had a thought: "Actually, you could do something. Be sure and site the hospital in Enniskillen." Foster said she scampered away quickly.

De Brun made no immediate decision on the Omagh/Enniskillen battle and instead her department embarked on its own in-house consultation, which took more than a year. She then announced that she was minded to go with the Enniskillen proposal. Some Sinn Féin members believed this had been the department's agenda long before devolution. The final decision was taken out of de Brun's hands by suspension, and the formal announcement was delivered by her direct rule successor, Des Browne.

On other issues de Brun won praise for an initiative that allowed renal patients to use Daisy Hill Hospital rather than having to travel to Dublin. In terms of practical measures, she also appointed a senior person in each trust with responsibility for cleanliness. Through cooperation at Executive level she was able to pass a healthcare Bill that introduced free nursing care. She also extended NHS funding throughout Northern Ireland for couples seeking *in vitro* fertilisation. She won praise for her sensitive handling of the organs scandal, which involved the admission by a number of hospitals that the organs of deceased babies had been retained without parents' permission. De Brun who inherited the problem apologised, ordered an inquiry and accepted the resultant recommendation. She also took hard decisions regarding the Royal Maternity Hospital and was delighted to announce the new cancer centre before she left office, a project that had been delayed for years.

Overall, however, there was disappointment that de Brun had not achieved more, a disappointment she shared, especially as she was denied the opportunity to complete the job. To be fair, she did run out of time, although others insisted that she was imprisoned by the department's bureaucratic tendencies. "There was a particular view in the medical profession," said a health sector source, "that she was a Shinner, that she was a socialist and when she got her feet under the table and got to know what end was up, she would kick ass and give the department a good shake-up and she was the one to do it, but it didn't happen."

Much of her time was taken up with laying the groundwork for future decisions and future goals. It was not until after de Brun left office that some of her work in terms of reducing waiting lists paid off. Her direct rule successor, Des Browne, gave her credit for this. She was disappointed, after all her effort and so many damning headlines, that she was not able to deliver the good news herself: "The work was interrupted and I regret very much I was denied the opportunity to see through the task." This applied to other areas of her brief as well. As one health official remarked, "Unfortunately, she was gone before the treading water had stopped."

Although progress was widely regarded as patchy on the health front, de Brun did make political strides. Before leaving office she finally shook hands with Ulster Unionist Dermot Nesbitt. "Things had moved on by then," he said.

Chapter 17

Restoration

Fed up with the political stalemate over guns and government, the SDLP's Bríd Rodgers took herself off to Italy for a week's holiday in early May 2000. She was enjoying her break on the Adriatic Coast when she received an unexpected telephone call from Teresa Higgins, who worked in her office back home. Higgins blurted out some unexpected news about the talks process: "They've reached an agreement. We're back in business!"

Rodgers was shocked. It had been less than three months since suspension. She, like most others, had expected Stormont to be frozen in time for quite a while. In the days that followed the February suspension there had been little sign of an end to the guns and government deadlock. The blame game had begun almost immediately and relations were strained between the governments. Dublin was angry over the unilateral suspension of the institutions by London, while Secretary of State Peter Mandelson was accused of mortgaging the Agreement to save the Ulster Unionist leader.

Following suspension, a mural had appeared on Divis Street in West Belfast. Beside an artist's impression of Mandelson, David Trimble and Ian Paisley were the words: "Wrecking the Agreement. Don't Let Them." Mandelson was also parodied as Pinocchio, with a rather long nose. The usually thin-skinned politician apparently did not take this to heart and, according to a senior republican, even ordered one of the posters for himself. That was the only lighthearted moment for Mandelson in the aftermath. Within days of the suspension, Sinn Féin would have what it termed the party's worst ever meeting with the Secretary of State. McGuinness privately admitted to using more colourful language with Mandelson than he had ever used with Trimble.

In the absence of devolution, Westminster Labour MPs Adam Ingram and George Howarth were charged with overseeing the ten departments. Ingram took Finance, Agriculture, Regional Development, Higher Education and Enterprise. Howarth got Health, Education, Social Development, Environment and Culture, Arts and Leisure. In the absence of devolution, Mandelson cut the Assembly members' wages by around £9,000, reducing salaries to just under £30,000. Cross-border bodies were allowed to continue operating on existing projects, but no new initiatives were to be undertaken. The unionists blamed the IRA, the IRA blamed the unionists and Seamus Mallon blamed them both: the "not an inch" versus the "not an ounce" gang, he called them.

The DUP declared the Agreement, and Trimble, a failure and called for his immediate resignation. This demand was ignored by Trimble. The day after suspension he accompanied Mallon to the Catholic St Patrick's Cathedral to attend a service for the 'disappeared' – victims of the Troubles whose bodies had never been found. Not for the first time their show of solidarity seemed at odds with the political events and the tensions whirling around them. Yet in spite of the difficulties, Trimble seemed wildly optimistic about the future following the suspension of the Assembly, insisting: "It's not terminal."

His remarks contrasted sharply with those made by Adams, who – perhaps mindful of new negotiations – suggested the peace process was in the "worst crisis of a crisis-ridden process". The IRA severed contact with the IICD in what was viewed as both a tantrum and a serious setback.

Conscious that his tactics had forced a shift from the IRA on the issue of decommissioning, and its intentions, Trimble looked forward to another review of the Agreement when the problems plaguing power-sharing could be dealt with and Stormont could be restored on a "sound basis". But nationalists and republicans, seething over enforced suspension, were suspicious of his intentions and feared he would use a review to renegotiate the Agreement. While his reputation was severely dented as far as nationalists were concerned, Trimble appeared to have improved his standing in the Ulster Unionist Council. Following suspension, he was able to block a motion tying the party's involvement in any future Executive to the retention of the name of the RUC. On the other hand, he had to refer any proposals to re-enter government back to another UUC meeting, and two prominent anti-Agreement unionists, Jeffrey Donaldson and Arlene Foster, were included in a new working group to devise future strategy for the review.

A month after suspension the political leaders departed for Washington to attend President Clinton's St Patrick's Day celebrations at the White House. Despite the pessimistic mood, there was a significant development in Washington. Trimble announced to a number of British, Irish and American correspondents in the National Press Club – with a view to out-manoeuvring republicans in the US capital – that he was prepared to get involved in another sequence leading to power-sharing without guns up front, provided there were clear and certain guarantees that decommissioning would happen. He paid dearly for this tactic, however. His press briefing took the media by surprise. His intention seems to have been to bounce republicans and put them on the defensive, but in doing so he also bounced himself into hot water with his party over his surprise announcement. Trimble had made his move without consulting senior members of his party, and certainly not MP Ken Maginnis, who was a member of the new strategy group. Maginnis heard the news in Belfast and immediately assumed the reports coming from Washington were inaccurate. When Trimble's nemesis, MP Jeffrey Donaldson, heard Trimble's position he was "gutted". The result of Trimble's Washington speech was that a leadership challenge was mounted within days of his return to Belfast. It was not Donaldson, however, who came up to the mark. The challenger was the MP for South Belfast, Martin Smyth, who at the age of sixty-nine was viewed by many as too old to take on the job, but was nonetheless considered a formidable stalking-horse.

When the UUC met for a showdown that March, the anti-Agreement camp failed to topple Trimble but did manage to seriously weaken his leadership. It was claimed that Donaldson punched the air in delight when it was announced that Smyth had won a credible 43% of the vote. Adding to his woes, Trimble failed to block the passing of a resolution that tied a return to power-sharing to the retention of the name of the RUC. Although he had won the vote on this, none of his opponents pledged loyalty to him. Trimble, looking dejected, denied he was either shattered or shackled.

Days later, his characteristic determination reappeared when he became the first unionist leader to appear on the popular RTÉ programme, "The Late, Late Show". "Just because you have a few difficulties doesn't mean you give up. This is too important to give up," he told the show's host, Gay Byrne. The unionist leader also explained why he had consistently refused to shake Gerry Adams' hand: "The origin of the handshake was to show there was no weapon in your hand. That is the symbolic aspect of it. Mr Adams' organisation doesn't have an empty hand yet."

Inevitably, the weapons issue dominated the agenda as negotiations continued amid low expectations and mixed messages. When accepting the St Angela's International Peace Award in Waterford, Mallon suggested there was still one more chance to save the Executive, a remark echoed by Adams a few days later. But Adams tempered his comments by repeating that the process was in "dire straits". While SDLP leader John Hume spoke about a "final push", John Taylor suggested there would be no return to power-sharing. The DUP's Nigel Dodds waded in too, calling it "wishful thinking and fantasy land".

The interminable row over guns and government seemed to have resurfaced with a vengeance. Observers expected a protracted stalemate as the British and Irish Prime Ministers slunk away from Hillsborough in April, yet again without any tangible progress having been made. Few paid any attention when Mandelson asserted that more imaginative ways would have to be found to solve the arms issue. In May, when Tony Blair and Bertie Ahern returned to Hillsborough Castle for more negotiations, the guns and government problem seemed intractable. Underlining this general perception was the fact that the May talks coincided with the start of a trial in Florida relating to charges of illegal IRA arms smuggling.

One SDLP source remembered having an inkling that a deal was taking shape after attending a meeting in Downing Street before the Hillsborough talks: "We knew there was going to be something happening from the IRA. We went to Downing Street and McGuinness and Adams were in Blair's office, using it as an office." However, there was no telling how long it would take and no guarantee it would actually work. Rodgers thought she was safe enough to go on holiday, glad to be away from Hillsborough Castle and a chance to unwind while waiting for Trimble and Adams to sort out their differences.

The talks proved more productive than many had anticipated; Trimble and Adams were both in the mood for a gamble. To the surprise of most observers – and Bríd Rodgers – there was a dramatic breakthrough at the Castle. Hammered out late in the evening of Friday, 5 May, the new compromise they reached was indeed imaginative on the arms issue. Under the terms of the deal the IRA would commit itself to putting weapons beyond use and, as a confidence-building measure, would allow two international inspectors to examine dumps regularly to ensure that the weapons were out of commission. In exchange, the institutions would be back in action by 22 May. As part of the sequence the UUC would also have to agree to the proposals, which included further demilitarisation, a timetable for police reform and a promise that all remaining prisoners who so qualified under the Good Friday Agreement would be released by 28 July. The plan was for the Agreement to be fully implemented by June 2001, a date effectively taken by unionists and others as a new deadline for complete decommissioning by the IRA.

The choreography was hard-won, but Mallon, for one, was wary. Annoyed at the way unionists had behaved in the negotiations he commented: "For two years we had a problem over decommissioning. One half-hour after decommissioning was effectively resolved, we had two more issues on the table." One well-placed source remembered that the arms problem was resolved around 3.00pm, but it was hours later, around 11.00pm, before they emerged with the deal. The two outstanding issues were flags and policing, and these would threaten to unravel the Hillsborough deal in the days that followed because the government subsequently made two moves that infuriated both the SDLP and Sinn Féin.

The policing issue concerned the extremely sensitive matter of the name of the police service. Unionists wanted to retain the title "Royal Ulster Constabulary". Trimble said he did not understand Mallon's surprise at these issues being raised, as his party's previous UUC meeting had also made the retention of the RUC name a precondition for power-sharing. He also failed to understand Mallon's objections to the name and felt he was merely trying to show he was a better nationalist than Sinn Féin. "This was a strategic mistake," Trimble claimed. Mallon found this notion very insulting, believing his stance was based on clear evidence of nationalist aversion to the RUC.

Trimble claimed Mallon had conveniently forgotten that it had been acknowledged in the talks that the retention of the name in one form or another was going to have to be addressed. A senior SDLP source said that during the talks at Hillsborough, Mallon insisted that retaining the name would not represent a new start to policing as promised under the Agreement, nor would it attract young Catholics to join the service. One SDLP source recalled a row in the castle's garden between the SDLP and Blair. The source said: "The British were saying, 'Can you offer us anything on this [the name]?'" One proposal that day was to have the RUC named in the legislation, so that the old and new would be linked in some way. One SDLP source said the party's position was clear: "We offered continuity but no ambiguity on this issue."

According to one source, Irish Foreign Minister Brian Cowen suggested to the SDLP that the issue be left "for another day". "Cowen said, 'We need to leave this over,' and Mallon gave him a look as if to say, 'Ah, come off it'." The SDLP source said his party wanted the issue addressed then and there to save grief later, but it was not amicably resolved and the row was pushed into the future. Mallon was extremely angry about this and has always blamed Mandelson. Mallon said he had obtained, through various meetings, a copy of the original policing legislation before Mandelson got to it. He claimed it held no reference to the name and that the "Mandelson theory" of linking the old and new name came later. He alleged that the Secretary of State wrote this in. "Mandelson came in and changed it before anybody saw it," Mallon asserted.

Mallon alleged that Mandelson was allowed to interfere and waste a few years:

> "Had it not been for Mandelson's destruction of Patten, it would have avoided the second reading of the House of Commons and the three-month committee stage and it would also have avoided the need at subsequent meetings to start to negotiate that which they had just legislated which involved completely new legislation, a new second reading and a new committee stage. In fact a total of 94 changes were made to Mandelson's original plans.

"Can you tell me of any other government in the world that writes legislation, has it then changed by the minister responsible for implementing it, puts it through Parliament and within a short period of time has to re-legislate through the whole Parliamentary process because of misjudgement by the Secretary of State? The mind boggles."

During the Hillsborough talks Mallon had also become suspicious about another side deal on the flags issue. He summoned legal advisor Brian Barrington and told him to bring with him a copy of the Good Friday Agreement and the Northern Ireland Act drafted to implement it. A proposal on the flags issue was not in the published terms for the Hillsborough deal, but shortly afterwards Mallon and other nationalist and republican negotiators were angered when they learned in Parliament about the Secretary of State's draft order, which gave him the power to set regulations regarding flag-flying on government buildings.

Mandelson defended his order, saying he simply wanted to prevent a situation where the new administration spent months shadow-boxing on the issue. He promised to consult the restored Assembly and the Executive and to use his power only if there were no compromise. But nationalists claimed this would prevent any compromise as unionists could now rely on a sympathetic Secretary of State to order the flying of the flag. Within four months of this, Mandelson produced a draft regulation to require the Union flag to fly alongside the European flag for seventeen designated days each year. Sinn Féin unsuccessfully challenged this regulation in the courts, while Trimble said he made clear to the government that he would not return to power-sharing without this concession.

There was further consternation when the new Police Bill was published. Nationalists were outraged, complaining it was a radical departure from the Patten proposals. For example, Patten had recommended a new name for the new service, but under the Mandelson plan a final decision on the name of the police force was long-fingered until September 2001, when the new service was due to come into effect. The RUC name would survive until at least then, and the Secretary of State would at that point have the final decision on the new name, after consultation with the police board. This move followed a letter sent by Mandelson to the Unionist party, reassuring its members that the government did not intend to disband the RUC.

Even armed with these apparent concessions on flags and policing, Trimble's ability to win over his party remained in doubt. The UUC meeting was set for 20 May, but forty-eight hours beforehand it was postponed to allow the leader an extra week to sell the proposals to the members, who were also being wooed by the Donaldson faction. Donaldson queried the arms inspections, which critics dismissed as a fudge on actual decommissioning. He also said he did not want Martin McGuinness in charge of his children's education while the IRA still had weapons and refused to decommission them. Ian Paisley also attacked the "repugnant deal", while Trimble sought and won public assurances from the Prime Minister that inspections would not be regarded as a substitute for actual decommissioning. Republicans publicly warned the government to stand firm against unionist pressure for more concessions, or risk losing the deal.

At the UUC meeting, Trimble told his party that the IRA offer on arms inspections would not have been made without unionists standing firm on suspension and that it was right to put republicans to the test again. He warned of the consequences if the proposals were rejected: more Dublin involvement in Northern Ireland affairs and unionism sidelined. Trimble was speaking from the stage in the Waterfront Hall, which had been dressed for that evening's presentation of Verdi's *Aida*, an epic tale set in ancient Egypt exploring the themes of jealousy and treachery; the main character is buried alive in the end. The stage, then, was literally set for a showdown. Standing amid the props, Donaldson tried to sell his plan, which Trimble had dismissed as an unworkable unionist wish-list. It proposed that the Ulster Unionists should only re-enter the Executive after confirmation that the IRA had commenced credible and verifiable decommissioning with an agreed timetable. After a bruising clash with his leader, a surly-looking Donaldson emerged from the Hall having lost the vote by only the narrowest of margins; Trimble won 53% backing for his plan to return to devolved government. It was hardly ideal. Such a slim margin was bound to spell further instability given the weakness of the unionist leadership's position.

President Bill Clinton, who was looking forward to a return visit to the North on the back of the vote, declared: "The wind is back in the sails of peace in Northern Ireland." But Sinn Féin, and others, were bent on taking the wind out of Trimble's sails when they learned he had told reporters that republicans needed to be "house-trained" before they could become bona fide democrats. When asked if his language compared Sinn Féin to dogs, Trimble responded: "That's your language, not mine." Sinn Féin members were furious. Bairbre de Brun, backed by McGuinness, denounced the remarks as disgraceful. "They were sectarian and they were racist," she said.

The remarks signalled that in the restored government relations would be, at best, fractious. More seriously, so did the murder of Edd McCoy, an alleged drug dealer shot dead in a bar in Dunmurry. His murder would soon be attributed to the Provisional IRA, based on security forces' intelligence. McCoy was killed within twenty-four hours of the Ulster Unionists agreeing to go back into government – without decommissioning. It too was not a good omen. Nevertheless, despite the evidence of ongoing IRA activity – which was bound to undermine unionist support for power-sharing with republicans – Taoiseach Bertie Ahern declared that the Assembly was "back for good".

Chapter 18
Power-sharing Struggle

It was a great show of unity. In the November rain, the First and Deputy First Ministers posed for photographs on the west lawn of the Stormont estate beside a new bronze statue entitled "Reconciliation". Set in a water garden, the statue, depicting a man and woman kneeling with arms outstretched in a compassionate embrace, was the work of Spanish sculptor Josefina de Vasconcellos. The artist was inspired by a story she had heard of a husband and wife, separated by war, who had found each other after years of searching. Replicas could already be found on the Berlin Wall, in Hiroshima and amid the ruins of Coventry Cathedral, all casualties of war; another was destined for Jerusalem. The inscription read: "These sculptures remind us that human dignity and love will triumph over disaster and bring nations together in respect and peace."

David Trimble and Seamus Mallon were accepting the statue from the acting Dean of Coventry on behalf of the people of Northern Ireland. As part of the ceremony, international visitors from as far away as Japan, Germany and Israel were invited to toss pebbles from their countries into the water garden. Sheltering from the autumn downpour under a marquee, Trimble spoke of building mutual understanding and recalled the words of Senator George Mitchell: "Signing the Good Friday Agreement was difficult, but more difficult still will be implementing it." Mallon pointedly reminded everyone that reconciliation, real reconciliation, was no easy task, but a noble outcome when the complexities of history and humanity were addressed honestly.

Trimble and Mallon, who had been sharing power for six months, performed their duty impeccably. Only a few present knew the truth, what the body language and the lack of eye contact hinted at: that they were fuming with one another, had spent their time before the ceremony at loggerheads and would soon return to their entrenched disagreement. One Stormont official remembered fretting beforehand that the growing strains in their relationship would be laid bare and the carefully planned peace and reconciliation ceremony would be ruined: "I was nervous about was going to happen. But they were both very professional."

The two ministers were increasingly burdened by the pressures of their roles as they grappled with a rather cumbersome bureaucratic department, personality clashes and conflicts over arms and policing. Trimble grimaced at the memory of his strained relationship with Mallon at that point. "Walking on egg shells. Time and time again," he recalled.

The Executive and the other institutions had been restored in May amid deep divisions within the Ulster Unionist party. As summer turned to autumn, Trimble was determined to achieve decommissioning and retain his leadership, and therefore felt he had no choice but to act. Unhappy with progress on the arms issue, the First Minister, just a few days before the ceremony, had signalled he would no longer sign papers nominating Martin McGuinness and Bairbre de Brun to attend NSMC meetings, thereby blocking their attendance. His tactic caused ructions within the administration, which had so far survived a turbulent summer marked by another violent protest at Drumcree, heated rows over highly sensitive policing legislation, the Real IRA's targeting of police stations and a bloody loyalist feud. Trimble's ban on Sinn Féin was the most serious crisis to date, and one that anti-Agreement unionists were hoping to exploit.

Although Peter Robinson and Nigel Dodds had returned to their desks at the same time as the other ministers, the DUP had adopted a new strategy of rotating ministers and were issuing threats of "whistle-blowing", which the other parties feared might be potentially disruptive. Civil servants were caught in the middle of these warring ministers, causing problems for the new head of the civil service, Gerry Loughran, who had taken over when Sir John Semple retired.

Loughran must have wondered how the administration would survive. It met none of the established criteria for stable coalition government: not all the parties had bought into the power-sharing system, as evidenced by the DUP's position; the ministerial jobs had been allocated on party electoral strength rather than by the usual horse-trading and agreement; there was no effective form of discipline or whip; and there was no agreed programme of government. While some ministers had arrived with a clear idea of what they wanted to achieve, others were just finding their feet and it was going to take some months to agree the Executive programme. Graham Gudgin, the First Minister's economic advisor, remembered that Trimble would grumble about the lack of ideas coming from the civil service, but Gudgin felt some sympathy for the officials, who were unsure of the ideology of their new coalition masters and whether it was capitalist or socialist. "I remember one senior civil servant asking, 'Could you give us a steer?'"

In response to these problems, Loughran – a rather more imperious character than his predecessor – decided to give some direction on the new administration. He suggested that an agenda for government, summarising a few key goals, should be published while the draft programme was being devised. This was done relatively quickly and in the first six months of the Executive, despite all the strains and the fire-fighting that Trimble and Mallon had to do over issues in the wider process, the administration did move forward.

As unionist and nationalist working together, the First and Deputy First ministers became important, living symbols of reconciliation to the wider world, jointly attending events and welcoming dignitaries. Side by side, they greeted Prince Charles in Armagh and laughed along with the Dalai Lama in Belfast's Waterfront Hall. The Buddhist spiritual leader had presented both men with *katags*, traditional Tibetan scarves. They posed for a photograph with these marvellous white garments, as Trimble called them, wrapped around their shoulders. "Looking at the faces of Seamus and myself," said Trimble, "it's difficult to say which is displaying the most embarrassment."

Trimble and Mallon had also made a return visit to Brussels, along with the Finance minister Mark Durkan, and met with the President of the European Commission, Romano Prodi, and other powerful commissioners. The purpose of the visit was to finalise EU funding and secure extra money for Northern Ireland to cement its fledgling administration. Durkan recalled making valuable contacts there and the administration subsequently announced £940 million in peace-funding. But critics, including Ian Paisley, claimed the aid would have come anyway and was not tied to the trip. Brian Feeney, *The Irish News* columnist, concluded the point of the mission was "simply to show they could actually go together".

The First and Deputy First Ministers managed to compromise on the make-up of the Civic Forum, one of the Good Friday Agreement bodies, and declared devolution was working well. By the autumn they and the other ministers agreed and launched a legislative programme, a draft budget and Programme for Government. Although civil servants had a significant role to play in writing the draft Programme for Government, there was also input from the parties, ministers and their advisors, particularly Colm Larkin on the SDLP side and Graham Gudgin on the Ulster Unionist side. The four parties of government were lacking in well-developed election manifestos for the new coalition, but the weighty document that became the Programme for Government was criticised as being too detailed, idealistic and cumbersome. Acknowledging imperfections in the document one civil servant said: "It was a compromise, remember. With twelve ministers and eleven departments, everybody wanted their bit in. It was very difficult."

The important commitments on tackling issues such as planning backlogs were lost in the minutiae and it became difficult to measure the Executive's success. There was a plethora of targets, some related to items voters were unlikely to get exercised about. One, for example, pledged the Department of Environment to "capturing and providing all significant topographic changes into mapping databases". There was some innovation, too, but a more streamlined document with a just few pledges on roads, hospital waiting lists and schools would have been more relevant to the public and would have helped voters to determine whether the Executive was working for them. Sir Reg Empey regretted the way the programme turned out: "We should have taken six to eight themes and delivered them, instead we had pages and pages. It was crazy. It was too technical and too bureaucratic."

The civil service had heavily influenced the Programme for Government and Trimble recalled that it was not until the later stages of power-sharing that the administration began to develop clear thoughts of its own. "Part of the reason we wanted a Programme for Government was … to ensure ministers from different parties would stick to an agreement," he said. Yet despite its flaws, it was, in some ways, a remarkable feat to get consensus on it relatively quickly. One official said a lot of people should take credit for this, adding: "For the parties to agree a Programme for Government in such a short time and to manage the intricacies of the Treasury, to give Mark Durkan his due, and to cut deals across departments, it was a huge achievement."

Some Assembly members grumbled that the October draft Budget came a week before the draft Programme for Government, creating a "cart before the horse position". Seamus Close, the Alliance member, complained in the chamber: "It is like buying the bricks before the architect has completed the plans for the house." It was not intended that way and lessons were learned: the sequence was reversed the following year.

At the news conference to unveil the draft programme, Trimble and Mallon were disappointed with the media's response, which they regarded as nit-picking. They had already concluded that the media was too focused on the big controversial political issues and generally disinterested in, or ignorant of, the bread-and-butter issues. Trimble and Mallon had trouble getting reporters to stick to issues of Health or Education at the press conferences that followed Executive meetings; Trimble usually ended up fielding questions on his party's difficulties. In the months ahead, these media events were sharply curtailed. Trimble's conclusion that the media was not interested in bread-and-butter-issues was underscored during one election campaign when not a single reporter showed up to his party's news conference on Health: "If they had turned up, they would have got a good story because our health spokesman refused to attend. That was Martin Smyth [the anti-Agreement MP]."

Despite Mallon's annoyance over the media's response to the draft programme, he managed to recount a humorous tale at the press conference. He described how, during the Sunningdale regime, he had escorted Prime Minister Brian Faulkner out of the chamber just as another member was physically assaulting the Finance minister. Mallon, turning to Trimble, joked: "Whatever else has happened to the both us, we have not been hit yet."

However, the fledgling Executive was soon hit – by crisis. The Executive ministers discovered, to their cost, that the administration's foundations had been built on two massive faultlines: policing and decommissioning. The police reform envisaged in the Good Friday Agreement was slowly taking shape, but the whole issue was marked by stark differences of opinion and interpretation between nationalists and unionists. Trimble and Mallon embodied these differences as they individually lobbied Blair's government in a bid to influence the policing legislation that was going through the House of Commons. For Mallon, policing was a critical issue if Northern Ireland was to achieve stability, and he was determined to stamp his authority on the new arrangements. He wanted to ensure that Catholic nationalists joined the new service, believing this to be the key to a stable society. For his part, Trimble recognised the benefits of redressing the historic imbalance in the police force, but he was not prepared to pay any price for it. He feared that too much change would unsettle unionism and further erode confidence in the Good Friday Agreement. Nationalists felt Trimble and many unionists were in denial about the nature of the Agreement and the changes that had been agreed in exchange for nationalist support for policing.

Their lopsided enthusiasm for the reforms was illustrated when the Deputy First Minister, alone, put out a statement welcoming the appointment of a new police oversight commissioner, a post recommended by the controversial Patten Commission. Indeed, the cracks at the centre started to appear in the first week of the administration, when it was reported that both the First and Deputy First Ministers had threatened to quit their posts over the policing issue.

In July, *The Irish News* quoted Labour sources as saying that David Trimble had threatened to resign as First Minister over the title of the police. This was true, but when contacted Trimble deflected the story with a claim that he understood it was Seamus Mallon who had threatened to resign. Mallon, aware that Trimble had vowed to quit, vehemently denied he had done so. When rumours persisted, Mallon issued a very public rebuke to Trimble, via an official statement from the Office of First and Deputy First Minister: "I am surprised that David Trimble has been drawn into disseminating stories which are completely untrue."

This episode was related to a political tug of war between the First and Deputy First Minister on the name of the police force, in the course of which Mallon became embroiled in a very public confrontation in the House of Commons with Secretary of State Peter Mandelson. At the Policing Bill's third reading, Mallon was furious because an amendment he had been promised was killed when the Parliamentary guillotine cut short a late Commons session. He had been assured that his amendment, dealing with the name of the police force, would be put into the legislation. This was to supersede a change that the Ulster Unionists had won during the committee stage, prior to the restoration of devolution, which clearly linked the RUC to the new police service and was designed to keep the old title alive. The SDLP accepted the RUC title being recorded in legislation, but wanted to ensure the name was consigned to history. Accordingly, Mallon's amendment made clear that the RUC title could not be used for operational purposes and defined such purposes. The SDLP feared a Derry/Londonderry situation developing over the name of the North's police force.

While Mallon was in Parliament, focusing on pushing his amendment through, Trimble got wind of the SDLP's plan and immediately went to see the Prime Minister, telling him very firmly: "Look, we made a deal on this and if you rat on me, we are away." The amendment was pulled. The first Mallon knew of this decision was on the floor of the Commons when the guillotine came down without his amendment passing. Rounding on Mandelson he barely concealed his contempt. Hansard reports the following quote: "I have seen much political chicanery on the issue. This is the third time that the Secretary of State has made deals and on the name of the police service…" Reflecting later on these events, Mallon stuck by his denial that he had threatened to quit and declared: "Blair was turned and Mandelson was already turned."

Trimble, on the other hand, felt it was the Deputy First Minister who was the guilty party and blamed Mallon for the episode, claiming he had ignored the fact that Ulster Unionists had returned to government on the condition of their amendment passing. But Mallon would insist he had not signed up to a position that would have left the operational name of the police unchanged. Trimble also suspected the SDLP was using policing as a battleground to show it was "greener" than Sinn Féin on the issue. "Instead of seeing this as a new dispensation in which they were going to work cooperatively with unionists, it was going to be a continuing of war against unionism by another means," he said.

Mallon found such accusations deeply offensive and wholly illogical. In a series of interviews soon after the confrontation in Parliament, he warned that failure to implement the Patten recommendations in full would have a very damaging effect on the whole psyche of the political process, the future of policing and nationalists' attitude towards the administration. "Government by consent requires policing by consent," he said. "The two cannot be divorced."

Mallon had worked hard to change the Policing Bill as soon as it was unveiled by the Secretary of State. He accused Mandelson of destroying Patten's recommendations and gutting the Bill. In discussions with the Secretary of State and others, Mallon insisted that the Bill, as it stood, was unacceptable. Mallon's legal advisor, Brian Barrington, who worked closely with the Deputy First Minister on the policing issue, was full of admiration, saying: "Mallon took no shit from Mandelson at all. We had [security minister] Adam Ingram telling us one thing and Mandelson telling us another." Barrington recalled Mallon being particularly disgusted when Mandelson suggested during one meeting that the SDLP would be on a par with Sinn Féin if it rejected the new policing service. Mallon, who held a deep contempt for Sinn Féin, was extremely insulted and leapt up from the table, furious, and indignant. The officials were sent out of the room, but one or two hovered near the door, listening to Mandelson and Mallon shout at each other.

While unionists generally regarded Mandelson as a sympathetic Secretary of State, Mallon and others in the SDLP could not stand him. In one meeting with the SDLP's Bríd Rodgers and Alex Attwood, the Secretary of State lost patience when a discussion on human rights veered onto the parades issue. As Attwood made his point, Mandelson became more impatient and, it was claimed, told his SDLP guests he was an important and busy man and if Attwood persisted in speaking to him in this way, he would have to send him down the hall to speak to his little dog, Bobby. Attwood refused to back down and when Mandelson repeated his line about being both important and busy, Attwood suggested that if he were so important, then he would have to call time on the meeting. At that point, Mandelson snapped, "Get out!" As Attwood and his colleague exited, Attwood heard Mandelson mutter that they had a lot to learn and shot back, "You have got a lot to learn, too."

Mallon particularly disliked Mandelson and could not understand the Prime Minister's faith in him, particularly after he had landed the government in so much bother over the Millenium Dome, at the time a troubled, controversial, debt-ridden New Labour project with which Mandelson had been closely associated when he was minister without portfolio. Curious about the relationship, Mallon observed Blair and Mandelson closely at the inaugural meeting of the BIC in London in December 1999. They and the other ministers were relaxing over lunch and it was the first time Mallon had seen the pair interact in a social context. "It was a joke," said Mallon. "And it wasn't a matter of Mandelson fawning over Blair. It was the opposite almost."

Mallon's hostility to Mandelson had grown stronger since then, mainly due to the problems of flags and policing. In a strange way, Mallon enjoyed battling with him. One of the young Turks in the SDLP nicknamed the Deputy First Minister "Gandalf", after the white-haired character in *The Lord of the Rings* who was very clever at confronting his enemies. A SDLP source recalled: "Mallon used to do this Gandalf thing in Mandelson's office. Mandelson hated cigarettes and Seamus would smoke in a way that only Seamus can. He would derive five times more smoke from one cigarette than any other mortal."

Eventually, Mallon would by-pass Mandelson and go straight to the Prime Minister. He vividly remembered knocking on the door of Chequers, the Prime Minister's country residence one Sunday morning, ready to complain about the Secretary of State. Mallon said he told the Prime Minister: "This fellow is going to destroy policing if you let him. He will destroy you on policing if you let him and he will destroy us on policing if you let him."

A SDLP source, recalling the Deputy First Minister's dogged determination, said:

The way they were. The first image of the power-sharing
Executive on devolution day, 2 December 1999. The
ministers are joined by the head of the civil service Sir
John Semple (far right).
(Picture: Paul Faith, courtesy of Irish News)

The SDLP's Carmel Hanna, MLA
for South Belfast, who succeeded
Sean Farren as Minister of
Employment and Learning.
(Picture: courtesy of Irish News)

The SDLP Agriculture minister
Bríd Rodgers with the Irish
Foreign Minister Brian Cowen
TD and her party leader MEP
John Hume, attending a
conference on the European Union
at the City Hotel, Derry.
(Picture: Margaret McLaughlin)

"The Brawl in the Hall" – A DUP man stands between Ian Paisley Jr and Mitchel McLaughlin (Sinn Féin MLA) and Alasdair McDonnell (SDLP MLA) as the DUP leader Ian Paisley looks on. (Picture: Bill Smyth)

The First Minister David Trimble does his best to ignore the cat-calling that descended into the "brawl in the hall" after his election as Deputy First Minister alongside Mark Durkan in November 2001. (Picture: Bill Smyth)

*Secretary of State John Reid and his new ministers Angela Smith and Des Browne
leave a press conference at Hillsborough after direct rule was announced in
October 2002. (Picture: Hugh Russell)*

*Sinn Féin Health minister Bairbre de Brun and North Belfast MLA Gerry Kelly in their
party offices with reporters during the "Stormontgate" raid by police. (Picture: Hugh Russell)*

Sinn Féin Education minister Martin McGuinness leaves Belfast High Court during a legal battle with the First Minister David Trimble. (Picture: Hugh Russell)

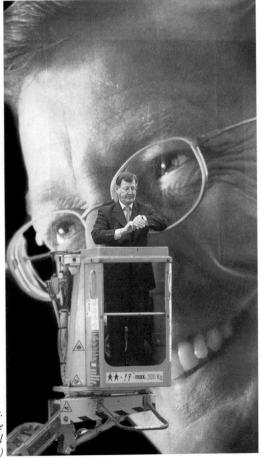

Watching his back.
The Ulster Unionist leader David Trimble launches his 2001 election poster at the Glengall Street headquarters. (Picture: Ann McManus)

The Sinn Féin leader Gerry Adams chats with the Ulster Unionist Enterprise minister Sir Reg Empey in the Cultúrlann as Janet Muller looks on. It was Sir Reg's first ministerial visit to the Falls Road. (Picture: Brendan Murphy)

Deputy First Minister Seamus Mallon in St James' Church of Ireland church hall on the Antrim Road. (Picture: Brendan Murphy)

The SDLP minister for Employment and Learning Sean Farren pictured at the Millfield site for the new Further Education College in Belfast.
(Picture: Niall Carson)

DUP leader Ian Paisley with a groundbreaking Sinn Féin statement calling on the IRA to put its weapons beyond use in October 2001.
(Picture: Ann McManus)

US President George W Bush greets First and Deputy First Ministers David Trimble and Mark Durkan at Speaker's Lunch, Capitol Hill, March 2002. (Picture: John Harrison)

Ulster Unionist Sports minister Michael McGimpsey on the speed ball at the Lisburn Boxing Club. (Picture: John F. Kelly)

Ulster Unionist Environment minister Sam Foster surveys Black Mountain with the West Belfast MP and Sinn Féin leader Gerry Adams. (Picture: Brendan Murphy)

Sinn Féin Education minister Martin McGuinness hands out diplomas to school children at the Bunscoil in Twinbrook in West Belfast. (Picture: Brendan Murphy)

"Mallon was very clear that without a new name, new badge and no union flag, you were never going to convince nationalists it was a new police service. He made that point again and again. But the British were under pressure because the unionists were so opposed to this."

Barry Turley, former SDLP director of communications, believed policing was the issue that caused the most damage to the relationship at the centre of the administration: "David Trimble and Seamus Mallon had a reasonable relationship in the early days because they both wanted it to work. Policing killed it – killed it. Policing broke any possibility of the centre ground holding."

Tension over policing was raging when the First and Deputy First Minister travelled to Washington that autumn for a three-day trip. They met with President Clinton at the White House on 13 September and discussed a range of issues, including policing. Mallon described it as a "bad meeting". He said he sat for a while in the Oval Office saying nothing while David Trimble gave a "dissertation" on the policing issue. "Clinton started to get an historical analysis of it all from Trimble," said Mallon. "And then at one point I said, 'Hold on lads, I am here and here is what I want to say.' You could see the colour going from [Trimble's] face and he made a number of attempts to [interrupt] and I said, 'Sorry, I'm not finished yet, you sit there until I am finished. You sit there until I have had my say, you have had your say.'"

In a lighter moment, Trimble and Mallon, knowing the President was anxious to return to Northern Ireland, thanked him for his support and invited him back. He privately accepted and plans were quietly put in place for the President's return.

Back home, there was a more immediate problem on the horizon. David Trimble faced a crucial test of his party's strength in a by-election following the death of Clifford Forsythe, Ulster Unionist MP for South Antrim. The DUP traditionally did not contest the safe Ulster Unionist seat, but the Agreement had shifted the sands in unionism and the party boldly parachuted former Mid-Ulster MP Willie McCrea into the constituency. Trimble's advisor, David Campbell, sought the Ulster Unionist nomination but lost to David Burnside, who no longer supported the Good Friday Agreement. With Burnside's selection, voters were effectively being asked to choose between two anti-Agreement unionist candidates. Ulster Unionists feared pro-Agreement unionists would stay home while anti-Agreement unionists would plump for the more united DUP. On the campaign trail in Glengormley, a man in a tracksuit and slippers summed up the party's dilemma when he hissed "traitor" at Trimble and derided Burnside as the "yes–no man".

Amid fears about the result, Mandelson produced his controversial draft regulation that required the Union flag to be flown on government buildings on seventeen designated days per year, angering the SDLP and Sinn Féin. The flags decision did not appear to have had much effect on the by-election result, however. The DUP snatched the seat on a low turnout, rocking both wings of the Ulster Unionist party and precipitating yet another challenge to Trimble's power-sharing policies. Policing, according to the DUP, had been a pressing issue on the doorsteps. Trimble said the result should be a wake-up call for the government, the SDLP, Sinn Féin and others over policing. In a message to nationalists, he said: "It is time they carried the weight instead of carelessly and needlessly throwing the burden to us."

At the Labour party conference in Brighton, Trimble again issued a stern warning that the Agreement was under real threat and could collapse in the face of nationalist demands on policing. But the SDLP continued to insist that policing had to change, while Sinn Féin argued that Patten was the compromise on its demand for the RUC to be disbanded. Like Mallon and his party, Sinn Féin and the IRA were studying the Policing Bill closely. The republican movement was deeply unhappy with the shape of the Bill and this began to threaten the deal on arms reached at Hillsborough in May. The restoration deal required a second arms inspection in September 2000, but republicans accused the British of failing to honour its pledges on policing. Concerns grew that the IRA was going to block a second arms inspection as a consequence.

Against this backdrop, anti-Agreement forces both inside and outside the Ulster Unionist party stepped up pressure on Trimble. The DUP prepared to table a motion of no-confidence in the First Minister in the hopes of chipping away at his power-base, while Trimble's internal party critics, led by Jeffrey Donaldson, organised another extraordinary meeting of the UUC. Speaking after a Stormont Executive meeting, David Trimble said he would not be panicked by the claims of an impending challenge, but others in the party expected him to react once again to the Paisley and Donaldson agendas. At the news conference reporters could not help but notice the tension between Trimble and Mallon. This followed the atmosphere noted at the second NSMC meeting in Dublin a few days earlier, where reporters felt there was a distinct chill in the air between the two men. At Stormont, a journalist suggested the pair were not getting along. Trimble said the issue was irrelevant to getting the job done and totally irrelevant to the business of the press conference, which was supposed to focus on Executive business, including the legislative programme. Mallon weakly laughed off suggestions their relationship was suffering: "Everybody seems to be drawing that conclusion." The lack of denial convinced reporters that the strained body language was an accurate reflection of a strained relationship.

Mark Durkan remembered that around that time insiders started to joke: "They're a bit like Bill and Hillary Clinton, they get along better in public than in private." Once, when Durkan was alone with President Clinton, waiting to take part in some event, the President raised the subject of Trimble and Mallon's difficult relationship. Durkan was about to repeat the joke – but bit his tongue when he remembered to whom he was speaking. But in an interview for this book, Trimble insisted it was not all bad. Joking that there were worse marriages, he added: "We had our ups and downs and we communicated and we worked together and sometimes there was a bit of tension in the relationship."

The reasons for this tension were complex, but it infected relations across the centre of the administration. Similarly, infighting in the Ulster Unionist party infected the Executive. Thirty-seven days after the South Antrim by-election and just weeks before policing legislation was due to pass, David Trimble faced Donaldson in another political duel over guns and government. It was preceded by a divisive party conference, during which Trimble was heckled as he stood in front of the conference banner, "Making Government Work". Trimble responded to his critics that day, saying there was no unionist utopia and warning dissidents to stop undermining the party, its leadership and its decisions. They took no heed. Republicans also did their bit to undermine the unionist leader when they murdered dissident republican John Joe O'Connor just days before the

UUC meeting. The Ballymurphy man was linked to the Real IRA and his murder was widely attributed to the Provisional IRA. The IRA denied involvement, but in the immediate aftermath Sinn Féin refused to condemn the killing. Whether the murder of O'Connor was a deliberate attempt by the republican leadership to further destabilise unionism or a coincidence of events stemming from friction between the Provisionals and the Real IRA is a matter of conjecture.

The IRA did, however, allow a second arms inspection just a few days before the UUC was due to meet. The IRA leadership also pledged to resume contact with the IICD once it was satisfied that the peace process would be advanced by such talks. The Trimble camp had mixed views on the move. On the one hand, they considered it a well-timed stunt to prevent the IRA from receiving the blame for the collapse of power-sharing. On the other, the Ulster Unionist leadership was able to point to some progress on the arms issue. Putting a positive spin on the move in a BBC "Newsnight" interview, Trimble said, "If, during the summer of 1940, Herr Hitler had said to Mr Churchill, 'You can send a team of inspectors to have a look at our arsenal', people would have thought that was a significant step." But he still faced complaints from Donaldson and his supporters that there was no detail on the number and amount of weapons that had been inspected. Donaldson wrote to members of the UUC seeking support for his motion to quit power-sharing by November 30 if there were no IRA decommissioning. Trimble dismissed the Donaldson motion as "a letter to Santa", and accused anti-Agreement unionists of undermining attempts to secure decommissioning.

On the eve of the conference, the Prime Minister visited Belfast in an attempt to shore up the unionist leadership once more. The First Minister, along with Mallon and Sir Reg Empey, toured the Harland and Wolff shipyard. Tony Blair confirmed that the shipyard, located in unionist-dominated east Belfast, would receive a Ministry of Defence contract to help secure its future. The £80 million order for two new vessels followed intensive lobbying by the Ulster Unionist Enterprise minister, Sir Reg Empey. The hope was that the good news would demonstrate the effectiveness of devolution. Earlier in the week Blair's government had moved again to satisfy unionists by actually passing the flags legislation it had previously promised.

Republicans insisted the IRA was in no mood to offer anything more on the arms issue at a time when the government was passing legislation on the Union flag, legislation that nationalists regarded as a breach of the Agreement. Gerry Adams claimed the Blair government had lost the plot over flags and policing and had failed to honour the agreed terms on demilitarisation. Following restoration of the Executive, republicans were annoyed when the Army checkpoint on the border at Cloghogue was removed, but surveillance equipment remained. In these uncertain circumstances, Adams was not going to throw away his best negotiating card.

On the unionist side the flags legislation provided little more than a fig-leaf for Trimble, whose deputy, John Taylor, was predicting that devolution would be over by Christmas. While Trimble wanted, and needed, a short-time frame for decommissioning, the IRA perhaps needed, and certainly wanted, to play it long. In a bid to avoid a damaging split and the loss of his leadership, Trimble attempted an eleventh-hour compromise with Jeffrey Donaldson, but he rejected Trimble's plan and once again the Council backed its leader by a narrow margin. Trimble emerged with 54% backing: hardly a massive vote of confidence. The UUC also decided to review the situation in the New Year.

Trimble had promised a comprehensive and phased response to the IRA's failure to decommission. He also demanded a more pro-active arms commission, deadlines for progress, a timetable for decommissioning and a moratorium on policing changes until peace was assured. Most crucially, in the absence of "reasonable" progress on decommissioning he intended to fulfil his threat to ban Sinn Féin from NSMC meetings. At the time he denied that he was bounced into this tactic by hardliners, claiming he would have implemented the ban anyway. Whatever the truth, a huge rift opened in the power-sharing Executive, precipitating what one nationalist termed "a slow death".

Mallon was apoplectic about Trimble's move to ban Sinn Féin, which he regarded as an attack on the Agreement and a deliberate provocation to nationalists. He condemned the ban and insisted there were no grounds for it and that the timing and methodology of decommissioning was a matter for the IICD. "These are not matters the Ulster Unionist Council can determine," he asserted. An angry Gerry Adams insisted his ministers did not need a note from Trimble to attend a meeting, and went on to say that Trimble had painted himself into Donaldson's corner. Some nationalists, already deeply suspicious of Trimble's aims, claimed this was his exit strategy from an administration he did not like, while avoiding blame. While the British and Irish governments engaged in crisis talks, Mallon demanded an immediate emergency meeting of the power-sharing Executive. This demand was backed by five other nationalist ministers, but Trimble refused, further infuriating Mallon.

Within days, on 3 November, Health Minister Bairbre de Brun, who had dubbed Trimble's actions anti-democratic and discriminatory, was scheduled to attend a NSMC food safety and health meeting in Enniskillen, along with the Dublin's Health minister Micheal Martin. De Brun accused the First Minister of playing politics with Health as the Enniskillen meeting had been called to discuss cancer services, public health and the use of emergency services across the island. A food safety campaign promoting the benefits of folic acid in combating *spina bifida* was also to be launched on the same day. The ministers intended to set the seal on the first meeting of the new all-Ireland Food Safety body and months of work had gone into the event. De Brun was determined it should proceed, even if it was on an unofficial basis, and Mallon concurred. In a blatant rebuke to Trimble's policy, Mallon issued a press statement announcing he would be attending: "I must protect the integrity and operation of these institutions."

The Irish government wanted to show solidarity with other nationalists, but at the same time was careful not to provoke David Trimble further. After discussing the issue at a Cabinet meeting, Taoiseach Bertie Ahern decided to send Micheal Martin to the meeting in Enniskillen. Dublin described the decision as a professional gesture rather than a defiant one. Trimble, however, hinted that he had made sure there would be no more such meetings after this one: "Had the Irish gone further … it might well have imperilled the NSMC."

In the absence of a unionist minister present, the meeting did not have the status of an NSMC meeting, but the launch was accomplished and a number of research papers on further cooperation were commissioned. Seamus Mallon sat through the event unsmiling and grim-faced. Afterwards he called on the Secretary of State to use his powers to intervene in the dispute and direct the First Minister to sign the nomination papers. De Brun did not rule out legal action; within days the party confirmed it was taking the matter to the courts.

There were renewed concerns of a second suspension in the New Year, but in the meantime the ministers went about their duties as best they could. Trimble and Mallon appeared together for Ministers' Question Time on the same day they launched the "Reconciliation" statue. The custom was that the First and Deputy First Minister sit together in the chamber and answer questions in turn. To facilitate this very public display of solidarity, they would alternate the side of the chamber on which they sat: first, David Trimble would join the SDLP benches, then on the next occasion Seamus Mallon would sit with the Ulster Unionists. It was at times like this, when the DUP were trying to undermine the Executive, that Trimble and Mallon found a common bond against a common enemy and officials observed that they would try to help one another out. Mindful of the row over the NSMC nominations, Sammy Wilson, DUP MLA for East Antrim, poked fun at the relationship between the two ministers, saying: "It's nice to see that the First Minister Mr Trimble and the Deputy First Minister Mr Mallon have kissed and made up and are now so happy together again." Equally sarcastic, Mallon responded, "I'm glad the Assembly Member recognises that the First Minister and I have a very good personal relationship. I'm also glad he recognises that within a political process there will be a divergence of opinion."

That divergence was most evident later that week behind closed doors in Room 21 when the Executive met for the first time since the First Minister had imposed his sanctions on Sinn Féin. Before going into the meeting, Sinn Féin Education Minister Martin McGuinness, in bullish form, insisted it would not be business as usual. On that point he had an ally in the Deputy First Minister. One SDLP source, recalling that Mallon played an important role, said: "He tried to ensure fair play even though he had no particular love for Sinn Féin. He ensured things were played right and he was meticulous about that."

The SDLP had formed the view that the First Minister, in correspondence, would avoid referring to the Sinn Féin Health and Education ministers, if he could. One SDLP source remembered: "He sometimes liked to get rid of references to Bairbre de Brun or Martin McGuinness. Mallon would never allow that. Trimble essentially wanted the Executive to be a coalition between the SDLP and the UUP. Mallon never bought that. He always tried to ensure de Brun, in particular, was treated fairly." Throughout the period of the ban Mallon would continue the ritual of signing nomination papers and pointedly send them to the First Minister's office for his signature. They never came back.

The official statement after the Executive meeting dealing with the ban was the height of understatement, suggesting there had been a "comprehensive exchange of views" on the NSMC. "Full and frank" was another anodyne description. "There was a little heat in that discussion," was how Trimble put it. Mallon did not recall a lot of what was said, but did remember it was a "tough meeting" with plenty of "squeaking" from Martin McGuinness as he tackled the First Minister. One insider recalled de Brun getting stuck into Trimble: "Bairbre nearly always took the lead and Bairbre in particular got somewhat heated on that." *The Irish News* reported that shouting could be heard from inside the room, but McGuinness said he could not recall losing his temper and insisted he merely expressed his views in a forthright manner: "Obviously, we made a case at the table, but it was done in a very civilised fashion." McGuinness was particularly annoyed as the ban was jeopardising decisions with Dublin, including proposals to tackle autism through a centre of excellence and a cross-border study on the link between social deprivation and underachievement.

Mallon continued his attacks on David Trimble at his party's annual conference in Newcastle later that month, describing the sanction as a body-blow to the institutions. He demanded that the sanction be lifted and told the IRA to re-engage with the decommissioning body and to stop using it as a bargaining chip in the process. He said space had to be created for the institutions to flourish. Appealing to the Ulster Unionists to commit fully to the institutions, Mallon urged the governments to carry the burden for the arms issue. He also declared his party's willingness to sign up to policing, if it was workable. This, he said, was up to the British government.

While the Secretary of State had told unionists he would press ahead with reforming the RUC, nationalists were still not satisfied that he was meeting the Patten requirements. The SDLP refused to support the Bill when it went through its final stage in the Commons on 30 November, delaying an historic breakthrough on policing that would continue to plague the political process. Although disappointed by the Bill, Mallon held hours of tough negotiations with the Prime Minister at Downing Street and said he would reserve judgement on the issue until he had seen the Police Implementation Plan. The Deputy First Minister felt he was making some headway in the run-up to Clinton's visit, which was to be a lap of honour for the outgoing President who once again wanted to put his seal of approval on the restored Executive, however beleaguered.

Both unionists and republicans tried to win Clinton's sympathy before he arrived at Stormont on 13 December. The IRA issued a statement insisting it was still committed to putting weapons beyond use, but not on British or unionist terms. David Trimble wrote a letter to President Clinton explaining why sanctions were necessary. Stormont's Great Hall was packed for his visit, even anti-Agreement unionists were in attendance, ready to press their case. Clinton worked the room, greeting members of each of the various parties, who stood in small clusters around the hall. Earlier, Sinn Féin had brought the former IRA veteran Joe Cahill into the hall to greet the President who had famously granted him a visa, paving the way for the IRA ceasefire. The President had balked when shown Cahill's *curriculum vitae*, which included a jail sentence for smuggling IRA arms and a conviction for murdering a RUC officer. Then Taoiseach, Albert Reynolds, who was pressing Cahill's case for a visa, reputedly said to Clinton: "What did you expect – a parish priest?" This time, Sinn Féin's plan to unite Cahill with Clinton was thwarted following a complaint that the old republican was not an Assembly Member; he was duly asked to leave. Undaunted, Cahill's friends shortly afterwards steered the President into a separate chamber where the pair were photographed shaking hands and exchanging reminiscences.

The DUP had an animated conversation with the Secretary of State, who was asked by Ian Paisley Jr why he was not wearing the "Save the RUC" badge he had been given by the party. Mandelson said he kept it pinned on the mirror in his bedroom. Peter Robinson then inquired how often the Secretary of State looked in the mirror. "Quite frequently,"

Mandelson replied. Ian Paisley good-naturedly pinned another RUC badge onto the Secretary of State's lapel. It was not the last time the badge came under scrutiny in this way. In 2002, when the Queen and the Duke of Edinburgh visited Assembly members in the Great Hall, the DUP's Jim Shannon was proudly wearing a similar "Save the RUC" badge, even though the force had been renamed and replaced with the new Police Service of Northern Ireland (PSNI). Bending down to get a closer look at the pin, Prince Philip looked up and declared: "Too late!"

For the Clinton visit, the main event was a keynote address by the President at the Odyssey Arena in Belfast, but behind the scenes a problem was unfolding. The President's schedule was running around an hour late and the First Minister was getting anxious because he had to catch a plane in London to make his connecting flight to Rome. He was due to attend an international conference in Palermo on tackling organised crime. He was also going to receive the Freedom of Palermo. Mallon, who had travelled to the Odyssey with Trimble and grabbed a coffee and a sandwich with him beforehand, had gleaned that the First Minister intended to leave the ceremony early rather than miss his flight. Mallon was horrified and told him: "You can't do it. You cannot get off the stage with the President of the United States in these circumstances."

Trimble insisted he had to go and had already explained the matter to both the President and the Prime Minister. Tony Blair, who was due to join the President on stage, also tried to dissuade him, even offering him a lift on his plane back to England. But Trimble thought this a "cloud-cuckoo-land idea" because he would not have arrived at Heathrow Airport on time, so he politely declined the Prime Minister's offer. Mallon recalled Blair coming up to him before the ceremony began. "Do you know about this?" Blair asked. Mallon said he did and that he had tried to persuade Trimble to stay, to no avail. According to Mallon the Prime Minister then uttered his disapproval at Trimble's plans: "'Stupid, stupid,' Blair kept saying to me *sotto voce*. And he said, 'He won't do it. He'll have more sense'." Mallon, who by now had a fair idea of how Trimble's mind worked, contradicted the Prime Minister: "You better believe it, mate. He'll do it."

Blair went on stage hopeful that he was right and Mallon was wrong. There were three chairs on the platform for the Prime Minister, Trimble and Mallon during Clinton's address, which was the last of the afternoon. From the audience Trimble's aide, David Kerr, watched anxiously as he saw his leader get increasingly fidgety and constantly check his watch. By now Clinton was in full flow, pressing the people of Northern Ireland to continue with the peace process, telling them how important it was for trouble spots around the world. But Kerr was distracted, watching his boss and all he could think was: "Don't do it. Don't do it."

Kerr, who was sitting with a party colleague, kept checking his own watch and muttered to his colleague: "He's going to get up. He's going to get up here. Please don't stand up. Please don't stand up." He spotted Trimble's close protection officer in the corner of the stage, waiting for the unionist leader to exit, if he wanted. Kerr retained vivid memories of Trimble's next move: "[David] sort of leans forward and sort of gestures to Blair, who is looking straight on, stony-faced as if he would kill Trimble if he got up." According to one source, an Ulster Unionist was watching the proceedings on television and, knowing Trimble was late for a plane, turned to his colleague and joked how it would be just like

Trimble to walk off the stage. "How embarrassing would that be?" he asked.

Not long after that, Trimble did get up and slip discreetly off the stage, leaving an empty chair behind while Clinton, who had earlier made a point about the importance of seizing the moment, was still talking. Kerr was appalled: "It was just bloody awful." Kerr was inundated with calls from reporters trying to find out what happened to Trimble. He laughed at the memory of it, although he was not amused at the time. Neither, according to Mallon, were some of the American Democrats backstage, who felt their President had been insulted. "They went spare. Absolutely bloody spare," he said. Mallon remembered being asked to go and calm some of Clinton's entourage. Trying to be sympathetic, Mallon commented: "'What the hell is he going to a conference in Sicily about the Mafia for?' And it was only then they found out why he was leaving." That made them even madder, said Mallon, who also recalled the President coming over and saying in a barbed way: "Not very popular today, am I?"

At the time, Trimble was taken aback as to why everyone was so upset. He had told the President beforehand that he had to leave. A source close to the UUP leader said: "He couldn't understand why people reacted the way they did. As far as he was concerned, if he had an appointment, he had to go, no matter what." Trimble admitted, in retrospect, that he should have announced to the audience that he was leaving and explained why. Mallon insisted that this would have been even more insulting to the President: "Oh, that would have been much worse!"

Trimble's dash to the airport was swift and within minutes of leaving the stage he had obtained his boarding pass and had been shuttled across the tarmac to the plane where he leapt up the stairs with the door closing behind him. "It was that tight," he said. Recalling the events, Trimble then ventured: "Do you know what the irony about this was? We got to Heathrow on time for the connection but the flight was two hours late."

Trimble insisted that his visit to Palermo was important because he made contact with a member of the Catholic clergy from Scotland, which led to members of the SDLP and other leading Catholics from Northern Ireland being invited to Gleneagles to discuss issues around crime and policing. "It was a worthwhile exercise," he maintained.

With Clinton coming and going with no apparent breakthroughs, Christmas 2000 became the new deadline to try to break the deadlock over arms and policing. There was, however, some good news emanating from Stormont, related to an initiative on the homeless. The SDLP's Barry Turley had been speaking to a homeless charity about the cost of ensuring that not a single person was sleeping rough on the street over the holidays. He went to colleague Damien McAteer, special advisor to the Finance minister Mark Durkan, and secured funding for the initiative. Turley believed it should have received more attention than it actually got: "The media were too obsessed with fights over things like Easter lilies to really notice."

Christmas came and went without any comfort for the politicians, either. No one was surprised when the talks broke up amid acrimony on 21 December. The Executive's problems once again spilled into the New Year.

Chapter 19
Caught in the Middle

Sir Christopher Meyer, the British Ambassador to Washington DC, had issued invitations to the city's political elite for a St Patrick's Day luncheon he was hosting. Everything was beautifully organised, but there was an embarrassing problem: only the First Minister's name featured on the invitations as an honoured guest; the Deputy First Minister's name had been omitted. It was a common error. Many outside the administration naturally assumed that the First Minister was the leader of Stormont's power-sharing Executive and that the Deputy First Minister was his number two. It was a problem that recurred throughout the lifetime of the Executive, and it never failed to raise hackles.

When the legislation defining their roles, first outlined in the Good Friday Agreement, was drawn up, the Irish government ensured the ministers were equal in law. According to a Dublin official: "Every time the First Minister was mentioned in the [Northern Ireland] Act, we made sure the Deputy First Minister was mentioned as well. David Trimble had no more power than Seamus Mallon." And so "jointery" was born, the rule that the First and Deputy First Minister of Northern Ireland were joined in decision-making and neither could hold office alone.

As far as Seamus Mallon was concerned, the two ministers were like Siamese twins: one could not move without the other. From the beginning he always made sure this dual status was reflected in every detail, not least the correspondence. After being installed in office in 1998, Mallon was annoyed to find letters of congratulations and other correspondence coming into the Office of First and Deputy First Minister addressed only to the First Minister. Whitehall officials in London, used to dealing with both a Prime Minister and a Scottish First Minister who had a more junior deputy, had to be educated on Northern Ireland's power structure. These officials were regularly asked to issue correspondence to both ministers. Even the office of the deputy Prime Minister, John Prescott, made the mistake.

At Stormont, the Deputy First Minister's Office was not content that the same letter be copied to it. Knowing how strongly Mallon felt about the issue, officials would politely request that the letter be re-sent in the correct format, addressed to both ministers. Mallon suspected that some in the British system deliberately ignored his right to be treated equally, which made him doubly determined to have his place. His suspicion was fuelled when the mistake was repeated well into the life of the administration. "Sometimes it was down to a lack of understanding," Mallon admitted, "[but] one or two occasions – and I'm not talking about John Prescott – it was quite deliberate." According to a senior source in the civil service, the UK system struggled with the concept of jointery and tended to regard Trimble as the main person in the administration: "Three years after devolution we were still writing to departments telling them they had to write to both the First and Deputy First Ministers. But the biggest problem was Number 10, they related exclusively to Trimble."

When the Ambassador's invitation to the Washington event arrived without the Deputy First Minister being mentioned, it was up to Gerry Loughran to inform Mallon of the oversight. Mallon seemed to take it in his stride. "That's grand," he said. "I am quite looking forward to getting a browse around Georgetown." Loughran, no doubt anticipating some trouble, was confused by his response and asked, "What do you mean?" Mallon repeated that he would be browsing around Georgetown – an upmarket district in Washington DC – adding, "I'll tell you what's more, most of the Irish-American lobby on the Hill will be browsing around Georgetown as well." The implied boycott alarmed Loughran, who feared the event could turn into a public relations disaster. He explained how it was too late to fix the invitations, that it was a genuine oversight and how dreadful Sir Christopher Meyer felt that the British embassy had made such an error. Mallon, a skilled poker player who knew when to play hard, when to bluff and when to quit, eventually gave in and attended the event. However, on his arrival at the ambassador's residence, he was greeted by Sir Christopher who, according to an observer, was suitably repentant, while Mallon was suitably forgiving. A witness to the meal that followed, in which Trimble and Mallon joined the ambassador at the head table, observed the tension, from starter to dessert, between the First and Deputy First Ministers. He remarked afterwards: "I've never seen such hatred over lunch."

Just like many a bride and groom, Trimble and Mallon had quickly discovered they had different ideas about the nature of their political marriage, their roles and precisely what was meant by "equality". A pattern had been set during the shadow period whereby Trimble would, on occasion, behave like a Prime Minister and Mallon would feel bound to object. "That was a constant issue for Seamus, trying to keep Trimble in check," said SDLP colleague, Mark Durkan. One insider recalled that the First Minister would send out memos to civil servants which had not been cleared by Mallon or sent on a joint basis. The Deputy First Minister's office would then send out a memo making clear that Trimble's memo was not agreed and therefore had no authority. "Trimble would go buck mad," said the source, "but there was nothing he could do. Mallon really ensured that Trimble did not get away with running the department on his own."

Evidence of Trimble's thinking on the issue was exhibited in his 1998 Waterfront Hall speech during the Clinton visit, when it was noted that the Shadow First Minister described himself as leader, not joint leader, of Northern Ireland. Even during the dark days of the Omagh bombing, when they were united in common cause, there was friction behind the scenes over jointery. They clashed when Trimble unilaterally declared that there should be a day of mourning for the victims without consulting or including his partner in government. "Mallon went mad and said it should have been a joint thing," recalled one source. Whether Trimble's propensity for solo runs was rooted in his impulsive nature, or a mindset of superiority, Mallon was not prepared to put up with what one insider called Trimble's "mother-hen bossy style".

Mallon's annoyance with Trimble over the day of mourning announcement was compounded by his anger at the Irish government – the first to breach the jointery rule. Mallon felt Dublin should have known better and was astonished when, shortly after the

First and Deputy First Ministers took up their posts, Taoiseach Bertie Ahern hosted talks with Trimble and did not include him. Others say Mallon was not entirely surprised by his treatment at the hands of the Irish government. As a northern nationalist, he shared some of the resentment felt by many of his compatriots towards the Republic's attitude to them post-partition. Sinn Féin MLA Alex Maskey, who took part in the Good Friday Agreement negotiations, formed the impression the SDLP man did not always have much faith in Dublin. "Partition damaged Mallon," said Maskey. Another member of the SDLP recalled sarcastic remarks from Mallon about going to Dublin "for cups of tea".

From whatever quarter the issue arose, Mallon pounced to defend the integrity of his joint office with Trimble. A Stormont official recalled: "They were joined in law and it was a marriage of equals. But there was a feeling on Seamus Mallon's part that others didn't see it like that." Their titles contributed greatly to the confusion. Trimble, some believed, took literally the word "First" in his title and focused on the word "Deputy" in Mallon's title. One Irish official concurred: "The biggest mistake was the description 'Deputy First Minister'. They should have been called 'Joint First Minister'."

The confusion was also apparent when the salaries were drawn up during the shadow period and Mallon was initially awarded a lower pay-scale. The NIO was immediately asked to rectify this and did so, but what was regarded by nationalists and others as an error proved the point for some unionists that the First Minister had a superior vote and therefore a superior status. Sir Reg Empey, who observed jointery at first hand when he endured a short stint as Acting First Minister, felt Mallon had a valid point about the equality issue and the plurality of the ministers, but insisted the larger electoral mandate also underscored the difference between the two posts, concluding, "Somebody has to go through the door first."

Over time, Trimble came to resent jointery and how it was operated. Mallon, equally convinced of the correctness of his position, became frustrated with the system. One insider recalled: "When Trimble was treated as the boss he was fine, but it drove Mallon round the bend." The rows over jointery would help to explain in part why Trimble described Mallon as a "nasty man" in Godson's *Himself Alone*. Mallon just shrugged off Trimble's description: "Sometimes I say what I think and I tend to do it in straight terms."

Trimble said he did not reject jointery out of hand, but suggested he had a broader interpretation of it than Mallon did, whom he felt was rigidly demanding it be applied to every little thing. He said part of the problem was that Mallon regarded everything as a "fresh negotiation". "I couldn't cope with that," said Trimble. "I wanted to deal with things on merit. Seamus wanted to do a deal on everything and consequently I found there just wasn't a meeting of minds," Trimble said. The SDLP's Denis Haughey summed up the differences in approach: "Trimble was inclined to behave as if he was Prime Minister and Seamus was John Prescott. Seamus was not having that. For Seamus, that was the big issue that superseded all others. We took the view that the ministers act in concert or not at all."

In order to understand how Mallon felt and the depth of his determination not to play second fiddle to David Trimble, it is important to examine the nature of the relationship between John Hume and Seamus Mallon over a number of years. While Trimble was haunted by the ghost of Faulkner, Mallon was almost certainly haunted by Hume. One

Ulster Unionist politician described Hume as the "spectre at the feast who never let Mallon breathe".

Hume gave up the post of Deputy First Minister, but stayed on as SDLP leader and appointed all his own ministers, who owed their positions to him, not to Mallon. Trimble remembered Mallon being caught out one day at the Executive table when his ministers did not back him on a particular issue, which did not appear to present a problem beforehand. "But when it came to the issue," said Trimble, "instead of it proceeding on the path as it was expected, the three SDLP ministers all raised problems. We had quite a difficult meeting." Trimble claimed that afterwards Mallon had turned to an official and, with some embarrassment, confided that he did not know there was going to be an issue. Trimble was not alone in thinking the ministers might have been more supportive of Mallon had he the authority to hire and fire them. Trimble thought so: "Hume gave Mallon no authority." When asked about the incident at the Executive table, Mallon said: "You're tipping the iceberg. I remember that day very well. There are other things that were done which would not have happened if I had the authority." Durkan could only recall an incident which involved disagreement over the format of Executive meetings, but did not think this had anything to do with interference from John Hume.

Mallon's long relationship with Hume no doubt shaped his attitude during his time as Deputy First Minister. SDLP sources said Mallon had been frustrated by years of playing second violin to the SDLP leader, at times being ignored or not consulted. He was therefore not about to repeat the experience with an Ulster Unionist leader. One official was struck by something Mallon used to say: "Mallon always made the point he was deputy to a Nobel Laureate in the SDLP and Deputy First Minister to a Nobel Laureate [at Stormont]."

To the general public, Hume and Mallon, two formidable politicians, seemed as one; indeed, there did not appear to be any strains in their relationship. Both were widely admired and seemed to complement one another perfectly. Hume was the deep thinker, the brilliant philosopher and the acknowledged architect of the peace process and the Agreement; Mallon was the shrewd pragmatist, the razor-sharp, instinctive politician, the careful compositor of the Agreement. Without a doubt, they were two remarkable men.

Both entered politics during the civil rights era of the 1960s and they shared a common commitment to non-violence, a profound belief in the political process as an alternative to armed insurrection and a dogged determination to achieve a resolution of the historic conflict. The formation of the SDLP gave them the means by which to achieve their aims. But with two such gifted politicians confined to the same party, where only one could be leader, friction was inevitable. Both jealously guarded their positions at the helm of the SDLP. It could be argued the party was doubly blessed and doubly cursed because it suffered a devastating loss at the polls when Hume and Mallon retired simultaneously.

Being John Hume's deputy for so many years must have been burdensome to Mallon. For no matter how brilliant an orator, how leader-like, how charismatic, or how sharp intellectually – and he was all these things and more – Mallon was doomed to be a deputy, perpetually walking in Hume's long shadow. He accepted the situation and did not, like some in other political parties, strive to oust Hume, whom he recognised as a talented, popular leader. Mallon insisted that, deep down, he always liked Hume and was always forthright with him: "Over a very long time I played it straight with him the whole way and any time I was going against him I went and told him." Despite this loyalty, SDLP sources say there was resentment at the way Hume treated him in return, going off on solo runs and failing, at times, to keep him informed; Mallon was once described as playing second fiddle in a one-man band. When asked about the challenging nature of the relationship, he would only say: "We are very different people."

It was, perhaps, Mallon's misfortune to be born just five months before John Hume, a colossus in twentieth-century Irish political history. Hume and Mallon were among the cream of a new generation of Irish nationalists who would seek to change the nature of the state in which they lived. They were the first generation to be schooled under the Education Act 1947, which introduced the Eleven-plus qualifying exam, allowing access to higher education for talented youngsters who otherwise could not afford it. At the SDLP's thirtieth anniversary gala, Mallon recalled that people said he and Hume had nothing in common. "But we do," he joked. "We both sat the Eleven-plus on the same day." It was tacit acknowledgement of their differences. In spite of the tensions they were a formidable team, but theirs was a complex partnership, marked by grudging respect, tension and rivalry. A veteran SDLP figure, when asked to characterise the Hume–Mallon relationship, laughed and said: "What relationship?" This source said the pair would moan about each other to various people in the party, but did go on to acknowledge that the two men did share a bond on a very human level: "There is something there because John will ring Seamus and say, 'I'm not feeling well, or cry on his shoulder'."

Another SDLP insider, who saw at first hand the nature of the relationship between Hume and Mallon, likened it to the famous song-writing duo, Paul McCartney and John Lennon. He suggested they were sometimes happy to be together, sharing the adulation, while at other times irritated at the attention the other was getting. "They had a very deep love for each other," the insider said, "but they pissed each other off. They were two big egos and it's not easy working that closely with anybody for thirty years. John and Seamus were afraid of each other, they needed each other, and hated the fact that they needed each other."

Neither man would be likely to accept such a description, but it was a perception formed by someone who worked closely with both of them. However, another SDLP member, who has known both men for years, did not recognise this characterisation. "Rubbish," he said. "Hume has no rapport with Mallon."

Mallon would have held the view that Hume, at times insecure, felt threatened by him. "I would not say there was resentment," he said. "There was suspicion. He was always a bit suspicious of me." The former SDLP leader and Hume's predecessor, the late Gerry Fitt, recalled a conversation he had with him years ago. Hume wondered who would succeed him as leader and Fitt named the obvious choice. Hume was aghast and said, "Sure Seamus Mallon couldn't lead the party. He's a manic depressive." Fitt had a characteristically colourful response to this remark. When the story was repeated to Mallon, he was at first incredulous and then laughed heartily at the notion that Hume, famous in political circles for his black moods, could think him a manic depressive.

Hume's decision to pursue secret talks with Gerry Adams, which led to the 1994 ceasefire, is probably the best example of the SDLP leader shutting out his deputy. He did not inform Mallon of the negotiations. The uneasy, rather distant partnership between

Hume and Mallon, exacerbated by friction over the Hume–Adams talks, became a talking point among journalists and party insiders. The nature of the their relationship was probably another reason why Hume left it to the last hour to give his deputy the job of Deputy First Minister. Hume's decision failed to free Mallon from the shadow of a party leader. He might have had a new platform from which to shine, but in reality, Mallon merely exchanged one political partner for another, one who was just as capable of going off on solo runs without consulting him. Even people in Trimble's own party complained about his failure to communicate with them.

Trimble claimed that he started out having quite frank conversations about his party's problems with Mallon, but felt he was less forthcoming about his own: "I was being frank about the problems with regard to the position in unionism and all the rest of it. Seamus was not saying anything to me. So I found the discussions uneven."

For Mallon's part, he found his frustrations had doubled because he now had both Hume and Trimble to deal with. Even if Trimble and Mallon had a shared view on jointery from the outset, it was never going to be an easy relationship. An "us and them" mentality was bound to occur, given the society in which they lived. It was a state of mind that may also have been encouraged by the physical space between their offices: initially the First and Deputy First Minister shared space in the West Wing of Parliament Buildings, with Trimble taking Brian Faulkner's old office and Mallon the one next door. But as time went on and devolution evolved, the number of staff and ministerial aides began to grow and it was felt the area was too confined to be comfortable. It was therefore proposed that the First Minister remain in the West Wing while the Deputy First Minister and his staff move to the East Wing. Mallon said he initially opposed the move, but was prevailed upon by senior civil servants to agree. It created what Sir Reg Empey called "a dumb-bell effect" and it was a decision Mallon would come to regret: "It wasn't good for the psychology of the process. If I had to do it again, I would have stayed."

Some civil servants in OFM/DFM felt torn between the two ministers, fearful of being seen to favour one or the other. "You had to give them the same attention," said one, "otherwise you would be seen to be in one person's pocket as opposed to the other." BBC business editor James Kerr remembered covering a trip to Paris by the ministers and being asked by an official after interviewing David Trimble to please interview Seamus Mallon also. When Kerr pointed out he had Mallon's speech and did not need them both, he was told by the official: "Yes you do – for the good of my health." Officials would also encourage reporters not to refer to Mallon as "Trimble's deputy".

When asked how the friction over jointery manifested itself, one source revealed: "Terse exchanges, dismissive remarks, refusal to cooperate – sometimes to the point of absurdity." Another insider, recalling the antics, declared: "You would be amazed at the amount of time that was wasted over petty things." Some ways of working were pretty straightforward and smoother once protocol was established. This involved the First and Deputy First Minister taking turns chairing Executive meetings, dividing ministerial questions in the Assembly – one took the odd numbers, the other the evens – and taking turns going to formal meetings in each other's offices. Sometimes Trimble and Mallon would pop into each other's offices informally, and some officials suggested the sequencing over office meetings was more of an issue for others in the respective East and West wings than it was the ministers themselves.

"Some people might have been exercised by where to meet," said one insider. Neither Trimble nor Mallon remembered it being an issue, although one official noted the First Minister always came to the Deputy First Minister's office next to Room 21 before the Executive meetings for their pre-Executive discussions, adding: "[The Deputy First Minister's Office] never counted those on the balance sheet, you know."

Press statements became an issue before protocol was established, whereby each had quotes of a similar length in the release to reflect their equal status and, where possible, both would be quoted on page one. Their names would go first on press releases in turn. Press officers would also encourage the media to ask each of them a question on the same subject before moving on, but that did not always go to plan. According to well-placed sources, including David Trimble, the number of words allocated to Seamus Mallon in a quote in a press release was counted to ensure equal time with the First Minister. One source insisted it was not as extreme as that, admitting: "It started off so and became less so. There were no protocols in place at first about how to handle this. The hardest part was clearing lines, trying to get the words right." There was also a protocol when they attended events. "Whenever they arrived at events we would make sure there were two people to meet and greet them," said one official. Another even recalled having to bring two pairs of scissors for a ribbon-cutting ceremony.

Finalising decisions under the jointery rule, which gave each minister a veto over the other, also proved problematic, particularly as both Trimble and Mallon had to agree the agenda for the Executive meetings in Room 21. If they could not agree on an issue, it would be long-fingered while a compromise was worked out. Mallon invoked his veto on occasion: "I was Deputy First Minister and I wasn't going to be sidelined and there were a number of times I would not let things go on the agenda because there had not been agreement. I had to do that on a couple of occasions." He cited as an example the Review of Public Administration, which was aimed at reducing bureaucracy in local government and streamlining local councils. "It's not that I was against it but I was not going to let it go on [the agenda] unless other things were dealt with," he said. In fact, both used their vetoes when it suited them and that slowed the wheels of government. "It wasn't an efficient system," said one insider. "It wasn't chronically inefficient, but it wasn't efficient."

Other departments were less forgiving, regarding the centre as a "black hole" into which documents or legislation could be cast adrift for months. The SDLP found the system was affected by Trimble's refusal to delegate, which "slowed things down", and by his propensity to change his mind. One SDLP member said: "People would say you couldn't have an agreement without David Trimble, but Mallon felt he couldn't have an agreement with David Trimble. He wouldn't follow through on it … He was inconsistent. He would say one thing one day and the next day something else. There were occasions when it was hard to get a decision out of him." Another SDLP source recalled: "Mallon couldn't bear the way Trimble couldn't agree anything, how he came and upset everything after he thought it was agreed. He got to dislike him more and more as time went on and I think in the beginning was prepared to give him a chance, but they just didn't get on." A senior official said Trimble would also get annoyed with the SDLP side of the house over decisions or agreements which did not work out as he expected.

Another divisive issue was Trimble's absence from Stormont. He was in demand internationally as a Nobel Laureate as well as attending at Westminster regularly, which meant he could be away a few days out of every week and not always available to agree or discuss policies. "An appalling problem" was how Mallon summed it up. Another official lamented: "Everything had to have two signatures and if he [Trimble] was not there, it could not be done." Nominations to the NSMC, for example, required dual signatures and these always seemed to be written at the last minute, according to insiders. A source at the centre said the best way to get agreement was to have Trimble and Mallon in the same room at the same time, without interference from others: "If you got them one at a time, you got two different answers. If one wanted to do x, the other wanted to do y. Sometimes I think they would just do the opposite because they knew the other wanted it. If they heard the other one didn't like it, they were even worse." Another civil servant recalled becoming exasperated by their behaviour: "They would engage when they got across the table, but doing it on paper was different. You'd be told, 'Change this paper' and you would be carrying it down the corridor to be told, 'Change it back again.' People did amazing work to try to keep things running."

The delay involved in securing a consensus decision between ministers with opposing views often frustrated civil servants. "That was the biggest difficulty about the office," said one. "You'd go to one and one would say 'yes' and the other would say 'no'. Then we'd decide we'd have to have a meeting, but you couldn't get them. And it would be put off for another week." One source recalled a classic example of this, which took place even before devolution, when four new permanent secretaries had to be appointed to the four new departments. The list went to Trimble and he agreed, but Mallon did not, said the insider. He recalled that an exasperated Gerry Loughran went to Mallon and challenged him: "Do you want permanent secretaries for your departments, or do you not?"

The source said doggedness was a trait both Trimble and Mallon shared: "Seamus was very stubborn, but it wasn't always Seamus." On a normal week it was possible to fill Trimble's diary three times over, and Mallon would become irritated when the First Minister took time out in the middle of the week to attend Westminster. "But he needed that outlet," said a source close to Trimble, "and he needed to get away from Northern Ireland where he could relax a bit."

Trimble found he was appreciated overseas in a way he was not, sometimes, in his own patch. "They lionised him in Spain," said a source close to him at Stormont. "Any time he got an invitation to Spain, he was keen to go." In the spring of 2000, Trimble flew to Palestine for a peace conference in Gaza to discuss Northern Ireland's peace process and meet with Israeli Prime Minister Ehud Barak. He also had a private meeting with the late Palestinian leader, Yasser Arafat, in Nablus. They discussed the talks about to be held at Camp David and Trimble, notably, told Arafat he should trust President Clinton and not just to see the United States as pro-Israel. Trimble began to be recognised when he travelled, although not always accurately. According to one Stormont insider: "One time in London he was in a black taxi and the driver said, 'Here mate, I know you, you're that John Hume, ain't ya?' He had a chuckle at that."

Mallon, who tried to curtail unnecessary trips to Westminster, would despair at how few opportunities he and the First Minister had to go out to visit people and promote the administration on the ground. "The pressures on his diary were huge," Mallon said. "To get outside of Belfast was difficult. To get to Derry was virtually impossible." When Trimble and Mallon did appear together, they were polite to each other and avoided the contentious issues in the office, such as policing, in much the same way other people in Northern Ireland tend to behave at work. Occasionally the First and Deputy First Minister would raise their voices at each other by telephone, or in their offices, but for the most part, according to various sources, their disagreements would be communicated through official channels and there were few face-to-face confrontations. One official said it was reasonably businesslike and the disagreements were not untypical of any government: "There were ups and downs over policing and decommissioning, but the majority of the time they got on fine."

An exception to this norm was a very public row in front of officials, which took place in the Washington home of a senior civil servant. The issue in question was protocol: Trimble wanted to include his party's representative in America, Anne Smith, in a White House meeting; Mallon objected because Smith was not part of the administration. "You could have cut the air with a knife," said one witness. Trimble backed down on this occasion, but according to one insider only after "they tore lumps out of each other". The pair managed to work together, nonetheless. Mallon said: "As two human beings, I tried to be aware of his problems and I like to think that he tried to be aware of mine."

An insider likened the pair to the fabled frog and scorpion: "They needed each other, but they couldn't help stinging each other." Mallon sometimes could not resist getting a rise out of the First Minister, and several sources recalled a few meetings between Trimble and Mallon that lasted only a matter of seconds or minutes. Trimble could not recall meetings being under a minute long, but some people do, including Mallon. "That happened," said the former Deputy First Minister. An SDLP member also recalled hearing about a meeting that lasted around nine seconds: "It was in Seamus' office and Trimble came in and Seamus immediately bit the head off him and Trimble got up and walked out."

Mallon liked to recount how he had once "locked" Trimble in his office in order to get a decision on an issue that had been dragging on for weeks. There were two doors in Mallon's office: an outer door through which civil servants and others entered, and another, adjoining door that would have been more convenient for officials but was generally kept locked. Trimble came to see Mallon and had not been in the room very long when he became irritated and tried to bolt, making a dash for the wrong door, the one that was locked. When he could not get out, he accused Mallon of locking him in. Mallon decided to take advantage of the situation, telling the First Minister, "Yeah you're locked in. You'll have a drink." When Trimble declined, saying it "was too early in the day," Mallon insisted. Trimble, irritated and red-faced, did have a drink and there was an agreement that day before Mallon "released" him. Mallon dined out on the joke, but Trimble had no recollection of the incident.

Some in the centre recalled Mallon could be both mischievous and difficult at the same time. One official remembered: "He took people apart quietly and would say to me afterwards chuckling, 'Well, what did you think of that?'" Others close to Mallon noted he was sometimes unwell, which contributed to his disgruntled disposition at times. But one civil servant said he admired Mallon's honesty: "He is a very straight guy. He can be very testy, but deep down I found he had integrity."

Various people found Trimble easy work with. One senior civil servant who worked with many direct rule ministers marvelled at his grasp of detail: "He had a first-class brain. He would skim through briefs. You could explain something to him in five minutes that you might have to spend an hour with others on, a very able man." This source said he never had a cross word from Trimble. "Any cross words were spoken by me," he said. An SDLP member who had a good working relationship with the First Minister said: "He was courteous and cooperative and willing to listen to a reasonable case." But, like Mallon, he too could have what one insider called "his strops". "Trimble lost it loads of times," said one person. "The finger-wagging would come out." However, the source thought that sometimes these were tactical and tended to occur around party people or politicians rather than civil servants.

While Trimble was known to want more powers into the centre, Mallon was cautious in that he believed it had become a sin-bin for issues other departments did not want to deal with and these were soaking up valuable time. One administrator said he would remove any issue that was not contentious, such as e-government, which is aimed at improving the way services are delivered by using more information technology. Another, lamenting that the centre had no time to mature, said, "There were so many odds and ends and it was slow, cumbersome and indecisive." Mallon found he was constrained by bureaucracy and yearned to be out in the community, promoting the Executive. Initially, Executive meetings were held once a week and that meant sorting through piles of briefing papers in a short period of time. Mallon eventually rebelled and demanded a synopsis sheet. He recalled: "We were getting these vast tomes of stuff, especially from Finance, and it would take you all week to read it. Of course it suited civil servants, but it wasn't the way to do it."

The civil servants were the "third person" in this political marriage, along with a plethora of advisors and two junior ministers. They could be likened, at times, to feuding in-laws. Aside from Trimble and Mallon, there were up to six advisors at any one time: three for the East Wing and three for the West Wing. There were also two junior ministers. All were vying with civil servants for face-time with the ministers, trying to get decisions or support for policies. Some civil servants resented the advisors, unique to devolution, and regarded them as a nuisance. "What you got," said one official, "was this seal around Trimble and Mallon and it was very hard for us to get to see them. And you had these papers going in the office and they were being vetted and these guys were changing papers and that led to friction."

Damien McAteer, Mark Durkan's advisor, felt civil servants saw advisors as "loose cannons" and did not always appreciate their role in bringing a different perspective, offering not just policy advice but driving initiatives and ideas and encouraging the minister to step outside the civil service mentality: "The system did not want people, who were temporary civil servants who had no line management, through to the permanent secretary." But an official dismissed ministerial advisors as generally "a precious breed". Another, who recalled feeling annoyed at their behaviour, said: "When we produced something, the advisors would go into a cluster and decide if they liked it or not. It was rare that both sides liked it. They would look at it from a party point of view. It was not normal Cabinet government and you were staggering on as best you could with the system you had got." Another complained of "six pairs of eyes looking at everything before it even reached the minister."

Not all civil servants felt this way, of course, and one who was regarded as "too friendly" recalled a senior mandarin telling him: "If you lie down with dogs, you get up with fleas." Like others in the administration, this civil servant found the advisors useful to bounce ideas off or consult with, but some complained advisors would get involved in decisions and elongate the process, or confuse it. Another civil servant wondered if tensions between the First and Deputy First Minister's office were not made worse by advisors, saying: "You could never be sure if it was the advisors who were stirring things up." In fairness to the advisors, issues were lobbed back to them if Trimble and Mallon would not agree. Sometimes aides would be useful in brokering a compromise, but this was time-consuming. One official cites the Single Equality Bill as an example: "David Trimble saw it as nothing more than a condition of British regulations, but Seamus and [later] Mark Durkan saw it as having a much more important status."

The SDLP advisor Colm Larkin was well-regarded by the First Minister's side and was considered particularly good at building relations between the East and West Wing. One SDLP source said Larkin was superb, adding: "He was fantastic at smoothing things over ... with Trimble's people." A few unionist insiders concurred and were sorry to see him leave, especially when Hugh Logue, who was considered very "green" by the unionists, remained. Larkin was responsible for the Executive and Logue for the NSMC, another irony of history: Logue was something of a bogeyman for unionists because in 1974 his remarks that the north-south structures in the Sunningdale Agreement would be the vehicle through which unionists would be 'trundled' into a united Ireland caused a furore among unionists who were already hostile to the deal.

Although they have been criticised, the advisors did generate some good ideas and did try to coordinate business across the departments. Their meetings made for strange bedfellows, though. David Trimble's aide, Mark Neale, would find himself across the table from Leo Green, Bairbre de Brún's aide. Green had served a prison sentence for shooting dead RUC Inspector Harry Cobb, a thirty-eight-year-old father of three, in 1977. Cobb's son was one of Neale's closest friends in Portadown, and he remembered finding it difficult attending meetings with him. "Leo Green shot my friend's father dead," said Neale. "When I went to meetings, he wasn't some abstract person there whom I'd met from Sinn Féin." Green said he had no idea of the connection and only learned of it when interviewed for this book. He seemed taken aback.

As well as the advisors, Trimble and Mallon had appointed two junior ministers immediately after devolution in December 1999, even before they had worked out a clearly defined role for them. Ulster Unionist Dermot Nesbitt, MLA for South Down, was appointed by Trimble, while Denis Haughey, MLA for Mid-Ulster, was given a post having worked for the party leader in Europe. The First and Deputy First Ministers liked the concept of the juniors, but failed to reach a deal on what responsibilities to give them. Trimble, who had fought for the centre to have an Economic Policy Unit (EPU) to keep an eye on Finance, seemed at times to want to put Nesbitt in charge of it, but the SDLP resisted this as the party did not want him challenging Durkan's role as Finance minister.

Neither Nesbitt nor Haughey was given a specific brief or power to take decisions, and this left them in a difficult position. One insider said some civil servants, realising their lack of authority, treated them accordingly. Without any defined role or power of decision, Nesbitt and Haughey clashed bitterly over issues such the equality agenda. "They fell out very quickly," said one source at the centre.

Nesbitt particularly annoyed the SDLP side of the administration. Once, according to an SDLP source, he tabled forty-four separate amendments to the Equality Commission's corporate plan: "Some were so pathetic, and everyone was just appalled. We didn't let him away with it but there were big long rows with him." What some in the SDLP regarded as minor details were matters of importance to Nesbitt and he insisted that any position he took on initiatives like this were both sensible and logical. The SDLP claimed he had an obsession with unemployment differentials between Catholics and Protestants and the reasons why Catholics were much more likely to be unemployed. One unionist in the administration, agreed with the SDLP that Nesbitt was obsessed, saying: "It was all he ever wanted to talk to me about." But while this unionist believed Nesbitt's stance on the differentials was correct, the SDLP vehemently disagreed with him. Nesbitt said he was diligent in accurately reflecting the issue, and the SDLP was constantly raising it when he felt it should be a dead issue. SDLP personnel in the administration thought he was wrong to conclude that the gap in Protestant and Catholic unemployment figures was due to the complexities of the labour market. The SDLP felt Nesbitt had ignored the significance of historic discrimination. The spat over this issue – and what if anything should be done about it – is said to have gone on for a year or more as memos flew back and forth.

Barrington said the debate was ridiculous because the Good Friday Agreement had committed the British government to progressively eliminating the unemployment gap between Catholic and Protestants: "What you had was the UUP trying to unpick the Good Friday Agreement on this issue. We were not going to back off on that." The SDLP eventually by-passed the centre and used the department it controlled, the Department of Learning and Employment, to tackle the issue, setting up a task force and special programmes in unemployment blackspots. "It was easier to do it that way," said Barrington. "Why row with Dermot when the key department was SDLP-controlled?" The arguments over the differential caused relations between the two junior ministers to deteriorate further.

On occasion, when they met in the SDLP junior minister's office, Haughey, frustrated by Nesbitt's insistence on a particular position, increasingly saw no point in continuing the meeting while Nesbitt kept insisting he was right. One insider described Nesbitt's firm stance in colourful terms: "He would just curl up like a hedgehog and refuse to give in." During some of these fruitless discussions in Haughey's office, Haughey would eventually leave the table, go to the other end of the room, put on his headphones and start typing at his computer, leaving Nesbitt, equally frustrated, to slope out of the room. "It was most embarrassing," said Nesbitt. Annoyed by this behaviour, Nesbitt became uncomfortable with meeting in Haughey's office. It was decided a neutral space would serve better to discuss what Nesbitt called "this issue that was so blooming sensitive". A civil servant found a small conference room, windowless and airless, in which they could meet.

Nesbitt and Haughey did manage to reach an agreement on the remit of the EPU, a source of friction within the administration that the advisors had failed to resolve. Neither side was entirely satisfied, but Haughey was happy that he was able to include in the deal a clause that the EPU would not subvert or undermine the role of the Minister of Finance and Personnel. Haughey and Nesbitt also managed to work together on some other initiatives, such as the victims strategy and the Children's Commissioner, one of the primary achievements of devolution. Even so, Haughey was much happier when Dermot Nesbitt was eventually promoted to Environment minister and was replaced by James Leslie.

In a somewhat ironic reflection of the problem, Trimble and Mallon never managed to agree to give the juniors decision-making powers. Loughran strove to find ways of improving the system, but no progress was made prior to suspension. Another problem that was not resolved was the amount of time taken up with trying to reach agreement in pre-Executive meetings. Trimble and Mallon would meet first with their own party ministers, and then meet with each other to make sure items and policy were agreed to avoid spats in Room 21. According to one official, half-an-hour was generally allocated for the Trimble/Mallon pre-meeting brief, but it was never enough time. Meetings would go on much longer, usually an hour, and that meant that fairly regularly the other ministers were kept waiting at the Executive table. Once, when the First and Deputy First Ministers were quite tardy, Bairbre de Brun gave out about people "swanning in half-an-hour late". At the next meeting Mallon said: 'I'm swanning in on time today."

Executive meetings tended to be dominated by Budget issues. Sometimes they would be dragged out by something raised under "Any Other Business" and on occasion could last for four hours, to the amazement of officials. "The Cabinet meetings in London," said one, "don't last four hours, but that is because the Prime Minister is the boss." In the Executive, on the other hand, power was blurred and one official recalled it was sometimes hard to tell where one minister's power started and the other's ended. The lesson of the East and West Wing – that Trimble could not act as a Prime Minister – was taught to civil servants, too, when they tried to model the Executive on the Cabinet office. "We were always trying to find ways to make collectivity work," the official said. "It was assumed the Executive was not going to work unless it had some sort of cohesion. It wasn't questioned as a principle [by ministers], but in practice people liked it when it suited them and didn't like it when it didn't. Everyone wanted a finger in everyone else's pie but didn't want fingers in their pie."

The reality was that there was no obligation in legislation that the Executive had to meet on a regular basis. The ministerial code of practice was not legally binding. Collective decisions became those that required either new legislation or a large expenditure, or involved more than one department. The departments were designed to be interlocking in order to force ministers to work together, but ministers could often do what they wished within their own silos. The same unspoken rule of avoiding the big political issues in the East and West Wing applied in Room 21 at the Executive table, where the political baggage was, for the most part, left at the door. "They could walk into Room 21," said one source, "and leave the other stuff behind and then walk out of Room 21 and go to war on it."

Some in the administration, including ministers, found it odd that they did not meet regularly, as ministers, to thrash out problems in the peace process. "You had this bizarre situation where David Trimble and Martin McGuinness were arguing in the media about decommissioning and then sitting down at the table and agreeing policy," said one person. Martin McGuinness felt that the absence of debate in Room 21 about wider political issues was a mistake and that the process could have benefited from debating sessions between the ministers on the difficult issues such as decommissioning. Sir Reg Empey said he was continually pointing out that talks on big political issues only came about when a crisis had formed: "Everything was left to the last minute." Others felt it would have been a recipe for gridlock. "Oh no," one official gasped, "then you'd have the baggage *in* the room. It would have dwarfed everything else." As Sam Foster recalled: "The Executive meetings could get tense at times. I wouldn't say hot and heavy, but it could be quite blunt and tetchy. On occasion you could easily have pulled the Executive to pieces."

Sometimes ministers would clash and revert to type over various things that had happened during the week. One official recalled: "It wasn't that serious and nobody walked out and it wasn't so harsh that it stopped business being done. It could be tetchy though, and it was time-consuming." The reality, said an insider, was that it was dreadfully dull in Room 21. He joked about "snoozing for Ulster". "Pretty much everything was agreed beforehand so you knew what the position was," he said.

There were moments of mirth, however. "What amazed me," said an official, "was the amount of laughter coming from the room." On one occasion David Trimble told the Executive about a poor Chinese immigrant who lived in his constituency. According to ministerial advisor Damien McAteer, Trimble recounted how the unfortunate man had been forced to slave for very long hours from early morning to late at night in unbearable conditions. "Durkan said something like, 'My God, he could get a job in here,' and everyone laughed."

Executive minutes are exempt, for now, under Freedom of Information, but there is believed to be only one occasion when a senior civil servant called time on an Executive meeting and asked government officials to leave because it had descended into heated debate about wider political matters, such as decommissioning. The civil servant in question was Gerry Loughran and it is believed to be the meeting where the ministers squared off over Trimble's ban on Sinn Féin. However, a number of sources said they could not remember for sure.

Whatever about the moment of mirth, the Executive was always under stress of one kind or another, and the system creaked and groaned beneath the weight of history and bureaucracy. The showdown over Trimble's ban on Sinn Féin was not confined to Room 21. It leaked out and spilled over into spring 2001, when it was clear that the Executive was dangerously close to unravelling.

Chapter 20
Things Fall Apart

David Trimble dashed down the corridor of Stormont's East Wing and popped his head around the door of the Deputy First Minister's office. "Can I have a word with you Seamus?" he inquired, his face flushed red. Trimble then charged in. It was around 10.20am on the morning of 8 May 2001 and the First Minister was due in the chamber in ten minutes. Seamus Mallon was being briefed by press officer Mark Larmour, who immediately offered the First Minister a cup of coffee. Trimble declined, saying: "This won't take long."

Trimble handed Mallon a piece of paper, and asked him to read it. The Deputy First Minister started to object and Trimble was about to reply but, pressed for time and not wanting an argument, he thought better of it and rushed off again to brief his Assembly team. Seamus Mallon sat reading the paper in disbelief. It was a personal statement from David Trimble.

Minutes later, Trimble was on his feet in the chamber, making the statement. A hush descended and members leaned forward to hear what the First Minister had to say. Trimble reminded everyone that it was one year and two days since the IRA had promised to initiate a process to put weapons beyond use. Since then the IRA had allowed a number of arms inspections, but there had been no actual destruction of weapons. As a consequence, Trimble was now putting the IRA and others on notice that if it failed to decommission, he would quit as First Minister on 1 July. Trimble indicated he was making his statement now in order to give the IRA time to engage with the IICD. His letter of resignation had just been lodged with the Speaker and would take effect on the date indicated if decommissioning did not take place. He said this would not cause the institutions to collapse, but would put the onus on republicans and others to preserve them.

Trimble was aware that Assembly rules dictated that the members had six weeks to re-elect a First and Deputy First minister and that in the interim period he could appoint a substitute to keep the administration ticking over. He was also aware that if a new First and Deputy First Minister could not be installed, the Secretary of State would be obliged to dissolve the Assembly and call fresh elections. That meant a new crisis would be looming by mid-August. Trimble said he took this step reluctantly, insisting he had worked hard to make the Agreement work, but the fundamental promise of decommissioning had not been delivered. Without such action, Trimble said, he feared that Northern Ireland would always be at the mercy of armed gangs: "It is for people to change. That change must occur." This was Trimble's way of keeping his promise to his party's ruling council, and to the electorate, that there could be no government if the guns issue were not addressed. Trimble had tried to contact the Prime Minister just minutes before he made his Assembly statement. He was not available so he spoke to the PM's chief-of-staff, Jonathan Powell, who lamented there was not really enough time to try to talk him out of it.

In the chamber that morning it was the DUP, not Sinn Féin, that forced the Speaker to call order over the statement. "Treat it with contempt!" Peter Robinson advised Lord Alderdice. His colleague, Nigel Dodds, wondered why Trimble was delaying his resignation. "Why does he not resign now?" he asked.

McGuinness declared Trimble's tactic a disaster. "I can say without fear of contradiction that if David Trimble persists with this line, we will never see decommissioning," he said. Mallon was also horrified, not least because he believed it was only with the cloak of the institutions around him that Trimble could grow stronger in his desperate efforts to fight off his critics. With characteristic understatement, Mallon declared, "It certainly doesn't make things any easier."

It did not escape anyone's notice that Trimble's statement came on the day Prime Minister Tony Blair announced the general election, which was now set for 7 June. Many concluded that Trimble simply did not want to be in government with Sinn Féin at election time while the IRA remained armed. When asked at a news conference whether he was panicking at the cusp of an election, Trimble gave his characteristic toothy laugh: "I'm not getting into that."

However he did confide, in an interview for this book, that the plan had been conceived earlier in the year, perhaps February or March, in a café in Massachusetts. Trimble and a few close confidants, including Professor Paul Bew of Queen's University, Belfast, were present and discussion arose as to how the Ulster Unionist leader and First Minister should approach the forthcoming Westminster elections. Trimble recalled that it was not so much the mechanism that was crucial in the discussions, but how to win back and build unionist confidence in the Agreement: "There had been such an erosion of confidence ... We needed to do something. We still took the [arms] issue seriously and we needed to achieve it."

Looking almost pleased with themselves after hearing Trimble's resignation threat, the DUP derided it as a pathetic election stunt. The election campaign had effectively begun, polarising the parties at a critical phase in the peace process. Within a month, Frank Millar, the well-informed London editor of *The Irish Times*, would declare that relations between the First and Deputy First Minister were now "poisonous". Their relationship, still reeling from the fallout over Trimble's ban on Sinn Féin ministers attending NSMC meetings, had reached a new low. It had been steadily deteriorating for some time, despite efforts since the New Year to find a resolution. It was increasingly looking like the centre would not hold.

Months earlier the Prime Ministers had met the parties in Downing Street, on 22 January, amid claims by Sinn Féin that a BIC meeting had been postponed because David Trimble had refused to sign the papers allowing Bairbre de Brun to attend. The biggest development that month was the removal of Secretary of State Peter Mandelson after he was caught up in a scandal over allegations that he had acted improperly in securing passports for two Indian businessmen. A government inquiry later found Mandelson not guilty of misconduct, but with a general election looming Tony Blair was not prepared to have his government tainted by scandal. Mandelson was replaced as Secretary of State by Dr John Reid, a Scottish political bruiser. Reid was not particularly popular, but he won a bit more respect among nationalists than Mandelson ever had. A republican source soon declared: "Reid was the spin doctor that Mandelson thought he was. Reid was much more astute."

Mallon was glad to see the back of Mandelson and his departure gave Mallon hope that he could fix the problems over policing. Amid the turmoil, the First and Deputy First Minister embarked on a trip to Paris, Dusseldorf and Berlin, with the mood between them rather sour. "Relations between them then were not that great," said one official. The purpose of the visit to Paris was to improve trade links between Northern Ireland and France. Sir Reg Empey, Enterprise Minister, also went along. Trimble described the visit as a significant milestone for devolution. The First and Deputy First Minister were guests of French President Jacques Chirac in the Elysée Palace. Trimble described it as a courtesy call, but Mallon remembered the First Minister speaking about the legacy of the past and talking very positively about the need for equality. "In those types of meetings," said Mallon, "there was no gallery and no playing to the gallery."

Their trip to Germany was cut short by events back home. They left Berlin to take part in consultations with the Prime Minister over a possible political deal. Before departing, Trimble said of IRA decommissioning: "I don't care how they do it, or where they do it … provided at the end of the process weapons are no longer usable."

The Taoiseach and the Prime Minister were reported to be making steady progress on the issue, but Sinn Féin's warning about spin proved to be accurate and there was no breakthrough. Nor was there good news for Trimble from the High Court, which ruled that he had acted unlawfully in banning the Sinn Féin ministers from the NSMC meetings. Trimble instructed his lawyers to appeal and hid his defeat by citing a few minor legal points in the judgement. He noted the judge had conceded that the First and Deputy First Minister had discretion over which ministers they nominated to represent the Executive. But crucially the judgement concluded that Trimble's refusal to nominate Sinn Féin in order to force IRA decommissioning was outside his discretion.

At that time the First and Deputy First Minister were also facing another court battle, this one with the DUP over the withholding of Executive papers, whilst the courts were also considering Sinn Féin's challenge to Mandelson's flags regulation. Trimble appealed the judgement on the north-south ban and refused to lift his sanctions against Martin McGuinness and Bairbre de Brun while the appeal was in process. A plenary meeting of the NSMC would soon have to be postponed because Ulster Unionists were refusing to attend.

In mid-February ninety-minute talks involving Tony Blair, Gerry Adams and Martin McGuinness failed to break the stalemate. There were sticking points over policing in particular, but nonetheless the government went ahead and launched a recruitment campaign for the new police service, which did not have the backing of either the SDLP or Sinn Féin.

Even though the process of administration was rife with tensions and divisions, the Executive was able to unite around the Programme for Government, which was formally ratified in the Assembly. Mallon was heartened by this progress, declaring: "This is the big picture." The Executive also rallied to other challenges, uniting to tackle a potentially devastating outbreak of foot-and-mouth disease in sheep and cattle. But breaking free of the political plague over decommissioning and sanctions was proving more difficult. Gerry Adams dubbed the administration "an apartheid Executive". This time there was no enthusiastic American president willing to give the process his time and energy. The right-wing Republican president George W. Bush was now settled in the White House and it was clear that he had considerably less interest in the process, although the Bush administration was still willing to assist. It was hosting the traditional St Patrick's Day festivities at the White House, for example.

In the days before the Washington trip, Mallon signalled that the differences between the SDLP and the government over policing were narrowing and related to operational matters, such as the phasing out of the RUC reserve and the future of Special Branch. He said an agreement was very close and hoped it would be reached by June. Before he left for Washington, Trimble also signalled that he would lift sanctions on the NSMC temporarily.

Despite these positive notes, the Trimble–Mallon relationship was still discordant and showed no sign of improvement. They travelled separately while in the USA, coming and going in their own cars during the three-day visit. One well-placed source could not recall them speaking to each other, outside of formal meetings, for the entire visit. Their formal engagements included the Speaker's lunch on Capitol Hill on 14 March and a meeting that same day with Secretary of State Colin Powell. They arrived separately for their meeting with Powell, according to a placed source, who said neither minister had spoken directly to the other in preparation for the meeting with Powell. When asked about these claims, Trimble replied: "Look, I mean, I very soon discovered that there was no need for small-talk."

Despite the personal friction, the pair were said to have given an impressive performance when they met Powell. "They were very effective," said an insider, "a brilliant team. They behaved like consummate professionals. They could agree and do things well and they were a good act with Powell. They talked about policing and security and you could not have put a cigarette paper between them." The pair also held a private meeting with the President on the margins of the White House reception on 16 March. During the trip Mallon stepped up pressure on the IRA, calling again for weapons to be put beyond use.

Back at Stormont the political battle within the Executive continued and in early April Martin McGuinness and Bairbre de Brun headed for Dublin to discuss the NSMC ban rather than attend an Executive meeting. The following month, de Brun launched a joint health report on cancer with her Dublin counterpart Micheal Martin. McGuinness and de Brun also met Seamus Mallon, as Deputy First Minister, to discuss the ban. When the Sinn Féin ministers travelled to Dublin weeks later for a high-profile meeting with their Dublin counterparts in Dublin Castle, Trimble vowed to take it up with the Taoiseach.

It was in the context of increasing tensions over sanctions and decommissioning that David Trimble announced his post-dated resignation that spring. It was not the best of circumstances for his appeal to Catholics to vote for his party in marginal seats to ensure the survival of the Agreement. Entering the general election campaign in 2001, the Ulster Unionists held the lion's share of the seats at Westminster: 10 of 18 seats. The DUP held just two, the anti-Agreement UK Unionist Robert McCartney one, and the SDLP and Sinn Féin the other five between them. But once-safe Ulster Unionist seats were now unpredictable due to divisions within unionism over the Agreement, the rise of Sinn Féin and the retirement of a number of veteran unionist MPs. The DUP and Ulster Unionists fought a bitter campaign against each other for the control of the unionist soul. The DUP claimed there would be meltdown for the UUP and urged voters to "stop the rot", citing the release of prisoners, the reform of the RUC and the lack of decommissioning as reasons not to vote UUP. Ian Paisley spoke of "bitter vinegar" for the Ulster Unionist party while David Trimble told voters he was absolutely determined to secure decommissioning this time.

Trimble spoke of his disappointment over policing and the slow progress on arms, but insisted that his party had achieved results in forcing suspension and had shown it had a bottom-line. He appealed for support to help him "stick at it" and pointed out all that had been achieved: a more stable Northern Ireland with a devolved Assembly involving nationalists who had previously spurned Stormont. "That makes the [unionist] future more secure," he declared in an address to business leaders.

However, Paisley's prophetic words about bitter vinegar came true. The Ulster Unionists lost five seats: three to the DUP in North Belfast, Strangford and East Londonderry, and two to Sinn Féin in Fermanagh–Tyrone and West Tyrone. The UUP gained North Down and reclaimed South Antrim from anti-Agreement unionists. Trimble felt that without his post-dated resignation letter, the result would have been much worse. Trimble himself suffered a bruising race against the DUP newcomer David Simpson, who was just 2,000 votes behind him in the end. There were shocking scenes as Trimble and his wife Daphne were kicked and pushed by angry DUP supporters when they left the polling station under a police escort.

There was speculation that this experience led Trimble to reconsider his decision to remain as Ulster Unionist leader. His aides dismissed this as inaccurate. However, when Secretary of State John Reid called to commiserate with him, he does not deny that he might have had harsh words for Reid. One unionist insider recalled hearing Trimble raising his voice and heatedly blaming the government for his electoral woes. Asked if he had shouted at Reid in that instance, he replied: "He might have got the rough end of it on that occasion."

The DUP were jubilant, sealing their achievement with a series of hardline speeches vowing to renegotiate the Agreement. Nigel Dodds described his victory in North Belfast as "one in the eye for the pan-nationalist front" and for David Trimble. As Peter Robinson spoke of binding the wounds in unionism, his supporters were singing "Cheerio, cheerio" at deflated Ulster Unionists. Inevitably parallels were drawn with the post-Sunningdale election, which saw the Ulster Unionist party defeated by the anti-Agreement forces.

On the nationalist side, Mallon had predicted that the election would be a watershed, that people were tired of fighting over the Agreement and just wanted to see it implemented. He also predicted the SDLP vote would prove rock-solid. Mallon was wrong. Before the election the SDLP held three seats: Newry and Armagh, Mallon's constituency; Foyle, where John Hume held sway; and South Down, Eddie McGrady's seat. Sinn Féin had two: Gerry Adams in West Belfast; and Martin McGuinness in Mid-

Ulster. The election proved to be a watershed for Sinn Féin, which swept the western counties of Fermanagh and Tyrone – it was a humiliation for the SDLP. Party leader John Hume looked shell-shocked as he emerged from Foyle, which he had successfully defended, in contrast to other constituencies. The SDLP was overtaken by Sinn Féin in a Westminster poll for the first time in its history. Sinn Féin had surpassed its rival party in both the number of seats and votes won. The SDLP failed to increase its holding. Although the SDLP had successfully defended its three seats, Sinn Féin's stock had risen from two seats to four. As well as West Belfast and Mid-Ulster, the party now had Fermanagh-South Tyrone and West Tyrone.

The Ulster Unionist party retained a precarious place as the largest party, but the SDLP was pushed from second into fourth place overall. Its share of the vote fell to 21%, a fraction below Sinn Féin's. Even Mallon, SDLP deputy leader and MP for Newry and Armagh, did not have an easy win. As the votes were counted he looked worried at times as Murphy ate into his majority. His lead over Sinn Féin was cut from around 10,000 to around 3,000. Eddie McGrady's vote proved more robust, although it too had dropped.

It was the defeat suffered by the SDLP Agriculture minister, Bríd Rodgers, that was the cruellest blow of all. Rodgers had quit Upper Bann for West Tyrone, where the party hoped her high profile and impressive performance in the battle against foot-and-mouth disease would prevent a victory by Sinn Féin MLA Pat Doherty, who chaired the Assembly's Enterprise committee. Rodgers had come late to the race and Sinn Féin supporters were not happy to see her. At one point in the campaign she was pelted with eggs, and when she arrived at the election count centre she was verbally abused by a baying mob. Her family had advised her not to stand, but she had come under pressure within the party and had agreed. "It was the biggest mistake of my political life," she confided later.

Trimble's threat to quit as First Minister had not delivered decommissioning and had not prevented the rise of the DUP. Post-election he found himself out of office and seemingly out of luck.

Chapter 21
Triumph and Disaster

It was fairly late in the evening, around 11.00pm, when Bríd Rodgers received a telephone call at home from her permanent secretary, Peter Small. "I have bad news," he said. There was a confirmed case of foot-and-mouth disease at an abattoir in Essex and a meeting was scheduled first thing in the morning with the chief veterinary officer, Dr Bob McCracken. As the outbreak had occurred in England, Rodgers was not unduly concerned by the information Small imparted to her. At that point she certainly had no inkling that events across the Irish Sea would turn her world upside-down and lead to the most important decision of her ministerial career. It was the first major non-political crisis to hit the administration, and it was Rodgers' remit to deal with it.

By the next day, 21 February 2001, the Agriculture minister knew exactly what she was facing and the devastating threat posed to Northern Ireland farmers if the disease spread to local farms. Dr McCracken outlined the situation and the possible outcomes. Many countries did not inoculate against the disease, while those countries that did were prevented from trading within the EU. It was an airborne virus, and with the high winds of February it could be transmitted across the Irish Sea. There was not much the minister could do about the weather, but after listening to McCracken's assessment she realised she could block imports of livestock and meat products from Great Britain. Rodgers knew closing the ports to goods from Britain would upset both the Ministry of Agriculture, Food and Fisheries (MAFF) in London and the Cabinet: neither would approve of her setting up an internal border within the United Kingdom. "MAFF were into damage limitation," said an insider, "and one of their concerns was if Northern Ireland wouldn't take products from Great Britain, what hope had they of persuading the French and Germans?"

Rodgers was more concerned with reaction in Northern Ireland than annoying the Prime Minister or Secretary of Agriculture Nick Brown. "I was made aware of the fact that the Northern Ireland Office and the British government were opposed to the closing of the ports because of the disruption to east-west trade," she said. The food retailers and other large companies had clout with central government and would have been aghast at any move to block their goods. "What happens if I don't close the ports?" Rodgers asked her advisors. She was warned that the disease could spread to Northern Ireland but that legally and procedurally her officials could not advise her to shut the ports. It was a political decision, requiring a ministerial instruction and was not without its risks. Insisting the devolved minister did not have the power to close the ports, MAFF threatened legal action if Rodgers defied the government. "Find me the power," Rodgers told her officials.

An old animal health act was found to justify the decision and Rodgers ordered her officials to ignore the pressure from London. "Just tell them we are closing the ports and that is that," she said. "What will it say to people about the new institutions if I don't act – that politicians can't do anything?" It was unlikely that any direct rule minister would have defied London in this way, as evidenced by the reaction of Secretary of State Sir Patrick Mayhew when the BSE crisis hit British beef. Mayhew refused to give in to local farmers' demands that Northern Ireland be exempt from the ban, in line with the Irish Republic. "I have no doubt in my mind," said Rodgers, "that had there been direct rule, the ports would not have been closed." As a nationalist minister in the devolved administration, Rodgers had no qualms about ignoring the government or creating an internal border within the UK. She also knew she would be judged on how she handled the crisis.

By 6.00pm on 21 February, just hours after her initial briefing, the ports were closed to vessels laden with meat and dairy products. The minister won praise for her brave decision – one that was widely credited with preventing the wholesale spread of the disease. Her defiance was challenged at the monthly meeting of the UK agriculture ministers in London, held soon after. One of the civil servants pointedly noted the government's displeasure and Nick Brown concurred, saying: "You were very bold."

"Well, I have to look after my own," Rodgers retorted, looking straight at Brown. Privately, Brown was more supportive, according to Rodgers. She said: "When we went outside, Nick Brown said to me, 'I'd have done the same in your position'."

As the crisis deepened in Britain and the government strived to protect the tourism and farming industries, Northern Ireland remained anxious to escape the scourge. As a precaution, Rodgers imposed restrictions on the movement and export of livestock and ordered that all animals imported from Britain in the previous month be traced. Non-essential farm visits were discouraged and disinfectant was widely distributed; the term "fortress farming" entered the vocabulary. Despite all her efforts, Rodger's worst fears were soon realised. On her way back from Brussels, where she had been battling to get the Northern Ireland beef ban lifted, she was informed about a suspect case in South Armagh. "I was quite shattered," she recalled, "because I thought we had escaped it."

By this time Northern Ireland's ports had been closed for one week and the minister was furious when she learned that someone may have brought infected sheep into Northern Ireland illegally following the outbreak in England. She called a news conference and disclosed that her officials had spent the day investigating Maurice Collins' border farm in Meigh, where a sheep had displayed signs of foot-and-mouth disease. In a statement issued through his solicitor Collins said he was cooperating with the authorities and denied ever owning, transporting, buying or selling the infected sheep found on his farm. He was never prosecuted. A central control room was set up at the Department to liaise with police, the industry and politicians. Farmers on both sides of the border were filled with apprehension as an exclusion zone was established around the property and the sheep immediately slaughtered, as a necessary precaution. The Irish government fretted. Tánaiste Mary Harney warned that the Irish economy could be brought to its knees if the disease spread, as it would not only affect agriculture but tourism too. In the North the president of the Ulster Farmers' Union, Douglas Rowe, spoke of dark days for the farming industry.

Subsequent tests proved positive and the cull widened to thousands of animals in the border area and then into County Louth when a farm in Proleek, a few miles from Meigh, was found to have a diseased animal. Fears grew as the slaughter spread. The cull became an extensive cross-border operation. It was essential that it was completed swiftly in order to prevent further outbreaks and to ensure that Brussels looked favourably on efforts to have the export ban on Northern Ireland livestock and other products lifted. But Rodgers encountered opposition from south Armagh farmers, who voiced their concerns when Department of Agriculture officials moved into the area. Initially, the objections appeared to centre on the disposal of carcasses and the need to ensure they were rendered rather than buried.

Rodgers despatched a senior Department official, Pat Toal, along with farming union representatives John Gilliland and Nigel McLaughlin to negotiate a resolution. In the course of their discussions it became clear that other issues were bothering the farmers, such as the financial impact of the cull and unfounded speculation that more compensation was being offered in the Republic. The Department also suspected that some farmers feared prosecution over the illegal trade in sheep; smuggling was considered to be common in South Armagh, as was the practise of claiming subsidies for sheep that did not exist. The concerned farmers sent a message to the minister, requesting to meet her directly. She agreed and suggested they come to see her at the department. The farmers insisted the minister come to visit them.

The Armagh cull was already two days behind the one in Louth, so Rodgers did not have time for a stand-off: a meeting was arranged in the Canal Court Hotel in Newry for noon the following day. At the hotel the minister met around fifty farmers from the south Armagh area. According to one observer some came in rather brash and aggressive, with a solicitor in tow. "They [some] were worried about what would happen," said Rodgers. "They asked me about amnesty."

As the meeting dragged on, the minister concluded she was getting nowhere. The farmers then suggested they would hold a public meeting that evening and get back to the minister in the morning. Rodger's patience snapped: "No. I can't wait until the morning. I am starting this cull at 2pm. I need to know in the next ten minutes." The minister knew that she might have a legal problem if she forced the farmers to cooperate with the cull and she could not afford a lengthy dispute. But she had an ace up her sleeve. While the farmers had brought the law with them, she had brought the media. According to one insider, the SDLP minister told the farmers: "I know what I need to do and I know what the Chief Medical Officer needs to do. It's ultimately down to you. [But] if you don't let me carry out this cull, I will tell the world why."

The farmers were not fools. They knew if they blocked the cull the entire Irish farming industry would blame them for the spread of the disease. After a brief discussion amongst themselves, they gave in and Rodgers returned triumphant to Stormont and her Executive colleagues. By now she was feeling good about being Agriculture minister. She concluded that it was just as well her portfolio had not gone to the DUP or Sinn Féin: a DUP minister might have engaged in a stand-off over the farmers' refusal to come to the Department, while a Sinn Féin minister, desiring their support, might have had difficulty standing up to the farmers. She also felt that a DUP minister might have had more difficulty cooperating openly with a Dublin minister.

Despite her own assessment of how she had managed the crisis, Rodgers faced criticism from some MLAs for her handling of the south Armagh farmers. She was accused of agreeing a side-deal that allowed some suspected of illegal activity to escape the law. This was vigorously denied, but there was a lingering suspicion when a loophole in the law ensured there were no prosecutions. Rodgers said this was coincidence, not conspiracy. The Department had been appealing for help to prosecute those involved in smuggling and a confidential hotline was set up to gather information to help police crack down on illegal livestock movements. A senior Department source recognised the genuine concerns of the DUP and others, who probably could not comprehend how Rodgers had persuaded the farmers without promises. "There was never any deal. There never could have been any deal. We were adamant anybody in breach of the rules would be prosecuted," the source said.

Rodgers rounded on her critics, as she had done early in the crisis, claiming they were trying to make political capital out of a very serious social and economic problem. However, the criticisms tailed off as the crisis deepened and politicians realised it was more prudent to support the minister. For her part, Rodgers was careful not to antagonise the chairman of her committee, Ian Paisley, who was quite capable of being a formidable opponent. When she met her committee, Paisley and the other members seemed more supportive, with one observer noting that the chairman was fair and diplomatic. Rodgers kept him informed and they spoke regularly about the crisis.

The Executive also pulled together on the issue, although there was some friction early on. Rodgers became suspicious that the Office of the First Minister – with whom she had clashed shortly after devolution over a farming relief scheme – was trying to take over the handling of foot-and-mouth. "Over my dead body," she had replied when her special advisor suggested Trimble wanted the centre to play the lead role. She had, after all, taken the job nobody wanted and she was not going to relinquish her power now. A senior official from OFM/DFM said an offer of assistance was misconstrued: "The Department of Agriculture was in 'ourselves alone' mode at that point. This was pure conspiracy theory. David Trimble and Seamus Mallon had no intention of taking it over."

Trimble blamed the misunderstanding on "oversensitive" officials. The early friction did not hamper cooperation, however, and soon the departments were pulling together. Rodgers felt this was in marked contrast to the British Cabinet where, she suspected, Nick Brown was being sidelined by the Prime Minister. Rodgers chaired an interdepartmental committee to co-ordinate cooperation across the Executive and reported to the First and Deputy First Ministers, in the process developing a good working relationship with Trimble, who turned out to be extremely cooperative. Her special advisor, Conall McDevitt, said of Trimble: "I found him very sharp. He would ask all the relevant questions. He was very down to earth and to the point. Apart from our own ministers, the minister I admired the most was David Trimble. During foot-and-mouth he saw immediately the need for Executive collectivity and the need to give Bríd the lead. That showed the best side of him."

In a show of public solidarity, Rodgers, flanked by the First and Deputy First Ministers, held a joint news conference after an emergency meeting of the Executive. The ministers appealed for vigilance across the community. Tangible signs of the efforts to avert the disease had reached Stormont, where disinfectant foot-bath mats were in place at the entrance doors. Tight controls were imposed to combat the disease and members of the public were asked to restrict their movements and avoid the countryside. A spirit of cooperation took hold on both sides of the border. Sporting and other events were cancelled in the North and in the Republic, where the annual St Patrick's Day parade was also postponed. Others were less willing to cancel their activities, notably the Belfast Giants ice hockey team and the Free Presbyterian Church, which was planning fiftieth anniversary celebrations in Belfast. The Reverend Ian Paisley, who chaired the Agriculture committee, firmly rejected criticism over his stance regarding the Church's celebrations. Assembly Speaker Lord Alderdice proceeded with his annual St Patrick's Day reception, insisting the event was in keeping with the guidelines; Rodgers declined her invitation to attend. She recalled initial reluctance on the part of the sports minister, Michael McGimpsey, to shut down the North West 200 that year, but she managed to persuade him that it was necessary. He credited the North West 200 club for recognising the risks posed by the event.

The foot-and-mouth crisis was a big test for the minister and for the power-sharing administration. The crisis also posed challenges for north-south relations, particularly as it worsened. The two Agriculture departments had a working relationship before devolution, but it became more formal thereafter. Rodgers had enjoyed a good relationship with her Dublin counterpart, Joe Walsh. In fact, he was among the first people she contacted about the Meigh outbreak. The southern economy was dependent on agriculture and he was particularly distressed to hear the outbreak had occurred on a border farm, as was the Taoiseach, who called a state of emergency. As the outbreak had originated in the north, it caused some resentment and underscored the territorial line between the two States, almost reinventing the Louth-Armagh border. "I remember a lot of tensions, as you would expect," said McDevitt. "The interests of north and south don't always coincide."

At the time, Rodgers was lobbying London and Brussels to have Northern Ireland excluded from the UK-wide ban. The outbreak was much worse in Great Britain and the minister was hoping Northern Ireland could quickly prove it was disease-free. This "regionalisation status" was a priority for local farming leaders, who worked alongside the minister to achieve it. While she was dismayed to hear about the outbreak in Louth, she was also frustrated to learn the Republic had been granted regionalisation status with great haste. Whereas Northern Ireland had to serve a thirty-day disease-free period, the ban in the Republic was lifted within forty-eight hours of the first outbreak, allowing twenty-five out of twenty-six of the Republic's counties to continue trading within the EU. Five of the six Northern Ireland counties had to wait much longer, illustrating in graphic terms the disadvantage Northern Ireland suffered as a region of the UK when it came to agricultural issues. Even unionist farmers shared the nationalist minister's disappointment.

This was another reason the cull in South Armagh needed to be completed swiftly. Following a tough meeting in Brussels between her officials, the chief veterinary officer Dr Bob McCracken and a powerful EU committee, it was agreed that Northern Ireland could move towards being treated as a separate region from the UK in relation to the disease. Provided there were no new outbreaks, this would take effect from 3 April 2001. While the Newry and Mourne district council area would remain under the UK ban because of the Meigh outbreak, it too could win regionalisation status once thirty days had passed from the initial outbreak without any new cases arising. "We had to wait, but we were lucky to get it," said a department insider. "Bríd put a lot of work in, developing relations in Brussels with [Commissioner] David Byrne and others." The minister was jubilant about the regionalisation status – a major victory for the devolved Assembly. A senior department insider said she deserved much credit for the victory, adding: "Bríd Rodgers broke the mould. Before that the UK line was our line."

But amidst efforts to achieve the exemption, the Taoiseach caused an uproar in Rodgers' department when he alleged that controls at ports in Northern Ireland were inadequate. The Irish Defence minister also criticised security at the border and Irish Natural Resources minister Hugh Byrne certainly did not help the matter when he was quoted demanding tougher measures against Britain and calling it "the leper of Europe". An angry and dismayed Rodgers protested to the Irish government in the strongest possible terms. In a statement the minister said the departments in Belfast and Dublin had been working closely together and no such concerns had been raised in any discussions. The minister pointed out that she had taken immediate and decisive action as soon as the cases in England were confirmed, closing the ports and imposing restriction on imports. "That was off the mark," said her special advisor Conail McDevitt, "and she saw that off."

"I was furious," said Rodgers. "I rang Joe Walsh and he said he had nothing to do with it and I invited him to Larne and he was happy enough with what we were doing." She travelled by helicopter to Ravensdale to examine operations south of the border. She got the red carpet treatment, but only after the scarlet mat was splashed with disinfectant. Walsh, in turn, came to her Dundonald House headquarters for an hour-long meeting. The two ministers held a joint news conference and warned of severe penalties for anyone involved in unauthorised livestock movement, a polite term for smuggling. "The big problem we all had," said McDevitt, "was the level of illegal trade and foot-and-mouth brought it to public attention." Cooperation between the departments helped in the battle against the disease and ultimately led to greater controls in animal trade.

The battle was a rollercoaster of hope and despair. When it appeared the disease was being stamped out, the mood lightened, especially when it was reported that spring that the Drumcree Orangemen had decided to suspend their protest in Portadown in a bid to halt the spread of the disease. "You've finally accomplished something," one insider joked to the minister, who had been dubbed "the witch of Drumcree" over her long opposition to the march in her constituency. McDevitt joked that if the disease persisted, she might even ban the march. "Impossible!" said another SDLP colleague. "Paisley doesn't get foot-and-mouth." Her press conferences gave way to lighter moments amidst the gloom. When she answered a reporter's question in Irish but kept using the word "fraud" in English, she was challenged by BBC agricultural correspondent Richard Wright on whether there was a word in Irish for fraud. She replied that Ireland was the land of saints and scholars until the English came and provided the word for fraud. In Brussels, she held court in Kitty O'Shea's Irish pub and joked about having to sit for hours under a Union flag at the top table for the British meat industry dinner.

But as quickly as the mood brightened, it darkened again. Despair returned when ten animals on a County Tyrone farm in Ardboe were found to have lesions consistent with the disease. What made it worse was that initial tests proved negative and that Easter weekend the minister had personally telephoned the farmer involved, Paddy Donnelly, with the good news. Their mutual delight was shortlived when further conclusive test results confirmed the disease. "That was devastating," said a department official, "because it carried the danger the whole thing could cascade out of control. It really set us back."

After receiving the initial all-clear, Rodgers headed to Donegal in celebratory mood for a break. She had just arrived through the front door when the telephone rang. It was Small, and he broke the news about Donnelly's farm. Rodgers was distraught. "That was the lowest ebb for her," said an industry source. "She was tired and distraught, feeling that she had let the farmer down and raised false hopes." She had to call a news conference. BBC correspondent Richard Wright met her the following morning for an interview. "She looked like she had been crying," he said.

The news was followed swiftly by reports of potential outbreaks close to the Donnelly farm, as well as at Cushendall in County Antrim. Thousands more animals had to be slaughtered, this time around the Ardboe area. The minister was also informed that a massive security operation was required to enforce an exclusion zone around the area, which would require assistance from the British Army. The minister was concerned about how local republicans would react to the Army moving in. She rang the area's MP, Martin McGuinness, who was also a fellow minister. She told the leading republican that she needed cooperation with the British Army. "What have you got to say about that?" she asked him. "If it has to be done, it has to be done," he told her. She was relieved by McGuinness' pragmatism.

For the farming community, the slaughter was heartbreaking and horrific. Animals were shot, the carcasses piled into a heap and burned. The flames could be seen for miles and the stench was overpowering. *The Irish News* reporter Billy Foley filed a graphic account of the cull: "It was a scene that would have left you numb. The twisted bodies of 19 animals lay dead … Tongues poked bolt straight from their mouths and eyes were wide open. Blood ran from their noses." In the midst of the despair that week, Rodgers stepped up restrictions, speaking with optimism while demanding vigilance. "We can beat this," she declared. "It is not a case of Doomsday yet." She tackled the disease wherever it was found and by early May the crisis appeared to have ended and disaster had turned to triumph. There was some criticism of Rodgers and her department in an independent report, which suggested some of the problems could have been avoided and communications could have been improved. The auditor's report claimed the department was too slow in bringing in the police and Army – understandable, perhaps, given the sensitivities in south Armagh and the reaction that might have followed. But overall her handling of the problem won her respect across the industry and in the Assembly. It was one of the reasons she was named the 2002 Politician of the Year in the annual Channel Four awards.

Rodgers had not anticipated accolades when she was given the post. In fact, when a party colleague had inquired which portfolio she would like, she had replied: "Anything but Agriculture!" During her years as an elected representative she had always passed agricultural matters over to her colleague, Denis Haughey. A source who observed her as she left the chamber after her selection was struck by her expression: "The look on her face said it all. This was a woman in deep shock." Even Paisley had spurned the department, having described it in the days before the selection as a poisoned chalice that would bring nothing but bad news, given the crisis already pertaining in Agriculture. Rodgers was all too aware that Agriculture had a number of disadvantages. In everything she attempted to achieve, the minister had two immediate hurdles to negotiate: getting policy agreed with a UK minister in London whose interests did not always converge with Northern Ireland's; and securing the agreement and support of the EU minister in Brussels.

When she arrived at the department for the first time, Rodgers met with Lord Dubs, the outgoing direct rule minister, and received a lesson in power politics. Technically he was still minister until midnight the following evening. Lord Dubs spoke to her about an initiative called "modulation" that the Labour government favoured. It meant that some of the subsidies that went directly to farmers would be slightly reduced to allow some funding to be diverted to rural development. There was no appetite for it among Northern Ireland farmers. "I won't be agreeing to it," Rodgers told him; Lord Dubs signed it into being at 11.55pm, minutes before power was transferred.

Her first choice would probably have been Education, as it was familiar territory to the former teacher. Rodgers said she would have been afraid to take a portfolio she did not know a lot about. "But in retrospect," she said, "I think it's much better to go into something that you don't know a lot about. Having gone to Agriculture with a clean sheet I was able to ask a myriad of questions." She spent the first few months quizzing everyone she met and engaging with the industry. Colleagues joked that she could not tell one end of a cow from another, but she would protest that she was the daughter of a Donegal small farmer and was not completely ignorant. "We had some land. My father had five cows, we had hens, we grew our own potatoes and our own corn and we even had a pig at one stage," she said. Rodgers took exception to claims by Ian Paisley Jr that she thought a hoggett was a baby pig. "That is rubbish!" she said, insisting her background in Donegal had taught her a hogget was a sheep. In fact, she was a country girl at heart with deep roots in rural Donegal.

Bríd Rodgers was born on 20 February 1935, and spent the first six weeks of her life in the village of Ardara, where her father was stationed as a Garda sergeant. Joe Stratford was a Galwayman who was among the first batch of new recruits to the Garda Síochána when the Irish Republic was formed. The Stratfords were Scottish Presbyterians who had crossed into Ireland to work in the big estates of the aristocracy. They had settled in Galway around the time of the plantation. Somewhere along the line, it is not clear when, one of them married a Roman Catholic and the family's destiny was altered.

Tom Stratford was raised on a small farm, but as his elder brother would inherit he joined the Gardaí and was posted to Bunbeg in Donegal, in the desolate wilds of north-west Ireland. Bunbeg, a harbour hamlet nestled where the Clady River met the sea, lay in the heart of the Gaeltacht. Stratford soon met and married local girl Josie Coll and it was in Ardra where the couple's second child, Bríd, was born.

Bríd was only six weeks old when her maternal grandfather died, leaving the young family several acres of land and a public house by the crossroads at the harbour. Decades later Teach Hudai Beag, as it was renamed, was a popular bar in Donegal and renowned for its traditional music. But in the 1930s it was a public house, a family home and a tavern all rolled into one. Bríd's mother, Josie, inherited it because her two brothers were pursuing their careers as doctors. Josie's mother had studied dentistry at University College Dublin and was the only woman in the class, but her plans were thwarted when she became ill with rheumatic fever. A specialist in Derry advised that she be taken out of school, as she would always be in bad health. "My mother accepted that," said Rodgers, who suspected old-fashioned chauvinism on the part of the doctor. "She lived until she was ninety-three and buried the whole damn lot of them and ran a pub in the meantime. My mother churned the butter. Almost everyone had one cow to supply the milk. The only people who didn't have cows were the doctor and the priest."

Rodgers had a carefree youth in Gweedore, where her first language was Irish. The area was rich in traditional culture, music and dancing and her childhood serenade was the fiddle music of Francie Mooney. Baba Dougan, the musical mother of the world-famous singing group Clannad, was a familiar figure. "There was no television so we had our own entertainment," said Rodgers. "We had the music and the *ceilidhs* and the melodeon, I think they call it the accordion now. That was our tradition."

Nature provided the art: a canvass of sea greeted her each morning and she took for granted the panoramic views of Donegal's off-shore islands, Tory, Inishfree and Inishmain. In the summertime the living was easy for a young child: unspoiled beaches in which to swim, fields to run through, Mount Errigal to climb and the River Clady to fish in. "It was freedom," she said. In those days, the pub and the church knitted village life together and being the daughter of a publican was good training for any politician: "You had to have the patience of a saint and you have to take insults as compliments and you had to have a thick skin and you had to work all the hours that God made and you had to settle rows."

Although memories of Partition were still fresh, she recalled no serious friction. "Politics was a kind of game between what side your parents were on in the civil war. That was about it," she said. Her father was Fianna Fáil; her mother Fine Gael, but made an exception for her first cousin, Cormac Breslin, who lived next door and was not only a Fianna Fáil TD but Speaker of the Dáil. Her mother would tell her about the Irish rebel leader, Michael Collins, and how Bríd's grandfather had proclaimed upon hearing the news of his death: "It's a sad day for Ireland."

Later, when she entered politics, Rodgers said in a television interview that her heroes were Collins the militarist, for his unwavering pragmatism, and Gandhi, the pacifist for his unwavering idealism. The comment was noted by Fine Gael and she became the first woman to speak at a Collins commemoration. She used her address that year, 1986, to denounce the violence of the Provisional IRA. The following year she faced a frightening encounter with masked republicans in Lurgan when she was driving home from a SDLP fund-raiser. There was rioting in the town because eight IRA men and one civilian had just been shot dead in Loughall by the security forces. Rodgers' car was attacked near the town's railway gates, at Lake Street, and a number of hooded men smashed one of the windows, injuring a woman in the back seat.

As a young girl, politics had held little appeal for Rodgers and in rural Gweedore religion was not an issue. The population was largely Catholic, with the exception of two Protestant families who were Irish-speakers and fully integrated into community life. The Protestant church was closer to Rodgers' family home than the Catholic St Mary's, a mile away. As a child, she and her friends would peer in the window of the mysterious St Patrick's. "We were just in awe of the church," she said. "There was this thing like a big eagle and it was the stand for the bible."

Education for girls as well as boys was important in her family. Rodgers was initially schooled in Bunbeg before moving, aged ten, to another primary school in Clady, run by a Master McGinley, who had a great name for producing results. There, Rodgers did all the scholarship exams and came second in Ireland in the Gaeltacht exam, beaten out of first by an older girl. Her parents expected their younger daughter to attend Mount Anville in Dublin, where her older sister, Maire, was already a boarder. But Bríd was set on attending St Louis' school in Monaghan with her friends. In the face of her determination, her parents relented.

The summer of 1947 was a watershed in Rodgers' life. She had just turned twelve when her father died suddenly that August, aged forty-five. A few weeks later, Josie Coll, with a heavy heart, sent her daughters back to school. The first months alone in a new school were heartbreaking for Bríd and she longed for home. Christmas brought her back to Gweedore and, refreshed by the comforts of home, she returned to school with a lighter step. "I loved Monaghan," said Rodgers. "People say your school days are the happiest of your life and you don't realise it until afterward, but I actually knew when I was there I was enjoying it."

As a class A student, Rodgers was schooled in Irish and through Irish learned Latin and French. She excelled in her studies and delighted in the after-school activities, such as opera, drama and games. She earned a scholarship to the National University, but as it was a Gaeltacht Scholarship she attended the campus in Galway, not in Dublin. This time she was determined to get to Dublin. She took the advice of a family friend and switched her course from French and Spanish to French and Italian, as Galway did not offer Italian but Dublin did. It worked. Sprung from convent school in the 1950s, Dublin offered freedom for Rodgers and her friends who went to dances, or hops as they called them, and to the cinema. Socialising was innocent: in those days the boys would have a pint, the girls a lemonade. At UCD she mixed with northern Catholics from Tyrone and Armagh, who would complain bitterly about discrimination in Northern Ireland. "They would tell us how you couldn't get a job and how it was all for Protestants and I thought they were exaggerating. I thought it just couldn't be that bad," she said.

However, Rodgers found out they were not exaggerating when she moved to Lurgan a few years later, in 1960, after she married Antoin Rodgers, a Gweedore man eight years her senior. Antoin courted her when he returned to Ireland from Africa, where he had worked as a dentist with the Medical Missionaries of Mary. Bríd had returned to Donegal, now in her twenties, and was working as a teacher in Falcarragh. Once she married she moved to Lurgan, where her new husband's practice was located, and described moving there as a culture shock. She recalled sitting in "mixed company" one evening when the abortion debate was raised: "I said my views would be coloured by the fact that I was a Catholic, and I got a kick under the table." She soon learned religion was a taboo subject.

The Rodgers were unprepared for the reaction when Antoin won the trophy in the local golf club in 1962 and had his named engraved on it. "I had polished it beautifully," said his wife, "and left the cup up, and all hell broke loose." Her husband, who had informed the other club members that his name would be engraved in Irish, was told it would have to be changed because the Lisburn members were laughing at them. "That's unfortunate," Antoin replied, "but you won't take it off with my permission and if you do take my name off, you won't put it back in English." His wife was equally annoyed. She said: "He signed his cheques in Irish and they never refused them." The story made the newspapers. Years later Bríd Rodgers would chide the electoral office for refusing to put a *fada* (accent) on her name on council ballot papers, even though there was no technical difficulty in doing so. She was heartened later on when her department's officials were sensitive to the use of both Irish and English, although she chose not to have all press releases translated as she believed the cost was prohibitive.

She was drawn into politics in the 1960s when, as a busy mother-of-three, she worked for the Campaign for Social Justice (CSJ). Rodgers and Antoin were asked by Dr Conn McCluskey of Dungannon if they would assist with gathering statistics on Catholic/Protestant employment in Lurgan. Rodgers helped to produce a pamphlet, *The Plain Truth*, which outlined alleged discrimination in employment. When the campaign gave way to the civil rights movement (NICRA), Rodgers joined in the demands for equality in housing and employment, as well as electoral reform. At her first NICRA meeting she was annoyed when she heard a man a deliver a republican rant. She whispered to her husband that the movement was about getting fair play for Catholics, not "this diatribe". Her husband told her to stand up and make her point. "My knees were literally knocking, but I spoke," she said.

Rodgers was not discouraged by the "chill" that attended her involvement in NICRA. She recalled that a Protestant doctor, whom she knew socially in the town, treated her very coolly when she brought her son to see him. "He would have known me on first-name terms, but he treated me like just another number," she said. When she led a march through the town in 1970, the hostility grew. According to Rodgers, a Bangor-based orthodontist from the unionist tradition quit working for her husband's practice on Saturdays, leaving a message with a woman employee who passed it on to Antoin. It read: "I won't be back. That Fenian bitch of a wife of yours disrupted the whole town on Saturday and I had trouble getting out." Bríd Rodgers was taken aback as she had given the man his lunch every Saturday. Her husband was equally annoyed. When the man rang again and asked the receptionist if he could return to finish his work so he could get paid, Rodgers had a message of his own to pass on: "If he wants to speak to me, he can speak to me. Until he speaks to me, he can go to hell."

The Rodgers' stance on civil rights cost them in financial terms, too, as their dental practice suffered a dramatic loss of clients. When the SDLP was formed in 1970, Bríd Rodgers declined to attend the first branch meeting. When John Hume rang to ask why, she told him: "I am waiting to be carted off to hospital." At the time she was eight months pregnant with her fifth child, Tom. Her first child, Mary, was born in 1961, followed swiftly by Anne, Seamus and Bríd. Her sixth and last child, Antoin, was born in 1973. But despite the pressures of motherhood, she was soon involved in the SDLP. Noting that a particular issue was not being addressed at the local council, she had written to Hume asking what the party intended to do about it. He sent back a one-line letter that read: "What are you doing about it?" She became the SDLP's branch secretary.

By then the Troubles were escalating and she almost quit Northern Ireland for good. While she was holidaying in Donegal, her home in Lurgan was burgled. "My handbags were searched and documents were strewn all over the place," said Bríd Rodgers, "But boxes of money belonging to the children were not touched." The Rodgers became convinced it was an intelligence-gathering operation by the security forces as the only items taken were six copies of the newly launched republican paper, *An Phoblacht*. Bríd Rodgers had been invited to write an article on civil rights by local republican J.B. O'Hagan, who had worked with her in the campaign. The Rodgers changed their minds about moving only at the last minute.

The young mother stuck with the SDLP, sharing her party's disappointment when Sunningdale failed. In 1976 Rodgers served as the party's vice-chairman, and in 1978 became chairman – the first woman to hold the post in an Irish political party. She held other posts too, including general secretary, and served on the Standing Advisory Commission on Human Rights. In 1983 she was appointed to the Irish Senate by Taoiseach Garret FitzGerald. When Rodgers retired from active politics, FitzGerald paid tribute to her at the SDLP's annual party conference, confiding to a delighted audience that he "had always been a bit in love with her".

Some members of the party resented her Senate appointment. She was not included in the party's delegation to the New Ireland Forum. In fact, no woman was appointed to the all-male delegation. However, by 1991 she was sufficiently prominent to warrant a place on the SDLP's negotiating team in the Brooke–Mayhew talks. Rodgers blazed a trail for many women in Northern Ireland politics and within the SDLP, never allowing herself to be put off by male chauvinism. By 1985 she had been elected to Craigavon Council, the same year the Anglo-Irish Agreement was signed. Unionist councillors, who dominated the Council, refused to engage in business as usual. Rodgers said she got a hard time about her involvement in civil rights and was overlooked for every committee appointment: "They absolutely ostracised me, but always nominated me for the police liaison committee, the one committee they knew I wouldn't go on." She appeared relieved when she gave up the Council in 1993, likening the majority of unionist councillors to the Bourbons: "learning nothing and forgetting nothing". She first stood for Westminster in 1987, taking on the Upper Bann MP and Ulster Unionist deputy leader Harold McCusker. Later she would do battle with his successor, David Trimble. In 1991–92 she won a place on the SDLP's negotiating team but, like most delegates, held out little hope of a resolution.

After the IRA ceasefire in 1994, Rodgers was among prominent SDLP members who demanded an immediate start to negotiations that included Sinn Féin. While the ceasefire marked an end to the war of attrition, a new battleground opened up over parades, the most famous dispute taking place at Drumcree, Portadown, in the heart of Upper Bann. Not for the first time, Rodgers was in the eye of the storm. Although she was a constitutional nationalist, her role in Drumcree had marked her out among unionists as very green. Within nationalism her stand brought plaudits and profile, and was one of the reasons she was appointed a minister in the power-sharing Executive. Another reason was the fact that the party needed to tick the gender-balance box. She chaired the party's negotiating team that helped to negotiate the Good Friday Agreement and was famously photographed through the window of Castle Buildings hugging a colleague in jubilation when the deal was agreed. It was the proudest day of her political career.

As a power-sharing minister in the Executive she enjoyed a good rapport with her officials: "I think I got the best permanent secretary in the business, very straight, very fair and extremely competent. From the first day we sort of had an understanding that he ran the department and I decided the policy and I let him get on with it." She made clear her intentions at a dinner in her private office with all the senior staff members:

> "I told them the one thing I wanted was to be kept informed about all the major issues, not the nitty-gritty. I wanted to be seen as the person who decided on policy issues, but I wasn't going to get in their way of running whatever section of the department they were running. I was very open and honest with them and I think they appreciated that."

When she chose her ministerial advisor, Rodgers opted for Dubliner Conail McDevitt, the SDLP's former director of publicity. "What do you know about agriculture?" she had asked McDevitt. "F— all," he said. She hired him anyway. "I had plenty of agricultural experts in the Department. What I needed was a political advisor, so I appointed someone with no agricultural experience but who had a very sharp political brain," she said. The pair of them muddled through the learning curve together.

Conail McDevitt's great-grandfather was republican socialist Danny McDevitt, who was a radical trade unionist at the turn of the century. His tailor's shop in Rosemary Street, Belfast, was known as "the Bounders' College" in the years before the Easter Rising and was a magnet for the city's radicals, who gathered to discuss politics. Irish rebel leader James Connolly had lodged with Danny McDevitt at 565 Falls Road when he came to Belfast. McDevitt was later interned, in 1919, at Ballykinlar and his sons became members of the IRA. At partition, Danny McDevitt was escorted to the border by the Royal Irish Constabulary and told never to return north. When Gerry Adams met McDevitt's great-grandson at the negotiations leading to the Good Friday Agreement, he told him he had a "good pedigree".

Rodgers sensed some nervousness in the Department about the arrival of her political advisor: "I know they were hugely suspicious at the beginning." In a meeting with her officials she made it clear that McDevitt's role was to advise her on policy matters and on political issues, and that he would not be interfering with the roles of officials. "It worked out extremely well," said Rodgers. "There was no tension I was aware of." But, like other political advisors, McDevitt did encounter resentment over his position. He clashed with civil servants on occasion and became known as "the Mouth from the South".

Rodgers, a natural-born politician, soon overcame any discomfort some officials may have felt about her own political baggage. One civil servant, who asked not to be named, was full of praise, saying: "She read her brief very well, worked very long hours and was a very astute lady." Her stamina for work, despite her age – she was sixty-four when she took office – became a talking point. Her younger officials sometimes struggled to keep up as her workload spilled into weekends. She reputedly went home sick only once during her tenure. On another occasion, when she took ill one morning in the ministerial car, she insisted on going into work. Her officials were concerned when she arrived, but, in fine form, she told them: "Don't worry gentlemen, I'm not pregnant."

Officials in her department said she was a joy to work with and paid tribute to her skills as a minister. Said one: "She was very good at keeping her eye on the big picture, where she wanted to get to, very good at saying, 'Just get it done'. If something did not get done, she would want to know why." When things did not work out, she accepted explanations "without grudges". Said the insider: "She never let an issue boil. So long as you went in and said, 'We have made a mess of something and here's what happened and here's how to fix it'."

In general the farming lobby welcomed her appointment, grateful to have a devolved minister. Less welcoming was a group of unionists in Portavogie, a County Down fishing village she visited soon after her appointment to announce new investment. The minister was pelted with eggs and confronted by a twenty-strong crowd of flag-waving protestors. Their banner read: "Portavogie supports Portadown Orangemen". They shouted insults at Rodgers: "Go home you Fenian bastard!" and "No Surrender!" The minister, huddled between two uniformed policemen, was escorted quickly towards the harbour, where she was again hit by a torrent of abuse and more eggs. Her hair and clothes were splattered. A protestor complained, by way of explanation, to a reporter: "When she stated her opening speech in the Assembly, she did it in Gaelic, a foreign language."

The attack was roundly condemned by the First and Deputy First Ministers. Rodgers dismissed the "rent-a-mob" and insisted she would not be intimidated from working to help everyone. She also hoped that in time people would recognise her efforts. She was greeted rather more warmly at the Balmoral Winter Fair and later won kudos among unionist farmers when she attended the agricultural fair with the Queen. She met the Republic's Agriculture minister, Joe Walsh, within a week of devolution, narrowly beaten to the title of first devolved minister to Dublin by the Enterprise minister, Sir Reg Empey.

The agriculture industry was undergoing its most depressed period for some time, plagued by the BSE crisis and the decline in the once thriving pig industry, which had reduced incomes substantially. Total farming income was reported to have plummeted by 75% in the previous five years. Rodgers appointed a steering committee, chaired by her permanent secretary, to develop a new vision for the industry. The difficulties facing the industry were underscored by Will Taylor, president of the Ulster Farmers' Union, who wrote to newspapers welcoming the first home-grown minister in almost thirty years. He noted that the day she accepted her nomination, it was reported that hill farmers in Northern Ireland were earning only £4 per week. But he urged the minister not to despair, pledging support from the industry, which was looking for a minister to make a strong case in Belfast, London and Brussels. He also urged her to prioritise the lifting of the beef ban by progressing Northern Ireland's case for low-risk status. Rodgers did put the issue high on her agenda and raised it in her very first meeting with Joe Walsh.

The farming lobby deeply appreciated the need for devolution and, in one of the more bizarre scenes in the administration's life, thousands of farmers descended on Stormont with their tractors and placards in January 2000 demanding assistance and complaining that they collectively owed the banks almost £500 million. What was surreal about the protest was that the Executive was days away from suspension; it was like appealing to a condemned man for help. Perhaps it was a measure of the extent of the crisis facing the industry, which saw farm incomes fall sharply by some 22% in 2000 alone.

Inside Stormont, Rodgers met five farming representatives while the rest of the protestors remained outside. According to the minister, word then arrived that the farmers wanted her to come outside to speak to them. Her officials were a bit hesitant; the permanent secretary instinctively trying to protect the minister. "Peter Small was the mother hen," said Rodgers. "I said, 'Peter, I will be alright. I've been through Drumcree. Drumcree is worse than this.' I think they were afraid of what I might say or promise. They were nervous, but they were supportive." One insider said his concern was the minister would have nothing to say and that this would be damaging. Peter Small offered to go with her, but she insisted she would do it alone.

From the steps of Stormont the new minister addressed the farmers, who were led by Taylor, the man who had praised the minister weeks earlier for showing a grasp of the complexities of the industry's problems. One observer was amused to see a banner stating that south Armagh farmers supported Paisley, and was also struck by the way unionists forgot themselves and clapped for Sinn Féin's Gerry McHugh, a member of the agriculture committee, when he berated the department and its officials. Rodgers won the farmers' respect that day, according to McDevitt and others, for coming out to speak to them. He claimed it helped build relations with farmers, particularly those from the unionist tradition. "They really saw that day that they didn't have 'the witch of Drumcree'," McDevitt said, "but they had a courageous, competent minister who was going to rise to the challenge." As the industry's respect grew, so did Rodgers' enjoyment of the job: "It was the first time I was in a position to affect people's lives."

Along with ministerial power came patronage, and in the summer of 2000 Rodgers was asked to make an appointment to the Rural Development Council. She was presented with a list of four people, three of whom were men. They were all suitable, but she chose the woman candidate, who went on to chair the council in 2003. As minister she made it clear that she also wanted to tackle the Department's historic employment imbalance; Catholics were under-represented. In this her attitude was in sharp contrast to Stormont's first Minister for Agriculture, Sir Edward Archdale. In 1925 *The Northern Whig* reported that Sir Edward was amused when a Fintona man had asked him how it was that his ministry employed "over 50 per cent Roman Catholics". The newspaper recorded: "He had 109 of a staff and so far as he knew there were four Roman Catholics. Three of these were civil servants, turned over to him, who he had to take when he began."

Rodgers restructured the department. Historically the department had formal ties to Queen's University's agriculture department, a potential conflict of interest. The link had been in place since partition, but on Rodgers' watch it was severed. "The link was no longer appropriate," said McDevitt. "It compromised independent research and there was broad consensus that change was required."

Following the death of one of Queen Elizabeth's relations, Rodgers caused a few ripples when she instructed that the Union flag be removed from a Department of Agriculture building in Dungannon, which was not covered by Mandelson's flags legislation. After consulting party colleagues she decided it should be flown at half-mast on Dundonald House only, her headquarters: "Some civil servants wanted to know who took the decision and why and caused a bit of a barney about it. But I just kept out of it and said nothing. It died a death."

While her confidence in her role grew over time, she admitted to being terrified the first time she had to go to the despatch box to answer questions in the chamber: "The first answer is prepared, but after that you are on your own and naturally, being new to it, I spent a lot of time the weekend before just going over all the stuff to make sure I was abreast of everything." It was difficult for her because her committee chairman, Paisley, was not only a formidable opponent but he knew more about agriculture than she did. Relations settled down after a while, however. She remembered that he challenged her about an enviable initiative that was being undertaken by the Irish government and demanded to know why she was not doing the same. She pointed out that her difficulty was she had to rely on a UK minister to represent Northern Ireland in Brussels: she wondered was the DUP leader suggesting a constitutional change?

Rodgers also got one over on the UK agriculture minister. Once a month the devolved ministers would meet with Nick Brown before the European Council of Ministers' meeting. It was an opportunity for Brown to discuss policy issues with all concerned and try to arrive at a common position. This was not always easy; sometimes each region had diverging interests.

At one such meeting, Brown tried to persuade the devolved ministers to agree to change the rules relating to farmers who were found to have been over-subsidised during the year. Farmers who had less than ninety cattle did not have to pay the claw-back, but Brown wanted to alter the regulations so all farmers were liable if they had been over-subsidised. Rodgers was determined to protect the smaller farmers' interests and found an ally in Welsh Agriculture minister Carwyn Jones, who was also conscious that the change was more likely to suit large farmers in Scotland and England than his own constituents. Rodgers recalled: "I had a wee chat with the Welsh minister and he was totally opposed to any change." At the meeting, Rodgers and Jones refused to agree to the change. A frustrated Brown turned to his permanent secretary and asked, "Well, what do we do now?" The official informed the minister that it could not be changed without agreement. Rodgers said the meeting was an eye-opener for the UK minister. "It was the first time he couldn't do what he liked," she said.

Previously, Brown had dealt with devolved ministers who were all in his party and thus subject to the party whip. They were less likely to challenge him as forcefully as Rodgers, who was not from the same party. A devolved Stormont gave the other regional Labour ministers a powerful ally in challenging UK decision-making. Eventually, the Northern Ireland and Welsh ministers did compromise on the issue, privately agreeing a joint approach. According to Rodgers: "I said to Carwyn, you say forty head and we'll agree to a thirty-head limit."

In office, Rodgers made the lifting of the beef ban in Northern Ireland a priority, as the farming community had beseeched her to do. It was a long-standing grievance that the region remained under the ban following the BSE crisis in the UK in the 1990s. The ban was catastrophic for the farming industry. Northern Ireland farmers protested that that incidence of BSE in their cattle was proportionally twenty-five times lower than in Britain and wanted to be treated the same as the Republic of Ireland, which did not fall under the ban. But the Ministry of Agriculture, Food and Fisheries wanted common UK status. "MAFF always made sure we knew our place," recalled Rodgers, who battled hard for regional status and believed she was making inroads until she was interrupted by suspension. It became an academic point whether she would have succeeded in achieving a BSE exemption for Northern Ireland if suspension hadn't cut short her tenure. Long after the suspension of devolution the row continued unabated, but most agree that a direct rule minister was not going to have the same flexibility to tackle London resistance. Consequently, Rodgers was best remembered for her battle against foot-and-mouth disease. A senior source in her Department was certain that without her decision to close the ports, the result would have been much worse:

> "The outbreak we eventually had would have occurred much earlier and in a much more traumatic way. That decision was key. It was very courageous. I wouldn't underestimate the pressure she was under at ministerial level not to do it. A direct rule minister would have found it impossible."

"She fought her corner and fought it well," said Ian Paisley Jr. But he was critical of the lack of substantive legislation coming through her Department, which he also condemned as too bureaucratic. He did praise her accessibility as a minister, however. An industry veteran struggled to find something negative to say and finally concluded that early efforts to help the fishing industry were perhaps overshadowed by the plight of farmers and the scourge of foot-and-mouth.

Devolution broke down barriers in the farming world, according to BBC correspondent Richard Wright. It paved the way for better relations between the Ulster Farmers' Union and nationalist politicians, even Sinn Féin. The DUP, said Wright, also benefited, enjoying a surge in support from being in control of the Agriculture committee. Rodgers' triumph over the foot-and-mouth crisis did not transfer to west Tyrone, where the SDLP underestimated the strength of sectarian voting in the 2001 general election, wrongly believing unionists and nationalists would unite with the farming minister to keep Sinn Féin out.

Unionism had always kept a close eye on Rodgers, waiting to catch her out. Robert Overend, a prominent pig farmer and a senior Orangeman with staunch unionist views, took her through her paces in daily briefings as an industry representative during the foot-and-mouth crisis. "He would try to confront Bríd and get the better of her," said McDevitt, "but eventually one day he just said, 'Ah heck, you are doing a great job'." It was a sweet moment; in sharp contrast to the one following suspension, when she was shown into her old office by her private secretary so she could brief the incoming direct rule minister. "It was one of the most awful experiences of my life," she said, "to hand over what I thought was my prerogative."

Chapter 22
Guns and Government

David Trimble stood on French soil on 1 July 2001, where battle-lines had once been drawn at the Somme, and hoped for a decisive victory in his political war with the IRA over decommissioning. He had arrived in France as First Minister of Northern Ireland, but overnight had been stripped of title, privilege and power. Wounded after the Westminster poll and considerably weaker without the armour of the First Minister's Office, Trimble stood quietly at Thiepval to commemorate the Battle of the Somme. But in an interview before retreating to Stormont, he lashed out at republicans and their refusal to destroy their weapons. He acknowledged his resignation had been risky but insisted his gamble would be worth it, if he could see the Agreement implemented and decommissioning achieved.

At Stormont, Seamus Mallon was asked if this was the beginning of the end for David Trimble. "Only David Trimble can answer that question," he replied. Although Trimble had resigned, Mallon still retained the functions of Office due to the quirks of the legislation governing jointery. Trimble was entitled to nominate an "alternative" First Minister to rule for a period of six weeks while the Assembly tried to reappoint the top posts. In his stead, Trimble nominated Sir Reg Empey – a sticking-plaster solution that meant the business of government could continue, at least temporarily.

In an Assembly debate the vehemently anti-Agreement UK Unionist Robert McCartney described the move as "Alice in Wonderland" politics and complained that the legislation was not designed for a "tactical" resignation, but rather for times when a First Minister was ill, or temporarily insane. "Or perhaps not temporarily," the DUP deputy leader Peter Robinson interjected pointedly. Lord Alderdice, a trained psychiatrist, noted that in those circumstances people might want to consult him.

Lord Alderdice then called upon the Deputy First Minister, who was in no mood for jokes, to make a personal statement. Mallon told the members that he recognised the real contribution David Trimble had made to devolution, but was disappointed that his actions had now destabilised the institutions and precipitated a crisis, one that PUP MLA David Ervine had dubbed "the daddy of all crises". Mallon expressed regret that the political process had been held to ransom, first by the failure to commence devolution and then by the failure to commence decommissioning. The Deputy First Minister said every crisis and interruption weakened the institutions still further. "Cynical party advantage," he vowed, "must not be allowed to threaten the Agreement."

Trimble was not in the chamber to respond to these words as he was in London. It was left to his Assembly colleague, John Taylor, to respond. Taylor blamed republicans for the problems in the Executive and warned that his party would press for Sinn Féin's expulsion from the Executive if the IRA failed to act within six weeks.

In London, Prime Minister Tony Blair and Taoiseach Bertie Ahern met for dinner to discuss how to tackle the latest crisis. They decided to spirit the parties away to an undisclosed location near Birmingham for secret talks aimed at breaking the stalemate. While this plan was unfolding, loyalist gunmen returned to their brutal ways. A Catholic teenager, Ciaran Cummings, was murdered while he waited for a lift to work, apparently in revenge for Sinn Féin's election success. Trimble sparked outrage when he suggested, erroneously, that the Antrim teenager might have been murdered by republicans in a drugs row. The Chief Constable moved quickly to dismiss this notion while nationalist ministers Martin McGuinness and Mark Durkan demanded an apology. A clearly embarrassed David Trimble, who appeared to have been briefed incorrectly by a party colleague, was forced to withdraw his remarks and apologise when pressed by the media. Within a few weeks another teenager, Gavin Brett, a Protestant, was gunned down by loyalists, who mistook him for a Catholic.

Newspaper headlines highlighted a fragile peace as ministers in the Executive laid bare the tensions in their relationships. Looking ahead to the talks planned by Blair and Ahern, Trimble made it known that he expected there would be but one item on the agenda: decommissioning. McGuinness, who had his own ideas about the talks, countered: "Poor David, he is living in a fantasy world." Nationalist agenda items included police reform and demilitarisation.

Despite efforts by government officials to keep the talks venue secret, it emerged that the negotiations would be held at Weston Park, the ancestral home of the Earls of Bradford on the borders of Shropshire and Staffordshire. The DUP was not invited to participate. However, buoyed by its election result and the increasingly precarious position of the Ulster Unionist leader, the party scornfully declared that the talks were doomed and any deal made without them would not stick.

The mood was glum at Weston Park when the talks began on 9 July with six parties taking part: the Ulster Unionists, the SDLP, Sinn Féin, Alliance, the Women's Coalition and the Progressive Unionist party. Soon one of this number was lost: the loyalist PUP pulled out within days, citing frustration with the process. Notably, the Ulster Unionist delegation included Jeffrey Donaldson, Trimble's arch critic. The discussions were overshadowed briefly by violence in North Belfast when scores of police officers were injured as they tried to clear the Catholic Ardoyne area to facilitate a Twelfth Orange parade. This was in contrast to the Drumcree protest, which had passed without violence days earlier. For Mallon, the confrontation in Ardoyne was a stark reminder that cross-community support for policing was critical to social stability. According to a party insider, Mallon arrived at Weston Park like a man obsessed and in a pretty severe state of agitation over the policing issue. "Mallon is deeply committed to policing," said the SDLP source. "He took it personally you know, getting it right. Policing was in many ways going to be the lynchpin in any system of government."

In the run-up to negotiations SDLP junior minister Denis Haughey remembered he had been unable to get Mallon to sign some papers on an e-government initiative he had been working on. Haughey went to Weston Park and, desperate to get his papers signed off, looked for an opportunity to do so. He thought he had found one when he spotted

Mallon stretched out on a sofa, but when he broached the subject, Mallon just waved him away. "Now I can understand why," said Haughey. "He was thinking, thinking, thinking his way through the difficulties and little things like e-government could come later."

Mallon was determined to get a deal on policing and wanted the matter settled before he left politics. He bristled at the suggestion that he was a man obsessed. "I wouldn't like to think I was obsessive about it," he said. "I knew what would hold and what wouldn't and I knew what was needed – and God knows the reason I knew what was needed was [that] I was dealing with it for so long and I had seen so much." After his own thirty-five-year battle for police reform, he was heartened by the Patten report and was bitterly disappointed when the Policing Bill failed to reflect its vision. But ever hopeful, he calculated that the Prime Minister would turn once he realised he was not getting anywhere with nationalists on the issue. Pressure had been mounting for the SDLP to sign up to policing, but Mallon would not be rushed. He was determined to get the various elements of the issue right and resented suggestions that his party was afraid to move on the issue without Sinn Féin. Having seen Sinn Féin's policing paper during the talks, Mallon concluded that republican demands were largely technical and that the Provisional movement was not yet ready to embrace policing. "The Shinners were always buying time," he said. "The Sinn Féin position was tactical, not a substantive position."

Trimble left Weston Park before the negotiations concluded. He departed when he realised there would be no breakthrough on the weapons issue and judged that Sinn Féin was demanding too much on policing. Consequently, the talks ended in acrimony with unionists blaming republicans and republicans insisting there was not enough on the table regarding policing. There was reason to believe that Weston Park had yielded some progress, however. In an interview given at the time, Mallon claimed a deal had been possible, pointing to progress on policing, demilitarisation and the protection on the Agreement's institutions. He agreed with Trimble, however, that there had been no movement on decommissioning.

In spite of his early leave-taking, Weston Park was memorable for Trimble because of Donaldson's contribution. Trimble spent some time in the garden, listening to what he called "serious music", while Donaldson took part in the talks. Trimble claimed Sinn Féin was impressed by Donaldson's participation and his commitment to inclusivity, if the IRA disarmed and disbanded. "McGuinness seemed to like him," said Trimble. It may well have been that republicans, now wary of Trimble and his ever-weakening position, viewed Donaldson as the better bet and a future Ulster Unionist leader.

While there was no agreement between republicans and unionists, Weston Park stood out because it marked a new low in relations between Sinn Féin and the SDLP, indeed the lowest point since the signing of the Good Friday Agreement. In the aftermath of the watershed election the animosity between the two parties was palpable. Martin McGuinness accused Mallon of carping at republicans. The *Observer* reported sharp exchanges during the talks between Mallon and McGuinness, who had called the Deputy First Minister "grumpy" during one interview. According to the newspaper, Mallon's patience snapped during talks with the Sinn Féin delegation and he shouted at the Education minister: "Don't talk to me like that, boy." An SDLP source described an incredibly bad atmosphere: "Adams was being unbelievably arrogant by going away in the middle of it all to make a speech and Trimble had gone off to a garden party and Mallon was just climbing the walls altogether."

The source recalled the Prime Minister trying to conquer the obstinacy of the SDLP, and Mallon, by focusing on party leader John Hume. In a divide-and-conquer strategy, Blair met Hume alone while the SDLP negotiators were tied up in another meeting, a move that particularly annoyed Mallon. On the last day, one talks insider recalled the party delegation being left in their room for most of the day: "By this stage, Seamus was pissed off, John was depressed and Mark was knackered." The situation changed, said the source, when Bríd Rodgers took charge and went to see the Irish government delegation to insist on a meeting; Dublin agreed. The SDLP then spent several fruitful hours with the Irish delegation, according to the insider: "We came out with what we needed on policing. Weston Park broke the back. It was in many ways a real low point, but it was also a high point."

At the time, however, Weston Park looked like a failure and the two governments attempted to put a gloss on the apparent stalemate by issuing a joint statement promising a comprehensive package of proposals based on the negotiations. While the package was prepared amid further contacts with the key players, Trimble made it clear that without guns being destroyed no unionist would volunteer for the position of First Minister. Even if he himself was minded to take that risk, it was clear that elements in his party would not permit it. Before the British-Irish proposals were unveiled, Donaldson, along with anti-Agreement unionist David Burnside, issued a statement withdrawing support for the current efforts to sustain power-sharing. The pair claimed that too many concessions were flowing to republicans in return for disarmament.

The governments' proposals – delayed by further secret efforts to persuade the IRA to move – were finally unveiled on 1 August. Backed by the White House, the proposals involved a number of key elements, such as rolling demilitarisation, including the demolition of the British Army base at Magherafelt. There was a promise to hold independent judicial inquiries into a number of controversial murders in which collusion was alleged between paramilitaries and security forces, including the murders of human rights lawyers Rosemary Nelson and Pat Finucane. These inquiries were demanded by the SDLP as a *quid pro quo* for signing up to policing. The proposals also included a pledge to revise policing legislation by October 2002 and a commitment to publish a revised implementation plan to reflect the Patten recommendations. The government committed itself to dealing with OTRs, or republicans who were "on the run" from the authorities. These suspects wanted to know that they could return home without fear of prosecution and the government promised to extend the prisoners' release scheme to accommodate them, a particularly controversial move in unionist circles, where it was regarded as an amnesty. Only two sentences in the ten-page proposals document focused on decommissioning, which was described as "indispensable" to the full implementation of the Agreement. The brevity was deliberate. It was hoped that republicans would act if it were not perceived as giving in to an overt demand for weapons.

The parties were given just days to respond to the document: haste was necessary as the deadline to find a Deputy First Minister was looming. The DUP leader Ian Paisley dismissed the Weston Park proposals as a last-ditch effort by a discredited government. Trimble, on the other hand, was careful not to reject them outright because he was waiting to see what the Provisional IRA would do next. The dissident Real IRA gave its reaction in no uncertain terms when it exploded a car bomb in West London, injuring seven people and causing extensive damage to nearby properties. The SDLP gave the package a cautious welcome. At a news conference with party leader John Hume and Education minister Sean Farren, Mallon suggested the party was inching towards accepting policing, but claimed the package was incomplete without the police implementation plan. Secretary of State John Reid had already briefed the SDLP on the plan, but this was extremely detailed and the party needed to study it closer and also wanted it published.

In its response, Sinn Féin focused on what unionism was going to do. The party said it was time the unionist leader embraced the Agreement whole-heartedly, accusing him of attempting to minimise and dilute its potential. Trimble, meanwhile, was concerned by the minimalist response from the IRA. He was not impressed when the IRA finally responded on 9 August with more words, but no actions. With barely any time left to meet the deadline for the re-election of the First and Deputy First Minister, the IRA announced it had agreed a scheme with the IICD to put weapons beyond use completely and verifiably. For unionists, this was too little, too late. While it was significant that the IRA had agreed the scheme, it was not clear when the group would carry out decommissioning. The organisation was still hinting that others had to do more first.

The following day, at 4.38pm, Secretary of State John Reid made his own move to buy more time. Rather than call an election to a new Assembly to deal with the stalemate – which may have been what republicans wanted in the aftermath of their Westminster successes – he signed a suspension order. Reid's suspension was different from the one Mandelson had signed in February 2000, and it was not foreseen by Trimble. This one was intended to last just twenty-four hours and was another bizarre technical device described as a "tactical suspension"; Trimble alleged it was thought up by someone at the NIO during the summer. It took effect at the stroke of midnight on Friday, 10 August and lasted until midnight the following evening. This tactical suspension allowed the clock to begin ticking again for another six weeks on the election of a First and Deputy First Minister. The hope was that this would give more time for the republican movement to decommission its weapons. The new deadline was 21 September.

Gerry Adams signalled the mood of republicans on the day after the suspension when he addressed thousands of people in Casement Park on a miserable, soaking wet Sunday. The event marked the twentieth anniversary of the 1981 hunger strike. As summer rain watered republicans, Adams vented his anger at the suspension and railed about "Humpty Dumpty" politics, insisting republicans would not bow to this kind of pressure. Before an audience that included his two ministers, Martin McGuinness and Bairbre de Brun, he rejected the claim made by the Secretary of State that a deal was within reach.

Despite the tone employed, Sir Reg Empey, the caretaker First Minister, appealed to republicans not to turn the current impasse over arms into a wrestling match with unionists. For his part, Empey now faced another six weeks in a post he did not relish, especially given the circumstances of his appointment. As alternative First Minister, Empey did not use the title, took no salary and was careful not to appear too comfortable in the role, running the centre mainly from his ministerial offices at Netherleigh. "I entered the First Minister's office once under duress," said Empey. "I didn't regard myself as First Minister. I did not feel legitimate. I was fulfilling a necessary function, not delivering new initiatives." This may explain why Mallon found Empey indecisive. On one occasion at least, however, Empey was extremely firm. He was asked to sign off some correspondence and noted that the First Minister's name, which normally comes to the left, had been put to the right and replaced by the Deputy First Minister's name. Empey objected to the change telling the official: "I'm sorry, sunshine, but even if it means that no other correspondence goes out of this office, I am not signing." It was during this time that he coined the phrase about the centre being a twin-headed monster: "It was slow, cumbersome and indecisive and suffocated the whole thing." But Empey also recognised it as a necessary form of administration. The staff liked his calm, polite approach. "He was a joy to work with," said one. "He brought his secretary Alison Coey flowers before he left."

In terms of the wider process, the extra time afforded to the Assembly proved to be rather more eventful than some might have imagined. With the Assembly's time-clock rewound, a series of events synchronised to create the conditions for an unprecedented move by republicans. Hours before the Sinn Féin leader delivered his defiant speech in Casement Park, three republicans suspected of being IRA members were detained in Colombia as they attempted to leave the country on false passports. The men denied any wrongdoing. Sinn Féin, puffed with election success, was deflated and immediately on the defensive. Initially its spokesmen floundered in the face of media questions about the party's relationship with the suspects, who were alleged to have been assisting FARC guerrillas with weapons training. The men were eventually identified as James Monaghan, Martin McCauley and Niall Connolly, and they repeatedly denied any wrongdoing, insisting they were in Colombia to study the peace process. Monaghan and McCauley had previous IRA convictions and were said to be IRA weapons experts. Connolly claimed to be Sinn Féin's representative in Cuba. Sinn Féin denied this, despite confirmation by Cuban officials who had anticipated a visit by Gerry Adams to the island. When Adams insisted that the three Irishmen had nothing to do with his party, David Trimble, who had his own sources of information, was scathing and dismissed the claims as "nauseating". "It's time Mr Adams had an encounter with the truth," said Trimble. Ulster Unionist minister Michael McGimpsey summed up the views of many unionists on the Colombian case when he said: "Unionists believe republicans are talking about peace and preparing for war."

While this storm was brewing, the IRA issued a second statement, on 14 August, withdrawing its plan on decommissioning and citing unionist rejection and British bad faith as the reasons. The statement suggested the Colombian allegations were an attempt by British "securocrats" to put pressure on republicans to disarm, or leave government. While the stand-off over arms deepened, there was a dramatic move by the SDLP on policing following the publication of the revised policing implementation plan on 17 August. While Sinn Féin immediately rejected the plan, complaining there was no outright ban on plastic bullets and citing the ongoing existence of Special Branch, the SDLP did not. On 21 August, John Hume and Seamus Mallon held a dramatic news conference at Stormont, during which they announced they were now satisfied that the spirit and substance of Patten was being delivered and, as a consequence, the party would take its seats on the policing board the following month.

Sinn Féin claimed the SDLP leadership was panicking following the election and as a result was breaking the nationalist consensus and settling for too little. But Mallon was firm that this was a chance to break the bitter legacy of the past: "No issue has been more difficult, more divisive and more controversial in the history of the north." Mallon also argued that without both sections of the population backing the police, Patten was only theory. "Do not let this opportunity slip," he pleaded, "because Patten will never be written again. We have one opportunity to get this right. Take that chance."

While Sinn Féin and the SDLP clashed over policing, the DUP and Ulster Unionists leaderships, both debating whether or not to join the policing boards, put aside their differences over power-sharing and the Agreement and met to discuss the issue. Any posturing about whether unionists would join the board was shortlived, and even as Stormont faced a slow death, a new institution was born: the cross-community Policing Board. Sinn Féin boycotted the board and Adams was criticised for suggesting new recruits to the service would be accorded the same treatment the republican movement gave to the RUC, "no more, no less".

At this time policing was undergoing another major test. In Ardoyne, loyalists were refusing to allow Catholic schoolgirls to pass through "their" area to reach Holy Cross primary school. The dispute, which saw loyalist adults shouting sectarian abuse at crying children as they were led along police lines, made world headlines and had a huge impact. Without security powers the Executive seemed impotent in the face of the crisis, as did the NIO, which did have security powers. In part the dispute was another symptom of a decaying political process at Stormont. Its domination of headlines around the globe came to an abrupt end, however, when it was overtaken by another event, one that would have massive implications for international affairs. The ripples from this act of terrorism hit the peace process and, some argue, altered its course.

Among the millions who witnessed the event live on television was Seamus Mallon, who watched it in his office at Stormont. He could hardly pull himself away from the images being broadcast when William Graham, veteran political correspondent for *The Irish News*, arrived for a pre-arranged interview about the crisis looming in the administration, which had just ten days left before its extra-time ran out. Graham was ushered in by Mallon's officials. He later gave a vivid account of the atmosphere in the office in an article he wrote for *The Irish News*. "This is the worst attack since Pearl Harbour," Mallon told Graham. It was 11 September 2000, just after 3.00pm in Belfast, and two aeroplanes had just flown into the twin towers of the World Trade Centre in New York. The first impact, on the South Tower, was followed swiftly by the crashing of a second plane, the moment of impact shown live on television. The second attack made clear that the crash was no accident but a devastating and deliberate attack. As a third plane headed for the Pentagon, Mallon instructed his officials to send condolences to the President Bush on behalf of the administration. His staff drew up a joint statement, to be sent by Mallon and Empey. The Executive's message of sympathy was echoed by other local politicians, including David Trimble and Gerry Adams in what was a rare show of unity.

By coincidence, Bush's advisor on Northern Ireland was in Belfast in a bid to move forward the peace process. Richard Haass' message could not have been clearer: terrorism had to be faced down wherever it was found. Post-Colombia and following 9/11, Haass challenged republicans to show they understood there was now zero-tolerance for illegal armed groups. In effect, the IRA was being asked to demonstrate it was on the side of the United States, and not in the same league as Al Qaeda, the perpetrators of the attacks on America. The Bush administration, along with many powerful politicians on Capitol Hill, was appalled by the recent allegations of IRA involvement with FARC guerrillas, a left-wing group that the right-wing US government vehemently opposed and believed to be involved in the cocaine trade. Sinn Féin feared a backlash from its lucrative but conservative Irish-American base, which had contributed millions of dollars to its coffers. It is believed an influential Irish-American who supported the peace process, had told Adams that, post-Colombia, the IRA needed to disarm if Sinn Féin were to rescue its reputation in the United States. The 9/11 attacks greatly magnified this need.

Haass echoed the call to disarm in a meeting with Adams on 11 September, the day the Twin Towers came under attack. Haass also strongly challenged Sinn Féin to move forward more quickly on issues such as decommissioning. He made clear his government was deeply upset about allegations coming out of Colombia, and Washington did not accept Sinn Féin's version of events. Days later Haass repeated his view that the three Irishmen in Colombia were not on vacation nor on a peace process mission. He suggested the republican involvement in Colombia was linked to terrorism.

"What 9/11 did," Haass would later declare, "was to bring about a sea-change in American thinking. There is simply zero tolerance in this country for terrorism of any sort." The mood in the United States had turned fearful as packages full of Anthrax, a deadly virus, were sent through the post to various targets. With American pressure escalating, republican defiance over decommissioning, which the leadership had appeared to be delaying as long as possible, began to shift – but not quickly enough to prevent another tactical suspension by Reid, which took place on 21 September. This latest suspension followed a fifty-minute meeting between Adams and Trimble, which apparently saw no breakthrough But this time there was some reason to hope the extra time would be productive. There had been a change in Sinn Féin's tone from the previous month. Sinn Féin sources were now suggesting that republicans were prepared to do everything they could to overcome difficulties. The IRA then issued a statement promising more intensive dialogue with the IICD, while insisting it had sent no one to Colombia.

Alongside tough talk from Haass, the US administration also employed gentle diplomacy in encouraging Sinn Féin. US ambassador to Dublin Richard Egan attended the Sinn Féin Ard Fheis on 4 October to hear Adams condemn the 9/11 attack. Adams was careful to distinguish the IRA's violent campaign from the incident, paralleling the movement with the US War of Independence in 1776. Egan's visit gave the IRA the cover it needed to proceed without being accused of acting under pressure. With P. O'Neill's pride cushioned, newspaper speculation intensified that republicans were finally going to decommission. There was also a claim that Martin McGuinness had returned to his role of IRA chief-of-staff, to ensure arms were destroyed. McGuinness dismissed the claims as an attempt to have him removed from Office, as such a role would, of course, be contrary to his post as Education minister.

Trimble and other critics were increasingly comparing Adams to Al Qaeda leader Osama

Bin Laden, and complaining bitterly that the government was differentiating between domestic and international terrorism. In the face of intensifying pressure, republicans did find some comfort in the increasingly difficult political climate for Trimble after he lost his court appeal against the ruling that he had acted unlawfully in banning Sinn Féin from NSMC meetings. Trimble suggested he would go to the House of Lords. "He can go where he likes," McGuinness declared. "He's not going to succeed." The subsequent weeks would prove McGuinness right, as Trimble was denied leave to appeal. But in another bid to bring matters to a head over the arms issue, Trimble had already found a new tactic to irritate republicans and other pro-Agreement elements. On 8 October he announced that his ministers would engage in a phased withdrawal from the Executive, if his Assembly motion failed to succeed in excluding Sinn Féin. Sinn Féin was already the target of a DUP exclusion motion that was waiting to be heard. Such a motion required SDLP support to succeed and the party had already indicated it would reject it. But at the same time, with the institutions in limbo, the party renewed its call for the IRA to save the Agreement by disarming.

Speaking later that week at the Tory party conference, Trimble showed impatience with the Prime Minister and his failure to deliver decommissioning while allowing Sinn Féin to continue in government. He accused Tony Blair of taking his eye off the ball on the arms issue and sliding into appeasement. He effectively accused Blair of ruining confidence in the Agreement by a flow of concessions that were "all one way". To many nationalists, Trimble was in denial about the nature of the Agreement and had confused entitlements with concessions. Blair was no doubt upset with Trimble, but kept his counsel as another round of intense discussions unfolded between Belfast, Dublin, London and Washington.

At Stormont on 18 October, Trimble stood on the steps with his three ministers, Sir Reg Empey, Michael McGimpsey and Sam Foster, and announced he had placed letters with the Speaker's Office signalling the Ulster Unionist ministers were vacating their offices.

Empey admitted to disagreeing with Trimble about the tactic and challenging him over the issue in internal party meetings. But Empey made clear he would not have defied the leader on the issue.

The DUP followed the Ulster Unionists out of the Executive. If the unionist places were not filled within days, the Executive was going to collapse. While the Ulster Unionists mocked the DUP for waiting for them before jumping, the SDLP's Mark Durkan said it was a pity that five good ministers, including the DUP ministers, were leaving the administration. It meant only Dermot Nesbitt remained – some speculated this was an oversight, others believed it was because he was a junior minister. The reality, in fact, was that the SDLP had become exasperated with his policy views and would have vetoed his reappointment had the institutions been restored, so he was left in place. Durkan joked pointedly that the team had quit the pitch, but left the mascot.

Adams condemned unionists for presenting the IRA with an ultimatum, saying: "I think we have learned in this process that all of these deadlines have been put up just to be broken." However, in a massive shift from "not a bullet, not an ounce", republicans realised there was no advantage in holding onto their weapons at that point, and finally made a move on 22 October. Adams, along with McGuinness and Joe Cahill, gathered at Conway Mill in West Belfast for what was billed as an historic press conference. Adams' language was subtle, but to the trained observer there was no mistaking the meaning of his words: it was time for the IRA to make a "groundbreaking" move on the arms issue to save the peace process from collapse and transform it. He would soon describe decommissioning as a patriotic act – language employed by Hume in January 2000 before the first suspension in a plea that went unheeded at the time.

Given the unprecedented nature of Adams' statement, the media immediately forgot about a statement made earlier in the day that had made clear that one of the Colombia accused, Naill Connolly, was in fact Sinn Féin's representative in Cuba. The party had, of course, denied this in the days immediately following the revelations, but Sinn Féin now blamed this on breakdown in internal party communications. Normally the media would have jumped on the news, but the admission quickly fell out of news bulletins, squeezed out by the even bigger story on decommissioning. An Irish government official commented acidly that Sinn Féin should get the "news management of the year" award. Cynics detected more Sinn Féin spin when McGuinness went to the USA and insisted decommissioning had nothing to do with 9/11.

Having claimed for years that decommissioning would never happen, the DUP seemed to give a contradictory response to it. Paisley was cautious, on the one hand, demanding to know what price had been paid for it, while, on the other, he rejected it as a massive effort to fool people. "There is nothing in it," said Paisley, who wanted to know if the war was over. His attitude did not stop the DUP from withdrawing their resignations from the Executive. Peter Robinson and Nigel Dodds were reappointed by Paisley as soon as the Ulster Unionist ministers returned to their posts, drawing jeers from the Trimble camp – "another example of the DUP piggybacking," said McGimpsey. Adams declared, with some cynicism, that the DUP's hokey-cokey politics provided light relief in difficult times. In his defense, Robinson insisted the policy of refusing to go to Room 21 would continue until the IRA disarmed and disbanded completely.

The DUP's dismissal of decommissioning was echoed from within Trimble's own party. Anti-Agreement MP Martin Smyth, who had unsuccessfully challenged Trimble's leadership the year before, was just as critical as Paisley, referring to decommissioning as "fool's gold". But these criticisms rang hollow with the pro-Agreement forces and for some simply exposed some unionists' distaste for power-sharing, regardless of the circumstances. The unionists' complaints were in marked contrast to the attitude of powerful figures, including President Bush, who was among the first to welcome the news. Trimble appeared buoyant and his deflated political fortunes, which had looked so bleak at the Somme, seemed solid once more. He had outwitted the "never, never, never" camp yet again and, perhaps due in part to the unforeseen occurrences in America, had appeared to have scored a victory in his battle of wills with the IRA over arms.

Chapter 23
Fostering Good Relations

Sam Foster edged towards the rather treacherous chasm, a rocky pit carved deep into the heart of Black Mountain in west Belfast. One unsteady move too close to the precipice and he risked slipping and falling to certain death. But he wanted to get a closer look at the sheer cliffs. As he stepped cautiously along the ledge he heard the rumbling tones of Gerry Adams and felt a reassuring arm around his waist. "Not too close, minister," Adams cautioned. "How kind," Foster thought to himself.

The irony of that moment was not lost on the unionist minister, who was once a "legitimate target" for the IRA and a sworn enemy of the republican leader who now stood at his side. As a member of the security forces, Foster was careful to check under his car every morning for IRA bomb devices. The minister pondered how times had changed as he absorbed the view, high above the city. To the east he could see Stormont and the Holywood hills and in between, rising up from the Lagan basin, a breathtaking view of Belfast City: lush green glens that melted into rows and rows of rooftops tilting down to the shimmering lough. From this distance, post-Troubles Belfast looked serene. He had to look a little harder to see the peace walls, the scars that served as reminders of the city's violent past and uneasy present.

During the Troubles, Foster could never have imagined being a Stormont minister, never mind having Gerry Adams express concern for his safety. As MP for West Belfast, Adams had invited Foster to his constituency to survey the mountain quarry, which was considered an environmental hazard by locals who were fearful that the beauty spot was being damaged irreparably. These claims were being refuted by the construction company that operated the quarry. Adams' invitation to visit was delivered during an Assembly session when he chided the Department of Environment for failing to stop the quarrying. Describing Foster as a "fair man", Adams, speaking in English and Irish, said: "[The minister] needs to decide if he will be remembered as the man who saved the Black Mountain, or as someone who made a molehill out of a mountain." Foster, in what was his first exchange with Adams, accepted the invitation, but added a barbed comment of his own: "We are all proud of the province, but we must not allow ourselves to become too sanctimonious. The countryside has been pockmarked for thirty years by terrorist activity. It is to be regretted that we did not receive united condemnation of that fact at the time." Foster went on to say he was a conservationist and recognised the importance of the Belfast hills. Before long he was standing on them, face to face with Adams about halfway up the mountain. "He had a great welcome for me," said Foster.

"You've brought the good weather with you," Adams grinned.

"I'm simply fulfilling my duty," said the minister rather seriously.

They agreed to travel together to the summit and Foster climbed into the front seat of the Land Rover, with Adams tucked in the back alongside SDLP MLA Joe Hendron and the minister's special advisor, Stephen Barr. It was a bit awkward. The affable Hendron broke the silence by recounting his latest visit to the wilds of Donegal, asking Adams if he was for the county soon. Adams lamented that he hardly had any time to go across to his new Donegal home. "It's a great place," said Adams. "I just love the walking there." Barr could not resist a jibe and chanced: "Would that be traditional routes, Gerry?" Hendron roared with laughter.

Foster, a high ranking Orangeman, was amused too, aware of the tensions around marching that had led to serious confrontation between the organisation and local residents groups over "traditional routes". The issue, or rather how to handle it, had split the Orange order, which was also divided on the question of the Good Friday Agreement. Foster had backed the deal in May 1998 and won a seat in the Assembly, representing Fermanagh-South Tyrone on a firmly pro-Agreement ticket. At the Twelfth celebrations that year, he was publicly rebuked at the field in Irvinestown. "Traitor!" an angry voice shouted as Foster read the Orange Order's annual Twelfth resolutions. County Grand Master Roy Kells had to intervene to stop the booing coming from some sections of the crowd. Foster, who held high positions in both the Order and the Royal Black Institution, was used to being treated with a certain respect on such occasions, but had anticipated trouble at Irvinestown that day. He sensed a coolness from some and felt the hostile stares of others as he mingled among the brethren. The worst was being accused of selling out. "I was very badly hurt by that," he said.

Foster knew the price of the Agreement and how unpopular it would prove. Even he had struggled with elements of the deal, particularly the release of IRA prisoners, as he had first-hand experience of the IRA's ruthlessness. In Enniskillen on Remembrance Sunday, 1987, he was standing close to the cenotaph when the IRA bomb exploded. There was a loud blast, then shocked silence, then shrieks and cries, dust and dirt and bricks flying around, and panic. Foster had walked away with only a few cuts, badly shaken and shocked. Others were not so fortunate. Eleven people lost their lives that day. His neighbour, Teddy Armstrong, was killed instantly; Foster struggled to recognise him as he lay bloated on the ground. Shell-shocked, Foster had helped rescue victims from the rubble, including the limp and almost lifeless body of Jim Dixon, forever maimed by the blast. Foster had walked amidst the debris and wondered, with a sickening feeling, if he was standing on the tomb of his pregnant daughter, Helen, and her two-year-old son. They, too, were at the cenotaph that day. It was an hour or two before he learned Helen and the boy were safe. His daughter had gone through similar anguish believing her mother had been killed. She was a few hundred yards from the cenotaph and had watched a woman dressed like her mother going towards the site where the bomb ignited. The woman perished and Helen only discovered later that her mother was safe.

Foster found a man and a woman trapped between a fallen gable wall and a steel rail and tried to lift them, but to no avail. He put his hand on the head of the woman and could see death rising through her body as her life ebbed away. He reached out and put his fingers under the bloodied face of the man beside her and placed a breathing apparatus into his mouth. "Keep his chin up, Sam," he was told by another helping the rescue effort.

"Let him breathe through that." Foster was wearing a light raincoat that day. It was blood-soaked. His memory, despite the passing years, was still clear: "The man was bleeding profusely into my hand and I can still feel to this day the dying jerk on the heel of my hand as he gave his last breath."

The day after the bomb, Foster travelled to Downing Street with a delegation led by his party colleague, Ken Maginnis, then MP for Fermanagh-South Tyrone. Prime Minister Margaret Thatcher sat and listened as Foster and the others recounted the devastation wreaked by the IRA. "She was very kind and very caring and very thoughtful," he said. But as he shook hands with Mrs Thatcher before leaving, the Prime Minister peered into his face: "You don't think I am doing as much as I should." Foster, equally direct, replied: "You are correct."

After the trauma of the many funerals, Foster relived the bombing for months afterwards because he was seconded to the Enniskillen Fund, interviewing scores of victims about their injuries and losses. He never received counselling. He was from a generation that tended to just get on with things. Even so, the burden of Enniskillen weighed heavily when Foster considered the Good Friday Agreement. He knew what it would mean: unionists sharing power with Sinn Féin, the political allies of the IRA. In spite of this, Foster chose to back the Agreement. When asked why, he told a colleague: "Because I'm tired of picking bits of my friends out of hedges."

But it was more than that. He realised republicans were not going to go away and there was a chance of a better future for Northern Ireland and its people. As a younger man he had opposed the Sunningdale power-sharing deal because he believed in majority rule. "For a long time I felt power-sharing was artificial and pretentious," he said. A generation on, Foster had come to realise that majority rule was not an option for Northern Ireland and he moved away from the notion that greater integration with Britain was the answer. The unionist majority in Northern Ireland had slumped from 70% to 55% as nationalists grew in number. Border unionists such as Foster were particularly conscious of being outnumbered. Foster had urged fellow unionists to be realistic, counselling: "You have to work with these people."

He stuck to the Agreement and supported party leader David Trimble in his attempts to restore devolution to Northern Ireland, provided decommissioning occurred. He remained loyal to his leader as the party split over the deal and when devolution was finally agreed Foster was rewarded with a post in the new power-sharing Executive. While there was resentment from some, there were good wishes from others. Trimble had wanted to appoint someone from the rural west, anxious that Stormont, in the urban east, did not become too distant from the general populace. As a senior member of the loyal orders, Foster carried some clout and had delivered unionist support in Fermanagh. He was delighted to be chosen, but was unsure. He took Trimble aside at the Waterfront Hall, after the party's ruling council agreed to enter devolution in December 1999, and suggested he might want to change his mind and choose someone else. "No," Trimble told him, "I've made up my mind. I want you."

At sixty-eight, Sam Foster was the oldest of the twelve Stormont ministers. With endearing modesty he admitted that the prospect of heading a department was extremely daunting. "I was frightened to death," he confessed. He was also aware of the deep animosity felt by many unionists towards the new administration: "There were pressures and lots of resentment about people like Martin McGuinness and Bairbre de Brun. It was a tense situation to be in. You felt you were waiting to be devoured by wolves." But despite the strains, Foster was determined to try. For him, power-sharing was an act of patriotism: "There were some issues I disliked and abhorred. But I felt for the benefit of Northern Ireland within the Union as a whole I should do it." He went to the first meeting of the power-sharing Executive with mixed emotions. He could not comprehend why Martin McGuinness and Bairbre de Brun would want to sit in a Northern Ireland government when the IRA had spent so many years trying to destroy the union. How could it work? he wondered. Foster dealt with his anxieties through humour and would often joke: "I'm fostering good relations." When he was handed the Environment portfolio he would also quip that he was a "green Unionist".

Foster's first weeks in office were painful. He had inherited a department with a small budget and big problems, including a massive backlog in both the planning system and environmental legislation. European standards had not been met and road safety was a growing problem. Waste management was badly in need of overhaul. Like planning, it was among a series of hot potatoes to be handled carefully. He was quickly overwhelmed by the amount of paperwork ministers were expected to read. On top of all this, his new department was in upheaval because it had been carved out of the old Department of Environment. Foster was in charge of the smaller-sized Department of Environment (DoE), while the DUP's Peter Robinson headed the fledgling Department of Regional Development (DRD). The shake-up had caused confusion and the DoE was forced to issue a press release clarifying the responsibilities of each of the new departments. These responsibilities overlapped – a deliberate attempt by the pro-Agreement architects to ensure the ministers had to work together on some issues. Foster's Department of Environment was responsible for local government, the protection of the countryside, environmental heritage, driver and vehicle licensing, sustainable development and waste management. It also had responsibility for planning control, but strategic planning remained with DRD. The DoE had road safety; DRD had the roads service. DoE was responsible for pollution, but DRD controlled water and sewage services.

Foster had previously served as Health spokesman for his party and undoubtedly would have been more content with that portfolio. Given his age, however, it was likely the massive department would have proven too much for him – a factor Trimble must have taken into account when considering his options. The minister faced a steep learning curve in trying to get to grips with complex issues. He fretted about how he would cope with the dreaded ministerial question time, a serious test of a minister's competence in mastering his or her brief. In fact, Foster always managed to get through question time without incident, but he was not alone among the ministers in finding the process nerve-wracking. "I didn't like it at all," he admitted. "It's quite theatrical." Foster wished he had been given the job fifteen years earlier, but found some comfort and joy when he made his first trip as minister to Enniskillen. Visiting his home county and exploring the Marble Arch Caves and other beauty spots were highlights of his time in office. However, soon after taking up his post, he became exhausted by the travel involved in having to commute from Enniskillen to Belfast every day, a three-and-a-half-hour round trip. His driver, Paul

Shilliday, who lived in Bangor, told him he had drawn the short straw. "This is no use to you or me," Foster told Shilliday after a week. The minister found lodgings in Belfast with a relation, Eileen Johnston, who lived near Stormont.

Eileen Johnston's husband, Charles, was Foster's cousin and he had been murdered in 1981, almost certainly by the IRA. The father-of-two was shot from behind as he left a car park near St Anne's Cathedral, close to his city centre travel firm. At his inquest the coroner suggested it was a case of mistaken identity as Charles, who had no political or security connections, closely resembled his brother, a former part-time member of the RUC. Despite her personal suffering, Eileen Johnston was supportive of Foster's decision to go to Stormont. He told her: "I can't reverse what happened to you, but if it can stop other people going through the same thing, I've done some good."

Foster, a churchgoer, tried to take a Christian attitude in all things. In fact, in his first Christmas message as minister he said the challenge ahead was for everyone to show Christian virtue at all times. Unlike some of his unionist colleagues, he was willing to shake hands with republicans, such as Martin McGuinness. "It is difficult, but I wouldn't be rude to anybody," he said. Foster was often described as a gentleman by politicians of all shades at Stormont. SDLP minister Bríd Rodgers found him very human and easy to talk to. "He had hardline views at times," she said, "but you knew where he was coming from. I found Sam to be a very decent, ordinary bloke you could have a joke with and chat to." Keen to improve relations with unionists, Gerry Adams was very friendly and cordial whenever he ran into Foster in the corridors. Foster laughed at the memory: "He would almost want to get his arms around you." Another unionist recalled: "I found it very difficult to get past him in the corridor. He wanted to shake my hand."

While Foster was nervous about handling a ministry, he was confident in his unionism and his ability to argue his case. In fact, he was vocal at the Executive table on issues about which he felt strongly and often challenged Sinn Féin on constitutional matters, such as the flying of the Union flag. Foster, said an insider, would regularly confront Sinn Féin ministers, particularly de Brun, over decommissioning. "Sam's central line was, 'Trust us, trust us. We've seen the light. Trust us. Why don't you give up your guns now?'" After heated exchanges at the Executive table following Trimble's NSMC ban on Sinn Féin in October 2000, Foster found himself alone with McGuinness in Room 21. He turned to the senior republican and said forthrightly: "You could get rid of all that terrible strife in the Executive if you had fulfilled your role by decommissioning." McGuiness looked at him and replied, "I'll tell you what, Sam, it's not that easy." Foster was struck by the tone of McGuinness' reply. "It made me think," he said.

The pair began to discuss their respective ideologies, with Foster insisting that McGuinness was in denial about his British identity: "You might deny what you are. But you are Britisher, just like me." McGuinness was taken aback: "What! I am a Britisher? I am an Irish republican." Foster went on: "I'm British-Irish and this island was once called Little Britain and there is British-Irish as there is British-Welsh, British-Scots, British-English. I am Irish and proud and I am also proud to be British." McGuinness had no comeback except to protest his Irishness and the circular discussion was left unresolved. Foster had an equally futile debate about the RUC with Sinn Féin's policing spokesman, Gerry Kelly, at a reception organised by the American consulate in Belfast. "It was blunt and straightforward," said Foster. "No punches were pulled. Mr Kelly has no love for the police. He had his mind made up about the RUC and I had mine made up."

Foster came from a family closely linked with the security forces, not uncommon among border Protestants in Fermanagh, where he was born on 7 December 1931. His father, Samuel, his mother, Maggie, and his brother, William, were en route to the village of Lisbellaw, having left Newtownbutler, when Sam's impending birth forced them to stop at the home of a relation in Lisnaskea. It was there, in the old railway gatehouse, that Samuel junior was born. Soon after his birth the family settled in the Tyrone village of Beragh, eight miles from Omagh. It was a humble existence for the Catholics and Protestants who lived in the village. In the nineteenth century the village had been described as "one long wide street of very mean houses whose tenants for the most part appear to be poor." Beragh, which is Scots-Irish for "place of peaks", had not altered much from that description when the Fosters arrived there in the hungry years of the Depression.

Sam Foster senior, a Lisbellaw man whose father came from a family of blacksmiths in the Clogher valley, worked at the local forge. The Fosters lived in a modest house in a small lane off the main street. There were three bedrooms upstairs, a sitting room and working kitchen in one room downstairs and an outdoor toilet. There was no running water. A bucket was kept at the back of the house and water was drawn from a nearby stream. Maggie Foster, born Johnston, had come from rural West Fermanagh. Her father was a steward at Florence Court, a vast eighteenth-century estate that had belonged to the Earls of Enniskillen. Maggie, too, had gone into service there as a young girl. Next to the splendour of Florence Court, with its landscaped lawns and fragrant rose gardens, Beragh must have seemed dull and drab, but she worked hard to make it a comfortable home for her family. "My mother could make a meal out of nothing in a wee scullery. I sometimes wonder how she did it," said Foster. One of his earliest memories was of being nursed at home by the open-grate fire after he took a bad chest, which his mother plastered with Vicks ointment, brown paper and red flannel. One visitor was the parish priest, who called in after tending to Fosters' Catholic neighbours. The priest would bring his dog with him and joke that it needed shoes from the forge.

At that time, it was only fifteen years since partition and the Fosters were staunch unionists, but relations with their Catholic neighbours were always friendly. Sam attended Hutton Memorial primary school in Beragh, along with his older brother, William, and his younger brother, George. (Later, George's son would marry Arlene Kelly, a Fermanagh-born Ulster Unionist who was vehemently opposed to the Agreement and to Trimble.) As a boy in Beragh, Sam was aware of politics and religion. His family was Church of Ireland and Sam senior was a staunch Orangeman, a member of the lodge outside Beragh. On Sundays the young Sam walked a mile towards Omagh to attend Sunday School in the Church of Ireland parish of Clogherney. He sang and learned his lessons and then walked home for lunch before attending Methodist Sunday School in Beragh in the afternoon.

His father was a member of the Ulster Special Constabulary, an auxiliary force established at Partition to counter the threat from the IRA when jobs were scarce and fears were plentiful. The USC was particularly loathed by nationalists, who regarded it as a Protestant or unionist militia. Samuel Foster senior would recount stories to his wide-eyed boys about the border battles he faced in 1921 when the IRA attacked Lisbellaw. He told them how village men had run to the tower at the parish church and rang the bells to warn of imminent danger. Sam and his brothers had a traditional unionist upbringing and looked forward to the thrills of the Twelfth, when their father would place his bright Orange sash over his best suit and play the side-drum in the Gortaclare pipe band. When he turned thirteen, Sam junior joined the Derryclavin pipe band, playing the side-drum and the pipes.

Sam Foster senior had expected that his sons would be blacksmiths, in the family tradition, and the boys often turned shoes for the horses after school when they were not gathering potatoes for the local farmers or running through the fields playing games. Sam junior, an above-average student, left the local primary school to attend Enniskillen Technical College at the age of twelve, but left after two years. "I could have gone on in school, but I was anxious to work," he explained. When the school principal inquired if he would be interested in a job as a dental technician he readily agreed, but the offer was withdrawn when the lad who was supposed to vacate the post stayed on. Instead, Foster went to work as a printer-compositor at the *Fermanagh Times*, a unionist journal that stopped printing in the early 1970s. He was employed there for the next twenty years, with the exception of a brief period when he worked for Thomas Johnstone Printers in Belfast's Great Victoria Street.

When he turned eighteen, Sam joined the Orange Order, like his father and grandfather before him. He devoted much time to the loyal orders and held a variety of positions, including Worshipful Master of his private lodge, District Master of Lisbellaw, Deputy Grand Master of Fermanagh Royal Arch Purple Chapter, and was a member of Grand Lodge. He also held senior positions in the Royal Black Institution and was Imperial Grand Lecturer for ten years. It was on a Twelfth, 12 July 1950, that Foster met his future wife, Dorothy. He had cycled to a dance in the Orange Hall at Monea when he spotted a pretty, slender girl with dark hair, high cheekbones and almond-shaped hazel eyes, not unlike his own. She was from Trory in Enniskillen, but was there because her boyfriend played in the dance band. Sammy, as she called him, persuaded her to dance and their courtship began. In 1952 they were married, both aged twenty, with their parents' approval. They honeymooned in Belfast, staying with a great aunt in Vernon Street, off Donegall Pass. *The Quiet Man*, starring John Wayne and Maureen O'Hara, was playing at the Curzon Cinema and they dashed out one night to see it.

Back in Enniskillen, they moved into their first home, a bungalow overlooking Lough Erne. They had three children: Mervyn, Helen and David. While Dorothy busied herself with the children, Foster remained the breadwinner and in his spare time was active in the Orange Order and pursued his studies with correspondence courses in English, or public speaking, or whatever subject interested him. In the 1960s he applied for a job as an education welfare officer with the Fermanagh Education Authority. In those days, before employment laws were introduced, it was common to lobby a local councillor for a job. Foster did not get the post; he noted that it went to a local Catholic. That experience left him with little sympathy for the civil rights movement when it flourished later that same decade: "[People] talk about discrimination here in Northern Ireland but there was a guy … who got the job over me."

Foster continued working at the *Fermanagh Times*, but later applied again for a position as a welfare officer in the local education authority. Once more he had competition, this time from an ex-serviceman. He got the job when councillors backed him by fourteen votes to seven, but a second vote had to be taken when there was some upset that his rival had been overlooked. Foster won the second vote by sixteen votes to nine, but he recalled some bad feeling over his appointment: "People didn't speak to me over it." He often recounted how a local nationalist put a sign up in his newspaper shop window that read: "The echoes of Remembrance day have barely died away when Fermanagh Education Authority employs an employed B-man ahead of an unemployed ex-serviceman." The jibe stuck in Foster's mind. The "B-man" referred to Foster's part-time job in the Ulster Special Constabulary (USC), or the "B-Specials" as it was known. He had joined, aged eighteen, more out of loyalty to the State than because of the wage he received. "I felt it was my duty to join, not to have a grudge against anyone but to ensure the border was guarded against the IRA."

Foster was on guard duty during the IRA's border campaign in 1956–1962. The IRA had begun to blow up bridges and had targeted the Territorial Army centre in Enniskillen. At times, Foster was out six nights out of seven, mounting road-checks or manning remote border posts, such as that at Swanlinbar: "We spent many cold nights lying around the customs posts staring out, two men and two rifles no communication, no nothing. If you were caught by someone else, you were very, very isolated." Nerves got the better of him one dark night when he was out guarding a makeshift bridge that had been hastily erected to replace one the IRA had just blown up. He and his companion heard "machine-gun fire" on the bridge. They were relieved, and amused, to find it was actually the noise made by a cyclist crossing the slots of the bridge at speed.

By the time the B-Specials were eventually wound up, in 1969, Foster had risen to the position of Platoon Sergeant. The Hunt Commission on policing recommended its abolition following clashes in the summer of 1969 between the B-Specials and Catholic nationalists in the Bogside in Derry. Foster was not involved in those clashes, which led to bitter complaints that the constabulary was ill-disciplined and ill-suited for dealing with street violence and crowd control. "We had to give all our weapons and equipment over," he recalled. Along with many unionists, he was annoyed by the decision: "I had never done anybody any wrong. I did my duty politely but firmly and I was upset. Lots of people were."

The USC was replaced with the Ulster Defence Regiment (UDR) and at first Foster was unsure about joining but, like many B-Specials, he was absorbed into the new force in 1970. The UDR failed to attract significant Catholic support, despite early promise. Its credibility was dented as far as nationalists were concerned when two members of the regiment were convicted of the murder of three members of the Miami Showband in 1975. Over the years other members have been accused of having links to loyalist paramilitaries, or have been convicted for other murders. Unionists have protested that these were minority elements out of the 40,000 men and women who served in the regiment for over twenty years before it was absorbed into the Royal Irish Regiment. These members were prime targets for the IRA. During the Troubles, around 200 serving UDR soldiers were killed, many when they were out of uniform, or after they had left the regiment.

Foster was undeterred by the threat from the IRA. He served in the UDR for eight years, rising rapidly through the ranks and eventually being promoted to Company Commander. He was in charge of B Company in the Fourth Battalion, the company responsible for Enniskillen and the south west of County Fermanagh, taking in Kinawley, Derrylin and Swanlinbar. "We had many scary nights along the border, especially along the Ballyconnell Road," he recalled. The worst incident occurred on 25 August 1972, when two of his colleagues were killed. It was reported that Jimmy Eames and Alfred Johnston were blown up when they checked a booby-trapped car abandoned by the IRA along the road at Cherrymount, just outside Enniskillen. Foster recalled that they were caught in the car bomb when they saw lights coming from the town and hid behind the vehicle. The floodlight turned out to be from an Army military truck heading to St Angelo airport. The military truck, said Foster, was the real target of the car bomb, but the UDR men were killed when it exploded. An eyewitness recalled a blinding flash when the 150-pound bomb ignited. Eames and Johnston were hurled through the air, their bodies ripped apart by the force of the blast.

Foster, who had heard the explosion from his Enniskillen home, immediately went to the scene: "It was a harrowing experience, no doubt about that. The two lads were picked up in pieces. I could see in the light of a torch just the top part of the body with no head and no legs and a flak jacket in the ditch." Both Eames and Johnston were married men, with children. Foster had the heartbreaking task of going to their homes, along with the local minister, to relay the news to their widows.

Dorothy Foster spent many nights fearful for the safety of her own husband who, like many UDR men, balanced his role as a part-time soldier with family and working life. He was constantly on his guard and would not get into his car in the morning without checking underneath it. He said: "I was very, very careful. I have enemies in the country but also [am] fairly well respected across the community." Bertie Kerr, a veteran unionist in the area, sometimes referred to Foster as "the most popular man in Fermanagh".

By the 1970s Foster had been promoted to the post of senior education welfare officer. His job dealt mainly with truancy and he was amused at some of the letters he received from parents seeking clemency for their offspring: "We'd get letters saying, 'Dear Sir, Johnny couldn't come to school yesterday because mammy was in bed with the doctor'." All the while he was interested in further education and had been pursuing a three-year course in social work part-time. In 1978 he had a chance to study full-time at the Ulster Polytechnic at Jordanstown. The course, which would have given him a qualification as a social worker, involved going to Liverpool for three months to work as a probation officer. At the age of forty-seven, he resigned from the UDR to pursue his studies as a mature student.

When he graduated he was offered a job in a special child care team in Birkenhead, a job he found both rewarding and challenging: "I was dealing with child abuse cases. It was difficult. I had some tough grinds." Dorothy said her husband was sometimes too soft-hearted for the job. The couple returned to Fermanagh after eighteen months in Birkenhead. He decided not to rejoin the UDR. After several approaches from Ulster Unionist Raymond Ferguson, Foster, a party member since he was eighteen, agreed to stand for the local council and was elected in 1981. Dorothy gave up on the notion of spending more time with her husband and, like many political wives, lamented how much of her husband's time was absorbed by politics. "He's very kind," she said. "He would go out of his way if someone rang him up. I would say, 'This is your day off', but he said, 'When you are in public life, you have to do it'." She said the only time he ever sat still was when he sat in front of the television to watch Manchester United play.

Foster spent twenty years on the council, where he had a reputation for being a hardliner on constitutional issues. He long remembered the time republican councillor John Joe McCusker compared him to a notorious Belfast unionist councillor, accusing him of being "the George Seawright of Fermanagh". When he served as chairman during 1995–1997, Foster tried to reach out to nationalists and prove his critics wrong. He hosted events for the GAA and welcomed Taoiseach John Bruton to the town hall, another watershed in unionist-nationalist relations. "We became quite good friends and exchanged Christmas cards for years after," he said.

Foster reluctantly resigned from the council when he became Minister of the Environment. He took the decision to quit his council seat only because he had no choice, due to conflict of interest: his department had the responsibility for overseeing the councils. Only one other minister took a similar decision and that was the Finance minister, Mark Durkan. Other ministers refused to give up their council seats as long as the Executive faced an uncertain future. Foster did not relinquish his seat immediately, but announced his resignation in February 2001, more than a year after he took up the ministerial post.

In fact, the Assembly was top-heavy with councillors and some believe this was the reason why Foster's Best Value Bill was diluted before it got to the floor of the Assembly. Foster introduced the Bill in July 2001 as an alternative framework for delivering council services, modelled on arrangements for Great Britain. All twenty-six district councils in Northern Ireland had voluntarily embraced the framework under direct rule, but Foster wanted to enshrine it in legislation to ensure that ratepayers' money was spent in a more transparent, accountable and efficient way. Best Value comprised the scrapping of Compulsory Competitive Tendering (CCT), whereby council contracts went to the lowest bidder. Instead, quality of service was to be weighed against price. The Bill was also to provide the local government auditor with more statutory powers and require councils to consult more with ratepayers. The Assembly committee was opposed to the Bill, however, with Assembly members complaining that it would limit the councils' flexibility. Some councillors felt it unnecessary and pointed out that replicating legislation in Great Britain was not appropriate given that councils in Northern Ireland had far less powers than local authorities. "We had to trim that [Bill] down. It was going to get a hammering on the chamber floor," Foster said.

The department was forced to come up with a compromise bill that, among other things, simply introduced a general duty of "best value" rather than repealing CCT. It also left the existing local government auditor in charge of monitoring improvements rather than creating a new best value inspection service. "Some MLAs took umbrage at the regulation," recalled Stephen Barr, who some months earlier been appointed a ministerial advisor.

At Stormont, Foster enjoyed a generally courteous relationship with the chairman of his Environment committee, Willie McCrea, a former DUP MP for Mid-Ulster and an anti-

Agreement political firebrand who would avoid addressing Sinn Féin committee members directly by having them called via the clerk, or by having everyone at the committee speak in turn on a given topic. Despite his fundamentalist politics, he kept the committee focused on environmental issues to avoid infighting over unionist and nationalist issues. McCrea was fiercely determined to keep the department on its toes: "There was a lot of friction between the department and the committee, make no mistake about it. Officials were going out of the place wiping the sweat off their brow." McCrea's committee regularly requested departmental papers, but was not always successful in obtaining them. Barr said this was because the committee was at times asking for documents that departmental officials deemed it was not entitled to. "Willie McCrea was certainly pushing the boundaries," said Barr, who was not alone in suspecting the DUP were simply looking for a means to embarrass the Ulster Unionist minister and his department.

Foster got on well with McCrea, but was conscious that he liked to get his way and that he was going to be critical wherever he could. "You knew all the time he was trying his best to undermine you," he said. Insiders said some department officials were contemptuous of McCrea's attitude. One recalled: "'Willie thinks he is the minister' was a phrase I would have heard in the DoE. Officials were concerned he was running riot with the committee." After years of direct rule, McCrea, along with many MLAs, was suspicious of civil servants whom, he claimed, often cast aside the views of politicians "during unrestrained reign" before devolution. He said: "I wanted accountable government. There was no cosy relationship between me as chairman and the minister … On occasion, officials came in and told me the department didn't like what we were doing and I said, 'So what?'"

McCrea insisted he was simply doing his job as a departmental watchdog, while being open and forthright with the minister. His perception was that it was officials not the minister who he needed to challenge on occasion:

> "I can remember one of the first times the permanent secretary came to the committee with the minister and he was answering all the questions and he said he had actually brought the minister to answer on this specific point and, as gracious as I possibly could, I reminded him that perhaps he hadn't fully understood what had happened with devolved government, that he hadn't brought the minister at all, the minister had brought him."

McCrea found Foster too reliant on his officials, saying: "I don't want to be ungracious or unkind, but he wouldn't have been regarded as the most effective minister." To this Foster retorted: "Willie McCrea's constant whinge reminded me of a creaky wheel on a wheel-barrow which required lubrication." Foster's special advisor disputed McCrea's contention, saying that Foster, although genial and well-liked, was no pushover and was wary of being manipulated. "Sam could look after himself," said Barr. Foster said he trusted his staff and that he took advice, initially because he was on a learning curve: "I did depend on them quite a bit. But if I felt something wasn't done, I wouldn't hesitate at all in saying, 'Look, this isn't good enough'."

The department was responsible for ensuring Northern Ireland legislation was kept in line with European directives. McCrea complained that the committee was not always given enough time to scrutinise these swathes of environmental legislation before they went to the Assembly. "If that happened," he said, "we made it abundantly clear that we weren't willing to put our stamp of approval on it." Much of this backlog was a result of direct rule, but it was a criticism levied by others, including Alliance leader and MLA David Ford. A member of the Environment committee, Ford also claimed the department failed on the bigger issues, such as waste management and planning. He liked to boast that he had forced an amendment to the Game Preservation Bill, against the department's wishes, increasing protection for Irish hares. Barr, on the other hand, was scathing about Ford's efforts: "This was pointless. No wild hares had been killed in years. The dogs are muzzled and the hares are released back into the wild. There wasn't a huge problem with the hare population." The minister also brushed the minor Alliance victory aside. "It annoyed the officials more than Sam," said Barr. "He wouldn't let it get to him."

As minister, Foster did not shy away from controversial decisions and annoyed his Ulster Unionist Executive colleagues, Sir Reg Empey and Michael McGimpsey, when he gave permission, after a number of court hearings had been won and lost, for the D-5 site to be developed for retail. The site encompassed a massive area within the Belfast harbour estate and the plan to develop it for retail had been opposed by the city's retailers, who complained it would damage the Belfast high street.

McCrea was critical that more was not done to deal with the planning backlog and other problems, many of which were inherited from direct rule. The planning backlog was exacerbated by the post-ceasefire building boom generated by the peace process. Foster regretted the lack of progress in transforming the planning service during devolution. The department was committed to reviewing planning processes in the 2001–2002 Programme for Government. "I wanted to get it by the scruff of the neck," said Foster, "but the civil servants kept on saying you couldn't do this or that. You were clamped all the time. You couldn't do what you wanted." He did initiate the Planning (Amendment) Bill and increased staffing to the service while in office.

Barr said no one disputed that planning needed a shake-up. "It was a mess," he agreed, pointing to a lack of accountability within the system. The department's planning service, after consulting local councils, made the decision, with the minister having final approval. Developers only had a right of appeal to the Planning Appeals Commission (PAC), which was unelected. In England, the local authorities took planning decisions and the appeal went to the minister, who was both elected and accountable. Barr felt that a major problem in getting planning overhauled was that the Executive lacked the political will to deal with the issue, and that OFM/DFM Bills took priority. He complained of difficulties getting even minimal planning bills onto the agenda, as Environment was well down the pecking order of departments. "The priorities were schools and hospitals," he said. He cited the fact that a Bill to make it illegal to keep an exotic wild animal as a pet, such as a tiger, was continually pushed down the list of priorities: "Certain Executive members talked a great game on planning ... but it was not a priority when action was required." A week before he left office, Foster did attempt to honour, in part, the commitment to overhaul planning. He launched a consultation paper aimed at delivering a future planning shake-up. It focused on the challenges ahead, including how to speed up decision-making and provide the public with a stronger, more effective voice in the process.

Waste management was another area needing reform and the failure to tackle this was another of McCrea's criticisms. It was one of the areas that made Environment a poisoned chalice for any minister, as the budget was largely taken up with wages and regulation costs. Before leaving office, Foster announced tougher sewage controls on the north coast and in North Down in a bid to meet European Directives. Foster can be credited with trying to make the department more accountable on the issue of waste management. He launched a new waste management strategy and, crucially, set up two new bodies to boost sustainable waste management in Northern Ireland, including an advisory board. Post-devolution, this measure haunted the department as it highlighted the fact that targets had not been met. Foster's initiative has made it difficult for the department to ignore the problem.

The minister and his committee also fought hard for more funding for the department, with some success. There was a 14% increase for the department, for example, in the 2000 Budget, while a proposed cut of £2 million in the Resource Grant for disadvantaged district councils was reversed. Foster also recruited more staff to deal with planning and environmental issues and accelerated plans for air quality.

The Environment committee clashed with the department over the issue of child safety on school buses, demanding seat belts and safety measures to prevent overcrowding. "The children are crowded in like sardines," said McCrea. "We wanted to ensure each child got a safety belt and rather than three children per seat, we had two children per seat. We did a very comprehensive report, but we were beaten because time ran out [due to suspension]." The department had concerns about the costs involved, but McCrea could not understand its attitude given the minister's commitment to road safety. "What's more dangerous than children crowded into a bus?" he asked. But Foster pointed out that it had been established that travelling by school bus was safer than walking to school, or passage in a family car.

McCrea acknowledged the minister's willingness to discuss issues with him and to attend the committee when asked, but argued that the department should have done more to increase penalties for drink-driving. "It seemed to me the legislation wasn't strong enough," he said. Foster had made road safety a priority when he took office. As a resident of Fermanagh, he was keenly aware of the dangers of the rural roads, where fatalities were all too common. He noted that during direct rule the number of road safety education officers had been reduced to ten. Having fought at the Executive table for extra finance for road safety, he secured £400,000 under the Executive Agenda for Government programme and doubled the number of officers to twenty, to ensure the message was given to as many schoolchildren as possible. In recognition of this, the Federated Institute of Road Safety Officers later made him an honorary member. Foster also launched a ten-year road safety strategy, seeking new ideas on how to tackle a problem that saw around 150 people killed annually. Road safety was one issue on which his department engaged with its Dublin counterpart. Although his department had no formal north-south body, there was scope for cooperation in terms of the environment, for example in ensuring that rivers were kept free from pollution, and in road safety. In fact, the Department shared costs on an all-island road safety campaign with its Dublin counterpart. The campaign involved a shocking film of a car crash in which a teenage boy, not wearing a seatbelt, is thrown violently against his girlfriend, killing her in the process. Foster was initially concerned that the film was too shocking, but was convinced by officials that it was necessary.

Foster was preparing to mark his first year in office when he began to feel unwell. He was relaxing at home after a hectic week when he suddenly suffered an uncontrollable spasm in his left arm. "I thought I was having a stroke," he recalled. Up until then he had had a quiver in his left arm, which jerked slightly every thirty seconds, but he thought it was related to a back operation he had had some years earlier. However, a medical examination confirmed it was much more serious. Foster was diagnosed with Parkinson's disease, what he would call "this damned illness". Foster was shattered by the news, but met the challenge with a quiet dignity. The disease took its toll on his confidence, however. Initially he had resisted having a ministerial aide, mainly because of the instability of the administration, but when Stephen Barr was finally appointed in January 2001, just after the minister was diagnosed with the disease, Foster was grateful to have the support. Barr recalled that at first the diagnosis was kept within a tight circle: "It would get him down and you knew he was capable of so much more and it was just frustrating for him."

A native of Portstewart, Stephen Barr had joined the administration from Westminster, where he had worked for the Ulster Unionist Parliamentary party. Barr had not voted in the Agreement referendum, but candidly admitted that, had he been living in Northern Ireland in 1998, he would have voted no on the issue of prisoner releases. But he also acknowledged that he would have been wrong to oppose the Agreement, which he came to view as a means of stabilising the union and undermining republican claims that unionism would not share power. "We nailed the lie that unionists didn't want a Fenian about the place," said Barr. "Nobody can say the Unionist party didn't try." Barr also changed his mind about the minister, whom he considered gruff at first, later realising that Foster's demeanour was actually due to shyness. Soon Barr found that Foster was very pleasant to work with and extremely down-to-earth. They had a good relationship. When he first went to Foster's home in Fermanagh, Barr half expected Foster to have his own country seat in line with the Stormont ministers of old and was pleasantly surprised to find the minister's home in Derrychara was on an ordinary housing estate. To Barr, it underscored the nature of the new administration and the depth of Foster's achievement in becoming a minister.

By the time he left office, this minister from a humble rural Fermanagh background had breakfasted with Tony Blair, whom he had found warm and engaging, and taken tea with Margaret Thatcher. He had been photographed with the Queen of England, with President Bill Clinton and with former South African president Nelson Mandela, whom he had met in Dublin along with John Hume, Gerry Adams and Martin McGuinness following the first suspension.

After the Parkinson's diagnosis, Foster struggled on for another year, but just before Christmas 2001 he told Trimble that he would willingly step aside if he wished to replace him. "The Parkinson's was battering my confidence," said Foster. "I knew it was getting worse." David Trimble agreed, but asked if Foster, who was about to mark his seventieth birthday, could hold on a little longer as he was planning a reshuffle in the New Year.

Foster's wife, Dorothy, was worried by this decision as she could see that the job was getting to be too much for her husband: "I could see him going downhill quite rapidly. There was an awful lot of pressure as minister. There were nights he went to bed at two and three in the morning and was then up again at six."

It was not until the following February, in 2002, that it was announced that Foster would be leaving, although there had been rumours circulating that he was planning to retire. He was sad to leave office, but it gave him more time to spend with his family. He continued to work on the police board, however, and was heartened in June 2002 when he was awarded a CBE in the Queen's Birthday Honours list.

Foster's replacement in Environment was junior minister Dermot Nesbitt, who was promoted from the Office of First and Deputy First Minister. As a relatively younger man, Nesbitt brought a new energy to the department and was, according to one insider, more demanding of his staff: "Dermot was more of a terrier, constantly pushing [civil servants] for answers. It was a bit of a wake-up. I think they knew there was a new sheriff in town." The new minister believed some in the department were resentful of devolved government, as they had been freer to pursue policies under direct rule. Some officials in the civil service were perceived to behave like politicians. Nesbitt, as an elected representative, soon made up his mind that there were three kinds of civil servants: the administrators who would carry out his policy; those who would explain why something could not be done; and those who would explain how to do something while setting out the risks. Nesbitt, who could be quite fastidious according to some who have worked with him, insisted on briefing papers being presented in a certain way and on at least one occasion sent a paper back to be improved. He was horrified at the lengthy briefing papers Foster had received. Nesbitt's preference was for a condensed note on one sheet of A4 paper, with a number of priorities set out and an update on progress. "I wanted to know the big picture," he said.

The Environment committee chairman noticed a change when Nesbitt took over. While he believed the minister was not there long enough to make an impact, he found his regime more accommodating: "He was more open to meeting the chair and the vice-chair and discuss issues at an early stage rather than at a crisis stage. We had humiliated the department on a number of issues and Dermot wasn't going to fall into that trap." Nesbitt recalled that his first meeting with the committee was "a bit fractious", but he treated it as a microcosm of the Assembly and tried to work with the committee and its chairman, Willie McCrea. "We had each other's mobiles," said Nesbitt.

One of the priorities Nesbitt set out on his A4 page was to have the Mournes declared a national park, but he found some resistance within the department: "Some officials said, 'You can't do that, you have to deal with the areas of outstanding natural beauty first'." The initiative became a casualty of direct rule.

The new minister was in the spotlight more than Foster, but not always for the right reasons. He got into a public row over a new integrated school in Carryduff. Nesbitt was en route from his home in Crossgar to Stormont in the ministerial car when he was caught up in traffic being directed by a policeman. The reason for this was that the road layout for the school had not been started, even though its completion was a condition of planning permission granted. After being briefed by an official, Nesbitt went public with his plans to put a stop order on the school, kicking off a farcical political storm in which the Alliance leader David Ford questioned his attitude. While Nesbitt might have been strictly correct in defending his department, it was not viewed as particularly good politics to be involved in a public row with an integrated school. The issue was resolved swiftly, but Nesbitt remained unapologetic: "What if someone had been killed or injured? The BBC would have been down on me like a tonne of bricks."

Planning also erupted into public controversy on Nesbitt's watch over plans to bulldoze a house in Belfast that had once been occupied by the renowned Irish poet Seamus Heaney. A media storm ensued when local campaigners tried to save the house, but failed. The difficulty was that the house was not listed and resources were already scarce for dealing with properties that were listed. It was also argued that Heaney had lived in several homes in Belfast. The house in question had been assessed and was not deemed suitable to be saved. Barr pointed out: "If you listed every house that someone famous had lived in, half of Belfast would be listed." Nonetheless, Nesbitt was criticised in some quarters for not stepping in with a "stop notice" to prevent the developer razing the property. For his part, Nesbitt said the legal advice received by the department did not support this as the property was not listed and the department risked being sued and having to pay compensation. One campaigner, who lived on the same street as the house, recalled: "I thought this was something devolution could do something about. I could have stood in my street and wept." Nesbitt insisted the fault did not lie with him, saying: "It wasn't a failure of devolution. It was a failure of the law." Pointing out that the house was in a poor state of repair, he added: "It was one thing to save it, another to fund it."

Like Foster before him, when he tried to reform planning he encountered resistance. He, too, pursued the issue of third-party planning appeals, based on the English model and also sought to criminalise planning, so that those who built without permission could be penalised in the courts. He was told by some civil servants why it could not be done: it would worsen the backlog that already existed in the system. He refused to take no for an answer. In June 2002 he outlined tough new legislation for those who flaunted planning laws, including the possibility of prison sentences. The proposed Bill also aimed to prevent a repeat of the Heaney house demolition by giving the department the power of spot-listing properties, so it could intervene quickly if a particular building was considered to be at risk. His efforts were interrupted by suspension, and when direct rule Labour minister Angela Smith took over the Environment mantle, he heard her utter the words of advice he had been given on why planning reform was a problem.

Nesbitt also raised hackles when he defended the British government's policy on Sellafield at a conference in Dublin, which was jointly organised by the Executive and the Irish government. The SDLP special advisor Conail McDevitt recalled: "He tried to back the British government line on behalf of the Northern Ireland Executive. We all went ballistic." The SDLP's South Down MP, Eddie McGrady, was a well-known critic of the nuclear power station and had long campaigned for its closure. That autumn Durkan had visited Amnesty International's *Rainbow Warrior* when it docked in Belfast and he too had called for the closure of Sellafield. When the SDLP heard of the position Nesbitt had adopted in Dublin, there was a challenge at the Executive table. "It was left to Bríd to ambush him at the Executive," McDevitt said.

Despite opposition from some environmentalists, Nesbitt was open to persuasion about nuclear power. Although it was not a risk-free option, it did not create the same level of emissions as other fuels that were linked to global warming. He also realised that alternative energy sources, such as wind power, would not be sufficient to cover energy demand. It was with an open mind, he said, that he visited the station in Cumbria. "Too many people based their decision on emotion not evidence," he maintained.

The waste management issue also came to a head during Nesbitt's term and caused friction between his department and the Department of Regional Development. The DoE regulated water and sewage standards, while the DRD was responsible for infrastructure and development. One of the challenges facing the departments was ensuring that the sewage and water systems were able to keep up with the speed of development. In the summer of 2002 Nesbitt's department became concerned that it could not meet the demands of developers and identified a number of hot-spots where it felt development would have to be suspended. Robinson said the people in his department "went ballistic" when they heard this and argued that it would be disastrous, not least for the people whose livelihoods depended on the building trade.

Nesbitt was receptive to a compromise and said he did not want to create a backlog of planning applications. He allowed those applications that had broad outline approval, but had been held back due to concerns over possible sewage pollution, to go to the decision stage. The two ministers made good progress in resolving the difficulties, but in a joint statement acknowledged they still had some way to go to ensure the sewage system in certain areas met EU and national standards. As part of a resolution, Nesbitt raised the issue at an Executive meeting:

> "It was decided that these developments could continue on the condition that when the Budget was drawn up in October 2002, there was a scheme to rectify sewage works and Robinson was obliged to give this to the Executive. I made it clear if [the compromise] was not forthcoming, it would be reviewed. I also made clear I would review the situation after seeing what Robinson brought forward."

He never did review it because direct rule interrupted. Nesbitt was extremely disappointed when Stormont closed. In some ways he was not surprised by the behaviour of republicans, but still believed there were some positive achievements. "I think we made good corporate decisions," he said. "I don't think any government will satisfy all the people. But anything that was done was done with the best intentions."

On his last day in office, he stayed late, anxious to sign off on some papers. He recalled that a few officials were working overtime with him. When they finally finished for the evening, one woman kindly wished the minister well, adding: "I hope you are back soon, we'll keep the seat warm."

Chapter 24
A New Order

Seamus Mallon went alone to Stormont's rather grim basement and made his way to the functional press conference room. He had spent the previous days in contemplation about his future. He had thought long and hard about the decision he was about to make. Having wrestled with the issue, he was satisfied he was doing the right thing. Aside perhaps from close family members, no one else was aware of what he was thinking; he had kept his own counsel regarding what he was about to say.

The press conference had been called for 18 September 2001, following the announcement that autumn that John Hume was retiring as leader of the SDLP. Mallon's reaction was generous. He paid tribute to Hume, praising his towering leadership. While acknowledging that they had had to overcome differences in temperament, Mallon stressed that Hume's contribution to politics had been enormous by any standard. Taoiseach Bertie Ahern described Hume as a "true Irish hero". Hume, still reeling from the disastrous general election results in June 2001, had been persuaded that the time had come to hand over the leadership. He had struggled with the issue of retirement for some time, even before the poor poll result, particularly as he was suffering from ill-health.

Speculation was rife concerning Hume's successor: would it be Mallon, his stalwart, long-serving deputy, or Mark Durkan, his protégé? A BBC "Hearts and Minds" poll indicated that Mallon was the popular choice with the electorate: he polled 41% to Durkan's 24%. Even among the younger generation of voters, Mallon's approval rating was higher than Durkan's. This no doubt brought Mallon some satisfaction as he pondered whether he was going to pursue the leadership.

For three days and three nights Mallon kept everyone guessing as to his intentions before appearing at the news conference alone. Barry Turley, the SDLP's director of communications, was convinced that Mallon would run and made a bet with a party colleague; he lost ten pounds.

Mallon had at last been freed from Hume's shadow – but the leader's decision had come too late for his deputy. Aged sixty-five, Mallon felt he was too old for the leader's post. "Had it been ten years earlier," Mallon said, "I would not be taking this decision." In an interview for *Room 21*, Mallon rejected suggestions that he did not want to lose to Durkan, insisting that had he pursued the leadership, he would have won it. But with time against him, Mallon had concluded that the SDLP needed a change. His decision meant the party had to seek not only a new leader but a new deputy leader. Mallon was retiring, having already signalled he would not be seeking re-election as MP for Newry and Armagh. As for Stormont, it would have to find a new Deputy First Minister. One

Stormont insider was not surprised. He had noted a change in Mallon during his time in office:

> "When he arrived he was happy and optimistic, full of self-deprecating humour. Then gradually, he was worn down by the treacle of the system, wading through the business of government."

Mallon admitted his decision was very difficult, and that he would miss the cut and thrust of politics. Asked how he thought unionists would remember him, the adjective he chose was "grumpy". But he added: "I played it straight and they know I played it hard. I don't think they could accuse me of not playing it straight."

His decision to end his political career removed from the field any serious leadership contender other than Mark Durkan. Some felt Mallon should have stayed on as a caretaker leader while Durkan took on the role of deputy, but Mallon had already calculated that a caretaker term would require five years, which in his mind would have meant running for European election in 2004. Given the workload he had carried for so many years, the intensity of the negotiations in which he had been involved and the unbearable strain of being a politician in Northern Ireland, Mallon no longer believed he had the energy to continue.

According to well-placed sources, Durkan had let it be known to Mallon that the opportunity was there for him to remain as Deputy First Minister. Apparently Mallon showed no enthusiasm for this scenario. No one stepped forward to challenge Durkan for the party leadership, and accordingly he was crowned leader. When asked about his victory in a radio interview some months later, he gave an unguarded answer, suggesting he would have preferred Mallon to have taken the post, but then adding quickly that no one had to "coax him to be leader". The Agriculture minister Bríd Rodgers, then aged sixty-six, had no qualms about age when the deputy leadership came up. After a tussle with a number of younger contenders, she won easily, succeeding Mallon.

After Mallon's retirement from political life, a portrait in oil by Belfast artist Rita Duffy was commissioned by the Assembly. The 5-feet (1.5m) high canvass was unveiled in a special ceremony in Stormont's Long Gallery hosted by the Speaker, Lord Alderdice, who observed that while the talented artist had done an excellent job, she had perhaps not quite captured Mallon's sense of fun. The Speaker did not fault the artist, insisting that Mallon was "too big a man" to convey in one image. Mallon recalled good days, precious days, during his time in office: "I remember them with affection."

In recognition of his position as the North's first Deputy First Minister, Mallon's portrait was hung in the formal dining room at Stormont. At the unveiling Mallon commented: "It's seldom that you are at your own hanging … I get a personal kind of pleasure from thinking of those who have to eat here and look at me with each spoonful."

Chapter 25
Mark Durkan: Power and Money

When Mark Durkan joined the Executive in December 1999 he enjoyed the double distinction of being the youngest and the "richest" minister. He was thirty-nine years old and nominally in charge of more than £8 billion.

Finance was not his first choice; Durkan had wanted Health. "At heart he is a social democrat and he wants to help everyone," said ministerial advisor and close friend Damien McAteer with a mischievous grin. "In another situation he would have been a priest or a social worker." Political considerations prevented Durkan from getting his first choice, or even his second – the Department of Regional Development. The SDLP selected Finance once the Ulster Unionists had settled on Enterprise, Trade and Investment as their first choice. The reason was clear: the Executive would have been unworkable with a DUP Finance minister because the role was in many ways the lynchpin of the Executive. The SDLP and others were concerned that if the DUP – which refused to attend Executive meetings or meet with Sinn Féin for one-to-one talks – controlled Finance, the system would be gridlocked and it would destroy any notion of corporate life in the Executive. "We were stuck with having to take it," said Durkan.

The anxiety about the DUP may have been misplaced. In an interview for *Room 21* the party's deputy leader, Peter Robinson, claimed that the DUP had never had any intention of taking Finance because it had no desire to deal with Sinn Féin. Moreover, the DUP, like other parties, viewed Finance as less attractive. It was considered an invisible ministry that offered little reward for much hard effort. McAteer summed it up best: "There's no glamour in it." Durkan was painfully aware of the disadvantages of his post. "Not sexy," was his curt conclusion about the department.

After thirty years of conflict, Durkan soon found the Budget was woefully inadequate for any administration hoping to improve public services. During the Troubles resources had been diverted into the security Budget, or used to rebuild infrastructure destroyed by the IRA. It was estimated that £14 billion was required to improve standards. Some public assets, such as the sewerage system, were literally crumbling. New schools, roads and hospitals were urgently needed if Northern Ireland was to prosper and compete with other European regions. A Confederation of British Industry report declared that Health needed £1 billion urgently, as did roads and transport, and that a staggering £3 billion was required to improve water and sewerage facilities. Like his direct rule predecessor, Durkan received little sympathy from the Treasury and had limited flexibility over how money would be distributed. He soon discovered that the Social Security budget immediately ate up £3 billion, or 33%, of the annual Budget. Health took another chunk, around 20%, while his own department's budget was around £110 million.

Early in the administration, Durkan had a frantic time negotiating the new open and accountable Budget procedure and said on one occasion he was constantly running between Room 21, talking to Executive ministers, and the Long Gallery, liaising with his Assembly committee. "Finance was a real work-horse," he said. But once the structure was in place, Durkan believed any future Finance minister would at least have an easier time of it: "I was the crash-test dummy for the Executive in many respects."

As well as Finance, Durkan also dealt with personnel issues, the 2001 census, the construction service, the rate collections agency, the valuation and lands office and law reform. He used to refer affectionately to the civil servants on the finance side as "the book-cookers". Durkan did not have the last word on annual spending plans: he had to win Executive and Assembly approval for his draft Budgets, and had much less autonomy than the Chancellor of the Exchequer in London. This need for consensus did not stop rival political parties whingeing about the Budget, however. To Durkan's annoyance, during debates various Assembly members would complain about Finance decisions approved by ministers from their own party. He would joke that he got all the blame for the unpopular decisions and none of the credit for the popular ones: "In our system responsibility-sharing means the other ministers get the credit for the good things and the Finance minister gets the blame for the not-so-good things."

Attempts by the Finance department to make sure it got some credit for big spending decisions led to friction between ministers on occasion as they jockeyed to announce good news. But despite the drawbacks, Durkan was conscious of the department's importance and the significant contribution it could make. Finance dominated the Executive meetings in Room 21, taking up at least half of the business on any given day. Mallon would occasionally remark: "If it wasn't for the filthy lucre, we'd have nothing to talk about."

Although Durkan had to get all the ministers at the table to agree the Budget in order to get it passed, he was in a strong position nonetheless. He oversaw the redistribution of unspent funds and had a key role in shaping finances through his draft Budgets. He consulted with all the ministers before deciding his plans, allowing him to set the agenda. "As Finance minister," he said, "your only power is the power of influence. You don't have the power of control." Achieving consensus was extremely difficult at times and Durkan had to field questions from ministers without any back-up at the Executive table, as he was allowed to bring in his staff in only when the Budget was being delivered. Money, or the "filthy lucre", was, naturally enough, at the root of a lot of infighting, angst and tension within the Executive. But those working within the system felt Durkan was adept at handling a tense situation. "Mark Durkan was the most impressive minister," said a senior civil servant. "He has a droll sense of humour and when things were getting hot and heavy, Mark would defuse it with a lighthearted comment."

His one-liners were legendary. Reflecting on his role as Finance minister, he once declared: "I enjoyed a good relationship with all the ministers. They laughed at my jokes and I laughed at their spending plans." Durkan was self-deprecating in his humour and could see the funny side of his propensity to deliver unwelcome news. He would grin as he delivered one of his favourite lines: "I don't suffer from depression, but I'm a carrier."

Despite his reputation for pithy one-liners he was also known for being verbose. "He is a nice guy in many ways," said Sam Foster, "but he talked too damn much. He took fifteen

minutes to tell you what he could have done in five." His speech patterns were unusual –
long-winded and pithy at the same time. On occasion, Durkan struggled to master the
twenty-second television soundbite. From his prolonged paragraphs sprung clever rhymes,
eloquent phrases and colourful analogies and at times he appeared to be a frustrated poet.
When the British and Irish governments published the controversial *Framework Document*
in 1995, he caused amusement with his declaration that unionists were acting as if the
paper was a "textually transmitted disease". On another occasion he accused anti-
Agreement unionists of "antics, pedantics and semantics".

Durkan could be a combative and powerful debater, but his nature was that of a
conciliator, according to party colleagues. This made him well-suited for the Finance post,
as did his ability to comprehend complex figures and long-term planning schedules. "A
brain with binoculars," was how the SDLP junior minister Denis Haughey described him.
And even though Finance was not his first choice, Durkan embraced it with enthusiasm.
"Durkan ate finance," recalled one official. "He loved it."

Indeed, he endured long hours and a 175-mile round trip, travelling from Derry to his
office in Bangor's Rathgael House. He was accompanied by Damien McAteer, a fellow
Derryman who was close to Fianna Fáil and who shared Durkan's sharp, analytical mind,
his passion for politics and his enthusiasm for getting things done. Both minister and
advisor found the journey arduous, but McAteer says he had trouble persuading Durkan
to stay in Belfast overnight rather than return to Derry. They tried various ways of
avoiding the journey. McAteer said that at one point they opted to work one very long day
until midnight or so, stay overnight and then follow it with a shorter day and a return to
Derry. "But we just ended up doing two very long days," said McAteer. Durkan would
spend the chauffeur-driven journey reading his brief and absorbing figures so efficiently
that some assumed he had a background in Finance. He would laugh: "People think that
just because I have two brothers who are accountants, I am an accountant-in-waiting. I'm
not."

In fact, Durkan was a career politician who had not graduated from university. He
studied politics and philosophy at Queen's University, but did not complete his degree as
he was increasingly drawn into politics. He was deputy president of the Student's Union
(1981–2) before becoming deputy president of the Union of Students in Ireland (1982–4)
and moving to Dublin. Adrian Colton, president of the Students Union at the time,
recalled that Durkan was popular among students: "He wasn't somebody obsessed with the
North – southerners were impressed he had a southern perspective on things as well."

In Dublin, Durkan helped lead a campaign against the Irish government's attempts to
remove health cards from thousands of young students. He was among a group of
protestors who squatted in Labour party headquarters for several days and remembered
how Michael D. Higgins, then party chairman and later a Dublin minister, sneaked in
quite early one morning hoping the protestors would still be napping.

Durkan missed the next protest because he had accepted a job offer from SDLP leader
John Hume after his 1983 election victory. When Durkan joined Hume's staff he was
known in the newspapers as "a student radical". While Hume has long been regarded as
his political mentor, Durkan was also greatly influenced by Ted Kennedy, the colourful US
senator and brother of the former president, John F. Kennedy. His 1985 internship with

Kennedy helped Durkan build contacts in the United States, including a close friendship with Nancy Soderberg, who went on to become staff director of the National Security Council. Kennedy's advice has always stuck with Durkan: "You should never go into any issue on any angle unless you know how you are going to get out of it." The Senator made the comment after the young Durkan advised him to get involved in a campaign to prevent the spread of the AIDS virus in the armed forces; there were brothels operating near army bases, putting soldiers at risk. Kennedy, who had a reputation as a womaniser, listened in bemusement as Durkan urged him to spearhead a campaign for safe sex. "Yeah," replied Kennedy with self-deprecating humour, "you can see me holding hearings on this and them saying in Wisconsin, 'Hey Martha, can you believe this guy?'"

Durkan learned his trade with Kennedy and Hume: two formidable politicians. For years Hume had groomed Durkan as his successor; by the age of thirty he was known within the party as the "Londonderry Heir", or "Derry Heir". Speculation about Hume's retirement went on for at least ten years before he actually quit active politics, which meant Durkan was forever deflecting questions about the succession with this comment: "One thing I have learned in politics is that 'up-and-comings' always get their come-uppance." Some regarded Durkan's protestations as a reluctance to enter the limelight, or a desire not to upset Hume by appearing too anxious or impatient for his job. Whatever his ambitions, the editor of the *Derry Journal* suggested Durkan was a man obsessed, one who "eats, sleeps and breathes politics".

Like Hume, Durkan was a Derryman, although he did not share his mentor's working-class roots. While Hume's mother had worked in a shirt factory, Durkan's Aunt Sally had owned one and his maternal grandfather was an industrious and successful businessman. John Mark Durkan was born into a close-knit, middle-class family in Derry on 26 June 1960. He was the youngest of seven children and his family called him Mark. His father, Brendan, was originally from Corporation Street in Belfast, but had been raised in Newry. Generations on the family still talked about the time a bullet was fired into the house on Corporation Street in the turbulent years following partition. Brendan was the son of a policeman, Patrick Durkan, who had served in the Royal Irish Constabulary (RIC) until Ireland was partitioned and the RUC was formed. Unlike his father, Brendan opted for a career in the RUC.

Mark Durkan laughed at the stories told about his father, who was reputedly a great man for the law, enforcing it in a pedantic way at times: "He was doing people for playing dominoes in the street." Brendan Durkan, like his son, was not without a sense of humour, however. One day one of his officers was trying to avoid being reprimanded and got his colleagues to pretend he had left the police station while he hid in the cupboard. But the sharp-eyed Inspector Durkan had spotted the policeman's bike and knew it was a lie. Brendan sat on for hours until the poor man was forced out of the cupboard in desperation.

In 1949 Brendan Durkan married Isobel Tinney, whose maiden name was also a source of amusement in the Durkan family. "Would you," asked Mark, "call your daughter Isobel if her last name was Tinney? Is a bell tinny!?" Isobel's family were involved in commerce and she worked in her father's factory, the Bayview Shirt Company. Her father also owned a pub, a shop and other property and she too had an eye for business. One of her uncles,

Denis McFeeley, was an eccentric character who owned the Carney Dance Hall, which attracted American servicemen from the US Navy in the 1940s. McFeeley got grief from some American sailors for serving black servicemen and was so incensed he hung a welcome sign outside his premises which read: "Black, white or candy-striped." He also wrote a letter of protest to the allied commander, US General Dwight D. Eisenhower, about the treatment of black servicemen.

For stories about his father Mark Durkan has had to rely on other people, as Brendan was killed tragically in 1961, shortly after his son's birth. The young policeman had just been appointed District Inspector for Armagh and had settled his family into 11 Victoria Street, Armagh, a house that came with the post. By coincidence, the man who had just vacated the premises was another Catholic RUC officer, John Gorman, who would go on to join the Ulster Unionist party and become deputy speaker in the 1998 Assembly. On the night he was killed, Brendan Durkan was driving his Morris Minor car near Stewartstown when he hit a sharp bend followed by a hump-backed bridge. He lost control and crashed into the river. His death certificate reported facial injuries and fresh water drowning. He was barely forty years of age.

With seven children to raise, Isobel Durkan, a devout Catholic, relied on her faith, a great inner strength and a loving family circle to see her through. When Brendan died, Anne, her oldest child, was around ten years old, while Mark, her youngest, was just ten months. In between came Mary, Patrick, Oonagh, Mo, and Brian. The family returned to Derry and, with some insurance money and an inheritance, Isobel purchased a detached, three-bedroom house in the rapidly developing Pennyburn estate. The Durkans lived in Troy Park, which in those days was peppered with both Catholic and Protestant families. Isobel Durkan was unusual among women in the district in that she could drive. She ferried her brood around the city in an old Austin Cambridge, which was in such a colourful state of disrepair that one of her sons nicknamed it Hercules, after the Greek god famed for his strength.

Mark was just five years old when his teacher asked the class to draw a picture of their fathers. Mark did not know what to draw, so his teacher suggested he think of something his father might have done. Having seen a man cut the hedge at home, the youngster drew this image, but stuck a policeman's hat on his hedge-cutter. When he was making his First Holy Communion, he joined the other pupils in cutting and pasting a "thank you" card for each of their parents. Mark addressed his card to both his mother and his father. Touched by the gesture, Isobel kept the card on display in her cabinet. His older brothers and sisters used to tease him that he was "Mama's wee treasure" and for a while tried giving him the nickname "treasure".

It did not stick and was soon replaced by another nickname, inspired by the politics of protest. As a consequence of gerrymandering in Derry, there were few houses being built within the city limits, leading to rapid population shifts to places like Pennyburn, to the point where the local Catholic school, St Patrick's, was flooded with children and struggling to cope. There were so many students moving into one primary class that some were kept back, among them Mark Durkan. One evening, Mo Durkan was checking her little brother's reading when she noticed he was not actually reading. He had read the book so often he was able to recite it. When their mother heard this, she went to the school to demand her son be moved into the class ahead, with children of his own age. The principal said this was not possible, and that she could take her son to another school if she wished.

Isobel Durkan decided the school was favouring some children over others based on who their parents were. She left the headmaster's office that day with Mark packed into "Hercules". On the way home, she stopped at the local priest's house and explained the problem. Father Gildea suggested she might place her son in one of the other Catholic schools in the city. "No," she informed the priest, "Mark will attend Christchurch, which is on the doorstep." The priest was aghast; Christchurch was a Church of Ireland school. Isobel Durkan quoted canon law at the priest, insisting she had no choice and that it was the responsibility of the Church to ensure her son received a religious education, which should be no problem as Christchurch was just opposite both the Catholic cathedral and the Bishop's house. For a few weeks Mark Durkan remained on "school strike" while the authorities worked out what to do. Word had spread and by now other angry parents were objecting to the state of affairs in St Patrick's, forcing the bishop and the schools inspector to intervene. At the time, talks were going on to resolve the troubles in the African state of Rhodesia, now Zimbabwe, where the white leader, Ian Smith, had seized control through a "unilateral declaration of independence" from Britain. Referring to the conflict there, the vexed Father Gildea tried to reassure Isobel Durkan that the problem over Mark's schooling could be resolved, saying: "After all, he's not Rhodesia." The name stuck. From then on and long after the "school strike" was settled and the boy had won his promotion to the proper class at Pennyburn, Mark was burdened with a new nickname. Father Gildea would greet him with the words: "Hello, Rhodesia."

Durkan, it seemed, was marked out for politics from an early age. Before the age of eight, he was holding a bucket of paste with which to post fly posters for a nationalist candidate who was battling fiercely against a unionist in a local election. His boyhood friends were the children of politicians Michael and Ivor Canavan, two brothers who were active in the civil rights movement. Ivor Canavan lived just yards from the Durkans and in 1973 stood for Alliance in the Sunningdale Assembly election against his brother, Michael, who was standing for the SDLP. Durkan said his friendship with Ivor Canavan's son may have caused another family friend to think his allegiance lay with Alliance rather than the SDLP. He said his support for the SDLP was not immediate, although when he was nine his mother took him to Shantallow, in Derry, where John Hume was campaigning: "He got out of his Volkswagen and made a speech. My mother was a big Hume supporter, but she used to say he needed more of a sense of humour."

In his formative years, Mark Durkan said there were times when he would have argued that the SDLP was not "red or green" enough – too weak in socialism and nationalism. While some of his schoolfriends from St Columb's supported Sinn Féin, he never did. He always had an aversion to violence in all its forms, including that of the IRA: "I don't think it is because I am a policeman's son, but I have always had this deep thing against violence. When the British soldiers came on the school bus, I found even people spitting at them repugnant."

It was as a student at Queen's University in Belfast that he made up his mind to support the SDLP. The catalyst was the hunger strike in 1981. Mark was twenty-one and Bobby Sands, who was not much older, was starving himself to death as protesting republican prisoners demanded political status. Durkan said he was appalled at the way groups he regarded as nothing more than fronts for Sinn Féin were being established on campus: "The hunger strike moved me off my perch. I felt the emotion and the impulse of it all as much as anybody else, but I could see how it was being used and how it was polarising the student population."

He began to canvass for the SDLP and in 1983 took leave from his Student Union post in Dublin to assist Hume in his successful bid for a Westminster seat. By February the following year Durkan had quit student life to work full-time for Hume. He soon won respect from others in the party for his quick mind and organisational skills, and helped manage Seamus Mallon's election victory in 1986 in Newry and Armagh and Eddie McGrady's successful win in South Down the following year. As a member of the SDLP, Durkan would occasionally meet senior RUC officers who knew his father. These included Sir Jack Hermon, the former chief constable, who would tease him about his background. "If your father had lived to be chief constable, there would have been none of that nonsense from the SDLP out of you," he told the young aspiring politician.

Brendan Durkan had been among a small number of Catholics who had served in the police force in the years before the start of the Troubles. Mark Durkan found that his father's job was raised during his time as a politician, although not often. He remembered having an argument with a Sinn Féin member at a polling station: "It ended up with him shouting at me, 'Your father beat the civil rights marchers off the streets in 1968'. Not only was my father dead [at that time], but, as my mother would say, he was that long dead he was tired dead." Durkan sometimes wondered what would have happened had his father lived. "Some of my aunts have told me my father was actually thinking of leaving the police back then and he had started looking for a farm near Newry. I don't know."

In 1990 Durkan began five years of service as SDLP chairman, during which time the party suffered financial hardship and violent attacks from loyalist terror groups. His role was mainly backroom and he indulged in strategy, spin-doctoring and election campaigns. In 1992 he went to South Africa to assist the ANC with elections. He was viewed as rather introverted for someone in public life. "His problem is that he is very shy," said one insider. Nevertheless Durkan eventually opted for front-line politics and was elected to Derry City Council in 1993, the same year he married his wife, Jackie, who also worked for Hume. During his council years he served on the Western Health and Education Services Council, building up a knowledge of health that later inspired him to want to become Health minister. Durkan gave up his Council post when he became Finance minister, an example others were reluctant to follow because they were unsure how long devolution would last. Durkan may have been over-confident in the ability of the institutions to survive, but did not feel he could do both jobs well. He was wedded firmly to the Agreement and in fact, as one of the central SDLP negotiators, wrote some key sections of it, along with Mallon and others. Durkan recalled it was he who insisted on the d'Hondt formula being applied in the selection of ministers: "I started off in a minority of one in the SDLP on that. John [Hume], Seamus [Mallon] and Denis [Haughey] said parties would negotiate to form the Executive in terms of voluntary coalition, but I argued this should be more formal."

For Durkan, d'Hondt was a way of ensuring coherence and cohesion and preventing unionists from refusing to share power with nationalists. The d'Hondt mathematical formula, which had originated in Belgium, could be confusing and some politicians joked that Durkan was the only one who actually understood it. He helped persuade Ulster Unionist negotiators, who were insisting on a committee-centred administration, to adopt a Cabinet-style government with ministers. Like Mallon, Durkan embraced the role of defending the spirit and letter of the Agreement. He directed the party's campaigns for a "Yes" vote in the referendum and the Assembly poll that saw the SDLP emerge with the lion's share of the nationalist vote. In subsequent negotiations he was central in designing the new departments at Stormont. It was no surprise when Hume appointed him to the Executive. As soon as he became Finance minister he promised fair treatment and value for money: "quality and equality" was how he put it.

Durkan was widely regarded as a tough but fair minister who approached his post in a non-partisan way. "If the SDLP, and in particular Durkan, had not got the Finance portfolio then I think the first Assembly would have been totally unworkable," said McAteer. His advisor may have been overstating the case, but was not alone in asserting that Durkan would have been among the most competent of the ministers to take on Finance. He enjoyed the kind of detail that is involved in the post and was intelligent enough to digest the complexities of the job. "He is a big details guy," said McAteer. "Some see that as a disadvantage, but in trying to turn the juggernaut that is Northern Ireland finance onto a more productive cycle, it is an essential requirement."

Within days of taking office, Durkan was in the spotlight, presenting the Executive's first Budget, although he acknowledged the figures were not his own. The Budget, he explained, had been inherited from direct rule. He calculated it was pointless to change it because no minister was going to settle for less than what had already been allocated. "Changes for the sake of it would have been an act of political joyriding," he reasoned. By New Year 2000, however, he had his first chance to shape spending due to the December monitoring round. These monitoring rounds arose every few months when departments that had under-spent their projected budget handed money back to the Finance department for redistribution. Durkan redirected the money enthusiastically and generally won plaudits during this early honeymoon period. With Executive approval, several million pounds was spent tackling the winter 'flu crisis.

This monitoring round was the first big test of the powers and role of the Department of Finance in relation to the Economic Policy Unit (EPU), which had been set up in the Office of the First and Deputy First Minister. Dermot Nesbitt was a junior minister whose Ulster Unionist party had demanded the creation of the unit during negotiations to decide departments. As a junior minister in the Office of First and Deputy First Minister, Nesbitt believed his role was to manage Budget decisions. The SDLP and Durkan held a different view, insisting that the EPU's function was to provide advice. Durkan recalled that Trimble's economic advisor, Graham Gudgin, along with Nesbitt, was keen on an enhanced role for the EPU: "They talked about it having equivalence with the Office of Budget Management in the White House." Given these different interpretations of the EPU's powers, Nesbitt inevitably clashed with Durkan from the start. According to Durkan, Nesbitt suffered under the misapprehension that he had some kind of veto over Finance and Budgets through the EPU. "He thought every time I sneezed, I was to show him the hanky," said Durkan. One unionist put it differently: "The EPU was supposed to give the Department of Finance advice, but it did not want it."

Durkan recalled that some papers he put forward to the Executive were not distributed: "They weren't circulated because Dermot wanted EPU in the script and for EPU in the script he meant himself." During one encounter with the Finance minister, Nesbitt became quite upset and accused Durkan of head-butting his way through the meeting. Nesbitt felt the Finance department and the SDLP minister were trying to shut out, or sideline, EPU. Nesbitt claimed he was entitled to monitor Finance through the EPU: "It was supposed to be joined up government wasn't it? It was very clear it was a check and balance, but it was neutered by the SDLP."

The EPU did win some changes to the first monitoring round, much to Durkan's chagrin. This early success was probably due in large part to Durkan's brief absence from Stormont, when he had to leave the office due to a family bereavement. His teenage niece, Deirdre Durkan, was killed tragically on 9 January 2000 in a road accident in Derry involving other family members. It was a devastating blow to the Durkan family. An Executive meeting was re-scheduled to allow the Finance minister to attend the funeral. Despite his grief, Durkan returned to work relatively quickly, throwing himself into his job and setting about devising a Budget that would match the Programme for Government, also being drafted at that time. But his efforts to find solace in his job were shortlived when the Executive was suspended within a few weeks.

Durkan used the suspension to figure out how he could get more money and more flexibility into his Budgets. He wanted to ensure that funds were spent efficiently and strategically – a key Treasury demand – otherwise, attempts to win more funding from London would be in vain. McAteer said Treasury officials already resented Northern Ireland's £8 billion-plus annual allocation, much of which was eaten up in advance by fixed costs: "The reality was, there was not much room for manoeuvre. Some of the services in Northern Ireland were already operating at the very backbone." Durkan had already ruled out, for the short-term at least, seeking income-raising tax powers for Stormont, similar to the Scottish model. The Edinburgh Parliament, for example, was free to vary income tax by 3%. Even if the Executive would agree such a move, there were fears the Treasury would simply substitute existing funding with the new money, with no net benefit to Northern Ireland. Durkan believed there were better ways to yield more money and when the suspension of Stormont ended, he returned to work determined to break the old spending patterns that had been formed under direct rule. It was an aim shared by Seamus Mallon who, during an Executive "away day" at Cultra, raised the notion of some funds being placed directly under Executive control. Durkan, who was already thinking along those lines, agreed: "I didn't like the idea that when money was budgeted to departments, they saw it as their money and resented handing it back to the centre."

By October 2000 Durkan had proposed a new initiative to coincide with his draft Budget, the first such budget to be unveiled by a home-grown minister in almost thirty years. This was the Executive's chance to distinguish itself from direct rule. The new initiative and draft Budget followed intensive discussions with all the ministers and represented the most important collective act undertaken by the Executive to date, although behind-the-scenes the Finance proposals had proven pretty divisive.

Frustrated that the departments were soaking up millions, Durkan was determined to boost efficiency, cut costs and redirect savings to worthy projects. He administered a shock to the other Executive members and their department heads, informing them he intended to claw-back a slice of funding from each of the ten departments. The money would then be put into five central funds, controlled by the Executive and known as the Executive Programme Funds (EPF). Initially the funds would be worth £16 million, but this would multiply to tens of millions within a year or two. Durkan told the ministers the EPF would have a number of advantages: departments would be encouraged to cooperate; money could be stored up for large projects that required long-term planning; there would be emergency funds available; the Executive could set its own priorities independent of departments and projects that otherwise would be overlooked could be developed. The EPF had various themes, the largest and most significant of which was an infrastructure fund that would improve roads and deliver big capital projects, such as a north-south gas pipeline. There was a fund on regeneration to tackle poverty, another to promote efficiency and another to promote innovation and technology. There was also a children's fund to provide for those in need or young people at risk. "What we were trying to do," said McAteer, "was to introduce new financial engineering to match the new political architecture."

Durkan claimed that without devolution and the EPF, important projects would never have been achieved. Mallon demanded that the EPF be used for the much-needed road improvement scheme between Newry and Dundalk, on the southern border. He was determined this should be done before he left office and was annoyed that the Department of Regional Development, headed by the DUP's Peter Robinson, had identified more pressing projects. McAteer soon learned that getting things done at the centre required sheer force of personality.

Robinson resisted Mallon's demands. He wrote to the Executive and to Mallon, in particular, explaining his position thus: "Look, I am not going to get into taking decisions on what might be politically a good road to build and I have asked my department to use objective criteria about where the priorities apply." In October 2001, just a few weeks before Mallon left office, the funds were announced for the £20 million north-south project. Durkan said that in order to get the requisite agreement from unionists, another £20 million in road improvements had to be spread beyond Newry and the border. "Peter Robinson had teed up the option of making [the scheme] from Belfast to the border and then the Ulster Unionists kind of trumped him by insisting on Larne to the border," he said.

Durkan and McAteer recalled ministers and their departments being rather resentful at first at having to give up some of their Budget. Asked who showed the most generosity, McAteer could think of no one in particular: "None of them [was] very good at it, quite frankly." McAteer had a notion that the permanent secretaries, whom he called "the apostles", were whispering in the ministers' ears: "I wouldn't do that minister, what we have we hold!" McAteer remembered that Sinn Féin and the DUP were particularly unhappy: "Bairbre de Brun opposed the Executive Programme Funds and she probably got the most out of them." Durkan confirmed this, saying both Sinn Féin ministers were unhappy: "Bairbre and Martin were iffy and dismissive and were just about quietened when I made clear that the infrastructure fund was not just about roads and rail, that we could siphon money off to Health and Education."

Regional Development Minister Peter Robinson concluded the EPF was a waste of time and effort, designed to give the First and Deputy First Minister some power and responsibility over funding. Robinson was not a lone voice on this either; Durkan said his attitude was characteristic of the other ministers: "They didn't like the idea that they would have to come up with bids for things and have to deal with other people in other departments." Even SDLP ministers, on occasion, would come in reflecting civil servants' briefs. Initially, the First Minister had his doubts, according to Durkan, and McAteer said he was initially less enthusiastic than Mallon before finally agreeing and then arguing the EPF should be run from the EPU in the centre office. This led to more friction. Trimble supported the logic of the funds: "It was to break down the silo mentality of the departments, which was the curse of the administration." McAteer recalled that other Ulster Unionists ministers, anxious about their own Budgets, were a bit suspicious of the EPF.

In a multi-party Executive where four parties are vying for credit, there was also an issue about who got to announce the funds. Trimble and Mallon had a row about this. Trimble wanted the Office of First and Deputy First Minister to announce the EPF; Mallon insisted it should come from the SDLP Finance minister. Mallon thought it was appropriate that Durkan make the announcement, as he had conceived of the idea, done a lot of the groundwork and understood the details. Trimble refused to agree and he was most annoyed when he later discovered that a decision allowing Durkan to make the announcement had been made after he left an Executive meeting early. The result, according to insiders, was a sharp exchange between Trimble and Mallon. A senior civil servant described it as a SDLP ambush: "The SDLP conspired in a subtle way to have Mark make the announcement. Sir Reg was not tipped off about this and at the Executive meeting he agreed. David Trimble hit the roof ... David huffed for quite a while after that." Asked about the row, Trimble said: "This was a reflection of the SDLP not being truly committed to partnership."

The EPF was controversial throughout the Executive as questions were asked, for example, about why some money was left in the Programme Funds rather than distributed immediately. There were other problems, too. Some ministers, who were still on a sharp learning curve, were relatively slow at tapping into the funding. The voluntary and community sectors were allowed to bid for a portion of the Children's Fund and initially proved more effective at acquiring the money than the government departments. Sinn Féin's Francie Molloy, who chaired the Finance committee, detected some impatience from Durkan when ministers sometimes failed to seize opportunities and think imaginatively: "He was trying to drive people to create new initiatives. You could see the frustration. I think he genuinely wanted to provide better services."

Looking back, Durkan believed the funds could have been better developed had the Executive continued in existence. He envisaged forming an Executive subcommittee to manage the funds and set out priorities around issues such as infrastructure: "That didn't happen, unfortunately. The problem with the EPF was that the other ministers opposed it and all came in saying the department knows best and we don't need those other funds."

When direct rule returned, the funds were dismantled one by one, to the dismay of Durkan and his supporters. By the time the funds were unveiled to coincide with the first Budget, it was also clear that the Executive, struggling to meet demand for improved public services, was facing hard choices and had decided to abandon idealism in favour of pragmatism. Despite an extra 5% in spending in real terms over the previous year, Durkan expressed disappointment that expenditure was markedly less than in England, Scotland and Wales.

The Executive agreed to a controversial initiative called Public Private Partnership (PPP), which parties such as Sinn Féin and the SDLP had previously opposed. This method of raising revenue was inherited from direct rule. It involved giving the private sector guaranteed low-cost government loans to build large capital projects, such as schools or hospitals. Critics claimed it mortgaged public assets for years to come and burdened future generations while giving private contractors a sweet deal. The Executive decided it was the only way some projects were ever going to be developed.

Durkan also set up a high-level working group to look at new ways of attracting private investment into Northern Ireland and to generate wealth. The group was to be jointly chaired by officials from his Department and the EPU in the Office of First and Deputy First Minister. Despite some negativity around the Executive funds and some criticism of PPP, Durkan was generally praised in the Assembly and in the media for delivering a polished performance with his draft Budget. There were significant gaps between the departments' financial bids and what they received, but there were increases across all the departments. Both Health and Education won rises of around 7%. Agriculture got a 16% rise while Regional Development got an extra 10%. Enterprise received just 1%, however, to the consternation of its minister, Sir Reg Empey.

Durkan acknowledged there were considerable gaps in what the departments asked for in their "wish lists" and what they received. Bairbre de Brun often made the point that the funding she received was inadequate to tackle deep-rooted problems. Health funding remained a particular issue and Durkan claimed to have done his best to meet the minister's demands. By the time Durkan left Finance in December 2001, the Health budget was 37% higher than it was in 1998–99. Unionists became quite resentful at how much money was directed towards de Brun's department and according to some insiders, on occasion Martin McGuinness politely distanced himself from some of her demands at the table, acknowledging that everyone was cash-strapped. Nonetheless, Durkan was relatively sympathetic to Health as it was one of the priorities, along with Education and roads, that had been identified by the Executive. The Finance minister became exasperated with the Ulster Unionist ministers' attitude to the Department of Health and Education as well as to the Department of Regional Development. He claimed they were more fixated with the fact that these departments were controlled by Sinn Féin and DUP ministers, respectively. "Michael McGimpsey and Reg Empey would come and say, 'This isn't fair. Why are you giving this to the DUP and Sinn Féin?' and I would say, 'You know, it isn't just Sinn Féin people who are going to get sick and need hospitals and home helps and it isn't just DUP people who need better roads to drive on. These are service priorities – forget who the ministers are'."

Empey and McGimpsey were entitled to argue for their departments, however, as any good minister would do. Trimble felt his ministers were irritated not by money going to schools and hospitals but by a perception their departments were losing out. It was acknowledged that McGimpsey's department, being new, did not initially have the expertise to put together bids and staff were eventually seconded to assist the minister in this. Durkan felt the Arts Minister and his unionist colleagues sometimes resented having to go through these Budget processes. Durkan recalled Ulster Unionists arguing that they should be getting funds because they were taking the risk for the Agreement, but the point did not wash with him. He likened this argument to the one he made to his mother when he was a boy and she was at the kitchen sink and, without turning around, refused when he asked for money for a bar of chocolate. When he asked again and she again refused, his demand got louder until finally he asked her: "Do you know who it is who's asking?"

Ulster Unionists occasionally accused Durkan of giving money to the DUP to stop them from carping. Robinson also claimed his department did well in the budget rounds because the pro-Agreement Finance minister wanted to prevent the DUP from becoming the "crying child" in the Executive. Durkan insisted it was simply a matter of priorities and roads happened to be one of them. Despite resentment behind the scenes, there was a remarkably warm exchange in the chamber, particularly between Durkan and the Regional Development minister. Robinson in fact congratulated Durkan on his Budget, remarking it would be "churlish" not to do so. Robinson joked that while the Chancellor in London traditionally drinks whiskey, his "abstemious" Stormont counterpart was drinking water. "I hope it is from the Department of Regional Development's Water Service," he said with a smile.

Robinson did criticise some aspects of the Budget, particularly funding for north-south bodies (an ongoing DUP theme), but expressed his appreciation for Durkan's "*modus operandi*". He acknowledged the Finance minister's ability to "stand back" from the political difficulties in the system and take a professional approach. Durkan was the one minister in the Executive who had the most contact with the DUP ministers, as they would meet him directly to discuss their spending needs. Durkan thanked Robinson for his remarks and reminded him that the Budget was collectively agreed, a theme he would return to, particularly when the Budget debate, which followed a month later, was markedly critical.

Durkan found himself on the defensive over his spending plans because it had become clear that they assumed an 8% rise in the regional rate bill for 2001–2. When Durkan countered that most of this could be traced back to direct rule, the Alliance MLA Seamus Close said this was inconsistent with his claims there would be no hand-me-down budget. Close added: "I feel we are being railroaded towards a vote on the Budget without proper scrutiny." Durkan was also stung by claims from the Alliance party that he had attempted to introduce a stealth tax. He insisted the rates rise was clearly flagged in the draft Budget statement. Alliance's criticism was echoed by Sinn Féin Finance committee chairman, Francie Molloy who claimed credit for branding the rates increases as the "Durkan tax". Whoever concocted the phrase, it was seized upon by both Sinn Féin and the DUP for political advantage. Durkan tried to stamp it out by pointing out that the entire Budget was collectively agreed by all the ministers in Room 21, including Sinn Féin, whose departments were benefiting. McAteer shared the minister's frustration, saying: "You had this absurd situation where you had Bairbre saying, 'I don't mind voting for rates increases as long as I get the money'." Durkan would soon declare: "Sinn Féin in the Assembly increasingly act like the DUP, as though agreed decisions have nothing to do with them."

At his party's annual conference a few weeks later, he launched an attack on his critics, summing up his difficulties thus: "The DUP do not participate in the Executive and then make ministerial announcements as though they did. On the other hand, Sinn Féin does participate properly but … Sinn Féin Assembly members oppose Executive decisions as though they didn't."

In an interview for *Room 21* he gave a fuller account of what happened with the rates situation. Durkan stated that he told the Executive, when drawing up the Budget, that it could opt for a 7 % rise as projected under direct rule, or select a lower rise of 5% or 6%. Initially the Executive agreed to stick to 7%, but as the Budget came to be agreed, three ministers rebelled and refused to sign off because they wanted more money. Durkan had to secure their approval, or the Budget negotiations would be a bust. Durkan said he informed the Executive that the only way they could have more money was through higher rates and that an extra 1% could be added to the rates rise to generate another £8 million. Durkan claimed Sinn Féin's Bairbre de Brun and Ulster Unionists Michael McGimpsey and Sir Reg Empey "demanded" the rates rise: "They said, 'We'll have that £8 million'."

The Executive meeting, Durkan said, was adjourned and the ministers in question went to another office to discuss what to do with the money. At first, according to Durkan, the two Ulster Unionists tried to block de Brun from getting anything, but Durkan balked at this and Health was given £3 million, while Enterprise and Culture, Arts and Leisure divided the remainder between them. Despite the controversy over the rates rises and complaints that it was being rushed through without proper committee scrutiny, Durkan's final Budget did win approval in the Assembly that December. It was passed by a majority of both unionists and nationalists following a nine-hour debate. Two amendments were tabled, resurrecting the stinging debate over rates rises. One amendment came from the DUP, which called for a rates reduction through the scrapping of funding to the north-south bodies and the Civic Forum. The DUP argued that without these bodies, there would be "savings" of £20 million, ignoring pro-Agreement claims that the institutions brought tangible benefits. The other amendment was tabled by Sinn Féin and demanded a reduction in the regional rate to match inflation levels. Both motions failed, but not without some heated debate that exposed faultlines in the administration.

The DUP Social Development Minister, Nigel Dodds, was among the first to speak. He used Sinn Féin's motion to undermine claims that the Executive operated through collective responsibility. Dodds said Sinn Féin's amendment proved this was not the case. His fellow minister, Peter Robinson, also accused republicans of "stitching-up" the Finance minister: "IRA/Sinn Féin is leading the Minister of Finance and Personnel to the end of the plank, and it will leave him there." Sinn Féin's Alex Maskey disputed the DUP's assertion that this spelled the end of collective responsibility, saying: "Any party in the Executive can hold a position that is contrary to that of others without causing a collapse." He also mocked the DUP's attempts to distance itself from the rates rise when its departments were benefiting. "Their hands are wringing wet," he said. Robinson rejected this, insisting his funds came from the block grant.

Maskey admitted that de Brun and McGuinness had been prepared to support the rate increase, but after wider consultation in the party it was decided that the inflation-busting rise was unacceptable. Maskey "reluctantly" suggested that the extra cash should be taken from the EPF "on a one-off basis". With this idea floating in the chamber, Maskey's praise for the "Trojan efforts" of Executive ministers in dealing with funding demands rang hollow with Durkan. Nor was the minister placated by praise from Francie Molloy for finding an extra £7 million for Health and another £1.3 million for Education. In fact, Durkan was most annoyed when Molloy declared that it was the Finance minister who carried the can for the Budget, even though it was the Executive's Budget. Molloy then noted that his committee had not taken a position with regard to the 8% regional rate rise, while making clear that the cross-party committee would have opposed the rise had it done so.

This state of affairs was another quirk in the system, which meant Executive ministers could do one thing and members of their party on committees could do another. Durkan could do little about this, except perhaps enjoy the part of Seamus Close's contribution that condemned the DUP and Sinn Féin. Close accused these parties of trying to absolve themselves of any responsibility for Executive finance decisions. "I have never seen so much wriggling, squirming and so many would-be Pontius Pilates," he said. Unlike Sinn Féin the DUP ministers, however, were not at the Executive to approve the Budget.

In his summation, Durkan himself was fairly measured, although he did say he was at a loss to understand how members who wanted more resources could demand that rates be cut back. He described occasions like this as "close encounters of the absurd kind". Later, in Room 21, Durkan was among those who made clear that ministers should stand by the collective decisions of the Executive.

While the Ulster Unionists did not, on this occasion, try to distance themselves so blatantly from the rates rise – unlike Sinn Féin – it was not long after the Executive discussion on the need for collectivity that Durkan became incensed with Sir Reg Empey and his ministerial colleague, Sam Foster. The two ministers voted against an Executive initiative on the Assembly floor, but insisted it was a genuine mistake. Out of habit they simply followed their party members through the division for the vote, forgetting they had to vote with the Executive on this one.

Given his anger at the way some politicians had tried to brand the rates rise a "Durkan tax", it was not surprising that by February 2001 Durkan had intervened to block the rates rise. The DUP called it a "rapid *volte-face*". Durkan announced that the proposed rise in commercial regional rates be cut in half, reduced from 6.6% to 3.3% following routine savings. Durkan also announced that the rate rise would be cut back from 8% to 7%. He denied there was any U-turn, insisting his decision was not the result of representations from others but unexpected revenue. Within a few weeks, he would also announce a new rate relief scheme. Durkan ignored further demands to cut the domestic rate as he judged it would be imprudent to annoy the Treasury, which was demanding higher, not lower, rates to bring Northern Ireland ratepayers in line with Great Britain.

The pressure for rates rises paralleled an ongoing debate about the formula used by the Treasury to determine how much funding Northern Ireland was entitled to receive. The annual funding was around £8 billion and included a subvention of around £4 billion, because the cost of administering Northern Ireland was much higher than the revenue the region yielded. The formula used by the Treasury had been devised by Joel Barnett when he was chief secretary of the Treasury in the 1970s, during the Labour government. The Barnett formula tied Northern Ireland into spending increases or decreases in the rest of the United Kingdom. For example, if there were a £1 billion allocation to Health in Great Britain, Northern Ireland would get a portion of this relative to its population. Historically, Northern Ireland, Scotland and Wales got more than their population share of Treasury funding to prevent disparity within UK regions. But that historic advantage has gradually diminished as Barnett is not based on need. While Northern Ireland does spend more per capita on delivering public services in comparison with England, it also suffers from greater poverty and unemployment. Although a 2000 spending review had highlighted deficiencies in Barnett, the Scottish Parliament preferred not to tamper with the system for fear of getting even less from the Treasury. Wales and Northern Ireland, on the other hand, became interested in reviewing Barnett.

Durkan continually argued with Treasury officials that Barnett needed to be reformed because it was out-dated and unfair. He pointed out that Northern Ireland's needs were higher than other areas of Great Britain and there were important structural differences in the way the public sectors operated in Northern Ireland as compared to England. For example, Northern Ireland received nothing for water and sewage expenditure under the Barnett formula as this service was privatised in Britain. Durkan also argued that the Executive could not match the rates of spending on Health in England. While recognising the benefits of finding a new formula, Durkan also recognised that any change would bring challenges. He warned his Assembly colleagues that the Treasury would demand its own price for replacing Barnett and that would be in the form of higher rates: "We will not get a free run at the rickety wheel when it comes to challenging the Barnett formula."

The Treasury was insisting that Northern Ireland was enjoying more spending per head than England and demanding that the Executive put its house in order and "reprioritise". The Treasury wanted spending to be more efficient, an aim shared by Durkan. He laid the foundations for the challenge of the Barnett formula and tried to end rows at the Executive table over whether Health needed funding by introducing Needs and Effectiveness surveys for several departments, including Health. Sinn Féin regarded the survey as an attempt to expose inefficiencies and prove that the department did not need all the money it was getting. This was underscored when Ulster Unionist MLA Alan McFarland tried to characterise the initiative as a "hit squad", reflecting Trimble's view that Health was inefficient. Durkan claimed his view was that Health needed the money and he wanted to demonstrate this fact to the Treasury.

Durkan knew that if Barnett were to be challenged, the administration would have to prove it needed more money and that it was spending what it had efficiently. He also wanted to settle the ongoing disagreement between Trimble and de Brun over how much money Health actually needed. But he was concerned by the Treasury's condition that in order for Stormont to win more money higher rates and water charges needed to be imposed. The Treasury saw rates increases as one way Northern Ireland could raise £300 million and its demands were ringing in Durkan's ears as he delivered his second draft Budget to the Assembly in September 2001. He did not call directly for water charges, but spoke instead of the Treasury's figures. Spelling out hard realities, he informed the

Assembly that his arguments about Northern Ireland's social deprivation were not making much headway with the Treasury because of the region's lower rates. Durkan stressed the need to break the old spending patterns inherited from direct rule and demanded more realism from departments. This time he managed to avoid criticism from members of his Finance committee about the lack of time to scrutinise the Budget. He unveiled his draft within a few weeks of the Assembly's return from its summer break, following the unveiling of the Programme for Government, which was announced by Sir Reg Empey in his capacity as caretaker First Minister, and by Deputy First Minister Seamus Mallon.

Durkan tried his best to prioritise the funding, with most of it going to Health, Education and roads. "They presented the most clear-cut cases for some increase," he explained.

But in juggling figures, the Department of Enterprise was now getting less than was previously indicated – the only department to get less than expected. Empey was most annoyed, despite Durkan's assertion it was a "slight decrease" following an anticipated slowdown in economic investment. Durkan noted that his department remained sensitive to any changes in the situation and that the Budget did not reflect spending on large projects in Empey's department, such as the north-south gas pipeline, which would be funded from the EPF. According to well-placed sources, Empey and Durkan had heated exchanges over his Budget allocations. In fact, it was Empey to whom Durkan was secretly referring when he once joked in the Assembly: "Does my Budget look big in this?"

Durkan privately complained that if the Ulster Unionists wanted big budget departments, they should have chosen better when the departments were up for selection. He said Empey was unable to show where he needed the money and it was not good enough to say it looked bad for the Northern Ireland economy if his budget was cut. The Budget was still between the draft stage and the final approval stage when Durkan's position came into question due to the retirement of Seamus Mallon.

When Mallon declined to stay on as Deputy First Minister under a new leadership, Durkan realised that as the new SDLP leader, he would have to take the post. Some senior civil servants suggested he could perform a dual role, taking on the Office of Deputy First Minister and retaining Finance, but he decided against this, believing jointery would complicate the Budget process. Instead, he held both positions for a number of weeks to ensure his second Budget went through the Assembly without interruption. He delivered a final monitoring round in December 2001, just before he handed over the reigns to Sean Farren, his SDLP colleague.

Although Durkan had taken Finance reluctantly, he also left it reluctantly. A senior civil servant got the impression he would have preferred Finance to the Office of Deputy First Minister: "Mark was excellent in Finance and he was far more comfortable in [that] role." In assessing Durkan's performance in Finance, Sinn Féin's Francie Molloy was largely positive. They generally had a good relationship. "I found him on a personal basis very compassionate and very thoughtful, particularly when there was a death in my family," Molloy said. Praising Durkan for his industriousness, his willingness to make the department accountable and his comprehensive understanding of Finance, Molloy said: "Certainly, I think the officials would have found it very difficult to bluff him. I'm not saying they would, but he would be up to scratch with this brief. He was also one of the few ministers in my view who understood the role of the committee."

He recalled that Durkan got annoyed when ministers failed to spend their allocations: "He didn't want it coming back unspent. He had difficulty with departments who did that and some of the worst offenders were his own ministers. You could see he didn't tolerate that very easily." But Molloy felt that Durkan should have stood up to the Treasury more forcefully on the issue of under-funding, saying, "Instead of arguing the case from the point of view of deprived communities, he started to give the Chancellor's view to the Assembly."

Durkan rejected the notion that he adopted the Treasury view, insisting he did stand up to the Treasury and consistently demanded more funding. He complained that Molloy was ignoring the realities, a view echoed by McAteer who said: "Durkan would go to the Treasury and ask for more money, but they just didn't want to know." Molloy also complained that the minister failed to decentralise the civil service – a stated aim in the programme of government. This is something the administration would likely have tackled had it not been interrupted.

Durkan's departure from Finance left Farren to manage the funding deficit and the extremely controversial water and rates issues. Freed from these controversies, Durkan would soon find himself with a whole new set of problems to tackle, the first of which was getting elected on a joint ticket with David Trimble. There was no question of a majority of nationalists voting for the pair, but Trimble had lost his majority in the Assembly and getting a majority of unionists to back the ticket became a challenge in itself. Decommissioning had paved the way for uninterrupted devolution, and Trimble's return as First Minister, alongside Durkan, in the autumn of 2001. But anti-Agreement unionists plotted to block it; in this they enjoyed a short-lived victory.

Chapter 26
A Dubliner in Stormont

Sean Farren thumped the desk several times in a fit of pique during a bad-tempered exchange in the debating chamber. The Minister for Employment and Learning had lost patience with members of his Assembly committee over the controversial issue of student tuition fees. He was frustrated because he believed the committee was trying to pre-empt his plans. He had made tuition fees a priority and although he supported the right of free education for all, the minister had signalled he was going to have to compromise. Around half of third-level students were contributing to their education costs, with the other half paying no fees at all due to low incomes. Fees could not be scrapped altogether, the minister suggested adding: "The most important thing is to ensure that students do not suffer hardship."

The minister had a student support budget of around £130 million for higher education, but found, in a multi-party Executive, he did not have the money to fulfil the SDLP pledge to abolish fees. Instead, he began to examine the possibility of reintroducing grants to assist those most in need. He initiated a review that included public consultation on the issue. While the review gripped politicians, it seemed to hold less interest for members of the public and received considerably fewer responses than a similar exercise conducted in Scotland.

Farren's committee had strong views on the issue. Many of the members shared a background in education similar to that of the minister, who had taken leave of absence from his lecturer's post at the University of Ulster in order to pursue politics full-time. The committee chairman, Ulster Unionist Esmond Birnie, was also on leave from Queen's University, where he lectured in economics; Women's Coalition MLA Professor Monica McWilliams came from the University of Ulster; and SDLP MLA Joe Byrne was a former lecturer at Omagh College. All of the members were extremely keen to help shape policy – an important part of the committee's remit. To the minister's chagrin, the committee members not only commissioned their own report, which pre-empted the ministerial review, but asked the Assembly to endorse its findings and pass a motion calling on the minister to implement them at the earliest opportunity. It was a clear challenge to Farren's authority and was viewed by some as an attempt to handcuff the minister, who was still a few months away from presenting his own proposals. The minister told the committee chairman that he would prefer the report to be debated without a vote, but the committee refused. On the day of the debate, Farren arrived at the Assembly chamber more than a little displeased.

In drawing up its report the committee had consulted widely and produced a paper with four options, ranging from no fees to a modified Scottish model whereby tuition fees were scrapped, some means-tested grants were introduced and graduates were asked to contribute a fixed amount in tax once they reached a certain income threshold. The committee had trouble agreeing which option to adopt and almost split over the issue after an intense debate, which ended in deadlock. Sinn Féin members refused to endorse the first draft because it did not reflect their party policy, which called for tuition fees to be scrapped. At one point the republicans threatened to issue a minority report. Twice the committee had to sit into the evening until a hard-won compromise was brokered: the modified Scottish option finally received the support of all committee members, pleasing the committee Chairman immensely. He saw it as an encouraging sign that the multi-party committee system could work.

However, the consensus began to fray on the morning of the debate when the SDLP member for East Derry, John Dallat, spoke against the report in a radio interview. Angry committee members suspected Dallat had been pressured by the minister or by his party and Dallat was attacked in the debating chamber, even by the gentle chairman of the committee, Esmond Birnie who had tried to mend fences with the department by recognising that resources were scarce and that the report was aspirational. He suggested the committee's preferred option need not be implemented all at once. The priority, said Chairman Esmond Birnie, would be to grant an extra £20 million for the 16,000 undergraduates who came from families with annual incomes below £23,000. "We are talking about bursaries of about £500 and £2,000," he said. As he detailed other elements of the package, such as extra student places, the minister listened in grim silence.

Farren then attempted to amend the committee's motion, asking only that the minister be required to consider the report. He made it clear he was not going to be bounced into the committee's recommendation, ignoring other views. "The report leaves some important questions unanswered, or inadequately answered," he said. The minister asserted that the report lacked detailed costings and pointed out that the complete abolition of fees would cost £35 million in a full year, a move that would benefit the well-off, and that this money would be better used to target resources for those who needed assistance. Farren spoke at length, picking holes in the committee's recommendations. He pointed out that the committee was recommending tuition fees be scrapped only for those students attending Northern Ireland universities, a factor he insisted would disadvantage the 33% of Northern Irish students who attended universities in Scotland, England and Wales. The committee's own special advisors had suggested this might be discriminatory, and certainly not compatible with the policy of Targeting Social Need. He did, however, pledge to pursue a no-fees policy across Great Britain in a meeting the following day with UK education ministers.

The committee members were in no mood to accept Farren's amendment. Sinn Féin's John Kelly was soon on his feet, attacking Dallat for "rubbishing his own report" and expressing disappointment the minister had not been more open to the proposal. He pointedly reminded the Assembly, and the minister, that SDLP leader John Hume would not have benefited from a university education if he had been asked to pay for it.

On the defensive, Dallat insisted he had merely pointed out concerns about the report which had to be discussed before ratification, but others on the committee continued to condemn him. Professor Monica McWilliams rebuked the minister's department for repeatedly ignoring requests by the committee for financial costings: "We received nothing so, if there is any fault it does not lie with the committee." McWilliams' attitude annoyed the minister: "Monica particularly irritated me because she knew better." But perhaps it was Mary Nelis' contribution that most irked Farren. The Sinn Féin MLA for Foyle hailed from working-class Derry and had little more than a primary school education. But she was an articulate speaker and bluntly told the minister it was up to him to find the finance for the policy, noting that student finance was not in the minister's financial bids that had been shown to the committee.

Farren lost his amendment by two votes. "I was annoyed, I must say," said Farren, "and I didn't conceal my anger at people who, in my view, were being opportunistic and were promoting the cause of those at the top end of the income scale and ignoring the benefits that were coming to those most in need."

According to Nelis, a bad-tempered Farren, suffering a proverbial bloody nose, crossed the floor and challenged Nelis, who was rather taken aback. "He came over and tackled me and said, 'What do you think you are at? You are not thinking about the students'." Farren could not recall the exchange. Nelis, who genuinely felt she had the students' interests at heart, concluded that the minister was arrogant: "His problem is, he comes from a nice middle-class background and he hasn't a baldy notion of the hardship students from working class areas endure."

In fact, the minister had worked his way through his post-graduate studies, supporting a wife and a baby with another on the way, and insisted he therefore understood only too well the difficulties facing students. He himself had worked and saved and believed in self-sacrifice. The debate turned out to be irrelevant. The committee was testing its strength in the new system at a time when it was not clear where the power lay. Birnie explained:

> "We wanted to establish in general terms the rights and prerogatives of the committee. It had been imagined we had created a dual monarchy of minister and committee with a dual veto and practice showed that was not the case. The fees issue demonstrated where the Executive authority really lay. Having said that I think the minister should be careful about over-riding a majority view in the committee and the Assembly."

Farren admitted he valued the Assembly's and the committee's approval. "I am vain enough to want to be clapped on the back occasionally," he said. Farren also felt that Sinn Féin was attempting to have it both ways: complaining loudly in the chamber about fees while acquiescing in the Executive. He recalled that de Brun had said nothing when he told the Executive that if he scrapped fees, the people in her West Belfast constituency would lose out to the wealthier people in Holywood. He claimed de Brun merely looked at him blankly: "It was see no evil, hear no evil. They said nothing except that Martin McGuinness was a bit concerned that if money was going to higher education he would lose out." De Brun challenged this account and insisted Sinn Féin did make its position on tuition fees known.

Members of his own party were pretty unhappy with his stance, he admitted, as were some student leaders. Farren was tackled at his party's annual conference and got into a terse exchange on the issue late in the evening. Despite the criticism, he remained unapologetic. His department, he said, had examined scrapping fees but could not justify the cost. He also insisted he did have the interests of poorer students at heart and was targeting social need rather than courting populist policies: "The idea of abolishing fees just to look as if you're doing something that is socialist, I mean it's crazy. It wasn't putting the least well-endowed first and it certainly wasn't targeting social need."

A few weeks after the rancorous debate, Farren announced the broad principles of his own plans, but took another three months before finalising them with the Executive and conducting further consultation. In March 2001 he announced a £65 million package that he described as a "realistic, affordable and targeted" response. He felt his three-year package represented a significant U-turn on direct rule policy. Indeed, Farren sensed some annoyance in London about the impact of devolution on education policy, recalling an encounter with Tessa Blackstone, the minister in charge of higher education. She was nicknamed "the Red Baroness" and Farren recalled that "She didn't like the idea of the system being broken up."

Farren abolished tuition fees, but only for certain vocational courses. He introduced means-tested bursaries worth up to £1,500 for full-time undergraduates and created 1,000 new places in higher education. He estimated that around 17,000 students would benefit from the bursaries. Farren raised the income threshold for those fee-paying students by 12%: anyone with a parental income of £20,000 or below would not pay; previously the cut-off threshold was £17,805. He also introduced 3,000 discretionary bursaries for students at further education colleges, one of the areas he was praised for assisting during his time as minister. Finally, he reintroduced childcare grants for third-level students on low incomes.

The minister failed to win over his committee, which complained the package did not go far enough. The committee pointed out that, on the minister's own estimate, only 2% more students would benefit from the rise in the income threshold. The committee did, however, welcome moves to accept its recommendation to streamline the administration of student loans into a one-stop shop. With hindsight, Birnie seemed sympathetic to Farren's plight about budget constraints: "Certainly he argued to the committee very strongly that he was finding it increasingly hard to defend having no up-front fees because the principle beneficiaries of that would be families from higher income backgrounds."

Looking back, Farren believed his communication skills may have lacked the necessary sales pitch, and may have come across as more like lecturing:

> "People said to me I didn't do very well. It is probably coming from an academic background. You see a case and you make a case and you kind of almost expect people to at least recognise the case. But politics is more about influencing and oiling people up the right way. But I was like, 'Why the hell can't you see the rationality of that?'"

"Principled but not good at the political sell," was how an SDLP colleague put it. However, his sometimes colourless approach was offset by an indepth knowledge of his brief. Education was a lifelong passion and Farren was one of the few ministers who got the post he wanted. "I probably would have taken Enterprise if I had the first choice but was well satisfied with higher education."

From the outset department officials had a healthy respect for his knowledge of education and employment issues and he developed a good working relationship with his staff, including Alan Shannon, his permanent secretary, who had a background in the prison service. "I found him upright and easy to work with," said Farren. "He knew people in London and knew how to get advice informally about things related to higher education."

As an educationalist, Farren may have seemed a natural choice for Education minister, but as an Irish-speaking Dubliner, he had farther to travel than some to get to Room 21.

He was born on 6 September 1939 and his mother, Mary, liked to remind him he arrived three days after the start of the Second World War. He was born in the Republic when Éamon de Valera's Fianna Fáil government was in power. The oldest of five children, he had two brothers and two sisters. His mother had worked as a civil servant until she married Joseph Farren, who worked in the family's gas appliance business. The couple and their children lived in Milltown, in suburban Dublin and the family's politics were Labour. His grandfather was a Labour councillor and his uncle a Labour senator. The young Sean grew up on stories about the 1916 Rising and the War of Independence. His father had been a member of Fianna Éireann, a republican youth organisation, and he would recount how he and his companions would steal the Post Office's bicycles so messages could not be passed as quickly as they might have, thus thwarting the efforts of the Black and Tans.

Farren travelled across Dublin by bus each day to attend Coláiste Mhuire, a Christian Brothers school in Parnell Square. It was there he learned Irish and played rugby and Gaelic games. His favourite subjects were English and History and he enjoyed his school years. He was an above-average student and earned a place at the National University of Ireland in 1960, opting to take an arts degree. Upon graduation, he indulged his passion for travel and taught overseas in St Paul's Secondary School in Sierra Leone. Later he went to the Dublin Institute Stavia in Switzerland, where he was able to improve his French. He then re-entered third-level education to study for a MA in Essex University. By then he had met his wife-to-be, Patricia, a Cavan woman. He was delivering a speech at a function in Dublin and they got talking afterwards and found they shared a mutual interest in travel. The couple married and had four children, Orla, Ciara, Niamh and Ronan.

Northern Catholics were more inclined to go south than the other way around, but the Farrens ended up in Northern Ireland. It was a matter of economic necessity: with a young family to support and the economic climate precarious, Farren came north of the border in the early 1970s to take up a post at the University of Ulster's Coleraine campus. He and his family moved to Portstewart, a seaside town that offered a relatively peaceful haven from the terrible violence that was taking hold in cities such as Belfast and Derry. Despite their safe distance from the Troubles, Farren found it impossible to ignore the political turmoil and when an opportunity arose to get involved with the newly formed SDLP, he took it. Within a year, he was on the party's Executive. His first foray into elected politics resulted in a seat on the unionist-dominated Coleraine Council. He and John Dallat, who was elected to the 1998 Assembly in East Derry, were the only two nationalists on the council. With characteristic understatement Farren recalled that the Council was not very warmly disposed towards power-sharing: "In the first year, I don't think either John or I were selected for committees, but we were allowed to attend, which we did, and we contributed. By the second, third and fourth year, I suppose, we were treated as if the horns had fallen off of us."

Farren was elected SDLP Chairman in 1981, a post he held for five years. It was a difficult period as the IRA hunger strikes had polarised unionists and nationalists, with violence spiralling. In 1982 the SDLP had the poorest election result in its history, just months after the death of hunger-striker Bobby Sands. The party was split on the question of standing for the 1982 elections to the Prior Assembly. Some members were opposed to fighting the election at all because the Assembly had no north-south linkages; others wanted to stand. "It was one of the most intense debates I have ever participated in," Farren recalled. "I voted in favour of contesting the elections, as did John Hume and Austin Currie, but there were other prominent names who didn't."

The compromise was that the SDLP would stand for election on an abstentionist ticket. Farren was duly elected to the 1982 Assembly for the constituency of North Antrim, the citadel of the DUP. In 1983 his home came under attack from loyalists who threw petrol bombs and daubed UVF symbols and other slogans on the wall. Like many people, at times he almost despaired at the political stalemate and violence that consumed Northern Ireland. He had long been regarded as a moderate within the SDLP, a staunch critic of, in his words, republican "Fascists" and unionist "bullies". In 1984 he fiercely attacked the mentality of political unionism, claiming it could never conceive of a situation where it did not dominate as top dog: "They can only think in religio-sectarian and not political terms." Farren also blamed republican violence for destroying any chance of Irish unity and sowing the seeds for generations of bitterness. He said republicans were as guilty as the DUP for spreading bigotry.

An intellectual nationalist, Farren has authored *The Politics of Irish Education 1920–1965* and *Paths to a Settlement in Northern Ireland*. He has long been a close ally of the SDLP leader John Hume, a statesman whom he admires and respects as one of the greatest politicians of the last century. His family is close to the Humes, and one party veteran liked to joke, tongue-in-cheek, that Farren was the only one who could stand to go on holiday with the ever-restless Hume. Along with the party leader, he took part in the 1988 talks with the Sinn Féin leadership, including Gerry Adams, Mitchel McLaughlin, Tom Hartley and Danny Morrison. The talks were doomed at that time because of the failure of the IRA to renounce violence, but he believed they provided a useful backdrop to the Hume-Adams talks which led to the 1994 IRA ceasefire.

Between 1979 and 2001 Farren stood in successive Westminster elections against DUP leader Ian Paisley. Six times he stood and six times he lost. He enjoyed himself nonetheless, particularly at the declaration, when he spoke in Irish – a source of annoyance for the DUP and amusement for the nationalist politician. Despite his losing streak, he steadily increased his share of the vote during those barren years.

While continuing to earn his living as a lecturer, he gradually built a public profile, serving as the SDLP's economic spokesman and taking part in negotiations. He was a member of the New Ireland Forum and later helped negotiate the Good Friday Agreement. During the multi-party talks he was particularly impressed with a meeting the parties had with the former South African president Nelson Mandela, who urged compromise during a seminar in Johannesburg aimed at encouraging negotiations. Mandela reminded the Northern Ireland politicians that he was sharing the room with white South Africans who had been responsible for his incarceration. He was the most impressive politician Farren had ever met. "His charisma was understatement and sincerity," said Farren. "His demeanour was so powerful in its simplicity."

Farren played a key role in the 1996–1998 negotiations to bring about the Good Friday Agreement, but struggled with the tedium of it. It was never a straight path; there were always obstacles to overcome and too often it was a case of one step forward and two steps back. On Good Friday, as he waited for the unionists to decide if they were going to accept the deal, his wife and a friend came to Castle Buildings with red roses, which they pinned to the lapels of the SDLP negotiators. Even as the party emerged triumphant with a deal finally agreed after so many wasted years, Farren was very conscious that half of unionism had not signed up. "The omens weren't terrific, but the referendum gave us great hope," he said philosophically.

In the 1998 Assembly poll he faced not one but two Paisleys, father and son. Finally, he out-polled a Paisley, with Ian Jr finishing 2,000 votes behind him. He was among those who insisted on steady progress on the decommissioning of weapons, describing it as an essential, potent symbol that politically motivated violence was over forever in Northern Ireland.

When he was finally made a minister after so many years of frustrating failure and stalemate, Farren relished every bit of his power, finding devolution both an educational and a liberating experience. In his first weeks in office he was asked by a former neighbour to open a new centre for religious studies in Armagh. "I had a plaque on the wall with my name on it, that was very nice," he said. He also made time, on quite short notice, to travel to Rathlin Island, which lay in his constituency, to launch a new video-conferencing facility that linked the village of Dunloy with the islanders, allowing them to learn Irish. This trip was particularly memorable for the department's press officer, Simon Burrowes, who was not only seasick but had to be put briefly in the boot of the car as there was not enough room to transport him with the others when the delegation got to the island. Not exactly the trappings of office Burrowes had expected, one might say.

Farren's department, the Department of Employment and Learning (DEL), was in the main carved out of the old departments of education and economic development. It was initially called the Department of Further and Higher Education and Training – whose initials (DFHET) became shorthand for "defeat." References to "defeat" began to grate with the minister and the name was changed. Farren settled on the Department of Learning and Employment but when he realised that spelled "dole" changed it to the Department Employment and Learning (DEL). He had responsibility for third-level education, training and employment as well as labour relations. He had a clear set of priorities when he took office, including more student support, more funding for university research, more places for students at university, more assistance for those who had dropped out of education and improving the labour market.

Farren was commended for his efforts in assisting mature students and ensuring that

Further Education colleges received a more equitable deal. In fact, Farren was generally credited with improving the lot of these Further Education colleges, who for years had to make do with second-rate facilities and inadequate funding. In May 2000 he announced a £5.5 million package for colleges, which encouraged greater collaboration between the institutions.

Farren regretted that more was not done to tackle labour relations and the issue of staffing problems for tribunals, but there were other priorities initially. His experience in juggling various issues was one of the reasons Farren was prepared to defend ten departments over six because it enabled ministers to focus time and attention on issues that were often overlooked in larger departments. "I was able to put the spotlight on the further education colleges for example and Michael McGimpsey was able to focus on sport and art."

There was a shortfall in research funding for local universities compared to Great Britain and Farren, conscious of this, introduced a special funding package called the Spur Initiative. It involved a £20 million allocation from the government, to be matched by private funding. While there was criticism that facilities were funded with private finance, new or improved facilities were granted to colleges in Belfast, Tyrone, Derry and Fermanagh, for example. "That is where he made a difference," said Birnie. "He did identify this tendency to treat further education as a Cinderella service and what happened during his time was, there was a substantial increase in funding." Birnie also believed Farren improved morale in the higher education sector: "He impressed people in that he quite literally went around so many places and attended so many functions. That was a contrast to direct rule where you hardly saw the minister."

While in office, Farren announced that the proposed Springvale Education Village had been approved, hailing it as a victory for devolution. The £70 million project, which would straddle the peaceline in West Belfast, had been promoted by the University of Ulster for a number of years and had President Bill Clinton's personal seal of approval. Unfortunately, the project later faltered when the University of Ulster decided to withdraw and Farren's successor in DEL announced a review to the disappointment of the local community.

Farren was a passionate advocate of north-south cooperation and although his department had no cross-border body, some modest steps were taken. In 2000 he attended a two-day jobs fair in New York with the Irish Minister for Health and Children, Micheal Martin. The ministers were trying to attract people back to Ireland, north and south, to help fill jobs: a remarkable turnaround from the years when America was the land of opportunity. He also made contact with Michael Woods, the Irish Minister for Education, and they agreed an agenda to be taken forward that included improving all-island links between the universities and facilitating lecturer exchanges. His department also supported a cross-border initiative to create a digital corridor between Armagh and Monaghan.

In the autumn of 2001, Farren's political path took a new turn. His bid to succeed Seamus Mallon as deputy leader of the SDLP failed (he was beaten easily by Bríd Rodgers), and he was promoted to the finance portfolio, which Durkan vacated when he took the post of Deputy First Minister. So it was that Farren left a department where he was familiar with all aspects of his portfolio and joined a department where he quickly had to learn a new more complex brief. He was replaced in DEL by Carmel Hanna, MLA for South Belfast.

Farren found finance a steep learning curve:

"Mark mastered it, I think, better than I did. I mastered the general concepts, but in terms of detail I wouldn't have had the same grasp. I don't think I spoke as long as Mark did when I presented it at the Executive table."

Some in the Executive found this a blessing. Farren's appointment came at an increasingly difficult time for finance. The Treasury had stepped up pressure on the Executive to increase rates. There were pressing issues over the antiquated state of the water treatment and sewerage infrastructure, which required a staggering £3 billion to bring it up to European standards. The Treasury wanted water charges, but this was a highly contentious political issue and no party particularly wanted to be saddled with blame. Farren saw the logic of having to pay for services and went further than his party would have liked in a speech to the Confederation of British Industry in April 2002. He annoyed his Executive colleagues in Room 21 by delivering his strongest hint yet that rates might rise. He spoke of hard choices and spelled out the unpalatable facts as he saw them: "If people want better public services, they will have to pay for them." The minister pointed to the deficit in infrastructure and said that without changes Northern Ireland would struggle to pay for health and other services, such as sewage facilities. He suggested water charges might be necessary to raise funds. His predecessor had already told the Assembly in 2001 that water charges could raise £300 million in revenue. Durkan had simply noted this, but Farren almost advocated it, causing quite a storm in and outside of Room 21.

The resulting headlines caused panic among some in the administration. Few issues have generated so much public debate in Northern Ireland in recent years as water charges. Farren's comments opened a rift in the Executive, with the Minister for Culture, Arts and Leisure firmly disputing in the media any notion that he would support water charges. At an Executive meeting McGimpsey also scolded Farren for his handling of the issue. Joe Byrne, the SDLP MLA, swiftly clarified that the minister was not reflecting party policy, thus leaving him stranded in a political mire.

Durkan sympathised with Farren's argument that he was reflecting economic realities and that a rating review was imminent, but Durkan was also annoyed at the way it had been handled and Farren was forced to clarify his remarks and issue a statement emphasising that he had no immediate plans for a major hike in the rates. Farren was unrepentant in retrospect, saying: "They were all annoyed. At the table, Michael McGimpsey said something like 'never again'. But there is no point in shirking the issues. Nobody likes paying, but you have to pay for these things."

Although the Executive ministers were not pleased, the Treasury most certainly was. It had made an offer to the department that it would allow more flexibility in its accounting rules on water infrastructure if the charges were implemented. This flexibility would give the finance minister an extra £50 million to play with. Durkan recalled: "The offer was made if we could show we were looking at this, water and rates. The Executive said, 'how do we show this?'" After some discussion the Executive agreed, in a classic "Yes, Minister" tactic that Farren could launch a review of rates, both industrial and domestic, and water charges. The Executive announced a review of rating policy in May 2002 and hoped it would take the heat off the administration if they were seen to be doing something, while actually doing very little. "Then in the summer of 2002," said Durkan, "the Treasury cottoned on to us and what we were trying to do, saying 'yes, we were looking at this' and we were going through the motions and having a public consultation and they knew we didn't have the heart or mind to do water charges."

Treasury minister Paul Boateng sent a sharp letter, stating firmly that the Executive had to make a commitment to take a decision by January 2003 and to make water self-financing by 2006–2007. According to Durkan, Boateng warned that the Executive would lose its flexible accounting concession and its £50 million if it did not comply. The Executive rejected the demand. The Treasury hardened its position further and began to threaten that it might not be so well disposed in the negotiations over the terms of Stormont's new borrowing power as part of the Reform and Reinvestment Initiative (RRI). No agreement had been reached with the Treasury at that point regarding the level the rates would have to reach before the borrowing power could be activated. (In fact, agreement was never reached due to suspension.) According to Durkan, the Executive considered Boateng's letter a second time in either August or September amid dark warnings that the Treasury might set the borrowing threshold high if the Executive did not respond to Boateng's demand. Durkan said his response was: "So be it!"

Post-devolution, Durkan was upset when the Treasury tried to give the impression that RRI was tied to water and rates charges. He claimed nothing of the sort had ever been agreed. He insisted that direct rule finance minister Ian Pearson also started the borrowing much earlier than he would have. It was Pearson, he said, who attached the £2 billion figure to the RRI over six years. The administration never agreed it.

While the Executive was rowing with the Treasury, Farren was in regular contact with DUP minister Peter Robinson at the Department of Regional Development (DRD) about the issue of how to fund the upgrade in water and sewerage infrastructure. After taking office, Robinson was informed of the state of the sewage system and was shocked by what he heard. He was careful of what he said at the time, but in an interview for this book revealed:

> "I went into the department and hardly slept for a week having been told how bad things were. I turned on the radio in the morning waiting to hear the streets [of Belfast] had collapsed under the city centre because the Victorian sewers had collapsed. I think many of us had been aware of the under-investment but what was hidden was the impact. It was literally dreadful and I saw photographs of the state of the sewage pipes in our city centre and that is why we had to push ahead."

Funding had been an issue in previous discussions with Durkan, but had not been resolved; both men offer differing accounts of what took place in their exchanges about water charges. Before devolution in 1999 water charges were notionally part of the regional rates bills paid by householders, which raised £300 million for Executive spending. A specific charge for water was part of this bill and was diverted to the Water Service, but the link was broken during direct rule. Robinson, along with his permanent secretary, Ronnie Spence, met Durkan in July 2000 to discuss the issue. Both Robinson and Durkan said they recognised the fact that without the link the Executive was unable to demonstrate to the Treasury that there was in fact a water charge in place, leading to pressure from central government that water bills be introduced to householders: in effect, the Northern Ireland public continued to pay for water without getting any credit for doing so. Durkan claimed that in the July meeting Robinson had wanted to convert the regional rates bill to a water charge, giving him control of the £300 million. Robinson had calculated that he would use this money to pay for upgrades in the water service and he would avoid costly rate increases through the introduction of efficiency savings and "a developer's contribution". For various reasons Durkan was not prepared to cede control of the regional rate to any other minister, never mind one outside of Room 21. The regional rate, said Durkan, was already being used for a range of services, including health and education. Durkan said when he briefed the other ministers about Robinson's proposal they were incensed: "They were saying, 'He has some cheek'."

Durkan was wary in his dealings with Robinson. Having been burned with the "Durkan tax" label, he had no intention of risking his party's popularity to bail out the DUP minister who would benefit from the investment while presumably attacking the Executive for imposing water charges. Robinson had ruled out privatising water as a means of investment. He had also determined that it was the responsibility of the Department of Environment and the Department of Finance to legislate for water charges and he was waiting for these departments to move. Durkan however wanted Robinson to come up with proposals.

While he disagreed with the way the Executive had approached the issue, Robinson might have been gratified by Farren's Confederation of British Industry speech because it tied the Executive into the charges issue, not him. Robinson had raised a number of concerns about the review paper, including its failure to take into account efficiency savings in the Water Service. Durkan said he told his finance minister: "Look, be careful, because if Robinson has plans on water, let him come forward with these issues. You shouldn't be walking the plank for him and nor should the Executive ... Where are his plans?"

Durkan had made the point at the Executive table, following Boateng's demands, that the ministers were not in a position to know if they could make water self-financing as the issue was Robinson's remit and he was not at the Executive table to explain how efficient or inefficient the Water Service was:

> "We weren't in control of the water service and that was a very basic reason why we didn't sign up to what the Treasury wanted. That was part of my challenge to Sean, that there were a number of games going on, with officials in DRD talking to officials in DFP, and he was going to find himself as the person who got knocked down in the middle of that junction."

Farren and Robinson never got a chance to resolve the matter because suspension intervened and direct rule ministers took control of plans to impose water charges.

Assessing Farren's performance in finance, the committee chairman, Sinn Féin's Francie Molloy, criticised his approach, accusing the minister of not doing enough to achieve a peace dividend from the Treasury. The SDLP said its demands for assistance were ignored and delivering the RRI was a feat in itself. Relations between Farren and Molloy were rather prickly. The Sinn Féin chairman sought a meeting with the minister about a remark he had made during a committee session when Molloy had challenged Farren about the possibility of water charges and demanded to know what happened to the money ring-fenced for water and sewage under direct rule. Farren was unable to hide his disdain for Sinn Féin and its brand of republicanism:

> "I very quickly retorted that if we hadn't been blowing ourselves up and killing each other and having to pay a lot of money in compensation to business people for destroyed businesses, maybe we would have had more money to put into public services. We do have to pay for our own misdeeds sometimes. He took that as a criticism of him and of course all the unionists around the table were smirking."

The pair did have a meeting the following morning, but Farren refused to apologise for his comment.

For his part, Molloy was not impressed with Farren's approach compared to that of his predecessor, whom he found much more willing to explain policies. "The pleasant approach that Mark Durkan had adopted very quickly went out the window," said Molloy, "and you had a very arrogant person who thought he was the only one who knew anything about finance and the rest of us were there for him to throw figures at."

In one of his last ministerial acts Farren did manage to outline a draft budget in the final week of the administration. Notably, it was the first time the Executive had agreed three-year spending plans. He described it as radical. There were 3% rises in spending and the minister asked the departments to consider a 1% reduction in running costs. The lion's share of the budget went to Health. Suspension stopped the clock before the budget won final approval.

In the Assembly's last session, on 14 October 2002, Farren announced a £144 million boost to public spending through the Executive Programme Funds. The money was aimed at improving health, education and transport, including a further £5 million for the purchase of new buses. At this session, Farren was the last of all the ministers to give an account of himself at question time, a part of the brief he particularly enjoyed. He told the Assembly he hoped that it would not be too long before devolution was back.

Chapter 27
The Brawl in the Hall

At first, the angry insults were barely audible in the Great Hall of Parliament Buildings, crowded as it was with reporters and politicians. But as David Trimble and Mark Durkan conducted their first official press conference after being elected First and Deputy First Ministers, there was no mistaking the words "Cheat!" and "Traitor!"

Trimble, looking flushed, had just left the debating chamber with Durkan beside him. As the First Minister spoke to the media about stable government, DUP members moved in on the two ministers and their circle of supporters, who included Ulster Unionist, SDLP and Sinn Féin Assembly members. The pro-Agreement forces stood their ground. A few feet away Ian Paisley, his right hand tucked into his double-breasted, navy, pinstriped jacket, was uncharacteristically silent while his son, Ian Jr, in a suit of the same cloth, heckled Trimble: "You're not credible by your own words!" DUP MLA Paul Berry, following Junior's lead, shouted, "Go and join your Provo friends!"

Trimble and Durkan did their best to ignore the catcalls, until Joan Carson, an Ulster Unionist matron representing Fermanagh–South Tyrone, let out a rather loud yelp and pitched forwards. Someone had pushed her from behind and the domino effect plunged the SDLP's Alasdair McDonnell and Sinn Féin's Mitchel McLaughlin into the DUP chorus section. McDonnell, a strapping Glens man, might have crushed Ian Jr had the DUP man not put his hands up to shield himself from the force. Scuffles ensued, with a number of rival Assembly members hanging onto each other as if playing a rather rough game of tug-o'-war, without the rope.

As tempers flared, the DUP moved forward calling out, "IRA scumbags". With those words, Sinn Féin's Alex Maskey was drawn into the fray. His party press officer, Ned Cohen, sensing trouble, stepped in with arms outstretched to prevent any serious clashes, aided by colleague McLaughlin, who had recovered his balance. McDonnell, still reeling from being shoved, looked around to see who was responsible, but his cool-headed colleagues trailed him away before he could discover who had kicked and pushed him. All the while Paisley Jr shouted with glee about the peace-loving party: "The SDLP is fighting!" Amid the turmoil, SDLP advisor Conail McDevitt had a sharp exchange with the DUP member for Lagan valley, Edwin Poots, and Paisley Jr shouted louder: "The SDLP is fighting!" Side by side in the Great Hall, the irresistible forces that craved change and the immovable ones that did not clashed.

"Gentlemen, please," Stormont's security men shouted as they moved in alongside a policeman, who sported a poppy in his cap and looked woefully outnumbered. More than a score of door-keepers were involved in calming the incident, which became known as the "brawl in the hall", although a perhaps more apt description came from the Sinn Féin member for Mid-Ulster, John Kelly, who dismissed the episode as a case of "hold me back, let me at him". Lord Alderdice later recalled that he had feared just such an interruption given the strength of feeling in the chamber and had worked hard to prevent scenes similar to those that typified previous administrations: "We managed to do that and then the doors opened. It was almost like a valve opened with people shooting out."

The trouble was defused when Trimble and Durkan headed off for a tea break, leaving the DUP at the microphones. The refreshments started with a photo-call as the two ministers settled into leather chairs. Trimble seemed a little shaken as he took his cup and saucer, his face still beetroot red. As he settled back in his armchair, crunching a chocolate biscuit, the photographer asked him to lean forward as he looked a little too comfortable. Trimble made a face as if to appear astonished by the suggestion after his ordeal in the Great Hall and Durkan joked: "We are meant to look comfortable after *that*?" The photographer took his shot and, temporarily blinded by the flashbulb, the First Minister leaned over to Durkan and jested that the first thing he would do when he got justice powers would be to alter the definition of assault to include the discharge of camera flashes within three metres of a person without their permission.

As the ministers got down to business with Gerry Loughran, head of the civil service, just yards away the DUP members were busily complaining about the "First and Deputy First Cheats". The DUP was deeply upset at losing an Assembly battle to block Trimble from returning as First Minister, this time alongside Durkan. When the happy couple emerged victorious from the chamber just before noon on 6 November 2001, it was too much for the anti-Agreement forces to bear, particularly as it came so soon after a sweet victory for them. For some weeks devolution had been disintegrating, with only nationalist ministers prepared to continue power-sharing. But an act of IRA decommissioning, finally carried out on 23 October 2001 had halted the collapse at the eleventh hour and convinced David Trimble and his Ulster Unionists to try again. Despite fierce opposition from internal party critics power-sharing had returned, but it was a far from straightforward process because Trimble had lost his Assembly majority and the rules, known as "parallel consent", stated that a majority of unionists as well as a majority of nationalists had to vote for the First and Deputy First Ministers. There was also the pressing matter of the looming deadline following the second tactical twenty-four-hour suspension in September. In a race against the clock to ensure the First and Deputy First Ministers were elected before the deadline, the Assembly Speaker had moved with haste and agreed to convene the Assembly on Friday, 2 November. The deadline expired at midnight the following evening.

Trimble was soon forced to accept that the possibility of obtaining a majority vote was slim. PUP MLAs David Ervine and Billy Hutchinson had warned him not to take for granted their support, while two Ulster Unionist members, Peter Weir and Pauline Armitage, were refusing to indicate how they would vote. Consequently, at the last minute Trimble decided to accept the Women's Coalition offer he had previously declined: that its two members would redesignate from "other" and one would become unionist in order to vote for him. This step was derided by anti-Agreement unionists as "political cross-dressing", but Jane Morrice, MLA for North Down, insisted that the motion was consistent with the diverse nature of the cross-community coalition and with the rules.

At the Assembly gathering a motion was passed to change the standing orders and allow the coalition to change their voting category. Accordingly, Jane Morrice redesignated from "other" to unionist, while Monica McWilliams switched to nationalist. Sir Reg Empey, as Acting First Minister, then proposed David Trimble and Mark Durkan for the two top posts, seconded by Seamus Mallon. The vote proceeded, but ended in humiliation for the pro-Agreement side. Trimble failed to get the majority he needed when Weir and Armitage, as feared, both voted against him. Support for the joint election on the nationalist side was 100%, but mustered just 49.2% on the unionist side. The Women's Coalition switch had bought him only one vote and Trimble was still one short.

The Speaker pledged to consult members about the next step as a triumphant "No" camp left the chamber that Friday afternoon. During the twenty-four hours that followed, pressure came on both the SDLP and Alliance leaders to find a resolution so that another motion could be tabled with the Speaker's Office, allowing for another vote. The NIO decided that if they got the motion to MLAs before the Saturday night deadline, with notice of a sitting on Monday, they could proceed.

Secretary of State John Reid, a Glaswegian with a reputation as a political heavyweight, initially turned his steely eye to the Alliance leader whose party had five pro-Agreement votes in the Assembly. Reid wanted David Ford to allow a few of his MLAs to emulate the example of the Women's Coalition and redesignate as unionists. It is thought Alliance was approached about this earlier as it was fairly clear to many observers that the vote was bound to fail; but the request was refused. Afterwards when he was again asked to redesignate, Ford suggested another route: instead of his party having to bend, why not change the rules? Ford had long regarded the "parallel consent" rule as discriminatory and argued that it did not give the same weight to the votes of "others" as it did to those designated unionist or nationalist.

The SDLP leader was hearing talk of a deal being struck between Reid and Ford, whereby the government would legislate on new rules and in turn Ford would be willing to redesignate temporarily. Trimble recalled that Reid was only promising to consult on a rule change, but Durkan was aghast at any such change and let Reid's office know that his party would not return to power-sharing on the basis of "unilateral" moves by the British to change the rules designed to protect the nationalist minority. His suspicions about a firm private deal having been worked out by Ford and Reid receded somewhat when he spoke to sources in the Alliance party, but he remained concerned about a side-deal.

The gap between the Alliance and the SDLP was underscored in a multi-party meeting at Castle Buildings the afternoon of the failed vote. Ford suggested the SDLP should redesignate from nationalist to unionist. But the SDLP leader took the view that, unlike his party, Alliance was pro-Union. That same Friday evening the Alliance party met at its headquarters. This was a difficult meeting for Ford because he faced opposition to redesignation from elements within his party. In a telephone conversation, Durkan told Reid that he should implement another brief tactical suspension if he had to, until the matter was resolved. Reid refused, saying he could not do this. Durkan claimed the reason given to him that night was that "the IRA campaign would resume". Durkan understood from this that IRA decommissioning had been secured with a promise from the British not to suspend the institutions again. Trimble, however, claimed Reid had ruled out a third tactical suspension because the NIO feared a judicial review from the DUP, challenging the decision.

Durkan's legal advice was that a tactical suspension would have been more constitutionally sound than Reid's plan of action. The Secretary of State was insisting that the election of a First and Deputy First Minister could take place outside the six-week deadline – provided it was clear to him before time ran out that an election was possible and imminent. The SDLP leader said he had an angry exchange with the Secretary of State after allegedly being told he had to give in, or the IRA would go back to war. Durkan claimed Reid told him to "live in the real world". According to Durkan, he retorted that he saw nothing real about side-deals and half-deals with the republican movement and what mattered was the Agreement, only to be told by Reid he would then call an election. "So be it," Durkan recalled telling the Secretary of State.

Reid refused to be interviewed for this book in order to confirm or deny the version of events recounted by Durkan.

A compromise was worked out the day after the failed vote, on Saturday, 3 November. Durkan spent the day holding out against rule changes, meeting his party at Parliament Buildings, where Alliance members had also gathered. Durkan learned that Ford wanted a motion signed by himself and Trimble that largely guaranteed that the rules would be reviewed and altered in exchange for temporary designation. "Again, I refused," Durkan recalled. "Reid tried again, talking to me, trying to sound calmer, more rational and then again chiding me about being so precious."

Trimble, who was at Gleneagles in Scotland for a conference on policing, telephoned Durkan that Saturday, urging him to go along with the motion. The Ulster Unionist, according to the SDLP leader, was in bullish form – in between conference sessions he was shooting clay pigeons, telling those who complimented his extremely accurate shot that he was imagining his targets were Jeffrey Donaldson and other internal party critics. Durkan was not in the mood for humour, however. His mood turned even blacker when he learned that afternoon that the Speaker's Office had in its possession a motion purporting to come from Trimble and Durkan, pledging rule changes. "I dug my heels in all the more," he said.

The most Durkan was willing to concede was a bland motion promising a review of the rules, without prejudice to the party's position and signed by the SDLP and Ulster Unionist chief whips. He had learned that the NIO was panicking about time running out and had couriers standing by, ready to whisk a motion, set for Monday, on an election of a First and Deputy First Minister to Assembly members before the midnight deadline. While Durkan was willing to agree to a review with no predetermined outcome, he decided not tell the NIO early in the day for fear the government would use the afternoon to squeeze him for firmer guarantees about rule changes. He gave nothing away, not even when Sinn Féin's Martin McGuinness came to see him, no doubt to ascertain his bottom-line. Around tea-time Jonathan Powell, the Prime Minister's chief-of-staff, telephoned him to plead his case, followed swiftly by the Prime Minister. It was then Durkan made his concession, accepting a bland motion in the name of the UUP and SDLP whips that called for a review of rules in exchange for the Alliance party redesignating for one week only. According to Durkan, a confused and relieved Blair asked him, "If you are willing to do that, then what is the problem?"

The motion, with notice of an Assembly meeting, was immediately dispatched by courier. Faced with the Assembly's collapse, Ford agreed to redesignate but in a BBC interview employed an unfortunate phrase about becoming "the back end of a pantomime horse". When the Assembly was reconvened on the Monday, just outside the six-week time limit, DUP lawyers were in court arguing for a judicial review on the grounds of abuse of procedure. The DUP contended that the Secretary of State must dissolve the Assembly and call a fresh election, as outlined in legislation because the deadline had passed. Reid's lawyers disputed this. As the arguments were being made in the High Court, there was some light relief at Stormont when the Speaker ruled on a complaint from the anti-Agreement Northern Ireland unionist Cedric Wilson that the PUP member Billy Hutchinson had used unparliamentary language when he had called him an "eejit" at the last session. In making his judgment, Lord Alderdice light-heartedly recalled a previous ruling made by Sir James Kilfedder, the Speaker of the ill-fated 1982 unionist-dominated Assembly, when a member complained that another was "acting the eejit." Sir James had replied caustically, "He's not acting."

There was more jocularity during the ensuing debate about rule changes when the UK Unionist Robert McCartney, who had heard the Alliance leader's BBC interview, took a swipe at him, saying of the Assembly: "I never thought the time would come when its future would depend upon the decision of a self-confessed horse's ass." McCartney's objections to the Alliance tactic, echoed by other anti-Agreement unionists, failed and Alliance members David Ford, Eileen Bell and Sean Neeson redesignated for voting purposes. Anti-Agreement unionists then found another blocking device under the rules and delayed the vote for a First and Deputy First Minister for a full twenty-four hours. Consequently, it was not until the following day, Tuesday, 6 November 2001, that David Trimble and Mark Durkan were finally elected, this time with 100% support from nationalists and 51.7% from unionists, thanks to the redesignations. The DUP's court challenge also failed, clearing the way for the new administration.

So it was that on 14 November 2001 David Trimble returned to Room 21 after an absence of about five months due to the row over decommissioning. He had already settled in his chair when Sinn Féin's Martin McGuinness burst through the door and took a seat a few feet away. The cameras were there to record the moment. This time, McGuinness took the correct place beside his nameplate, shaking Gerry Loughran's hand as he settled into his seat. Before McGuinness even thought of stretching out a hand to the First Minister, Trimble good-naturedly scolded: "No stunts for the cameras." The ministers and officials giggled like schoolchildren back for another term and when McGuinness said it was good to see the First Minister back after his absence, Trimble was relaxed enough to joke: "My bid for freedom failed."

Trimble was delighted and relieved to be back in office, having outwitted opposition unionists yet again, and achieving what anti-Agreement unionists said was impossible: an IRA act of decommissioning witnessed by an international observer. The First Minister was also relieved that Mallon was not sitting beside him this time, believing relations would improve with Durkan as Deputy First Minister. But then again, Trimble had once been glad to hear Mallon was taking the job over Hume, only to admit: "I subsequently changed my mind."

Chapter 28
"Government by Correspondence"

While the anti-Agreement forces had lost yet another battle in their bid for supremacy in Northern Ireland politics, the pro-Agreement forces still had good reason to fear them. The DUP had returned to ministerial office, but was seeking another opportunity to strike.

Despite an act of decommissioning by the IRA, the DUP's hopes of future triumph remained high following the June 2001 Westminster poll, a turning-point in the fight for the soul of unionism. The election – which had seen the DUP win an unprecedented five Westminster seats, three of them at the expense of the Ulster Unionist party – had vindicated the DUP's approach: taking up their ministerial posts with all the advantages that brought, but staying out of Room 21 while accusing Trimble of treachery. The DUP had a right to two places in the Executive and seized them, but vowed never to have direct dealings with Sinn Féin ministers. They called it "government in opposition". Sir Reg Empey scoffed at this notion: "At no time did the DUP sensibly challenge government authority except on paper. The Executive functioned in spite of them." Part of the DUP tactic was to challenge the Executive while delivering professional and effective service within their departments. Talk of wrecking was, in the main, replaced with more temperate language, which was seen to be more in line with the popular mood shortly after devolution. Apart from verbally attacking the Agreement and Trimble's Ulster Unionists, the DUP ministers seemed determined to steer clear of controversy over the handling of their portfolios.

The SDLP's Mark Durkan coined his own term for this tactic: "government by correspondence". He said: "The DUP engaged in a correspondence course with the Executive. They would send their papers for approval and receive the papers of other ministers." Dodds was dismissive of Durkan's description, saying all governments operate through correspondence, but Durkan countered with an anecdote to illustrate his point. On taking office as Finance minister he had despatched letters to all the ministers, inviting their views on issues of common concern. He lightheartedly told an official that the new DUP ministers, Peter Robinson and Nigel Dodds, would be the first to respond. "Peter and Nigel replied almost by return post," Durkan remarked with satisfaction. The SDLP would call this enthusiasm; the DUP, efficiency.

Empey considered Durkan's description an apt one, as Executive minutes and other papers were despatched to the DUP for information purposes or commentary. "They did not come in through the door, but they stuffed notes under the door," said Empey, speaking metaphorically. "For their department to work, they had to get permission from the Executive for the budget. They met the Finance minister. The media let them off the hook." In terms of relations with the Executive, Robinson said ministers had no need to pay homage to the centre as they were chiefs in their own fiefdoms, unaccountable to the First and Deputy First Ministers who could neither summon them nor sack them for non-cooperation. "I had complete control of my department," said Robinson, "I didn't need to correspond." He did, however, find it useful, as did Dodds. In effect, the DUP and the Executive ministers were co-dependent. The DUP departments needed money, their departments overlapped with others and everyone in Northern Ireland required the services offered by the DUP-controlled departments, such as roads or housing. The DUP ministers went to Durkan, not to the Executive as a whole, for funding and this concerned him as he was the one minister they would meet regularly: "I was determined not to be treated as some kind of hole in the wall for cash withdrawals from the Executive. Any discussions I would have with the Executive I would have related to the DUP ministers, but there were no proxy negotiations."

The DUP were mocked by the pro-Agreement parties for having one foot inside and one foot outside the administration – "hokey-cokey politics" as Gerry Adams called it. They were ridiculed not just for taking ministerial posts but for sitting on committees with Sinn Féin members, some of whom were former IRA prisoners. Paisley himself chaired the Agriculture committee, sitting with Sinn Féin's Gerry McHugh, Francie Molloy and Pat Doherty. Reputedly a senior figure on the IRA Army Council in his time, Doherty had one thing in common with Paisley: they were both known in some circles as "Papa Doc". During his time on the agriculture committee, Molloy recalled Ian Paisley Jr dragging his father away when the republican, in front of cameras, attempted to confirm dates with Paisley senior for a committee meeting. Molloy thought Paisley had a surface charm and was a fair and effective committee chairman. The republican recalled a lighter moment when a committee discussion turned to the decommissioning of fishing vessels: "The minister and the civil servants were saying that decommissioning didn't mean destruction and I said, 'That's what we have been for saying for years'."

Sinn Féin's Pat Doherty chaired the Enterprise committee and, speaking in the Assembly, had this to say about the behaviour of certain DUP members on his committee: "They take part in the debates, involve themselves in the dialogue and speak through the chairperson, who happens to be a member of Sinn Féin. Mr [Gregory] Campbell tries not to get into the debate, but when he has to, he does so regularly." Robinson and Dodds served for a time on the Finance committee, which was chaired by Sinn Féin's Francie Molloy, who praised their contribution and their intelligence. He recalled they would be very conscious of not being seen to be friendly and would always pull back: "I found [Robinson] a very good person to have on the committee. He was pragmatic. There was no messing. I think Dodds found it more difficult not to engage with people. He's naturally social."

Paisley defended the DUP's position of sharing committees with Sinn Féin by insisting his party did not speak to, or acknowledge "Sinn Féin/IRA". Paisley said his solution for dealing with Sinn Féin members was to point at the republican committee members with a pen. Willie McCrea, chairman of the Environment committee, got round the problem by operating through the clerk, or simply letting each member speak in turn without actually calling on anybody. Sinn Féin's Francie Molloy, who served briefly on McCrea's committee, was impressed with the way he accepted ideas across the committee if they were sound. "McCrea wasn't as bad as he was painted," he insisted.

In the shadow period, Peter Robinson sat on the multi-party Stormont Commission alongside Molloy. It was chaired by Lord Alderdice and was responsible for looking after the estate. Lord Alderdice took the commission to London to observe Parliamentary procedure and he hosted a dinner at the House of Lords during the shadow period. "We all stayed in the same hotel," Molloy recalled. "We travelled in taxis together and we dined around the table together. There was no sort of problem in that situation at all." When asked about the Stormont Commission's visit to London, Robinson said there was no engagement with Sinn Féin. Speaking in the spring of 2005, he said: "I have never to this moment in time had one word of conversation with any Sinn Féin member … I do my business and give them a wide berth. Just recently at Oxford University Martin McGuinness and I were both speaking and he spent at least half of his speech complaining that I wouldn't speak to him and I had to spend half my speech explaining why."

Despite condemnation from the pro-Agreement parties, who complained of contradictions in their position, the DUP was undeterred, grasping the devolution balloon and floating it to new heights, all the while keeping up the pressure. David Trimble branded the DUP hypocrites: "The DUP have no problem exercising Executive authority along with Sinn Féin. They want the system to work, but they also want to snipe at the UUP."

While the pro-Agreement parties were unimpressed with the DUP's antics, there was no lack of respect for the abilities of Robinson and Dodds, two of Paisley's key lieutenants. Robinson, the pragmatic deputy to the dogmatic Paisley, was noted for his sharp mind, sharp suits and sharp personality. He had a deep loathing for the republican movement and would sometimes recount a personal story about his old school pal, Harry Beggs, who was killed by an IRA bomb in 1971 as he was leaving his workplace after a woefully inadequate warning. "That was my introduction to terrorism," Robinson would say. "I got involved in active politics because of Harry Beggs."

Nationalists and republicans despised Robinson almost as much as they despised Paisley. Some nationalists regarded him as a sinister figure following his brief association with the Ulster Resistance, an organisation dating to the early days of the intense campaign against the Anglo-Irish Agreement. Robinson was at Paisley's side at the launch of Ulster Resistance in the Ulster Hall. The group was noted for the red berets worn by its militant members. The party formally ended its links with the organisation in 1987. The previous year Robinson was involved in an invasion of Clontibret, County Monaghan. A policeman was injured in the incursion by loyalists, some of whom were armed with cudgels and iron bars. Robinson said he was simply trying to highlight the gaping hole in border security. Whatever his reasons, he was arrested by the Gardaí and his fine was paid anonymously to secure his release from prison.

In those days Robinson's nut-brown hair was carefully parted to the side and he always seemed to be frowning behind his steel-framed spectacles. With the advent of the 1990s came a new image: spiky hair, bespoke suits and trendy glasses. When the BBC's "Hearts and Minds" programme profiled him, a talking point was his collection of 200 shirts and around 400 ties. An Ulster Unionist who watched the programme was aghast: "Anyone who has 200 shirts neatly laid out in his chest of drawers has to have, dare I say, some sort of obsession about order." Robinson's hobby was Japanese Koi Carp, an exotic fish that he bred in his pond. Most of his passion was poured into politics, however.

Robinson was generally regarded as prickly, cold, and dour. His supporters said he was actually quite shy. His humour was heavy with biting sarcasm, rather than witty repartee. His strengths were his ruthless dedication, his industriousness and his organisational skills. He was credited with transforming the DUP into a modern, slick, professional political machine. As time went on, Robinson was increasingly seen as the politician who might be able to deliver a stable agreement between unionism and nationalism. But his critics dismissed this.

Although Robinson is a powerful figure in the DUP, Paisley, ever the charismatic leader despite his age, remained firmly in charge. Along with Dodds, Robinson was at the forefront of multi-party negotiations in 1996–7 until the DUP pulled out over Sinn Féin's inclusion, leaving Trimble's Ulster Unionist party to negotiate the Good Friday Agreement. Robinson helped spearhead the party's campaign against the Good Friday Agreement and the promise of devolution, despite his growing irritation with direct rule – an exasperation he did not attempt to hide. "Always having to beg or argue for even the smallest of changes. It was frustrating," he said.

Robinson's wife, Iris, whom he married in 1970, shared his political outlook. Both were councillors in the DUP-dominated Castlereagh Council, a Robinson fiefdom where the local sports centre was named in his honour. As Paisley's lieutenant, Robinson won his own power-base in 1979 when, in a surprise victory, he ousted Vanguard leader William Craig. He beat his wife to Westminster by some twenty-two years. She was one of the new DUP MPs elected in 2001, after seeing off an Ulster Unionist representative. The Robinsons no doubt took some satisfaction from defeating the Ulster Unionist party, who were traditionally viewed as the "Big House, fur coat" establishment unionists.

Nigel Dodds was also victorious in the 2001 Westminster poll. He took North Belfast from the Ulster Unionists, bolstering his own position within the DUP. Dodds and Robinson were close friends for years, sharing a common desire for devolution and a loathing of Sinn Féin and the IRA. Dodds' hostility deepened when the IRA tried to kill his police bodyguards as he and his wife, Diane, visited their ailing son, Andrew, at the Royal Belfast Hospital for Sick Children in December 1996. Dodds' police bodyguards challenged the two gunmen and one officer was shot in the foot in the ensuing scuffle. Andrew, whose ailments included spina bifida, was one of three children the couple had, along with Mark and Robyn. Andrew died at the age of eight and the family was devastated by the loss of a boy so full of life. They found comfort in their Christian faith; Dodds was a member of Paisley's Free Presbyterian Church.

Dodds, who was originally from Londonderry but had moved to Fermanagh as a young boy, shared Robinson's working-class roots, industriousness and talent for party politics, but boasted a more formidable education, having attended Portora School in Enniskillen and Cambridge University, where he earned a double first in law before training as a barrister at Queen's University, Belfast.

Dodds joined the DUP amid the turmoil surrounding the 1981 IRA hunger strike, attracted by the party's "robust" stance and its work on bread-and-butter issues. He had served as a barrister only eighteen months before quitting to work full-time with the DUP, thinking he could return to the law in future. He never did. Dodds stuck with politics out of conviction and was much respected by the DUP leader. Paisley made sure the talented and loyal veteran councillor, who had been his aide in Europe for years, was not overlooked when the Executive ministers were nominated.

In Robinson's analysis the Executive gave the DUP power, profile and position:

> "I don't recommend this form of government, but I made use of it. I was able to do what no collective responsible government would allow to happen, namely to use the megaphone. For the first time you had a minister publicly stating how badly off his department was, the state of our water or sewage system, the state of our roads. If we wanted funding, we literally wound it up. To some extent we became the crying child they had to lift."

While Ulster Unionists complained that the DUP's "crying child" routine was providing them with a bigger slice of the Budget when they ought instead to be punished for their non-cooperation, the Finance minister insisted the DUP's whines were not an issue for him. He said Robinson got money for roads because that was a priority. But Francie Molloy, speaking as Finance committee chairman, shared the view that the DUP did better by putting a list of demands while refusing to come to the table.

The DUP had their own problems with anti-Agreement unionists and had to manage party policies carefully. The starkest example of dissent came on 4 February 2000 when the Agriculture committee, led by Ian Paisley, made a visit to the County Down village of Portavogie to investigate problems in the fishing industry and meet with local representatives. The delegation was met by an angry protest in the loyalist village. At first the hostility was directed at the Sinn Féin members as the committee's minibus rolled past. "Go on, ye bastards!" the protestors shouted, throwing eggs. There were scuffles and two protestors were arrested. The DUP's Gardiner Kane was among the members who were on the mini-bus, but the committee chairman and his son, Ian Jr, had travelled separately in a police vehicle. Inside the meeting, the DUP and Sinn Féin sat around the same table, answering questions and talking to local representatives. Outside, the protestors became increasingly agitated. Sinn Féin's Francie Molloy said the police advised him to remain inside, but to his surprise it was the DUP that was the target this time. As DUP members emerged they were challenged over their presence in the village with Sinn Féin.

Ian Jr argued with two women and for once a Paisley was out-shouted. "I was doing my job," Ian Jr protested. "If they [Sinn Féin] want to follow in our wake, that is up to them." A woman holding a child jabbed her finger into the DUP man's face and shouted: "You sit on the television and youse wouldn't be with them [there]. Youse wouldn't be in their company!" "So I should run away?" Paisley Jr wanted to know. Another woman jumped in: "I think you should have walked away! We are your voters!" He again retorted: "Yes, and I'm here to try to keep your husbands in jobs and try to get work!"

It was perhaps not surprising the Portavogie people reacted the way they did. Only a few weeks earlier the DUP had condemned the terms under which the Ulster Unionists had agreed to share power with Sinn Féin following the Mitchell review. "No amount of spin or hype can make a devastatingly immoral or corrupt capitulation into a good deal for unionists," said Robinson. Paisley was quoted in the media as having threatened to wreck the Executive, although Robinson, not for the first time, blamed media spin, insisting that the party was not out to wreck the Assembly. What seemed clear was that Paisley had not anticipated a backlash in Portavogie. Molloy observed: "He was shook up. The denials of his son … and his explanation weren't being accepted at all. For the first time, people had [seen] through the issue that Paisley and the DUP weren't working alongside Sinn Féin."

The DUP tried to play down the episode, but some of their Assembly opponents whispered that it had caused friction in the party and had led to questions about the strategy of having ministers half-in and half-out of the Executive. The DUP denied this was ever the case. Robinson said the leader was supportive of the decision to retain ministerial places adding: "There were people in the party, but maybe more outside the party, who were angry at the decision and I think we took the right decision."

The party adopted a new tactic a few months later when the institutions, having been suspended, were restored in spring 2000. When asked why the tactic had changed, Robinson said there was a suggestion from "some people" that the DUP should withdraw their ministers, but he felt, along with others in the party, that the tactic of "ministers in opposition" remained the best strategy, once they continued to make a clear point about their objection to Sinn Féin in government. Robinson went on:

> "We consulted massively throughout the party and we had the most in-depth consultation and it went down to the single member and every element of our organisation was discussing it and they felt we should hang in but make the point in some other way. And we came up with the notion of rotating revolving ministers."

He insisted Portavogie had no bearing on this decision: "Ian Paisley, by the time he was two miles down the road, it had washed off him and he had forgotten all about it." Robinson suggested another event had more bearing, but he could not recall what it was. Possibly it was the May 28 murder of Edd McCoy, which security forces attributed to the Provisional IRA. He also said the leader was not among those who had demanded the party pull out altogether. Dodds said he agreed with staying in, but advocated the new tactic of rotation to demonstrate the DUP approach was not the same as that of the other parties.

The DUP unveiled its plan of opposition after a meeting of its party Executive in East Belfast on 31 May 2000 as the pro-Agreement parties were plotting the restoration of devolution. The party dismissed the IRA's agreement to allow international inspectors into its arms dumps as a stunt, and claimed restoration did not have the consent of the unionist people. Consequently, they would protest through a system of rotating ministers. Robinson and Dodds would be replaced in office if a DUP motion to have Sinn Féin excluded failed to be passed. Potentially, this in itself could have proved quite disruptive, but the DUP were not specific about how often the rotations would take place. Paisley seemed to be relishing the power of deciding the rotation. In a bizarre metaphor for a fundamentalist Protestant who had attacked the Vatican vociferously most of his life, he declared: "I'm the boss of this game … I am the Pope in this matter. I make the cardinals."

The DUP further escalated tensions with the Executive by declaring its ministers would be whistle-blowers who would uncover and reveal what was going on at the heart of government. The pro-Agreement ministers were angered by this. The First and Deputy First Ministers had been particularly anxious to do something about the DUP but could not determine between them what the best tactic would be: drawing the DUP into the system further, or pushing them out? In December 1999 they had toyed with an "all or nothing approach", but Trimble did not feel it was right to shut out the DUP for non-cooperation while Sinn Féin remained inside, without IRA decommissioning. The Ulster Unionists and the SDLP could have excluded the DUP and warned Sinn Féin that they would be next if, after a reasonable period, there was no decommissioning, but that option was not taken up. The pro-Agreement ministers concluded that punishing DUP departments would be counterproductive. Refusing their departments' funds would only punish ordinary people across Northern Ireland, a tactic the DUP would surely have exploited. Consequently, the Executive had to live with the DUP taking money, and often the credit, for initiatives supported by the Executive.

In the early stages of devolution Trimble and Mallon had settled for a measured response, excluding the DUP from BIC meetings because they would not attend NSMC discussions. In retrospect, Trimble felt it would have been better to allow them to go the BIC, thereby absorbing the DUP further into the system. At the time, however, the First and Deputy First Ministers felt they had no choice but to react when the DUP upped the ante in June 2000, after the Executive was restored. "Not to respond," said Trimble, "would be to put at risk the integrity of the institutions." Accordingly, the First and Deputy First ministers, backed by the other ministers, announced that Executive papers would be withheld from the DUP until they received answers from the party regarding comments that its ministers would not be bound by the ministerial code. Trimble subsequently clarified that the DUP would not get the Executive papers as a matter of course, but would only receive those papers the Executive deemed necessary for them to carry out their functions. They would not, for example, receive papers relating to other departments.

The DUP ministers were summoned to a meeting with Trimble and Mallon, but refused to attend, instructing their officials not to provide any information to OFM/DFM without prior approval. Robinson then accused Trimble and Mallon of behaving like schoolchildren with "high-handed, panic-stricken behaviour". While condemning Trimble and Mallon for "petty" behaviour, the DUP taunted the Executive: "Throw us out!" The DUP ministers' lawyers had informed them that officials in their departments could be instructed by no one other than them. Civil servants were put in an awkward position and some felt torn between loyalty to their department and to the administration as a whole. It was handled sensibly, but one official in the Department of Regional Development recalled some of his counterparts in other areas of government being careful not to tell him things lest the DUP take advantage of the information. He resented being treated as if he was in another camp.

Robinson had some sympathy for those civil servants caught in the middle. The head of the civil service, Gerry Loughran, was getting instructions from OFM/DFM while at the same time being responsible for the civil servants who had to work through the internal friction. A senior civil servant recalled Mallon being particularly resentful at the way the DUP worked the system, believing it was playing with peace for party political advantage. The source recalled briefing the Deputy First Minister about a letter being sent to Robinson and laughed at the memory of Mallon spitting out the words: "Oh, it's 'Dear Peter', is it?"

The DUP went to court to demand their right to Executive papers, all the while protesting that no one could accuse them of leaking confidential information. This was odd given the DUP's threat to expose the Executive. Had the DUP spoken out of turn at a news conference and not meant to provoke the battle? Or, having deliberately provoked the battle in order to undermine Trimble, were their protestations for legal reasons? A DUP source suggested the latter was the case: "Taking on the DUP, taking us to court, whilst not lifting a finger against Sinn Féin, [that] would have backfired on Trimble."

The DUP initially lost its High Court bid, but this decision was overturned on appeal in March 2002 during the Trimble–Durkan era. In a defiant letter to the DUP ministers, the First and Deputy First Minister said they would continue to protect the integrity of the institutions and DUP ministers would not receive Executive papers as of right.

While the DUP won in the courts, its July 2000 motion to exclude Sinn Féin from the Executive was defeated in the Assembly when it failed to win backing from both a majority of unionists and a majority of nationalists. No one was surprised by this outcome. "A political stunt," Trimble had called it. Even the DUP knew the motion was doomed from the start, but it was a clever piece of theatre aimed at embarrassing Trimble. Most of the pro-Agreement Assembly members stayed away, leaving rows of empty benches. The cameras remained to capture the DUP drama, which was made possible because Ulster Unionists Peter Weir and Pauline Armitage signed a petition of concern, giving the DUP and its allies the requisite unionist majority to force the debate.

During the debate, Paisley accused Tony Blair of treachery, condemned the Ulster Unionists and the SDLP for failing to exclude Sinn Féin, dismissed the IRA arms inspections as a worthless stunt and complained about a catalogue of beatings and shootings by republicans. Anticipating a complaint that he was hypocritically ignoring loyalist crimes, he said he condemned those as well, but it was a red herring because they were not in government. He also said Sinn Féin was not fit for office – prompting Sinn Féin's Pat Doherty to attack the DUP motion as a waste of time and a symptom of the internal battle within unionism. He recalled the DUP's own past misdeeds, accusing the party of hypocrisy. He listed its members' involvement on Assembly committees with Sinn Féin. The SDLP's Alban Maginness said the debate was pointless and detected little appetite on the part of Robinson or Dodds to quit office and play "musical chairs". "The lure of office seems to have taken its toll," he said.

Alliance member Seamus Close did not take issue with the DUP's demand for an end to paramilitary bone-crushing, but he did challenge claims that the debate was a waste of time, declaring it a "glorious opportunity" to expose the hypocrisy of the DUP. He accused the DUP of political opportunism and feeding on fear because it could not cope with peace: "Like bats in the sunlight, they cannot survive when progress is being made."

Trimble made a similar point before stinging the DUP: "The truth of the matter is that if the DUP really wanted to stop the Assembly, it could have done so by now." He said the DUP had missed just such an opportunity a few weeks earlier. Why had they not objected, he asked, to the accelerated passage of the Appropriations Bill? Had they done so, he asserted, the administration would have run out of money by mid-August and would have been brought to a crashing halt, forcing an immediate return to direct rule. Trimble said it would only have required one member to object to the Bill's speedy passage. This prompted objections; Trimble was accused of trying to give the impression such a halt would be permanent.

In retrospect, both Robinson and Dodds dismissed the notion that they had missed an opportunity and suggested there was nothing to be gained from disrupting departments financially. Dodds said he did not believe that devolution would have been halted: London would have found a way to get around the problem. "We were always determined that we would not let the people's business be interrupted, or have anything happen in terms of departmental action that would impact adversely on ordinary people," he said. When his motion failed Paisley announced he was replacing Robinson and Dodds with two substitutes, Gregory Campbell, MLA for East Londonderry, and Maurice Morrow, the member from Fermanagh-South Tyrone. Campbell was the better known of the two. He had famously featured in a 1985 "Real Lives" documentary that profiled him and Sinn Féin's Martin McGuinness. The film was controversial in that it was accused of softening McGuinness' image while portraying Campbell, polishing his legally held weapon, as belligerent.

When the rotation policy was first announced the pro-Agreement ministers feared it would be particularly disruptive and some imagined that the party might be replacing ministers regularly with different personalities. But there were only ever two substitutes. Campbell and Morrow served sixteen months, from July 2000 to November 2001 – about the same amount of time as Robinson and Dodds ran the departments. "We actually found that secretaries of state rotated more than we did," Robinson grinned.

Overall, the DUP ministers were generally credited with managing their departments efficiently. Some in the pro-Agreement camp insisted others were trying to flatter the DUP into power-sharing, but even their detractors grudgingly praised their efforts, particularly Robinson, Dodds and Campbell for their performance in the despatch box, for mastering their briefs and for how they handled their civil servants. Robinson recalled that some civil servants seemed to prefer direct rule and he wasted no time making clear there was a new regime. "I think Robinson ran a fairly tight ship," said his SDLP committee chairman, Alban Maginness. "I think he expected his civil servants to click their heels and used his reputation to his advantage."

Robinson, in particular, won rave reviews for his performance. Alban Maginness praised him as being professional, efficient and innovative. Both Robinson and Campbell had good relations with their committee. Recognising the value of having his committee on-side, Robinson regularly lunched with Maginness and the committee deputy chairman, Ulster Unionist Alan McFarland. Both Maginness and McFarland said the committee should be credited with the strategies launched as much as the minister. "The committee was so involved in every decision," said McFarland, who said he got on "fairly well" with the minister. Maginness felt Robinson was genuinely concerned with doing a good job for everybody and did not detect any sectarian policies. Maginness was pleasantly surprised at how well he got on with Robinson: "His image is that he is formidable and unapproachable. In fact, I found him quite an engaging individual. He has a cold exterior, but once you got to know him, you found him quite warm." When it was put to him that some people would be astonished to learn that, he laughed, saying, "I was astonished myself." Maginness found Campbell shyer, and less confident than Robinson: "He was a gentle sort of person. You know what he is like in public, a bit waspish, but in private, more caring.

Dodds' relations with his committee were rather less smooth, which may be in part explained by electoral and party tensions. Dodds' chairman was the Ulster Unionist Fred Cobain, who was a rival for power in the North Belfast constituency, as were other members of his committee, the PUP's Billy Hutchinson and Sinn Féin's Gerry Kelly. Dodds said he found the committee unnecessarily combative at times. In support of this he cited their threats to throw out the Housing Bill, which had been floating around during direct rule and dealt with issues such as problem neighbours. "There was a lot of rhetoric about the Housing Bill, quite frankly" said Dodds, "that it wasn't far-reaching enough and it was a conglomeration of things. It wasn't all that controversial a piece of legislation and was dealing with things that had been on the table for years. I think in the end people thought why say no to something because something else is not in front of you. It was common sense and it was accepted."

During his tenure, Morrow also clashed with his committee. This occurred when he circulated proposals for an above-inflation rise in Housing Executive rents. Fred Cobain, Ulster Unionist chairman of the Social Development committee, and other members of the committee called a news conference and attacked the minister. Morrow was put on the defensive and argued that he had not made up his mind about the proposals, which were aimed at dealing with a shortfall in the housing budget. The rises were not imposed and the DUP made it a policy to restrict rises to inflation levels.

Campbell, like Robinson, got on well with his committee and was credited for his handling of the flood crisis, which occurred almost immediately he took up office. Robinson teased him about the disasters that had befallen his department: first a flood and then a plague. He had just been sworn in and was in his first briefing when thunder and lightning started in the late afternoon. By the next morning the rain had caused severe flooding – a symptom of the antiquated sewage system in Belfast. The flooding affected the staunchly nationalist lower Ormeau Road in South Belfast, as well as part of unionist-dominated East Belfast. Campbell was invited to both areas by local MLAs, but going to the Lower Ormeau Road was potentially problematic. At the same time, Campbell knew he could not go to one area and ignore the other. The nationalist representative of the Lower Ormeau who had extended the invitation to the minister, the SDLP's Alasdair McDonnell, made it clear that he was not out to embarrass Campbell, or "stitch him up". Campbell admitted to being nervous, but trusted McDonnell and agreed to visit the Lower Ormeau and the Ravenhill area. He told the SDLP politician he would leave the area if anything untoward occurred. His fears were unfounded. The nationalist residents appreciated his gesture and the media was there to capture the moment. In fact, in one house Campbell was speaking to a man who was standing in front of a hunger strike memorial on his wall. The minister could see a press photographer trying to get a shot of this. Campbell recalled:

> "There was this ludicrous situation where the photographer was inching around to get me in line and I was inching the other way and this guy is talking about his carpet and there is this sort of dance going on."

The photographer did not get the clear shot he wanted, but the man with the ruined carpet got a promise that something would be done about the repeat flooding. Campbell secured around £5 million from the Executive Programme Fund for a series of preventive measures, which included improving drainage.

Campbell's announcement about free travel for the elderly was much less straightforward and exposed the deep tensions between the Executive and the DUP departments. At the time, the warfare over ministerial papers was well underway. Had the DUP been at the Executive table, there would have been no more than the usual tensions surrounding such announcements. But with the DUP in "opposition" mode, the Executive was determined they would get no credit for the scheme. The proposal was contained in the Programme for Government, but the DUP's Peter Robinson claimed it was his idea, and had long been a goal of his and was in his party's manifesto. Finance minister Mark Durkan claimed his party had come up with the idea, as the scheme was already available in the Republic and elsewhere and that Seamus Mallon had pushed the idea at the Executive table. In fact, Mallon had joked that he would have to declare a conflict of interest as he was eligible.

The Finance minister was due to announce the money in the Assembly, a fact Campbell was aware of because Durkan had telephoned him to inform him about it. Campbell had no intention of pre-empting Durkan, but when Trimble and Mallon gave a news conference and mentioned that the funding was forthcoming, Campbell no longer felt bound by confidentiality. The problem for the First and Deputy First Minister was they could not answer detailed questions on the scheme. Campbell could and did, on radio, and there followed a slanging match about who should get credit.

In Regional Development, Robinson and Campbell were singled out for making improvements to roads and rail, achievements supported and helped by the Executive, which had made these issues a priority. The Toome bypass was constructed during devolution, as was the Strabane bypass. More than £100 million was poured into railways for new tracks and the purchase of twenty-eight new trains. "That was the highest investment ever in terms of our railways," said Robinson. The DUP minister was appalled on his first visit to Coleraine to open a new integrated transport system, "which meant a train and a bus going through the same building." "The train," said Robinson, "was a rust-bucket with graffiti up the side. It was appalling – and the buses! We had the oldest fleet not just in the British Isles but beyond it." In office, the DUP launched a Railway Task Force, a Regional Transport Strategy and a new Quality Bus Corridor between Saintfield and Carryduff to reduce traffic congestion. The concept was inherited from direct rule and was designed to improve journey times by providing buses with their own lanes during rush-hour traffic; Robinson modified it to include bicycles and taxis. Robinson regretted that his plans for a light railway system were dropped after suspension. It was replaced with a guided bus service, even though Robinson had gone all the way to France and Germany to view systems and concluded light rail was the best way to proceed.

In Social Development there was less scope for high-profile initiatives, but Dodds and Morrow took credit, along with the Executive, for the Warm Homes scheme. As a Belfast councillor, Dodds focused on introducing measures to tackle problems that direct rule had ignored. He cracked down on illegal street traders and, along with Robinson, insisted civil servants find a way to introduce a simple measure – called alley-gating – to deal with glue-sniffing and anti-social behaviour in alleyways, which was a common complaint among their urban constituents. On the DUP's insistence, civil servants found a way to make alley-gates legal and the result was that a pilot scheme was introduced post-suspension.

Cobain complained that Dodds was typical of most ministers in that he was not radical, arguing he could detect no difference from direct rule. But Dodds countered that had he told the Treasury he wanted to radically increase benefits, for example, and taken them out of line with the rest of the UK, it would have backfired on Northern Ireland: "The Treasury would have loved us to break the parity and would have said, 'You are on your own', and it would have been disastrous." Dodds was also accused of dodging pressure for Sunday betting, but he said he had other priorities in terms of legislation and there was no great lobby of vested interests. The issue would no doubt have caused a backlash among his party supporters, however. Dodds said his priority in office was to establish a much better relationship between the government and voluntary sector to end the *ad hoc* funding and bring more financial stability. He argued that the framework he launched in February 2000 led to a task force on the future of the voluntary sector, post-suspension.

At loggerheads with the Executive over the site for a £200 million shopping development, Dodds over-ruled the Planning Appeals Commission, which did not want it sited at Victoria Square, and ignored claims by the Executive in correspondence that it was not his decision to take: "That was a bit of a trial of strength between DSD and the other departments. It became clear we had the final say." He maintained he was right to take the decision based on urban regeneration and had he not acted the development would have been delayed even further. Speaking in 2005, he said: "The site would still be sitting in its old state if I hadn't acted."

The DUP may have hated this form of devolution, but the party loved devolution. After all, every politician wants power. On first taking their posts, both Robinson and Dodds had read from their own pledge of office, each promising to be "a servant of all". Opinion was divided on whether the DUP always lived up to the promise. Robinson met delegations that included Sinn Féin members, but he was attacked publicly by Sinn Féin MLA John Kelly when he refused to shake hands with the local Assembly member at the launch of the Toome bypass project. "If he can't be a minister for all he should resign," said Kelly, echoing Robinson's devolution pledge. But Robinson was unrepentant: "If there is no dismantling of the terrorist organisation, I can't sit down with Sinn Féin."

When a virus, known as cryptosporidium, infected the water supply in parts of West Belfast and Lisburn, Campbell came under fire for not meeting directly with the Executive and the Sinn Féin Health minister, who shared responsibility for dealing with the issue. Casualty wards began to fill up with victims suffering from stomach cramps and diarrhoea and residents had to boil their water. While Bairbre de Brun tried to deal with the medical crisis, Campbell was tasked with identifying the source of the bug because the water service fell under his remit. He annoyed the Executive when he declined to attend a meeting in Room 21 to discuss the crisis, sending the chief executive of the Water Service, Robert Martin, in his stead. He was accused of hiding behind his officials. Campbell also declined a meeting with the Sinn Féin MP for West Belfast, Gerry Adams, but did give an account of the problem in the Assembly.

As ministers, the DUP delegates also pledged to use every opportunity to prevent Northern Ireland being conveyed to a United Ireland. But this did not stop them engaging in some limited north-south cooperation. Robinson insisted DUP policy was that its ministers were open to practical cooperation, although Dodds and Morrow had much less scope for cross-border cooperation in Social Development. Dodds' department cooperated with its southern counterpart on social security fraud and Robinson had encounters with Dublin ministers, but only outside the formal structures of the NSMC, claiming it was made up of unaccountable bodies that posed a threat to the union. The DUP's attitude to Dublin had evolved since the day in 1965 when the young Ian Paisley had thrown snowballs at Taoiseach Sean Lemass. But at that point, the DUP leader had yet to have a meeting with an Irish Prime Minister.

Given this state of affairs, one reporter was astounded when Robinson, as guest speaker at the influential Council for Foreign Relations in New York in 2004, insisted he never had a problem with accountable, practical relations with Dublin. The Ulster Unionist John Taylor apparently had the same reaction at a dinner years earlier, hosted by the former *Sunday Times* editor Andrew Neill, who had pressed Robinson about his attitude to Dublin. In reply, the DUP deputy leader said he had no problem going to the Irish capital. "Will it be during the day or during the night, Peter?" Taylor enquired.

Later, as Regional Development minister, Robinson stressed his party's north-south approach when he finally agreed to his first formal interview with the staunch nationalist daily, *The Irish News*. The newspaper was one of his most caustic critics. Robinson had long tried to put the embarrassing Clontibret episode behind him, but for years afterward, on the anniversary of the incursion, a reporter from *The Irish News* would be assigned to ring him and question him about it. Each time he would decline to comment. Reporter Liz Trainor began her generally positive report by recounting the tale of Clontibret. She also described how she found it ironic that the minister had kept her waiting because there were Dublin officials in his office. The report was not a negative attack on the minister, however. Twice during the interview Robinson told Trainor that people were missing the point of his attitude to north-south relations, which he put into two categories: the political issues with implications for the constitution; and common-sense cooperation between neighbouring states. He said that, as a unionist, he was not ready to put up the white flag on the former, but had no problem with the latter. "Good practical politics, I was happy to do that," he declared. At one point Robinson even sounded like John Hume when he said practical working relationships benefited everyone and threatened no one.

During his time in office, Robinson went to Dublin and shared a platform with the Dublin transport minister. "I had gone to Dublin ready to offer defences," he said, "but nobody seemed interested I would be speaking with a Dublin minister."

Richard Bullick, Robinson's special advisor, said his party never felt it was missing out by not being wholly in the Executive. The only really disruptive issue was the legal case. He said: "We never had a sense there was a particularly negative outcome. To be honest, everybody played the game and they didn't run the system to disadvantage us and we didn't disadvantage the smooth running of government." Bullick did suggest, however, that long-term planning was more difficult during the rotation: "With Peter, maybe there was more long-term planning when he came in and maybe more fundamental change in the department as to how business was done and how things were approached." But others in the administration felt it would have been better served with all the ministers working together. Certainly Trimble's Ulster Unionists would have had moral support at the table, constitutionally speaking, and the institutions would probably have held wider appeal and authority as a result.

The system never gave up hope that the DUP would eventually embrace the Executive. Similarly, there was some nervousness about the damage the DUP might do. The party got a fair wind from the scrupulously impartial Speaker, Lord Alderdice. Once when Secretary of State Mo Mowlam pressed him to end a debate, probably because the DUP were spewing vitriol about the process, he refused to budge: "She wanted to bring the shutters down on the Assembly, basically when it was in session, and she kept sending in letters to say, 'Close it down, close it down'." The Speaker knew Ian Paisley's party and others wanted to have their say and allowed them to do so.

Despite the tensions created by the DUP's "hokey-cokey" stance, behind the scenes the administration ran relatively smoothly due in no small part to the efforts of civil servants, who were caught in the middle of the warring tribes. The SDLP's John Dallat had once issued a grim warning that the DUP's rotation strategy might well herald the road to ruin for the DUP. It was anything but that. More prophetic was Dodds' prediction, issued around the same time: "The reality is, support will continue to seep away from David Trimble on a steady basis."

Chapter 29
No King of the Castle

Despite the problems posed by power-sharing, David Trimble and Mark Durkan saw a second chance for good relations, a chance for the centre to hold through a better, stronger relationship between the First and Deputy First Minister. Trimble and Mallon had been torn apart not just by personality clashes and a bureaucratic system but more particularly by the explosive issues of policing and decommissioning. Things were different this time round, however.

The twin burdens of policing and decommissioning had been eased considerably when Trimble and Durkan began to share power. There had finally been an act of decommissioning by the IRA, and the SDLP's gut-wrenching negotiations over policing had concluded with the party signing up to the new Police Service of Northern Ireland (PSNI), thereby ending a source of tension between the party and the Ulster Unionists. In the Prime Minister's words, this offered a realistic hope of stable government.

One insider recalled that Trimble respected Durkan's intellect and had been impressed by the way he handled the complexities of Finance, and he quickly noticed a change in atmosphere with the arrival of the new Deputy First Minister: "I did not see the relationship disintegrate at all and they were civil to each other. It was less intense, the issues were less intense." Trimble said he had always wanted a better relationship at the centre, even during Mallon's term. He insisted the problem was not with jointery per se, but the way the SDLP constantly focused on "the fine print". A source in the First Minister's office recalled him trying very hard to make the partnership work, saying: "With Mallon, I could see him biting his tongue quite often and with Durkan I think he tried very hard to get a good relationship through a series of one-to-one meetings." For his part, Durkan – who is often credited with conceiving the idea of joint First and Deputy First Ministers – was also determined to improve the relationship at the centre: "We tried to have a better chemistry. There were big issues we needed to work out and if we ended up having just another personality clash or stand-off it wasn't going to say much for the whole concept of jointery."

For a while the chemistry was better and there was something of a honeymoon period in the early days of the Trimble–Durkan regime. When the perennial issue of jointery resurfaced, for the sake of harmony Durkan initially opted for a more laid-back approach. He wanted to improve not just the way the Office of First and Deputy First Minister operated but also how it related to the other departments, which sometimes tended to see OFM/DFM as "the opposition" rather than the Assembly and its committees. As Deputy First Minister, Mallon had toiled to make the centre work, but in some ways it was easier for Durkan: he was younger, fitter and more energetic and did not carry the same baggage as Mallon regarding Hume's leadership. He had also entered the administration when devolution had been operating for a time, while Mallon had suffered the problems of the shadow period, which had worn him down.

One potential conflict was easily avoided early on when both Trimble and Durkan opted for the same principal private secretary, Dr Bill Smith. The head of the civil service no doubt feared he had another row on his hands when he informed Trimble that Durkan wanted to employ Smith as well, only to be told: "Well, I'm the First Minister." But Trimble and Loughran need not have worried because Durkan took the news in his stride. He was not going to fight about it and had calculated that since he got on well with Smith, it would perhaps help him foster better relations between the East and West Wings. In fact, Durkan had such good relations with Trimble's staff that he joked: "I think I had a better relationship with them than the First Minister." Durkan's attitude was a key component in his working relationship with Trimble. A natural conciliator, according to colleagues, Durkan decided at the outset that Trimble was not always deliberately trying to upset him personally and would tell himself: "People are doing things that annoy me, not to annoy me. Let's not turn a slight into a stand-off." He was also undergoing a personal trauma which gave him a different perspective on getting involved in disputes with his new partner. Durkan's mother Isobel, who had been suffering from a stroke, had just been diagnosed with terminal cancer, and he had learned the news only the day before his election to Deputy First Minister. He clung to the advice Isobel had given him when he went to see her in hospital after his election as SDLP leader: "Sanity, not vanity."

In the days that followed their election, officials were reporting a better working relationship. Their press operation was certainly anxious to tell reporters that the chemistry had improved and correspondents were soon talking about how the leaders regularly breakfasted together. Although the importance of this may have been exaggerated – the meetings were not sustained regularly over a long period – Trimble did notice the improvement immediately and noted less tension between the EPU and the Finance Department. "There was clearly a difference," he said.

Durkan's advisor, Damien McAteer, also remembered a congenial start, although he still had to remind officials in meetings with the Treasury that Durkan should not be regarded as Trimble's deputy. In an early show of unity, the two ministers travelled to Downing Street together, something Durkan felt was important because, like Mallon, he was wary of the First Minister's regular solo trips to Number 10. In his first meeting as SDLP leader with Blair, Durkan recalled telling him that he must meet with both ministers together to underscore the joint nature of the administration. The Prime Minister's reaction, according to Durkan, was: "It is not me who insisted on doing it this way."

In his meeting Durkan took the opportunity to demand more resources for the new administration to underwrite the peace process. He had long believed it was not good enough for the government to close army bases as part of a demilitarisation plan and leave no means of economic development. He said he had talked about a peace dividend, an idea he had raised as far back as the Good Friday Agreement negotiations, but the proposal had not been taken up. Durkan told Blair that former security force land and bases must be returned to the Executive, which did not have the resources to fund its Programme for Government, even if every minister tightened his or her belt. Effectively, he wanted the

Prime Minister to help him turn swords into ploughshares.

Blair took what Durkan had said seriously and followed up their discussion with a joint meeting involving both the First and Deputy First Ministers, at which the issue of a peace dividend was discussed again. Blair could see that the First Minister was keen and no doubt wanted to encourage the new relationship at the heart of the institutions of the Agreement, a significant part of his legacy. The discussions led to a unique plan that would become known as the Reinvestment and Reform Initiative (RRI). Trimble was so enthusiastic about it that he later described it as the most important initiative to come out of the devolved administration. Durkan had conceived the plan as Finance minister. One of its most important elements was a borrowing facility from the Treasury.

Before it was unveiled in Belfast's Odyssey Arena by the Prime Minister and the Chancellor, the RRI was worked on for some months by two of Trimble and Durkan's most trusted advisors. These were David Campbell, Trimble's shy, cerebral chief-of-staff, who was so quiet that a colleague likened him to a "Trappist monk", and the more loquacious Damien McAteer, a whiz at economics, who had served as Durkan's advisor in Finance. By coincidence, McAteer was a cousin of Aidan McAteer, McGuinness' special advisor. McAteer described Campbell as one "one of the smarter guys on the block". He was viewed as having Trimble's ear and he frequently travelled to Downing Street with him. McAteer, deeply committed to the initiative, referred to former army bases as "dynamos for generation". These advisors were tasked with liaising with Stormont's Department of Finance and Treasury officials about the initiative. Although it had Blair's backing, McAteer remembered he still had to battle with the Treasury to get the borrowing facility and remembered terse exchanges between Belfast and London:

> "[the Treasury] were extremely difficult on everything. The distinct impression you got was they didn't want us there, that Northern Ireland was a burdensome liability. It was Trimble and Durkan who persuaded Blair that the military bases and the Maze prison should be the first endowment of a peace dividend to be followed up by further endowments free of charge."

Trimble however recalled the Treasury was quite helpful and keen to make special arrangements to fund the infrastructure deficit. McAteer did form the view the Chancellor was well-disposed to the RRI and recalled a woman on Gordon Brown's staff telling him at the Odyssey Arena in Belfast when it was launched, that the Chancellor wrote his own speech for the occasion: "(She) said 'he wouldn't let anybody write this. He is fully committed'." In his speech, Brown declared: "In the place of the symbols of the old conflict and despair, there will be symbols of new progress and hope. Barracks and prison will be replaced by businesses and prosperity."

Ebrington Barracks and the former Maze prison were among the former bases and jails gifted to the Executive. The package also involved the Assembly immediately obtaining a £200 million loan to enable it to tackle its infrastructure deficit in terms of roads, schools and hospitals. No figure was put on how much money would be obtained in the longer term. But a principle was established that any future borrowings made would be based on higher rates. In other words to access the Treasury gilts, the Executive would have to raise more revenue. The ability to leverage rate rises gave the Executive the incentive to raise them, one of the Treasury's aims. If, in the words of Mark Twain, nothing is certain but death and taxes, then it was inevitable that higher rates were on the way. The question was when. Durkan disputed that rates increases were inevitable and insisted this remained a decision for a future Executive and Assembly "We could well choose not to raise rates," he said, but did not dispute that the Treasury post-devolution tried to give the impression water and rates charges were automatic under the scheme.

According to Durkan the initiative was still evolving when the Prime Minister and Chancellor came to Belfast in the Spring of 2002 to put their seal on the RRI. While the broad outline of RRI was announced by Brown in May, 2002, attempts were made to iron out the details in subsequent weeks and months. From the outset, a new Strategic Investment Board (SIB) was envisaged to help manage the new funds in partnership with the private sector, together with trade unionists and individuals from the public and voluntary sectors, along the lines of the Republic's very successful "social partnership" programme. Durkan believed the SIB could help ensure collective responsibility around decision-making. He was anxious to avoid a repeat of the rates rise row which had occurred when Sinn Féin tried to distance themselves from the Executive's proposed rates hike by dubbing it the "Durkan tax" in the Assembly. One commentator called this "selective, not collective" responsibility.

The Executive set up a working group to take forward proposals on the shape of the SIB, its remit, structures and relationship with the Executive. It took several months to report but it was estimated that £6 billion would be required over a decade to cover the investment deficit in infrastructure. Generally speaking the First and Deputy First Minister worked well on the issue, although Durkan recalled a few differences, particularly over where the money should go. Trimble initially mentioned the £100 million Ulster Canal, which was a pet project of his and Culture Minister Michael McGimpsey. But Durkan was adamant the money should fund a new regional cancer centre and remembered telling Trimble, not for the first time, that he should not see it as money for a Sinn Féin department, but funds for the health sector which affected everyone. Trimble said he was ultimately content to have the funding go to the cancer centre.

By mid-summer, as details of the RRI were being worked out, the First and Deputy First Ministers announced that the total package the Executive had to spend on infrastructure amounted to £275 million. Around £125 million came from borrowing and a further £75 million followed an agreement with the Treasury to relax accounting rules which freed up money within the existing Northern Ireland block funding. The remaining £75 million derived from Executive Programme Funds. Departments scrambled to get their share. It was not all good news, however, as the First and Deputy First Minister had to defend their initiative against criticism from various quarters about impending rates rises. Trade union leaders were amongst the most critical and claimed the RRI was being presented as a gift when it would have to be paid for from a local revenue stream in the form of higher rates. While the Treasury was demanding this, Trimble told the Assembly that spring there would be no sharp rates rises within the next two years. The Executive also made it clear that the rates were being reviewed and would remain within the existing pattern until then. In fact, the review had the advantage of showing the Treasury that the Executive was taking their demands for rates rises seriously, while not actually doing anything immediately. The theory was that the SIB would be able to sweat more money out of the assets and there would be greater efficiencies in the system to help negate any rates increases.

Although interrupted by the suspension of devolution and later taken forward by direct rule in a way that horrified Durkan, the RRI was an example of what the First and Deputy First Minister could achieve when working together. As the two ministers united to forge the initiative, Durkan made other efforts to foster good relations with Trimble and the unionist population. In February 2002, he put his name to a joint statement with Trimble, expressing sympathy on the death of the Queen's sister, Princess Margaret, and the following month repeated the move on the death of the Queen Mother. The two ministers also attended her funeral service. Durkan said he would have expected as much of Trimble if for example the Irish head of state had passed away. Durkan was a bit concerned about the reaction, but the only criticism he remembered centred on the fact that Trimble wore a blue shirt, instead of a sober white one, like him. Durkan, surprised by this, said: "I thought I couldn't win, but it was actually David Trimble who couldn't win."

Trimble was heartened when Durkan joined him for lunch with the Queen at Hillsborough hosted by the Secretary of State. This was shortly after he took up office. A cameraman, who was brought in to take pictures, described a stilted conversation between the Queen and the Deputy First Minister. "It was an awkward moment. She said to Mark Durkan that she was in Derry that day and he said, 'I was in Derry today. I'm from there', and she just looked at him like 'who cares?'"

Durkan remembered having to slip out a side door because he had to leave early to go to a meeting in Dublin and did not want the media reporting that he had snubbed the Queen. His decision to take part in the lunch was made easier by the fact Sinn Féin had refrained from protesting her visit. The party adopted what Lord Alderdice, the Assembly speaker, called an attitude of "dignified detachment" when the Queen and the Duke of Edinburgh visited Stormont the following spring to mark her Golden Jubilee. It was her first visit to Stormont since 1953 when she came to Parliament Buildings shortly after the Coronation. The Northern Ireland Office, still reeling from "the brawl in the hall" at Stormont, was anxious that the event go well. Sinn Féin stayed away and the First and Deputy First Ministers led the monarch in turn around the hall to greet unionists lined up on the right, nationalists on the left and others in between.

The First and Deputy First Minister embarked on official visits of their own while they were in joint office. They made a joint visit to the Scottish Parliament, and officially opened the Northern Ireland Executive's new European office in Brussels in January 2002, along with junior ministers Dermot Nesbitt and Denis Haughey. They then opened the Northern Ireland bureau in Washington the following month. This was swiftly followed by a joint visit to Washington for St Patrick's Day celebrations which had become an annual pilgrimage for many Northern Ireland politicians.

They were invited to the White House, but Durkan said he drew the line at attempts to have Trimble and himself achieve similar status with the Taoiseach Bertie Ahern who was feted by US President George W. Bush as a head of state when they both took part in the traditional Shamrock ceremony with the President. "I thought it was us getting above ourselves," Durkan said. "We were not heads of state. We were heads of a regional administration." However, protocol was not the big problem about the trip, which saw the two ministers visiting US Secretary of State General Colin Powell and Condoleezza Rice, then Bush's national security advisor. The problem that marked the trip came from another, unexpected quarter and involved an ill-judged remark attributed to Trimble at his party's annual conference some days before.

Trimble was juggling his duties as First Minister and leader of a chronically divided party when he sat down on the eve of conference to read a draft of his speech. He was struck by a phrase written by his aide, Steven King, which referred to the Irish Republic as a "pathetic, sectarian state". Trimble planned to delete the word "pathetic". Regrettably, however, when he informed King of this the following morning, before he delivered the speech, his aide grinned at him and said: "Too late. It's already gone out."

Reporters seized on this description of the Irish Republic. Trimble, instead of distancing himself from what he himself considered to be "not the best-judged term," dug in, even though he had not used the word in his own address. The result was a storm of protest from Irish nationalists and republicans. Trimble thought this an over-reaction, but Durkan, too, was annoyed and made his protest through "the proper channels," as he put it. Publicly, he called the remarks gratuitously offensive, and "unbecoming of a political leader."

The SDLP Finance minister Sean Farren, who hailed from Dublin, suggested Trimble's remarks said more about unionist insecurities than the Irish Republic, and called for their withdrawal. The speech was also controversial because it included demands for a border poll. The remarks were still hanging in the air as Trimble and Durkan made their way to Washington for what was potentially an uncomfortable reception at the residence of the Irish ambassador. Trimble hesitated about going, but Durkan pointed out it would add to the damage in relations and he agreed to the visit, provided they arrived together. The Taoiseach had already made his address by the time the two ministers turned up, but despite this the evening went well and Trimble's remarks seemed to have been forgiven if not forgotten. Durkan recalled: "The damage was all back in the black box until the following morning."

It was at the ceremony for the Global Citizens Award that the *détente* became strained again. The award was being presented to the First Minister and his wife by a foundation linked to the wealthy Irish-American Dunphy family. Everything went smoothly until the question and answer panel discussion afterwards, when Trimble floundered as the issue of his remarks was raised. Durkan was dismayed when the First Minister failed to let the matter rest. "He waded right back in," he said.

To justify his remarks, Trimble said the recent abortion referendum in the Republic was a sectarian vote and quoted from an old work, *States of Ireland* by Conor Cruise O'Brien, which was published in 1972. Durkan judging this to be both irresponsible and insensitive felt compelled to disagree, if for no other reason than to stop Trimble proceeding. "I had to say something," he explained. "I had no choice. I made clear I would never find myself in a position where I was relying on a 30-minute quote from Conor Cruise O'Brien, never mind a 30-year-old one."

It was not just nationalists who were annoyed. Sir Reg Empey was also mortified as he was in the United States trying to drum up investment for Northern Ireland. "It is not language I would have used," said Empey. "It is outdated because the Republic has moved on. …We had an Irish-American under-secretary in the Department of Commerce with whom I was doing business. It was awkward. I would go on a radio show in New York and you get all this tossed about. What do you say?"

The issue resurfaced back home when the ministers returned to their first Executive meeting. It was reported that the decibels were rather high as Martin McGuinness and Trimble "verbally wrestled" over the First Minister's remarks. One insider recalled "quite a ding-dong". In retrospect, when asked to explain why he did not let the matter drop quietly in the US, Trimble suggested it was "an academic tendency to explain".

The new administration did make some progress on some thorny issues. Within a few months of taking office, the two ministers launched a consultation process within the Assembly about the terms of reference for the Review of Public Administration (RPA). This was aimed at streamlining local government and reducing some of the bureaucracy in the system. The Programme for Government had pledged to launch the Review by spring 2002, and by June they had agreed the panel to spearhead the initiative. But Durkan was anxious to have more joint visits within Northern Ireland with the First Minister. Like Mallon, he felt it was vital that the First and Deputy First Ministers go out together to community events but these were difficult to schedule as Trimble was in demand both at home and abroad. They did, however, manage to jointly launch the inaugural Holocaust Memorial Event in Belfast and they travelled to Durkan's constituency together where they visited Foyle Search and Rescue and other venues. The press release described their visit to the "North West" and in their respective quotes, Trimble referred to Londonderry and Durkan to Derry.

There was, throughout devolution, an issue within the Office of First Minister and Deputy First Minister about what to do about the city's controversial name. As a unionist Trimble preferred to use the official title, while both Mallon and Durkan preferred Derry which was favoured by nationalists. It became a bit contentious when the Executive held its first meeting in the city in a bid to move government away from Stormont and bring it closer to the people. Trimble objected when he saw that only Derry was mentioned in the press release. But Durkan protested that the meeting was being held in a school called "First Derry School." A similar controversy raged over the use of the term in an answer to a ministerial question. Without agreement the member's question remained unanswered for months. An official recalled that the question was in fact never answered because devolution was suspended.

This was minor compared to other disputes that were unfolding. It may have been too much to expect dramatic change or a friction-free zone at the centre. The nature of politics dictates there is going to be some tensions. "Two saints would have trouble getting along in this system," commented one insider. When Durkan was asked if he agreed with this, he laughed and joked: "I'd have to be there with another saint first." Trimble, too, was amused by the notion of a joint administration requiring two saints and pointed out that Rome created an empire with joint consuls, adding: "Mind you they had an interesting rule. They each commanded on different days."

Accordingly, the relationship at the centre began to come under pressure. Durkan said his patience with Trimble and his "solo runs" snapped some months into the administration, when he decided he was taking no more "slights". Some in his party were beginning to grumble that he was too soft on the unionist First Minister. Durkan, feeling as if his goodwill was being taken for granted and abused, began to object. "There were a few issues where I did start telling people where to get off," he said.

"Durkan drew a line in the sand," McAteer recalled. "Trimble saw himself as a strong unionist and Durkan as a strong nationalist and people thought when Mallon left that Durkan would be a pushover, but Durkan was far from a pushover." A source close to Trimble lamenting the down-turn in relations, said: "Trimble and Durkan both started to play politics with each other and both of them expected better of each other."

Efforts to resolve the Holy Cross school conflict, the dark drama being played out in the streets of North Belfast, caused more strain. The previous devolved ministers, Sir Reg Empey and Seamus Mallon, had been working on a long-term resolution when they left office. Both Mallon and Empey had been supportive of those trying to resolve the dispute over the summer. When the protest resumed in September, they jointly condemned what they called the protestors' unacceptable intimidation and abuse of the children en route to Holy Cross. They concluded that it was not just a problem for North Belfast, but it was "everyone's problem". The Executive had appointed a Senior Liaison Officer for North Belfast to encourage dialogue and a resolution and Mallon and Empey were involved in a number of meetings to try to end the dispute.

The new First and Deputy First Ministers picked up the initiative after they took office. The Executive had no responsibility for security, which was a reserved matter, but could not ignore the dispute as it impacted on devolved areas such as social housing, education and community relations and also created negative international publicity. The centre office was credited with helping to get the loyalist protest suspended. Aware that the Glenbryn residents' committee was meeting to consider calling off the protest, which had become an embarrassing public relations disaster for the community, Trimble and Durkan sent them a letter on 23 November 2001. Signed by both ministers, it committed their joint office to meeting some of the committee's concerns provided the protest ended, with no resumption.

The residents had a number of issues they wanted addressed, including more financial support for the area. But the most controversial issue fell under the heading, "community safety". They wanted a new wall to be built on the Ardoyne interface and a new road realignment. This was controversial because the Catholic parents did not want another "peace" wall, believing this was no solution to the community relations problem. They also had objections to the road realignment at the Ardoyne-Alliance Avenue intersection near the school, and were anxious to have an unobstructed view of their children on the school route.

The Trimble/Durkan letter made clear that any changes of this nature to the Ardoyne intersection would have to be subject to agreement on the design and that "possible" road alignment would also be subject to agreement. Emotions were running high on both sides and rows began almost about the nature of the offer and exactly what was promised. That is where the East and West Wing began to split down the middle on the issue.

Durkan, along with others from the Deputy First Minister's office, insisted that no cast-iron promises were made and that it was always made clear both sides would have to agree to the community safety aspects of the deal. These sources do not tend to blame Trimble for the friction but his advisor, David McNarry. Durkan claimed McNarry was making promises to the community, but did not have the authority to speak for the joint office and that led to friction: "The big problem was McNarry running his own channels and his own lines and people were coming in to us and saying McNarry assured of this and McNarry wasn't acting on behalf of OFM/DFM. He had his own twilight zone operating."

McNarry, who was sympathetic to the Glenbryn residents demand for a wall and road realignment complained about interference from civil servants and alleged Durkan was either indecisive or reneged on agreements as soon as he came under pressure from nationalist residents. Durkan said McNarry wrongly presumed there was agreement when issues had not been finalised.

Durkan said one problem was that advisors were working away in both wings to try to get the matter settled and by the time it came to a meeting with Trimble, the First Minister was upset by what he had heard. "Trimble would go on into a rage," said Durkan, "and make accusations and then when it came to meeting with the community groups, Trimble wasn't there."

But Trimble recalled that both he and Durkan were hands-on in dealing with the dispute and pointed to meetings he had with residents from Ardoyne and Ballysillan. According to Durkan, Trimble would sometimes be represented by new junior minister James Leslie, but the First Minister did not regard Leslie's actions as having his authority. "Trimble felt free to change any understanding that Leslie had been part of," he said.

Durkan remembered being accused of acting in bad faith but insisted that he always stuck to the initial line which was that agreement was necessary between the two sides of the dispute if the community safety initiatives were to proceed.

In early January, after some progress in the dispute, there were renewed scenes of violence. In a joint statement, Trimble and Durkan appealed for calm and patience as they attempted to implement new measures. They said it was vital that work being carried out by the Roads Service and other government agencies should not be disrupted. The following day, 10 January, they issued an appeal for restraint and common sense following a vicious attack on property at the nearby Our Lady of Mercy School in North Belfast. They asked their officials to arrange urgent talks between the area's community activists and its Assembly representatives. The situation in north Belfast deteriorated within a few days, however, when a Catholic postal worker, Daniel McColgan was shot dead by loyalist paramilitaries. The murder was jointly condemned by the First and Deputy First Minister as a loyalist paramilitary threat against Catholic teachers and postal workers.

The situation calmed down, relatively speaking, for a few months after that, but outstanding issues around the dispute remained unresolved, even though the protest itself had ended before Christmas, until the matter went to arbitration and a report was drawn up by the Quakers. Trimble felt the administration's involvement was useful despite some of the friction caused by it at the centre of the administration. "We were a bit reluctant to get involved in the first place," he said, "because we did not want to be seen to be grandstanding or exploiting issues and we arranged at an early stage for officials to look at it and developed an approach to defuse the initial dispute over access and then to look at more significant underlying problems." He pointed, for instance, to their efforts in creating the North Belfast Community Project to help tackle inner-city problems.

In the spring of 2002, the embers of Holy Cross were still smouldering when another potential inferno ignited, this time inflicting further damage to relations between Trimble and Durkan. The interface between the Catholic enclave of the Short Strand and the Protestant Cluan Place in East Belfast erupted, with shades of the kind of early clashes that marked the outbreak of the Troubles in 1969. Short Strand residents maintained they had been attacked by loyalist paramilitaries. On the loyalist side, it was claimed republicans from the area had attacked the residents of Cluan Place, which lies in the shadow of the peace wall, and put them out of their homes. As arguments raged about who started the dispute, the violence continued.

Typical of Northern Ireland society at large, Trimble and Durkan did not agree on the causes of this local conflict. Trimble blamed republicans and the IRA and Durkan felt this was unfair, believing the First Minister was ignoring the loyalist paramilitary role in the trouble. He also thought it inappropriate for the First Minister to takes sides so publicly. He very firmly attacked suggestions the attacks were tit-for-tat, and said the problem in the Short Strand was a systematic attack on the community by loyalists. In a remark that some thought was pointed at Trimble, Durkan said he understood people's anger that the situation had been "misrepresented by those who should know better". Durkan said he was sceptical about promises by the Loyalist Commission of "no first strike". Each visited the area separately. Trimble said this was because of security considerations and that police could not guarantee his safety in the Short Strand. He went alone to Cluan Place and Durkan went on his own to the Short Strand, although Durkan did also meet a group of women from the Protestant side of the dispute at Parliament Buildings. He was also due to go to a community centre to meet both sides in the dispute but had to cancel when his mother died. Durkan, when interviewed for *Room 21*, said he was not aware that Trimble was interested in travelling together to the controversial interface. "He didn't really tell me at the time that he wanted to," he said.

Their separate visits sent the wrong signal, but to their credit, they got there ahead of Secretary of State John Reid who actually had responsibility for security. Reid was pictured beside a sign at the Cluan Place interface that read: "Welcome to hell."

It was the tension over the Short Strand that became a turning point in their relationship, according to some insiders. The early chemistry began to fizzle out. Some in the First Minister's office formed the view that Durkan was indecisive and difficult to prise a decision out of. "He was known as Hamlet," said one official, "the young prince who couldn't make up his mind." Brian Barrington, Durkan's advisor, disputed the comments describing them as "sour grapes" from people around Trimble over the efforts to get the Holy Cross dispute resolved. In his own defence, Durkan said: "[Trimble's side] decided they couldn't get a decision when they couldn't get the one they wanted."

Rows over community relations seemed to mark the administration because neither side could agree on the publication of a report on the issue drawn up by an academic, Jeremy Harbinson. His report also bounced around for months. Barrington said his party had a different aim – to try to bring Catholics and Protestants closer together, integrate and have a tighter knit society – while the Ulster Unionists were only interested in solving the interface problem. He remembered someone from Trimble's side telling him that the

Ulster Unionists had problems with the approach to community relations identified in Harbinson:

> "He told us the bottom-line was that they were not really up for this shared future stuff. Trimble saw it all as being about getting people not to riot at interfaces and we saw it as getting a more integrated society in the north. Interfaces were symptoms of the problem. They [the unionists] saw it as the problem itself. A divided community, they were happy with that."

Trimble advisor David McNarry complained about the report and its "focus on integrated housing estates". "This is complete nonsense. ... The communities in Northern Ireland aren't ready for it. We sent Harbinson away three or four times for a re-write," he said. As the Ulster Unionists demanded a re-write, the SDLP began to press for its publication. "We weren't happy with that," McNarry revealed. "We just were not going to sign off."

The "Shared Future" document, based on the Harbinson report, was not published until direct rule returned. Trimble pointed out that it was rewritten several times during devolution and that he regarded the SDLP's focus on integrated communities as "esoteric" given the friction at the interface where people were not ready for integration.

The head of the civil service was by now distraught over another issue: getting the First and Deputy First Minister to move to Stormont Castle on the estate. It was once the home of Northern Ireland's first Prime Minister, Lord Craigavon. This was an issue that had been on-going since the early days of the Trimble-Mallon era. These two ministers began to realise that the East and West Wings were getting increasingly crowded with staff, even though many officials still worked down the hill at Castle Buildings. Naturally, there was a desire to have all the staff in the one place, if possible, and Trimble and Mallon found a common solution: Stormont Castle, at the foot of Parliament Buildings which would do nicely. The problem was it already had a tenant, Peter Mandelson, the Secretary of State for Northern Ireland. Trimble felt it would be appropriate for the new administration and Mallon, having no love for Mandelson, and anxious for more space, went along with the notion. Together they raised concerns about the "presentational" aspect of Mandelson and his ministers occupying both the Castle and Castle Buildings as the new devolved administration took root. In a joint memo, they noted that it was sensitive territory as the NIO still had reserve powers, but added: "We do wonder about the message that is given if you continue to hold...two of the three most prestigious buildings on the Stormont estate." Loughran used his influence and obtained the Castle site for Trimble and Mallon. But he had no sooner got the Castle when the pair cooled on the idea.

They became concerned about moving away from the legislature and wanted to keep their offices in Parliament Buildings. Mallon had a number of concerns including the lack of canteen facilities in Stormont Castle. The issue came to a head during the short-lived Mallon-Empey era when Loughran, frustrated by delay, reminded them that £7 million had been spent renovating and refurbishing the Castle and the NIO was now pressing the devolved administration to take up the accommodation. Trimble claimed he was willing to go part-time but Mallon remained reluctant and while some staff were transferred to the Castle, the two ministers were still in Parliament Buildings when Durkan arrived.

Durkan shared Trimble's concerns about moving to the Castle and being cut off from the Assembly. Loughran however did persuade the Executive to leave Room 21. By the summer of 2002 the Executive was holding its meetings in the Castle.

Trimble and Durkan inherited another problem that had also dogged the Mallon–Trimble regime: the question of jointery and the threat posed to it by Trimble's solo runs to Downing Street. A serious issue arose when Durkan got wind that on one of his personal visits to Downing Street, Trimble had spoken to Tony Blair and Jonathan Powell, the Prime Minister's chief-of-staff, about who should replace the head of the civil service, Gerry Loughran, who was due to retire in the autumn of 2002. According to Durkan, Trimble rated a certain individual in the NIO and was thinking also about recruiting someone from outside the Northern Ireland Civil Service, perhaps preferring someone from the Home Service. Durkan deemed Trimble's discussions with Downing Street as not only a breach of protocol in terms of recruitment but also of jointery. Durkan accused the Prime Minister and his official of ignoring the political sensitivities in a bid to show Trimble how supportive they were of him. "This was their way of humouring David," he said.

Durkan said Trimble was challenged about sounding people out for the post when it was raised in a meeting involving himself, the First Minister and Gerry Loughran: "[Trimble] tried first of all to deny it and said this was all nonsense and then ended up protesting at the end of the meeting. As he slunk off he just said, 'This is terrible, that you can't have a private conversation any more'."

Trimble said he had casually raised the issue with the Prime Minister in the course of a meeting about another issue as he had come to the conclusion that the Northern Ireland Civil Service had been cut off from "modern best practice." He thought the system, after years of direct rule, would benefit from an outsider's perspective. He said he just wanted to broaden the pool of potential candidates to replace Loughran.

Yet another issue inherited from the Trimble–Mallon era was the Children's Commissioner proposal. Trimble and Durkan clashed over this initiative, although both were committed to achieving a children's commissioner for Northern Ireland. It had been proposed that the role be created to address children's needs, with a particular emphasis on disadvantaged children or those at risk. The OFM/DFM consulted on the matter. A Children's Commissioner had been appointed by the newly created Welsh Assembly and during the consultation there also had been a Private Member's Bill from the Women's Coalition pressing the case. The Executive, however, had to agree powers for the commissioner and this led to some friction not just within the Executive but between the devolved administration and the Northern Ireland Office, which was not keen on the Children's Commission having, for example, powers of entry. The Ulster Unionists and SDLP claimed Sinn Féin ministers also raised concerns about some far-reaching powers for the Commissioner, including the right to investigate a child's past. It was alleged McGuinness and de Brun were taking their cue from civil servants concerned about the impact it would have on the powers of their respective departments. Introducing the second stage of the Bill in July 2002, junior minister Denis Haughey said the OFM/DFM believed it was essential that the commissioner should have a retrospective power to investigate because the abuse or neglect sometimes took time to resolve and complaints were not made for some years after the trauma.

Generally the centre worked well on the issue, but the most contentious point was getting the NIO to agree to the Commissioner having powers of entry, something the new Children's Commissioner in Wales did not have. Durkan recalled a stand-up row with Trimble in Belfast City Airport when the First Minister accused him of "getting uppity": "He upbraided me because he thought he had a line worked out with the Northern Ireland Office," said Durkan, who claimed Trimble was willing to accept limits that he would not, on how much power to give the commissioner in terms of juvenile justice. Durkan said he was not prepared "to blink" on the issue in negotiations with the NIO and felt Trimble had breached jointery by trying to do his own deal with the Secretary of State. "He was as usual having his own wee foray and his own wee chat with Reid," Durkan said. Trimble suggested this was an "over-egged" account and that his concern was to get the best possible deal. Trimble also had concerns about the SDLP's approach to the negotiations.

When the Bill was introduced in June 2002, it reflected a hard-won victory for the devolved administration in getting the NIO to concede world-leading robust powers for the commissioner. By September it was passing through the committee stage by which time relations were not terribly warm between Trimble and Durkan. The Deputy First Minister's mother had died after a long illness. Durkan, naturally was in emotional turmoil and was annoyed at the way Trimble reacted. When Isobel Durkan died, Trimble had been at the Earth Summit in South Africa along with the Taoiseach and Prime Minister. Durkan recalled receiving messages of sympathy from Blair and Ahern in Johannesburg, but nothing from Trimble.

On their first day back in Stormont together, the pair were scheduled to meet in Durkan's office. Durkan recalled Trimble behaving oddly:

> "He came in with his hands in his pocket and just said 'well', and I just decided, 'I am not doing this for you'. He looked out the window and he said, 'well, it is good you are here'. I said, 'well, there is nothing else for it in the circumstances' and again he kind of shifted from one foot to the other and both hands in his pocket and said, 'you're back, anyway' and I said, 'you are back yourself'."

Durkan was disgusted when Trimble moved on to talk about his trip without expressing any sympathy. He felt no better when the First Minister read out a formal statement of condolences, penned by a civil servant, in the Assembly during question time later that day. "He didn't make it personal. He just read it as if he were answering a question," said Durkan.

Durkan contrasted Trimble's behaviour on this occasion with an earlier conversation he had in July with the First Minister who was quite sympathetic when he heard Durkan's mother was going into a hospice. Trimble confided that he had been through the same experience with his own mother. Durkan was struck at the way Trimble could sometimes, but not always, relate on an emotional level. "Sometimes he had it and other times he didn't. He is very left-handed with people," he said.

Just like Mallon, Durkan struggled with Trimble's mysterious personality. He remembered another time he and Trimble visited the Hospital for Sick Children together and how awkward that could be for two shy ministers who were meeting people facing trauma:

> "David could be brusque and he was talking more to the management than the nurses and carers but I remember him talking to one young fellow who was in hospital and telling him of when he was a wee boy and had been in hospital and what had happened to him. He had banged his head and he joked that 'a lot of people say that explains a lot since'. I thought again, 'you have it, why don't you show it?' I think he is shy actually. I am shy and I can sympathise with him sometimes."

In spite of any empathy he may have felt, Durkan had hardened in his attitude towards the First Minister and was determined to challenge Trimble on every issue he felt necessary. One soon came along. In fact, the First and Deputy First Minister were heading for a clash in the autumn of 2002 over new UK transport legislation.

Dermot Nesbitt, the new Environment minister, was enthusiastic about a new initiative from the Department of Transport in London. It proposed that British motorists in England, Scotland and Wales could adorn their car license plates with either the Union flag or their region's emblem, for example, the Scottish saltire or the Welsh dragon. Nesbitt wanted to include Northern Ireland in the legislation. According to Durkan, Nesbitt informed him about a potential legal problem if Northern Ireland was left out. Durkan was sceptical about this and demanded to see the legal advice. He was also sceptical when Nesbitt rang him on his mobile and assured him the only emblem allowed would be the St Patrick's Cross because he considered it neutral as it featured on the new police badge. The Deputy First Minister believed that an MP in Westminster, probably a unionist, was bound to table an amendment demanding that Northern Ireland motorists be given the same rights as the rest of the UK to have the choice of the Union flag.

Durkan thought it was a "mad" idea to have flags on license plates in Northern Ireland where it would only stir up divisions. He ignored Nesbitt's note on the issue, as it did not include the legal advice. But Trimble shared Nesbitt's enthusiasm for the initiative and wrote to Alastair Darling about it, acknowledging Durkan's reluctance but stressing the importance of including Northern Ireland in the legislation. When Durkan found out that Trimble had "unilaterally" written to Darling, he was most annoyed. He wrote his own letter to Darling. Durkan set out the case against and making clear it would not have the wholehearted support of the Stormont administration, even if it was only the St Patrick's Cross as Nesbitt had suggested. Durkan alleged that Trimble then wrote a second letter to Darling insisting that he wanted Northern Ireland motorists to have the choice of the Union flag as well as St Patrick's Cross. Trimble disputed this, and said his recollection is that he did not write again and that he was content with Nesbitt's proposal.

Either way, Durkan's early good intentions not to fight with Trimble were now firmly cast aside. As they approached the first anniversary of their partnership, Durkan prepared for battle. "We were heading for a big bust up," he said.

No doubt the issue would have turned into a public row had events not intervened.

Chapter 30
Stormontgate

The Minister of Environment, Dermot Nesbitt, was standing on the steps outside Parliament Buildings, attending an early morning photo-call, when he spied the convoy. A line of more than half-a-dozen police Land Rovers was ascending the hill towards him in close formation. Nesbitt watched as the fleet circled Carson's statue and then sped off to the left, in the direction of the West Wing. Curious to know what was happening, he despatched Stephen Barr, his ministerial aide, to find out. "It was basically my last act as advisor," said Barr, who had soon reported to his boss that the police – around thirty officers in black boiler suits and baseball caps – were there to raid the offices of Sinn Féin. Nesbitt, who was attending an Environment conference at Parliament Buildings that day, was one of the few politicians to witness first-hand the events as Stormont was fairly deserted, not just because of the early hour: most members worked in their constituency offices on Fridays, which was where many were to be found on the morning of 4 October 2002.

The Speaker of the House was 3,000 miles away and five hours behind by the transatlantic time-clock. It was the early hours of the morning in Ottawa, Canada, when the telephone rang in his hotel room. Lord Alderdice was wakened by a member of his staff in Belfast, who informed him of the raid. Apologising for the late hour, the official – who had just been informed by the police they were coming to the estate – felt certain the Speaker would want to know what was happening. Lord Alderdice was deeply upset when he heard the news, particularly when further details emerged about the number of police and how the raid was conducted, all witnessed by UTV reporter Fearghal McKinney and his camera crew, acting on a tip-off. McKinney was preparing to take his daughter to school shortly after 8.30am when a source telephoned him with the news. He scrambled to get a camera crew to Stormont and managed to arrive in time for what appeared to be the second wave of police searches; no one was there to capture the first part of the operation. McKinney would not say who his source was, but insisted republican claims that the police tipped him off are incorrect. The information, he maintained, came from someone who was at Stormont that day.

As the incident unfolded, Lord Alderdice telephoned the chief constable in Belfast and expressed his displeasure. "I'm most unhappy about this," he told Hugh Orde. By now, Lord Alderdice had been in touch with the Assembly's head of security and the Clerk, Arthur Moir, and was aghast that the police could simply barge into Parliament Buildings, home to a democratically elected legislative Assembly with certain privileges, rights and entitlements. Lord Alderdice felt the police had not shown due respect for this fact. "I have no doubt," he said, "that there was intelligence about the gathering of material on the

Stormont Estate and I have no doubt about that. In that context, addressing Stormont as part of their investigations was not necessarily inappropriate. The question was how." The Speaker was very conscious that when the Queen delivered her annual speech to Parliament, she did not go to the House of Commons. No monarch had been in the Commons since Charles I. "Why?" he asked, before answering his own question in an interview, recalling the events of the seventeenth century at the time of Charles I. When the monarch marched to Parliament to arrest some members, he was told by the Speaker, 'Your Majesty, I have neither eyes to see nor ears to hear, save such as this chamber gives me.' Lord Alderdice noted that the King withdrew, adding:

> "When the force of the state comes up against the Parliament, the Parliament is separate from the Executive. The Speaker has to stand up for the rights of the legislative Assembly and say to the Executive side, 'No, you can't do that'. So I was following in a tradition that goes back to Speakers in the time of Charles I by saying, 'No, you can't do this, it is not the way to do it'. If you have got a problem, come and talk to the Speaker about it, but don't come marching in without a by-your-leave."

Lord Alderdice said he doubted his presence at the Assembly that day would have prevented the police raid: "I don't think I would have actually stood in front of a police officer and had him walk over me."

After making his protest to Orde, Lord Alderdice said the Chief Constable was anxious to discuss the situation and told him: "Come straight from the airport to my office. We need to talk about this." Alderdice found the Chief Constable very helpful and sympathetic: "He made it very clear that he did not think it was handled in a proper way either." Indeed, the incident led to a long series of discussions between the Speaker's officials and police about protocol and how such a situation should be handled in future. In the aftermath, the Chief Constable apologised for the way it was handled. As the full details of the raid made international headlines, it became a talking point at the Canadian Parliament. Said Alderdice: "The Parliamentarians were shocked that such a thing could happen and they said, 'There is no way that the Mounties would come into the Ottawa parliament in that kind of way without proper consultation with the Speaker and so on'."

As the raid was taking place, Sinn Féin minister Bairbre de Brun was on the scene, scolding the police officers. She was accompanied by her party colleague, Gerry Kelly, a former IRA prisoner and MLA for North Belfast. By around 10.20am, police were still searching the Sinn Féin offices, but were now being watched by de Brun, Kelly and a crowd of reporters and film crews, who had been invited into the office. At Kelly's invitation, they raced through the entrance to the West Wing, with one cameraman almost strangling himself when he got caught in the revolving doors. Kelly, who had once led an escape from the Maze prison, now headed a thirty-strong entourage, guiding them towards the lift. A dozen or so piled in amid a policeman's objections. The Sinn Féin MLA retorted: "You don't tell me what to do." When the lift stalled, an excited voice suggested the power had been cut and urged everyone to head for the stairs. This led to further chaos. "As the crowd went up the stairs, an equally excited PSNI raiding team were trying to get down," recalled reporter Steven McCaffery. De Brun then berated the police, saying: "Oh, you decide to go when the media arrive."

The First Minister's inquisitive advisor, David McNarry, had by now joined the press pack and Kelly, in a lighter moment, suggested to him that he must be moonlighting. As the cameras rolled, Kelly then told the reporters of dirty tricks by police, who took away just a few documents and a couple of computer disks in a small plastic bag. Coincidentally, the warrant for the search was signed by a Justice of the Peace named P. O'Neill, the pseudonym used by the IRA.

There were also dawn raids in other areas, mainly in the north and west of the city. The most serious allegations appeared to centre on documents taken from the NIO, which housed sensitive security information. A woman and three men were arrested during the raids. These included a former NIO employee and Denis Donaldson, who worked in the Sinn Féin office at Stormont and had been imprisoned with the republican hunger striker, Bobby Sands. Sinn Féin said that three out of the four detainees worked on a party policy group relating to policing and justice. Police sources said the raids were investigating espionage involving around a thousand documents.

The Stormont search lasted only a few hours, but the repercussions were felt for years. Even on the day of the raid there was speculation the Executive was going to be suspended. It was, said one commentator, a matter of "when, not if". Few doubted the gravity of the event. "Everybody knew it was serious," said the Enterprise minister, Sir Reg Empey. Sinn Féin claimed the raid was political, that the government had already calculated another suspension was looming and the spying allegations were being used as a pretext for suspension.

The six months leading up to Stormontgate had been nothing if not eventful. There had been a second substantial act of decommissioning in April 2002, when General de Chastelain and his fellow arms commissioners announced they had witnessed the IRA put a "varied and substantial quantity of ammunition, arms and explosive material beyond use." Reaction was similar to that which marked the first event. The Ulster Unionist leader welcomed the move and insisted his critics had been wrong when they alleged decommissioning would happen only once. "My only regret," said David Trimble, "is the IRA chooses not to make known the precise nature of what they have decommissioned." Anti-Agreement unionists however were no more satisfied with the second act of decommissioning than they were with the first. They dismissed the move as a stunt and demanded more information.

After the act of decommissioning it emerged that the IRA had honoured its republican dead in a special ceremony, which some interpreted as a sign the conflict was coming to a close. These two moves might have strengthened Trimble's hand over his unionist critics had it not been for another event that had happened just days earlier, not in Room 21 at Stormont, but in Room 220 at Castlereagh police headquarters, where sensitive Special Branch files were stored. On St Patrick's night, while most of the Northern Ireland politicians were in Washington celebrating the occasion, there was a break-in at Castlereagh. Initially, there were suspicions that it was an inside job, but by the end of the month, after a number of arrests had been made, republicans were on the defensive, issuing denials of involvement. Security sources were now alleging that the IRA, assisted by an insider, was behind the break-in. Sinn Féin's Martin McGuinness rejected this. Blaming "securocrats", he said: "I am absolutely convinced the IRA was not involved." There were further strenuous denials, from the IRA as well as from Sinn Féin figures, but the allegations persisted. When republicans were accused of targeting politicians using documents stolen from Castlereagh, Adams appeared indignant. "What hit list?" he demanded to know. "Who is circulating what - who said this? Have you seen it, can you prove it? Who killed Cock Robin? We are talking about James Bond in *From Russia With Love*. It's nonsense."

Adams' remarks further muddied the waters, as did claims in the media, which were attributed to senior security sources. One report had security sources describing the recently up-dated "hit-list" as intelligence-gathering rather than targeting, citing the fact that the details relating to former Tory politicians were already in the public domain. But another newspaper carried the names of various unionists who had been told by police that they had been targeted. One pro-Agreement unionist who received such a warning from the police was not particularly alarmed; he did not believe the Provisional IRA was about to start killing unionist politicians.

A return to violence was not so much the issue as the notion that, if the allegations regarding Castlereagh were accurate, one party in the political process still had a private army at its disposal that was acting illegally and challenging the authority and stability of the state. As a consequence, anti-Agreement unionists, post-decommissioning, found in Castlereagh an opportunity to once again question power-sharing with Sinn Féin. Jeffrey Donaldson MP persuaded the Ulster Unionist Executive to pass a motion expressing grave concerns about IRA activity in Colombia, its alleged involvement in Castlereagh and IRA gun-running in Florida. Under pressure from internal party critics, Trimble sought a motion in the Assembly at the end of April, asking the Secretary of State to make a determination on the ceasefire. Trimble believed the government had information it was not disclosing and wanted to force the Secretary of State's hand. His partner in government, Mark Durkan, had a lot less faith in the intelligence services than the Ulster Unionist leader and wanted hard evidence about the Castlereagh break-in. Furthermore, Durkan deemed it inappropriate to use the Assembly to press the Secretary of State for a determination. "That is not the Assembly's job," he declared.

Durkan would have been criticised by his own supporters if he had signed up for the motion because there had been no such motion the previous summer when loyalist paramilitaries were pipe-bombing Catholic homes. The matter put further strain on relations between Trimble and Durkan. The First Minister felt there was clear evidence that the IRA ceasefire had been breached in Colombia, but without support from the SDLP, the motion failed. The DUP tabled its own motion, seeking exclusion instead. Trimble and the DUP clashed over whether asking the Secretary of State to make a determination would do any good. The Secretary of State meanwhile attempted to reassure unionists that breaches of the ceasefire were not being ignored. On 1 May, Reid tried to assuage unionist opinion. He told the Commons that a ceasefire was not enough, that the peace process was on trial and that the Castlereagh break-in was a matter of grave concern.

Unionist confidence continued to wane however and the following month, the Ulster Unionist party's internal divisions were once again exposed. At a meeting of the party's

Executive, anti-Agreement unionists demanded a withdrawal of ministers by 1 July. Trimble opposed this, arguing that it was up to the Prime Minister to act and sanction Sinn Féin. He comfortably defeated the motion. But to the horror of Durkan and other pro-Agreement parties, he hardened his position after the meeting and warned that he might again quit as First Minister, if it "meant saving the Good Friday Agreement". While acknowledging that the deal remained the last hope for Northern Ireland, Trimble warned that circumstances could force his resignation. "If it is necessary, I'm quite happy to do it," he said.

He again appealed to Blair to act to avoid a "catastrophic lack of confidence" in the peace process. Trimble's comment that the NIO and Downing Street still lacked the courage to "tell the truth" indicated he was not getting the response he desired. Trimble called for "modest restraints", including the arrest of paramilitaries suspected of causing disturbances at interfaces that summer. He cautioned there were dangers ahead for the institutions, warning that ongoing street violence could wreck devolution. He blamed the IRA for most of the violence and demanded an end to paramilitary activity. While welcoming Sinn Féin Lord Mayor Alex Maskey's break from tradition to honour the Somme dead, it was, as far as Trimble was concerned, a half-measure. He complained that only those loyalists who had flouted the terms of their licence had been returned to prison and further alleged that the law had been subordinated for political purposes.

Trimble showed signs of being under pressure that summer. In a television interview with BBC's "Hearts and Minds", he struggled to keep his cool with presenter Noel Thompson. Criticism was escalating and at one point a loyalist website called for a picket of the "traitor's house". It was the kind of jibe that Trimble had been putting up with for years, but he showed grit when asked if he intended to lead the party into the Assembly election, declaring: "It is not just a question of intending to lead. I will lead the party. There is a job to be finished here. I intend to finish it."

Sinn Féin's Martin McGuinness claimed Trimble's concern was not Castlereagh but the Assembly election scheduled for spring 2003. He alleged the First Minister was planning to collapse power-sharing before then in order to embrace an anti-Sinn Féin agenda. McGuinness insisted republicans wanted to make peace "among ourselves" as well as with Trimble, but spoke of difficulties due to the ongoing "unresolved dispute" within the leadership of unionism. The impression from those words was that republicans were not determined to keep Trimble perpetually weak. Rather McGuinness' comments suggested the republican leadership was thinking about doing more to address his concerns regarding continuing paramilitary activity, but could not decide whether it was worth gambling on him. Certainly a senior Belfast republican said this was an issue and that they did not trust him to deliver. Even moderate nationalists were showing little faith in Trimble, questioning his real motives on power-sharing and the Agreement. "Nationalists are fed up with him," said the SDLP minister Bríd Rodgers. "Mr Trimble is fast being seen as the biggest threat to our new institutions." She accused Trimble of wanting an "each way" on the peace process.

Trimble, for his part, felt let down by the SDLP, believing nationalists were in denial about the true extent of IRA activity. He did not share their patience for giving republicanism time to change while awaiting concrete evidence of alleged IRA misdeeds.

As tensions were mounting, the IRA signalled that it was preparing to lay to rest its past by apologising to its victims, although this was selective in that it ruled out combatants in the security forces. Trimble however wanted more than words and again appealed for Blair to become the guardian of the Agreement. In the House of Commons in July, he hoped the government would issue a "red card" against the republican movement and was disappointed by the Secretary of State's "yellow card" speech. John Reid merely warned republicans that any further IRA activity would not be tolerated, specifically mentioning targeting and intelligence-gathering. While Reid's speech fell short of Trimble's demand for action, the government tried to balance this by delivering on one of Trimble's demands, promising to return with proposals for a ceasefire monitor to assess paramilitary activity independently. Republicans were angered by Reid's tone and his focus on them, coming, as it did, just a few days after loyalists murdered nineteen-year-old Catholic teenager Gerard Lawlor in North Belfast.

On the back of Reid's statement the Prime Minister offered more rhetoric, promising a motion to exclude Sinn Féin if the IRA breached its ceasefire – something unionists believed had long since happened. Trimble noted Blair's "unambiguous statement" that action would be taken, but was privately disappointed with the lack of action as assaults rained down on him from all sides: his partners in government, his internal party critics and his DUP opponents. But the matter was not as black-and-white as Trimble presented it. *The Observer* recorded that within the space of five hours on Sunday, 21 July there was one murder, four attempted murders, one wounding and two incidents of sectarian rioting in the north of the city. It also calculated that violence so far that year had amounted to ninety-six shootings, sixty-nine bombings and eighty-six explosive devices. Loyalists were responsible for the majority of these incidents. Both the SDLP and Sinn Féin wanted unionists to do more to tackle the ongoing campaign of violence being waged by some loyalist paramilitaries in the UDA. Trimble had encouraged members of his party to work with the Loyalist Commission, involving paramilitary leaders and others in a bid to stabilise loyalism. Nonetheless, nationalists felt that unionists were engaged in double standards and were more tolerant of loyalist misbehaviour

The Executive was growing increasingly unstable. This in some ways paralleled events on the ground. Under a siege, of sorts, from the DUP, the Executive won a battle for survival when Ian Paisley's party challenged the legitimacy of the First and Deputy First Ministers. This legal challenge stemmed from the day Trimble and Durkan were elected outside the six-week deadline set down in legislation. The DUP took its case all the way to the House of Lords and lost, but the decision was close enough – three to two – and was described by Peter Robinson as a hair's breadth escape for the Secretary of State and the First Minister. The Lords were persuaded by the Secretary of State's argument that as long as he had reason to believe, before his deadline ran out, that the two ministers would be jointly elected, then he was not obliged to call an Assembly poll.

The Ulster Unionists challenged the DUP to leave their Stormont ministries following their embarrassing defeat in the House of Lords. Ian Paisley refused. Hearing yet more mere promises from Blair, Paisley declared Trimble had "lost the plot" as it seemed both the First Minister and Prime Minister intended to keep Sinn Féin on board at any price. Trimble was determined to prove Paisley wrong. He began consulting widely within unionism about his party's next move and how much time he was prepared to give the government to respond. Sir Reg Empey, who was regarded as one of the party's most fervent supporters of the Agreement, spoke of a moral dilemma in sharing power with Sinn Féin.

Durkan was horrified by Trimble's tactics and called for the pro-Agreement parties to come together in an implementation group to try to manage the problems affecting the institutions. He said collapsing power-sharing was not the answer and would only serve to encourage, not discourage, the paramilitaries. Seamus Mallon weighed in and summed up the concerns of most nationalists when he expressed suspicion that unionism did not want Sinn Féin excluded as a consequence of something they had done, but as a political objective.

Hardline republicans, sensing the Agreement and its institutions were in jeopardy, stepped up their own campaign to undermine it. The Real IRA, which had been responsible for the Omagh bombing, murdered fifty-one-year-old Protestant David Caldwell, a civilian worker, who died when a booby-trap bomb exploded at the Territorial Army base in Limavady Road. Martin McGuinness condemned the killing and heaped abuse on the "militarily incompetent" Real IRA. The First and Deputy First Ministers issued a joint statement condemning the murder.

The pro-Agreement Executive members were united briefly when they supported and attended a Belfast rally against sectarianism that was organised by the trades unions. As August drew to a close, Trimble seemed more confident that devolution would last, even as his internal critics were circling once again. At a joint news conference with Durkan, he declared: "I can't see that there is any serious doubt in that." Trimble pointed out that even those purporting to be anti-Agreement remained part of the administration. He expressed confidence in retaining his leadership. Subsequently, he delighted moderates and nationalists with his remark that he was supporting the County Armagh team in its bid for the All-Ireland GAA championship at Croke Park. Armagh played in a bright orange kit, leading Trimble to joke: "I have been a supporter of Orangemen from Armagh for some time." He wished the team well, while preparing for a contest of his own: another meeting of the Ulster Unionist ruling council.

The UUC meeting had been called for 21 September. In the run-up to the meeting Trimble argued against Donaldson's demands for a power-sharing deadline to be imposed on republicans: "It's all very well to say 'set a deadline', but you have to take public opinion with you." He wrote to council delegates, arguing against an immediate withdrawal from the institutions. He urged party members to recognise the social and economic benefits of devolution and insisted that an independent paramilitary ceasefire monitor was a useful way to put pressure on the IRA. A negative report, he said, would force the government to act. While a battle of wills raged in the Ulster Unionist party, the loyalist paramilitary feud escalated.

Sensing his leadership might be lost, Trimble tried to reach a compromise with Donaldson. There was no agreement. Before the meeting Donaldson warned that the status quo was not an option. The leader and his nemesis each put their own motions to the Council at the showdown in a South Belfast hotel. The meeting did not go well for Trimble. Former supporters turned on him and he cut a deal with the anti-Agreement wing rather than risk being toppled. Donaldson looked satisfied; Trimble looked shaken.

"Move closer, Jeffrey," he said, as the unionists sat down to address the waiting media, which was not fooled by the show of unity. Trimble's weakness had been exposed that day and many insiders felt Trimble would have lost had he not moved towards Donaldson's position. The party decided to pull out of power-sharing by January 2003, and to withdraw immediately from north-south institutions. The UUP was echoing the DUP by demanding talks to discuss a "viable basis" for governing Northern Ireland.

The Deputy First Minister showed no public sympathy for Trimble's position, warning that his party would not tolerate unionist attempts to "turn the clock back". Trimble protested that he remained committed to the Good Friday Agreement, but Sinn Féin's Martin McGuinness was scathing. "David Trimble is no more than a front for the rejectionists, who are now in control," he said. Gerry Adams complained that unionists had once again pocketed concessions on the arms issue and made more impossible demands, claiming that if the IRA marched naked to Parliament Buildings, it would still not be enough for some unionists. He railed against unionism and its inability to accept change. Trimble countered that it was the republican failure to change that was at issue. He said Sinn Féin was crying crocodile tears while the IRA's nocturnal activities posed the most serious threat.

While the DUP renewed its call for renegotiations, the British and Irish governments announced talks to "take stock". The DUP failed to pass a motion calling for fresh elections in the Assembly, where the business of government continued. In the thick of the crisis, the Assembly Finance minister announced that the Executive had agreed a three-year draft Budget for the first time, allowing for 3% increases in spending overall, and a matching Programme for Government was also unveiled.

With unionists withdrawing from the north-south institutions, Durkan was said to be weighing his options, one of which was pulling out of the Executive immediately rather than waiting for the unionists to collapse Stormont in January. Trimble accused the SDLP of hysterical over-reaction. The First and Deputy First Ministers turned on each other in public. Each blamed the other for ignoring the violence of the paramilitaries from their own side of the community.

The centre was barely holding when Stormontgate erupted on 4 October. At the time, the Secretary of State was in Blackpool at the Labour party conference, where former US President Bill Clinton was a special guest. The day before, Reid had delivered yet another tough message to republicans, warning that they could not continue to ride two horses, but had to make the journey to democracy. It was the second such message since July.

Following the raid, Empey was furious to learn that one of the men arrested, William Mackessy, had worked in his office and he had been given no warning. The suspect had, in fact, been transferred from the NIO to the headquarters of the Industrial Development Board (now Invest Northern Ireland). Empey claimed that, as a messenger, Mackessy would, on occasion, have had the keys to IDB House, where the minister sometimes worked. Sir Empey claimed the man had in fact served in his private office on 8 September. After the raid, staff informed him that Mackessy was among those arrested:

> "I was sitting there open-mouthed and then I sent for his file. His file was clear.
> I asked Reid's private office for an explanation as to why we were not advised

[about him]. We never received a response. I felt the NIO must have known what was happening, but they couldn't prove it either because they hadn't sufficient evidence or witnesses wouldn't testify. It was our understanding witnesses wouldn't testify. So they shipped him out quite deliberately. They got him out of the road."

Sir Empey was not sure if he had ever spoken to, or encountered the suspect: "I might have done, I don't know."

All of those arrested protested their innocence. Gerry Adams and Bairbre de Brun were among those present at Denis Donaldson's initial court hearing, which was held amid tight security. The court heard that police had uncovered highly sensitive documents in a rucksack at Donaldson's home, which, it was claimed, contained personal details of known loyalists and serving police officers, as well as documents of a restricted nature originating from government offices. His co-accused, Fiona Farrelly, was accused of being in possession of a laptop computer "which could be useful to terrorists" and also having the personal details of full-time employees of the Northern Ireland prison service. Charges against her were later withdrawn. On 9 October, William Mackessy was charged with two counts of having documents likely to be of use to terrorists. Ciaran Kearney, Donaldson's son-in-law, was charged on five counts of possession of information likely to be of use to terrorists. In early 2004, some of the charges against Kearney and Donaldson were withdrawn due to lack of evidence. "The Special Branch fantasy of a Stormont spy-ring has finally been disproved," said Kearney on the day. Although a number of charges against these individuals were subsequently withdrawn due to lack of evidence, they still face a total of seven charges connected with this affair.

Sinn Féin claimed Stormontgate was a political red-herring, designed to ensure unionism did not get the blame for the suspension, which had become inevitable after the Council decision in September. Sinn Féin alleged that Stormont had been raided merely to ensure that the Assembly and the party were very clearly tied into the spying allegations, both at home and abroad. The newspaper, *An Phoblacht*, carried the headline: "Spies, spooks and Special Branch," and alleged securocrats in Special Branch were attempting to marginalise Sinn Féin, in order to prevent further changes to policing, by demonising the IRA and creating "McCarthy-type hysteria". The newspaper alleged a "witch-hunt" against Catholic civil servants and wondered why the DUP, which had at times been in possession of confidential information over the years, had never been punished. Sinn Féin also demanded to know why police had not conducted a more thorough search of the party's office. When a computer disk was returned to Sinn Féin within days, McGuinness brandished it at a news conference in the Great Hall, challenging the authorities to explain why other material in the office was ignored and declaring his opposition to any activity that would undermine "the people's institutions". Nothing incriminating was found at Sinn Féin's Stormont office.

Once more the First and Deputy First Minister found themselves on opposing sides. In the immediate aftermath there was confusion within nationalism, traditionally suspicious of the police and MI5, about what was actually going on. The SDLP's Assembly team met a few days after the raid and, according to an insider, some members were angry at the way it had been handled by police, leading to questions about the party's continued involvement on the policing board. A source said Joe Byrne, who sat on the board, told the Assembly team there should be no knee-jerk reaction.

Trimble was upset that he had not been informed earlier that the government suspected an IRA spy-ring was operating at Stormont. He declared that the government must now act, pointing to the promises given in Parliament in July. With his party demanding Sinn Féin's removal from office and a get-tough policy on republicans, Trimble accused Sinn Féin of a massive political conspiracy, ten times worse than Watergate. "The immediate future of the Assembly is unclear," he said, "but there are a number of nuclear options." At the same time he publicly chided Jeffrey Donaldson for predicting collapse and, quoting former Prime Minister Clement Atlee, declared: "A period of silence from you would be helpful."

The First Minister met the Prime Minister on 8 October. He gave Blair one week to act, after which he would withdraw from power-sharing. Blair knew Trimble meant it. The First Minister did not want suspension, which would remove all the parties from office; he wanted power-sharing to continue without Sinn Féin. Blair weighed his options. He could suspend the institutions, or he could do what Trimble wanted and have Sinn Féin excluded. The Good Friday Agreement allowed for Sinn Féin's exclusion if a majority of nationalists and a majority of unionists agreed. Getting the unionists to agree was easy, but the SDLP, which commanded a nationalist majority at Stormont, were not going to be persuaded quite so easily, and certainly not without evidence of actual wrong-doing. With Trimble's deadline looming, Blair met the SDLP leader in Downing Street and sounded him out. Durkan recalled that the Prime Minister asked him if he would back a motion of exclusion. "I said, 'Are you putting a motion for exclusion?" Blair replied: 'I asked you first.'" Durkan maintained he had no basis for such a motion and told him he had no intention of signing up to one. "[It's] not on," he told Blair.

The conversation, according to Durkan, then turned to the possibility of the Secretary of State proposing a motion and evidence for exclusion. Durkan claimed the Prime Minister told him he had evidence, but there was no point in putting it if the SDLP were not going to vote for exclusion. The Prime Minster, he said, referred to the allegations surrounding Stormontgate and "other things" in the background, trying to make a cumulative argument for exclusion. But Durkan demanded to know why had had not heard of this evidence before, if it represented grounds for exclusion. According to Durkan, Blair repeated his central point: "He said, 'We won't table one unless you say you would support it,' and I said, 'It doesn't sound to me that you have strong evidence or conviction on this.' [Blair] knew where we stood on this." Durkan said that in subsequent negotiations when Blair pressed him about voluntary coalition with the DUP and Ulster Unionists, he challenged Blair, telling him that there would be no point as the government would continue to undermine the SDLP with secret negotiations with Sinn Féin. "The Prime Minister told me, 'You are very cynical. We'll have to do something about your cynicism, Mark.' I told him to check the record."

Without convincing evidence, Durkan was not prepared to turn what he called a serious crisis into an historic disaster and exclude Sinn Féin from the Executive – a move that risked the breakdown of the IRA ceasefire. Although Durkan acknowledged that continued unionist involvement in power-sharing was untenable in the circumstances, the

SDLP had long maintained it would not abandon the inclusive nature of the Executive, as outlined by the Good Friday Agreement. Durkan argued this was not out of fear of the electorate – or a need to keep the nationalist consensus, noting that his party had broken from republicans on the policing issue. In November 2002 Durkan told the story of Blair's private proposal for an exclusion motion in an interview with the BBC's "Inside Politics" programme. A republican suggested that by doing so, he had opened a "hornet's nest". Downing Street tried to play down the significance of the conversation, suggesting Blair was obliged to explore all options. It was debatable whether Blair was going through the motions, or whether he would actually have gone down the route he outlined to Durkan. One SDLP source said the Prime Minister was hoping to shift the blame for exclusion away from his own government, which was not prepared to take the risk of falling out with the IRA: "He was trying to get Mark to take the heat, but at the same time he wouldn't do it himself. The Prime Minister admitted to Durkan that he wouldn't do it himself."

As time went on, some in the SDLP became more convinced that there was some substance to the spying allegations, but could not prove it. At the time of the raid, there was considerable confusion. What was clear was that this problem would not be solved by an act of decommissioning. What little trust there had been within the Executive evaporated after Stormontgate: unionists firmly believed republicans had acted in bad faith.

The events at Stormont coincided with the start of the trial of three alleged IRA men in Colombia, and a savage attack on a man who was beaten with a sledge-hammer by ten masked men in South Armagh. Burdened with these developments, claims surrounding Castlereagh and the weakening position of the Ulster Unionist leader, the Assembly began to sink. The Ulster Unionist party felt a mixture of resignation and disillusion, but no shock. Stephen Barr recalled: "Within the party there had always been people asking questions: are Sinn Féin serious? Is the war over and is this for real?" The pro-Agreement wing felt badly let down by republicans. "We played the game," said Barr.

For the DUP, it was a case of "I told you so". Initially the DUP demanded all Assembly business be suspended so the crisis could be debated. Someone stuck a sign outside a window at Stormont, punctuated with a pound sign and posing the question: "Why is the DUP still here£". Within a few days and after a debate on the crisis, the DUP announced it was abandoning ship, perhaps sensing that Stormont was doomed. "The process is in tatters," one member declared.

In his last days as First Minister, and accompanied by Stormont minister Michael McGimpsey, Trimble went to see Taoiseach Bertie Ahern in Dublin. The two unionist ministers made clear to Ahern that suspension was not right, that the exclusion of Sinn Féin was the only fair way to proceed. But on Sunday, 13 October, John Reid telephoned Gerry Adams with the news that he was suspending the institutions the following morning. He made the announcement at Hillsborough, just ahead of Trimble's 15 October deadline and just as five suspected IRA men appeared in a Dublin court following arrests that weekend. When Reid signed the order suspending Stormont, twenty-two pieces of legislation were in the pipeline. The institutions were frozen at midnight on 14 October: history in the un-making.

Reid was pictured that same day with his new direct rule line-up, all careful to look glum. He dismissed speculation about joint authority and the notion of the First and Deputy First Ministers reverting to shadow mode, which was thought to be Trimble's desire. He said his preference was for devolution. But Empey formed the view that Dr Reid was relishing being a Secretary of State with all the powers that devolution had given the Assembly: "I got the clear impression that John saw he was going to be emperor and he was going to be an interventionist Secretary of State, not like Paul Murphy." As it happened, he did not get the chance. Events in London saw Reid returned to Westminster, where he took up the post of Secretary of Health. In the days after Stormontgate, Reid was of the view that suspension was going to last a few years, given the fallout still to come from Castlereagh, Colombia and Stormontgate. "It's chronic," he was said to have commented privately.

The parallels with Sunningdale could not be ignored. The Sunningdale Executive was abandoned on 28 May 1974 after violent unrest and polarising of the unionist and nationalist communities. Now, the devolved Executive, forged on the cusp of a new millennium with so much hope and optimism, had been irreparably damaged by Stormontgate. Whether real or imagined, Stormontgate ultimately destroyed what little trust had been built up between unionists and nationalists. The Executive met for the last time on 3 October 2002, the day before the raid on Sinn Féin's office. Whereas the final death throes of Sunningdale were accompanied by public rioting, the forces that overcame the millennium Stormont were much quieter: there was barely a whimper when it ceased. "There was just," said Sir Reg Empey, "this smouldering resentment."

Postscript

One year after Stormontgate, Tony Blair looked around the table at the stony faces of David Trimble and his party delegation. It was the Prime Minister's first meeting with the Ulster Unionist leadership since their disastrous Assembly election of November 2003. Conducted just days earlier, the Assembly poll had delivered stunning victories for the DUP and Sinn Féin, leaving the Ulster Unionists and the SDLP trailing in third and fourth places, respectively. This forfeited any claim the UUP and SDLP may have laid to speaking for the majority unionist and nationalist communities – and any claim David Trimble or Mark Durkan once had to the First and Deputy First Ministers' posts. Trimble had long warned Blair of this "nightmare scenario", a view shared by his old partner in government, Seamus Mallon, who believed Northern Ireland was heading for a dangerous balkanisation, with the unionist and nationalist extremes carving up the region as they pleased.

Blair knew Trimble had been humiliated and furthermore that Trimble blamed him and the Labour government's handling of the peace process. Trimble had warned the Prime Minister time and again what would happen to the UUP if he did not insist that republicans put an end to all IRA activity and embrace a purely democratic future.

Now the Ulster Unionists, at their lowest ebb, joined the Prime Minister at the table in his office at Number 10 Downing Street. Blair was determined to acknowledge the Ulster Unionist contribution to the peace process and how it had suffered as a result. He also wanted to focus attention on what should happen post-election to move the process forward. But as the Ulster Unionist delegation waited for him to speak, Blair, perhaps gathering his thoughts, had an expression that Trimble took to be a grin. "Why are you laughing?" Trimble, not remotely amused, demanded to know.

Blair was taken aback, and one Downing Street source felt Trimble had perhaps misinterpreted Blair's body language. Dermot Nesbitt felt Blair was lost for words in the face of accusing stares from unionists and recalled the Prime Minister grinning, in a disarming way, shrugging his shoulders in a manner that suggested: "What else can I say?"

Nesbitt felt it eased the mood.

Blair had tried in vain to restore devolution after Stormontgate, but it all went spectacularly wrong when his carefully choreographed deal fell apart. It was the Prime Minister himself who had set the tone for the post-Stormontgate negotiations. Three days after the Assembly's suspension on 14 October 2002, Blair had visited Belfast and delivered his "fork-in-the-road" speech. He declared the IRA was the primary impediment to progress, insisting the process could not move forward while the organisation remained armed and active. Signalling his impatience with republicans, Blair insisted they had to choose between democracy and violence and called for a bold move, a quantum leap, from the IRA, one that went beyond decommissioning. Although he did not use the word disbandment, his words suggested he wanted the IRA to shut up shop for good: "We cannot carry on with the IRA half in and half out of this process. Not just because it isn't right any more. It won't work any more."

The Prime Minister contended that minus the threat of violence, the peace process would be on an unstoppable course. He coined a new phrase for a new phase in the process: acts of completion. Thus the emphasis moved from words to actions. Blair promised to complete the implementation of the Agreement if republicans completed their transition.

Trimble welcomed Blair's speech because it put the blame for the stalemate on the IRA. Republicans did not reject the Prime Minister's demands, but used the opportunity to outline what the government had to do if the IRA were to leave the stage: conclude the demilitarisation process, provide more policing reform, safeguard the institutions, introduce more measures on equality, human rights and justice, and agree an effective amnesty for republicans on the run from the law.

In spite of the fact that the Prime Minister had ruled out "inch by inch" negotiations, it took almost a year before Blair had both unionists and republicans signed up to yet another deal aimed at restoring devolution. This followed an aborted attempt at a deal in spring 2003, when Trimble rejected an offer from republicans, deeming it insufficient. At the time it was whispered that there was discontent within the republican camp regarding the failure to conclude a deal at that point. Some saw it as a missed opportunity. One republican source suggested there was friction among the republican leadership and claimed that Martin McGuinness was annoyed that the deal involving acts of completion had not been done then. McGuinness, said the source, saw clearly the benefits of power-sharing and felt that Gerry Adams, who was perhaps less enthusiastic about the Executive, had been too cautious about taking risks in the negotiations and delivering a conclusive end to the IRA and a new beginning to policing. McGuinness denied this was the case: "There's not a blade of grass between Gerry Adams and me." The same republican source insisted there was a feeling that spring that the republican leadership had "blown it".

If Adams was being cautious, it may have been because there were tensions within the ranks of the IRA. It had begun to dawn on grass-roots republicans that the process ultimately meant the end of the IRA, with no guarantees of a united Ireland on the horizon.

While managing the IRA may well have been part of the problem, there could also have been a difference of opinion on future strategy, a disagreement that went beyond the question of the continued existence of the IRA and its right to retain "armed struggle" as a viable option for achieving its goals. Perhaps Adams did not share McGuinness' enthusiasm for a return to Stormont as the best means of securing Irish unity. There was, after all, Plan B – to force the British and Irish governments to conclude that Northern Ireland was unworkable in its present state and to forge a deal over the heads of unionists that would effectively deliver joint authority. If that were in fact the plan, then republicans might have been offering just enough compromise to deflect blame, leaving the unionists at the mercy of two resentful governments.

Those who support this theory point out that Gerry Adams had not taken a ministerial portfolio, choosing instead to focus on building Sinn Féin as an all-Ireland party. Adams rarely attended Assembly debates and his visits to Parliament were relatively infrequent. There was a suspicion that Adams saw risks in power-sharing, in settling for Stormont and equality within the state. If Northern Ireland worked as a separate entity, why would anyone need, or demand, a united Ireland? Is that a question republicans asked themselves at this time? Did republicans wonder whether making Northern Ireland work was in their best interests when there was no guarantee it would be a stepping-stone to Irish unity? Might republicans have concluded their best interests lay in proving the state was dysfunctional, incapable of accommodating nationalists, calculating the two governments would be forced to impose an all-Ireland agenda? Perhaps republicans were always hedging their bets – keeping devolution as Plan A and joint authority as Plan B?

What is clear is that by autumn 2003 the threads of the spring devolution deal had been re-woven and all sides believed they had reached an understanding regarding what was required. Their agreement was due to be unveiled in a series of choreographed steps on 21 October 2003, but it came apart at the seams within a few hours that day, for reasons that are still not entirely clear. The SDLP's Mark Durkan summed it up succinctly: "There was hype in the morning, hope in the afternoon and a debacle in the evening."

The choreographed day crucially began with confirmation from the government, at 7.00am, that an Assembly election would take place on 26 November 2003. This prompted the Sinn Féin leader to call a news conference in the Balmoral Hotel in Belfast and issue a statement on republican intentions. Adams declared that the full implementation of the Agreement, by parties and governments, would allow republicans to pursue their objectives peacefully, thus providing "full and final closure of the conflict". Adams also expressed republican opposition to the use or threat of force for any political means. The IRA then made its statement, asserting that Adams' remarks accurately reflected the organisation's position.

However, the cross-referencing was a bit complex for unionists, who were seeking clear, unequivocal statements from the IRA. Anti-Agreement unionists dismissed the words as nothing new, insisting they needed deeds, not conditional statements. When the statements from Adams and the IRA failed to lift the unionist mood, Trimble and his party knew their only hope lay in what the IICD and General John de Chastelain had to say about IRA decommissioning.

This particular nut had been cracked, as Martin McGuinness would say, in terms of securing IRA cooperation with the IICD, and General de Chastelain and his two IICD colleagues were working closely with an IRA representative following two acts of decommissioning. Despite this "action", unionists were dissatisfied. They demanded to see the decommissioning for themselves, complaining that the process was too confidential. As a result, "transparent decommissioning" became the panacea for building unionist confidence. Trimble hoped that republicans' words – matched by visible action – would transform attitudes in unionism and create the conditions necessary to strengthen his party's mandate and restore devolution. Republicans, on the other hand – perhaps anxious not to unsettle their own supporters with any whiff of surrender – wanted a veiled process involving only the IICD, as outlined in the Good Friday Agreement.

A few hours after Adams' Balmoral Hotel speech, the Ulster Unionist leader had still not responded. It was planned that Trimble would speak after General de Chastelain's statement – not before. This turned out to be critical.

Trimble and a coterie of influential UUP members gathered at their headquarters in East Belfast to await the next, crucial step in the sequencing. Those present included Sir Reg Empey, Michael McGimpsey and Lady Sylvia Hermon, MP for North Down. The Ulster Unionists, who had been expecting transparent decommissioning, were dismayed as they watched the live press conference unfold. While the General did announce that he had witnessed a third – and substantial – act of decommissioning by the IRA, and gave more detail than ever before, he also declared he was bound by the IRA's insistence on confidentiality. The more questions directed at the General from reporters, the more obvious it became that he had little to say. With each word he uttered, the sense of despair at unionist headquarters increased. "There was pandemonium," recalled one unionist.

General de Chastelain was a soldier, not a politician. As a man of his word, he was not going to spin, or break a confidence – much as he may have liked to. Although he was able to say that what he had witnessed was a considerably larger event than previous acts of decommissioning, there was no gloss as he talked about witnessing the destruction of light, medium and heavy ordnance, including explosives, automatic weapons and other materials. The General's fellow arms commissioner, American Andrew Sens, realised the public relations disaster that was unfolding and tried to make the presentation more positive by suggesting that the amount of weapons put beyond use could have caused death and destruction on a huge scale had they been used. His efforts were in vain.

As a group of reporters assembled at UUP headquarters waiting to hear a prepared statement on power-sharing from Trimble, the party leader and his fellow Ulster Unionists were gathered around a conference table in glum silence. The eerie calm was broken by McGimpsey's rhetorical question: "David, we can't go with this?" The Ulster Unionists concluded it was not too late to the pull the plug on the deal, and on Trimble's prepared statement on power-sharing. Accordingly, Trimble went and told the media that the sequence was on hold. Even in retrospect, McGimpsey did not feel it would have been better to have gone ahead with a flawed deal than none at all – but felt an earlier, better opportunity had been missed in the spring of that year.

Having called off the choreography, Trimble went to Hillsborough for several hours of talks with the government and Sinn Féin in the hope of fixing the problem. No resolution was achieved, however; the IRA refused point-blank to allow an inventory of decommissioned weapons to be published. Nor was the issue resolved in the days that followed. Instead, Adams warned of profound difficulties following Trimble's refusal to proceed and insisted he could do no more. The Prime Minister – not wanting to alienate Adams and perhaps now impatient with Trimble's change of mind – refused to call off the Assembly poll.

On the night of the failed deal a Sinn Féin source privately tried to suggest Trimble had double-crossed republicans. Perhaps this was how republicans genuinely saw the problem: they had delivered decommissioning and Trimble had failed to deliver his party. However, a white-faced Trimble looked like a man in deep shock that evening, and certainly did not have the demeanour of a cocky politician who had put one over on his opponent.

Others suspected republicans had double-crossed Trimble for cynical party advantage, knowingly delivering a deal that was good enough for Blair but not for the UUP. Those who espouse this theory believe the real republican agenda, post-ceasefire, was to expose unionism as being incapable of compromise. By this reckoning, republicans had sought to break the umbilical cord between the British government and the Ulster Unionists, severing the close links between London and unionism. To do this, London had to become frustrated with the Ulster Unionist leadership, thereby pushing unionists further towards an all-Ireland state. Essentially a weak UUP would mean a weak state – a state republicans had vowed to destroy. If this was the plan, Trimble proved problematic because he showed flexibility, willingness to compromise and a belief in power-sharing. As a result he had strengthened relations with London and the Prime Minister, who at times tried to protect him. Trimble's determination to avoid alienating London and to avoid joint authority was based on his belief that if Northern Ireland worked, its place within the union would be more secure and nationalists would settle for equality within the state, perhaps abandoning demands for all-Ireland state.

Republicans might have decided Trimble was no longer a convenient bedfellow, that he was too clever, too unpredictable and too close to Downing Street. Certainly they were frustrated that he exploited his weak standing within unionism to gain London's backing for his position and to slow some changes unpalatable to unionists, even as he pledged support for power-sharing. If Sinn Féin had both a Plan A and a Plan B, the party might have decided Trimble did not fit into either of them. Sinn Féin might have concluded that as long as Blair had a unionist leader who appeared willing to share power, he would not implement the Agreement in full for fear of losing pro-Agreement unionism. Perhaps Sinn Féin decided that Trimble was not going to deliver stable devolution, but would continue to block Plan B. Had republicans decided the DUP was a better bet: strong enough to bring about power-sharing; or inflexible enough to alienate Blair and force him to make changes over the heads of unionists, just as Margaret Thatcher had done in 1985 through the Anglo-Irish Agreement? Did republicans engineer an election in November 2003 that would bring the DUP to power? And to what end – to tame Ian Paisley's party by wooing them into power-sharing, or to split unionism once again between the fundamentalists and the pragmatists?

Were republicans that calculating – or merely reactive?

It may have been a case of Trimble expecting the maximum and Sinn Féin delivering the minimum. Trimble may have relied too heavily on the Prime Minister and his chief negotiator, Jonathan Powell, thus failing to pin down the precise details of the decommissioning element. One republican suggested Trimble knew the parameters of what was agreed, while another wondered, from that remark, if he knew every detail. Trimble said it was not true that he knew the parameters; rather, he said, he made republicans aware of the parameters of what was required. He likened the scenario to the Mitchell Review when he told republicans "that things were only sustainable if they followed through." Trimble also suggested he was not told details by Sinn Féin as the leadership was indicating the decisions on detail would be taken by others, suggesting Sinn Féin was always hiding behind the IRA. Said Trimble: "I developed a response to that [by saying] that this has to be happen and if it doesn't happen then that is going to happen and it is tied down as far as I am concerned and if they didn't deliver it [the sequencing] wouldn't continue." For this reason, Trimble said he insisted on speaking only after Adams and General de Chastelain, leaving him with the option of calling off the choreography if republicans failed to deliver.

There were signs even before the sequencing was put in motion that all was not well – signs others seemed to read clearly. Taoiseach Bertie Ahern was reported to have become anxious about the decommissioning element and, fearful it was not going to be enough for Trimble, had tried in vain to get the sequencing postponed while it was sorted out.

Sinn Féin has always insisted, and continues to insist, that it wanted power-sharing to work while the unionists did not. Some republicans have admitted privately to making mistakes, but they still largely blame Trimble for the failure of devolution because he either would not or could not deliver unionism. They complain that Trimble was too weak, too impulsive and too willing to swing through Stormont's revolving doors and quit power-sharing. Republicans insist they were always suspicious of Trimble's motives, believing his real goal was power-sharing with the SDLP alone. They feel he did not want power-sharing with Sinn Féin, therefore his strategy all along was based on giving London and Dublin the impression of being agreeable while hoping republicans would fail to pass the democratic test. Trimble, republicans claim, intended to proceed in an Executive without them. They further claim that he never fully embraced the Agreement.

Did the fault lie primarily with David Trimble? Perhaps the real fault lay ultimately with Tony Blair: was he prepared to pay any price for power-sharing and settle too quickly for less than was required by unionists; were his fine words about choosing between war and peace merely spin to be discarded as soon as the republicans blinked slightly; or did he simply accept that the transition from peace to democracy was going to take longer than unionists realised? Some might conclude that blame lay with all the players, that there was a complex combination of errors on all sides, which resulted in the suspension of power-sharing.

It is a matter for historians to debate.

In truth, Adams and McGuinness were formidable opponents. These were the politicians George W. Bush had once privately described as "the hard dudes". While pursuing peace, they also fought the old battles, just as unionists did, trying to gain maximum advantage. Whether or not they sought to create crisis, they certainly knew how to turn it to their advantage. Trimble made gains from turning some crises to his own advantage also, having achieved three acts of decommissioning. However, it was Sinn Féin and the DUP, not the Ulster Unionists, who gained electorally from this.

Sinn Féin won sympathy among nationalists as the "thwarted peacemakers" by continuing to insist that the fault lay with Trimble and "bigoted unionism". The party's key arguments have proved persuasive at the polls: Trimble failed to embrace the process; Trimble tried to turn the devolution tap on and off when it suited him; Trimble could have obtained his goals had he committed himself wholeheartedly to power-sharing. A common charge was that Trimble failed to sell the Agreement to his people. This accusation Trimble found particularly galling. He insisted that it was his backing for the deal that split his party and cost him electorally.

A more accurate criticism, perhaps, is that he may have been simply a poor salesman – too honest and too quick to point out the flaws in his product. His critics said this was because he did not believe in it, or his belief in it came too late. Brian Feeney of *The Irish*

News put it another away, maintaining that Trimble would privately tell the Sinn Féin leadership that he wanted the process to work, but would publicly speak and act as if he was an anti-Agreement unionist, wrongly believing this would bring him safety when it actually had the opposite effect, sowing confusion and contempt. Ian Paisley summed up Trimble's dilemma in an Assembly debate in April 2002: "Every time the leader of the Ulster Unionist party indicts the IRA, he is indicting himself."

Trimble had a thornier problem than the leaders of nationalism, whose people were supportive of the Agreement. Trimble faced unionist opposition to the Agreement from day one: he had a formidable task persuading unionists to share power while the IRA remained armed. Consequently, he ended up fighting a war on two fronts, one with Sinn Féin and one with the DUP and other anti-Agreement unionists within his own party. Faulkner's burden, it could be argued, was lighter as he did not have to make peace with Sinn Féin.

Sam Foster echoed many unionists' thoughts when he blamed republicans for the problems within the process. He derided their insatiable demands and their failure to abandon their violent past and adhere to the Mitchell Principles. However, he acknowledged his party, too, had make mistakes: "We spent too much time trying to define the negative and not projecting the positive – the fact that in 1997 republicans were saying 'No Stormont', but there was Stormont resurrected with the government flag flying and legislation going through with Royal assent." A senior member of the DUP stated frankly that Trimble's failure was a failure of salesmanship. The DUP, he said, painted a black picture of the political process and the Agreement, while Trimble (perhaps more accurately) painted it grey instead of white. The DUP man declared: "Go for government completely and absolutely, no-holds-barred, and the people will either love you or hate you totally."

The DUP, some have argued, played a relatively minor role in bringing down Stormont compared to that played by the pro-Agreement politicians. After all, a house divided cannot stand. James Kelly, the *Irish News* columnist who chronicled the battles between unionists and republicans, concluded the faultline was the gap between expectations following the signing of the Agreement. The unionist and republican leaderships had wildly different ideas about the timescale for the dissolution of the IRA: Trimble wanted a short timescale; the IRA wanted time. While Kelly concluded that Trimble did not always help himself, he expressed some sympathy for his position: "David Trimble did his best and the IRA did not help him at critical times."

Trimble's supporters insisted he was right to be sceptical. Trimble himself was quick to point out that Sinn Féin abstained on the day of the Good Friday Agreement vote and noted that at a subsequent Ard Fheis the party endorsed the leadership's strategy rather than the Agreement itself.

How, then, could he be sure of their intentions? How was he supposed to build trust amid reports the IRA was still recruiting? Amid allegations of gun-running in Colombia? Amid court proceedings pertaining to the Florida gun-smuggling operation? And amid the alleged involvement of the IRA in the Castlereagh break-in? All of these elements naturally undermined the process. Republicans have attempted to blame the securocrats for these allegations, but many do not accept this. One might ask, however: were these events, in the republican mind, a consequence of unionist scepticism and lack of enthusiasm for power-sharing – or justification for it?

As for Stormontgate, just what were republicans up to? Was there a covert IRA spying operation at Stormont? Or was it drawn into the controversy in order to create a context for suspicion? One veteran republican said the description of "a spy ring" was over-the-top. He claimed that the "spying" was in fact the leadership's way of managing the situation – all part of the "constructive ambiguity" used by the republican leadership to keep the IRA involved in the peace process and in power-sharing at Stormont while partition was still in place: "It was nudge nudge, wink wink, 'See we are in here and the lads are still here'. That kind of nonsense. That's my view on it." But it was not just unionists who refused to accept this benign explanation. Over time some senior members of the SDLP became convinced the IRA was, in fact, engaged in a spying operation.

Whatever the truth, Trimble entered the election of 2003 at a serious disadvantage. The collapsed deal tainted him: instead of looking like a weak negotiator, he looked like a seriously bad one. What is more, unionist voters went to the polls with memories of Stormontgate still fresh in their minds. Trimble was unable to exploit the success of securing three acts of decommissioning and sounded as negative as the DUP when he pointed up the lack of detail in the arms process. A more effective strategy might have been to focus on the trustworthiness of the IICD and to argue that even the DUP had not questioned General de Chastelain's integrity.

While devastating, the poll result was not as bad as some in the UUP had feared. Although the DUP overtook the Ulster Unionists, the party remained only a few seats behind Ian Paisley's party. The DUP won 30 seats; the Ulster Unionists 27. However, this was followed by the defection of three Ulster Unionists to the DUP, changing the score to 33 for the DUP and 24 for the Ulster Unionists. Trimble's nemesis, MP Jeffrey Donaldson, now an Assembly member, realised he could not beat Trimble and so joined the team that could, defecting to the DUP taking with him two other Assembly members.

Even then, the UUP might have had a chance of recovery at the Westminster polls had Trimble quit the leadership at that point and allowed a new team to take control. But Trimble refused to go. He reasoned that he was now in a position to rebuild, noting that his party had fared better at the November 2003 poll than the SDLP, which had been humiliated into fourth place and had struggled to get 16 elected, many seats only coming its way on the last count. Trimble decided to view the election result as a sign that his party was well-placed for a comeback, and was convinced he was the person to lead the charge. Lord Deedes, a Conservative peer, once spoke with admiration of Trimble's determination never to give up: "Anyone can bicycle downwind. It's bicycling uphill, upwind that tests a man, and by that test Trimble scores." But one embittered party colleague, a pro-Agreement unionist and one-time Trimble supporter, held it was not determination that kept Trimble going: "It was arrogance, arrogance. Arrogance kept him going." Others were kinder. "Trimble's mistake," said a loyal supporter, "was that he mistook stubbornness for perserverance."

In time, Trimble came to regret his decision not to quit the leadership after the Assembly poll of 2003. Instead he held on until the Westminster poll of 2005, when he endured a crushing defeat – much worse than that of the Assembly election. He not only lost his own seat in Upper Bann to the DUP but his party lost all its seats bar one.

Trimble's leadership came to an end, but he maintained he had lasted longer than other unionist leaders and, in his view, had accomplished more. His supporters insist history will credit him. The DUP deputy leader Peter Robinson has criticised Trimble for corrupting and prejudicing the Union, but Trimble's supporters insist he secured the Union, put country before party, for which actions history will judge him kindly, whatever his personal flaws. Michael McGimpsey insisted:

> "We did the right thing. Northern Ireland is a more prosperous, peaceful society than at any other time since Carson. It was about peace and that's the reality. You can say what you like about David Trimble. He produced a strong union based on the consent principle, a more stable, prosperous union."

While Trimble was often compared to Faulkner, there are also parallels with Faulkner's SDLP partner, Lord Fitt. Both lost their tribes through the delicate art of compromise and both reached perhaps not dissimilar conclusions about the Union. Fitt never felt concerned about being in the nationalist minority at Stormont and Westminster in the late 1960s, having decided that the Union was doomed as long as unionists refused to accept and apply British standards of equality and democracy to Northern Ireland. Later, Trimble realised that the Union would only be strengthened when nationalists themselves believed they had achieved those standards, hence his much-overlooked statement in 1998 that he envisaged a pluralist Parliament for a pluralist people. Alex Kane, the Ulster Unionist commentator, concluded that Trimble had been good for unionism, even though, as leader, he had to endure being a human punchbag:

> "He shifted unionism from the margins, where it had been almost semi-comatose for two decades and put it back in the heart of UK politics. It's not fair to say he did not entirely embrace the Good Friday Agreement. There are occasions when more solid movement from the IRA would have made our job easier."

As for the others who stepped into Room 21 in 1999, their fortunes since then have been mixed. Seamus Mallon retired as an MP in 2005 and bade farewell to Westminster. The SDLP's Dominic Bradley fought to defend the seat, but failed, and it was taken by Sinn Féin MLA Conor Murphy. This was yet another body-blow to the party that had delivered the Agreement in 1998. But the SDLP did have other successes in the 2005 poll, which gave cause for optimism: the party kept its South Down seat and gained a seat in South Belfast. Crucially, Mark Durkan successfully defended Foyle, John Hume's old seat, against a concerted attack by Sinn Féin; in the words of Foyle Ulster Unionist Earl Storey, Durkan stopped a juggernaut. Professionally, this was a turning-point for Durkan, allowing him to emerge from Hume's shadow. Personally, 2005 was also a memorable year for Durkan as he and his wife celebrated the birth of their first and much longed for baby, Dearbháil Sarah Isobel Durkan, who was born on 10 January.

Bríd Rodgers retired in 2003, devastated by the party's worst-ever election, but took great satisfaction from the 2005 results, which came just a few months after she celebrated her seventieth birthday.

Sean Farren continued to wage unsuccessful battles with Ian Paisley in elections in North Antrim. In the 2005 general election he was outpolled by Sinn Féin's candidate. He remains a firm champion of the Good Friday Agreement and continues to serve as senior negotiator for the party, under Durkan's leadership.

Michael McGimpsey faced the disappointment of losing his bid for Westminster in 2005. The South Belfast seat went to the SDLP's Alasdair McDonnell, who succeeded Rodgers as deputy leader of the party. McGimpsey came third in the bruising race for South Belfast, behind the DUP candidate. McGimpsey's loss was, in part, due to his party's continued in-fighting. The out-going Ulster Unionist MP Martin Smyth, an anti-Agreement unionist, was pictured in the DUP campaign literature along with former Ulster Unionist leader Lord Molyneaux. McGimpsey, who had been tipped as a possible successor to David Trimble, declined to stand for the leadership.

After Trimble's departure, Sir Reg Empey was elected leader of the Ulster Unionist Party. In June 2005 Empey won the leadership in a too-close-for-comfort contest with the North Down Ulster Unionist Alan McFarland: the vote was 321 to 287. A few months later he surprised some observers when he aligned himself with the DUP leader Ian Paisley in support of a controversial Orange march; violence erupted when the march was re-routed by the Parades Commission.

After retiring from the Executive, Sam Foster continued to work on the policing board.

Bairbre de Brun's fortunes rose after suspension. She was elected to the European Parliament, snatching a seat vacated by the former SDLP leader John Hume in 2004. Northern Ireland's first woman MEP went on to spend much of her time in Brussels and Strasbourg.

Martin McGuinness retained his Mid-Ulster seat and continued to negotiate on behalf of his party. He was instrumental in persuading the IRA to issue a statement pledging to enter a new mode and to complete the decommissioning of all of its weapons.

The DUP leader Ian Paisley was dogged with health problems in 2004 – in his own words he had walked in Death's shadow. Nonetheless, he recovered and lived to celebrate his party's 2005 election win, when the DUP took 9 seats out of a possible 18 in Northern Ireland.

The former DUP ministers Peter Robinson, Nigel Dodds and Gregory Campbell consolidated their positions as MPs in the 2005 Westminster poll. Speculation continued about the likely successor to the DUP leader Ian Paisley: Robinson, or Dodds?

The burden of history Seamus Mallon spoke of has fallen on the two parties that have benefited most from the failure of devolution. Ian Paisley and Gerry Adams, as leaders of their respective tribes, may be carrying that load for some time. Their attempt at a deal, without having exchanged a single word with one other, fell apart in December 2004. Despite some optimism that a deal would be concluded in December 2004, their "comprehensive agreement", which envisaged a return to power-sharing by spring 2005, faltered when the IRA refused to meet Ian Paisley's demand for photographic evidence of decommissioning. Ten days after the talks breakdown the Northern Bank was robbed of around £30 million in one of the biggest bank robberies in history. The IRA was blamed and questions were once again raised about the organisation's motives and intentions.

In the aftermath of the raid Sinn Féin came under increasing pressure to bring about an end to the IRA. That pressure was stepped up dramatically when Belfastman Robert McCartney was beaten to death in Belfast city centre by members of the IRA after he came to the aid of an associate. McCartney's murder highlighted Sinn Féin's refusal to join the policing board or cooperate with the police, and served as a grim reminder of the problems plaguing the process.

In April 2005 Gerry Adams called on the IRA to embrace purely political means to achieve their ends. His call came one day after the general election was called and cynics dismissed it as an election ploy aimed at bolstering Sinn Féin. While electoral advantage was surely a consideration, Adams had no doubt realised the process was going nowhere without such a move.

On 28 August 2005 the IRA finally issued the statement that unionists and others had been demanding for years. The IRA leadership formally declared an end to its armed campaign and all IRA units were ordered to dump arms and pursue peaceful, political means. It pledged that the decommissioning process would be completed in a verifiable way, with a Catholic priest and a Protestant minister invited to witness and attest that weapons had been put beyond use.

On 26 September General John de Chastelain and his two fellow commissioners on the IICD announced the completion of IRA decommissioning. The commission was accompanied by two church witnesses: the Reverend Harold Good, former President of the Methodist Church, and the Redemptorist priest Father Alec Reid, who had played a role in delivering the IRA ceasefire of 1994. The two witnesses stated they were certain, utterly certain, about the exactitude of the IICD report, having spent many days watching the painstaking way General de Chastelain went about the task: "The experience of seeing this with our own eyes on a minute-to-minute basis provided us with evidence so clear and incontrovertible, it demonstrated to us that beyond any show of doubt the arms of the IRA have now been decommissioned."

The IRA statement unlocked the process of demilitarisation, but not the door to Room 21. Based on the DUP's reaction to the decommissioning statement, that room will remain closed for some time. The DUP expressed doubt that IRA decommissioning had been completed, despite acknowledging that a significant act of decommissioning had taken place.

Paisley has insisted on a protracted testing period, claiming in August 2005 that power-sharing was at least two years away.

Despite the rise of the DUP, the Agreement has not been altered fundamentally by subsequent negotiations. The deal that was almost concluded in December 2004 did not differ radically from the Good Friday Agreement. The DUP had promised a fair deal, but its critics claimed it delivered a fairly similar deal: the three-stranded approach is intact, albeit with some tweaking. Some of the changes made in the comprehensive agreement merely envisaged putting into statute what had been anticipated in the Agreement about Assembly powers and the ministerial code of practice, ensuring ministers were not just honour-bound but legally bound to stick to it. Trimble insisted this was going to happen anyway and the process was interrupted by suspension – adding that the code of practice was being observed by the Executive as a matter of convention.

While the Ulster Unionists insisted the DUP won little, the SDLP claimed Sinn Féin negotiated a poor deal, which watered down the powers of nationalist ministers to take decisions independent of unionists. One Dublin official said that Sinn Féin's negotiating position tended to be the SDLP demands plus 10 per cent, but the SDLP was not involved in proposing changes and Sinn Féin faltered. The acid test, he said, was this: would Bairbre de Brun, as Health minister, have been able to proceed with her decision on the Royal Victoria Hospital in any future administration with her committee, the Assembly and other ministers at the Executive objecting? According to this official, and others within the administration, the answer is no, or probably not.

The Agreement has not died, but without devolution it is not fully alive either.

Stormont gave the Agreement a heartbeat. But it was too short-lived for the community to feel a sense of loss at its collapse; direct rule had been the norm for too long for there to be any serious objection to its return. It seems the people of Northern Ireland have simply got used to the "democratic deficit".

During its existence, the administration proved wrong the notion that unionists and nationalists could not work together in a devolved institution. Graham Gudgin, who had not supported the Agreement when it was signed, witnessed many meetings in Room 21 and was forced to conclude: "Except for one or two tense moments over the IRA's failure to decommission, the Executive worked constructively and harmoniously." However, the Assembly was not helped by the geographic divisions between the East and West Wings, which some believed fuelled the "us and them" mentality within the administration between the Ulster Unionists and the SDLP. One former official in the Faulkner–Fitt Sunningdale administration noted that at least those two leaders saw their administration sinking from the same window.

The Executive was condemned for not being radical enough. Some observers felt it lost touch with the people too quickly as it became embroiled in the arguments about guns and government. "Energy was diverted to 'big politics' and the arguments put people off and distracted from the real business on the hill," said the SDLP's Barry Turley. He recalled his party had not wanted to make the new start at Stormont and had argued for a new, purpose-built, city centre facility: "The SDLP never wanted to go to Stormont and felt it immediately cut the politicians off from the people. We wanted to be in Belfast."

In the final analysis, what did the Executive achieve? Its critics say very little, but in the circumstances it could be argued that it was an achievement for the Executive to survive as long as it did. If nothing else, the ministers proved that power-sharing could work, that, despite all the problems, unionists and nationalists could sit down and agree budgets and programmes and reach common ground. Without devolution, it has been argued, the foot-and-mouth crisis of 2001 would have been far worse. Projects and decisions that had been delayed for years were addressed during devolution, for example, the Toome by-pass was built, the Royal became the site for a new maternity hospital and plans for new cancer centre proceeded. The Children's Commissioner was another concrete example of how devolution could make a real difference. It also delivered free bus-passes for the elderly and student grants for the less well-off – even if the ideal of no tuition fees failed to materialise. It is unlikely a Labour minister would have had the courage to abolish the Eleven-plus in search of a better alternative.

In terms of economics, the devolved Assembly also delivered on a number of fronts. Demands from the business community for the merger of the economic development agencies –the IDB, Ledu, and IRTU – were finally attended to and met. Northern Ireland had fallen behind in terms of expenditure for trains, schools and other infrastructure and these areas were identified as priorities, although efforts to address them were interrupted by suspension. In terms of north-south cooperation, the Executive also delivered the biggest ever cross-border project in the shape of the north-south gas pipeline, which is now coming to fruition and bringing benefits to homes on both sides of the border – even if civil servants claimed it did not represent value for money, a fact that has yet to be proved. A new all-Ireland centre for autism is another example of successful cooperation. More importantly, perhaps, unionism became more comfortable with cross-border cooperation. "I think we made some good corporate decisions," said Sam Foster. "I don't think any government will satisfy all the people, but anything that was done was done with the best intentions."

The Executive shied away from difficult issues, such as water rates, but this would have been addressed in the second term; the Executive had initiated a rates review in its final months. Damien McAteer, Mark Durkan's advisor, said the Executive was eclipsed before it was given a chance to shine. As Durkan put it, it never got to drive at full speed because there was always another bump, another corner to negotiate. According to McAteer, "In the first term people were just finding their feet, but I think within two or three terms, it would have really taken off." The Reform and Reinvestment Initiative and the Strategic Investment Board, forged in the latter days of the administration and designed to inject some dynamism into it and provide solutions to infrastructure problems, simply were not operational long enough to prove their worth under devolution.

When power-sharing failed, the Women's Coalition MLA Monica McWilliams said the people of Northern Ireland were the losers. Simon Jenkins, the former *Times* columnist, wrote that Parliament Buildings should become a museum exhibit, a shrine to sectarianism and the threat of bigotry, a monument to Britain's political ineptitude. In a strange irony, it has fallen to Ian Paisley and Gerry Adams to prove Stormont can work. If the IRA does truly dissolve and embrace solely political means, then a massive hurdle will have been overcome. This will leave unionism with a challenge of its own: does it want to share power with republicans under any circumstance? A post-devolution survey showed one in five voters did not want any form of devolution that included Sinn Féin. It will take time to build trust.

The challenge is to convince unionists across Northern Ireland that direct rule is a poor second to devolution, and to ensure that nationalists do not become too comfortable either with a "greener" version of direct rule or joint authority, should Sinn Féin's Plan B come to pass. As the architect of the Good Friday Agreement, John Hume has his own perspective on the potential of power-sharing. Speaking in his party conference in 2005, Hume declared that only when unionists and nationalists were working together in a devolved administration for the common good would there be healing, and true reconciliation.

SOURCE LIST

BOOKS
Godson, Dean, *Himself Alone* (Harper Collins)

McDonald, Henry, *Trimble* (Bloomsbury)

Elliott, Sydney and Flackes, WD, *Northern Ireland: A Political Directory 1966-1999* (Blackstaff Press)

McKittrick, David; Kelters, Seamus; Feeney, Brian; and Thornton, Chris, *Lost Lives, the stories of the men, women and children who died as a result of the Northern Ireland Troubles* (Mainstream Publishing)

Adams, Gerry, *Hope and History* (Brandon Books)

Millar, Frank, *The Price of Peace* (Liffey Press)

Clarke, Liam and Johnson, Kathryn, *Martin McGuinness: From Guns to Government* (Mainstream Publishing)

NEWSPAPERS
The Irish News, The Irish Times, The Belfast Telegraph, Ulster News Letter, Observer, Irish Examiner, The Guardian.

INTERVIEWEES*
The ministers: David Trimble; Seamus Mallon; Mark Durkan; Bríd Rodgers; Sean Farren; Carmel Hanna; Denis Haughey (junior minister); Michael McGimpsey; Sam Foster; Dermot Nesbitt; Sir Reg Empey; Sinn Féin's Bairbre de Brun and Martin McGuinness; the DUP's Peter Robinson, Nigel Dodds, and Gregory Campbell.

Members of the Assembly interviewed included: the Ulster Unionists Danny Kennedy, Esmond Birnie, Alan McFarland, Fred Cobain; the DUP's Sammy Wilson, the Reverend William McCrea, Ian Paisley Jr; the SDLP's Patricia Lewsley, Alban Maginness, John Dallat, Joe Byrne, John Fee, Alex Attwood, Eamon O'Neill; Joe Hendron; Sinn Féin's Pat Doherty, Francie Molloy, Barry McElduff; Alex Maskey; Mary Nelis; the Alliance leader David Ford; Lord Alderdice, the former speaker; deputy leader Eileen Bell; John Kelly.

Party officials and advisors interviewed included: the SDLP's Brian Barrington, Damien McAteer, Colm Larkin, Hugh Logue, Conail McDevitt; the Ulster Unionist advisors Graham Gudgin, David McNarry, Mark Neale, Stephen Barr; Sinn Féin's Aidan McAteer, Leo Green; DUP special advisor Richard Bullick.

Also Ulster Unionist MP Jeffrey Donaldson; David Kerr, formerly UUP director of communications; and Barry Turley, formerly SDLP director of communications; Fianna Fáil's Mary O'Rourke; Wilfred Mulryne, Methodist College; Lord Fitt; Gearoid Ó Caireallain; Brian Walker, Arts Council.

* *A number of interviewees from parties and within the administration preferred to remain anonymous.*

MEMBERS OF THE 1998 ASSEMBLY

Gerry Adams, Sinn Féin
Ian Adamson, UUP
Fraser Agnew, UUAP
Lord Alderdice, Speaker
Pauline Armitage, (elected UUP later became Independent Unionist)
Billy Armstrong, UUP
Alex Attwood, SDLP
Roy Beggs, Jr, UUP
Billy Bell, UUP
Eileen Bell, Alliance
Paul Berry, DUP
Tom Benson, UUP*
Esmond Birnie, UUP
Norman Boyd, NIUP
PJ Bradley, SDLP
Joe Byrne, SDLP
Gregory Campbell, DUP
Mervyn Carrick, DUP
Joan Carson, UUP
Seamus Close, Alliance
Wilson Clyde, DUP
Fred Cobain, UUP
Robert Coulter, UUP
John Dallat, SDLP
Duncan Shipley-Dalton, UUP
Ivan Davis, UUP
Bairbre de Brun, SF
Nigel Dodds, DUP
Arthur Doherty, SDLP**
Pat Doherty, SF
Boyd Douglas, UUAP
Mark Durkan, SDLP
Sir Reg Empey, UUP
David Ervine, PUP
Sean Farren, SDLP
John Fee, SDLP
David Ford, Alliance
Sam Foster, UUP
Tommy Gallagher, SDLP
Oliver Gibson, DUP
Michelle Gildernew, SF
Sir John Gorman, UUP
Carmel Hanna, SDLP

Denis Haughey, SDLP
William Hay, DUP
Joe Hendron, SDLP
David Hilditch, DUP
John Hume, SDLP***
Derek Hussey, UUP
Billy Hutchinson, PUP
Roger Hutchinson, (elected UKUP, later joined DUP)
Gardiner Kane, (elected DUP, later Ind Unionist)
Gerry Kelly, SF
John Kelly, SF
Danny Kennedy, UUP
James Leslie, UUP
Patricia Lewsley, SDLP
Alban Maginness, SDLP
Seamus Mallon, SDLP
Alex Maskey, SF
Kieran McCarthy, Alliance
Robert McCartney, UKUP
David McClarty, UUP
Rev William McCrea, DUP
Donovan McClelland, SDLP
Alasdair McDonnell, SDLP
Barry McElduff, SF
Alan McFarland, UUP
Michael McGimpsey, UUP
Eddie McGrady, SDLP
Martin McGuinness, SF
Gerry McHugh, SF
Mitchel McLaughlin, SF
Eugene McMenamin, SDLP
Pat McNamee, SF
Monica McWilliams, NIWC
Francie Molloy, SF
Conor Murphy, SF
Mick Murphy, SF
Jane Morrice, NIWC
Maurice Morrow, DUP

Sean Neeson, Alliance
Mary Nelis, SF
Dermot Nesbitt, UUP
Danny O'Connor, SDLP
Dara O'Hagan, SF
Eamonn O'Neill, SDLP
Ian Paisley, DUP
Ian Paisley, Jr, DUP
Edwin Poots, DUP
Sue Ramsey, SF
Iris Robinson, DUP
Ken Robinson, UUP
Mark Robinson, DUP
Peter Robinson, DUP
Patrick Roche, NIUP
Bríd Rodgers, SDLP
George Savage, UUP
Jim Shannon, DUP
Lord Kilclooney, UUP
John Tierney, SDLP
David Trimble, UUP
Denis Watson, UUAP
Peter Weir, UUP (later joined DUP)
Jim Wells, DUP
Cedric Wilson, NIUP
Jim Wilson, UUP
Sammy Wilson, DUP

*Tom Benson died in office and was replaced by nominee, Tom Hamilton
**Arthur Doherty died in office and was replaced by nominee Michael Coyle
***John Hume retired and was replaced by nominee Annie Courtney
****NIUP members were originally elected on a UK Unionist party ticket

INDEX